CAPITAL AND INTEREST

VOLUME I | History and Critique
of Interest Theories

Eugen von Böhm-Bawerk

Eugen von Böhm-Bawerk

CAPITAL
AND INTEREST

VOLUME I | History and Critique
of Interest Theories

TRANSLATED BY GEORGE D. HUNCKE
AND HANS F. SENNHOLZ

LIBERTARIAN PRESS
SOUTH HOLLAND, ILLINOIS

LIBRARY OF CONGRESS CATALOG CARD NUMBER: 58-5555

PRINTED IN THE UNITED STATES OF AMERICA

BIOGRAPHICAL SKETCH

OF EUGEN VON BÖHM-BAWERK

EUGEN VON BÖHM-BAWERK (February 12, 1851, Brünn, Austria-August 27, 1914, Vienna, Austria) was one of Austria's foremost economists and statesmen. His enduring fame rests on his lifelong defense of the science of economics and his stout resistance against the rising flood of interventionism and socialism. He was one of the first to see clearly the imminent destruction of our civilization through Marxism and all its related schemes of socialism. Böhm-Bawerk was a brilliant critic who also had the rare gifts of an originator.

He studied law at the University of Vienna and political science in Heidelberg, Leipzig, and Jena. In 1881 he was appointed professor of economics at the University of Innsbruck where he developed and defended the economic principles that Carl Menger and the classical economists had outlined.

His name as a statesman is associated with the best period of Austrian financial history. In 1889 he entered the Austrian Finance Department, where his abilities as an economist were needed for a projected currency reform. He was vice-chairman of the commission which led to the adoption of the gold standard with the krone as the unit. He was minister of finance in 1895, then again in 1897 and for the third time from 1900 to 1904. His tenure of office was characterized by far-sighted management, balanced budgets, stable currency and a successful conversion of the public debt. He also succeeded in abolishing the age-old special privilege of government subsidies to exporters of sugar. All this was achieved in spite of rising economic nationalism which was working continuously toward the disintegration of the Austro-Hungarian union. It was achieved in spite of the fact that Böhm-Bawerk was not associated with any political party. In 1904 he resigned from his position in protest against army irregularities in budgetary estimates and thereafter devoted his life to writing and teaching economics at the University of Vienna.

As an economist he won great fame by an unusual combination of qualities—extraordinary learning, independence of thought and judgment, dialectical skill, power of penetrating criticism, and mastery of exposition and illustration. An indefatigable scholar, he was marked by the ability always to go to the core of the subject. He showed lively interest in the problems of the Western democracies and in the controversies carried on in English and American journals to which he frequently contributed.

His labors were prodigious. In his famous treatise, *Capital and Interest,* he not only expounded a complete theory of distribution but also a theory of social cooperation which exerted a profound influence on the thought of other economists. His most important works are the following:

1. KAPITAL UND KAPITALZINS comprising three volumes:

   I *Geschichte und Kritik der Kapitalzins-Theorien*
   (first edition, 1884; second edition, 1900; third edition, 1914; fourth edition, 1921)

   II *Positive Theorie des Kapitales*
   (first edition, 1889; second edition, 1902; third edition, 1909-1912; fourth edition, 1921)

   III *Exkurse zur "Positiven Theorie des Kapitales"*
   (Printed as appendices to the third edition of *Positive Theorie des Kapitales* in 1909-1912; printed as separate volume in 1921)

2. *Rechte und Verhältnisse vom Standpunkte der volkswirtschaftlichen Güterlehre,* Innsbruck, 1881

3. "Grundzüge der Theorie des wirtschaftlichen Güterwerts," in Conrad's *Jahrbücher für Nationalökonomie und Statistik,* new series, volume 13, 1886, pp. 1-88 and 477-541; reprinted in the "School of Economics Series of Scarce Tracts in Economic and Political Science," number 11, London, 1932

4. "The Austrian Economists," in the *Annals of the American Academy of Political and Social Science,* volume 1, 1891, pp. 361-384

5. "The Historical vs. the Deductive Method in Political Economy," in the *Annals of the American Academy of Political and Social Science,* volume 1, 1891, pp. 244-271

6. "Wert, Kosten und Grenznutzen," in Conrad's *Jahrbücher für Nationalökonomie und Statistik,* series III, 1892, pp. 321-367

7. "Der letzte Masstab des Güterwertes," in *Zeitschrift für Volkswirtschaft, Sozialpolitik und Verwaltung,* volume III, 1894, pp. 185-230; English translation under the title "The Ultimate Standard of Value," in the *Annals of the American Academy of Political and Social Science,* volume v, number 2

8. "The Positive Theory of Capital and Its Critics," published as a series of essays in the *Quarterly Journal of Economics* in 1895 and 1896 under the titles:

   "Professor Clark's Views on the Genesis of Capital," volume IX, pp. 113-131

   "General Walker Against *Capital and Interest,*" volume IX, pp. 235-256

"The Views of Mr. White, Mr. Bilgram, Professor Mac-Vane and Mr. Hawley," volume x, pp. 121-155

9. "Zum Abschluss des Marxschen Systems," in *Staatswirtschaftliche Arbeiten, Festgaben für Karl Knies,* Berlin, 1896, published in English under the title "Karl Marx and the Close of His System" by T. Fisher Unwin, London, 1898, and by Augustus M. Kelley, New York, 1949

10. "Einige strittige Fragen der Kapitalstheorie," Vienna, 1899, in *Zeitschrift für Volkswirtschaft, Sozialpolitik und Verwaltung,* volume VIII

11. "Macht oder ökonomisches Gesetz?" in *Zeitschrift für Volkswirtschaft, Sozialpolitik und Verwaltung,* volume XXIII, 1914, pp. 205-271, published in English under the title "Control or Economic Law?" by Consumers-Producers Economic Service, South Holland, Illinois, 1951

12. "Unsere passive Handelsbilanz," in *Neue Freie Presse,* issues of January 6, 8 and 9, 1914

F. X. Weiss has collected the more important minor works of Böhm-Bawerk in *Gesammelte Schriften,* two volumes, Vienna 1924-1926.

HANS F. SENNHOLZ

IN BÖHM-BAWERK'S lifetime there were in the original German three editions of *Capital and Interest,* and after his death there was an unchanged fourth edition. There were originally two volumes, the *general* title of which was *Capital and Interest.* The *specific* title to the first volume which appeared in 1884 was *History and Critique of Interest Theories.* The *specific* title to the second volume which appeared in 1889 was *Positive Theory of Capital.*

In 1890 William Smart, an economist living at Edinburgh, prepared a translation of Volume I of the first edition under the title *Capital and Interest;* observe that he used the *general* title which Böhm-Bawerk had adopted, rather than the specific title which covered Volume I, namely, *History and Critique of Interest Theories.* In 1891 William Smart prepared a translation of Volume II of the first edition, under the specific title, *Positive Theory of Capital.* For Volume I he used the general title; for Volume II, the specific title.

The publication of *Capital and Interest* by Böhm-Bawerk was a significant event in the history of economic literature, and in the following years the problems he discussed became some of the most active subjects of economic thought. Böhm-Bawerk published a substantially revised second edition of Volume I in 1900; of Volume II in 1902. A third and final edition of Volume I was published in 1914; of Volume II, half in 1909 and the remainder in 1912. (The material now known as Volume III first appeared in the two installments of the third edition of Volume II, namely, half in 1909 and the remainder in 1912). There was a posthumous edition in 1921 of the three volumes; Volumes I and II contained a foreword by Böhm-Bawerk's contemporary and brother-in-law, Friedrich von Wieser. The only English translations heretofore available have been those by William Smart of the long-superseded first edition.

In the last German edition the two volumes became three volumes, all under the general title *Capital and Interest,* with the specific subtitles *History and Critique of Interest Theories, Positive Theory of Capital,* and *Further Essays on Capital and Interest.*

The chronological order of the various editions of *Capital and Interest* is shown graphically as follows (excluding translations into languages other than English):

CAPITAL AND INTEREST

	HISTORY AND CRITIQUE OF INTEREST THEORIES (Volume I)	POSITIVE THEORY OF CAPITAL (Volume II)	FURTHER ESSAYS ON CAPITAL AND INTEREST (Volume III)
1884	First		
1889		First	
1890	English Translation (Smart) (Titled: "Capital & Interest")		
1891		English Translation (Smart)	
1900	Second		
1902		Second	
1909		Half of Third	Half of First
		(in one binding)	
1912		Remainder of Third	Remainder of First
		(in one binding)	
1914	Third		
1921 (posthumous)	Fourth	Fourth	Second (called Fourth)
	(Verlag von Gustav Fischer, now Stuttgart, Germany)		
1959	English Translation		
	(Libertarian Press, South Holland, Illinois)		

In the English-speaking world, primarily because of the *general* title selected for Volume I by Smart, the title situation in regard to Böhm-Bawerk's work is confused. In this new edition we are following the German fourth edition, with the following titles:

CAPITAL AND INTEREST
(in three volumes)

Volume I History and Critique of Interest Theories

Volume II Positive Theory of Capital

Volume III Further Essays on Capital and Interest

The preferable way to end the confusion of the titles is to subordinate the general title and identify the three volumes primarily by their specific titles. The specific titles are descriptive. Volume I is a painstaking history and critique. Volume II presents Böhm-Bawerk's own theory of capital and of interest; that is why he put in the adjective, *Positive,* to contrast the contents of Volume II with the critique in Volume I. Then he felt it necessary to do a substantial amount of further explaining and of rebuttal of current criticisms of his views, and so Volume III, *Further Essays on Capital and Interest,* came into existence.

These three volumes of Böhm-Bawerk are classics. Like all true classics, they are "readable," and the present-day English-speaking reader will not find himself in insurmountable difficulties if he turns directly to Chapter I of Volume I and reads without omissions, keeping in mind the slightly ironical comment of a famous scientist that, of course, later chapters will not be understandable if the earlier chapters have not been read.

Böhm-Bawerk published the three volumes serially, and each new edition had some changes. The then current circumstances justified the writing of separate prefaces to each edition. Collectively, these prefaces occupy many pages. As they are not particularly helpful to nontechnical readers, they have been printed in smaller type, and have been relegated to the back of the book.

It is important that the reader pay attention to the definitions of terms which appear near the end of Chapter I. The page heading in the German edition reads *Grundbegriffe* which may be translated into English as "Basic Terms." In this country the term "interest" is popularly limited to the return on loan money, but in *Capital and Interest* the term "interest" has the customary broader economic meaning. See pages *4-7* in Chapter I.

It is, of course, ideal if classics in economics are read in natural sequence: Adam Smith, Ricardo, John Stuart Mill, etc. To do all such reading is practically the task of a lifetime. But it is not necessary to do such reading before reading Böhm-Bawerk. If there is to be any antecedent reading, it is recommended that it be the classic by Böhm-Bawerk's contemporary, Carl Menger, entitled *Principles of Economics,* published in English by The Free Press, Glencoe, Illinois, 1950. This book was the earliest that thoroughly and simply described the real foundation of economic science, namely, a correct understanding of "value," involving the idea of marginal utility.

In the opinion of the publisher, the so-called Austrian school in Vienna, together with certain contemporaries in England and Switzerland, were the real classicists in economics. As that name, however, is inseparably connected with Adam Smith and David Ricardo and others in the famous English tradition, the only suitable term to be used for Menger and Böhm-Bawerk and their associates and successors is Neo-Classicists. Among the Neo-Classicists, the great names are the Englishman William Stanley Jevons, the Swiss Leon Walras and, among the Austrians, Menger, Böhm-Bawerk, Wieser and, after them, Ludwig von

Mises and Friedrich A. von Hayek, both presently (1958) living in the United States.

In the January 1891 issue of *The Annals of the American Academy of Political and Social Science* Böhm-Bawerk, in an article entitled "The Austrian Economists," wrote:

> . . . The most important and the most famous doctrines of the classical economists are either no longer tenable at all, or are tenable only after essential alterations and additions . . .

And a little later he wrote:

> . . . Political economy is even yet one of the youngest sciences and it was still younger in the time of the classical economy, which in spite of its name "classical," given as the event proved, too soon, was only an incipient embryonic science. It has never happened in any other case that the whole of a science was discovered, at the first attempt, even by the greatest genius; and so it is not surprising that the whole of political economy was not discovered, even by the classical school. Their greatest fault was that they were forerunners; our greatest advantage is that we come after. We who are richer by the fruits of a century's research than were our predecessors, need not work by different methods, but simply work better than they . . .

One of the things which will interest the average American reader of this work is the long history of economic thought; how rudimentary its beginnings were; what a mass of error it was necessary to clear away as unsound; and how much has been contributed by economists in the non-English-speaking nations.

The translators of Volume I are George D. Huncke, formerly head of the Foreign Language Department of the Andrew Jackson High School of New York City, and Hans F. Sennholz, professor of economics at Grove City College, Pennsylvania. The division of labor has been that Mr. Huncke was responsible for translation into idiomatic English, and Dr. Sennholz for the accurate translation of technical terms and the conformity of the translation to the composite thought of Böhm-Bawerk.

The translator of Volume II is Mr. Huncke. Dr. Sennholz acted as consulting economist.

The translator of Volume III is Dr. Sennholz.

The publisher is immeasurably indebted to Dr. Ludwig von Mises, visiting professor of economics at the Graduate School of Business Administration of New York University, for many and valuable suggestions and encouragement. Without those, this translation would not have been attempted.

LIBERTARIAN PRESS

South Holland, Illinois, U.S.A., 1958

TRANSLATORS' PREFACE

THE TRANSLATORS have faced difficulties of which they hope little trace is to be discerned by the reader. Their chief obstacle was the necessity for the dismemberment of the ponderous and involved sentences and paragraphs that are characteristic of the writings of German scientists in general and of Böhm-Bawerk in particular. They sanguinely hope that they have achieved some measure of success in presenting his text in style and thought units which are more consonant with the spirit of our language and the mental habits of readers of English. A few other knotty problems have been treated in translators' footnotes, but every effort has been made to hold these to a minimum, whether they deal with linguistic or economic questions. Böhm-Bawerk's prefaces, which have small significance presently, and his footnotes have been relegated to the back pages of this book in order to remove deterrents to the early and uninterrupted perusal of the text proper.

GEORGE D. HUNCKE
HANS F. SENNHOLZ

CONTENTS

Contents

Contents

APPENDIX

Recent Literature on Interest
(1884 to 1914)   *355*

I

THE PROBLEM OF INTEREST

1. What the Theoretical Problem of Interest Deals With

WHOEVER is the owner of a capital sum is ordinarily able to derive from it a permanent net income which goes under the scientific name of interest in the broad sense of the term.

This income is distinguished by certain notable characteristics.

It arises independently of any personal act of the capitalist. It accrues to him even though he has not moved a finger in creating it, and therefore seems in a peculiar sense to arise from capital or, to use a very old metaphor, to be begotten by it. It can be derived from any capital, no matter what be the kind of goods of which the capital consists, from naturally fruitful, as well as from barren goods, from perishable as well as from durable goods, from replaceable as well as from irreplaceable goods, from money as well as from commodities. And, finally, it flows without ever exhausting the capital from which it arises, and therefore without any necessary limit to its continuance. It is, if one may use such an expression in mundane matters, capable of everlasting life.

And so the phenomenon of interest presents, on the whole, the remarkable picture of a lifeless thing, capital, producing an everlasting and inexhaustible supply of goods. And this remarkable phenomenon appears in economic life with such perfect regularity that the very concept of capital has often been founded upon it. Thus Hermann, in his *Staatswirtschaftliche Untersuchungen* defines capital as "wealth which produces a constant flow of income without itself suffering any diminution in exchange value."[1]*

Whence and why does the capitalist receive this endless and effortless flow of wealth? These words contain the problem of the theory of interest. That problem will be solved when the actual fact of the drawing of interest, together with all its essential characteristics, is fully described and explained. But the explanation must be complete both in compass and in depth. In compass, inasmuch as all forms and varieties of interest will be explained. In depth, inasmuch as the explanation must be carried

* Footnotes are in the rear of this volume.

without a break to the very limits of economic research; that is to say, to those final, simple acknowledged facts which the science of economics itself regards as axiomatic and does not profess to prove, facts on which economics rests, and the further explanation of which, if it be demanded, must be furnished by related sciences, especially psychology and the natural sciences.

2. How the Theoretical Problem Differs from the Social Problem of Interest

THE "theoretical" problem of interest must be sharply differentiated from the "social" problem of interest. While the former asks only why interest exists, the latter asks whether it is entitled to exist, whether it is just, is right, is useful, is good and therefore whether it is to be retained, modified or abolished. While the theoretical problem deals exclusively with the causes of interest, the social problem deals principally with its effects. And while the theoretical problem is concerned only with the truth, the social problem is attentive primarily to expediency.

But this differentiation between the two problems is no sharper than that which applies to the arguments that are urged on behalf of each, and to the exactness of the proof which is presented in the respective fields. In one case the argument is concerned only with truth or falsehood, while in the other it is concerned for the most part with expediency. While there is but one answer to the *wherefore* of interest, and one which compels acknowledgment in the mind of anyone who applies the laws of logic correctly, it is largely a matter of opinion whether interest is just, right and useful. The most cogent argumentation on this point, though it may convince many who thought otherwise, will never convert all of them. Let us suppose, for instance, that by the soundest of reasoning it were established that the abolition of interest would inevitably be followed by a decline in the material welfare of the civilized world. The argument would still have no weight with the person who, applying a standard of his own, lays no great store by material welfare anyway. For such a person would doubtless argue that earthly life is but a short moment in comparison with eternity, and that the material wealth to which interest ministers, will hinder rather than help man in the attainment of his eternal destiny.

Prudence urgently demands that these two fundamentally different problems be sharply differentiated in scientific investigation. It cannot be denied that they stand in close relation to each other. Indeed, it appears to me that there is no better way of coming to a correct decision on the question whether interest be a good thing, than by a correct understanding of the causes which have given rise to it. But this relationship entitles us only to correlate the results of our investigations, not to confuse the investigations themselves.

3. The Dangers of Confusing the Theoretical Problem and the Social Problem

CONFUSING these investigations will, in fact, endanger the correct solution of both problems, and that on several grounds. In the social question, if both problems are attacked at the same time, all sorts of wishes and inclinations and passions naturally come into play, and they will then only too easily enter into the theoretical part of the inquiry and lower one of the scales of the balance. It could possibly be the scale which would have remained the lighter if it had been weighted only with dispassionate reason. There is truth in the old proverb which maintains that we readily believe that which we wish to believe. And if our judgment on the theoretical problem of interest is distorted, it will naturally influence our judgment on the practical question.

Considerations like these show that an unjustifiable use may be made of arguments which are in themselves justifiable. The man who confuses the two problems, or even mistakes one for the other and who, by following the same procedure with respect to both, renders the same verdict, may easily confuse both groups of arguments and allow each group to exercise an influence on his total judgment. He will let his judgment as to the causes of the phenomenon of interest be guided, to some extent, by principles of expediency, a procedure which is wholly bad; and he will let his judgment as to the desirability of interest as an institution be to some extent directly guided by purely theoretical considerations, a procedure which *may* at least be bad. It is easily possible, for instance, that where the two problems are being confused, a person who perceives the existence of interest to bring with it an increase in production, will for that reason be more inclined to agree with a theory which regards interest as arising from the productive power of capital. Or it may happen that someone may be led to the theoretical conviction that the existence of interest is due to a reduction in wages caused by competition between capital and labor. Such a person may on that account condemn the institution of interest without further ado, and advocate its abolition. Either conclusion is as improper as the other. Whether the existence of interest be attended by results that are useful or harmful to production has absolutely nothing to do with the question of why interest exists. And the knowledge of the source from which interest springs cannot, on the other hand, supply the slightest grounds for judging whether interest should be retained or abolished. Be the fountainhead of interest as it may, and even though its waters be somewhat muddied, yet may the abolition of interest be resolved upon only if and because the welfare and the proper interests of society are furthered thereby.

The precaution of separating the two problems in the scientific treatment of them has been overlooked by many writers. And although this oversight has been the source of many errors, misunderstandings and prejudices, we hardly have the right to complain of it. For it was only in the wake of the practical problem of interest that the course was charted toward the theoretical problem and its scientific treatment. Because of the merging of the two problems, to be sure, the theoretical problem has been investigated under conditions which were not conducive to ascertainment of the truth. But had it not been for that merging, the problem would have failed to be investigated at all by many able writers. It is all the more important to derive profit for the future from such experiences in the past.

It is my deliberate intent to limit the task to which the following pages will be devoted to that of a critical history of the theoretical problem of interest. I shall try to set down, in the course of their historical development, the various attempts at scientific research into the nature and origin of interest and to subject to critical examination the various views that have been taken of the question. I shall, on the other hand, treat of judgments as to the justice, usefulness or propriety of interest only to the extent that it may seem indispensable to do so, in order to winnow out the theoretical kernel they may contain.

In spite of that self-imposed restraint I need fear no dearth of material for this work—material either for the history or for my critique. For a whole literature has been amassed on the subject of interest, a literature which in mere extent is equalled by that of few of the branches of political economy, and by that of none in the variety of opinions presented. Not one theory of interest, nor even two or three, but an ample dozen of such theories bear witness to the zeal with which economists have devoted themselves to the investigation of this remarkable problem.

Whether these efforts were as successful as they were zealous may with some reason be doubted. And it is at least a fact that of the numerous opinions which have been advanced as to the nature and origin of interest no single one has been able to win undivided approval. Even though each of them, as might be expected, has inspired the faith of utter conviction in a greater or smaller circle of adherents, yet each was sufficiently open to objections to prevent the achievement of a completely victorious decision. At the same time, even those theories which could win the support of only weak minorities proved tenacious enough to escape complete extinction. And so the present (1884) status of the theory of interest is characterized by a motley collection of the most varied opinions, of which none is able to achieve victory and none is willing to admit defeat, and whose very numbers indicate to the impartial mind what a mass of error they must necessarily contain.

I venture to hope that the following pages may serve to move us a little closer to that unity which is today a distant prospect indeed.

4. *Preliminary Explanation of Some Basic Concepts*

BEFORE I can devote myself to my actual task, I must reach an understanding with the reader concerning a few concepts and distinctions of which we shall have to make frequent use in the pages to come.

Because our science, unfortunately, exhibits wide variance in its terminology, the word "capital" has many meanings. For the purposes of this critical inquiry I shall confine myself to the one which defines capital as consisting of a *complex of produced means of acquisition,* that is to say, a complex of goods which came into existence as the result of a previous process of production, and which are destined, not for immediate consumption, but for the acquisition of further goods. We therefore exclude from our concept of capital any objects of immediate consumption on the one hand, and all land (as not produced) on the other.

I do not intend, for the present, to justify my preference for this particular definition, except to urge two reasons of expediency. In the first place, it is in harmony with the terminology of at least a substantial majority of the writers whose views I shall have to set forth; in the second place, this delimitation of the concept of capital conforms most closely to the limitations of the problem with which we wish to deal. For it is not our intention to investigate the theory of land rent, but only to pursue the theoretical explanation of that kind of acquisition of goods which is derived from a complex of other goods, excepting land. I shall reserve a more detailed development of the concept of capital for the second and positive volume of this work.

Within the general concept of capital, moreover, there are two shades of meaning which must be distinguished. There is the social concept of capital, which embraces the social means of acquisition, and only those. And there is the private concept of capital, which includes all goods by means of which an individual acquires wealth, no matter whether, in terms of national economy, they are a means of acquisition or a means of enjoyment, that is to say, whether they are goods for production or goods for consumption. The books owned by a rental library would, for instance, fall within the definition of private capital, but not that of social capital. Social capital, then, is identical (if we except those few objects of immediate consumption which are loaned out for a consideration to foreign countries) with a nation's *produced means of production.* The theory of interest is concerned with both these shades of meaning of the term "capital." It ought really to deal principally with the concept of private capital, because interest represents a form of acquisition of private wealth. Special circumstances, however, have brought it about that in most discussions of interest the social concept of capital primarily engages our attention. For that reason we shall ordinarily have the social concept of capital in mind when we use the word "capital" without modification.

The revenue which is derived from capital I may refer to as *interest,* using the latter word in its broader meaning.

Now interest makes its appearance in many different forms.

In the first place, we have to distinguish between gross interest and net interest. The former represents a mixture of heterogeneous revenues, which are only outwardly a unified whole. It includes the gross return from the employment of capital which consists only in part of true interest, since there are also present other elements such as replacement of

5

the part of the capital which has been expended, all kinds of current expenditures, repairs, insurance premiums, etc. Similarly, rent income which the owner receives as the rent for a house is a gross interest, from which we must deduct a certain proportion for current maintenance costs and for eventual replacement of the house which the passage of time will in the end destroy, if we are to determine the true income derived from the capital. The net interest, on the other hand, is this very "true income" on capital, which is revealed after the elimination of those heterogeneous elements included in the gross interest. The theory of interest is of course concerned with the explanation of net interest.

Furthermore, we must distinguish between *originary interest* and *contract* or *loan interest*.

In the hands of one who uses capital for production, the utility of that capital is demonstrated by the fact that the sum of the products created with its help is regularly of greater value than the sum of the costs of the goods expended in the course of production. The excess value constitutes a certain gain, which we wish to designate as the *originary interest*.

The owner of capital, however, often forgoes earning the originary interest himself, and prefers to hand over his capital to another for temporary use in return for a fixed compensation. This compensation bears various names in common speech. It is called hire or rent if the capital consists of durable goods. It is called interest if the capital consists of perishable or fungible (replaceable) goods. All these kinds of compensation may properly be grouped under the single category of *contract* or *loan interest*.

While the concept of loan interest is extremely simple, the concept of originary interest requires closer definition. For it is not at all unreasonable to doubt whether the entire excess of proceeds over costs that is realized by an entrepreneur from a process of production should be credited to his capital. Certainly it should not be, if the entrepreneur simultaneously occupies the position of a worker in his own enterprise, for in that case part of that "excess" is a mere wage of the entrepreneur for work performed. But even if he does not personally participate in the labor of production, he contributes a certain measure of personal effort, either by reason of the intellectual effort represented by his supervision, or by his formulating policies for the business to follow, or at the very least because of the act of will by which he determines that his means of production shall be enlisted in the service of that particular enterprise. And so the question arises whether we should not, in view of these considerations, distinguish two components in the total excess of proceeds realized by the enterprise. One component would be the result of contributing capital—the originary interest, as it were, and the other the result of the entrepreneur's effort.

Opinions on this point are divided. Most economists make some such distinction. They separate the total excess of proceeds of a productive enterprise into interest and entrepreneur's profit. Of course it cannot be determined with mathematical accuracy how much has been contributed to the total excess by the material factor, capital, and how much by the personal factor, the entrepreneur's activity. And yet, in order to be able to separate the two contributions and set them down in actual figures, we look elsewhere to borrow a measuring device. We seek to establish what income is ordinarily derived from a given capital sum. This is most readily determined by reference to the usual rate of interest on loans, with due regard to complete safety. And so we credit to capital such portion of the total excess of proceeds from the enterprise as is equal to an amount derived by applying the customary rate of interest to the capital invested in that enterprise, and we credit the balance to the activity of the entrepreneur, and call it entrepreneur's profit. If, for instance, an enterprise in which a capital of $100,000 has been invested makes a surplus in a given year of $9,000, and if, furthermore, the customary rate of interest is 5%, then $5,000 is considered originary interest and the remaining $4,000 as entrepreneur's profit.

On the other hand, there are many economists who hold that such a division is inadmissible, and that so-called entrepreneur's profit and originary interest constitute a homogeneous whole.[2]

The decision as to which of these opinions is the correct one constitutes an independent problem of no small difficulty—the problem of the entrepreneur's profit.

The difficulties which surround our special subject, the problem of interest, are so great that I can have no desire to increase them by introducing the complication of a second difficult problem. I shall therefore purposely refrain from investigating or deciding the problem of the entrepreneur's profit. I shall treat as interest only that which is conceded by all parties to be of the nature of interest. By that is meant loan interest in its entirety,[3] and originary interest of an enterprise to the extent that it corresponds to the revenue computed at customary interest rates on the capital employed in the enterprise. The question of whether the so-called entrepreneur's profit is or is not income on capital I shall intentionally leave open. Fortunately the circumstances are such that I may do so without prejudice to our investigation. At the worst, just those phenomena which are generally agreed upon as being definitely classifiable as interest are the ones which predominate so heavily, both in number and in their possession of the characteristics of interest, that from them we can determine with assurance the nature and origin of interest without being first compelled to settle the question of that controversial borderline.

I trust I need not state with any special emphasis that I do not consider the few remarks above an exhaustive or even an entirely correct exposition of the principles of the theory of capital. My only concern was to establish, with a minimum of delay, a serviceable and reliable terminology to serve as a basis of mutual understanding between author and reader for the critical and historical portions of this book.

II

THE OPPOSITION TO LOAN INTEREST
ON THE PART OF THE
ANCIENT PHILOSOPHERS AND
THE CANONISTS

1. Early Preoccupation with Loan Interest

IT HAS often been remarked that not only our knowledge of
interesting subjects, but also our curiosity regarding them develops
only gradually. A phenomenon, when it first attracts attention, is very
rarely fully comprehended. Nor do we recognize the multiplicity of
interrelated details, and make them the subject of one comprehensive
inquiry. More frequently we are first stimulated to thoughtfulness by
some particularly striking instance, and it is only gradually that the
less striking phenomena come to be recognized as belonging to the same
group, and are included in the compass of the growing problem.

This has been the case with the phenomenon of interest. It first
became the object of question only in the form of loan interest, and
for fully two thousand years the nature of loan interest had been discussed and theorized on, before any one thought it necessary to put
the other question which first gave the problem of interest its complete
and proper range, namely, the question of the why and whence of
originary interest.

It is easy to see why this should be so. The thing about interest
that specially challenges our attention is its effortless genesis from a
mother wealth, which seems to have the power of procreation. This
characteristic is so prominent in loan interest, and where that loan
interest is derived from sums of money that are by nature barren, it
appears so positively arresting, that it must excite question even where
no systematic reflection has been devoted to it. Originary interest, on
the other hand, though admittedly not obtained *through* the labor of

8

the capitalist-entrepreneur, is certainly obtained *with the cooperation of* that labor. It was easy for the superficial observer to confuse the two, or at any rate to fail to differentiate between them with sufficient clarity to recognize the presence in originary interest, as well as in loan interest, of the strange element of acquisition of wealth without labor. Before this could be recognized, and thus before the interest problem could attain its proper compass, it was necessary that capital itself, and its employment in economic life, attain much wider development, and that some beginning be made of a systematic investigation into the sources of income. And this investigation could not be one that was content to point out the obvious and striking manifestations of the phenomenon; it had to cast light on its more inconspicuous forms as well. But these conditions were not fulfilled until some thousands of years after men had first expressed their wonder at loan interest "born of barren money."

The history of the interest problem, therefore, begins with a very long period in which *loan interest* alone is the subject of investigation. This period begins in very ancient times, and extends into the eighteenth century of our era. It is filled with the conflict between two opposing doctrines, of which the elder is hostile to interest and the later one defends it. The course of the dispute gave rise to an interesting chapter in the history of civilization, but it also exerted an influence of great importance on the practical development of our economic life and of our jurisprudence. Of that influence we may see many traces even in our own day. But the whole period, notwithstanding its length and the great number of writers who flourished in it, was rather barren with respect to any development of the theoretical interest problem. The attack was directed, as we shall see, not against the stronghold of the problem, but against an outpost of it which, from a theoretical standpoint, was of comparatively subordinate importance. Theory was too much the bond servant of practice. It was not so much a matter of investigating the nature of loan interest for its own sake, as it was of finding in theory some justification for an opinion on the goodness or badness of interest, which opinion was already firmly rooted in religious, moral, or economic conviction. Since, moreover, this controversy was at its height during the heyday of scholasticism, it can well be imagined that the growth in number of arguments and counter-arguments was by no means a measure of the growth in knowledge of the subject itself.

I shall therefore not waste many words in describing these earliest phases in the development of our problem; and I consider this all the more permissible because there are already several treatises, some of them excellent, relating to that period. In them the reader can find much more detail than is necessary or even appropriate for our purpose.[1] We begin, then, with some account of the movement which opposed loan interest.

9

2. Hostility to Interest in the Earlier Periods of Civilization

ROSCHER has aptly remarked that throughout the lower stages of economic development there regularly appears a lively aversion to the taking of interest. Credit still plays but a small part in production. Almost all loans are for consumption, and are, as a rule, loans to people in distress. The creditor is usually rich, the debtor poor, and the former appears in the hateful light of a man who squeezes from the little that the poor man has, something, in the shape of interest, that he can add to his own superfluous riches. It is not to be wondered at, then, that both the ancient world and especially the Christian Middle Ages were exceedingly unfavorable to interest. For the ancient world, in spite of some economic development, never worked out very much of a credit system, and the Middle Ages, after the decay of Roman culture, suffered a relapse in industry, as in so many other fields, to the circumstances of primitive times.

Both periods have left us documentary records of this aversion to interest.

3. The Legal Prohibition of Interest in the Ancient World

THE hostile expressions of the ancient world are not few in number, but they are of trifling importance for the development of theory. They consist, in part, of a number of legislative acts forbidding the taking of interest, some of which date back to very early times.[2] The rest are more or less incidental utterances of philosophers or philosophizing writers.

The legal prohibitions of interest may, of course, be taken as evidence of a strong and widespread conviction that the taking of interest was, as a practical thing, to be condemned, but it can scarcely be said that they were founded on any distinct theory. At any rate, no such theory has been handed down to us. The philosophers, moreover, such as Plato, Aristotle, the two Catos, Cicero, Seneca, Plautus, and others, usually touch on the subject too cursorily to give any foundation in theory for their unfavorable judgment. In addition, the context often makes it doubtful whether they object to interest on the ground of a peculiar fault inherent in interest itself, or only because it usually results in an increase of the riches they despise.[3]

One passage in ancient literature has, in my opinion, a direct value for the history of theory, inasmuch as it allows us to infer what really was the opinion of its author on the economic nature of interest. I have in mind the oft quoted passage in the first book of Aristotle's *Politics*. He says there (III, 23): "Of the two sorts of money-making one, as I have just said, is a part of household management, the other is retail trade: the former necessary and honorable, the latter a kind of exchange which is justly censured; for it is unnatural, and a mode by which men

10

gain from one another. The most hated sort, and with the greatest reason, is usury, which makes a gain out of money itself, and not from the natural use of it. For money was intended to be used in exchange, but not to increase at interest. And this term usury, which means the birth of money from money, is applied to the breeding of money, because the offspring resembles the parent. Wherefore of all modes of making money this is the most unnatural." [Jowett's *Translation* p. 19.]

This represents a contribution to theory which may be summed up as follows. Money is by nature incapable of bearing fruit. The lender's gain therefore cannot come from any economic power inherent in money, but only from a defrauding of the borrower. Interest is therefore a gain got by abuse and injustice.

That the writers of old pagan times did not go more deeply into the question admits of a very simple explanation. The question was then no longer a practical one. In course of time the authority of the state had become reconciled to the taking of interest. In Attica interest had for long been free from legal restriction. The universal empire of Rome, without formally rescinding those severe laws which had entirely forbidden the taking of interest, had first condoned, then formally sanctioned it by the institution of legal rates.[4] The fact was that economic relations had become too complicated to be fitted into a system naturally so limited as that of gratuitous credit. Merchants and practical men were certainly unanimously in favor of interest. In such circumstances, to write *in favor of* it was needless, to write *against* it was hopeless; and it is a most significant indication of this state of affairs that almost the only quarter in which interest was still rather resignedly censured was in the works of philosophical writers.

4. The Christian Church Renews the Prohibition of Interest

THE writers of the Christian Middle Ages had more occasion to treat the subject thoroughly.

The dark days which preceded and followed the break-up of the Roman Empire had brought a reaction in economic matters, which, in its turn, had the natural result of strengthening the old hostile feeling against interest. The characteristic spirit of Christianity worked in the same direction. The exploitation of poor debtors by rich creditors must have appeared in a peculiarly hateful light to one whose religion taught him to look upon gentleness and charity as among the greatest virtues, and to think little of the goods of this world. But what had most influence was that, in the sacred writings of the New Testament, certain passages had been found which, as usually interpreted, seemed to contain a direct divine prohibition of the taking of interest. This was particularly true of the famous passage in Luke: ". . . lend, hoping for nothing again."[5] The powerful support which the spirit of the time, already hostile to interest, thus found in the express utterance of divine authority, gave it the power once more to influence legislation its way. The Christian church lent its arm. Step by step it managed to introduce

11

the prohibition into legislation. At first the taking of interest was forbidden only by the church, and to the clergy only. Then it was forbidden to the laity also, but still the prohibition came only from the church. At last secular legislation succumbed to the church's influence and adopted its severe statutes, thus abrogating the Roman law.[6]

For fifteen hundred years this turn of affairs gave abundant support to those writers who were hostile to interest. The old pagan philosophers had been able to fling their denunciations out into the world without supplying much proof, because they were neither inclined nor able to give them practical effect. As a "Platonic" utterance by idealists their criticism did not have sufficient weight in the world of practical affairs to be either seriously opposed or seriously defended. But now the matter had become practical again. At first it was a matter of seeing to it that the Word of God be made victorious on earth, and once that had been assured, it became necessary to defend the righteousness of the new laws against the attacks which immediately followed. This task naturally fell to the theological and legal literature of the church, and a movement set in which manifested itself in literary activity on the subject of loan interest and which accompanied the canonical prohibition from its earliest rise to its remotest manifestations late in the eighteenth century.

The twelfth century of our era saw a noteworthy change in the character of this literature. Before that century the controversy was confined mainly to the theologians, and even the way in which it was conducted was essentially theological. To prove the unrighteousness of loan interest writers appealed to God and His revelation, to passages of Holy Writ, to the injunctions of neighborly love, of righteousness, and so on. Only rarely, and then in the most general terms, did they urge legal and economic considerations. It is the fathers of the church who express themselves in greatest detail on the subject, although even their treatment can scarcely be called detailed (*see the following text*).

After the twelfth century, however, the discussion was conducted on a more and more scientific basis. Proofs from Scripture were bolstered by citing as authorities reverend fathers of the church, canonists and philosophers—even pagan philosophers—by quoting old and new laws, by deducing from the *jus divinum* (divine law), from the *jus humanum* (human law), and—what is particularly important for us as touching the economic side of the matter—from the *jus naturale* (natural law). And now the lawyers begin to take a more active part in the movement alongside the theologians, first the canonists and then the legists.

The more extended and more careful attention which these writers gave to the subject is chiefly due to the fact that the prohibition of interest pressed more heavily as time went on, and needed to be more strongly defended against the opposition of the trade which it oppressed. The prohibition had originally been imposed under economic conditions so primitive that it could be easily borne. Moreover, during the earlier centuries the prohibition had so little external force at its command that where the man of practical affairs felt hampered by the restraint, he could disregard it without much danger. But later, as industry and commerce grew, the ever increasing necessity for credit made the hampering effects of the prohibition increasingly vexatious. At the same time, the prohibition became more keenly felt as it extended to wider circles, and as its transgression was punished more severely. Thus it was inevitable that its encounters with the economic world should become doubly numerous and doubly serious. Its most natural ally, public opinion, which had originally stood most loyally at its side, now began to withdraw its support. There was urgent need of assistance from theory, and this assistance was readily obtained from the growing science.[7]

Of these two phases of the canonist writings on the subject, the first is almost without value for the history of theory. Its theologizing and moralizing is restricted almost entirely to expressing abhorrence of the taking of interest and to proving its case by citing authorities.[8]

The second phase is of greater importance, although it owes that importance neither to the number of its writers nor to the very numerous arguments they introduced.[9] For the work that had been genuinely original with a few was soon slavishly repeated by the many, and the treasury of arguments collected by the earlier writers soon began to reappear, an inviolable legacy, in the works of all later authors. Most of the arguments are mere citing of authorities or are of a moralizing character, or have no force whatever. Only a comparatively small number of them, mostly deductions from the *jus naturale,* can lay claim to any theoretical interest. Even if many of these arguments should appear to a reader of today to be little calculated to carry conviction, still it should not be forgotten that at that time it was not their office to convince. What was to be believed already stood fixed and fast. The one convincing argument was the Word of God, and that Word, as they understood it, had condemned interest. Any rational arguments along this line which might be discovered were little more than a desirable bit of trimming which, since it did not have to bear the burden of proof, could well be less substantially woven than the main fabric.[10]

I shall very briefly state those rational arguments that have an interest for us, and verify them by one or two quotations from such writers as have given them clear and effective expression.

5. *The Theoretical Foundations of Canonistic Doctrines*

TO BEGIN with, we are confronted by the argument of the barrenness of money. It is the same consideration as was urged by Aristotle, only the canonists emphasize more strongly the theoretically important point that the taking of interest constitutes a parasitic battening on fruits produced through the industry of others. Thus says Gonzalez Tellez:[11] ". . . So then, as money breeds no money, it is contrary to nature to take anything beyond the sum lent, *and it may with more propriety be said that it is taken from industry than from money,* for money certainly does not breed, as Aristotle has related." Covarruvias speaks in still plainer terms:[12] "The fourth reason is that money brings forth no fruit from itself, nor gives birth to anything. On this account it is inadmissible and unfair to take anything over and above the sum loaned for the use of that sum since this would be not so much taken from money, which brings forth no fruit, *as from the industry of another.*"

The consumption of money and of other kinds of goods that are loaned furnished a second argument "in accordance with natural law." This argument was very clearly urged by as early a writer as Thomas Aquinas. He contends that there are certain things the use of which consists in the consumption of the articles themselves, such as grain and wine. On that account the use of these things cannot be separated from the articles themselves, and if the use is to be transferred, the article itself must necessarily be transferred with it. Therefore, when an article of this sort is lent, the title to it will always be transferred as well. Now it would be patently unjust if a man should sell wine, and yet, as a separate thing, sell the *use* of the wine, too. In so doing he would either be selling the same article twice, or he would be selling something which does not exist. Exactly in the same way is it unjust for a man to lend things of this sort at interest. Here also he is asking two prices for *one* article; he is demanding that it be replaced by a similar article and is also asking a price for the use of the article. That we call interest or usury. Since the use of *money,* too, consists in consuming or spending it, it is inadmissible in itself, on the same grounds, to ask a price for the use of money.[13] According to this reasoning interest appears as a price filched or extorted for a thing that does not really exist, the separate and independent "use" of consumable goods.

A similar conclusion is arrived at by a third recurring and stereotyped argument. The goods loaned pass over into the property of the debtor. Therefore the use of the goods for which the lender collects interest is the use of another person's goods, and from that the lender cannot draw a gain without injustice. Thus Gonzalez Tellez says: "For the creditor who gains from a *thing belonging to another person* enriches himself at the expense of another." Even more outspoken are the words of Vaconius Vacuna:[14] "Therefore he who gets fruit from that money, whether it be pieces of money or anything else, *gets it from a thing which does not belong to him, and it is therefore just as if he were to steal it.*"

It was, I believe, Thomas Aquinas who first added to the canonists' repertoire the strange argument that interest is to be regarded as the hypocritical and underhand price asked for a possession common to all, namely, time. The usurers who receive more, by the amount of their interest, than they have given, seek a pretext to make the business transaction seem fair. This pretext is offered them by time. They claim that time is recognized as the equivalent for which they receive the surplus income which is the interest. That this is their intention is evident from the fact that they increase or reduce the amount of interest they demand, according to whether the time for which a loan is given is longer or shorter. But time is a common possession that belongs to

14

no one in particular, but is given to all equally by God. When, therefore, the usurer would charge a price for time, as though it were property received from him, he defrauds his neighbor, to whom the time which he sells already belongs as much as it does to him, the seller, and he defrauds God, for whose free gift he demands a price.[15]

Let us sum up. In the eyes of the canonists loan interest is simply an income which the lender extracts by fraud or force from the resources of the borrower. The lender collects in interest fruits which barren money cannot bear. He sells a "use" which does not exist, or a use which already belongs to the borrower. And finally, he sells time, which belongs to the borrower just as much as it does to the lender and to all men. In short, regard it as we may, interest always appears as a parasitic gain, extorted or filched from the defrauded borrower.

This condemnation was not visited upon the interest that accrues from the lending of durable goods, such as houses, furniture, etc. Nor did it affect the originary interest acquired under the owner's own management. That this originary interest might be an income distinct from that due to the entrepreneur for his services, was but little noticed, especially at the beginning of the period. And, so far as it was noticed, little thought was given to it. At any rate, this kind of interest was not condemned as a matter of principle. Thus, for instance, the canonist Zabarella[16] deplores the existence of loan interest for the reason, among others, that the agriculturists, looking for a "more certain" income, would be tempted to put their money out at interest rather than employ it in production, and would thus jeopardize the food supply of the people. This represents a line of thought which evidently sees nothing objectionable in investing capital in agriculture, and drawing income from it. It was not even considered necessary that the owner of capital should operate it personally, so long as he did not let the ownership of it out of his hands; thus interest obtained from a silent partnership was at least not forbidden.[17] And the case in which one man intrusts another with a sum of money, but retains the ownership of it, is decided by the stern Thomas Aquinas to the effect that such a man may unhesitatingly appropriate the income which arises from that sum of money. He will not lack a just title to it, "for he, as it were, receives the fruit of his own estate"—not, as St. Thomas carefully adds, a fruit that springs directly from the coins, but a fruit that springs from those things that have been obtained in just exchange for the coins.[18]

Where exception is, nevertheless, taken to interest obtained through personal exertions, (and this does occur often), the exception is not so much to that income as such, but rather to some concrete and objectionable manner of getting it, such as business conducted in an avaricious or even fraudulent way, or forbidden traffic in money, and the like.

III

THE DEFENSE OF LOAN INTEREST

FROM THE SIXTEENTH TILL THE

EIGHTEENTH CENTURY. THE

DECLINE OF CANON DOCTRINE

1. Resistance of Economic Practice
to the Canonistic Prohibition of Interest

THE canonistic doctrine of interest enjoyed its highest degree of public esteem during the period which began sometime during the thirteenth century. Its principles at that time held almost undisputed sway in legislation, temporal as well as spiritual. Pope Clement V, at the Council of Vienna in 1311, was in a position to go so far as to threaten with excommunication those secular magistrates who passed laws favorable to interest, or who failed to repeal such laws, where already passed, within three months.[1] Nor were the laws inspired by the canonical doctrine content with opposing interest in its naked and undisguised form; by the aid of much ingenious casuistry they had even taken measures to prosecute it under many, if not all, of the disguises by which the prohibition could be evaded.[2] Finally, literature no less than legislation fell under the sway of the canon doctrine, and for centuries not a trace of opposition to the principle of the prohibition dared show itself.

There was only one opponent that the canonistic doctrine had never been entirely able to subdue, and that was economic practice itself. In the face of all the penalties of earth and heaven which were provided, interest continued to be offered and taken. This was done partly without disguise, partly under the manifold forms which the inventive spirit of business men had devised for slipping through the meshes of the prohibitionist laws in spite of all their casuistry. And the more flourishing the economic condition of a country, the more strongly did practice oppose the dominant theory.

In this battle it was the more stubborn contestant who gained the victory, and that contestant was this very economic practice whose existence was endangered by the prohibition.

2. Numerous Exceptions

AN EARLY success, not marked by much outward circumstance but actually of great importance, was obtained even when canonistic doctrine was still at the height of its prestige. Too weak to hazard open war against the principle of prohibition, the business world yet managed to prevent the enactment of laws which carried the principle to its ultimate conclusions, and so establish a number of direct and indirect exceptions.

The following may be regarded as among the direct exceptions: the privileges of the public pawn brokerages (*Monts de Pitié*), the toleration of transactions by other kinds of banks, and the very extensive indulgence shown to the usury practices of the Jews—an indulgence which was here and there extended, at least by secular legislation, into formal legal permission.[3]

And there were many indirect exceptions, such as the buying of annuities, the taking of land in mortgage for money loaned, the use of bills of exchange, partnership arrangements, and above all, the possibility of getting indemnification from the borrower for the time interval involved in deferred payments (*damnum emergens* and *lucrum cessans*). In and of itself this interval or *interesse* would have entitled the lender to compensation only in the case of culpable negligence (called *mora*) on the part of the borrower to fulfill his contractual obligations; and the existence and extent of the *interesse* would have had to be proven in each case. But this difficulty was avoided, although under protest of the stricter canonists, by the introduction of two contract clauses. Under one clause the borrower agreed beforehand that the lender should be released from the obligation of proving the borrower's *mora;* and under the other a definite amount was agreed on in advance as the indemnification the lender was to receive. The practical result was that the loan was made nominally without interest, but that the creditor actually received, by virtue of the clause relating to *interesse,* a regular percentage for the whole period of the loan, the borrower having been technically put in *mora* for that period.[4]

Results like these in practice eventually brought in their train corresponding modifications in principle.

To the attentive observer of men and things it must in time have become questionable whether the constant and ever increasing resistance of practical life really had its root, as the canonists affirmed, only in human wickedness and hardness of heart. Those who took the trouble to go more deeply into the technicalities of carrying on business inevitably recognized that practice not only would not, but that it could not dispense with interest. They perceived that interest is the soul of credit, and that where credit is to exist to any considerable extent interest cannot be prohibited, and that suppressing interest means suppressing at least nine-tenths of all credit transactions. In a word, the conclusion was forced upon them that even in an incompletely developed system of economy interest is an organic necessity. It was inevitable that the recognition of such facts, which had long been commonplaces among practical men, should in the end force its way into the circles of the theorists. When it did, the effects which it exerted there were varied.

One party retained unshaken the theoretical conviction that loan interest was a parasitic gain, admitting of no defense before any strict tribunal. But it consented to a practical compromise with the imperfection of man, on which it laid the blame for the obstinate vitality of loan interest. From the standpoint of an ideal order of society, it contended interest cannot be permitted, but since man is so imperfect it cannot conveniently be eradicated, and so it is better to tolerate it within certain limits. This was the view taken by several of the great reformers, including such men as Zwingli,[5] and Luther in his later days (although earlier he had been a relentless enemy of usury),[6] and, with still more reservations, Melanchton.[7]

It naturally had a great effect on public opinion, and indirectly also on the later development of law, that such influential men as these declared for tolerance in the matter of loan interest. However, as they were guided in their conduct not by principles, but altogether by motives of expediency, their views have no great significance in the history of theory, and we need not pursue them further.

But another party of thinking and observing men did go further. Convinced by experience of the necessity of loan interest, they began to re-examine the theoretical foundations of the prohibition, and finding that these were not valid, they commenced to write in opposition to the canonistic doctrine, basing their opposition on principles. This opposition begins about the middle of the sixteenth century, rapidly gathers impetus and power in the course of the seventeenth, and towards its end obtains so distinct an ascendency that during the next hundred years it has to do battle only with a few isolated writers and straggling proponents of the canonistic doctrine. And if, after the end of the eighteenth century, any one had professed to defend that doctrine with the old specific arguments, he would have been thought too eccentric to be taken seriously.

3. Beginnings of Opposition, as a Principle

THE first champions of the new school were the reformer Calvin, and the French jurist Dumoulin (Carolus Molinaeus).

Calvin has defined his attitude towards our question in a letter to his friend Oekolampadius.[8] In this letter he treats it, not in detail perhaps, but certainly with decision. At the outset he rejects the usual scriptural foundation for the prohibition, seeking to show that, of the writings customarily adduced in its support, some are to be differently interpreted, and some have lost their validity because of the entirely changed circumstances.[9] The scriptural authority for the prohibition being thus disposed of, Calvin turns to the rational arguments usually given to support it. Its strongest argument, that of the barrenness of money (*pecunia non parit pecuniam*), he finds of "little weight." It is with money as it is with a house or a field. The roof and walls of a house cannot, properly speaking, beget money, but through exchange of the use of the house for money a legitimate money gain may be drawn from the house. In the same way money can be made fruitful. Since land is purchased for money, it is quite correct to think of the money as producing other sums of money in the shape of the yearly revenues from the land. Unemployed money is barren, to be sure, but the borrower does not let it lie unemployed. The borrower therefore is not defrauded by having to pay interest. He pays it *ex proventu*, that is to say, out of the gain that he makes with the money.

Calvin would have the whole question judged in a reasonable spirit, and he illustrates in detail by an example, how the lender's claim to interest may, from this point of view, be well grounded.

A rich man who has plenty of landed property and general income, but little ready money, applies for a money loan to one who is far less wealthy, but has more ready money. The lender could use the money to purchase land for himself, or he could request that the land bought with his money be hypothecated to him till the debt is wiped out. If, instead of doing so, he contents himself with the interest, the fruit of the money, how can he be condemned, when the other much harder bargain is regarded as fair? As Calvin vigorously expresses it, that were a childish game to play with God, *"et quid aliud est quam puerorum instar ludere cum Deo, cum de rebus ex verbis nudis, ac non ex eo quod inest in re ipsa judicatur?"**

He concludes then, that the taking of interest cannot be universally condemned. But neither is it to be universally permitted, but only so far as it does not run counter to fairness and charity. The application of this principle necessitates the listing of a number of exceptions in which interest is not to be allowed. The most noteworthy of these are: that no interest should be demanded of persons in urgent need; that due consideration should be shown to the "poor brethren"; that the "welfare of the state" should be considered; and that the maximum rate of interest established by the laws should in no case be exceeded.

As Calvin is the first theologian, so Molinaeus is the first jurist to oppose the canonistic prohibition on theoretical grounds. Both writers agree in their principles, but they differ in their manner of stating them as widely as do their professions. Calvin goes directly to the heart of the matter as he sees it, without bothering to refute secondary objections. His convictions are based on impressions rather than on dialectical argumentation. Molinaeus, on the other hand, is inexhaustible in distinctions and casuistry. He is no less indefatigable than his opponents when he pursues them in all their scholastic turnings and twistings, in

---

* Translators' note: "and what is it but playing, like children, with God, if one's judgment of a thing is based on the bare words, instead of on the nature of the thing itself?"

19

order to confute them formally and point by point. Moreover, although more cautious in expression than the impetuous Calvin, he is quite as frank, pithy, and straightforward.

The principal work of Molinaeus on the subject is the *Tractatus contractuum et usurarum redituumque pecunia constitutorum,*[10] published in 1546. The first part of it shows strong though perhaps accidental resemblance to Calvin's line of argument. After a few introductory definitions, he turns to the examination of the *jus divinum* (the law of God), and finds that the relevant passages of Holy Writ are misinterpreted. They are not intended to forbid the taking of interest in general, but only such interest as violates the laws of charity and brotherly love. And then he, too, introduces the effective illustration used by Calvin of the rich man who purchases land with borrowed money.[11] But as he proceeds, his reasoning becomes much fuller than that of Calvin. He points out in detail (*No. 75*) that in almost every loan there is involved an *interesse* of the creditor—some injury caused or some use foregone —the compensation for which is just and economically necessary. This compensation, he says, is interest, is *usura,* in the right and proper sense of the word. The laws of Justinian which allow interest, and limit only its amount, are consequently not only not unjust, but actually in the interest of the borrower, inasmuch as the payment of a moderate interest gives him the chance of a greater gain (*No. 76*).

Later (*No. 528 ff.*) Molinaeus reviews the chief arguments of the canonists against interest, and refutes them in detail.

To the old objection of Thomas Aquinas, that the lender who takes interest is either selling the same thing twice, or selling something that has no existence at all (*see foregoing p. 14*), Molinaeus answers that the use of money is a thing independent of the capital sum, and consequently may be sold independently. We must not regard only the first immediate spending of the money as its use. That may consist in the subsequent employment of those goods that are acquired or preserved by means of the borrowed money (*Nos. 510, 530*). It was also maintained that, along with the money itself, its use passed over into the legal property of the borrower, and that he therefore is paying for his own property when he pays interest. To this Molinaeus answers (*No. 530*) that I am quite justified in selling another man's property if it be a debt due me, and that this is exactly the case with loans. "*Usus pecuniae mihi pure a te debitae est mihi pure a te debitus, ergo vel tibi vendere possum.*"*

Finally, to the argument which urges the natural barrenness of money Molinaeus replies (*No. 530*) that the everyday experience of business life shows that the use of any considerable sum of money yields a service of no trifling importance, and that this service, even in legal language, is designated as the "fruit" of money. To argue that money of itself can bring forth no fruit is not to the point, for land, too, brings forth nothing of itself without expense, exertion, and human industry. And

---

* Translators' note: "The use of money which you owe me is simply something I own and can therefore sell to you."

quite in the same way money, when assisted by human effort, brings forth notable fruit. The rest of the polemic against the canonists has little theoretical interest.

On the basis of this comprehensive consideration of the subject, Molinaeus in conclusion formulates his thesis (*No. 535*) as follows: *"First of all, it is necessary and useful that a certain practice of taking interest be retained and permitted . . ."* The contrary opinion, that interest in itself is absolutely reprehensible, is foolish, pernicious, and superstitious (*Stulta illa et non minus perniciosa quam superstitiosa opinio de usura de se absoluta mala*) (*No. 534*).

In these words Molinaeus had taken a stand most violently opposed to the church's doctrine. To modify his position in some degree, (a Catholic might find it very advisable to do so from purely material considerations), he made certain practical concessions without, however, yielding anything in principle. The most important of these is that, on grounds of expediency, and on account of prevailing abuses, he acquiesces in the church's prohibition (as appropriate to the day and age) of interest pure and simple in the shape of undisguised usury, wishing to retain only the milder and more humane practice of the purchase of annuities which, however, he rightly looks on as a genuine species of interest transaction.[12]

Calvin and Molinaeus remained for a long time entirely alone in their position, and the reason for this is quite apparent. To pronounce that to be right which the church, the law, and the world of scholars had condemned with one voice, and opposed with arguments drawn from every conceivable source, required not only a rare independence of intellect but an equally rare strength of character with the fortitude to risk suspicion and persecution. The fate of the leaders of this movement showed clearly enough that these consequences did actually follow. Calvin, of course, aroused the ire of the Catholic world for additional and quite different causes. But Molinaeus, too, had much to suffer, for he himself was exiled, and his book, carefully and moderately though it was written, was put on the Index. Nevertheless the book had marked success, was read, quoted, and published again and again, and so scattered a seed destined to bear fruit in the end.[13]

Aside from the immediate disciples of Calvin, who naturally agreed with the views of their master, there were few writers in the sixteenth century who ventured to argue in favor of interest on economic grounds. Among them may be specially mentioned the humanist Camerarius,[14] Bornitz,[15] and above all, Besold.

Besold argues ably and at length against the canonistic doctrine in the dissertations entitled *Quaestiones aliquot de usuris,* (1598), the work with which he began his very prolific career as a writer.[16] He ascribes the origin of interest to the institutions of trade and commerce, in which money ceases to be barren. And as every man must be allowed to pursue his own advantage, so far as that is possible without injury to others, natural justice is not inconsistent with the taking of interest. Like Molinaeus, whom he often quotes with approval, he adduces on behalf of loan interest the analogy between such a loan for interest and hire for pay. A loan at interest is related to a loan not at interest exactly as any perfectly permissible hiring for a consideration is related to a borrowing without any obligation to make payment (*commodatum*). He is very keenly aware that the rate of loan interest must at all times correspond to the rate of originary interest, the latter, indeed, being the basis and the source of the former. And he maintains that in those places where the use of money customarily results in greater gain, a higher limit of loan interest should be allowed (*p. 32 f.*). Finally, he is as little impressed by the passages in Holy Writ which have been interpreted as forbidding interest (*p. 38 ff.*), as by the arguments of the "philosophers," for he feels that the latter must appear quite untenable to anyone who looks at the matter from the proper standpoint (*p. 32*).

From this short abstract it will be seen that Besold is a frank and able follower of Molinaeus. As his numerous quotations[17] show, he took the better part of his doctrine from Molinaeus, but it would be difficult to find in his writings any indication that he had progressed beyond the point attained by his exemplar.[18]

This is true to even greater degree of the great English philosopher Bacon, who wrote on the subject almost contemporaneously with Besold. He is not misled by the old ideas of the "unnaturalness" of interest. He has enough intellectual freedom and sufficient grasp of the needs of economic life to weigh impartially its advantages and disadvantages, and to pronounce interest an economic necessity. Nevertheless he tolerates it only on the ground of expediency. "Since of necessity men must give and take money on loan, and since they are so hard of heart (sintque tam duro corde) that they will not lend it otherwise, there is nothing for it but that interest should be permitted."[19]

4. Victory in The Netherlands of School of Economists Who Approved of Interest

IN THE course of the seventeenth century the new doctrine made far greater advances, and the earliest of these were in the Netherlands. There the conditions were peculiarly favorable to its further development. During the political and religious troubles which prevailed when the young free state was born, men had learned to emancipate themselves from the shackles of a slavish subservience to authority. There was the additional circumstance that the decaying theory of the fathers of the church and of the scholasticists nowhere came into sharper conflict with the needs of actual life than in the Netherlands, where a highly developed economy had created for itself a complete system of credit and banking. There, consequently, transactions involving interest were common and regular; and there, moreover, temporal legislation had long since yielded to the pressure of practice and allowed the taking of interest.[20] In such circumstances a theory which pronounced interest to be a godless defrauding of the debtor was unnatural, and inevitably doomed to a premature end.

Hugo Grotius may be regarded as a forerunner of the change. In his attitude towards our subject he is peculiarly Janus-faced. On the one hand, he clearly recognizes as untenable the position taken by those who base their theory of interest on natural right, as the canonists had done. He sees no force in the argument of the barrenness of money, for "houses also, and other things barren by nature, have been made productive by the skill of man." To the argument that the use of money, consisting as it does in its being spent, cannot be separated from money itself, and therefore cannot be paid for independently, he finds an apt rejoinder and, speaking generally, the arguments which represent interest as contrary to natural right appear to him "not of a kind to compel assent" (*non talia ut assensum extorqueant*). But, on the other hand, he considers the passages in Holy Writ forbidding interest to be undoubtedly binding. So that in his conclusions he remains, in principle at least, on the side of the canonists. But in practice he does recede from the principle of the prohibition of interest by allowing and approving many kinds of compensation for loss, for renunciation of profit, for lender's trouble and risk,[21] compensations that might be termed akin to interest. And so Grotius vacillates between the old and the new doctrine.[22]

Undecided views like his were speedily left behind. In a few years the economists openly threw overboard not only the rationalistic basis of the prohibition as he had done, but the prohibition itself. The decisive point was reached shortly before the year 1640. As if the age-old barriers of restraint had all been torn down in one day, there burst forth a perfect flood of writings in which interest was defended with the utmost vigor, and the flood did not abate till the principle of interest, in the Netherlands at least, had conquered. In this abundant literature the first place, both in time and in rank, belongs to that of the celebrated Claudius Salmasius. Of his writings, begun in 1638 and continued at short intervals, the most important are: *De usuris,* 1638; *de modo usurarum,* 1639; *de foenore trapezitico,* 1640. To these may be added a shorter controversial work which appeared under the pseudonym of Alexius a Massalia, and which was entitled, *Diatriba de mutuo, mutuum non esse alienationem,* (1640).[23] These writings, almost by themselves, determined the direction and substance of the theory of interest for more than a hundred years, and even in the doctrine of today, as we shall see, we may recognize many traces of them. His doctrine therefore deserves thorough consideration.

The views of Salmasius on interest are summarized most concisely in the eighth chapter of his book, *De usuris.* He begins by developing his own theory of interest. Interest is a payment for the use of sums of money lent. Lending belongs to that class of legal transactions in which the use of a thing is made over by its owner to another person. If the thing is not perishable, and if the use that is transferred is not to be paid for, the legal transaction is a *commodatum;* if it is to be paid for, the transaction is a *locatio conductio.* If it is a perishable or a fungible thing, and the use is not to be paid for, it is a loan bearing no interest (*mutuum*); if to be paid for, it is a loan at interest (*foenus*).

The interest-bearing loan accordingly stands to the loan which bears no interest in exactly the same relation as the *locatio* to the *commodatum,* and is just as legitimate.[24]

The only conceivable ground for judging otherwise about the propriety of payment in the case of the *commodatum* (where a non-perishable good, such as a house is lent) than about a *mutuum* might be the different nature of the "use" in the two cases. In the latter case a perishable or fungible good is transferred and the use consists in complete consumption, and it might be objected that in such a case the use of a thing could not be separated from the thing itself. But to this Salmasius has two answers. In the first place, such an argument would lead to the condemnation and abolition of the non-interest-bearing loan as well, inasmuch as it is impossible, in the case of a perishable thing, to transfer a "use" whose existence is denied, even if *no* interest is asked for it. In the second place, the perishable nature of loaned goods rather constitutes an additional reason why the loan should be paid for. For in the case of hire (*locatio*) the lender can take back his property at any moment, because he remains the owner of it. In the case of the loan he cannot do so, because his property is destroyed in its consumption. Consequently the lender of money suffers delays, anxieties, and losses, and by reason of these the claim to compensation in the case of the loan is even more consistent with fairness, than it is in that of the *commodatum.*

After thus stating his own position Salmasius devoted himself to refuting the arguments of his opponents point by point. As we read these refutations we begin to understand how Salmasius succeeded so brilliantly in doing what Molinaeus a hundred years before had failed to do, namely to convince his contemporaries. They are extremely effective pieces of writing, veritable gems of sparkling polemic. The materials for them, it must be confessed, had in great part been provided by his predecessors, especially by Molinaeus.[25] But the happy manner in which Salmasius employs these materials, and the many pithy sallies with which he enriches them, places his polemic far above anything that had gone before.

It may not be unwelcome to some of my readers to have a few detailed examples of Salmasius's style. They will serve to give a more accurate idea of the spirit in which people were accustomed to deal with our problem in the seventeenth century, and far into the eighteenth, and to make the reader better acquainted with a writer who is today very often quoted but extremely seldom read. I therefore give in footnote 26 in his own words one or two passages from the polemic.[26]

What follows has less bearing on the history of theory. First comes a long-winded, and, it must be confessed, for all its subtlety a very lame attempt to prove that in the loan there is no alienation of the thing lent —a subject to which the whole *Diatriba de mutuo* is devoted. Then follows the reply to some of the arguments of the canonists relating to fairness and expediency. One such argument is that it is unfair to the borrower, who immediately assumes the risk of the principal sum lent him, to burden him with interest in addition, and to make him hand over the fruit of the money to another who takes no risk. Then there is the contention that usury would lead to the neglect of agriculture, commerce, and the other *bonae artes,* to the injury of the common weal, and so on. In replying to this latter argument Salmasius gets an opportunity to commend the virtues of competition. The more capitalists there are, the better; their competition will lower the rate of interest. Then, from the ninth chapter onwards, with an extraordinary display of intelligence and erudition, with many passages full of striking eloquence, but also with endless prolixity, comes the refutation of the argument that interest is "unnatural." Quite at the end (*De usuris, chap.* xx), the question is finally put whether interest, thus sanctioned by the *jus naturale,* is also consistent with the *jus divinum,* and this naturally is answered in the affirmative.

Those are the essential features of Salmasius's doctrine. Not only did it mark an advance, but it remained for a long time the very forefront of that advance. For more than a hundred years further development was confined to its adoption in wider circles, the repetition of it with more or less skillful variations, and the adaptation of its arguments to the fashion of the time. But there was no essential advance on Salmasius till the time of Smith and Turgot.

As the number of those who accepted the doctrine represented by Salmasius increased, so did the number of those who adhered to the canonistic doctrine diminish. This defection, as may be easily understood, went on more rapidly in Protestant countries and in those speaking Germanic languages, and progressed more slowly in countries purely Catholic and in those speaking the Romance tongues.

In the Netherlands, as I have already said, the works of Salmasius were almost immediately followed by a whole series of writings of similar tenor. As early a date as 1640 marks the appearance of works of Kloppenburg, Boxhorn, Maresius, Graswinckel.[27] A little later, about 1644, the *Tafelhalterstreit*[28] gave rise to a fiery feud between the two parties, and in 1658 this ended in a practical victory for the supporters of interest. Within the next few years, the renowned and influential lawyer Gerhard Noodt rose to a position of special prominence among the increasingly numerous adherents of the new theory. In his *Libri tres de foenore et usuris,* he discusses the whole question of interest very thoroughly, displaying great knowledge of his subject and its literature.[29] After that there are fewer and fewer expressions of hostility to interest, especially from professional men; still, they do occur sporadically right on into the second half of the eighteenth century.[30]

5. *Gradual Spread of Ideas Favorable to Interest in Germany*

IN GERMANY, where political economy during the seventeenth and even the eighteenth century showed only meager development, the Salmasian doctrine gained acceptance but slowly and quite unsensationally, nothing being added in the course of that acceptance. It was quite obvious that practice was the force to which the revolution in opinion on German soil was due. Theory meanwhile lagged clumsily behind the reform in public opinion and in legislation. Half a century before the first German jurist, in the person of Besold, had rendered a verdict in favor of interest, the taking of interest, or at least the demanding of a fixed *interesse* arranged in advance (which in practice came to the same thing), had been pronounced permissible in Germany by the law of many localities.[31] And when in 1654 German imperial legislation followed this example,[32] few theorists had yet gone over to the side of Besold and Salmasius. As late as 1629 it was possible for an Adam Contzen to demand that lenders at interest should be punished by criminal law like thieves, and that all Jews should be hunted out of the country as *venenatae bestiae*.[33] Not till the end of the seventeenth century do the theorists begin to become more generally convinced of the legitimacy of interest. When such prominent men as Pufendorf[34] and Leibnitz[35] espoused the new doctrine they hastened its victory, and in the course of the eighteenth century it was at last gradually removed from the field of controversy.

That is the position we find it occupying in the pages of the two great cameralists who flourished at the end of our period, Justi and Sonnenfels. Justi's *Staatswirtschaft*[36] does not contain a single line relating to the great question on which in former times so many bulky volumes had been written. Neither, to be sure, is there a single line that could be taken as setting forth a theory of interest. He tacitly assumes it to be a matter of course that interest is paid for a loan; and if in one or two short remarks (*Vol. I, Sec. 268*) he inveighs against usury, he understands by that—still tacitly—only excessive interest.

Sonnenfels is not so silent on the subject as Justi. But even he, in the earlier editions of his *Handlungswissenschaft*[37] never once touches on the controversy as to the theoretical legitimacy of interest. In the fifth edition (published in 1787) he refers to it, indeed, but in the tone which one usually adopts towards issues long since settled. In a mere footnote on p. 496, he dismisses with a few resolute words the prohibition of the canonists, ridicules their absurd proofs, and finds it preposterous to forbid 6% interest on money, when 100% can be made if the money is changed into commodities.

Sonnenfels's contempt for the canonistic doctrine carries all the more weight, since he has nothing good to say of interest in other respects. Influenced by Forbonnais, he finds that interest originates in a damming of the circulation of money by hoarding capitalists, out of whose hands it can be attracted only by paying tribute in the shape of interest.[38] He ascribes to it many injurious effects, claiming that it makes commodities dear, reduces the profits of industriousness, and allows the owner of money to share in those profits.[39] Indeed, in one place he speaks of the capitalists as that class of persons "who do no work, and draw their nourishment from the sweat of those who do."[40]

But side by side with expressions such as these we encounter the accepted Salmasian doctrine. In one place, quite in the spirit of Salmasius, Sonnenfels adduces as arguments for the capitalists' claim, the deprivation of their money, their risk, and the gain they might have made by the purchase of productive things.[41] In another place he recognizes that a lowering of the legal rate is not an effective means of controlling the evil of high interest.[42] Then again he finds that, since the above mentioned conditions which determine interest are variable, a fixed legal rate is generally unsuitable as being either superfluous or harmful.[43]

The double circumstance of Justi's complete silence and Sonnenfels's inconsistent loquacity on the same subject seems to me to be a very characteristic proof of two things. The first is, that when these men wrote, the Salmasian doctrine had already secured so firm a footing in Germany that even the writers who felt the most hostile towards interest could no longer think of going back to the strict canonistic standpoint. The second is, conversely, that up to that time the acceptance of the Salmasian doctrine had been unaccompanied by any further development of it.

6. Development of Ideas on Interest in England

ENGLAND appears to have been the country where the throwing off of the canonistic doctrine was attended with the least literary excitement. Because of the rapid rise of its commerce and industry, its economy was at an early date amenable to the institution of interest and its legislation had early given way to the needs of industrial life. Henry VIII had by 1545 abrogated the prohibition of interest, and replaced it by a simple legal rate. For a short time, it is true, the prohibition was reimposed under Edward VI, but in 1571 it was once more repealed by Queen Elizabeth, and this time for ever.[44] And so the theorctical question whether loan interest was justifiable or not was settled as a matter of practice before there was any economic literature, and when one at last emerged, the question, being settled, was of little concern. All the more, however, was attention riveted upon a new controversial question raised by the change in legislation. That was the question whether there should be a legal rate at all, and if so, what that rate should be. These circumstances have left their stamp on England's interest literature of the seventeenth and eighteenth centuries. We find numerous and heated discussions as to the height of the interest rate, as to its advantages and disadvantages, and as to the advisability or inadvisability, of limiting it by law. But they only rarely touched upon the question of its justifiability, and then as a rule, merely in cursory fashion. One or two short samples of this stage in the development of the problem will suffice.

Mention has already been made of Bacon, who flourished very shortly after the age of the prohibition, and who declared himself in favor of interest for very matter-of-fact, practical reasons.[45] Some twenty years later even Sir Thomas Culpeper, a violent opponent of interest, does not venture to put forward the canonistic arguments under his own name, but characteristically passes over the subject with the remark that he leaves it to the theologians to prove the injustice of interest, and that he himself intends only to show how much evil it causes.[46] And then he goes on to attack not so much interest in general, as high interest rates only.[47]

In the same way another writer very unfavorably disposed towards interest, a certain Josiah Child, refuses to discuss its justice and simply refers[48] the reader who wishes more information to an older and apparently anonymous work, which had appeared in 1634 under the title of *The English Usurer.* Furthermore, he frequently calls interest the "price of money," and by this definition certainly betrays no deep insight into its nature. He expresses his opinion in passing, that it enriches the creditor at the expense of the debtor, but nevertheless contents himself with pleading for a reduction in the legal rate, not for entire abolition.[49]

His opponent, North, who favors interest, conceives of it, quite in the manner of Salmasius, as a "rent for stock," similar to land rent, but cannot say anything more, in explanation of either of them, than that owners hire out their superfluous land and capital to such as are in need of them.[50]

Petty and Vaughan injected an interesting thought into the discussion by certain remarks casually tossed out, but not carefully carried to a conclusion. Those remarks drew a parallel between interest, which is paid out because of a difference in time, and the premium collected by exchange-brokers, which is paid out because of a difference in place. We shall perceive the same thought making its appearance a hundred years later, and being worked out in greater detail by Galiani and Turgot. In fact, we may say that this thought is the very first hint of an idea which, after still another century, gave rise to a modern theory of interest which ultimately attained a broad and systematic formulation, the so-called "Agio" theory of interest.[51] In this connection it is fitting that we speak at some length of the philosopher, John Locke.

Locke has left a very remarkable tract on the origin of loan interest. He begins with a few propositions that remind one very much of the canonists' standpoint. "Money,"[52] he says, "is a barren thing, and produces nothing, but by compact transfers that profit that was the reward of one man's labour into another man's pocket." Nevertheless Locke finds that loan interest is justified. To prove this, and to bridge over his own paradox, he uses the complete analogy that exists between loan interest and land rent. The proximate cause of both is unequal distribution. One has more money than he needs and another has less, and so the former finds a "tenant" for his money[53] just as the landlord finds a tenant for his land, because he has too much land, while the other has too little.

But why does the borrower consent to pay interest for the money lent? Again, for the same reason as the tenant consents to pay rent for the use of land. For money—of course only through the industry of the borrower, as Locke expressly adds—is able, when employed in trade, to "produce" more than 6% for the borrower, just as land, "through the labor of the tenant," is able to produce more fruit than the amount of its rent. Even if the interest which the capitalist draws from the loan is thus to be regarded as the fruit of another man's labor, this is true only to the same degree as it is true of rent. Indeed, it is true to a lesser degree. For the payment of land rent usually leaves the tenant a much smaller proportion of the fruit of his industry than the borrower of money has left over, after paying the interest, out of the income made with the money. And so Locke comes to this conclusion: "Borrowing money upon use is not only, by the necessity of affairs and the constitution of human society, unavoidable to some men; but to receive profit from the loan of money is as equitable and lawful as receiving rent for land, and more tolerable to the borrower, . . ." (*p. 37*).

It can scarcely be maintained that this theory is particularly happy. There is too marked a contrast between its starting point and its conclusion. If it be true that loan interest transfers the hard-earned wage of the man who works into the pocket of another man who does nothing, and whose money besides is a "barren thing," it is absolutely inconsistent to say that loan interest is nevertheless "equitable and lawful." There is undoubtedly an analogy between interest and land rent, but this could logically have led only to the conclusion that land rent is as much to be condemned as is interest. Locke's theory would have presented sufficient support for such an extension of a condemnation of interest to a condemnation of ground rent, since he expressly declares rent also to be the fruit of another man's industry. But with Locke the legitimacy of rent appears to have been beyond question.

But, however unsatisfactory Locke's theory of interest may be, there is *one* circumstance at any rate that confers on it an important interest for the history of theory. In the background stands the proposition that human labor produces all wealth. In the present case Locke has not so much expressed the proposition as made use of it, and has, indeed, made a rather unhappy use of it. But in another place he has given it clear utterance where he says, "For it is labor indeed that puts the difference of value on everything."[54] We shall see how important a bearing this proposition was to have on the later development of the interest problem.[55]

A certain affinity to Locke's conception of loan interest is shown somewhat later by Sir James Steuart. "The interest," he writes, "they pay for the money borrowed is inconsiderable when compared with the value *created* (as it were) by the proper employment of *their time and talents.*"

"If it be said, that this is a vague assertion, supported by no proof, I answer, that the *value of a man's work* may be estimated *by the proportion between the manufacture* when brought to market *and the first matter.*"[56]

The words I have emphasized indicate that Steuart, like Locke, regards the whole increment of value got by production as the product of the borrower's labor, and loan interest, therefore, as a fruit of that labor.

If, however, both Locke and Steuart were quite uncertain as to the nature of that which we call today the originary interest harvested by the borrower, they were far from making any mistake about the fact that loan interest has its origin and its foundation in this originary interest. Thus Steuart in one place writes, "In proportion, therefore, to the advantages to be reaped from borrowed money, the borrowers offer more or less for the use of it."[57]

Generally speaking, in England the literature on the subject took great pains to discuss the connection between loan interest and originary interest. In doing so it certainly did not surpass the Salmasian doctrine in clearness as to principles, but it did enrich it by extending the knowledge of details. A favorite subject of inquiry was whether a high loan interest is the cause or the effect of a high originary interest. Hume comes to the decision that they exert reciprocal influence. "It is needless," he says, "to inquire which of these circumstances, to wit, *low interest or low profits,** is the cause and which the effect. They both arise from an extensive commerce, and mutually forward each other. No man will accept of low profits where he can have high interest; and no man will accept of low interest where he can have high profits."[58]

Of more value than this somewhat superficial opinion is another discovery associated with the name of Hume. It was he who first clearly distinguished the concept of money from that of capital, and showed that the interest rate in a country does not depend on the amount of currency that the country possesses, but on the amount of its riches and stocks.[59] But it was not till a later period that this important discovery was put to good use in the investigation of the source of originary interest.

How strange the once widespread doctrine of the canonists had in the meantime become to the seasoned English businessman of the eighteenth century may be seen by the manner in which Bentham could treat the subject, in his *Defense of Usury*. It was not published, to be sure, until 1787, but it should be noted that there is no longer any serious attempt to justify the taking of interest. The arguments of the ancient writers and of the canonists are mentioned only because they offer a welcome butt for his witticisms. Aristotle, as the originator of the argument of the sterility of money, is the target of these bantering words, "Notwithstanding the enormous pains he had bestowed on the subject of generation, he had never been able to discover in any piece of money any organs for generating any other such piece" (*Letter*. x).[60]

7. Backwardness of the Romance Countries

ITALY stood immediately under the eye of the Roman Church, but was also the first country in Europe to know the full flower of a lively trade and commerce. It was therefore inevitably the first to find the pressure of the canonistic prohibition unbearable. Its reaction to that

* Translators' note: The older British and especially the classical economists applied the term "profit" to the gross difference between the price at which a commodity is sold and the costs expended in its production, exclusive of interest on the capital invested.

Böhm-Bawerk and later economists conceive of this excess of gross receipts over expenditures as a complex which includes the remuneration for the entrepreneur's own labor employed in the process of production, interest on the capital invested, and entrepreneurial profit proper. See Böhm-Bawerk's statement in Note 57 to Chapter XII.

prohibition gave due weight to both demands arising from its dual obligations. For while it is true that nowhere in Europe was the prohibition of interest in actual practice more completely disregarded, it is also true that nowhere in Europe was the day so long deferred when the theorists ventured openly to oppose the church's statute.

Everything that could be done to evade the ostensibly valid prohibition was done, and it seems that almost anything could so be done, that was necessary for actual practice. The most convenient forms of evasion were offered by the traffic in bills of exchange—a traffic which had its home in Italy—and by the stipulation of *interesse* as "indemnification." Temporal legislation offered ready and willing assistance to such evasion from a very early period by allowing interest to be contractually arranged in advance, at a fixed rate or percentage on the capital lent. The only limitation consisted in fixing a maximum rate which was not to be exceeded.[61]

On the other hand, no Italian writer appears to have made any open attack on the theory of the canonistic doctrine before the eighteenth century. Galiani in 1750 mentions Salmasius as the first to make a complete statement of doctrine in favor of interest. And the only mention of the subject he can find in Italian literature previous to that time, is the quarrel which had shortly before flared up between the Marquis Maffei and the preaching monk, Fra Daniello Concina.[62] When other prominent writers of the same period cite notable predecessors, they mention principally Salmasius, and after him some other foreigners, such as Locke, Hume, Montesquieu and Forbonnais; but the earliest name among native writers to be mentioned is that of Marquis Maffei.[63] In Italy too, then, it was none other than Salmasius who became the pioneer among writers to champion interest.

The tardy acceptance which his doctrine met in that country does not appear to have been attended by any special enrichment. There is only one writer who can be excepted from this criticism, and that is Galiani. But he deals with the question of the nature and legitimacy of loan interest in a way that is altogether peculiar.

If interest, he says,[64] really were what it is usually taken to be, that is, a gain or an advantage which the lender obtains with his money, then it would indeed be reprehensible, for "any gain, be it great or small, that is yielded by naturally barren money, is objectionable; nor can anyone call such a gain the fruit of exertion, for the one who puts forth the exertion is the borrower, not the lender" (*p. 244*).

But interest, Galiani goes on to say, is not a true surplus at all; it is only a supplement which is needed to equalize service and counterservice. As a matter of justice, service and counter-service should be of equal value. Since value is the relation in which things stand to our needs, we should be quite mistaken, were we to seek for such an equivalence in an equality of weight, or in number of pieces, or in external form. What is required is simply an equality of use. Now in this respect present and future sums of money, though equal in amount, still are not equal in value just as in bill transactions equally large sums of money are not of equal value at different places. And just as the charge for exchange (*cambio*),

31

notwithstanding that it seems to be a premium (*soprapiù*), is in truth an equalization, which when added either to the local or to the foreign money, establishes the equality of real value between the two, in just the same way loan interest is nothing but the equalization of the difference between the value of present and future sums of money (*p. 243 ff.*).

In this interesting idea Galiani has hit on a new method of justifying loan interest, and one which relieves him of the necessity of following a certain doubtful line of argument that his predecessors had been obliged to take. Salmasius and his followers, to avoid the reproach of destroying the equality between service and counter-service, had been obliged to attempt to prove that in consumable goods, (possibly in articles actually already consumed at the beginning of the loan period), there is an enduring use which may be separately transferred, and for which a separate remuneration, namely interest, is rightly claimed. This line of reasoning, always somewhat embarrassing, was rendered superfluous by the new turn which Galiani now gave to the argument.

But unfortunately the inference which Galiani draws from this idea is very unsatisfactory. The only reason why present sums of money are regularly more valuable than future sums, he says, is the difference in the degree of security. A claim to future payment of a sum of money is exposed to many dangers, and on that account is less valued than an equally large present sum. In so far as interest is paid to balance these dangers, it appears in the light of an insurance premium. Galiani gives this conception very strong expression by speaking in one place of the "so-called fruit of money" as a price of heartbeats (*prezzo del batticuore*) (*p. 247*); and at another time he says in so many words that that thing called the fruit of money might be more properly called the price of insurance (*prezzo dell' assicurazione*) (*p. 252*). This was of course a complete misunderstanding of the nature of loan interest.

The way in which later Italian authors of the eighteenth century treated the interest problem is less worthy of notice. Even the more prominent among them, such as Genovesi[65] and Beccaria,[66] as also those who wrote monographs on the subject, like Vasco,[67] follow for the most part in the tracks of the Salmasian doctrine, which had by that time become traditional.

The most worthy of mention among those is Beccaria. He draws a sharp distinction between *interesse* and *usura*. The former is the immediate use of a thing, the latter is the use of a use (*l'utilità dell' utilità*). All goods render an immediate use (*interesse*). The special *interesse* of money consists of the use which may be rendered by the goods it represents, for money is the common measure and representative of the value of all other goods. Since, in particular, every sum of money represents or may represent, a definite piece of land, it follows that the *interesse* of the money is represented by the annual return of that land. Consequently it varies with the amount of this return, and the average rate of money-*interesse* is equal to the average return of the land (*p. 116 ff.*).

In this analysis the word *interesse* evidently means what we should call originary interest, and in it accordingly we can recognize an attempt, although a very primitive one, to explain the existence and amount of originary interest by the possibility of a purchase of land. As we shall see later, however, the same thought had already, some years before, been accorded much fuller treatment by another writer.

In one place Beccaria also touches on the influence of time, first advanced by Galiani, and speaks of the analogy between exchange interest, which is an *interesse* of place, and loan interest, which is an *interesse* of time (*p. 122*), but he passes over it much more cursorily.

Catholic France in the meantime lagged behind, both in theory and practice. Its laws against interest enjoyed for centuries the reputation of being the severest in Europe. At a time when it had become common practice in other countries either to allow the taking of interest quite openly, or to allow it under the very transparent disguise of previously arranged *interesse,* Louis XIV thought fit to renew the existing prohibition, and to extend it in such a way that even interest for commercial debts was forbidden,[68] Lyons being the only market exempted. A century later, when in other countries the long obsolete prohibitions of interest were scoffed at in the tone of a Sonnenfels or a Bentham they remained in force and in baleful activity among the law courts of France. It was only in the year 1789, when so many other institutions that still breathed the spirit of the middle ages were cleared away, that this one, too, was abolished. By a law dated October 12, 1789 the prohibition of interest was formally rescinded, and in its place a maximum interest rate of 5% was enacted.

French theory, like French legislation, adhered most tenaciously to the strict canonistic point of view. We have already seen how little success Molinaeus had in the middle of the sixteenth century. At the end of that century a writer as enlightened in other respects as Jean Bodinus finds the laws against interest fully justified; he praises the wisdom of the legislators who enact them, and considers it safest to extirpate interest root and branch (*usurarum non modo radices sed etiam fibras omnes amputare*).[69] In the seventeenth century, it is true, the Frenchman Salmasius wrote brilliantly on the side of interest, but he wrote outside of France. In the course of the eighteenth century the number of advocates of interest increases. A writer by the name of Law already contends for the abrogation of all restrictions on interest transactions, including the fixed rate.[70] Melon pronounces interest an absolute social necessity, and leaves it to the theologians to reconcile their moral scruples with that necessity.[71] Montesquieu declares that lending a man money without interest is admittedly a very good deed, but it is one that can only be a matter of religious consideration, and not of civil law.[72] But there were still writers who opposed such ideas, and contended for the old strict doctrine.

Among these late champions of the canonistic tenets there are two who are particularly prominent, the highly esteemed jurist Pothier and the physiocrat Mirabeau.

Pothier succeeded in culling the most tenable arguments from the chaotic repertory of the canonists, and working them up with great skill and acumen into a doctrine in which they really became very effective. The gist of it is contained in that characteristic passage which has already attracted the attention of several writers on our subject.[73]

Pothier was seconded with more zeal than success by Mirabeau, the author of *Philosophie rurale*.[74] Mirabeau's lucubrations on interest are among the most confused that have ever been written on this subject. He is a fanatical opponent of loan interest, and inexhaustible in points to be urged against it. He presents the argument, among others, that there is no possible justification for lending out money at interest. In the first place, there is no natural use for money, it is merely a symbol. "But to derive a profit from its merely *representative* character means searching in a mirror for the figure that is reflected there." Nor can the possessors of money avail themselves of the argument that they must live on the proceeds of their money. Their recourse is merely to convert their money into other goods and then gain their living from hiring out those goods! And finally he argues that there is no wear and tear in the case of money, as there is with houses, furniture and the like. Therefore a charge for wear and tear would also be unjust.[75]

Probably the reader will think these arguments weak enough. But Mirabeau, in his blind zeal, sinks even lower. He cannot help recognizing that the debtor, by his use of the money (*emploi*), is able to obtain the means to pay interest for the capital borrowed, but even this he turns into an argument against interest. He points out that the borrower must always suffer injury, because it is impossible to establish an equality between interest and *emploi*. One does not know how much agriculture will yield to the borrowing farmer. Unforeseen accidents happen, and on that account (!) the borrower will always (!) lose.[76] But there is more to come! In one place he notes the very natural fact that any private person prefers taking interest to paying it. From this he deduces, *in all seriousness,* that the paying of interest must be harmful to the borrower![77]

Fortified by reasoning like this, Mirabeau is rigorous indeed in his condemnation of money interest. "All in all," he says,[78] "money interest ruins society by putting incomes into the hands of people who are neither owners of land, nor producers, nor industrial workers, and these people can be compared only to hornets, who live by plundering the hoards of the bees of society."

But for all that, Mirabeau cannot deny that interest is justified in certain cases. Sorely against his inclination, therefore, he is compelled to violate the principle of the prohibition in favor of a few exceptions, the selection of which is based on quite arbitrary and untenable distinctions.[79]

Seldom can there have been a more rewarding task than was the refutation of this doctrine in the second half of the eighteenth century. Long since a prey to internal decay, detested by some and derided by others, forced to seek support in such pitiful scientific props, this theory had long outlived its day, and now lingered on into a later age, like a crumbling ruin. This highly gratifying task was taken up by Turgot, and performed with a skill which was as remarkable as its results were brilliant. His *Mémoire sur les prêts d'argent*[80] is a worthy companion-piece to Salmasius's writings on usury. It is true that the research economist of today will find in his reasoning some good arguments, and not a few bad ones. But, good and bad alike, they are presented with so much intelligence and acumen, with such rhetorical and dialectical skill, and with such strikingly turned phrasing, that we can easily understand how the effect on his times could have been nothing less than triumphant.

As the charm of his work lies not so much in the ideas themselves —which for the most part coincide with the traditional arguments of his predecessors—as in the charming way in which they are put, it would repay us to go thoroughly into the contents of the *Mémoire* only if a great deal of it were reproduced in his own words, which space forbids. I shall restrict myself, therefore, to bringing out some of the more striking features of Turgot's treatment.

The weightiest justification of interest, in his opinion, is the right of property which the creditor has in his own money. By virtue thereof he has an "inviolable" right to dispose of his money as he will, and to impose such conditions on its alienation and hire as seem advisable to him, such as the payment of interest (*Sec. 23 f.*). This is an obviously distorted argument which, if it proved the legitimacy of interest at all, could just as well be used to justify a usurious interest of 100%.

Turgot dismisses the argument based on the barrennness of money with the same arguments as those advanced by his predecessors (*Sec. 25*).

He gives special attention to Pothier's argument quoted above. Pothier's thesis is that, in justice, service and counter-service should be equal to each other, and that this is not true of a loan at interest. Turgot answers by saying that objects which are exchanged freely and without fraud or force always have, in a certain sense, equal value. To the vexatious argument that, in the case of a perishable thing, it is not possible to conceive of any use separate from the thing itself, he answers by charging his opponents with legalistic hairsplitting and insufferable metaphysical abstraction, and Turgot draws the old and favorite analogy between the hiring of money and some durable thing like a diamond. "What!" he says, "Am I to pay for the trifling use that I make of a piece of furniture or a trinket, and then be told that it is a crime to charge me anything for the immense advantage that I get from the use of a sum of money for the same length of time? And all because the subtle intellect of a lawyer can separate the use of a thing from the thing itself in one case, and not in the other! That is really too ridiculous!" (*P. 128.*)

But a moment later Turgot himself resorts to metaphysical abstraction and legalistic hairsplitting. To refute the argument that the debtor becomes a proprietor of the borrowed money, and that its use consequently belongs to him, he invents a property in the value of the money, and distinguishes it from the property in the piece of metal. The latter, he admits, passes over to the debtor, but the former, he claims, remains with the creditor.

Turgot concludes with some very remarkable passages in which he follows Galiani's example by emphasizing the influence of time on the valuation of goods. In one place he draws the parallel already familiar to us between exchanges and loans. Just as in exchange transactions we give less money in one place to receive a greater sum in another place, so in loan transactions we give less money at one point in time to receive more money at another point in time. The reason for both phenomena is that the difference of time, like that of place, produces a real difference in the value of money (*Sec. 23*). On another occasion he alludes to the universally recognized difference that exists between the value of a present sum and the value of a sum obtainable only at a future period (*Sec. 27*). And a little later he exclaims, "If these gentlemen suppose that a sum of 1000 francs and a promise of 1000 francs possess exactly the same value, they are making a still more absurd supposition, for if these two things were of equal value, why should any one borrow at all?"

Unfortunately, however, Turgot has not followed out this pregnant idea. It is, I might say, strewn in among his other arguments, without having any organic connection with them. Properly speaking, it really contradicts them. For if only interest and the replacement of capital together constitute the equivalent of capital that was lent, the interest is then part of a whole which is equivalent to the principle sum. In that case, how can it be a payment for a separate use of the principal sum, as Turgot has just taken so much trouble to prove?

We may look on Turgot's controversy with Pothier as the closing act of the three hundred years' war which jurisprudence and economics had waged against the old canonistic doctrine of interest. After Turgot that doctrine disappeared from the sphere of economics. Within the sphere of theology it dragged out a semblance of life for some twenty years longer, until finally, in our own century, even that came to an end. When the Roman Penitentiary* pronounced the taking of interest to be allowable, even without any peculiar title, the church itself had confirmed the defeat of its erstwhile doctrine.[81]

8. An Appraisal

LET us pause for a moment and look back appraisingly over the period we have just reviewed. What are its results? What progress did science make during this period towards the elucidation of the interest problem?

The ancients and the canonists had said, "Loan interest is an unjust defrauding of the borrower by the lender, for money is barren, and, furthermore, there is no special 'use' of money which the lender may justly sell for a separate remuneration." This was contradicted by

---

* Translators' note: In the Roman Catholic Church the Penitentiary was a court under a cardinal who was appointed by the Pope and who bore the title Grand Penitentiary. This court examined cases of conscience and rendered decisions.

the new doctrine which said, "Loan interest is just, for in the first place, money is *not* barren because, when properly employed, it is capable of producing a gain, the prospect of which the lender renounces in favor of the borrower; and in the second place, there *is* a use of capital which is separable from capital itself, and which may be sold separately from it."

Let us disregard for the time being the latter more formal point, for it will come up again later in another connection. The central idea of the new doctrine is the suggestion that capital produces fruits for him who employs it. After an immense expenditure of ingenuity, dialectics, polemics, and verbiage, there emerges from the new doctrine a thought which is basically the same idea that Adam Smith, in his wonderfully simple way, expressed shortly afterwards in the few words that contain his solution of the whole question as to whether interest is justifiable or not. "As something can everywhere be made by the use of money, something ought everywhere to be paid for the use of it."[82] Translated into our modern terminology, this idea would run, *"There is loan interest because there is originary interest."*

What the theory of Salmasius and his followers amounts to then is essentially this, that they explain contract or loan interest *by establishing the fact of the existence of originary interest.*

How much did the elucidation of the interest problem gain by this? That the gain was not inconsiderable is attested by the fact that the intellectual labor of centuries was needed to secure credence for the new doctrine, in the face of hostile impressions and prejudices. But just as certain is it that, when this explanation was given, much remained still to be done. The problem of interest was not solved, its solution was only postponed. To the question, "Why does the lender get from his loaned capital a permanent income not due to work?" the answer was given, "Because he could have obtained it if he had employed the capital himself." But why could he have obtained this income himself? This question obviously required an answer before any progress could be claimed toward a solution of the true origin of interest. But in the period we are discussing, that question not only was not answered, it was not even asked!

All attempts at explanation got as far as the fact that the man who has a capital sum in hand can make a gain with it. But here they go lame. They accept this as a fact, without the slightest attempt at any further explanation of the fact itself; thus Molinaeus, with his proposition that money, assisted by human exertion, brings forth fruit, and with his appeal to everyday experience; thus Salmasius himself, with his delightful plea for the fruitfulness of money, in which, however, he simply invokes the fact without explaining it; and thus, too, even the latest and most advanced economists of the whole period—such men as Locke, Law, Hume, James Steuart, Justi, Sonnenfels. Now and then they advance extremely clear and thorough statements of how loan interest is bound to emerge from the possibility of a gain, and how in the amount of that gain it must find the measure of its own amount.[83] But not one of them ever achieves the question as to the why and wherefore of that originary interest.[84]

What Salmasius and his time achieved for the interest problem can best be evaluated by comparing that problem with the problem of land rent. Salmasius, though badly handicapped by attendant, even if irrelevant circumstances, accomplished for the interest problem the thing which it had never been necessary to accomplish in the case of the land rent problem, just because it was too self-evident. He proved that the lessee pays the stipulated rent because the leasehold yields that rent. But he did not accomplish, and did not attempt to accomplish for the interest problem the one thing that required scientific effort in the case of land rent. He did not explain why the leasehold, even if it remain in the hands of its owner, still yields that rent.

So all that had been accomplished in the period we have just been considering was to drive an advanced outpost back to the main position, as it were. The problem of loan interest is pursued till it coincides with the general problem of interest. But the main position is not captured or even attacked. At the end of the period the heart of the interest problem is virtually untouched.

And yet the period was not quite barren of results with respect to the solution of the chief problem. It at least prepared the way for future research by clearly delineating the objective, originary interest, which had until then been obscured, but which was now brought clearly into view. The fact that every one who works with a capital makes a gain had long been known. But it was a long time before any one clearly distinguished the nature of this gain, and there was a tendency to ascribe the whole of it to the entrepreneur's activity. Thus Locke himself regards the interest which the borrower pays to the lender as the "fruit of another man's labor," and though he concedes that the borrowed money employed in business may produce fruit, he expressly ascribes the possibility of this to the exertion of the borrower. Now in the course of justifying loan interest, there had developed a tendency to lay more stress on the influence of capital in the production of such "fruits." It was, therefore, inevitable that it would eventually be clearly recognized that a part of the entrepreneur's income constituted a type of income *sui generis,* one to be strictly differentiated from the product of his labor, in other words, a genuine yield derived from capital. The first stirrings of a recognition of this thought are discernible in the writings of Molinaeus and Salmasius; its complete acknowledgment stands out in perfect clarity at the end of the period in the pages of Hume and others. But once attention had been called to the phenomenon of originary interest, it became an absolute certainty that, sooner or later, people would begin to ask about the causes of this phenomenon. And at that point the history of the problem of interest entered on a new epoch.

IV

TURGOT'S FRUCTIFICATION THEORY

1. Prior to Turgot Conditions Unfavorable to Research Concerning Originary Interest

SO FAR as my knowledge of economic literature goes, I am bound to consider Turgot the first to attempt a scientific explanation of originary interest, and accordingly the first to propound the problem with any recognition of its full extent.

Before his day the times had been quite unfavorable to any scientific investigation into originary interest. Only a very short time previously had people come to a clear consciousness that in this matter they had to deal with an independent branch of income, possessing a nature peculiar to itself. But, more important still, there was present in the external conditions of the age nothing which might act as an agent to precipitate an investigation into that nature. The problem of loan interest had been treated at such an early period, because loan interest had been attacked as a fact of everyday practical life, and as the bone of contention which had from the beginning caused hostility and a conflict of interests between the parties to the loan contract, the creditors and the debtors. It was an entirely different matter with respect to originary interest. People had scarcely learned to distinguish it with certainty from the reward due to the entrepreneur's personal labor, and in any case they still regarded it with indifference. The power of capital was as yet insignificant. It can hardly be said that any antagonism had yet developed between capital and labor, the two parties concerned in originary interest, and at all events it had not developed into an opposition of classes. So far, therefore, no one was hostile to this form of income, and consequently no one had any occasion to defend it against attack from without or to make any thorough inquiry into its nature. If under such circumstances any one took it into his head to do so, it would have to be some lover of system for whom the urge to theorize supplied the incentive which the external conditions did not. But up to that time there had been no genuine systematizer of that sort in economics.

The physiocrats were the first to offer a real system. For a long time, however, even they ignored our problem. Quesnay, the founder of the school, was so far from understanding the nature of originary interest that he considered it replacement costs—a kind of reserve for losses from which the shrinkage due to wearing out of capital or to unforeseen accidents was to be defrayed, rather than a net income of the capitalist.[1]

Mercier de la Rivière[2] comes closer to the truth, in that he recognizes that capital produces a net yield. But he restricts himself to proving that agriculture must meet the compelling necessity of such a yield, if it is not to be abandoned for other pursuits. He does not go on to ask why capital in general yields interest. Neither does Mirabeau who, as we know, wrote on the subject of interest very extensively, but also very badly.[3]

2. Turgot the First to Expound a General Theory of Interest

IT WAS Turgot, then, the greatest of the physiocrats, who was also first among them to seek for a fuller explanation of the fact of originary interest. Even his way of treating the problem is modest and naive enough, and it is easy to see that it was no fiery zeal for a great social problem that forced his pen into his hand, but only the need for clear consistency in his ideas. But it was a need that would be content with an explanation which did not have to be very profound, provided only it was cast in plausible form.

In the *Mémoire sur les prêts d'argent* already known to us, Turgot deals with the question of loan interest exclusively. His more comprehensive theory of interest is developed in his chief work, *Réflexions sur la formation et la distribution des richesses.*[4] Or let us rather say, it is not so much developed as contained in it. For Turgot does not formally raise the question as to the origin of interest, nor does he accord the question any connected treatment. What we find is a number of separate paragraphs (*Secs. 57, 58, 59, 61, 63, 68, and 71*), into which he has strewn a series of observations, out of which we have to construct for ourselves his theory of the origin of interest.[5]

His theory bases the explanation of all interest on the fact that the owner of any capital employed in a fruitful field always has the option of a different field. That is to say, he can use it for the purchase of land which is then capable of yielding him land rent. Because Turgot makes land the standard fruitful field, I propose to designate his theory briefly as the "Fructification Theory."

3. Character of Turgot's Argument

THE argument is as follows. The possession of land guarantees a permanent income without labor, in the shape of land rent. But since movable goods, even when independent of land, also can be used, and so also acquire independent value, we may compare the value of these two classes of goods and may evaluate land in terms of movable goods, and may exchange it for them. The exchange price, as in the case of all goods, depends on the relation of supply and demand (*Sec. 57*). At any time it forms a multiple of the yearly income that may be drawn from the land, and it very often gets its designation from this circumstance. A piece of land, we say, is sold for twenty or thirty or forty years' purchase, if the price amounts to twenty or thirty or forty times the annual rent of the land. The particular multiple, again, depends on the relation of supply and demand; that is, whether more or fewer people wish to buy or sell land (*Sec. 58*).

By virtue of these circumstances every sum of money, and any capital, in whatever form, is the equivalent of a piece of land yielding an income equal to a certain percentage of the capital sum (*Sec. 59*).

Since in this way the owner of capital can make it yield a permanent yearly income by buying land with it, he will not be inclined to invest his capital in an industrial (*Sec. 61*), agricultural (*Sec. 63*), or commercial (*Sec. 68*) enterprise, unless he can expect just as large a net return as he could obtain through the purchase of land over and above reimbursement of his expense and compensation for his trouble. On that account capital, in all these branches of employment, *must* yield an income.

This is the primary explanation of the economic necessity of originary interest. Loan interest is derived from it in the simple way described below. The entrepreneur without capital is gladly willing, and economically may be well prepared to pay to the man who entrusts him with a capital some part of the gain which the borrowed capital yields (*Sec. 71*). Thus, all forms of interest are, in the last analysis, the necessary consequence of the circumstance that any capital can be exchanged for a piece of land which yields rent.

It will be noticed that throughout this line of thought Turgot's foundation is a circumstance which had for some centuries been the recourse of the defenders of loan interest, from Calvin on. But Turgot makes an essentially different and much more thorough-going use of this circumstance. Whereas his predecessors availed themselves of it occasionally, and by way of illustration, Turgot uses it as the pivotal point of his system. Whereas they did not consider it the sole cause of loan interest, but gave it equal rank with other sources of income, such as commerce, industry, etc., Turgot puts it by itself in first position. Finally be it said, that whereas they had used it only to explain loan interest, Turgot advances it as the explanation of the entire phenomenon of interest. And so Turgot, although he used only old materials, constructed a new doctrine, the first general theory of interest.[6]

4. Defects of Turgot's Theory

AS FOR the scientific value of this theory, the fate which has befallen it is very significant. I cannot recollect ever reading a formal refutation of it. But a tacit verdict as to its inadequacy is implicit in the fact that efforts were continued to seek other explanations. It seemed too plausible to be refuted, but too shallow to inspire confidence. It produced the feeling that it had not penetrated to the very root of interest, even though it seemed impossible to give an exact accounting of its shortcomings.

To give such an accounting even at this late date seems to me by no means a work of supererogation. In doing so I shall be doing something more than merely fulfilling a formal duty which I imposed on myself when I undertook to write a *critical* history of theory. For by pointing out where and how Turgot failed, I hope to make perfectly clear what the heart of the problem is toward which every earnest attempt at solution must be directed. Perhaps I can thus prepare the way for the profitable pursuit of our future task. The example of a very gifted writer of our own day shows that we are not yet so far past Turgot's line of thought as we might perhaps suppose.[7]

Turgot's explanation of interest is unsatisfactory because its course is a circle. The circle is concealed only by the fact that Turgot breaks off his explanation at the very point where the next step would inevitably have brought him back to the point from which he started.

The case, according to Turgot, is as follows. "A definite capital must yield a definite interest, because it may buy a piece of land yielding a definite rent. Let us take a concrete example. A capital of $10,000 must yield $500 interest, because with $10,000 a man can buy a piece of land which will return a rent of $500."[8]

But the possibility of such a purchase as Turgot envisions is not in itself an ultimate and clearly obvious fact. So we are forced to inquire further and ask: "Why can a person with a capital of $10,000 buy a rent-producing piece of land in general and a piece of land producing a rent of $500 in particular?" Even Turgot feels that this question may be put, and must be put, for he attempts to give an answer to it. He refers us to the relation of demand and supply, which always determines (he claims) the relation of the price of capital to that of land.[9]

But does this exhaust the questions we wish to ask, and those it is our duty to ask? Certainly not. The man who, when asked what determines a certain price, answers, "Demand and supply," offers a husk for a kernel. The answer may be allowable in a hundred cases, where it can be assumed that the one who asks the question knows sufficiently well what the kernel is, and can himself supply it. But it is not sufficient when the thing we seek is the explanation of a problem which has not yet been satisfactorily explained. If it were sufficient, we might simply say, "Well now, the problem of interest is always concerned with phenomena of price. It is a fact that the borrower pays a price for the 'use of capital,' and it is a fact that the price of the finished product exceeds the price of all the goods from which it is produced, and that there is always an excess left over for the entrepreneur." And so we could settle the whole problem of interest by pronouncing a formula, to the effect that supply and demand so regulate the price of all goods

42

that there is always a net yield left over for the capitalist. But certainly no one would regard it as a satisfactory explanation.

We must therefore ask further, "What deeper causes lie behind demand and supply, and govern their movements in such a way that a capital of $10,000 can regularly be exchanged for a rent-producing piece of land in general, and a piece of land producing a $500 rent in particular?" To this question Turgot gives no answer, unless we accept as such the somewhat vague words at the beginning of Sec. 57, which, even then, could by no means be termed satisfactory. He says, "Those who had a great deal of movable wealth were in a position to employ it not only in the cultivation of land, but also in different industries. The ease with which this movable wealth could be amassed and made use of, quite independently of land, made it possible to value the pieces of land themselves, and compare their value with that of movable wealth."

But if we continue with Turgot's explanation just a little way beyond the point where he left off prematurely, we shall discover that this interest, which purports to be explainable as the result of the exchange relation between land and capital, is in reality the cause of this exchange relation. That is to say, whether it is twenty or thirty or forty times the annual rent that is asked or offered for a piece of land depends chiefly on the percentage which the capital that buys it would obtain if otherwise employed. A piece of land which yields $500 rent will be worth $10,000 if and because the rate of interest on capital amounts to 5%. It will be worth $5,000 if and because the interest rate is 10%. It will be worth $20,000 if and because capital bears only 2½% interest. Thus, instead of the existence and the rate of interest being explained by the exchange relation between land and capital, this exchange relation on the contrary must itself be explained by the existence and the rate of interest. Nothing has been accomplished, therefore, toward the explanation of interest, because the whole argument has moved in a circle.

I should be content to terminate my remarks on Turgot's doctrine at this point, if I did not feel myself in duty bound to be especially careful in all cases involving the nature of reciprocal action between economic phenomena. For I know that it is exceedingly difficult to determine with certainty which is the starting point of a chain of reciprocal causes and effects. And I am aware also that in deciding on such points, we are particularly exposed to the pitfalls of dialectics. And so I should not like to force on the reader the opinion that Turgot was in error without offering one more proof and thus removing the last scintilla of doubt. I am particularly anxious to do so, because that proof offers a welcome opportunity of shedding a clearer light on the nature of our problem.

Barring misfortune, a piece of land will yield its rent for a practically infinite series of years. The possession of it assures the owner and his heirs the price of the yearly use, not for twenty or forty times only, but for many hundred times, nay, for almost an infinite number of times. But as a matter of common experience this infinite series of uses which, added together, represent a colossal sum of income, is regularly sold for

43

a fraction of that sum—for twenty to forty times the year's use. And that is a fact which demands explanation.

Nor is such explanation furnished by a superficial reference to the state of demand and supply. For if demand and supply are at all times in such a position that this striking result is brought about, then its regular recurrence must have deeper roots, and these deeper roots demand investigation.

In passing I should like to refute a hypothesis which might come to mind, to the effect that the reason for the low purchase price is that the owner takes into consideration only such a number of uses as he himself may hope to obtain from the land, and ignores anything beyond. Since man's average life span, and therefore that of landowners, too, has not varied very much in historical times, the ratio of the value of land to the rent of land would, if that hypothesis were true, have had to remain fairly constant. But this is by no means the case. Indeed, we see that ratio varying from ten to fifty fold, according to the varying rate of interest at given times.

There must, therefore, be another reason for that striking phenomenon. I think I can count on general agreement when I maintain that the true reason for it lies in the fact that in placing a valuation on a piece of land we include a *discounting process* in our calculations. Though we are purchasing many hundred years' use of the land our valuation is fixed at only twenty years' use if the prevailing interest rate is 5%, and to twenty-five years' use if the interest rate is 4%. The reason is that we place only a discounted value on future uses. In terms of present value, future uses are scaled down *pro rata temporis et usurarum,* that is to say, in proportion to or in accordance with the remoteness of the time and of the uses. In doing so we follow the same principle as governs our estimation of the present capital value of a limited or a perpetual claim to rents.

If this is so (and I do not think anyone will question it), then the capital valuation of land on which Turgot relied to explain the phenomenon of interest is itself nothing more than one of the many forms in which we encounter the phenomenon of interest in economic life. For that phenomenon is protean. Sometimes it is an explicit payment of loan interest; sometimes it is payment of hire which leaves a "net use" to the owner after making an allowance for wear and tear; sometimes it is a difference in price between product and costs, the difference accruing to the entrepreneur as an excess of proceeds; sometimes it is a deduction in advance by the creditor from the amount of the loan granted to the debtor; sometimes it is an increase in the purchase price when payment is deferred; sometimes it is a reduction in the purchase price because claims, prerogatives, and privileges are paid for before they are due; and sometimes, finally, (to mention an instance closely related and indeed, essentially the same) it is a reduction in the purchase price, granted because certain uses, inseparable from a piece of land, are available only at a later date.

To base an explanation of the originary interest that capital obtains

in commerce and industry on the possibility of acquiring land in exchange for definite sums of capital means only to invoke one form of
the phenomenon of interest to explain a second, while we still lack an
explanation of the first. Why do we obtain originary interest? Why do
we discount the value of future rates of payment or rates of use? These
are evidently only two different forms of the same question, and we
register no progress toward its solution if our explanation begins by
answering it in its first form, only to pull up short before the second.

V

ADAM SMITH AND THE DEVELOPMENT

OF THE INTEREST PROBLEM

1. Adam Smith Had No Clearly Defined Theory Regarding Interest

IT HAS never, I think, been the good fortune of any founder of a scientific system to think out to the very end even the more important ideas that constitute his system. The strength and lifetime of no single man are sufficient for that. It is enough if some few ideas, those great pillars which support the weight of the edifice of the system, are disclosed down to their fundaments, and if their ramifications and interlacings are exposed. It is a great deal if, over and above that, equal care is bestowed on a few other favored parts of the system. Even the most comprehensive of intellects will have to be content to erect a structure consisting in large measure of uncertainties, and to incorporate in his system thoughts which have been subjected to only a cursory examination, for the simple reason that there was not time to make an exhaustive one. We must keep these considerations before us if we would rightly appreciate Adam Smith's attitude towards our problem.

Adam Smith has not overlooked the problem of interest, but neither has he elaborated it. He deals with it as a great thinker may deal with an important subject which he encounters often, but which he fails to examine thoroughly for lack of time or opportunity. He adopted an explanation which, while manifest, is also vague. The more indefinite it is, the less does it oblige him to strict consistency. While a versatile mind like Adam Smith's could not but be aware of the varieties of possible approach to the problem, yet he lacked the yardstick which a distinct theory of his own would have afforded. And so he was guilty of quite a few equivocal and contradictory statements. Thus we have the peculiar phenomenon that, while Adam Smith did not formulate any distinct theory of interest, the germs of almost all the later and conflicting theories are more or less recognizable in his scattered observations. This is true of Adam Smith with respect to several other questions.

The line of thought which seems to commend itself principally to him as explaining originary interest appears twice and in very similar wording in the sixth and eighth chapters of Book I of the *Wealth of Nations*. It might be summed up in the statement that there must be income from capital, because otherwise the capitalist would have no motive for spending his capital in the productive employment of laborers.[1]

Generalizations like these can, of course, make no claim to the status of a complete theory.[2] For there is no reasoned attempt in them to show what we are to consider the effective connecting links between the psychological motive of the capitalist's self-interest and the final determination of market prices which, by leaving a difference between costs and proceeds, permit of originary interest. But if we consider those expressions in conjunction with a later passage,[3] in which Smith sharply contrasts the "future profit"* that rewards the investor with the "present enjoyment" of immediate consumption, we may recognize the first germs of that theory which Senior later worked out under the name of the abstinence theory.

2. Smith's Contradictory Statements Contain the Germs of the Most Important Later Theories

ADAM SMITH asserts the necessity of originary interest without furnishing much support for the assertion. In the same way he avoids making any systematic investigation into the important question of the source of the income received by the capitalist entrepreneur. He contents himself with making a few passing observations on the subject. In fact, in several passages he offers two contradictory versions of the source of this income. According to one, it arises from the circumstance that the buyer, in order to meet the capitalist's claim to originary interest, must consent to pay more for goods than the value which these goods acquire from the labor expended on them. Accordingly, the source of interest is an unexplained increase in value of the product over that created by labor. According to the other version, interest is a deduction which the capitalist makes in his own favor from the return that is accorded to labor, so that the workers do not receive the full value created by them, but are obliged to share it with the capitalist. According to this version, originary interest is a part of the value created by labor and withheld by the capitalist.

Both versions are to be found in a great number of passages, and these passages, oddly enough, sometimes stand quite close to each other. This applies especially to those in the sixth chapter of the first book.

Adam Smith, speaking of a mythical age when land was not yet privately owned and accumulation of capital had not yet begun, remarks that at that time *the amount of labor* required for the production of goods *alone* determined their price. He continues: "As soon as stock has accumulated in the hands of particular persons, some of them will naturally employ it in setting to work industrious people, whom they will

---

* Translators' note: For the classical notion of "profit" see translators' footnote in Chapter III, page 30.

supply with materials and subsistence, in order to make a profit by the sale of their work, or by what their labour adds to the value of the materials. In exchanging the complete manufacture either for money, for labour, or for other goods, *over and above* what may be sufficient to pay the price of the materials and the wages of the workmen, *something must be given for the profits of the undertaker of the work, who hazards his stock in this adventure."*

This sentence, especially when read in the light of the contrary statement in the preceding paragraph (that, under primitive conditions, labor is the sole determinant of price), very clearly expresses the opinion that the capitalist's claim to interest causes an increase in the price of the product, and is met from this increase. But Adam Smith immediately goes on to say: *"The value which the workman adds to the material,* therefore, resolves itself in this case into two parts, of which the one pays the wages, the other the profits of the employer upon the whole stock of materials and wages which he advanced." Here again the price of the product is considered to be determined by the quantity of labor expended exclusively, and the claim to interest is said to be met from a part of the return which the worker has produced.

We meet the same contradiction in even more striking form, one page further on. "In this state of things," says Adam Smith, "the whole produce of labour does not always belong to the labourer. He must, in most cases, share it with the owner of the stock which employs him." This is clearly a paraphrase of the second version. But *immediately* thereafter he says: "Neither is the quantity of labour commonly employed in acquiring or producing any commodity, the only circumstance which can regulate the quantity which it ought commonly to purchase, command, or exchange for. *An additional quantity,* it is evident, *must be due for the profits* of the stock which advanced the wages and furnished the materials of that labour." He could not have said more plainly that the effect of the claim to interest is an increase in price which makes curtailment of the wages of labor unnecessary!

Later on he alternates between the two versions. He says, in Book I, Chapter VI, toward the end, "As in a civilized country there are but few commodities of which *the exchangeable value arises from labour only,* rent and *profit* contributing largely to that of the far greater part of them, so the annual produce of its labour will always be sufficient to purchase, or command a much greater quantity of labour than was employed in raising, preparing, and bringing that produce to market" (*First version*).

Then in Chapter VIII of the same book he says, "The produce of almost all other labour is liable to the like deduction of profit. In all arts and manufactures the greater part of the workmen stand in need of a master to advance them the materials of their work, and their wages and maintenance till it be completed. *He shares in the produce of their labor, or in the value* which it adds to the materials upon which it is bestowed; and in this share consists his profit" (*Second version*).

---

* Translators' note: The italics are Böhm-Bawerk's.

And in Chapter XI we read: "High or low wages and *profit are the causes of high or low price;* high or low rent is the effect of it" (*First version*).

Contradictions like these on the part of such an eminent thinker admit, I think, of only one explanation. Adam Smith had not thoroughly thought out the problem of interest and so acted in a manner quite usual when one deals with a subject which he has but imperfectly mastered. That is to say, he was not very particular in his choice of expressions, but unconcernedly allowed himself to be swayed by the changing impressions which the subject may have made and was bound to make on him.

Adam Smith, then, has no perfected theory of interest.[4] But the suggestions he tossed out were all destined to fall on fruitful soil. His casual remark on the necessity of interest was developed later into the abstinence theory. In the same way the two versions he gave of the source of interest were taken up by his followers, were logically developed, and exalted to become principles underlying independent theories. The one, the principle that interest is paid out of an additional value which the employment of capital calls into existence, furnished the foundation for the later productivity theories. The other, that interest is paid out of the return to labor, formed the basis of the socialist theories of interest. Thus the most important of later theories can trace their pedigrees back to Adam Smith.

3. Theoretical and Socio-Political Neutrality of Smith's Ideas on Interest

THE position taken by Adam Smith towards the question of interest may be termed one of complete neutrality. He is neutral in his theoretical exposition, for he places the germs of distinct theories beside each other without revealing any marked preference for any one of them. And he is neutral in his practical judgment, for he maintains the same reserve, or rather the same contradictory hesitancy, both in praise and in censure of interest. Sometimes he commends the capitalists as benefactors of the human race, and as authors of enduring blessings;[5] sometimes he represents them as a class who live on deductions from the product of other people's labor, and manifestly compares them to people "who love to reap where they never sowed."[6]

In Adam Smith's time the relation of theory and practice still made it possible to observe such neutrality, but his followers soon could no longer do so. Changed circumstances made it necessary for them to show their colors on the interest question, and that necessity was certainly not to the disadvantage of our science.

The special requirements of economic theory could no longer be satisfied with information that was less than unassailable. Adam Smith had spent his life in laying down the foundation of his system. His followers, finding the foundations laid, now had time to take up those questions that had been passed over. The inquiry into the related problems of land rent and wages had reached a stage which furnished a strong inducement to pursue the problem of interest. There was a very complete theory of land rent and there was a theory of wages scarcely less complete. Nothing was more natural than that systematic thinkers should now begin to ask in earnest about the third great branch of income—the whence and wherefore of the income derived from the possession of capital.

4. Growing Practical Importance of Interest Problem Enlivens the Discussion

BUT finally the demands of practical life also began to require an answer to this question. Capital had gradually become a power. The machine had appeared on the scene and had won its great triumphs, and everywhere it was helping to extend business on a grand scale, and to give production more and more of a capitalist character. But this very introduction of machinery had begun to reveal a conflict which had been injected into economic life with the development of capital, and which daily grew in importance. This was the conflict between capital and labor.

In the days of the handicrafts the business man and the wage-earner, the master and the apprentice, belonged not so much to different social classes, as simply to different generations. What the one was, the other could, and normally would become. Though their interests might for a time conflict, yet on the whole the feeling prevailed that they belonged to the same profession. The large capitalist enterprise presented an entirely different situation. The entrepreneur who contributed the capital had seldom or never been a workman; the workman who contributed his thews and sinews would seldom or never become an entrepreneur. They were working at the same trade, like master and apprentice, but they were not only, like the latter, of different rank, they were of different kinds. They belonged to groups whose interests diverged as widely as their persons. The machine had illustrated how violently the interests of capital and labor could collide. The same machines which had born golden fruit for the capitalist entrepreneur had, upon their very introduction, deprived thousands of workers of their bread. But even after the first hardships were over there remained antagonism enough and to spare. It is true that capitalist and laborer shared the yield of enterprise, but in such fashion that the worker usually received little, very little indeed, while the entrepreneur received much. The worker's discontent with his small share was not lessened, as in the case of the handicraft assistant, by the prospect that he would himself one day enjoy the lion's share. For in a large enterprise the worker had no such prospect. On the contrary, his discontent was aggravated by the knowledge that for his meager wage he did the harder work, while the entrepreneur gained his generous share with far less exertion, and often even without any personal exertion whatever. As Smith's system gained wide circulation, one concept, suggested by recurrent passages, became broadly manifest. It was the concept that, fundamentally, it was the workers' labor which created the products from which the entrepreneur derived his profits. Once this thought began to heighten the consciousness of the wide disparity in interests, and the sharp contrast in fortunes of capitalist and worker, it was inevitable that an advocate from among the "fourth estate" should raise again that question which had been raised centuries before. Then it had been raised in favor of the debtor with respect to loan interest. Now the question was raised with respect to originary interest. And the question was, *Is it just?* Is it just that the capitalist entrepreneur, even though he does not raise a finger, shall yet receive, in the guise of interest, a large portion of that which has been created by the workers' toil? Or should not the workers receive the entire product?

From the turn of the eighteenth century on, this question was raised, at first softly, then more and more loudly. And it is to that fact that the interest theory owes its unusual and enduring vitality. So long as the problem interested theorists alone, and was of importance only for purposes of theory, it might have slumbered on undisturbed. But it was now elevated to the rank of a great social problem which economics was neither able nor disposed to ignore. And so the inquiries into the nature of originary interest became as numerous and pressing after Adam Smith's day, as they had been scanty and inadequate before it.

It must also be admitted that they were as divergent as they were numerous. Before Adam Smith the scientific opinion of each era had been represented by one single theory. After him, opinion was divided into a number of theories which conflicted with each other at the outset, and have maintained that conflict with rare persistence to this very day. Ordinarily, new theories supplant the old, and the latter gradually abandon the field. But in the present case, each new theory of interest succeeded only in winning a position *beside* the old which contrived stubbornly to maintain their own positions. Under these circumstances the course of development since Adam Smith's time presents not so much the picture of a progressive reform as that of a schismatic accumulation of theories.

5. Divergences of Post-Smithian Literature; Five Principal Classifications

THE problem now before us is clearly defined by the nature of the subject. It will consist in following the development of all the divergent systems from their origin down to the present time, and in trying to form a critical opinion on the value, or lack of value, of each. As the development from Adam Smith onwards follows different lines simultaneously, I consider it more to the purpose to abandon my chronological arrangement, and to group the material according to theories.

To this end I shall try first of all to make a methodical survey of the whole mass of literature which will engage our attention. The quickest method is to center our attention on the characteristic essential question which the problem poses. As a prism affects a beam of light, so that central question will serve to break down our theory of interest, and make its varied multiplicity immediately apparent.

What we have to explain is the fact that, when capital is productively employed, there regularly is left over in the hands of the entrepreneur a surplus proportional to the amount of the capital employed. This surplus owes its existence to the circumstance that the value of the goods produced with the assistance of capital is regularly greater than the value of the goods consumed in their production. The question accordingly is, *Why is there this constant surplus value?*

To this question Turgot had answered, "There must be a surplus, because otherwise the capitalists would employ their capital in the purchase of land." Adam Smith had answered, "There must be a surplus, because otherwise the capitalist would have no interest in employing his capital productively."

We have already pronounced both answers inadequate. What then are the answers given by later writers?

To begin with, they appear to me to follow five different lines.

One group is content with the answers given by Turgot and Smith, and stands by them. This line of explanation was still a favorite at the beginning of the 19th century, but has been gradually abandoned since then. I shall group these answers together under the name of the *colorless theories.*

A second group says, *Capital produces the surplus.* This school, amply represented in economic literature, may be conveniently called that of the *productivity theories.* I may note here that in their later development we shall find the productivity theories splitting up into several sub-classifications, including productivity theories in the narrower sense, which assume a direct production of surplus on the part of capital, and use theories, which explain the origin of interest by the roundabout way of calling the productive use of capital a special element of cost, which, like every other element of cost, demands compensation.

A third group answers, *Surplus value is the equivalent of one element of cost which enters as a constituent into the price, namely, abstinence.* For in devoting his capital to production, the capitalist must give up the present enjoyment of it. This postponement of enjoyment, this abstinence, is a sacrifice, and as such is a constituent element in the costs of production which demands compensation. I shall call this the *abstinence theory.*

A fourth group sees in surplus value *the wage for work contributed by the capitalist.* For this doctrine, which has numerous sub-classifications, I shall use the name *remuneration theory.*

Finally, a fifth group, and one which for the most part belongs to the socialist parties, answers, *Surplus value does not correspond to any natural surplus whatever, but has its origin simply in the curtailment of the just wage of the workers.* I shall call this the *exploitation theory.*

These are the principal classifications. They are certainly numerous enough, yet the list falls far short of exhausting the many variants of the interest theory which actually exist. We shall see, rather, that many of the principal classes divide again into a multitude of essentially different types, and that in many cases elements of several theories are united in a new and strange combination. And it will be observed, finally, that within one and the same theoretical type the variations in the formulating of the common fundamental principle are often so pronounced, and so characteristic, that there would be some justification for recognizing the individual shades of difference as separate theories. The fact that the outstanding minds in the field of economics have labored along so many different paths to discover the truth bears eloquent testimony to the importance as well as the difficulty of their task.

We shall begin with a survey of the *colorless theories.*

VI

THE COLORLESS THEORIES

THE question of interest had long been the object of contemptuous neglect. But the revolution spoken of at the end of the preceding chapter was destined to elevate it to the position of a social problem of the first rank. And yet the break with the past was not so abrupt, but that a number of writers still remained content with the somewhat patriarchal treatment that the subject had received at the hands of Turgot and Adam Smith. It would be a great mistake to suppose that these successors were mere imitators, nothing but second and third-rate writers. Of course they included the usual crowd of mediocre writers, men who always appear in the wake of a pioneering genius, and find their mission in popularizing the new doctrine. But besides these we find many a distinguished thinker who had neglected our problem from motives similar to those of Adam Smith.

It may readily be seen that the writers whom I shall call "colorless" expressed opinions on the subject of interest which could hardly be expected to exert any great influence on the development of the theory as a whole. This circumstance will justify me in passing rapidly over the majority of them, and giving a complete account only of the few who may arouse our interest either by their personality or by the individuality of their doctrine.

1. Large Number of Colorless Writers
Among Earlier German Economists

ANY one familiar with the state of German economics at the end of the eighteenth and the beginning of the nineteenth century will not be astonished to find it marked by the presence of a singularly large number of "colorless" writers. Their indifference to the subject is not without a certain variety. Some who remain faithful to Adam Smith copy his vague hints concerning interest almost literally, in particular his remark that, if there were no interest, the capitalist would have no inducement to employ his capital productively. This is true of such men as Sartorius,[1] Lueder,[2] and Kraus.[3] Some, such as Hufeland[4] and Seutter,[5] ring the changes on the fundamental ideas, and treat it more freely.

Others take interest for granted and waste no words on an explanation of it. These include Pölitz,[6] and, somewhat later, Murhard.[7] Still others advance explanations that are certainly individual, but so superficial and meaningless, that they can scarcely lay claim to the honorable name of theories. One of these is Schmalz, who argues in a circle, explaining the existence of originary interest by the fact that it is possible to lend out capital at interest.[8]

Count Cancrin's explanation of the matter is extraordinarily naive. I should like to quote the short quaintly curious passage in his own words: "Every one knows," he says,[9] "that money bears interest. But why? *If two owners of capital goods wish to exchange their products, each of them is disposed to demand for the labor of storing, and by way of gain, as great a sum in excess of the intrinsic value of the product as the other will grant him; necessity, however, makes them meet each other half way.* But money represents capital goods; with capital goods a net income can be made; hence, interest."

The words printed in italics are meant to explain the existence of originary interest, the others the existence of loan interest; and the author considers this explanation so adequate that in a later passage he refers to it with complacency, saying, "Why capital bears interest, at a definite rate in the case of money values, and as reflected in the prices of commodities in the case of capital goods, has already been discussed." (*p. 103*)!

There are a few authors who place greater emphasis on those passages in Adam Smith which hold that interest is a share in the product of labor accruing to the capitalist.

One of these writers, Count Soden,[10] sharply contrasts capital as the mere material to which "productive power" is applied, with the productive power itself. He traces interest to the fact that the owner of "capital material" is able to "put the power of others in motion for himself, and therefore to share the income from this power with the isolated producer, the wage earner" (*Vol. I, p. 65*). That such sharing does take place Soden regards as a self-evident consequence of competition. Without taking the trouble to make a formal explanation, he repeatedly intimates that the smaller number of capitalists, as compared with the great number of wage earners, must always make it possible for the capitalist to buy wage-labor at a price which leaves him a surplus (*pp. 61, 138*). He thoroughly approves of this (*e.g., p. 65 ff.*), and consequently advises against attempting to raise wages by legal regulation. "For if the price is so regulated that the owner of the material cannot extract a gain from the power of others, he will allow all material which he cannot himself work up to lie dormant" (*p. 140*). Soden, however, wishes that the "price" of wages should be brought up to their "true value." Just what wage corresponds to this true value remains very obscure, in spite of the thorough discussion which the author devotes to the question of the value of productive power (*p. 132 ff.*). The only thing certain is that, in his opinion, even when the productive power is compensated at its *full* value, there must still remain an excess of proceeds for the capitalist.

The impression one gets from all this is that the first part of the argument, where interest is explained to be income from the power of others, would lead us to expect a very different conclusion from the one set forth in the second part. Nor can we escape the feeling that the reasons given for this change of front are much too vague to be satisfactory.

Lotz lays himself open to similar criticism.

This ingenious writer, in his *Handbuch der Staatswirtschaftslehre,* Erlangen, 1821, goes exhaustively into the subject of interest. He argues with great vigor against the doctrine which Say had in the meantime put forward, that capital possesses an independent productive power. "In and of itself all capital is dead," and "there is no truth in the assertion that it performs independent labor." It is, on the contrary, nothing but a tool of human labor (*Vol.* I, *p. 65 f.*). In a very notable passage he subsequently takes a point of view which is very significant in its bearing on originary interest.

If capital is only an instrument for furthering labor, and itself does no labor, says Lotz, then the capitalist "has no claim on the yield of labor, and on the amount of goods gained or produced by it, beyond that expended in furnishing the capital. Or, to put it more plainly, he has no claim beyond the amount expended for the laborer's subsistence, for the raw material supplied him, and for the tools that are worn out by the worker during his work. *This, strictly speaking, would really be the adequate compensation to capital* which the capitalist may claim from the laborer who works for him. Furthermore, it is really the appropriate measure of the quantity of goods produced by the laborer, or won from nature, which might of right belong to the capitalist. Accordingly, there can be no question of interest, in the correct sense of the word, that is to say, of *the payment to the capitalist, in consideration of his supplying the capital, of a wage which affords him a surplus over and above the goods so supplied. If labor yields more than the amount of the capitalist's expenditure, that yield and all the income derived from it, really belongs to the laborer alone,* as the wage of his labor. For it is not, in point of fact, the capitalist who creates the laborer's products. On the contrary, all that the laborer has produced with the assistance of capital, or that he has wrung from nature, belongs to him. Or, if the power which is operative in the worker at his work be looked upon as a natural fund belonging to the entire industrial mass of mankind, then all that the laborer produces belongs to humanity as a whole" (*p. 487 f.*).

In this penetrating and remarkable passage Lotz comes very close to the later exploitation theory of the socialists. But suddenly he vitiates the force of his argument, and swings back into the old colorless explanation of Adam Smith by going on to say, "If, however, the capitalist were limited to a mere replacement of such portion of his accumulated goods as he may have furnished to the worker during his work, and for his work—if, I repeat, the capitalist were thus harshly treated, he would scarcely decide to advance anything from his stock to the worker to further that work. He would perhaps never decide to accumulate capital at all. For many a capital sum would never be accumulated, if the accumulator did not expect compensation for the trouble of this accumulating in the shape of the prospective interest. Now the worker has none of the prerequisites and necessaries indispensable to the exercise of his power. And if he is to hope and expect that owners will consent to furnish their capital, and so make it possible or easier for him to exert the productive power that resides in him, then he must of necessity submit to the surrender of part of the product of his labor to the capitalist."

Lotz then proceeds to expand this vague explanation by suggesting, in justification of the capitalist's claim, that without the support of capital the work which produces the return to be divided could never have been done at all by the laborer, or, at any rate, not done so well. This consideration furnishes a yardstick for the "true and appropriate extent" of interest. It should be calculated in proportion to the support which the worker has enjoyed at his work by reason of the employment of capital. In explaining this method of calculation by several examples, Lotz shows how nearly the extremes may meet. A few pages earlier he said that the whole "yield of labor, and all the income that is derived from it, really belongs to the laborer alone, as the wage of his labor." But now he goes on to show how under certain circumstances the owner of a labor-saving machine may justly claim nine-tenths of the total yield!

It is easy to see that the contrast here between the starting-point and the conclusion is even more violent than it is with Soden, and that the argument which is invoked to bridge the gap is no sounder. Basically it says nothing more than that the capitalist would like to get interest, and that the worker may well consent to its being deducted. But how far this "explanation" is from being really a theory of interest is strikingly illustrated by comparison with the land rent problem. Lotz's explanation does for the problem of interest exactly what would be done for the problem of rent, if one were to say that landowners must obtain land rent, because otherwise they would prefer to let their land lie fallow, and that the agricultural laborers may well consent to the deduction of rent, because without the cooperation of the soil the return to be divided could not have been produced at all, or at any rate not produced so well! Lotz apparently never had the remotest idea that such an explanation left the essence of the problem quite untouched.[11]

Finally, there was one group of colorless writers which wavered between Adam Smith's view and the productivity theory which Say had in the meantime put forward. They accepted some features of each, but did not expand any of them into a complete theory. From Say these authors usually adopted the recognition of capital as an independent factor of production, or at the very least the one or the other of Say's expressions suggesting the "productive power" of capital. From Adam Smith they took the reference to the motive of the capitalist's self-interest. But one and all of them avoided any precise formulation of the interest problem.

In this group we find Jakob,[12] who at times recognizes as the ultimate source of all useful things only nature and industrial activity (*Sec. 49*), and attributes interest to a capability on the part of labor to produce a surplus product (*Secs. 275, 280*). But at other times he defines interest as *"that which is produced by a capital in excess of its own value"* (*Sec. 277*), calls capital (*Sec. 770*) a "productive instrument" (a typical Say phrase) and often speaks of the owners of capital as immediate producers, who are entitled to share in the original division of the product because of the direct share which they have had in the production of goods through the contribution of their capital.[13] Then we have Fulda,[14] who looks upon capital as a special, though secondary, source of wealth, and likens it to a machine which, when efficiently operated, produces not only enough for its own maintenance, but also a surplus. But he does not attempt to give any explanation of this at all (*Sec. 135*). Then there is Eiselen,[15] who betrays the lack of clarity in his own thinking by the fact that he first recognizes only two ultimate sources of wealth, nature and labor (*p. 11*), and then later lists nature, labor and capital as "fundamental powers of production," which, in cooperation, create the value of all products (*Sec. 372*). Eiselen, moreover, finds that the function of capital is to increase the yield of labor and of natural powers (*Sec. 497 et al.*), but in the end he can find nothing better to say in explanation of interest than that interest is necessary as an incentive to the accumulation of capital (*Sec. 491;* similarly *Secs. 517, 555, et al.*).

Besides these we meet in the same group the gallant old master Rau. It is singular that Rau, to the very end of his long scientific career, ignored the imposing number of distinct theories of interest which he had seen arise, and clung to the simple explanation that had been customary in the days of his youth. Even in the eighth and last edition of his *Volkswirtschaftslehre,* which appeared in 1868, he restricted himself to a few cursory remarks on the interest problem, containing in substance the old self-interest motive introduced by Adam Smith. "If he (the capitalist) is to decide to save wealth, to accumulate it, and to employ it as capital, he must get an advantage of another sort, namely, a yearly income lasting as long as his capital lasts. In this way the possession of a capital becomes for an individual . . . the source of an income which is called interest on capital or on stock, or originary interest."[16]

The rich development which the literature on interest had undergone before 1868 has left scarcely a trace in Rau's works. Of Say's productivity theory he has adopted only the single feature that, like Say, he recognizes capital to be an independent source of wealth. But he immediately weakens this concession by rejecting as inappropriate the expression "productive service," which Say used for the cooperation of this source of wealth, and classing capital as a "dead auxiliary," in contrast to the wealth-producing forces (*Vol.* I, *Sec. 84*). And on one occasion, in a footnote, he quotes Senior's abstinence theory, but without adding a single word either of agreement or censure (*Vol.* I, *Sec. 228*).

2. English Colorless Writers

WHEN we turn from Germany to England, our attention is first claimed by Ricardo.

In the case of this distinguished thinker we find the same phenomenon we have already noticed in the case of Adam Smith. Without advancing a theory of his own, Ricardo, too, exerted strong influence on the development of the interest theory. Yet I am forced to classify him with the "colorless" writers. It is true that he treats the subject of interest at some length, but he treats it only as a self-evident, or almost self-evident phenomenon, and its origin is accorded only a few cursory remarks. But he takes up at all the greater length a number of concrete questions of detail. And although he treats these questions most thoroughly and intelligently, he does so in such a way that their investigation throws no light on the primary theoretical question. But exactly as in the case of Adam Smith, his doctrine contains propositions on which distinct theories could have been built, if only they had been carried out to a conclusion. In fact, distinct theories were subsequently built on them, and not the least part of their support consists in the authority of Ricardo, to whom the advocates of these theories were fond of referring as their spiritual father.

The passages in which Ricardo makes reference to interest are very numerous. Apart from scattered observations, they are to be found principally in chapters I, VI, VII, and XXI of his *Principles of Political Economy and Taxation.*[17] The contents of these passages can best be surveyed, so far as need be, by dividing them into three groups. The first group will comprise Ricardo's direct observations on the origin of interest; the second, his views on the causes that determine the rates; and the third, his views on the connection of interest with the value of goods. It should be premised, however, that Ricardo, like the majority of English writers, makes no distinction between originary interest and entrepreneur's profit, but includes both in the word "profit."*

The first group is very thinly represented. It contains a few random remarks to the effect that there must be interest, because otherwise capitalists would have no inducement to accumulate capital.[18] These remarks are clearly akin to analogous utterances by Adam Smith, with which we are familiar, and are subject to the same criticism. There is some warrant for recognizing them as the earliest germs from which the abstinence theory was later developed, but in themselves they do not represent a theory.

The same can be said of another observation of Ricardo's which should be mentioned here. Ricardo says at one point that where production demands employment of capital for a longer period, the value of the goods produced must be greater than the value of goods which

---

* Translators' note: In the terminology of the time, profit was more loosely defined, but included originary interest (see translators' footnote p. 30). The irrelevancy of other elements has induced the translators to use the more restricted and more exact term "interest" rather than "profit" in subsequent instances.

have required exactly the same amount of labor, but where the employment of capital has extended over a shorter period. And he concludes, "The difference in value . . . is only a *just compensation for the time that the profits were withheld.*"[19] One might possibly find in these words a still more direct resemblance to the abstinence theory, but even they do not contain any finished theory.

Ricardo's views on the rate of interest, contained principally in chapters VI and XXI, are very interesting because of their originality as well as their completeness. As they arise out of his theory of land rent, it will be necessary to give some account of that theory.

According to Ricardo, when a country is first settled, the most fruitful lands are placed under cultivation. So long as there is a superfluity of land of the "first quality" no rent is paid to the owner of the land, and the whole revenue reverts to the cultivators as the wage of their labor and the income on their capital.

Later on, as population increases, the increasing demand for agricultural products requires an increase in cultivation. This increase is of two kinds. Sometimes lands of inferior quality, theretofore despised, are added to those under cultivation; sometimes the lands of first quality already under cultivation are tilled more intensively and farmed with a greater expenditure of capital and labor. Assuming that the state of agricultural technique remains unchanged, the increase in agricultural products is in both cases obtained only at increased cost, and the capital and labor last employed are consequently less productive. And this decrease in productiveness continues as the more favorable opportunities for cultivation are successively exhausted, and the less favorable sites must be utilized.

A disparity in yield marks the difference between the better and the less advantageous locations of the agricultural capital that helps produce that yield. But capital as such cannot permanently be subjected to such a disparity. For competition among capitalists soon equalizes the rate of earning for all capital employed in agriculture. And indeed, the measure is furnished by the earning rate of the capital employed in the least productive location. The result is that if, because of superior quality present in the cooperating forces of the soil, a more favorably located capital returns a surplus yield, that surplus falls into the lap of the owner in the guise of land rent.

The extent of interest and wages taken together is thus always determined by the total yield of the least productively employed capital, for this yield pays no rent, and is distributed entirely as interest and wages.

Now of these two factors, one, the wages of labor, follows a definite law. Wages are necessarily at all times equal to the amount of the necessary cost of subsistence of the worker. They are high if the value of the means of subsistence is high, and low if the value of the means of subsistence is low. As the capitalist receives what is left over, interest finds its own rate determined by the *rate of wages* prevailing at any given time. For Ricardo this connection between interest and wages constitutes the true law of interest. He emphasizes it in a great many passages, and contrasts it with the view entertained by earlier economists and particularly by Adam Smith, to the effect that the extent of yield is determined by the amount of the capital sums employed, and by the competition among them.

By virtue of this law, Ricardo now goes on to argue, interest must tend to fall steadily when there is a rise in economic development. For in order to obtain means of subsistence for the increasing population, use must be made of land areas that are ever less favorable for cultivation, and the diminishing product, after deduction of the wages of labor, leaves progressively less interest. Although the amount of the product diminishes, its value concededly does not. For, according to Ricardo's well-known law, the value of products is at all times determined by the quantity of labor employed in their production. Therefore if, at a later time, the labor of ten men produces only 35 tons of wheat, while at an earlier period it had produced 45 tons, the 35 tons will now have exactly the same value as the 45 tons had before, because both represent the same quantity of labor, namely, the labor of ten men for one year. But now of course the value of a ton of wheat will rise. The amount which the worker requires for his subsistence will necessarily rise with it, and as a further result, his wages must also rise. But if, for the same value which the smaller quantity of the product represents, a higher wage must be paid to labor, there is naturally a smaller residual amount for interest.

If cultivation were extended to lands so unfruitful that the entire product obtained were required for the laborer's subsistence, then interest would fall to zero. But that is impossible, because the expectation of gain is the only motive for the accumulation of capital, and this motive becomes weaker as interest diminishes. Hence, even before zero is reached, further accumulation of capital ceases and with it the advance of wealth and of population.

The competition of capitalists, which Adam Smith considers so important, can, according to Ricardo, only temporarily lower the rate of interest, because the increased quantity of capital at first raises wages in conformity with the well-known wage fund theory. But very soon the laboring population increases in proportion to the increased demand for labor, and wages tend to sink to the former rate and interest to rise. A permanent reduction of interest is brought about by only one situation. That is the situation which arises when the means of support necessary for the increased population can be obtained only by the cultivation of less productive lands and at increased cost. As a result, the diminished product leaves a smaller surplus after paying the necessary wages of labor. It is not the result of competition, however, but of the enforced recourse to less fruitful production. Only from time to time does the tendency of interest to sink with progressive economic development experience a check through improvements in agricultural technique, which make it possible to attain the same magnitude of production with less labor than before.

Reduced to its essence, this theory of Ricardo's explains the rate of interest *by the rate of wages;* the rate of wages is the cause, the rate of interest the effect.[20]

Criticism may approach this theory from different angles. Of course, it has no validity whatever for those who hold Ricardo's rent theory to be fundamentally untrue.[21] Further, that portion of the argument which is based on the wage fund theory is open to all the objections that can be raised to that theory. I shall disregard, however, all those objections which relate to any presuppositions underlying the interest theory, and direct my criticism simply to the theory itself.

If, then, we grant the correctness of the rent theory and of the wage fund theory, is the rate of interest, or for that matter, the very existence of interest, really explained by Ricardo's theory?

The answer is "No!" because Ricardo has mistaken what are simply *accompanying circumstances* of the phenomenon for its *cause.* The matter stands as follows.

It is quite correct to say that wages, interest, and the proceeds of production, after deduction of possible land rent, are inseparably related. It is quite correct to say that the excess of proceeds over cost can never amount to more, and never to less, than the difference between proceeds and wages. But it is incorrect to interpret this relationship to mean that the amount of the proceeds and the amount of the wages are the determining factors and that the amount of interest is simply the factor determined by them. While Ricardo declared the rate of interest to be a result of the rate of wages he might just as well have declared the rate of wages to be a result of the rate of interest. He did not do so because he rightly recognized that the rate of wages rests on independent grounds, and grounds peculiar to the factor of labor. But what Ricardo recognized in the case of wages he overlooked in the case of interest. The rate of interest, too, is determined by considerations arising out of circumstances peculiar to itself. Capital does not simply take what is left over; it knows how to exact its own proper share. Now a real explanation of interest would have to set forth those considerations which were marshalled on the side of the factor "capital," and which oppose the absorption of interest by wages just as effectually as, e.g., consideration for the laborer's necessary subsistence opposes the absorption of wages by interest. But Ricardo fails entirely to set forth the specific grounds that determine the rate of interest.

Only once does he take notice of the existence of any such grounds, when he remarks that such interest can never sink to zero, because if it did, the motive for the accumulation of capital, and with it the accumulation itself, would come to an end.[22] This thought, logically expanded, might have afforded material for a really original theory of interest, but it is not followed up by Ricardo. He continues to look for the circumstances that determine the rate of interest exclusively in the field of the competing factors. Incessantly shifting, he cites as determinants of the rate of interest any or all of several factors. These include the rate of wages, the degree of productivity of the most unproductive labor, and sometimes even (with a tinge of physiocracy, but still in harmony with the whole doctrine just expounded) the natural fruitfulness of the soil.[23]

To be sure, this criticism of Ricardo gives the appearance of being itself open to a very obvious objection. If, as we have assumed with Ricardo in the whole course of our argument, wages lay claim to an absolutely determined quantity, namely, an amount equal to the cost of subsistence, it would seem, in consequence, that the amount which is left over for interest is so strictly determined, that there is no room for the operation of any independent motive on the side of interest. Let us say that the distributable yield of production is 25 tons. If the workers occupied in producing these 25 tons require 20 tons, then the share of capital, it would seem, is certainly fixed at 5 tons, and cannot be altered through the operation of any motive which may be active on behalf of capital.

This conceivable counterargument, however, will not hold. For, (to keep entirely to Ricardo's line of thought) the return which the least productive labor yields is not fixed but elastic, and is capable of being affected by the peremptory claims of capital and of labor. The claims of the worker can and in fact do prevent cultivation being extended to a point at which labor does not obtain even its own cost of subsistence. But the claims of capital are no less capable of preventing an excessive extension of the limits of cultivation, and they also, in actual fact, do prevent it. For instance, suppose that the motives to which interest, generally speaking, owes its origin, and which Ricardo unfortunately does so little to explain, demand for a given capital a yield of 30 tons, and that the workers employed by this capital need for their combined subsistence 80 tons. Then cultivation will have to cease at the point where the labor of so many men as can live on 80 tons produces 110 tons. If the "motives of accumulation" demanded only 10 tons, then cultivation could be extended to the point where the least productive labor produced 90 tons. The cultivation of land less productive than that will always be economically impossible, and this will define the limit for the expansion of population for the time being.

The attentive reader will readily perceive that the result remains the same, if we vary the terms of our observation and consider the value, instead of the amount of the product and wages. In that case, indeed, the value of the return becomes a fixed quantity (*foregoing, pp. 60-61*) and wages an elastic quantity; and the proposition expressed above would change only in wording, not in meaning, and run thus: cultivation must cease at that point where the wages of labor, increased by the rising costs of cultivation, leave the capitalist too little of the value of the product to satisfy his claims to interest.

Ricardo himself admits, as we have seen, that the claims of capital may exert this limiting influence in the very extreme case where interest threatens to disappear altogether. But naturally, the conditions to which we may attribute the fact that interest exists at all are conditions which are operative not only in extreme cases, but at all times. They do not merely prevent the entire disappearance of interest, but support it constantly in its competition with the other factors, and help to determine the rate it attains. So that interest, no less than wages, may be said to stem from independent motives. To have ignored those motives completely is the decisive blunder committed by Ricardo.

The peculiar nature of this blunder also explains most naturally the otherwise astonishing phenomenon, that the comprehensive investigations which so distinguished a thinker as Ricardo devoted to the question of the rate of interest were marked by such complete absence of progress toward the solution of the principal question, the causes of that interest.

Finally, there is a third group of observations relating to interest, which is interwoven with Ricardo's views on the value of goods. This is a subject which generally gives writers opportunity to express themselves directly or indirectly on the source of interest. Does the capitalist's demand for interest make the exchange value of goods higher than it would otherwise have been, or not? If it does, interest is paid out of a special "surplus value," without despoiling those who own the cooperating productive powers, or, more specifically, the wage-earners. If it does not, it is got at the expense of the other participants. In connection with his utterances on this subject Ricardo also expressed the opinion that an addition is made to the value of goods by the employment of capital. But he does express himself somewhat cautiously.

He distinguishes between two different epochs of history. In the first, the primitive epoch, when there is very little capital and no private ownership of land, the exchange value of goods is determined exclusively by the quantity of labor expended on them.[24] In the second epoch, to which modern economy belongs, the employment of capital introduces a modification. In return for the capital employed by them in production, the entrepreneur capitalists demand the usual rate of interest, applied to the amount of capital for the length of time during which it is employed. But the amount of capital and the duration of its employment vary in the different fields of production, and the amount of interest demanded varies with them. One field requires more rapidly circulating capital, which is quickly replaced in the value of the product; another requires more fixed capital, with further variation with respect to durability, the rapidity of replacement in the value of the products being in inverse ratio to the durability. Now the varying claims to interest are equalized by the fact that, where a relatively greater part in the production of goods has been played by capital, those goods have a relatively high exchange value.[25]

In this passage one can see that Ricardo decidedly inclines to the view that interest arises out of a special surplus value. But that impression of decisiveness on the part of Ricardo is not a little weakened by certain other passages. There are, for instance, numerous passages where Ricardo advances the thought that there is a connection between interest and wages, and that the increase of one factor involves the loss or curtailment of the other; on the other hand, there is the enunciation above of the pure "labor principle" of the primitive epoch of economy, which is inconsistent with either. It must be said too, that he is much more interested and cordial in his exposition of this latter principle than in that of its capitalist modification, a circumstance which cannot but arouse the suspicion that he considered that original state of things the natural one. In fact, the later socialist writers have represented the "labor principle" as Ricardo's real opinion, and his capitalist modification as a mere illogical intrusion into the master's writings.[26]

And so we see Ricardo, too, taking an undecided position on the question of the source of interest. His hesitation is not so marked as that of his master, Adam Smith, but he is undecided enough to warrant his retention in the ranks of the colorless theorists.[27]

Ricardo's great contemporary, Malthus, did not express himself much more decidedly than Ricardo on the subject of interest. Yet there are some utterances in his writings which allow us to separate him from the entirely colorless writers, and class him among the adherents of the productivity theory.

The epithet "colorless" applies, however, all the more appropriately to Torrens.[28] The views of this pretentious and not very farsighted writer on the subject of interest are set forth, for the most part, in the course of a polemic against Malthus. The latter had shortly before promulgated the theory that interest forms a constituent portion of the costs of production, and therefore of the natural price of goods. In opposition, Torrens quite correctly, but at intolerable length, points out that interest represents a surplus over costs, not a part of them. He himself, however, has nothing better to put in place of Malthus's theory.

He makes a distinction between market price and natural price. Market price is what we must give in exchange in order to obtain an article on the market. Natural price is what we must give in order to obtain an article "from the great warehouse of nature," and is the same thing as the cost of production. By that expression Torrens means "the amount of capital, or the quantity of accumulated labor expended in production" (*p. 34*). This market price and natural price do not by any means, as is usually affirmed, tend, on the average, to find a common level. Quite the reverse is true. For interest constitutes no part of the cost of production, and therefore no element of natural price. But market price must always return the customary rate of interest to the entrepreneur, if the enterprise is to continue. Hence market price must in principle, and at all times, exceed natural price, and in fact, exceed it by an amount equivalent to the customary rate of interest (*p. 50 ff.*).

Torrens has thus eliminated interest from the determinants of natural price, and put it instead among the determinants of market price. This change, it is easy to see, is purely formal and amounts to no more than the use of a different terminology. The economists whom he attacked had meant that interest is a determinant of the average price of goods, and had called this average or permanent price "natural price." Torrens means exactly the same thing, only he calls the permanent price the "market price," and reserves the name of natural price for something that is not a price at all, namely, the capital expended in production.

Be they natural prices or be they market prices, the actual prices of goods do leave over a surplus, which we have agreed to call originary interest. The question still remains as to why this interest exists, and to the solution of that central question Torrens has contributed virtually nothing. He evidently considers interest to be a thing so self-explanatory that any detailed explanation of it is quite unnecessary. He contents himself with a few vaguely suggestive stereotyped phrases. And these, moreover, contradict each other because the lines of thought suggested lead in different directions. One of these clichés is the often recurring observation that the capitalist must receive interest, otherwise he would have no inducement to accumulate capital, or to invest it in a productive undertaking (*pp. 53 and 392*). Another cliché pointing in quite a different direction, is the statement that interest is a "new creation" produced by the employment of capital.[29] But how it is "created" we are not told. He puts us off with a slogan instead of a theory.

But probably no member of the English school has been so unhappy in his treatment of the subject or done the theory of interest such a disservice as McCulloch.[30] He hovers about the fringes of a number of divergent opinions. He penetrates just far enough into each to become involved in glaring self-contradictions, but he does not expand any one of them sufficiently to form a theory that even approaches consistency. He makes just one exception to this rule, but the theory which he does develop is the most absurd that could possibly occur to a serious thinker. True, he abandons it in later editions of his own work and yet not without allowing traces of it to remain which are as widely at variance with facts as they are inconsistent with the context in which they appear. Thus McCulloch's utterances on the subject are a veritable nosegay of incompleteness, indecision and contradiction.

Since McCulloch's views have nevertheless attained extensive circulation, and command a certain respect, I cannot shirk the rather unpleasant task of justifying these strictures.

McCulloch starts with the proposition that labor is the only source of wealth. The value of goods is determined by the quantity of labor required for their production. This is true not only of primitive conditions, but also of modern economic life, where capital, as well as direct labor, is employed in production. For capital itself is nothing but the product of previous labor. It is only necessary to add to the labor which is contained in the capital the labor immediately expended, and the sum of these determines the value of all products.[31] Consequently it is labor alone, even in modern economic life, which constitutes the entire cost of production.[32]

But only a few lines before this definition of costs as "identical with the quantity of labor," McCulloch includes interest, as well as labor, among costs;[33] and almost immediately after saying that the *quantity* of labor alone determines value, he shows how a rise in the *wages* of labor, in conjunction with a fall in interest, alters the exchange value of goods. He asserts that it raises the value of those goods which are produced by the use of capital possessing less than average durability and reduces the value of those goods which are produced by the use of capital possessing more than average durability.[34]

And again McCulloch does not scruple to define interest as an "excess of produce," as a "surplus," as "the portion of the produce of industry accruing to the capitalist after all the produce expended by him in production is fully replaced." In short, he defines it as a *surplus pure and simple,* although not long before he pronounced it a constituent part of the costs. His contradictions run almost one to every sentence!

Nevertheless McCulloch is at great pains, at least in the first edition of his *Principles,* to appear consistent. To this end he avails himself of a theory by which he attributes interest to labor. Interest is, as he emphasizes with italics on page 291 of his first edition, "only another name for the wages of accumulated labor." This explanation supplies him with the goad that enables him to bend to the yoke of his law even those cases where interest exerts an influence on the value of goods. And that law proclaimed that the value of all goods is determined by labor. But alas for the development of that explanation!

"Suppose," he says,[35] "that a cask of new wine, which cost £50, is put into a cellar, and that, at the end of twelve months, it is worth £55, the question is: Should the £5 of additional value, given to the wine, be considered as a compensation for the *time* the £50 worth of capital has been locked up, or should it be considered as the value of additional labour actually laid out on the wine?" McCulloch decides in favor of the latter view, because this increase in value takes place only in the case of an immature wine, "on which, therefore, a change or effect is to be produced," and not in the case of a wine which has already arrived at maturity. This seems to him "to prove incontrovertibly, that the additional value, acquired by the wine during the period it has been kept in the cellar, is not a compensation or return for time, but for the effect or change that has been produced on it. Time cannot of itself produce effect; it merely affords space for really efficient causes to operate, and it is therefore clear it can have nothing to do with value."

With these words and with almost startling naiveté, McCulloch concludes his proof. He seems to have no suspicion of the enormous difference between what he was supposed to prove and what he did prove. What he wished to prove was that the additional value was caused by an addition of labor, of human activity; what he did prove at most is that the additional value was not the effect of time, but of some kind of "change" in the wine. But that this change itself was effected by an addition of labor not only is not proven, but was ruled out as a possibility by the very premises of his hypothetical case. For during the whole intervening time the wine lay untouched in the cellar.

However, he himself seems to be somewhat aware of the weakness of this first proof. For in order *"still better* to illustrate this proposition," he piles one example upon another. But the more conclusively these are intended to demonstrate his thesis, the more damaging appear the enormities they contain.

In the next illustration[36] he puts the case of an individual who has two capital sums, "one consisting of £1000 worth of new wine, and the other consisting of £900 worth of leather, and £100 worth of money. Suppose now that the wine is put into a cellar, and that the £100 is paid to a shoemaker, who is employed to convert the leather into shoes. At the end of a year, this capitalist will have two equivalent values, perhaps £1100 worth of wine and £1100 worth of shoes." Therefore, concludes McCulloch, the two cases are parallel, and both shoes and wine are the result of equal quantities of labor.

Without doubt! But does that prove what McCulloch meant to prove, namely, that the additional value of the wine was the result of human labor expended on it? Not in the least. Yes, the two cases *are* parallel! In fact, they are parallel in one additional respect, namely, in that each includes an increment in value of £100 which is left unexplained by McCulloch. The leather was worth £900. The £100 in money was exchanged for labor of equal value, and that labor presumably added £100 in value to the raw material. Therefore the total product, the shoes, should be worth £1000. But instead it is worth £1100! Whence the surplus value? Surely not from the labor of the shoemaker? For in that case the shoemaker, who was paid £100 in wages, would have added to the leather a surplus value of £200, and the capitalist in this instance would have obtained a yield of 100%, which is contrary to the hypothesis. Whence then comes the surplus value? McCulloch gives no explanation in the example of the leather, and still less, therefore, in the example of the wine, for that was to have been explained by the analogy furnished by the example of the leather.

But McCulloch is indefatigable. "The case of timber," he says, "affords a still better example! Let us suppose that a tree which is now worth £25 or £30 was planted a hundred years ago at an expense of one shilling; it may be easily shown that the present value of the tree is owing entirely to the quantity of labour laid out upon it. A tree is at once a piece of timber, and a machine for manufacturing timber; and though the original cost of this machine be but small, yet, as it is not liable to waste or decay, the capital vested in it will, at the end of a distant period, have operated a considerable effect, or, in other words, have produced a considerable value. If we suppose that a machine, which cost only one shilling, had been invented a hundred years since; that this machine was indestructible, and, consequently, required no repairs; and that it had, all the while, been employed in the weaving of a quantity of yarn, gratuitously produced by nature, which was only now finished, this cloth might now be worth £25 or £30; but, whatever value it may be possessed of, it is evident (!) it must have derived it entirely from the continued agency of the machine or, in other words, from the quantity of labour expended on its production."[37]

That is to say, a tree has cost a few hours' labor, worth a shilling. At the present moment the same tree, without other human labor being expended on it in the interval, is worth not one shilling, but £25 or £30. And McCulloch advances this not to refute, but to prove the proposition that the value of goods is invariably measured by the quantity of labor which their production has cost. Further commentary is super-fluous![38]

In the later editions of his *Principles* McCulloch has dropped all these impossible illustrations of the proposition that interest is the wage of labor.[39] At the corresponding point in the fifth edition, pages 292-294, he mentions the illustration of the wine, which evidently causes him a certain amount of embarrassment. But he contents himself with the negative statement that surplus value is not produced by the activity of natural powers, as natural powers work gratuitously. The only positive statement he makes is, that the increment of value is a *result of the profit* which accrues to the capital required for carrying on the process. But he makes no further explanation of the nature of that profit. On page 277, however, the proposition that interest is only another name for the "wages of anterior labor" remains unaltered.

I may conclude this criticism by quoting two more statements by McCulloch, which will illustrate his untrustworthiness in matters of theory.

As if to render the chaos of his incoherent opinions quite complete, McCulloch also takes up Adam Smith's well-known self-interest argument.[40] And as if not content with the confusion prevailing in his own doctrine of interest, and anxious to throw his own tolerably clear theory of wages into the same confusion, he pronounces the laborer himself to be a capital, a machine, and calls his wages a profit of capital which he receives in addition to a sum for wear and tear of the "machine called man"![41]

Passing by another set of writers like Whately, Chalmers and Jones, who contribute nothing of great consequence to our subject, we come to MacLeod.[42]

This eccentric scholar is remarkable for the ingenuousness with which he treats the interest problem, and this not only in the fifties but even on into the seventies of the nineteenth century, although the problem of interest had in the meantime assumed far greater proportions. For MacLeod there is absolutely no problem. An excess of proceeds is simply a self-evident and necessary fact. The price of commodities sold, the hire of capital goods loaned out, the interest on sums of money borrowed, "must" yield the "necessary" surplus in excess of costs, amortization and compensation for risk.[43] Why they should do so fails to elicit from MacLeod even the most superficial inquiry.

When MacLeod does describe the origin of loan interest, he designedly chooses the specific conditions of his illustration in such a way that he can present an increase from the capital loaned as a natural and self-evident matter. Thus he has the capitalist lend seed and sheep,[44] but he regards it as no less self-evident that an "increase" should occur, even when the capital is of a type which does not consist of naturally fruitful objects. He seems to be innocent of the slightest notion that anyone might maintain that interest is not self-evident, or might even question its justifiability. And he exhibits this innocence in spite of the wide circulation of socialist ideas in his time. To him it is "perfectly clear" that when a man employs his own capital in trade he is entitled to retain for his own use all the profits resulting from such operations, whether these profits be 20%, 100%, or 1,000%. If any one of superior powers of invention were to employ his capital in producing a machine, he might realize "immense profits" and accumulate a "splendid fortune," and "no one in the ordinary possession of his senses" would grudge it him.[45]

At the same time MacLeod is a severe critic of the interest theories of other economists. He rejects the doctrine that interest is a constituent of the costs of production.[46] He disputes Ricardo's statement that the rate of interest is conditioned by the rate of wages.[47] He condemns alike McCulloch's strange remuneration theory and Senior's shrewd abstinence theory.[48] And yet even these critical attacks did not inspire him to formulate a positive opinion of his own which might displace the ones he rejects.

This appears to me to be due to two peculiarities of his doctrine. The first of these is the extraordinary vagueness of his notion of capital. Capital, in its original and primary sense, he takes to mean "circulating power." It is only in a "secondary and metaphorical sense" that it is applied to commodities. But when so applied it embraces things as heterogeneous as tools and merchandise, skills, capacities, education, land, and good character.[49] That *is* a conglomeration, to be sure, which makes it difficult to place the income from such varied sources in a single category and explain them by a well-defined theory. The second of his peculiarities is the exaggerated opinion he entertains of the theoretical value of the formula of supply and demand as an explanation of the various phenomena of price. If he could only succeed in bringing any phenomenon of value into some relationship to the question of supply and demand (or, as he likes to express it in his own terminology, to the relation between the "intensity of the service performed and the power of the buyer over the seller"), then he thought that he had done enough. And so he may have really thought it sufficient to say of interest: "All value proceeds exclusively from demand; and all profit arises from the value of a product exceeding its cost of production."[50]

3. Relatively Few Colorless Doctrines in France

WHILE in Germany and England there were comparatively many prominent writers who, for some considerable time, took an undecided attitude on the interest problem, we have only a few "colorless" writers to record in the literature of France. The principal reason for this difference is that in France J. B. Say, one of the first to disseminate Adam Smith's doctrine, himself propounded a definite theory of interest which achieved popularity simultaneously with Adam Smith's doctrine, while in Germany and England Adam Smith himself, and after him Ricardo, remained for a long time at the head of the general development of economic literature. And both of these, as we know, neglected the interest problem.

In the French literature of that period there are, then, only three names which I intend to mention, two of whom antedate J. B. Say. Those three are Germain Garnier, Canard, and Droz.

Garnier,[51] still half entangled in the doctrine of the physiocrats, asserts as they do that the earth is the one source of all wealth, and labor the instrument by which man obtains it from that source (*p. 9 f.*). He identifies capital with the "advances," that is to say, the sums which the entrepreneur must advance. And he defines interest as the indemnification received for those advances (*p. 35*). In one place he adds significance to his definition by saying that interest is an "indemnification for a deprivation and a risk" (*indemnité d'une privation et d'un risque, p. 27*). But he avoids going any deeper into the matter.

If I am to give a picture of Canard's conception of interest,[52] I must refer briefly to the general principles of his doctrine.

In the labor of man Canard sees the means of his support and development. A part of human labor must be expended, merely that man may live. Canard calls that "necessary labor." But fortunately that does not require the whole labor of man. The remainder, or "superfluous labor," may be employed in the production of goods which exceed man's immediate necessities and which create for their producer a claim to command, by way of exchange, the same amount of labor as the production of these goods required. Labor is thus the source of all exchange value; goods which have value in exchange are nothing but an accumulation of superfluous labor (*accumulation de travail superflu*).

It is to the possibility of accumulating superfluous labor that humanity owes all economic progress. Through such accumulation lands are made fruitful, machines are built, and all the thousand and one means are obtained which serve to increase the product of human labor.

Now the accumulation of superfluous labor is also the source of all rents. It may yield these rents by being employed in three ways. The first is the clearing and improving of land, the net return arising from which is land rent (*rente foncière*). The second is in the acquisition of personal skills, the learning of an art or a trade. The skilled labor (*travail appris*) which is the result of such an expenditure must yield, in addition to the wage of "natural" labor, a rent of the fund of labor which had to be sacrificed in the acquisition of the knowledge. Finally, all the products of labor that proceed from these first two "sources of rent" must be correspondingly distributed, to the end that they may be employed by individuals in the satisfaction of their wants. This requires that a third class of owners must invest "superfluous labor" in the institutions of commerce. This accumulated labor also must bear a rent, the *rente mobilière,* commonly called money interest.

But why accumulated labor in these three forms should bear rent is a question to which Canard gives no real answer. He accepts land rent as a natural fact not requiring explanation.[53] The same is true of industrial rent, (*rente industrielle*), with respect to which he is content to say that "skilled labor" *must* produce the rent of the capital that has been devoted to the acquisition of knowledge (*p. 10*). And with respect to *rente mobilière,* our originary interest, he summons before us a number of details, so marshalled as to suggest that they are being presented as the accompaniment of an explanation; then he allows them to degenerate into mere embellishments of a proposition which is, after all, no explanation at all. "Hence commerce, like the other two sources of rent, presupposes an accumulation of superfluous labor which must, in consequence, bear a rent" (*qui doit "par conséquent" produire une rente, p. 12*). But there is nothing whatever to justify this *par conséquent,* unless Canard, perhaps, considers that the bare fact of labor having been accumulated is sufficient ground for its obtaining a rent, and so far he has not said so. He has said, it is true, that all rents are traceable to accumulated labor, but he has not said that all accumulated labor must bear a rent. And there is a vast difference between the two. And there would certainly have been a vast difference, too, between making the assertion and proving it.

If we take into consideration an exposition which appears later (*p. 13 ff.*) to the effect that each of the three kinds of rent must be equivalent to the others, then undoubtedly we can deduce a certain explanation of interest. Canard, incidentally, did not state this explicitly, but it is an explanation which would agree in essence with Turgot's fructification theory. For if it is a matter of simple fact that capital invested in land bears rent, then all capital, even if otherwise invested, must also bear rent, or else everybody would prefer to invest in land. This is Canard's only explanation, and if he does not state it, it may at least be read between the lines. But we have already shown its inadequacy in our discussion of Turgot.

Droz,[54] some thirty years later, had to choose between the English view, according to which labor is the sole productive power, and the theory of Say, according to which capital represents an independent productive power. However, he finds flaws in both views and accepts neither, but advances a third to the effect that saving (*l'épargne*) rather than capital constitutes an elementary productive power. He thus recognizes three productive powers: the labor of nature, the labor of man, and the saving which accumulates capital (*p. 69 ff.*).

If this line of thought, which belongs, basically, to the doctrine of production, had been extended by Droz into the sphere of distribution and availed of as a basis for a closer analysis of the nature of income, he would probably have arrived at a distinctive theory of interest. But he did not go far enough for that. In his distribution theory he devotes almost all his attention to contract or loan interest, which offers little to be explained, and in a few words disposes of originary interest, which demands that everything be explained. In those few words he avoids any semblance of profound research into the nature of interest by treating it as loan interest which the capitalist pays to himself (*p. 267 f.*). And so, in spite of the fine running start provided by the originality of his creation of that productive power, "saving," his actual leap failed to carry him clear of the field of "colorless" writers.

VII

THE PRODUCTIVITY THEORIES

A. PRELIMINARY SURVEY

SOME of the immediate successors of Adam Smith began to explain interest as a result of the *productive power of capital.* J. B. Say led the way in 1803. One year later Lord Lauderdale took the same stand, though independently of Say. The new explanation found acceptance. It was taken up by gradually widening circles of economists, and worked out by them with greater care, branching out at the same time along widely divergent lines. Although attacked from many sides, chiefly by the socialists, the productivity theory has managed to hold its own. Indeed, at the present time (1884) the majority of such writers as are not entirely opposed to interest, subscribes to one or another variant of it.

The idea that capital produces its own interest, whether true or false, seems at least to be clear and simple. It might be expected, therefore, that the theories built on that fundamental idea would be marked by the especial definitiveness and lucidity of their line of thought. But that expectation fails completely to find fulfillment. For the most important concepts, which constitute the material that the productivity theories must manipulate, reveal, unfortunately, the flaws of indistinctness and ambiguity, and consequently we encounter a superabundance of obscurity, error, confusion and fallacious conclusions of every sort. These occur in such profusion that I dare not take the risk of letting my reader meet the various productivity theories without any preparation, lest I force him to orient himself anew each time, and to do so after he is already in midstream on the current of exposition concerning each particular theory. I must therefore bespeak my reader's indulgence, while I set down a few preliminary observations which are intended to delimit and illuminate the theater of operations for my exposition and critique of the productivity theories.

I think it is especially necessary to clarify two things. The first is the meaning or, more properly, the multiplicity of meanings of the expression "productivity or productive power of capital." The second is the nature of the theoretical function assigned by these theories to that productivity.

73

1. Ambiguity of the Term, "Productivity of Capital"

THE first question is, "What is meant by saying, 'Capital is productive'?"

In its commonest and weakest sense, the expression may be taken to mean merely that capital serves for the production of goods, as distinguished from serving for the immediate satisfaction of wants. In that event we are conferring upon capital the rank of a "productive" entity only in one particular sense. I mean the same sense which appears in our general division of all goods into "producers' and consumers' goods." And even if the degree of productive effect were so slight that the value produced failed to equal the value of the capital expended in the producing, yet even that slight degree would justify us in conferring the title of "productive." But it is clear from the first, that a power which has productivity in this sense alone is completely incapable of accounting for the rise of originary interest.

The adherents of the productivity theories do, as a matter of fact, invest the term with a stronger meaning. Expressly or tacitly they understand it as meaning that, by the aid of capital, *more* is produced, that is to say, that capital is the cause of a special productive surplus result.

But this meaning is further subdivided. The words "to produce more" or "a productive surplus result" may mean one of two things. They may mean either that capital produces more *goods* or that it produces more *value,* and these are by no means identical. To keep the two as distinct in name as they are in fact, I shall designate the capacity of capital to produce more goods as its *physical* or *technical productivity,* and its capacity to produce more value as its *productivity of value.* It is perhaps not unnecessary to say that, at the present stage, I am leaving the question entirely open, as to whether capital actually possesses such capacities or not. I am merely recording the different meanings which may be given, and have been given, to the statement that "capital is productive."

Physical productivity manifests itself in an increased quantity or, possibly, in an improved quality of the product. I might illustrate it by the well-known example given by Roscher: "Let us imagine a nation of fisher-folk, without private ownership or capital, dwelling naked in caves, and living on fish caught by hand in pools left by the ebbing tide. All the workers here may be considered equal, and each man is presumed to catch and eat 3 fish per day. But now one prudent man limits his consumption to 2 fish per day for 100 days, lays up in this way a stock of 100 fish, and makes use of this stock to enable him to apply his whole labor-power for 50 days to the making of a boat and a net. With the aid of this capital he catches 30 fish a day from that time on."[1]

In this instance the physical productivity of capital manifests itself in the fact that the fisher, with the aid of capital, catches more fish than he would otherwise have caught, namely, 30 instead of 3. Or, to put it more correctly, he catches somewhat fewer than 30 instead of 3.

For the 30 fish which are now caught in a day are the result of more than one day's work. To calculate properly, we must add to the labor of catching fish a quota of the labor that went into the making of boat and net. If, for instance, 50 days of labor were required to make the boat and the net, and if the boat and the net last for 100 days, then the 3,000 fish which are caught in the 100 days, appear as the result of 150 days' labor. The surplus production then, due to the employment of capital, is represented for the whole period by $3,000 - 450 = 2,550$ fish, or for each single day by $20 - 3 = 17$ fish. This surplus production is a manifestation of the physical productivity of capital.

Now how would the production by capital of "more value" be manifested? The expression "to produce more value" is, in its turn, ambiguous because the "more" may be measured by various standards. It may mean that, by the aid of capital, a value is produced which is greater than the value that could be produced without the aid of capital. In the foregoing illustration it may mean that the 20 fish caught in a day's labor with the aid of capital are of more value than the 3 fish which were got when no capital was employed. But the expression may also mean that, with the aid of capital, a value is produced which is greater than the *value of the capital itself.* In other words, it may mean that the capital gives a productive return greater than its own value, so that there remains a surplus value over and above the value of the capital consumed in the production. To put it in terms of our illustration, the fisher equipped with boat and net catches 2,700 more fish in 100 days than he would have caught without boat and net. These 2,700 fish are to be termed the (gross) return of the employment of capital and, according to this alternative interpretation of the expression, these 2,700 fish are of more value than the boat and net themselves, so that after boat and net are worn out, there still remains a surplus of value.

Of these two possible meanings those writers who ascribe to capital a productivity of value usually have the latter in mind. When, therefore, I use the expression "productivity of value" without qualification, I shall mean the capacity of capital to produce value exceeding its own value.

Thus we have for the apparently simple proposition, that "capital is productive," no fewer than four interpretations which are clearly distinguishable from each other. In order to place them in proper perspective, I should like to array them side by side. The proposition may signify any of the following:

1] Capital has the capacity of serving to produce goods.

2] Capital has the power of serving to produce *more goods* than could be produced without it.

3] Capital has the power of serving to produce *greater value* than could be produced without it.

4] Capital has the power to produce *value greater than that which it possesses itself.*[2]

It should be self-evident that such widely differing ideas, even if

75

they can, perchance, be designated by identical terms to summarize them, must not be considered identical. Even less permissible would it be to consider them interchangeable in one or more given syllogisms. For instance, it should be self-evident that even though I may have demonstrated a capacity on the part of capital *to produce goods at all,* or a capacity to produce *a greater quantity of goods,* I am still not entitled to consider that I have established its power to produce *more value* than could have been produced without its assistance, or to produce a *value in excess of that which the capital itself possesses.* To substitute the latter two concepts in a demonstration which may have established the correctness of a syllogism involving the former two would obviously be tantamount to proffering a sophism, where a logically sound proof cannot be found. Obvious as this observation may seem, I nevertheless feel constrained to make it—indeed, to emphasize it—because nothing is commoner among the proponents of the productivity theories than the arbitrary interchange of those concepts.

2. Nature of Theoretical Task Confronting the Productivity Theories

I NOW come to the second point, of which at this introductory stage I am very anxious to give a clear statement, namely, the nature of the theoretical task assigned to the productive power of capital by the productivity theories.

This task may be very simply described in the words, *the productivity theories propose to explain interest and claim they do explain interest as a result of the productive power of capital.* But these simple words encompass many meanings which deserve more detailed consideration.

The matter calling for explanation is originary interest. Now there is no question that contract interest (loan interest) is founded in all essential respects on originary interest, and can be easily dealt with in a secondary explanation, once originary interest has been satisfactorily explained. The explanation may therefore be limited to *originary interest.* The facts which form the basis of originary interest may be briefly described as follows.

Wherever capital is employed in production, experience shows that, in the normal course of events, the proceeds (or the share in the proceeds) which the capital creates for its owner have a greater value than the sum of the capital goods consumed in obtaining them.

This phenomenon occurs both in those comparatively rare cases where capital is the sole factor in obtaining proceeds (we cite the case of the new wine which, by lying in storage, becomes changed into matured and better wine) and in the much more common cases where capital cooperates with other factors of production, such as land and labor. For compelling reasons that do not concern us here, men engaged in economic enterprises are accustomed to divide the total product into separate shares, even though it results from undivided cooperation. One share is attributed to capital as a specific return on capital, one share is attributed to nature, as produce of the ground, produce of the mine, etc., and one share, finally, is attributed to the labor which cooperates, as the yield of labor.*

Whether the shares, as they are allotted in practical economic life to the individual factors in production, correspond exactly to the quotas which they have, respectively, *contributed to the total production* is a much disputed question. I must not prejudge that question here, and that is why I have chosen the noncommittal expressions that appear here. Moreover, it is to be noted that the phenomenon of surplus values is manifest not only in the excess of each attributed *share* of the return over the source to which that share is attributed, but also in the excess of the totality of the goods produced over the goods that produce them, *as a whole.* The sum of the means of production (labor, capital, and services of land) employed in making a product has, as a rule, a lower exchange value than is possessed by that which is subsequently their finished product. And this feature makes it difficult to regard as the source of the phenomenon of "surplus value" the mere circumstance that there has been an apportionment of credits within the total return.

Now experience shows that the particular quota of the total product which falls to the share of capital, that is to say, the gross yield of capital, is normally of greater value than the capital expended in its acquisition. Therefore, an excess of value, a "surplus value," arises which remains in the hands of the owner of the capital, and constitutes his originary interest.

The theorist, then, who professes to explain interest must explain the emergence of surplus value. The problem, more exactly stated, can therefore be contained in the question, "Why is the gross return to capital regularly of greater value than the portions of capital, which are consumed in acquiring that return?" Or the question can be worded, *"Why is there a constant difference in value between the capital expended and its return?"*[3] The *productivity theories* propose to *explain,* and say they do *explain,* this difference in value as a result of the *productive power of capital.*

Now, to *explain* means to reveal the complete and compelling nature of the causes of that productive power, not merely to mention one of the conditions upon which, in addition to other unexplained conditions, it depends. To prove that surplus value could not exist without a productive power inherent in capital would no more be explaining surplus value by means of the productive power of capital, than it would be an explanation of land rent, if I proved that the latter could not exist except for the fertility of the soil. Nor (to cite another analogy) would it be an explanation of rain, if I demonstrated that water could not fall to earth, except for the fact that water is subject to the law of gravity.

If surplus value is to be accounted for by the productive power of capital, it is necessary to establish, as obvious or incontrovertible, the

---

* Translators' note: The next paragraph appears as a footnote in Böhm-Bawerk's fourth edition.

fact that the productive power of capital is of such a nature that it can, all by itself, furnish a complete and compelling reason for the rise of surplus value. Or it might be proved that it furnishes such a reason when it operates in conjunction with certain other factors. *But in that case those other factors would also have to be included in the explanation.*

This condition could, conceivably, be met in any one of three ways.

The first of these would be to show that it is an obvious or an irrefutable contention that there is inherent in capital a power *whose very function is to create value,* a power by which capital breathes value, like an economic soul as it were, into the goods which it participates in producing. This would be a productivity of value in the most literal and explicit sense.

A second way would be to show that it is an obvious or an irrefutable contention that capital, by its services, promotes the acquisition of goods in greater quantity or of greater usefulness. But it would also have to be obvious at the same time that those *more plentiful or more useful goods must also be of higher value* than the capital consumed in their production. This would be physical productivity resulting in surplus value as a self-evident consequence.

A third way, finally, would be to show that it is an obvious or an irrefutable contention that capital, by its services, promotes the acquisition of goods in greater quantity or of greater usefulness, and to prove also, *simultaneously and expressly,* two points. The first is that the more plentiful and better goods must be worth more than the capital expended in producing them, and the second, *why* that is so. This would be physical productivity with the creation of surplus value as its deliberately announced objective.

These are, in my opinion, the only combinations of conditions under which the productive power of capital could be demonstrated to be an adequate reason for the rise of surplus value. Any attempt to prove the productivity of capital, except along one of these three lines, would be foredoomed to failure. If, for instance, reliance is placed on the physical productivity of capital without showing it to be self-evident, or without expressly proving that a surplus value accompanies the increased amount of goods, then such productivity would clearly *not* be an adequate cause of surplus value.

3. *Catalogue of Conceivable Productivity Theories*

IN THEIR historical development, the actual productivity theories exhibited a variety quite equal to that of the foregoing array of possible productivity theories. Each of the possible types of explanation has its representative in economic history. The great internal differences that mark the various typical lines of thought strongly suggest that, for the purpose of our description and critique, we should arrange those theories in groups. The grouping will be based on the lines of demarcation previously drawn, but will not follow them quite exactly. Those productivity theories which represent the first two types have so much in common that they may conveniently be treated as a single category. But within the group which comprises the third type we find such important differences that further subdivision seems to be appropriate.

1] There are productivity theories of the first type which maintain that there is inherent in capital a straightforward capacity to produce value. And there are the theories of the second type which, although they take their departure from the concept of physical productivity, nevertheless profess the belief that the phenomenon of surplus value is a necessary and inevitable corollary of that productivity. Both these types of theory have one point in common. That point is that without any intermediate or explanatory transition they leap from the assertion of a productive power to the conclusion of a surplus value. They simply state that capital is productive. Then they do, to be sure, tack on a description of its productive activity, though in this respect they are guilty of superficiality. But then they conclude very hastily by crediting the surplus value to the productivity which they have merely asserted to be present. I shall group these doctrines together under the name of the *naive productivity theories.* The paucity of their arguments, which is characteristic of them, is often so pronounced that we are left in doubt as to whether a given author is to be classed under type one or type two. And that constitutes an additional reason for assigning these two groups, which tend to merge, to a single category in our study of the history of theories.

2] Then there is a second group of theories which make the physical productivity of capital their starting point, but do not regard it as self-evident that the production of greater quantities is a necessary concomitant of the creation of surplus value. Therefore they feel it is necessary to extend their explanation into the sphere of value. I shall call these the *motivated productivity theories.* They all exhibit one characteristic feature in common, in that they assert and describe the productive power of capital, and then add a more or less successful line of argument to prove not only that this productive power of capital must lead to the existence of a surplus value, which accrues to the capitalist, but also why it must do so.

3] A third group of theories may be said to represent a branching off from the foregoing groups. Like the latter, they make their point of departure the physical productivity of capital. But the chief emphasis of their explanation is on the independent existence, activity, and sacrifice of the *uses* of capital. These I shall call the *use theories.* Since they recognize the productive power of capital only as a condition of surplus value, but not as the principal cause of its existence, they do not fully merit the name of productivity theories. Therefore I prefer to segregate them from the latter and devote a separate chapter to them.

B. THE NAIVE PRODUCTIVITY THEORIES

1. Founded by J. B. Say. His Doctrine.

THE founder of these theories is J. B. Say.

It is one of my least welcome tasks as a historian of economic doctrine to state Say's views on the origin of interest. He is a master of polished and rounded sentences, and he contrives to impart the appearance of clarity to his opinions, but as a matter of actual fact he fails completely to give clear cut expression to what he thinks, and the numerous remarks which comprise the scattered fragments of his interest theory unfortunately abound with contradictions that are by no means inconsequential. After careful examination I find it impossible to interpret them as the emanations of a single theory which the writer keeps consistently in mind. Say seems rather to vacillate between two theories, neither of which he expounds with any especial clarity, but which we, at any rate, must differentiate. One of them is essentially a naive productivity theory, the other contains the first germs of the use theories. And so, despite the obscurity of his views, Say occupies a pre-eminent position in the history of the theories of interest. He constitutes a sort of junction point at which two of the most important theoretical branches of economic science begin their respective courses.

One who would convey Say's views can make use of only one of his two principal works, which are his *Traité d'Economie Politique*[4] and the *Cours Complet d'Economie Politique Pratique.*[5] We must rely almost exclusively on the former, because the *Cours Complet* sidesteps practically every opportunity to make any significant statement.

According to Say, *all* goods come into existence through the cooperation of three factors, namely, nature (*agents naturels*), capital, and human labor power (*faculté industrielle*). These factors appear as the productive funds from which all the goods of a nation emanate, and which constitute its basic wealth (*fortune*).[6] The goods do not arise directly from these funds. Instead, each fund first produces "productive services" (*services productifs*), and only out of these do the actual products come into existence.

The productive services consist in either an activity (*action*) or in labor (*travail*) of the fund. The industrial fund (*fonds industriel*) provides its service through the labor of man engaged in production; nature supplies hers through the activity of natural forces, the action of the earth, the air, the water, the sun, etc.;[7] but how capital provides its productive service is a matter on which we receive much less explicit information. On one occasion Say makes the statement, vague though it is, in his *Traité,* that "capital must, so to speak, collaborate with human activity, and it is this collaboration which I call the productive service of capital" (*c'est ce concours que je nomme le service productif des capitaux*).[8] He does, to be sure, promise a more complete explanation, which is to be forthcoming later, of the productive activity of capital.

But when he fulfills the promise he does no more than describe the changes (*transformations*) which capital undergoes in the course of production.[9] Nor does the *Cours Complet* give a complete picture of the service of capital. It simply states that capital works when it is employed in productive operations (*on fait travailler un capital, lorsqu' on l'emploie dans des opérations productives;* I, *p. 239*). We learn only indirectly, from frequently recurring comparisons, that Say thinks of the service of capital as being strictly analogous to those of human labor and of the forces of nature. We shall soon see the evil results of the vague manner in which Say applies the ambiguous word "service" to the cooperation of capital.

There are certain natural agents which have not become private property, and which thus render their productive service gratuitously. To this class belong such forces as the sea, the wind, physical and chemical reactions, and the like. The services of the other factors, which are human labor-power, capital and appropriated natural agents (especially land), require that their owners be compensated. The compensation comes out of the value of the goods produced by the services, and that value is divided among all those who have cooperated in its production by contributing the productive services of their respective funds. The proportion in which this value is divided is determined entirely by the relation of supply and demand with respect to the several kinds of services. The function of distribution is performed by the entrepreneur, who buys the services necessary to production, and pays for them at the market price. In this way the productive services acquire a value which is to be clearly distinguished from the value of the fund from which they emanate.[10]

Now these "services" constitute the true income (*revenu*) of their owners. They are what a fund actually yields to its owner. If he sells them or, in the course of production, changes them into products, that means only that the income has undergone a change of form.

But all income is of three kinds, corresponding to the threefold character of the productive services. It is partly income of labor (*profit de l'industrie*), partly land rent (*profit du fonds de terre*), partly interest (*profit,* or *revenu du capital*). The inter-relationship of the three branches of income presents an analogy as complete as that of the different categories of productive service.[11] Each represents the price of a productive service, which the entrepreneur has used to create a product.

This exposition of Say offers an apparently plausible explanation of interest. Capital renders productive services for which the owner must be paid, and that payment is interest. The plausibility is still further heightened by the obvious comparison of interest with wages. Capital works just as man does, and so its labor must receive its reward just as man's labor does. Interest is a faithful copy of wages.

But if we examine this parallel more closely, we begin to discover Say's difficulties and, in consequence, his contradictions.

If the productive services of capital are to be paid for with an amount of value taken out of the value of the product, it is first of all necessary that there be present in the product an amount of value which is available for that purpose. And the obvious question which it is the duty of the interest theory to answer is, *Why is such an amount of value always present?* Let us put it concretely, and ask, "Why is it that products created with the cooperation of capital regularly possess a value so high that, after payment of the market price for the other cooperating productive services, labor and use of land, there still remains enough value to pay for the services of capital?" "And why, moreover, is it just enough to pay these services in proportion to the amount of capital and the duration of its employment?"

Let us suppose that the production of a commodity necessitates labor and use of land to the value of $100, and that it takes just so long to make the commodity that the capital of $100 advanced to purchase those services is replaced after one year. Why, then, is the commodity worth not $100, but more, say $105? And if another commodity has cost exactly the same amount for labor and use of land, but has taken twice as long to make, why is it worth not $100, nor $105, but $110, which is the sum required as adequate payment for the productive services of the $100 of capital over a period of two years?[12]

It will be readily perceived that this is a formulation, *in the terms of Say's theory,* of the question of surplus value. Now that question is the very essence of the interest problem. But nothing that we have as yet heard from Say has reached that essence. Indeed, we are only approaching it now.

With respect to the reason for the existence of that surplus value, Say is by no means as unambiguous as can be desired. His remarks may be divided into two groups which are sharply contradictory.

In one group Say represents capital as endowed with the power of creating value. The value exists because capital has created it, and the productive services of capital are remunerated *because* the surplus value necessary for this purpose is created. Here, then, the payment for the productive services of capital is the *result* of the existence of surplus value.

In the second group Say reverses the causal relation, by representing the payment of the services of capital as the *cause* of the existence of surplus value. Products have value because, and only because, the owners of the productive services from which they arise demand payment. And specifically, these products have a sufficiently high value to yield a surplus of interest, because the cooperation of capital is not to be had for nothing.

While the first group contains numerous passages where Say speaks in a general way of a *faculté productive* and a *pouvoir productif* of capital, I find more significance in a controversial note in the fourth chapter of the first book of his *Traité* (*p. 71, note 2*). He is arguing against Adam Smith who, he says, fails to understand the true nature of the productive power of capital when he ascribes the value created by means of capital to the labor by which that capital itself was originally produced. He illustrates by taking the case of an oil press. "Smith is mistaken," he says. "The product of this preceding labor is, if you will, the value of the press itself. *But the value that is daily produced by the press is another and entirely new value,* just as the rental value of a piece of ground is a separate value from that of the piece of ground itself, for it is a value which may be consumed without diminishing the value of the ground." And then Say goes on to say, *"If capital did not possess inherent productive power,* independent of the labor that created it (*si un capital n'avait pas en lui-même une faculté productive indépendente de celle du travail qui l'a créé*), what explanation is there for the fact that a capital produces in perpetuity an income which is independent of the industrial activity which employs it?" Capital, then, creates value, and its capability of doing so is the *cause* of interest. Similarly Say says in another place, "Le capital employé paie les services rendus, *et les services rendus produisent la valeur* qui remplace le capital employé."[13]

My first remarks with respect to the second group concern an observation which does not, indeed, directly refer to interest, but cannot escape being applied to it by analogy. "Those natural powers," says Say,[14] "which are susceptible of appropriation become funds productive of value because they do not cooperate gratuitously." Furthermore, he repeatedly states that the price of products depends on the amount of remuneration paid to the productive services which cooperated in their making. "A product will therefore be dearer in the same degree as its production requires, not only more productive services, but productive services that are *more highly compensated (plus fortement rétribués)*. The price of a product will rise in such measure as it reflects three factors —the degree to which the consumers feel a need for the product, the abundance of their media of exchange, and *the rate of compensation which the sellers of the productive services can demand*.[15]

Finally, I should like to cite a striking passage from Chapter VIII of Book II, because of its bearing on the subject of interest. "The impossibility of obtaining a product without the cooperation of a capital compels the consumer to pay for the product a price high enough for the entrepreneur, who assumes the work of producing, to buy the services of that necessary instrument." This is in direct contradiction to the passage first quoted,[16] in which the compensation of the capitalist was explained by the existence of the surplus value "created." For in this instance the existence of the surplus value is explained by the necessity for compensating the capitalist. It is in harmony with this latter concept, too, that Say conceives of interest as a constituent of the costs of production.[17]

Contradictions like these are the perfectly natural result of the uncertainty shown by Say in his whole theory of value. He succumbs to the blandishments of the Adam Smith-Ricardo theory of costs quite as often as he inveighs against it. It is very significant of this uncertainty that Say in the passages already quoted (*Traité, pp. 315, 316*) contends that the value of products arises from the value of the services which produce them, and then advances the diametrically opposed argument, that the value of the productive funds arises from the value of the

83

products which are obtained from them (*Leur valeur—des fonds productifs —vient donc de la valeur du produit qui peut en sortir*).[18] We shall return later to this important passage.

What has been said is perhaps sufficient to show that no injustice is done to Say in assuming that he had not himself any clear view as to the ultimate reason for interest, but vacillated between two opinions. According to the one opinion interest comes into existence because capital produces it; according to the other, because "productive services of capital" are a constituent of cost, and require compensation.

Between the two views there is strong and real antagonism, stronger than might appear at first sight. The one treats the phenomenon of interest as primarily a problem of production, the other treats it as a problem of distribution. The one concludes its explanation by calling it simply a fact of production that capital produces surplus value, and that therefore there is surplus value, and that there is no occasion for further question. The other theory places only incidental reliance on the cooperation of capital in production, which it of course presupposes. But its center of gravity, as it were, lies in factors which concern the relationships underlying the cooperative determination of value and price. Say's first opinion places him in the ranks of the adherents of the pure productivity theories, while his second marks him as a forerunner of the very interesting and important use theories.[19]

In accordance with the plan of procedure which I announced previously, I shall omit any discussion at this point of Say's use theory in order to follow the subsequent development of the naive productivity theory. There was really no development, in the strict sense of the word. The most conspicuous feature of the naive productivity theories is the silence in which they pass over the causal relation between the productive power of capital and its alleged effect, the "surplus value" of products. Thus there is no substance to develop, and the historical course of these theories is therefore nothing but a somewhat monotonous series of variations on the simple idea that capital produces surplus value. No true development can be expected until we reach the succeeding stage, that of the motivated productivity theories.

2. Say's Followers in Germany

THE naive productivity theory enlisted the greatest number of its adherents in Germany, and the next greatest in France and Italy. The English economists, whose bent does not seem favorable to any theory of productivity, and who, moreover, had possessed a motivated productivity theory ever since the time of Lord Lauderdale, completely vaulted over the naive phase of the productivity theory.

Say's catchword, the productivity of capital, quickly won acceptance in Germany. Even though no systematic interest theory was immediately founded on it, it soon became customary to recognize capital as a third and independent factor of production, beside nature and labor, and to set up a parallel between that "threesome" and the one composed of the three branches of income—rent of land, wages of labor, and interest on capital. A few writers who follow this line somewhat hesitantly, and even inject additional concepts of a different origin of interest, have already been mentioned in the chapter on the colorless theories.

But it was not long before Say's opinions came to be more firmly relied upon as the explanation of interest. The first to do so was Schön.[20] The explanation he gives is very short. He first claims for capital, in fairly modest words, the character of being a "third particular source of wealth, although an indirect source" (*p. 47*). But at the same time he considers it proved and evident that capital must produce a certain rate of interest. For "the yield belongs originally to those who cooperated towards its making" (*p. 82*), and *"it is clear* that national production must set aside as many distinct kinds of income as there are categories of productive powers and instruments" (*p. 87*). Any further proof is, quite characteristically, not considered necessary. Even the occasion of his altercation with Adam Smith fails to elicit from him any more detailed reasoning on behalf of his own view. He is content to find fault with Adam Smith in general terms for regarding only the immediate workers as participants in production, and for overlooking the productive character of capital and land. He terms this an oversight which led Smith into the mistake of thinking that originary interest is the result of a curtailment of the wages of labor (*pp. 85 ff.*).

Riedel espouses the new doctrine in greater detail and very decisively.[21] He devotes a special paragraph to an exposition of it under the title of *Productivity of Capital,* and in the course thereof he says, "The *productivity* which capital generally possesses when it is employed *is manifest from the fact that material values* which have been employed, with a view to production, in aiding nature and labor, not only are, as a rule, replaced, but also *assist in creating a surplus of material values, which surplus would not have been brought into existence without them."* At another point he says, "Whenever the use of capital results in the creation of material values exceeding the value of the aid which nature and labor have furnished, that result must be termed 'the product of capital.' " And at still another place we find, "It is always incorrect to credit the product of capital to those operative forces which capital needs as a condition precedent to employment, that is to say, to nature and labor. *Capital is an independent force,* no less than they are, and is in most cases no less necessary to them, than they are to capital" (*Chap.* I, *Sec. 366*).

It is very significant that Riedel finds the productive power of capital "manifest" because of the creation of excess value. In his view it is so self-evident that surplus value and productive power belong inseparably to each other, that from the fact of surplus value he deduces the productive power of capital as its only conceivable cause. We need not, under these circumstances, be surprised that Riedel considers that he has accounted completely for the existence of originary interest when he has simply mentioned the catchword, "productivity of capital," nor that he dispenses with any detailed explanation of it elsewhere.

But the writer who probably did more than any other to popularize the productivity theory in Germany is Wilhelm Roscher.

This distinguished scholar, whose most signal merits certainly do not lie in the sphere of precise theoretical research, has unfortunately devoted very little care to the systematic working out of the doctrine of interest. This is apparent, upon even superficial examination, from all sorts of glaring misconceptions and incongruities. Thus in Section 179 of his great work[22] he defines interest as the *price* of the use of capital, although this definition evidently applies only to contract interest and not to originary interest. And yet in the same paragraph Roscher calls the latter a "kind of interest." Again, in his Section 148 he asserts that the original amount of all branches of income (including, therefore, the amount of originary interest) "obviously" determines the amount of contract interest. And yet in his Section 183 he solves the problem of the rate of interest, not by reference to originary interest, which supplies a criterion, but to loan interest, which does not. According to Roscher, the price of the use of capital depends, to begin with, on the supply of and demand for "circulating capitals" and that demand, furthermore, depends "on the number of borrowers and *their ability to pay, especially of non-capitalists,* such as landowners and laborers." Thus Roscher's statement would seem to imply that the rate of interest is determined in the first instance by the state of the market with respect to loan interest, and secondarily by conditions affecting originary interest, by virtue of the law of equalization of interest in all kinds of employment. It is commonly accepted that the very opposite condition obtains. Finally it may be said that where his research touches the field of theory, Roscher does not treat the highly important theoretical question of the origin of interest at all. He merely touches on it superficially in the course of a discussion of its legitimacy which appears in a practical supplement dealing with the political aspects of interest.

To judge by the contents of the following observations, which are a medley of the naive productivity theory and of Senior's abstinence theory, Roscher is an eclectic. In Section 189 he ascribes to capital "real productivity," and in the note to it he commends the Greek expression τοκος (meaning "that to which birth is given") as "very appropriate" for interest. In a later note he argues heatedly against Marx, and his "latest relapse into the old heresy of the nonproductivity of capital," adducing as convincing proof of its productivity such things as the increase in value of cigars, wine, cheese, or any goods "which, through simple postponement of consumption, may attain a considerably higher value, both use value and exchange value, without the slightest additional labor." In the same paragraph he illustrates this by the well-known example of the fisher who first catches three fish a day by hand, then saves up a stock of 100 fish, makes a boat and net while living on his stock, and thereafter catches 30 fish a day with the help of this capital.

In all these instances Roscher's view evidently is that capital produces surplus value directly by its own peculiar power. Nor does he trouble to look for any more intricate explanation of the origin of surplus value. I cannot, therefore, avoid classing him among the naive productivity theorists.

As already pointed out, however, he has not kept exclusively to this view, but has both in form and in substance coordinated the abstinence theory with it. He cites as a second and "indubitable" foundation of interest the "real sacrifice which resides in abstinence from the personal consumption of capital." He calls special attention to the fact that, in the determination of the price for the use of the boat, the 150 days' privation on the part of the fisherman would be a weighty consideration, and he says that we can call interest a reward for abstinence, just as we call the wage of labor a reward for industry. In other respects, too, there are many ill-concealed contradictions. These include Roscher's assumption of the independent productive power of capital, which is utterly inconsistent with his Section 183, in which he declares the "use value of capital to be in most cases synonymous with the skill *of the laborer* and the abundance *of the natural powers"* which are connected with it.

Evidently the authoritative character which the respected name of Roscher enjoys among German economists has redounded to the benefit of his interest theory. For although that theory can lay but slight claim indeed to the cardinal theoretic virtues of unity, consistency and profundity, yet it has met with acceptance and imitation in many quarters.

I venture to pass over a goodly number of German writers who since Roscher's time have simply repeated the doctrine of the productive power of capital, without adding anything to it.[23] Of these Friedrich Kleinwächter may be mentioned as one who has worked at the doctrine, if not with much more success, at least with greater thoroughness and care.[24]

3. Say's Followers in France and Italy

IN France Say's productivity theory won as much popularity as it did in Germany. As a theory it became a veritable "fashion," and even the violent attacks made on it by the socialists during the forties, especially by Proudhon, did but little to prevent its spread. It is singular, however, that it was seldom accepted by the French writers in unalloyed purity. Almost all who adopted it added elements taken from one or more theories inconsistent with it. This was the case (to name only a few of the most influential writers) with Rossi and Molinari, with Joseph Garnier, and most recently with Cauwés and Leroy-Beaulieu.[25]

Since the productivity theory underwent no essential change at the hands of these economists, I need not go into any detailed statement of their views, especially since we shall meet the most prominent of them among the eclectics in a later chapter.

I shall mention only one particularly striking statement of the last-named writer, to illustrate how great a hold the productivity theory has on French economists even today, and in the face of abundant criticism by the socialists. In his *Essai sur la répartition des richesses,* the most highly respected monograph to appear in France on the distribution of wealth and a book which went through two editions within two years, Leroy-Beaulieu writes, *"Capital begets (engendre) capital, that is incontestable."* And a little later he guards against the possibility that this might be interpreted to mean that capital begets interest (*engendre un intérêt*) only in some legal sense, or through the arbitrariness of the law, by saying, *"This is true naturally and factually, and in this case the law has only copied nature"* (*c'est naturellement, matériellement; les lois n'ont fait ici que copier la nature*).[26]

From the Italian literature on this phase of our subject I shall, in conclusion, cite but one writer instead of many. But his method of treatment, with its simplicity in form coupled with obscurity in substance, may be taken as typical of the naive productivity theory. I refer to the widely read Scialoja.[27]

This writer makes the assumption that the factors of production, among which he reckons capital (*p. 39*), *share with or transfer to* their products their own "virtual" or "potential" value, which is based on their capacity for production. And then he assumes, further, that the part which each factor takes in the *production* of value is also the measure which governs the division of the product among the cooperating factors. Thus in the distribution each factor receives as much value as it has created, even though it is not possible to measure the amount *a priori* in exact figures (*p. 100*). In conformity with that assumption he then declares originary interest to be that "portion" of the total excess of proceeds accruing to the entrepreneur *"which represents the productive activity of capital during the period of production"* (*p. 125*).

4. Critique of the Naive Productivity Theories

BEFORE turning from exposition to criticism, I must once more point out the distinction between those two branches of the naive productivity theory which I previously combined in my historical presentation. All the views already examined agree in attributing surplus value to the productive power of capital, without showing any reason why that should be so. But, as I stated at the beginning of this chapter, this unanimity of nomenclature may in truth embrace two essentially different ideas. The productive power of capital referred to may be construed to mean, in the literal sense, productivity of value, i.e., a capacity on the part of capital to produce value directly; or it may be construed to mean merely physical productivity, i.e., a capacity on the part of capital to produce an especially large quantity or an especially high quality of goods. In this case no reason is implied for the creation of surplus value, because it is regarded as perfectly self-evident that the large quantity or the high quality must necessarily contain such surplus value.

In stating their doctrine, most of the naive productivity theorists are so sparing of words that it is easier to say what they *may have* thought than what they actually *did* think, and often we can only conjecture whether a given writer held the one view or the other. Thus Say's "productive power" is equally open to either interpretation, and the same may be said of Riedel's "productivity." Scialoja and Kleinwächter, however, seem to incline more to the literal construction, while Roscher, with his illustration of the increased catch of fish, seems to demand the physical construction. In any case, it is not of much importance to determine which of these views each writer holds, for if we submit each of the only two conceivable views to criticism, each will get its due.

Both variants of the naive productivity theory fall far short of satisfying the demands which may reasonably be made of a theory purporting to be a scientific explanation of interest.

After the violent critical attacks that have been directed against the productivity theory by the socialist and the "socio-political" school, its inadequacy has been so generally felt, at least among German economists, that any attempt by me to disprove its thesis will find me beating a dead horse. Still it is a duty which I cannot shirk. The theories of which we are speaking have been treated with such a lack of thoroughness and such hastiness of judgment that I, as a critic, am under the greater compulsion to avoid a similar blunder. But my chief reason is that I mean to attack the naive productivity theory with arguments which are essentially different from the arguments of socialist criticism, and which seem to me to go more nearly to the heart of the matter.

Let us begin with the first form.

5. *Untenability of the First Variant of the Productivity Theory*

WE are asked to believe that interest owes its existence to the fact that capital possesses the peculiar power of creating value. The question that inevitably arises is, "What proofs are there that capital actually possesses such a power?" An unproved assurance that it does so certainly cannot offer sufficient foundation for a serious scientific theory.

If we run through the writings of the naive productivity theorists, we shall find in them a great many proofs of physical productivity, but almost nothing that could be interpreted as an attempt to prove that there is a direct value-creating power inherent in capital. They assert it, but they do not take the trouble to prove it, beyond mentioning the fact that the productive employment of capital is regularly followed by a surplus of value and so implying that we have empirical proof of the power of capital to produce value. Even this, however, is mentioned only very cursorily. It is put most plainly, perhaps, by Say in the passage previously quoted (*page 83*). He asks, "How could capital be a perpetual source of independent income, if it did not possess independent productive power?" And to Riedel, we recall, the productive power of capital "is manifest" in the existence of surplus values.[28]

Now how convincing is this empirical proof? Does the fact that the employment of capital is regularly followed by the appearance of surplus value actually furnish adequate proof that capital possesses a power to create value?

Certainly not! No more than the regular rising of the barometer in the mountains after a summer snowfall proves that there is inherent in summer snow a power to cause a column of mercury to rise. That, incidentally, is a naive theory which is often heard from the lips of the mountaineers.

The scientific blunder here is obvious. A mere hypothesis is taken for a proven fact. In both cases experience presents us with the juxtaposition of two facts, *the unknown cause of which is the object of inquiry.* There are in both cases a great many conceivable causes for the effect in question. So in both cases it was and is possible to advance a great many hypotheses as to the actual cause. To ascribe the rising barometer to a specific power of the summer snow, or the surplus value of the products of capital to a specific power inherent in capital to create value, is to select only one of many possible hypotheses. We are the more convinced that both are mere hypotheses, since nothing is known in other respects as to the existence of the "powers" referred to. They *had to be postulated* for the specific purpose of explaining the phenomena in question.

But the cases we have compared resemble each other not only in being examples of mere hypotheses, but in being examples of bad hypotheses. The credibility of a hypothesis depends on whether it finds support outside the body of data which has suggested it, and particularly, whether it is inherently probable. That this is not the case as regards the naive hypothesis of the mountaineer is well known, and therefore no educated man believes in the fairy story that the rise of the column of mercury is caused by some mysterious power of the summer snow. But the hypothesis of a value-creating power in capital has no stronger case. On the one hand, it is supported by no single fact of importance from any other quarter—*it is an entirely unaccredited hypothesis.* Furthermore, it contradicts the nature of things—*it is an impossible hypothesis.*

Literally to ascribe to capital a power of producing value is to misunderstand the essential nature of value, and to misunderstand the essential nature of production completely. *Value* is not produced at all, and cannot be produced. We never produce anything but forms, shapes of materials, combinations of material, that is to say, things, goods. These goods can of course be *goods possessing value,* but they do not bring value with them ready made, as something inherent that results from production. They only *acquire* value from the wants and satisfactions of the economic world. Value has its source not in the past of goods, but in their future. It does not come out of the workshop where goods came into existence, but out of the wants which they will satisfy. Value cannot be forged like a hammer, nor woven like a piece of linen. If it could, our industries would be spared those frightful convulsions called crises, which have no other cause than that quantities of products, though manufactured to technical perfection, cannot achieve the value expected. The most that production can do is to create goods in the hope that, according to the anticipated relations of demand and supply, they will be of value. Its action might be compared to that of the bleacher. Just as the bleacher lays his linen in the sunshine, so production applies its activity to the things and in the places that promise to make its products valuable. But it no more creates the value than the bleacher creates the sunshine.

I do not believe it necessary to amass any more positive proofs in support of my proposition. I think it too self-evident to require them. But it may not be superfluous to defend it against some considerations that at first sight—but only at first sight—seem to oppose it.

It is a familiar fact that the value of goods bears some relation to the cost of their production. And even though there may be no clear recognition of just what that relation is, the impression is nevertheless created that the value of goods stems from the circumstances of their production. But it must not be forgotten that this connection is valid only subject to certain presuppositions. In formulating the law of the value of costs, one of these presuppositions is usually expressly stated, while the other is usually tacitly assumed, yet neither of them has anything at all to do with production. The first presupposition is that the goods produced are *useful,* and the second is that, as compared with the demand for them, they are *scarce,* and continue to be so.

It is very simple to demonstrate that these two circumstances which stand so modestly in the background of the law of costs, and not the costs themselves, are the truly ruling determinants of value. So long as costs are expended on the production of goods which are sufficiently useful and scarce, so long, therefore, as the costs themselves are in harmony with the usefulness and scarcity of the goods, just so long do they remain in harmony with the value of the goods and appear to govern it. But as soon as costs are expended on goods which are not useful enough or scarce enough, as, for instance, on the making of watches which will not run or on the raising of timber in districts where there is a natural superfluity of wood, or on making an oversupply of good watches, then the value no longer covers the costs, and goods no longer even seem to derive their value from the circumstances of their production.

There is another plausible objection. My opponents may admit that we produce, in the first instance, goods only. But since without the production of goods there would be no value, it is evident that by creating goods we also create value. When a man produces goods of the value of $1,000, it is quite evident that he has occasioned the existence of $1,000 of value which would never have existed without the production. This appears to offer palpable proof of the correctness of the proposition that the value, too, comes into existence through production.

Certainly this proposition is, in a sense, correct, but in a quite different sense from that which it has in the question at issue. It is correct in the sense that production is *one* cause of value. It is not correct in the sense that production is *the* cause of value. That is to say, it is not correct in the sense that the full and complete complex of causes

91

required to account for the existence of value is to be found in the circumstances of production.

There is a world of difference between these two senses and I should like to illustrate that more clearly. If a field is turned up by a steam plough, it is indisputable that the steam plough is one cause of the grain produced, and at the same time is one cause of the value of the grain produced. But it is equally indisputable that the emergence of value on the part of the grain is very far from being fully explained by saying that the steam plough has produced it. One cause of the existence of the grain, and hence of the value of the grain, was certainly the sunshine. But if I should ask why a bushel of grain possesses a value of three dollars, would anybody think it an adequate answer to say that the sunshine produced the value? Or when the old question is raised, whether talents are innate or acquired, who would decide that they are innate on the strength of the argument that, if man were not born there would be no talents and that, consequently, there is no doubt that birth is the cause of talents?

And now let us apply this to our present problem. Our productivity friends are wrong because they desire too strongly to be right. If they had been content to speak of a value-creating power of capital in the sense that capital supplies *one* cause of the emergence of value, there would have been no grounds for objection. To be sure, next to nothing would have been done towards explaining surplus value. It would only be saying explicitly what practically goes without saying, and in the nature of things our theorists would have been compelled to go on to explain the other and less obvious contributing causes of excess value. Instead of that, they imagine that they have given *the* cause of the existence of value. They assume that in the words, "Capital, by virtue of its productive power, creates value or excess value," they have given such a conclusive and complete explanation of its existence that no further explanation of any kind is needed. And that is their blunder.

What has been said finds another important and useful application, and I offer that application here, although it is not concentrated against the productivity theory. What is sauce for the goose is sauce for the gander, and if capital can possess no value-creating power because value is not "created," then for the same reason no other element of production, be it land or be it human labor, possesses such a power. This has escaped the notice of that large school of economists which directs the sharpest weapons of its criticism against the assumption that land or capital has any value-creating power, only to be even more emphatic in claiming that very power for labor.[29]

In my opinion those critics have overturned one idol only to set up another in its place. They have attacked a broad prejudice only to embrace a narrower one. The privilege of creating value belongs as little to human labor as to any other factor. Labor, like capital, creates goods, and goods only; and only the economic conditions which they are meant to serve can arouse and then fulfill the expectation that those goods will have value. The partial, though by no means complete, correlation between quantity of labor and value of product is caused by things quite apart from any "value-creating" property of labor, which does not and cannot exist. I hinted at those things (quite cursorily, to be sure) when I spoke of the incidental connection between costs and value.

All these prejudices have been a deplorable hindrance to the development of theory. They have misled theorists into accepting far-too-easy solutions to the most difficult problems in economics. If the creation of value was to be explained, they followed up the chain of causes a little way (often a very little way), only to come to a contented stop at the erroneous and prejudiced decision that capital or labor had created the value. In so doing they gave up searching further for the true causes, and made no attempt to pursue the problem into those depths where the real difficulties lie.

6. *The Second Variant of the Productivity Theory Similarly Untenable*

NOW let us turn to the second interpretation of which the naive productivity theory is capable. Here the productive power ascribed to capital is, in the first instance, to be understood as physical productivity only, that is to say, a capacity on the part of capital to furnish assistance which results in the production of more goods or of better goods than could be obtained without its help. But it is assumed as self-evident that the increased product, besides replacing the costs of capital expended, must include a surplus of value. Just how convincing is this interpretation?

I grant without ado that capital actually possesses the physical productivity ascribed to it, that is to say, that more goods can actually be produced with its help than without.[30] I will also grant (although here the conclusion is not quite so inescapable) that the greater amount of goods produced with the help of capital has higher value than the smaller amount of goods produced without it. But there is not one single feature in the whole set of circumstances to indicate that this greater amount of goods must be worth more *than the capital consumed in its production.* And that is the feature of the phenomenon of excess value which has to be explained.

To put it in terms of Roscher's familiar illustration, I readily admit and understand that with the assistance of a boat and net one catches 30 fish a day, while without this capital one would have caught only 3. I readily admit and understand, furthermore, that the 30 fish are of higher value than the 3 were. But that the 30 fish must be worth more *than the pro rata portion of boat and net which is worn out in catching them* is an assumption which the conditions of the problem do not prepare us for, or even cause to appear tenable, to say nothing of making it obvious. If we did not know from experience that the value of the return to capital is regularly greater than the value of the substance of capital consumed, the naive productivity theory would not furnish a single reason for regarding such a result as necessary. It might very well be quite otherwise. Why should not capital goods that yield a great return be highly valued on that very account and indeed, so highly that their capital value would be equal to the value of the abundance of goods which they yield? Why, for instance, should not a boat and net which, during the time that they last, help to procure an extra return of 2,700 fish be considered exactly equal in value to those 2,700 fish? But in that event, in spite of the physical productivity, there would be no excess value.

Strangely enough, some of the most prominent representatives of the naive productivity theory make definite statements which would lead us to expect just such a result, namely, the absence of an excess value. Several of our authors assert unequivocally that the value of capital goods has a tendency to coincide with the value of their products. Thus Say writes (*Traité, p. 338*) that the value of the productive funds arises from the value of the product which may come from them. Riedel in Section 91 of his *Nationalökonomie* develops in detail the proposition that "the value of means of production" (hence of concrete quantities of capital) "depends substantially on their productive ability, or on a capacity, guaranteed under the immutable principles of production, for performing a greater or a lesser service in the producing of material values." And Roscher says in Section 149 of his *Grundlagen,* "Moreover, land has this in common with other means of production, that its *price is essentially conditioned by that of its products.*"

What then if, in accordance with these views, the value of capital goods accommodates itself entirely to the value of the product, and becomes exactly equal to it? And why should it not? But in that case where would be the excess value?[31]

Even though excess value may actually be a concomitant of the physical productivity of capital, it is certainly not a self-evident one, and any theory which, without a word of explanation, accepts it as such does not meet the scientific requirements of a theory.

7. Summary

LET us sum up. Whichever of the two meanings we give to the expression "productive power," the naive productivity theory breaks down. If it maintains that there is a direct value-creating power inherent in capital, it maintains an impossibility. There is no power in any element of production whatsoever, which can infuse value immediately or necessarily into its products. A factor of production can never be an ultimate source of value. Wherever value makes its appearance it has its ultimate cause in the relation of human needs to the means of satisfying them. Any tenable explanation of interest must go back to this ultimate source. But the hypothesis that there exists a value-creating power is an attempt to gloss over this last and most difficult part of the explanation by means of a completely untenable assumption.

If, however, the writers we are discussing understand by productivity merely physical productivity, then they are mistaken in treating excess value as a concomitant phenomenon which can be taken for granted. By failing to supply a word of explanation for the ostensibly axiomatic, the theory fails to furnish the most important and the most difficult part of the solution.

It is, however, very easy to understand how the naive productivity theory enlisted so many adherents in spite of these defects. It is impossible to deny that at first blush it appears unusually beguiling. It is undeniable that capital helps to produce, and helps to produce "more." At the same time we see that, at the end of every productive activity in which capital takes part, there remains a "surplus" for the entrepreneur, and that the amount of this surplus bears a regular proportion to the amount of capital employed, and to the duration of its employment. In these circumstances nothing really is more natural than to connect the existence of this surplus with the productive power that resides in capital. It would have been almost a miracle if the productivity theory had *not* been advanced.

How long one remains under the influence of this theory depends on how soon one begins to reflect critically on the meaning of the word "productive." As long as one does not reflect, the theory appears to be an exact representation of the facts. It is a theory which, one might say with Leroy-Beaulieu, *n'a fait ici que copier la nature* (has merely copied nature). But if one does reflect, the theory shows itself to be a web of dialectical sophistry, achieved through the misuse of that ambiguous term, the "productive surplus yield" of capital.

That is why the naive productivity theory is, I might say, the predestined interest theory of a primitive and immature stage of economics. But it is also predestined to disappear as soon as that science ceases to be "naive." That it finds such wide acceptance among economists even now is certainly no cause for pride.

C. THE MOTIVATED PRODUCTIVITY THEORIES

1. General Characteristics

THE motivated productivity theories agree with the naive theories in regarding the productive power of capital as the ultimate source of interest. But in the working out of this fundamental idea they show a twofold advance. In the first place, they shun the mysticism of "value-creating powers," and, with their feet on the solid ground of fact, they always mean physical productivity when they speak of the "productivity of capital." In the second place, they do not consider it to be self-evident that physical productiveness must be accompanied by excess value. They therefore insert a characteristic middle term, which has the special function of giving reasons *why* the increased quantity of *products* must result in an excess *value.*

2. *Necessity for Detailed Analysis of the Several Doctrines*

OF COURSE the scientific value of all such theories depends on whether or not the middle term will bear investigation. And since the writers of this group differ very widely with respect to this middle term, I shall be obliged to individualize my exposition and critique of their several doctrines in this chapter to a far greater degree than was necessary in the case of the almost uniform "naive" theories. In doing so I certainly impose on myself and on my readers no small burden, but it would be impossible to spare us both without sacrificing honest and sound criticism. When a writer has anything particular to say, the honest critic must allow him to say it in particular, and must answer him in particular. The particular must not be dismissed with generalities.

The succession of motivated productivity theories begins with Lord Lauderdale.[32]

In the history of the theory of interest Lauderdale occupies a rather important place. He recognizes, as none of his predecessors did, that there is a great problem here which calls for solution. He first states the problem formally and explicitly by asking: "What is the nature of profit, and how does it originate?" His appraisal of the few writers who had expressed themselves on the subject of originary interest before his time is well considered. He is, moreover, the first to present a connected and complete theory, and one that is unified in form, rather than a series of scattered observations.

He introduces his interest theory by denying Adam Smith's premise and declaring that capital is a third original source of wealth, the others being land and labor (*p. 121*). Later on he examines very thoroughly the method by which it operates as a source of wealth (*pp. 154-206*); and at the very beginning he recognizes the importance and difficulty of the interest problem, and takes occasion, in a remarkable passage, to pose the problem formally.[33]

He is not satisfied with the views of his precedessors. He expressly rejects the doctrine of Locke and of Adam Smith, who are inclined to derive interest from the increment of value which the worker produces by expending labor on capital goods. He rejects Turgot's doctrine too, which, much too superficially, connects interest with the possibility of obtaining rent by the purchase of land.

Lauderdale then formulates his own theory in these words: "In every instance where capital is so employed as to produce a profit, it uniformly arises, either from its *supplanting* a portion of labour, which would otherwise be performed by the hand of man, or from its *performing* a portion of labour, which is beyond the reach of the personal exertion of man to accomplish" (*p. 161*).

In thus proclaiming the *power of capital to supplant labor* as the cause of interest, Lauderdale refers, under a somewhat altered name, to the same thing as we agreed to call the physical productivity of capital.

And, as a matter of fact, Lauderdale himself, many times and with emphasis, calls capital "productive" and "producing."[34]

Still the chief question remains, "In what way does interest originate from the power of capital to supplant labor?" According to later statements by Lauderdale, it does so because the owner of a capital good is able to secure for himself as his share, either wholly or at least in part, the wages of those workers who are replaced by the capital.

"Supposing, for example," says Lauderdale, in one of the many illustrations by which he tries to confirm the correctness of his theory,[35] "one man with a loom should be capable of making three pair of stockings a day, and that it should require six knitters to perform the same work with equal elegance, in the same time; it is obvious, that the proprietor of the loom might demand for making his three pair of stockings the wages of five knitters, and that he would receive them; because the consumer, by dealing with him rather than the knitters, would save in the purchase of the stockings the wages of one knitter" (*p. 165*).

Lauderdale himself is very prompt in meeting one obvious objection. "The small profit which the proprietors of machinery generally acquire, when compared with the wages of labour, which the machine supplants, may perhaps create a suspicion of the rectitude of this opinion. Some fire engines, for instance, draw more water from a coal pit in one day than could be conveyed on the shoulders of 300 men, even assisted by the machinery of buckets; and a fire engine undoubtedly performs its labour at a much smaller expense than the amount of the wages of those whose labour it thus supplants. This is, in truth, the case with all machinery."

But this phenomenon, Lauderdale explains, should not mislead us. It simply arises from the fact that the excess of proceeds obtainable for the use of any machine is also subject to the universal regulator of prices, the relation of supply and demand. "The case of a patent, or exclusive privilege of the use of a machine . . . will tend further to illustrate this.

"If such a privilege is given for the invention of a machine which performs, by the labour of one man, a quantity of work that used to take the labour of four; as the possession of the exclusive privilege prevents any competition in doing the work but what proceeds from the labour of the four workmen, their wages, as long as the patent continues, must obviously form the measure of the patentee's charge—that is, to secure employment, he has only to charge a little less than the wages of the labour which the machine supplants. But when the patent expires, other machines of the same nature are brought into competition; and then his charge must be regulated on the same principle as every other, according to the abundance of machines, or (what is the same thing), according to the facility of procuring machines, in proportion to the demand for them."

In this way Lauderdale thinks he has conclusively established that the cause and source of interest lies in a saving of labor, or of the wages of labor.

Has he really succeeded in establishing this? Has Lauderdale in the foregoing passages really explained the origin of interest? A careful examination of his arguments will very soon enable us to answer this question in the negative.

No fault can be found with the starting point that he takes for his argument. It may be quite correct (to continue Lauderdale's own illustration) to say that one man with a knitting loom can turn out as many stockings in a day as six hand knitters. It is also quite correct to say that if the loom is a monopoly, its owner may easily secure for its day's work the wage of five knitters or, of course, in the case of unlimited competition, a correspondingly smaller amount. And thus, after deducting the wages of the man who tends the machine, there remains as the owner's share four days' wages of labor or under free competition correspondingly less, but always something. It has indeed been shown that the capitalist receives a value.

But this amount received by the capitalist is not the thing that was to be explained, the *net* interest or "profit." It is only the *gross return* for the use of capital. The five men's wages which the capitalist charges or the four that he retains after paying the man who operates the machine are the total income that he makes with the machine. In order to get the net return contained in that income, we must obviously deduct the wear and tear of the machine itself. But Lauderdale, whose whole course of reasoning is always directed toward "profit," either overlooked this, thus confusing gross and net interest, or he considered it quite self-evident that, after deducting from gross interest a proportion for wear and tear, something would be left as net interest. In the first case he made an outright error, and in the second case he has assumed without proof the very point which is the most difficult, indeed the only difficult point to explain, which is that, after deduction from the gross return of capital as much of the capital as has been consumed, something must be left over as excess value, and why it is left over. And that point is, of course, the question which constitutes the essence of the interest problem.

As everything turns on this point, let me put it in its clearest light by means of figures. Suppose, for convenience, that each laborer gets $10 a day, and that the machine will last one year before it is entirely worn out. Then the gross yield of the machine for a year will be represented by 40×365 or $14,600. To ascertain the net interest included in that amount we must evidently deduct the whole capital value of the machine now completely worn out by one year's work. How much will the capital value be? This evidently is the determining factor. If the capital value is less than $14,600, there is a remainder of net interest left over. If it is equal to or higher than $14,600, there can be none.

Now on this decisive point Lauderdale has neither furnished any proof nor even made any assumption. No feature of his theory prevents our assuming that the capital value of the machine amounts to an even $14,600. On the contrary, if we think of the machine as Lauderdale does, as a monopoly, there is a certain justification for our expecting its price to be very high. I grant that experience goes to show that machines and capital goods in general, be their monopoly price ever so high, can never cost quite so much as they yield. But we learn that only from experience, and not from Lauderdale. The important thing is that Lauderdale has not said a word in explanation of that empirical fact. And so he has left the heart of the interest problem untouched.

In the variation of the illustration in which Lauderdale assumes unrestricted competition, it is true that we might consider the value of the machine as fixed (relatively at least) by the amount of its cost of production. But here again we are assailed by doubts as to the other determining factor, the amount of the gross yield. Let us say that the machine cost $10,000 and that $10,000 is presumably its capital value. Then the presence or absence of any net interest depends on whether the daily gross yield of the machine exceeds $\frac{\$10,000}{365}$ or not. Will it exceed that? All that Lauderdale says on this point is that the claim of the capitalist "must be regulated on the same principle as everything else," the relation of supply and demand. In other words, he says nothing at all.

And yet it was very necessary to say something and, moreover, to prove what was said. For it is not in the least self-evident that the gross yield is higher than the capital value of the machine, if that value is depressed by free competition to the amount of its cost. The same unrestricted competition which exerts its influence on the use of the machine also depresses the value of the *products* of capital (in this case, the stockings) and thus reduces the gross return of the machine. Now as long as the machine produces more than it costs, there remains an excess of proceeds for the entrepreneur, and the existence of an excess, one would think, would act as an inducement to further multiplication of the machines till such time as, through the increased competition, the extra income vanishes. Why should competition cease any earlier? Why, for instance, should it stop when the gross yield of a machine which costs $10,000 has sunk to $11,000 or $10,500, when a net interest of 10% or 5% is thereby assured? That calls for complete explanation, and Lauderdale has not said a word about it.

His explanation has therefore shot wide of the mark. What it actually explains is something that needed no explanation, namely, the fact that capital brings in a gross return, a gross interest. But the thing that sorely needed explanation, namely, the remainder of net return included in the gross return, remains as obscure as before.

The test by which Lauderdale attempts to confirm the accuracy of his theory, and on which he lays great weight, fails to change our judgment. He shows that whenever a machine fails to save labor (when, for instance, the machine takes three days to make a pair of stockings while the hand worker does the same in two days) there is no "profit." This, according to Lauderdale, is clear proof that "profit" derives from the power of capital to replace labor. (*P. 164 f.*)

The test is inconclusive. It does admittedly prove that the capacity of the machine to replace labor is a prerequisite for a Lauderdalian "profit" or excess of proceeds. It might be pointed out, incidentally, that this is rather self-evident, since without that quality the machine would have no usefulness at all, and could not even be called a good. But the test falls far short of proving that we may regard that capacity of the machine as the complete explanation of interest. Lauderdale might just as well have used a fully comparable test to prove the truth of a diametrically opposite contention. He could have proved that interest derives from the activity of the workman who operates the machine. For if no one operates the machine it stands idle, and an idle machine will never yield what Lauderdale calls a "profit." Does that mean the workman produced the interest?

I have purposely taken rather great care to point out the blunders into which Lauderdale's method of explanation leads him, because the criticism applies not to Lauderdale alone, but to all those who, in trying to trace interest to the productivity of capital, have been led astray on the same false trail. And we shall see that the number of those I have thus condemned in advance is not small, and embraces many a famous name.

Lauderdale found his first important follower, though by no means his disciple, in Malthus.[36]

With his well-known love of exact definition Malthus carefully stated the nature of interest. "The profits of capital consist of the difference between the value of a commodity produced and the value of the advances necessary to produce it" (*p. 293*). "The rate of profit," he continues more exactly than euphoniously, "is the proportion which the difference between the value of the commodity produced and the value of the advances necessary to produce it bears to the value of the advances" (*p. 294*). "It varies with the variations of the value of the advances compared with the value of the product."

Definitions like these might lead us to expect the obvious query, "Why must there be this difference between the value of the advances and the value of the product?" Unfortunately Malthus does not go on to put this question in so many words. He devoted all his care to his inquiry into the rate of interest, and only a few rather inadequate remarks to the subject of its origin.

In the most detailed of these, Malthus, quite in the style of Lauderdale, refers to the productive power of capital. By means of certain advances in the way of machinery, food, and materials, the laborer is made capable of performing eight or ten times as much work as he could have performed without such assistance. At first blush that might seem to entitle the capitalist to the entire difference between the effectiveness of unassisted labor and that of labor so assisted. But the increased productivity of labor produces an increased supply of goods which results in a reduction in their prices. As a consequence the remuneration for the capital advanced would soon be reduced to "what was necessary, in the existing state of society, to bring the articles, to the production of which they were applied, to the market." Since neither the exertion nor the skill of the laborer is materially greater than when he works unassisted, his wage will remain about the same. "It is not, therefore," continues Malthus, defining his point of view more clearly, if somewhat disputatiously, "quite correct to represent, as Adam Smith does, the profits of capital as a deduction from the produce of labor. They are only a fair remuneration for that part of the production contributed by the capitalist, estimated exactly in the same way as the contribution of the laborer."[37]

In this analysis the reader will have no difficulty in recognizing the principal ideas of Lauderdale's productivity theory. Though they are expressed in somewhat modified form and with somewhat less precision, there is only one feature that points in another direction, and that is the emphasis, however slight, on the point that the pressure of competition must always leave a share for the capitalist, "as much as may be necessary to bring the articles, to the production of which the capital was applied, to market." To be sure, Malthus has not said anything concerning the reason for this new feature, so delicately hinted at. But the fact that he mentions it at all reveals a definite feeling on his part that, in the formation of originary interest, something besides the productivity of capital must be operative.

The same idea is expressed more forcibly in Malthus's direct statement that interest is a *constituent part of the costs of production.*[38]

The formal enunciation of this proposition, to which Adam Smith and Ricardo inclined without expressly stating it,[39] turned out to be a literary event of some importance. It started a very stimulating controversy which was carried on for some decades with great vigor, first in England, and then in other countries. And this controversy made a great, if indirect, contribution to the development of the interest theory. For when economists were heatedly discussing whether originary interest belonged to the costs of production or not, they were inevitably led to make a more thorough investigation into its nature and origin.

The proposition that interest is a constituent portion of the costs of production is one concerning which the verdict rendered by the economic theorist will be basically different from that handed down by the historian of economic doctrine. The former will condemn it as a gross blunder. Torrens[40] did so in Malthus's own time. More recently Pierstorff repeated the condemnation in terms that are harsh—much too harsh in my estimation.[41] They condemn it because originary interest is not a sacrifice that production requires, but a share in its fruits. Calling it a sacrifice was possible only as the result of a rather flagrant confusion of the "social" concept of interest with the "individual" point of view of the single entrepreneur who, of course, feels the payment of interest on borrowed capital as a sacrifice.

But even in this distorted form, the proposition contains a highly significant thought, which suggests a remedy for the inadequacies of the productivity theory, and which Malthus evidently had in mind. It is the thought that the sacrifices of production are not limited to the labor which is employed in production, whether that labor be applied directly, or contributed indirectly as embodied in capital goods. For a separate sacrifice is demanded of the capitalist, and that, too, calls for compensation. Malthus, of course, was not yet able to furnish a specific designation for the nature of this sacrifice. Yet in this somewhat unusual mention of originary interest as a constituent of costs, the economic historian will recognize an interesting connecting link. On one side of the gap, which here is bridged, are found such early intimations as those of Adam Smith, to the effect that the capitalist must have a return because he would otherwise have no interest in the accumulation of capital. At the other end of the bridge the historian encounters several later and more precise theories which recognize, among the constituents, some element of sacrifice which demands compensation. This element goes under different names. J. B. Say calls it "productive services," Hermann prefers "use of capital," and Senior's name for it is "abstinence." Malthus's delicate premonitory tones of those later doctrines of course lacked the volume necessary to drown the coarser notes of the Lauderdalian song of the productivity of capital.

But that neither the one explanation nor the other ever really became part and parcel of the basic theory of Malthus is shown by his remarks on the rate of originary interest (*p. 294 ff.*). Instead of deriving the current rate of interest, as one would naturally expect, from the interplay of those same forces that bring interest into existence, he explains it as determined by utterly foreign influences, namely, the rate of wages on the one hand and the price of products on the other.

He calculates in the following manner. Excess of proceeds is the difference between the value of the costs advanced by the capitalist and the value of the product. The rate of this net yield will, accordingly, be greater, the less the value of the costs and the greater the value of the product. But as the greatest and most important portion of the costs consists in wages of labor, we have as the two determinants which influence the rate of net yield the rate of wages on the one hand, and the price of products on the other.

However logical this explanation may seem, it is easy to show that it does not go to the heart of the matter at all. Perhaps I may be allowed to make use of a comparison. Let us suppose that we wish to designate what determines the distance between the car of a balloon and the balloon itself. It is immediately apparent that the measure of the distance is the length of the rope that fastens the car to the balloon. What should we say if someone were to conduct the investigation thus: "The distance is equal to the difference between the absolute height of the balloon and that of the car, and is therefore increased by everything that increases the absolute height of the balloon and diminishes the absolute height of the car, and is diminished by anything that diminishes the absolute height of the balloon and increases the absolute height of the car"? And now suppose the one offering the explanation should invoke the assistance of all the possible factors that could influence the absolute elevation of the balloon and of the car, such as the density of the atmosphere, the weight of the silk and of the car, the number of persons in the car, the specific gravity of the gases employed to fill it—everything excepting the length of rope!

That is exactly Malthus's method of procedure. For page after page of research he inquires why wages are high or low. He inveighs indefatigably against Ricardo, arguing that the difficulty or ease of agricultural production is not the only cause of a high or a low wage, but that on the contrary, the abundance of capital which accompanies the demand for labor exerts its influence on wages. He is equally tireless in assuring us that the relation of supply and demand for products, by raising or lowering their price, is the cause of a high or a low rate of originary interest. But he forgets to put the simplest question of all—the question on which everything hinges: *What power is it that keeps wages of labor and price of products apart* in such a way that, no matter what be their absolute height, there is still an interval between them which is filled up by interest?

Only once, and then very vaguely (even more faintly than Ricardo on a similar occasion) does Malthus hint at the existence of a power of this sort, when he remarks that the gradual diminution of the excess of proceeds must, in the long run, bring "the power and the will to accumulate capital" to a standstill.[42] But he is just as impotent as is Ricardo to exploit this element in order to explain the amount of the excess.

Finally, Malthus's explanation is completely vitiated by his inability to adduce any more significant reason for the prices of products (one of his two determining factors) than the relation of supply and demand.[43] Thereby his theory ensconces itself in a position which is, I grant, unassailable, but where at the same time it ceases to say anything. That the rate of interest is influenced by the relation between the demand for and the supply of certain goods is, considering the fact that interest is itself a price, or a difference in price, altogether too obvious.[44]

After Malthus, the only protagonist of the theory of the productive power of capital in England was Read.[45] As Read, however, adopted elements from other theories, we shall meet him again among the eclectics. But very similar views are to be found somewhat later in the writings of a few celebrated American economists, particularly Henry Carey and Peshine Smith.

Carey offers one of the very worst examples of confused thinking on our subject, where there has already been a great deal of confusion.[46] What he says on interest is a tissue of incredibly clumsy and thoughtless mistakes of such a nature that it is almost inconceivable how they could ever have won such esteem in the scientific world. I should not express this opinion in such severe terms if it were not that Carey's interest theory even now, in 1884, enjoys a reputation which I consider very ill deserved. It is one of those theories which, to my mind, cast discredit not only on their authors, but on the science that is misled into credulous acceptance of them. His theory is to be condemned, not so much because of its errors as because of the unpardonable kind of errors it contains. My readers may decide, on the basis of what follows, whether or not I am judging too harshly.

Carey has not cast his views on the source of interest in the form of any abstract formulation. It is his favorite plan to explain economic phenomena by portraying simple situations out of a Robinson Crusoe society. In the present case, too, he is content to draw a picture of the origin of interest, leaving us to discover his opinion concerning its causes only by means of the characteristic features with which he endows the event. It is from such pictures that we have to piece together Carey's theory.

Professedly he deals with our subject in the forty-first chapter of his *Principles,* under the title, "Wage, Profit, and Interest." After a few introductory words the following picture appears in the first paragraph:

"Friday had no canoe, nor had he acquired the mental capital required for producing such an instrument. Had Crusoe owned one, and had Friday desired to borrow it, the former might thus have answered him: 'Fish abound at some little distance from the shore, whereas they are scarce in our immediate neighborhood. Working without the help of my canoe, you will scarcely, with all your labor, obtain the food required for the preservation of life; whereas, with it, you will, with half your time, take as many fish as will supply us both. Give me three-fourths of all your take, and you shall have the remainder for your services. This will secure you an abundant supply of food—leaving much of your time unoccupied, to be applied to giving yourself better shelter and better clothing.' Hard as this might seem, Friday would have accepted the offer—profiting by Crusoe's capital, though paying dearly for its use."[47]

Up to this point one can see that Carey's theory is a fairly faithful copy of Lauderdale's. Like him, Carey starts as Lauderdale does by making capital the cause of a productive surplus result. That is the reason why the capitalist receives a price for the use of his capital. And that price, as appears from many passages, is without further examination identified by Carey, as it was by Lauderdale, with interest, although obviously it represents only the *gross return for the use* of the capital. It is immaterial that Carey, unlike Lauderdale, does not regard capital as an independent factor of production, but only as an instrument of production.[48] The essential feature remains that the surplus result from the production, which accompanies the employment of capital, is represented to be the cause of interest.

But while Lauderdale is open only to the one charge of having confused gross and net use, Carey plays fast and loose with a long line of concepts. Not only does he confuse net and gross use, but he confuses these two concepts in turn with capital goods themselves, and not only occasionally, but consistently. That is to say, he deliberately identifies the causes of a high or low *interest* with the causes of a high or low *value of capital goods,* and deduces a direct correlation between interest rate and value of capital goods!

This almost incredible confusion of ideas pervades every passage in which Carey treats of interest. In order to submit a statement of his argument I shall use his Chapter VI (on Value) and his Chapter XLI (on

Wage, Profit, and Interest), in which he expresses himself most coherently on the subject.

According to Carey's well-known theory of value, the value of all goods is determined by the amount of the costs required for their reproduction. Progressive economic development, which means simply man's progressive mastery over nature, enables man to replace the goods he needs at a steadily decreasing cost. This is true of many things, including those tools that form man's capital, and capital therefore reveals a tendency to fall steadily in value with the advance of civilization. "The quantity of labor required for reproducing existing capital and further extending the quantity of capital diminishes with every stage of progress. Past accumulations tend steadily to decline in value, labor rising not less steadily when compared with them."[49]

A concomitant, as well as a resultant of the decrease in the value of capital, is a fall in the price paid for its use. This proposition is not actually proven by Carey, for he evidently thinks it too self-evident, and so indeed it is, if it is rightly understood. But he embodies it, like a previously established principle, in his pictures of Crusoe's economic development. He relates how the owner of the first axe could have demanded for the loan of it more than half the wood that could be felled with it, while later, when better axes could be acquired at a cheaper price, a relatively lower price was paid for their use.[50]

On these preliminary facts, then, Carey founds his great law of interest, which runs as follows. With advancing economic civilization, *the rate of originary interest falls, while the absolute quantity of originary interest rises.* The way in which Carey arrives at this law can be adequately appreciated only through reading his own words. The reader will, I trust, pardon the somewhat lengthy literal quotation that follows.

"Little as was the work that could be done with the help of an axe of stone, its service to the owner had been very great. It was, therefore, clear to him, that the man to whom he lent it should pay him largely for its use. He could, too, as we readily see, well afford to do so. Cutting with it more wood in a day than without it he could cut in a month, he would profit by its help, were he allowed but a tenth of his labor's products. Being permitted to retain a fourth, he finds his wages much increased, notwithstanding the large *proportion* claimed as profit by his neighbor capitalist.

"The bronze axe being next obtained, and proving far more useful, its owner being asked to grant its use is now, however, required to recollect, that not only had the productiveness of labor greatly increased, *but the quantity required to be given to the production of an axe had also greatly decreased*—capital thus declining in its power over labor, as labor increased in its power for the reproduction of capital. He, therefore, limits himself to demanding two-thirds of the price of the more potent instrument . . . This arrangement being made, the effects of the earlier and later distribution are as follows:

105

	Total Product	Laborer's Share	Capitalist's Share
First distribution	4	1	3
Second distribution	8	2.66	5.33

"The axe of iron next coming, a new distribution is required, the cost of reproduction having again diminished, while labor has again increased in its proportions as compared with capital. The new tool cuts twice as much as had been cut by the one of bronze, and yet its owner finds himself compelled to be content with claiming half the product; the following figures now presenting a comparative view of the several modes of distribution:

	Total Product	Laborer's Share	Capitalist's Share
First distribution	4	1	3
Second distribution	8	2.66	5.33
Third distribution	16	8	8

"The axe of iron next coming, a new distribution is required, the doubled, with further diminution in the cost of reproduction; and now the capitalist is obliged to content himself with a less proportion, the distribution being as follows:

	Total Product	Laborer's Share	Capitalist's Share
Fourth distribution	32	19.20	12.80

"The laborer's share has increased, and—the total product having largely increased—the augmentation of his quantity is very great. That of the capitalist has diminished in proportion; but—the product having so much increased—this reduction of proportion has been accompanied by a large increase of quantity. Both thus profit greatly by the improvements that have been affected. With every further movement in the same direction, the same results continue to be obtained—the proportion of the laborer increasing with every increase in the productiveness of effort—*the proportion of the capitalist as steadily diminishing,** with constant increase of quantity and equally constant tendency towards equality among the various portions of which society is composed.

"Such is the great law governing the distribution of labor's products. Of all recorded in the book of science, it is perhaps the most beautiful, being, as it is, that one in virtue of which there is established a perfect harmony of real and true interests among the various classes of mankind."[51]

I beg the reader to pause for a moment at this point of the quotation, and to determine exactly what it is that Carey has asserted up to this point and what he has graphically presented, if not, strictly speaking, proven. The object of Carey's inquiry was the price paid for the use

* Translators' note: Italics are Böhm-Bawerk's.

of the axe, that is to say, its hire. The amount of this hire was compared with the amount of the *total product which a worker could obtain
with the help of the axe*. The result of repeated comparisons is the
proposition that, with advancing civilization, the hire paid for capital
is an ever decreasing proportion of that total return. That and nothing
else is the substance of the law which Carey has so far expounded and
proven, and which he is fond of abridging in the words, "The proportion
of the capitalist falls."

Let us hear Carey further. "That the law here given as regards the
return to capital invested in axes is equally true in reference to all other
descriptions of capital will be obvious to the reader upon slight reflection." He demonstrates its efficacy first in the reduction of the rent
of old houses, and about that there is nothing in particular to say, and
then goes on. "So, too, with money. Brutus charged almost *50%* interest
for its use, and in the days of *Henry VIII the proportion* allotted by
law to the lender was *10%*.* Since then it has steadily declined, 4%
having become so much the *established rate* in England that property
is uniformly estimated at 25 years' purchase of the rent; so large, nevertheless, having been the increase in the powers of man that the present
receiver of a twenty-fifth can command an amount of convenience and
of comfort twice greater than could have been obtained by his predecessors who received a tenth. In this *decline in the proportion charged
for the use of capital** we find the highest proof of man's improved
condition."[52]

With these words Carey has suddenly done a bold about-face. He
suddenly speaks as if the proof adduced in the preceding passages had
referred to the *rate of interest,* and he now begins and continues to treat
it as an established fact that the diminution of the *value of capital*
brings about a reduction of the *rate of interest!*[53]

This change of front rests on as bare-faced a bit of legerdemain as
can well be imagined. In the whole course of the preceding argument
Carey did not say a single word about the rate of interest, much less
make it the subject of any proof. To apply that argument to the rate
of interest Carey has now to perpetuate a double perversion—the first,
of the concept of "use"; the second, of the concept of "proportion."

In the course of his argument he continually employed the phrase
"use of capital" in the sense of "gross use." He who hires out an axe,
sells its gross use, and the price which he receives for it is a hire or
gross interest. But now all at once he employs the word "use" in the
sense of "net use," the use to which net money interest corresponds.
While the argument, therefore, did demonstrate that gross interest has a
tendency to fall relatively, Carey distorts the conclusion of his argument
in such a way as to make it appear that net use has this tendency.

But the second perversion is even more violent.

In the course of the argument the word "proportion" always referred to the relation between the amount of the interest and *the total*

---

* Translators' note: Italics are Böhm-Bawerk's.

product of the labor performed with the help of capital. But now, in his application of the argument, Carey substitutes a new interpretation of the word "proportion" and makes it express a relation between the amount of the use and *the value of the capital,* in other words, the rate of interest. He speaks of a *"proportion of 10%,"* by which he no longer means, as formerly, 10% of the product obtained by the assistance of the capital lent, but 10% of the capital. And in the fall of the interest rate from 10% to 4%, (in "the decline in the proportion charged for the use of capital"), he sees a simple application of the law just proved without the faintest realization that the "proportion" spoken of earlier meant something quite different from that now referred to.

In case the reader may think that this criticism is mere hairsplitting, I should like to ask him to consider the following concrete illustration, which I adapt as closely as possible to Carey's line of argument.

Suppose that with a steel axe a worker, in a year's time, can cut down 1,000 trees. If only one such axe is to be had, and no other of the same kind can be made, its owner may ask and receive for the transference of its use a large part of the total product, say one-half. Thanks to the monopoly, the capital value which the single axe attains in these circumstances will also be high. It may, for instance, amount to the value of as many trunks as a man can fell with it in two years, that is, 2,000 trunks. The price of 500 trees which is paid for the year's use of the axe represents in this case a proportion of 50% of the total yearly product, but a proportion of only 25% of the value of the capital. This by itself proves that the two proportions are not identical. But let us go a bit further.

Later on people learn to manufacture steel axes in any quantity desired. The capital value of the axes falls to the amount of the costs of reproduction at the time. If those costs are equal to 18 days of labor, a steel axe will be worth about as much as 50 trees, since the felling of 50 trees also costs 18 days' labor. Naturally, if the owner lets out the axe for hire, he will now be content with a much smaller proportion of the 1,000 trees that represent the year's work. Instead of receiving the half, as before, he now gets at the most a twentieth, or 50 trees. These 50 trees represent, on the one hand, *5% of the total product,* and on the other hand, *100% of the capital value* of the axe.

What does this prove? Whereas one proportion, namely 50% of the gross return, represented only 25% of the capital value of the axe, now a smaller proportion, namely, 5% of the gross return, represents 100% of the capital value. In other words, while the proportion of the owner's return fell to a tenth part of the original distributive share, the rate of interest represented by this proportion rose fourfold. That indicates the utter fallacy of any assumption that the proportions which Carey lightly confuses with one another should even run parallel, and the equally complete failure of Carey's law of the "falling of the capitalist's proportion" to show what he intended it to show, namely, the course of the rate of interest.

It scarcely needs to be argued any further that Carey's contributions to the explanation of interest are entirely worthless. The real problem, the answer to the question why the yield falling to the share of capital is worth more than the capital consumed in obtaining it, is not even touched, and the inept sham solution which Carey offers cannot meet even the most superficial tests. That such a specious solution did, nevertheless, find admission into the writings of many highly respected economists of our own and other nations is proof of the very small degree of thoroughness and discrimination which is devoted to the important material with which we must deal.

His pupil, E. Peshine Smith, is little, if any, sounder than Carey himself. His *Manual of Political Economy* (1853) obtained wide circulation in Germany in Stöpel's translation.[54]

Peshine Smith finds the origin of interest in a partnership between workman and capitalist. The object of the partnership is "to change the form of the commodities contributed by the capitalist, and increase their value by combining them with a new infusion of labor." The return, "the new thing produced," is divided, and divided in such a way that the capitalist receives more than the replacement of the capital he has contributed, and so makes a gain. Smith obviously considers it self-evident that it must be so. For without taking the trouble to offer a formal explanation, he is content to point out, in quite general terms, that the bargain must promote the interests of both, and that "both the capitalist and the laborer expect to derive their respective shares in the advantages of their partnership." Beyond this he simply cites the facts: "In point of fact," he says, "they do so, however long may be the series of transformations and exchanges before the division is made" (*p.* 77).

A purely formal distinction of interest emerges according to which member of the partnership, the capitalist or the laborer, assumes the risk. In the former case "the share in the product which the workman obtains is called wages; and the difference in value between the materials as turned over to the workman, ... the deterioration of the tools employed, and the finished product is termed profits.[55] If the workman takes the risk upon himself, that share which he gives to the capitalist, in addition to replacing the capital he borrowed, is called rent" (*p.* 77).

In this passage Smith introduces interest as an integral part of his system. Yet the superficial way in which he evades any deeper explanation of it clearly shows that he has not grasped his problem at all. Yet what he has said up to this point, if not of much importance, is not incorrect.

But even this modest praise cannot be given to what follows, where he goes on to examine the influence which the growth of capital exerts on the *rate* of interest. Here he copies faithfully not only Carey's method of exposition and his final conclusions, but even all his errors and blunders.

Smith begins, quite in Carey's style, by introducing a couple of economic pictures drawn from primitive conditions. A savage goes to the owner of a stone axe, and gets permission to use the axe on condition that he build 1 canoe for the owner of the axe, as well as 1 for himself. A generation passes away, and copper axes are substituted, by the aid of which three times as much work can be done as with the stone axe. Of the 6 canoes that the worker now builds in the same time as he formerly built 2, he may retain 4 for himself, while 2 are claimed by the capitalist. The share of the laborer has thus increased both in proportion and in quantity; that of the capitalist has also increased in quantity, but has decreased in relative proportion, for it has fallen from a half to a third of the product. Finally, in a still later era, the excellent "American axes" of the present day come into use. With them three times as much work can now be done as formerly was done with the copper axes, and of the 18 canoes, or other products of labor, which the borrower of an axe can now make, he will have to pay 4 for the use of the axe, and 14 are left him as the share of his labor. In this case again the share of the worker has increased proportionally, and that of the capitalist has diminished.

Having arrived at this point, Smith begins to apply his rules to modern economic life and its forms.

First, the form of contract used by the savage is replaced by the modern loan contract.

"The cases we have put represent the capitalist agreeing to make a fixed payment out of the product of the capital which is entrusted to the laborer, and of the mechanical force of the latter. In so doing he runs a risk that the laborer may not exert himself to his full ability, and that the residue after payment of wages, upon which he depends for *profits,* may be less than he calculates. To insure himself against this contingency, he naturally seeks to bargain for less wages than he is confident that the earnest and honest exertion of the workman's strength would enable him to pay, without impairing his expected *profit.* The workman, on the contrary, knowing what he can do, and unwilling to submit to any reduction, prefers to guarantee the profit which the capitalist desires, taking upon himself the risk that the product will leave a margin broad enough to provide for the wages which the capitalist is afraid to guarantee. The contract thus becomes one of hiring capital."

The careful reader will note that in these words not only has the old form of contract been replaced by the new, to which there can be no objection, but also, and quite unexpectedly, the price of the use, which was previously under discussion and which was a gross interest, has now been replaced by the "profit" (net interest). And to that there are very serious objections.

But Peshine Smith goes still further. Without hesitation he substitutes for the proportion of the *product* the proportion of the *capital,* or the *rate of interest.* Carey had fallen into this confusion blindly; Smith walks into it deliberately, which is still stranger and still more difficult to excuse. "Men reckon their gains by a comparison between what they previously possessed and what is added to it. The capitalist reckons his profits not by his proportion of the product which has been won by the combination with labor, but by the ratio which the increment bears to the previous stock. He says he has made so much per cent on his capital; he rents it for so much per cent for a year. *The difference is one of arithmetical notation, not of fact. When his proportion of the product is small, it being composed of the original capital and the increment, the ratio of the latter to the capital will also be small"* (*p. 82*).*

So a small proportion of the product and a small rate of interest are substantially identical and merely different arithmetical notations for the same thing! To permit the reader to appraise this strange doctrine I need only remind him of the illustration I submitted to refute Carey. We there saw that half of the product may represent 25% of the capital, and that a twentieth part of the product may represent 100% of the capital. This does seem something more than a mere difference in arithmetical notation!

By substituting one term for another in this way, Smith is finally able to proclaim Carey's "great law" that as civilization advances the share of the capitalist, that is, the rate of interest falls. And he is able to verify it by the historical fact that in rich countries the rate of interest does fall. At the same time his own example illustrates how a relatively true proposition may be deduced from very false reasoning.

The unassuming but conscientious and thorough-going way in which the German scholar, v. Thünen, dealt with our problem[56] furnishes a pleasant contrast to the superficiality of the American writers.

Like Carey, Thünen investigates the origin of interest genetically. He goes back to primitive economic relations, follows the first beginnings of the accumulation of capital, and inquires into the manner and methods by which capital comes into existence in these circumstances, as well as the laws under which it develops. Before beginning the inquiry itself he is careful to establish with minute exactness all the assumptions of fact with which he starts, as well as the terminology he means to use (*pp. 74-90*). This is valuable to Thünen as a means of checking on his own work, and is a characteristic mark of his conscientious thoroughness.

I gather from his introduction that Thünen postulates a people living in a latitude of tropical fruitfulness, equipped with all the capacity, knowledge, and skill of civilization, but as yet absolutely without capital, and without communication with other peoples, so that the accumulation of capital must ensue from within, and without external influence. Land has as yet no exchange value. All men are equal in position, equally capable, and equally saving, and earn their living by labor.

The standard of value which Thünen makes use of for the scope of his inquiry is the laborer's means of subsistence, taking as a unit the hundredth part of the means of subsistence required by a laborer for one year. The year's need he calls S, the hundredth part he calls c; so that $S = 100c$.

"Suppose," he begins (*p. 90*), "that the worker, if diligent and

---

* Translators' note: Italics are Böhm-Bawerk's.

saving, can produce by the labor of his hands 10% more than he requires for his necessary subsistence, say 110c in a year. Then, after deducting what he must spend for his own support, he has 10c left over.

"In the course of 10 years he can accumulate a store on which he can live for a year without working. Or he can devote his labor for a whole year to the making of useful tools, that is to say, to the creation of capital.

"Let us follow him now in the labor that creates the capital.

"With a fragment of flint he fashions wood into a bow and arrow, a fish bone serving as an arrowhead. From the stalk of the plantain, or the fibrous covering of the cocoanut, he makes cord and string, of which he uses the one to string the bow, and the other to make fishing nets.

"In the following year he applies himself again to the production of means of subsistence, but he is now provided with a bow, arrows, and nets. With the help of those tools his work is much more remunerative, the product of his work much greater.

"Suppose that in this way the result of his work, after deducting what he must spend to keep the tools in good condition, rises from 110 to 150c, then he can lay by 50c in a year, and he needs to devote only two years to the production of the means of subsistence, in order to spend another whole year making bows and nets.

"Now he himself can make no use of these, since the tools made in the previous year are sufficient for his needs; but he can lend them to a worker who until then had worked without capital.

"This second worker has been producing 110c. If he borrows capital on which the laborer who made it expended a year's labor, his production, if he maintains and returns the tools in their original condition, will amount to 150c.[57] The extra production got by means of capital amounts therefore to 40c.

"This worker can consequently pay a rent of 40c for the borrowed capital, and this sum the worker who produced the capital draws in perpetuity for his one year's labor.

"Here we have the origin and the basis of interest, and its relation to capital. The relation of the wage of labor to the amount of rent which that same labor creates when directed to the creation of capital goods is the relation between capital and interest.

"In the present case the wage of a year's work is 110c, the rent brought in by the capital which resulted from a year's labor is 40c.

"The ratio therefore is 110c : 40c = 100 : 36.4, and the rate of interest is 36.4%."

The passage that follows refers not so much to the origin as to the rate of interest, and I shall make only a brief abstract of such of the leading ideas as may illustrate Thünen's concept still further.

According to Thünen, as capital increases, its productive efficiency declines, each new increment of capital increasing the product of human labor by a smaller margin than is true of the increment immediately preceding. Thus, if the first capital increased the return to labor by 40c, or from 110c to 150c, the capital next applied will bring a further increase of only 36c, the third only 32.4c, and so on. There are two reasons for this.

"1] If the most efficient of the tools, machines, etc., which constitute capital, are available in sufficient quantity, then any further production of capital is compelled . . . to concern itself with less efficient tools."

"2] In agriculture the increase in capital, if that increase is all to find employment, leads to the cultivation of less fertile and less favorably situated parcels, or to a more intensive cultivation that necessitates greater costs. And in such cases the capital last employed brings a smaller return than that which found employment earlier."[58]

As the return produced by the efficiency of capital declines, the price that a borrower is willing and able to pay for the use of the capital also declines, and in the same proportion. And since two different rates of interest cannot prevail side by side, one for the capital first applied and another for the capital applied later, the interest on capital as a whole is governed by "the use of that portion of capital which is last applied" (*p. 100*). Under these conditions the rate of interest tends to sink with the increase of capital, and the consequent reduction in interest redounds to the benefit of the worker, inasmuch as it raises the wage of his labor (*p. 101*).

It is apparent that Thünen very definitely makes the productive efficiency of capital his starting point. Not only is this productive efficiency the origin of interest, but the prevailing degree of that efficiency at any given time exactly determines the rate of interest.

Now the value of this theory depends altogether on its ability to show the connection between the greater productiveness of labor supported by capital and the obtaining of excess value by the owner of capital.

Thünen happily keeps clear of two dangerous pitfalls. He does not invent a fabulous value-creating power of capital. He simply ascribes to capital a property which it actually possesses, and that is the ability to promote the production of more *products,* or in other words, physical productivity. Secondly, he has escaped the blunder that lies in confusing gross interest with net interest. What he calls net interest, the 40c, 36c, 32.4c which the capitalist receives, is really net interest, because the debtor is expressly obligated to restore the capital unimpaired. (*See p. 91, towards the end.*)

But by that very stipulation Thünen's interest theory becomes vulnerable elsewhere.

The thought process which the Thünen theory employs might be said to progress by the following stages from the physical productivity of capital to the acquisition of excess value by the capitalist.

1] *"Labor supported by capital can turn out a greater quantity of products."* This assumption is indubitably correct.

2] In Thünen's illustration *the excess which results from the employment of capital consists of two components.* They are, *first,* the 40c, 36c, 32.4c, which the capitalist receives in means of subsistence, and

113

second, the replacement of the capital goods consumed in its employment. Nothing less than the *sum of these two components* constitutes the gross return from the employment of capital.

The interpolation of a little calculation of my own will show that this important proposition, although not plainly stated by Thünen, is really contained in his doctrine. According to Thünen, a year's labor unassisted by capital produces 110*c*. A year's labor assisted by capital is sufficient, not only to renew the capital to the extent that it has undergone wear and tear, but also to produce 150*c* besides. The difference between the two results, which represents the excess due to the employment of capital, thus actually amounts to 40*c* *plus* the upkeep of the capital. It must be admitted that Thünen rather relegates the existence of the second component to the background. He makes no further mention of it, except in two passages on page 91, and ignores it as a factor in the subsequent compilation of his tables (*pp. 98, 110 etc.*). The accuracy of these tables is thus markedly impaired. For it is reasonable to suppose that by the time capitals representing six or ten years' labor are being employed, the yearly labor required to replace them will necessarily absorb a considerable portion of the total labor power of the user.

3] *The excess production resulting from the employment of capital*[59] (replacement plus 40*c* or 36*c* or 32.4*c*, as the case may be) *is obtained by the capitalist as such.* I consider this assumption of Thünen's correct, on the whole, even though "price wars" may often modify the share of the capitalist in individual cases.

4] *This gross excess production by capital which the capitalist receives is regularly more valuable than the capital goods consumed in producing it,* so that a net yield, an excess value, a net *interest* remains. This proposition forms the natural conclusion to Thünen's thought process. He failed to formulate it in general terms just as he failed to formulate his previous theses. But at the conclusion of his concrete illustration the amount received by the capitalist regularly exceeds the amount given by him. And since his chosen example is avowedly typical, we have to all intents and purposes the equivalent of an express formulation of the principle. And there is further reason for so regarding it, since it was *imperative* for him to assert and to explain the existence of a permanent excess of the return to capital over the sacrifice by capital, if he had any intention of explaining interest, which consists in this very excess value.

At this point we come to the last and the decisive stage in Thünen's thought process, which so far has proven essentially unexceptionable. But just at this critical point the weakness of his theory betrays itself.

If we are asked, "What reasons and what explanation does Thünen give for the existence of this excess value?" we are compelled to answer, that he does not explain it at all, but assumes it. Indeed, the decisive assumption slipped in at that very inconspicuous point where Thünen says that the possession of a capital enables the worker to produce a surplus product of 40*c*, 36*c*, and so on, *after deduction of what is necessary to return the capital "in equally good condition" and "equal in value."*

If we look more closely at this apparently harmless proposition, we find that it contains the assumption that capital possesses two powers. The first is, to reproduce itself and its own value, and the second is, to produce something more beyond that. If it is true, as is here assumed, that the product of capital is always a sum of which one constituent alone is equal to the whole sacrifice of capital, then it is self-evident that the whole sum must be worth more than that sacrifice, and in that case Thünen is quite right to dispense with any further explanation. But the question is whether Thünen was justified in assuming any such efficiency on the part of capital.

To my mind this question definitely requires an answer in the negative. It is true that, in the first of the concrete situations which Thünen imagines, such an assumption may appear to us quite plausible. It does not seem improper to assume that the hunter equipped with bow and arrows is able to bring down 40 more head of game than he could without those weapons or even to assume in addition that he could find time besides, to keep his bow and arrows in good condition, or to renew them, so that his renewed capital would be worth as much at the end of the year as it was at the beginning. But are we entitled to make analogous suppositions in regard to a complicated economy? Can we do so with respect to a condition in which capital is so varied, and the division of labor so complex, that the capital cannot be renewed by the individual laborer who has been using it? If this laborer must *pay* for the renewal of the capital, is it then self-evident that the excess in products obtained with the help of capital will exceed the costs of renewal, or in other words, the value of the capital consumed?

Certainly not. There are, on the contrary, two conceivable possibilities by which the excess value might be swept away. In the first place, it is conceivable that the great productive use assured by possession of the capital will so greatly increase the valuation of that capital, that it equals that of the prospective product. Bows and arrows which, during the whole term of their existence, make it possible to bring down an excess 100 head of game could conceivably have a valuation equal to those 100 head. In that case the hunter, in order to replace the weapons worn out, would be obliged to pay the maker of the weapons the whole surplus return of 100 head or their value, and would have nothing left out of which to pay any surplus value, that is to say, interest to the man who lent him the weapons.

In the second place, it is conceivable that the competition in the making of weapons is so keen that it depresses their price below that very high valuation. In that case will not that same competition necessarily lower the claims which the capitalist can impose when lending the weapons? Lauderdale assumed such a depressing factor, and so did Carey and our experience of economic life leaves no doubt that it is present. So again I ask, as I did in the case of Lauderdale, "Why is it impossible for the depressing effect of competition on the capitalist's share to be so great that it lowers its value to the value of the capital itself? What prevents the production and employment of so great a quantity of a given capital good that its employment returns just enough to replace the capital and no more? If that were to happen, the excess value, and with it the interest, would disappear.

In short, I can see three possible changes in the relationship between the value of the product and that of the capital which produces that product. Either the value of the product raises the value of the capital good to the height of its own value, or the value of the capital good, by reason of competition, lowers the value of the capital yield to *its* level, or as a third possibility, the share of capital in the product remains at a level higher than that of the capital good. Thünen assumes the third of these possibilities without proving or explaining it, and the lack of explanation is the truly vital fault. And so the whole phenomenon which his inquiry set out to explain, the phenomenon of interest, remains unexplained because Thünen has treated it as an assumption.

Our final judgment must, therefore, be expressed as follows. Thünen gives a version of the productivity theory which is more subtle, better thought out, more thorough, than that of any of his predecessors, but he too stumbles at the most critical step. Where the problem is to deduce *excess value* from the physical productivity of capital, from the surplus in products, he includes among his assumptions the thing he has to explain.[60]

Thünen's method marks an apogee of solid and well-considered investigation. Unfortunately his high standards were not long maintained, even in the literature of his own nation. In his successors, Glaser[61] and Roesler,[62] who wrote along the same line, we note a distinct falling off in thoroughness of conception and strictness of method.*

In the interval, however, the productivity theorists had become the object of serious and weighty attacks. Rodbertus, writing in a vein of calm, objective criticism, had accused them of confusing questions of distribution with questions of production, pointing out that, in assuming the portion of the total product which is obtained as originary interest to be a specific product of capital, they were merely returning to their starting point. At the same time he enunciated his own formula that the sole source of all wealth was labor. Then Lassalle and Marx had delivered variations on this theme, each in his own way, the one with vehemence and wit, the other bluntly and ruthlessly.

These attacks elicited a reply from the camp of the productivity theorists, with which I shall conclude a chapter already overlong. Though the scholar who wrote it was still youthful, it deserves our full consideration for at least two reasons. One is the position of its author, for he was a member of the Staatswissenschaftliches Seminar in Jena. There he was in close professional contact with the men who were at that time the guiding spirits of the "historical school" in Germany and therefore he may well be regarded as representative of the views of that

* Translators' note: In the German editions of 1884, 1900, 1914, and 1921 Professor Böhm-Bawerk devoted several pages to these two writers. In the 1890 English edition he wished to have them omitted as of little importance. In accordance with his wish, they are omitted from the present edition.

school. Another reason lies in the circumstances which occasioned his reply. For, since it is written with full knowledge of Marx's fulminations in *Das Kapital* against the doctrine of the productivity of capital, we are justified in expecting that its author, after mature critical consideration, would be in a position to muster the best and most convincing arguments that could be urged in favor of the productivity theory.

This reply is to be found in two essays by K. Strasburger, published in 1871 in Hildebrand's *Jahrbücher für Nationalökonomie und Statistik*.[63]

The gist of Strasburger's theory is summarized in the second of these essays as follows:[64]

"Capital enlists the services of certain forces of nature which, though they are available to all, can nevertheless be turned to account for production of a given kind only if they have the help of capital. Not everyone has the means of harnessing these forces of nature. The man who works with a small capital must expend his energies on tasks which these forces of nature perform for the man who is amply supplied with capital. *Therefore, the activity of the forces of nature, when it is procured through the agency of capital, is no gift of nature. In any exchange transaction it is taken into account. And the man who possesses no capital must pay the product of his own labor to the capitalist for the services rendered by the forces of nature. Capital therefore does produce value,* but its role in production is utterly different from that of labor."

And a little further on, in the course of page 329, he says: "What has already been said will show what we mean by the productivity of capital. *Capital produces value by harnessing the forces of nature for work which otherwise would have to be done by man.* The productivity of capital then, is characterized by the fact that its activity in production is distinct from that of the labor of living men. We have said that the service rendered by the forces of nature is considered, in an exchange, as an equivalent of human labor. Marx maintains the contrary. He thinks that, if one worker is assisted by the forces of nature more than another, then he creates more use value, the quantity of his products is greater, but that the action of the forces of nature does not raise the exchange value of the commodities he produces. To refute this view one need only remember what we have already stated, namely, that not everyone possesses the same means of commanding the forces of nature. Those who do not possess capital must buy its work by means of their own labor. Or if they work with the help of another man's capital, they must allow him a share of the value produced. This share of the value newly produced is originary interest, and the drawing of a certain income by the capitalist is inherent in the nature of capital."

If we condense the substance of these words still further, our explanation will run somewhat as follows. While it is true that the forces of nature are in themselves gratuitous, it is often only with the help of capital that they can be utilized. Now since capital is available only in limited quantity, its owners are in a position to obtain payment for the cooperation of the forces of nature which their capital renders avail-

117

able. This payment is originary interest. Hence, *the necessity of paying the capitalist for the cooperation of the forces of nature* is the explanation for originary interest.

Just how efficaciously does this explanation explain?

Strasburger's premises may be readily conceded. I grant at once that many forces of nature can be utilized only through the mediation of capital; and I also grant that, because the amount of capital is limited, the owner of it can often get paid for the cooperation of the forces of nature thus made available. But what I cannot grant is that these premises in any way account for the origin of interest. It is a hasty and unjustified assumption on the part of Strasburger that the existence of *interest* is the conclusion to be drawn from these premises, inasmuch as these premises, by their very nature, must lead to entirely different economic phenomena. It should not be too difficult to expose Strasburger's error.

There are but two alternatives. Either capital can be had only in such limited quantity that the capitalist can obtain payment for the forces of nature made available, or it can be had in unlimited quantity. Since Strasburger's theory assumes the former, let us proceed on that basis. What, then, is the nature of the economic process by which the capitalist can obtain that payment for the forces of nature?

It would be a hasty return to our starting point to answer "Simply by pocketing the interest." Even brief consideration will make it clear, that if interest does result from compensation for the forces of nature, it can make its appearance only as a secondary result of more complicated economic processes. That is to say, since the forces of nature depend on capital, it is obvious they can be utilized only at the same time as the services of capital itself are utilized. But since capital was created by the expenditure of labor, and in the course of being used is either consumed at once or wears itself out gradually, it is clear that, wherever the services of capital are used, the labor that was put into the capital must be paid for also. Therefore the compensation of the forces of nature can accrue to the capitalist only as a constituent portion of a *gross return* which, in addition to such compensation, contains a further payment for the expenditure of labor.

It would be more exact to say that the economic process by which the capitalist receives the compensation for his forces of nature is the sale of the services of his capital at a price higher than that which represents the expenditure of labor made in producing the concrete capital goods in question. If a machine which lasts for a year is made at the expenditure of 365 days of labor, and if the customary day's wage is $15, then selling the daily services of the machine for $15 would only just pay for the labor that was put into the machine, and leave nothing over for the forces of nature which it makes available. No payment for these forces occurs until the daily services of the machine are paid for at a rate in excess of $15, say $20 per day.

Now this general process may be operative according to several different methods. One of them is in force when the owner of the capital uses it himself in production as an entrepreneur. Then the compensation of the total services of capital consists in that portion of the product which remains after deducting the other expenses of production, such as use of ground and direct labor. This constitutes the "gross yield of capital." If this gross yield amounts to $20 a day and if $15 pays for the labor which created as much of the capital good as is used up in a day, then the excess of $5 a day represents the compensation for the forces of nature. It must not be taken for granted, however, that this excess is *originary interest.* That will be decided later.

A second and more direct method is in force where capital is hired out, and its services paid for in that manner. If our machine is hired out for $20 a day, then in exactly the same way $15 will represent the payment of the labor expended in making the machine, and the excess of $5 again represents the compensation for the forces of nature.

But there is still a third method of selling the services of capital, namely, by selling the *capital good itself.* Economically speaking, this is tantamount to a single sale covering the total services which that capital is able to perform.[65] But will the capitalist in this case be satisfied with nothing more than compensation for the labor that was put into the machine? Will he not also demand compensation for the forces of nature which he makes available for use? Of course he will. There is absolutely no reason why he should be compensated for them in a piecemeal sale of the machine's services, and not in the case of a single sale, especially in view of Strasburger's assumption, which we accepted, that the quantity of capital is so limited that he can compel such compensation.

How will the forces of nature be compensated for in this case? Quite naturally by selling at a price in excess of the amount which represents the customary payment of the labor employed in making the machine. Thus, if the machine cost 365 days of labor at $15 a day, its purchase price will amount to *more* than $365 \times $15 = $5,475$. And since there is no reason why, in a single sale of the services of capital, the forces of nature should be compensated for at a cheaper rate than in a piecemeal sale, we can again assume compensation for the forces of nature at 33.3% of the labor payment. Consequently, the capital price will amount to $5,475 + $1,825 = $7,300$.

Now what about interest when these assumptions are made? There is no difficulty in answering that. When the owner of the machine employs it in his own enterprise, or hires it out, he draws $20 a day for its services during the year which it lasts. That yields a total income of $365 \times $20 = $7,300$. But since the machine wears out in a year and its capital value amounts to exactly $7,300, there remains as excess, as pure interest, *exactly nothing.* And so, although the capitalist has been paid for the forces of nature, there is no interest. That is a clear proof that the reason for interest must be something other than compensation for the forces of nature.

I anticipate a counterobjection at this point. It will be urged that it is not possible for the value of capital goods to remain so high that its sales price will yield its producer a premium for the forces of nature. For then the production of capital would be too remunerative, and would certainly cause competition that, in the long run, would depress the value of the capital goods to the value of the labor employed in their production. Let us suppose that a machine costing 365 days' labor should fetch a price of $7,300 by reason of the inclusion in such price of compensation for the forces of nature which it makes available. If the usual wage in other branches of employment were $15 a day, then the labor applied to the making of such machines would be more remunerative than any other kind of labor. As a consequence there would be a great rush into this branch of production, and more and more of those machines would be manufactured, until the increased competition lowered their price to $5,475 per machine. Thus the yield obtained from them would be depressed to the normal standard.

I concede at once the possibility of such an occurrence. But I counter with a question of my own. Let us grant that the machines are so numerous, and competition so strong that their producer is forced to be satisfied with a sales price that represents a bare compensation for his labor, and allows *nothing for the use* of the forces of nature which he makes available. If that is true of a sale, how should hiring out these machines, or employing them himself, enable him all at once to obtain something for the forces of nature? You cannot have your cake and eat it! Either the machines are scarce or they are numerous. If they are scarce enough to make them worth a charge for the forces of nature, their scarcity is as advantageous for selling as it is for hiring, and in the absence of complicating factors the capital value of the machines will rise to the point of absorption of gross interest. If the machines are made in such quantity that the pressure of competition precludes a charge for the forces of nature, then that condition, too, will be as true for the hiring as for the selling, and, again barring any irrelevant complicating factor, gross interest will fall to the point where it is once more absorbed in the cost of replacement.

3. Final Conclusions

IT IS an odd coincidence that the motivated productivity theories, after almost seventy years' development, should end at nearly the same point as that from which they started. What Strasburger teaches in the year 1871 is essentially almost exactly what Lauderdale taught in 1804. The "power of capital to replace labor" which, because of the scarcity of that power, and in proportion to the scarcity, yields compensation for the capitalist, is different only in name from the forces of nature which are made available through the possession of capital and which, likewise in the measure of the scarcity of capital, exact compensation. Both Strasburger and Lauderdale confuse gross interest and capital value on the one hand with net interest on the other. Both are guilty of the same misinterpretation of the true effects of the premises they assumed, and of the same neglect of the true causes of the phenomenon they seek to explain.

This return to the starting point demonstrates the utter futility of the events that lie between. That futility was no coincidence. It was not simply an unfortunate chance that no one uttered the "Open sesame!" which would draw the veil of the productivity of capital and reveal the key to the mystery of the origin of interest. The magic word remained unspoken because no foot had made the first step on the road to truth. It was hopeless from the outset to attempt to explain interest wholly and entirely on the basis of a productive power of capital. If only there were a power that could make a "surplus value" grow, as wheat grows in the field! But there is no such power. The only thing that productive power can do is to create a large quantity of a product, thereby creating, at most, *much* value, but never excess value. Interest is a surplus, a remainder when "value of consumed capital" is deducted from "product of capital." The productive power of capital may increase the minuend, but in and of itself it cannot do so without at the same time increasing the subtrahend to the same degree. For productive power is undeniably the basis and measure of the value of the capital in which it resides. If one can produce nothing with a capital good, the capital good is worth nothing. If one can produce little with it, it is worth little, if one can produce much with it, it is worth much. Indeed, the increase in its value is in direct proportion to the increase in quantity of its product, as well as in direct proportion to the increase in value of its product. And so, even if the productive power be ever so great, it can only increase the product, that is to say, the minuend, and even increase it enormously; but for all of that, the capital consumed, that is to say, the subtrahend, will increase just as much, and there will be no remainder, no excess value.

I beg to be allowed, in conclusion, one more comparison. If a flash-board is lowered into a running stream, the level of water below the flashboard will be lower than it is above the flashboard. If asked why the level is higher above the flashboard than below, would any one imagine the water-volume of the stream to be the cause? Certainly not! For although the volume makes the water level above the flashboard *high,* it also tends, as far as it is a factor, to make the water level below the flashboard just as high. The volume is the reason why the water level is "high," but the reason for the "high*er*" is not the volume of water, but the flashboard.

Now what the water-volume is to the difference in water level, the productive power of capital is to excess value. It may be an adequate reason why the value of the product of capital is high, but it cannot be the adequate reason why the product is higher in value than the capital itself, since it feeds and raises the level of the capital in the same way as it does that of the product. The true cause of the "excess" is in this case too—a barrier, and one which is not even mentioned by the productivity theories proper. It has been sought by other theories in various guises—sometimes in that of a sacrifice of work devoted to the creation of capital, sometimes in that of the sacrifice of a use, sometimes in that of the sacrifice of abstinence, sometimes simply in the exploiting pressure of the capitalist on labor. But so far as we have gone, there has been no satisfactory recognition of its nature and action.[66]

VIII

THE USE THEORIES

1. General Characteristics

THE use theories are an offshoot of the productivity theories, but the offshoot soon acquired an independent character of its own. The point of contact between the two groups is the very idea which wrecked the productivity theories proper, namely, the recognition of an exact causal connection between the value of products and the value of their means of production. If, as economists began to acknowledge, it is a sound principle that the value of the product is identical with the value of the means of production expended in making it, then every attempt to explain "excess value" by the productive power of capital must fail. For the higher such a power might raise the value of the product, the higher would it necessarily raise the value of the capital. But the second of these values, by the terms of the principle itself, is identical with the first. The one would perforce cling to the other with the fidelity of a shadow, and there would be no possibility of the slightest gap between them.

Nevertheless there is a gap. Why?

The line of reasoning just set forth almost automatically suggested a new explanation. For if, on the one hand, it is true that the value of every product is identical with the value of the means of production sacrificed in making it, and if, on the other hand, it is observed that nevertheless the product of capital regularly possesses greater value than the capital goods thus sacrificed, then the conviction is almost inescapable that perhaps those capital goods do not represent the entire sacrifice that is made to produce the consumers' good. Perhaps there is something else that must be expended in addition to the capital goods—a something which absorbs a fraction of the value of the consumers' good. And that fraction constitutes the very "excess value" which is so puzzling.

And such a something was indeed sought and found. In fact, we might say that more than one was found. Three distinct opinions developed as to its nature, and the fundamental idea they had in common gave rise to three distinct theories, the *use theory,* the *abstinence theory,* and the *remuneration theory.** Of these, the one that adhered most closely to the productivity theories and at first seemed to be merely an extension of them, is the use theory.

* Translators' Note: See footnote on first page of Remuneration Theory, Chapter X.

122

The use theory is founded on the principle that the *use* of capital is a quality of the latter independent of its substance. The *use* of capital has an independent nature and independent value. To obtain a return on capital it is not enough to sacrifice the substance of capital alone; the "use" of the capital employed must be sacrificed as well during the period of production. Since the value of the product is, by definition, equal to the sum of the values of the means of production spent in producing it, and since, in conformity with this principle, it requires the sum of the substance of capital and the use of capital to equal the value of the product, this latter value naturally must be greater than the value of the substance of the capital by itself. In this way the phenomenon of excess value is explained. That component part of value which goes under the name "excess value" corresponds to that component part of sacrifice which goes under the name "use of capital."

This theory of course assumes that capital is productive, but it makes the assumption with no special emphasis and without suggesting complex implications. It assumes no more than that the reinforcement by capital of a given amount of labor assists in obtaining a product greater in quantity than that which labor, unsupported by capital, could obtain. It is not even necessary that the capitalist process of production *on the whole,* embracing as it does both the making *and* the employing of capital, should be profitable.[1] If, for instance, one fisherman makes a net at a cost of 100 days' labor, and with the net catches 500 fish in the 100 days during which the net lasts, while another fisherman without any net has been able to catch 3 fish a day for the 200 days, the total process has obviously been an unprofitable one. Despite the use of capital, only 500 fish were caught with 200 days' labor, while without capital 600 fish could have been caught. Nevertheless according to the use theory, and also as a matter of actual fact, the net once made must bear interest. For, once made, it helps to catch more fish than could be caught without a net and this fact causes the excess return of 200 fish to be credited to the net. But it is so credited only to the net plus the use thereof. A part of the yield, say 190 fish or their value, will be credited to the substance of the net, and the remainder to the use of the net. And so we get an excess value and an interest.

If this very modest degree of physical productivity on the part of capital is sufficient, according to the use theory, to cause excess value, then it is self-evident that this theory in no way assumes a direct *productivity of value.* Indeed, if it is rightly understood, the theory excludes such a power.

But this relation between the use theories and the productive power of capital will not be found stated so clearly in the writings of their representatives as I take the pains to do. The reverse is more likely to be the case. For a long time expositions of the use theory itself were replete with references to the productive power of capital. And these were couched in terms that leave us in doubt as to whether the author who was explaining excess value placed greater reliance on the productive power of capital or on the style of argumentation peculiar to the use theorists. The divorce of the use theory from the productivity theory and its development to independent clarity ensued only gradually.[2] My procedure in the subsequent pages of this chapter will be to begin with a presentation of the history of the use theories. My appraisal of them will be twofold. Such discussion as applies to individual shortcomings of the several theories will be interpolated at once into the historical presentation. My critical estimate of the whole movement will then follow in a section summarizing my conclusions.

A. HISTORICAL STATEMENT OF USE THEORIES

1. J. B. Say, the Founder of the Use Theory

THE development of the use theory is associated for the most part with three names. J. B. Say first suggested it, Hermann's detailed exposition of the nature and essence of the uses put the theory on a firm foundation, Menger developed it to the most advanced point which, in my opinion, it is capable of attaining. All the intervening writers take one or other of these as their model, and although some of them are quite meritorious, they are of secondary importance in comparison with those three.

Contemplation of a list of such writers reveals two striking facts. The first is that, with the single exception of Say, the working out of the use theory has been done entirely by German economists. And the other is that in Germany this theory seems to have enjoyed the marked preference of our most thorough and acute thinkers. At least we find the best names among them represented here in conspicuously large numbers. We have already considered at length the doctrine of Say, the founder of this school.[3]

Say's references to the productivity theory and the use theory are so thoroughly intertwined that neither seems to receive greater deference than the other, and the historian of theory has no alternative but to consider Say the representative of both theories. As a basis for what is to follow, I shall recapitulate very briefly his line of thought in so far as it applies to the use theory.

The productive fund termed capital renders productive services. These services possess economic independence, and are subjects of independent valuation and sale. These services are indispensable for production, and at the same time are not to be obtained from their owners without compensation. Therefore the prices of all products of capital must adjust themselves, subject to the operation of supply and demand, in such a way, that in addition to compensating the other factors in production, they include the ordinary compensation due these productive services. Thus the "excess value" of the products of capital, and with it interest, originates with the necessity of paying independently for that independent sacrifice in production known as the "services of capital."

The most signal weakness of this doctrine, apart from its being continually interspersed with contradictory expressions borrowed from the naive productivity theory, is the nebulousness which surrounds Say's concept of productive services. A writer who makes the independent existence and remuneration of such services the axis on which his interest theory turns is certainly bound to state with complete clarity just what he means by those services. Not only has Say failed to do so, as we have already seen, but the few clues that he does give point in an entirely wrong direction.

Say repeatedly draws an analogy between the services of capital on the one hand, and human labor as well as the activity of the "natural fund" on the other. That leads us to believe that Say would have us understand that "productive services of capital" means the *activity of the forces of nature* which reside in capital goods, such as the physical movements of a draught animal or of a machine, the thermal potential of coal, and so on. But if that is what he means, then the whole argument is on the wrong track. For such activity is nothing more nor less than what I have elsewhere called the "renditions of services" of goods;[4] it is what the current language of our German economists, deficient as it is in significance and clarity, terms the "use" of capital. But that, be it noted, means the *gross* use of capital. That service is remunerated by the undiminished *gross* return, sometimes called the "hire" or "rent" of capital goods. In a word, it is the basis of gross interest, not of net interest with which we are concerned. If that is what Say actually meant by his *services productifs,* then his whole theory has missed the mark, for the necessity of paying for productive services accounts only for gross interest, not net interest. But it is net interest that requires explanation. But if by the *services productifs* he meant something else, he has left us absolutely in the dark regarding the nature of that "something else." As a result, the theory founded on its existence is, to say the least, incomplete.

In any case, then, Say's theory is imperfect. Yet it pointed out a new way which, if properly followed, led much nearer the heart of the interest problem than did the sterile productivity theories proper.

The first two writers to follow Say can scarcely be said to have done much towards any such development. In fact, one of them, Storch by name, represents a marked retrogression from even the modest heights attained by Say's theory.

Storch[5] bears some external resemblance to Say, whom he quotes frequently, but he takes over none of the arguments that Say submits to prove his results, nor does he supply any of his own to take their place. It is characteristic of the futility with which Storch attacks our problem, that he does not explain loan interest through originary interest, but *vice versa.*

He starts by saying (*p. 212*) that capital is a "source of production," although a secondary source, along with nature and labor, the two primary sources of goods. The sources of production often belong to various persons. Hence it is only through a loan-contract, which makes them available to someone capable of uniting them in productive cooperation, that they become sources of income. For this they receive remuneration, and this remuneration constitutes income to the lender. "The price of a loaned piece of land is called rent; the price of loaned labor is called wages; the price of a loaned capital is sometimes called interest, sometimes hire."[6]

After Storch has thus given us to understand that lending out productive powers is the regular way of getting an income, he adds, by way of postscript, that the owner can also obtain an income by employing productive powers himself. "A man who cultivates his own garden at his own expense unites in his own hands the land, the labor and the capital. *Nevertheless* (the word is significant of Storch's point of view) he draws from the first, land rent; from the second, subsistence; from the third, interest on capital." The sale of his products must return to him a value which is at least equivalent to the remuneration he would have got from the land, labor, and capital if he had lent them out. Otherwise he would stop cultivating the garden and lend out his productive powers.[7]

But why should it be possible to get remuneration for productive powers that are loaned out and specifically for capital so loaned?

That is another question that Storch makes no great effort to answer. "Since every man," he says on page 266, "is compelled to eat before he can obtain a product, *the poor* are dependent on *the rich,* and can neither live nor work if they do not receive some of the food already in existence, which they promise to replace when they have completed their product. *These loans cannot be gratuitous,* for if they were, the advantage would be entirely on the side of the poor man, and the rich would have no interest whatever in making the bargain. *So to get their consent, an agreement had to be reached, by which the owner of the accumulated surplus or capital draws interest or an excess of proceeds* in proportion to the amount of the capital advanced." This is an explanation which, for scientific precision, leaves just about everything to be desired.

Of a second follower of Say, Nebenius, it can at least be said that the theory suffered no deterioration in his hands.

In his excellent work on public credit,[8] Nebenius devoted brief consideration to our subject, and gave a somewhat eclectic explanation of it. In the main he follows Say's use theory. He accepts Say's category of the productive services of capital,[9] and bases interest on the fact that these services attain exchange value. In proof of his contention he adduces as a new factor the consideration that "painful privations and exertions" are required for the accumulation of capital.[10] We can also detect echoes of the productivity theory. Thus on one occasion he remarks that the hire which the borrower has to pay for a capital which he employs to advantage may be considered as *the fruit of the capital itself* (*p. 21*); and on another occasion he emphasizes the fact that, "in the reciprocal valuation by which the hire is determined, it is the *productive power of the capital* that constitutes the controlling factor" (*p. 22*).

Nebenius, however, does not enter into a complete explanation of his interest theory. Nor does he analyze the nature of the productive services of capital since he obviously accepts the category as an established principle handed down by Say.

At this point I wish to mention a third writer who wrote considerably later (long after Hermann) but never got beyond Say's standpoint. I refer to Carl Marlo and his *System der Weltökonomie.*[11]

The imposing plan of this work, and the supreme importance which, in the light of its purpose, the interest problem must have had for it, are in sharp contrast to the extremely scant attention which the problem actually received. One may search these ponderous tomes in vain for any connected and thorough inquiry into the origin of interest, or indeed for any genuine interest theory at all. Marlo engaged in polemics against those with whom he differed, especially the proponents of the doctrine that labor is the sole source of value.[12] Had he not thus in some degree defined his position negatively, his positive assertions would hardly suffice to orient us even superficially as to his views, let alone induct the uninitiated into the essential inwardness of the problem.

Marlo's views are a mixture of use and productivity theories derived from Say. He recognizes, with special emphasis on the necessity of their working together,[13] two sources of wealth, power of nature and power of labor, and thinks of capital as "developed power of nature."[14] There are two kinds of income to correspond to these two powers—interest and wages. "Interest is the compensation for the productive or consumptive use of wealth." "If we apply forms of wealth as instruments of work, they contribute to production, and so render a *service.* If we apply them to purposes of consumption we not only consume the wealth itself, but also the service which they might have rendered if productively employed. If we employ the wealth of others, we must compensate the owners for the productive service which it is capable of rendering. Such compensation is called *interest* or *rent.* If we employ our own goods, we ourselves draw the interest which they bear."[15] Alas! What a sorry summary of Say's old theory!

This pitiable repetition of old arguments strikes us as still stranger when we consider that in the interval a great stride forward had been taken toward perfecting the use theory by Hermann's *Staatswirtschaftliche Untersuchungen,* published in 1832.

2. Hermann's Detailed Exposition of the Use Theory

THIS work is the second milestone in the development of the use theory. Out of Say's scanty and contradictory suggestions, which he adopted with laudatory acknowledgments,[16] Hermann contrived to erect an imposing theory, with foundations soundly laid, and details carefully worked out. To Hermann's great credit be it said that this well-constructed theory became "flesh of his flesh and bone of his bone." It permeates the whole of his lengthy work from end to end. There is not a chapter in it which fails to devote considerable space to its statement or its application. There is not a passage in it where the author allows himself to be untrue to the position to which his acceptance of the use theory commits him.

In what follows, I shall outline the principal points of Hermann's theory although it certainly deserves our more thorough acquaintance. In doing so I shall confine myself for the most part to the second edition of the *Staatswirtschaftliche Untersuchungen* in which the theory is substantially unchanged, but the form more trenchant and the details more copious.[17]

The foundation of Hermann's theory is his conception of the independent use of goods. Quite in contrast to Say, who tries to gloss over the nature of his *services productifs* with a few analogies and metaphors, Hermann takes all possible care in explaining his fundamental concept.

He introduces it first in his theory of goods, where he speaks of the different kinds of usefulness that goods may have. "Usefulness may be transitory or it may be durable. It is partly the nature of the goods, partly the nature of their use that determines this point. Transitory, often momentary, usefulness marks freshly cooked food, and many kinds of drink. The performance of a service has only a momentary use value, yet its result may be permanent, as in the case of instruction or a physician's advice. Land, dwellings, tools, books, money, have a durable use value. *Their use, for the time that they last, can be conceived of as a good in itself, and may acquire exchange value of its own which we call interest.*"

However, not only durable goods, but transitory and consumable goods as well, are capable of affording a durable use. Since this proposition is of cardinal importance in Hermann's theory, I give his exposition of it in his own words.

"Technical processes are able, despite changes and combinations in the usefulness of goods, to preserve the sum of their exchange values undiminished, so that goods, although successively taking on new shapes, still continue unchanged in value. Iron ore, coal, and labor, in the form of pig iron, acquire a combined usefulness to which all three contribute chemical and mechanical elements. If, then, the pig iron possesses the exchange value of the three exchange goods employed, the earlier sum of goods persists, bound up qualitatively in the new usefulness, and added together quantitatively in the exchange value.

"Through this change of form, technical processes add economic durability and permanence to goods of transitory material. This persistence of usefulness and of exchange value which is given to otherwise transitory goods by technical change of form is of the greatest economic importance. The amount of durable useful goods thereby becomes very much greater. *Even goods of perishable material and of only temporary use, by constantly changing their shape while retaining their exchange value, can acquire permanence for their use. Thus, as in the case of durable goods, so also goods which change their form qualitatively, while retaining their exchange value, have a use which may be conceived of as a good in itself, a use which may itself acquire exchange value.*"[18] I shall return to this notable passage later on.

Hermann then makes use of this analysis to introduce his concept of capital, which is based altogether on that of use.

"Lasting or durable goods, and perishable goods which retain their value while changing their form, may thus be brought under one and the same concept, for they are the durable basis of a use which has exchange value. Such goods we call *capital.*"[19]

The bridge between this introductory definition and Hermann's interest theory proper is the proposition that in economic life the uses of capital do regularly possess the exchange value of which, as independent entities, they are capable. Hermann does not treat this proposition with an emphasis commensurate with its importance. Although everything else depends on it, he neither enunciates it in due form, nor supports it in detail. There is supporting evidence, but it must be read between the lines. It amounts to this, that the "uses" possess exchange value because they are *economic goods.* That is a bit of information which is concise indeed, but acceptable without further commentary.[20]

His explanation of interest then proceeds as follows.

In virtually every productive process the uses of capital which possess exchange value form an indispensable portion of the cost of production. That cost consists of three parts. The first is the *outlay* of the entrepreneur, that is to say, the expenditure of previously existing wealth such as primary, secondary, and auxiliary materials, also his own labor and that of others, as well as wear and tear of workshops, tools, etc. The second is the application of thought and care by the entrepreneur in initiating and conducting the enterprise. The third is the use of such fixed and floating capital as is necessary to production not only throughout the time it is employed in the productive process itself, but also thereafter until the product is sold.[21]

Economically speaking, the price of the product must cover the total costs of production. Therefore, that price must be high enough to cover "not only the outlays, but also the sacrifice of the entrepreneur as represented by the uses of capital, and by his thought and care." Or, as it is usually expressed, the price must yield an *excess of proceeds* (originary interest and entrepreneurial wage) over and above the compensation for outlays. In further elucidation, Hermann goes on to say that this excess of proceeds "is by no means a merely fortuitous result of price competition." Rather we should say that the excess of proceeds is as much a "compensation for goods possessing exchange value that are really sacrificed in the product as the outlays are. The only difference is that the entrepreneur makes these outlays in order to procure and retain certain extraneous productive elements, whereas the use of necessary capital and the conduct of the business constitute his own contribution to the work, made while it is in progress. He makes use of the outlays in order to obtain the maximum remuneration for his own contribution. That remuneration is the excess of proceeds" (*p. 314*).

To make this explanation of interest complete, there is one thing still wanting, and that is to show why, in production, there must be a sacrifice of the uses of capital, as well as of the outlays of capital. Hermann does so in another passage, where he points out at the same time and in great detail, that all products can ultimately be traced to the exertions of labor and the uses of capital. In the course of it he makes such interesting statements about the character of the "use of goods," as he conceives it, that it may be well to give this passage verbatim.

In an analysis of the sacrifices that are required for the production of salt fish, he enumerates labor of catching, use and wear and tear of tools and boats, labor of procuring salt; and again the use of all kinds of tools, casks, and the like. Then he further analyzes the boat, listing wood, iron, cordage, labor, use of tools, and analyzes the wood still further as comprising use of the forest and labor, and also the iron as representing use of the mine, and so on. "But this succession of labors and uses is not the sum total of the sacrifices made in producing salt fish. For one must also take into account the period of time during which each element of exchange value is embodied in the product. For from the moment when a labor or a use is employed in the making of a product, no independent ultimate disposition of it is possible. It cannot be used by itself, but can only cooperate in the making of the product and in its delivery to the consumer. A proper appreciation of this function depends upon a realization of the fact that labor and uses become quantitative components of liquid capital, as soon as they are employed in production, and that they do so at the exchange value they possessed at the time they were first employed. *It is this value which makes them liquid capital, but it is also this same value which is renounced, so far as the use of it in any other respect is concerned, until such time as the product is paid for by the purchaser.* Such liquid capital in the course of its acquisition, adaptation, storage and shipment adds ever new labors and uses and itself becomes wealth. With all these accretions, it becomes the object of use in the hands of the ultimate purchaser. *What the buyer must pay for is not simply the renunciation of that use which the entrepreneur might have made of the wealth for his own gratification. It is actually a new and peculiar use which is conveyed to him along with the wealth itself. It is the putting together and keeping together, the storing and keeping ready for use, of all the technical elements of production,* from the acquisition of its first basis in natural goods, on through all technical changes and commercial processes, till the product is delivered in the place, at the time, and in the quantity desired. *This holding together of the technical elements of the product is the service, the objective use of liquid capital.*"[22]

If we compare the form which Hermann has given to the use theory with the doctrine of Say, we find them alike in general outline. Both recognize the existence of independent work done by capital. In the use of capital in production, both see a sacrifice independent of and separate from the expenditure of the substance of capital. And both explain interest as the necessary compensation for this independent sacrifice. Still, Hermann's doctrine shows a substantial advance beyond Say's. Say had, in fact, given the mere outlines of a theory, but within that outline most important features were left blank. His *services productifs* are nothing but an ambiguous name, and the very important consideration of how the sacrifice of these services constitutes an independent sacrifice in production (independent, that is, of the substance of capital sacrificed) is virtually left to the reader's imagination. It took Hermann's true German thoroughness, in elaborating and clarifying these two cardinal points, to add firm substance to the outlines received from Say, and invest them with the rank of a solid theory.

A negative merit in Hermann, but one not to be underestimated, is his punctilious avoidance of the secondary explanations (explaining interest by productivity) that are so objectionable in Say. He too, to be sure, uses the expression "productivity of capital," but in a sense that, if not happy, is at least not misleading.[23]

It must be admitted that Hermann did not manage to keep his formulation of the use theory entirely free from inconsistency. Specifically, even he leaves us in doubt as to the nature of the connection between the exchange value of the uses of capital and the price of the products of capital. Is the price of products high because the exchange value of uses is high? Or, on the contrary, is the exchange value of the uses high because the price of products is high? This point involves Say in the wildest contradictions,[24] and Hermann did not make it entirely clear either. In the passage just cited and in many others, he obviously inclines to the former view, and so represents the price of products as affected by the value of the uses of capital.[25] But at the same time there is no paucity of passages which presuppose just the opposite. Thus (*p. 296*) he remarks that the determination of the price of products "is itself the first to exert a retroactive influence on the price of the labors and uses." A similar instance occurs on another occasion when he is speaking of production processes involving intermediate products. In such a case, he says, it is not the cost of the primary elements which determine the price of the intermediate products derived from them. It is rather the price of the finished product which has that function. It was reserved for Menger to make this difficult question clear.

Thus far we have examined only Hermann's doctrine of the origin of interest. But we cannot ignore the highly original views that he propounds on the causes of the varying *rate* of interest.

Hermann starts from the proposition already established, that "the total quantity of products," resolved into its simple constituents, is "a sum of labors and uses of capital." If we adhere to that principle, our next conclusion must clearly be that all acts of exchange must consist in the exchange of labors and uses of capital possessed by one person for labors and uses possessed by another, such labors and uses being either direct or embodied in products. Whatever a man receives for his own labor in the form of the labors and uses of others is the exchange value of his labor, or his wage. And "whatever a man receives in the form of labors and uses of others when he offers his own uses for sale, forms the exchange value of these uses, or interest on his capital." The sum of wages of labor and interest on capital must therefore, measure the total quantity of all products coming to market. In this connection it must be remembered that for Hermann the term "capital" includes land.

On what, then, does the rate of originary interest depend, or, (which is the same thing) the rate of exchange value of the uses of capital? First, naturally, it depends on the amount of other men's labors and uses obtainable for them. But this itself, again, depends on the reciprocal ratio between demand for and supply of the two components of the total product, labors and uses. Every increase in the supply of labor tends to diminish wages and to raise originary interest, and every increase in the supply of uses, to raise wages and lower interest. But again, the supply of either of these two factors may be increased by two circumstances, either by an increase in the amount available or by an increase in its productiveness. These circumstances become operative in the following way.

"If the *amount* of capital increases, more uses are offered for sale, more equivalent values are sought for them. Now these equivalent values can be only labors or uses. If, in exchange for the increased uses, other uses of capital are demanded, a greater amount of equivalent values is actually available. Since, then, supply and demand are equally increased, the exchange value of the uses cannot alter. But if, as is here assumed, the total quantity of labor is not increased, then the owners of capital find, for the increased amount of uses which they seek to exchange against labor, only the same amount of labor as before. That is to say, they get an unsatisfactory equivalent value. The exchange value of uses will therefore fall in comparison with labor, or, conversely, the labor with the same expenditure will buy more uses. In the exchange of use against use the capitalists now receive the same equivalent value as formerly, but in the exchange of uses against labor they receive less. The amount of originary interest, in proportion to the total capital, must decrease, or in other words, the rate of originary interest must fall. The total quantity of goods produced is indeed increased, but the increase has been divided between capitalists and laborers."

"*If the productiveness of capital increases,* or if in the same time it furnishes more means of satisfying wants, the owners of capital offer for sale more useful goods than before, and demand greater equivalent values. They obtain these values to the extent that each one seeks other uses in exchange for his own increased use. In this instance the supply has risen with the demand, and so the exchange value must remain unaltered, in the sense that the uses of equal capitals for equal times are being exchanged. However, the magnitude of these uses in terms of usefulness is greater than before. But if the assumption is valid, that labor is not increased, then not all the uses with which the capitalist wishes to buy labor will command their former equivalent value. That inevitably raises the competitive demand for labor, and lowers the exchange value of uses as against labor. The laborers now receive more uses for the same amount of labor as before, and therefore find themselves better off. The owners of capital do not enjoy the whole fruit of the increased productiveness of capital, but are compelled to share it with the workers. But the lowering of the exchange value of the uses does not cause the owners of capital any loss, since the reduced value still commands more means of gratification than did the higher value formerly."

For similar reasons which need not be further detailed, Hermann shows that the rate of interest rises if the amount or the productiveness of labor increases.

The most striking feature in this theory certainly is that Hermann attributes a decline in interest to an increase in the productive power of capital. This places him in direct opposition, on the one hand, to Ricardo and his school, who considered the principal cause of a decline in the rate of interest to be the *decrease* in the productiveness of capital which results when it must be employed on inferior land. On the other hand, Hermann opposes the productivity theorists also, since the very nature of their theory presupposes direct correlation between the degree of productivity and the rate of interest.[26]

Whether or not Hermann's use theory is essentially tenable or not, is a question I prefer to leave open for the present. But his use of it to explain the interest rate can be proven fallacious, I think, even at the present stage of our inquiries.

For it appears to me that in this part of his doctrine Hermann failed to distinguish adequately between two things that must be very clearly distinguished, namely, *the ratio between the total excess of proceeds and total wage, and the ratio between the amount of interest and its capital,* that is to say, *the rate of interest.* Hermann's argument furnishes an excellent explanation and proof of a rise or fall in the total excess of proceeds in proportion to wages of labor. But it explains and proves nothing with respect to the rate of interest.

The source of his error is apparent. Hermann sets up an abstraction, by the terms of which he recognizes in products only the labors and uses which created them. This abstraction of his is ordinarily well justified, but he extends it to a field to which it is not applicable, the field of exchange value. Being accustomed to treat uses and labors as symbols representative of all goods, Hermann thought he was justified in dealing exclusively with those symbols, to determine whether a given quantity has high or low exchange value. He reasons that uses and labors are symbols representative of all goods and that a use which purchases the same amount of uses as before, but a smaller amount of labors, therefore has a low exchange value. That is wrong. The exchange value of a good (in the sense of "power in exchange," which is the sense in which Hermann always uses the word) is measured, not only by the quantities of one or two definite kinds of goods that can be got in exchange for it, but by the average of all goods. These include all products, each one having equal rights with the good called "labor" and the good called "use of capital." That is what we mean by exchange value in practical life and in economics, and that is what Hermann himself means, too. On page 432 he says expressly, "Where the goods to be priced are so heterogeneous, we cannot justify the establishment of an average price, such as was required for the determination of exchange value. And yet that does not mean that an exchange value is inconceivable. But we arrive at it by considering all the average prices which a given good commands in the same market, in all goods. *It is a series of comparisons of the same good with many other goods.* We shall call the exchange value of a good, as thus determined, the '*real value*' of the good, to distinguish it from the average amount of the money prices, or the money value."

Now it is not difficult to show that the power in exchange of the use of capital as against products, by no means follows the same line as does its power in exchange as against other uses and labors. For instance, if the productiveness of all uses and labors exactly doubles, the reciprocal power in exchange of uses and labors is not disturbed. However, the power in exchange of both as against the products which result from them is very seriously disturbed. It doubles!

Determination of the rate of interest is obviously a matter of the ratio of the exchange power of the uses of capital to the exchange power of a very definite kind of goods, namely, that capital good which furnishes the "use." If the power in exchange of the use of a machine is a twentieth of the exchange power of the product machine, then the use of the machine "buys" $100, while the machine itself obtains $2,000 as its equivalent value, and this ratio is expressed as a 5% rate of interest. But if the exchange value of the use of a machine is a tenth of that of the machine, the former buys $200 while the latter buys $2,000, and the ratio is expressed as a 10% rate of interest.

There is no reason at all for assuming that the exchange value of capital goods is determined in one way, and that of other goods in another way. Moreover, we have seen that the exchange value of products, in terms of uses, generally can vary in a ratio utterly different from that which applies to the exchange value of uses and labors *in terms of each other*. Therefore it follows that the ratio between the power in exchange of the uses of capital and the power in exchange of capital goods (in other words, the rate of interest) may take a course different from that followed by the ratio of exchange value between uses and labor. Hermann's rule therefore is not adequately established.[27]

I should like to conclude with a few words on the position that Hermann assumes towards the "productivity of capital." I have already said that he often uses the expression, but by no means in the sense which it has in the productivity theory. He is so far from believing that interest is produced directly by capital, that he maintains high productive power to be a cause of low interest. He expressly denies (*p. 542*) that originary interest is a compensation for "dead use." He asserts, on the contrary, that capital remains barren in the absence of "plan, care, supervision and intellectual activity generally." Incidentally, he did not himself attach any particularly clear significance to the expression "productivity." His definition reads, "The sum total of possible ways of employing capital, and the *relation of the product to the expenditure,* constitute what is called the productivity of capital."[28] Does he mean by this the relation of the *value* of the product to the *value* of the expenditure? In that case high productivity would occur only in the event of high interest. But in actual fact, it certainly brings about low interest! Or does he mean the relation of the *quantity* of the product to the *quantity* of the expenditure? But in economic life quantity is not a determining factor at all. Or does he mean the relation of the *quantity* of the product to the *value* of the expenditure? But quantity and value are incommensurable. The short of it seems to be that Hermann's definition will not stand strict interpretation. On the whole, it is just possible that he may have had in mind a kind of physical productivity.

In Germany many writers of note accepted Hermann's use theory, and even fostered it assiduously.

One very clear-headed follower of his is Bernhardi.[29] He did not develop the theory any further, but merely quoted Hermann's doctrine incidentally, and expressed agreement with it.[30] But he demonstrated originality and profundity in several fine critical works which were directed principally against the English school.[31] He also censures the school that stands at the opposite extreme, the blind productivity theorists, and excoriates that "strange contradiction" which ascribes living and independent activity to a dead instrument (*p. 307*).

Mangoldt is a follower of Hermann who deviates from him only in unimportant details.[32] Thus he attributes even less importance to the "productivity of capital" in the formation of interest, and even finds fault with that expression 'as incorrect. Yet he does not scruple to use it himself "for the sake of brevity."[33] Furthermore, while Hermann maintains that the rate of interest varies in inverse ratio to the productivity of capital, Mangoldt would have it in direct ratio and indeed, he accepts Thünen's formula, that this direct ratio applies to "the portion of capital most recently invested."

Similarly Mithoff, in his account of the economic distribution of wealth, published in *Schönbergs Handbuch,* follows Hermann in all essential respects.[34]

Schäffle takes a peculiar position with respect to the use theory. He was one of the most prominent representatives of the critical movement which the rise of "scientific" socialism brought into being, and so was one of the first to participate in the seething ferment which inevitably resulted from the clash between two schools of thought which were so violently at odds. That ferment left some highly characteristic traces in his utterances on the subject of interest. I shall show later that we can discern in Schäffle's writings no fewer than three distinctly different kinds of explanation for the phenomenon of interest. One of them belongs to the older school, and two to the later "critical" conception. The first of them is closely akin to the use theories.

In his earlier work, *Das Gesellschaftliche System der menschlichen Wirtschaft,*[35] Schäffle states his entire theory of interest in terms of the use theory. Originary interest is with him a yield of the "use of capital," loan interest is a price paid for use, its rate depending on the supply of and demand for the uses of loan capital, the uses are an independent element of costs, and so on. But there are unmistakable signs that he is on the point of renouncing the theory he professes. He repeatedly employs the word "use" in a sense that is far removed from Hermann's. He defines the use of capital as a *functioning of the individual as an economic entity by means of wealth,* as a utilization of wealth for fruitful production, as a "dedication," an "employment" of wealth, a "fulfilling of a function" on the part of the entrepreneur.[36] These expressions reveal a conception of "use" as an element of production which is rather a personal emanation of the entrepreneur than an objective manifestation of capital. And this impression is confirmed by the fact that Schäffle repeatedly speaks of originary interest as the premium of an economic *vocation.* And he inveighs against the view that interest is a *product* of the use of capital contributed to the process of production (*Vol. II, p. 389*). He charges Hermann with having colored his theory too strongly with the idea of independent productivity on the part of capital (*Vol. II, p. 459*). But, on the other hand, he often employs the word "use" in such a way that it can be interpreted only in the objective sense we find in Hermann, as for instance, when he speaks of the supply of and demand for the *uses of loan capital.* On one occasion he explicitly admits that there is present in use not only the personal element, but also an *objective* one, which he calls "utilization of capital" (*Vol. II. p. 458*). And despite his condemnation of Hermann, he himself does not scruple now and then to ascribe "fruitfulness" to the use of capital. Thus he neither entirely accepts the basis of the use theory nor entirely rejects it.

Even in his later systematic work, *Bau und Leben des sozialen Körpers,*[37] Schäffle's views did not resolve themselves into a clarified and consistent theory. While he advanced beyond the old use theory in one respect, in another he approached it more closely. For he still classifies the phenomenon empirically familiar as interest, under the formula "return for the use of capital," which use at all times retains an economic value. In this connection he abandons the subjective meaning of use, and now treats it unequivocally as a purely objective element contributed by goods. He speaks of the uses as "functions of goods," as "equivalents of useful materials in living labor," as "living energies of impersonal social substances." Even in the socialist state this objective use would retain its independent value, and thereby preserve its capacity to yield interest. The phenomenon of interest can disappear only if, in the socialist state, the community, as sole owner of capital goods, should contribute the valuable use of capital gratuitously, in which case the return from it would redound to the advantage of the entire social body (*Vol. III, p. 491 f.*). On the other hand, Schäffle rather diverges from the old use theory by refusing to recognize the use of capital as an ultimate and original element in production, and insisting that all costs of production originate from labor alone (*Vol. III, pp. 273, 274*).

That commits him to another line of explanation, which I shall have occasion to discuss at length in another connection.

The aforementioned followers of Hermann may be said to have promulgated his theory rather than developed it. But Knies may fairly claim to have improved it in certain essential respects. He made no change in its fundamental ideas, but he did give those fundamental ideas much clearer and more unambiguous expression than had Hermann himself. And such clarification was a service of which Hermann's theory was sorely in need, as may be perceived from the frequency with which it was misunderstood. For instance Schäffle, as I have already remarked, considered Hermann a productivity theorist. But it is more significant still that Knies himself thought of Hermann as an opponent rather than a forerunner.[38]

Knies was not originally an adherent of the use theory. In his *Erörterungen über den Kredit*[39] published in 1859, he expressed the view that credit transactions are barter transactions, or according to circumstances, buying transactions, in which one service is rendered in the present as the equivalent of another service to be rendered in the future (*p. 568*). The logical consequence of that principle would have been the conclusion that interest is not to be regarded as an equivalent of a use transferred in the loan, but as a partial equivalent of the total loan itself, which is something Galiani had said long before.[40] But Knies expressly disavowed this view later, since he saw no need of such an innovation, but was, on the contrary, aware of many considerations that could be urged against it.[41] Subsequently, he loosed a detailed polemic in which he spoke of the consideration which had been accorded to the difference in value of present and future goods of the same class by reason of the greater urgency of immediate need. He went on to say quite unequivocally, that such consideration might perhaps be termed "not entirely unfruitful," but that it could certainly not suffice to explain the fundamental character of the phenomenon of interest.[42]

Instead, Knies laid down an exceptionally lucid and consistently logical use theory in his comprehensive *Geld und Kredit*.[43] Although the purpose of this work was avowedly restricted to an inquiry into loan interest, Knies treats the subject so generally that his views on originary interest may easily be inferred from those he expresses on loan interest.

Basically he agrees with Hermann. Like him, Knies conceives of the use of a good as "a use which lasts throughout a period of time which is itself initiated and terminated at definitive moments of time." This use must be clearly differentiated from the good itself which is the "bearer of the use." Furthermore, the use possesses economic independence. A question of great importance for the use theory is the question, whether an independent use and its transfer are conceivable and practicable in the case of *perishable goods*. To that question Knies devotes a searching inquiry, which ends with an answer definitely in the affirmative.[44] Another cardinal question of the use theory is whether and why the independent use of capital necessarily possesses exchange value, and whether and why it also must follow that such use will obtain compensation in the form of interest. Hermann, although he cannot be said to have ignored the question, couched his answer in terms so unassuming and unemphatic, that it is not infrequently overlooked completely.[45] Knies, however, after thorough rationalization, concludes that "the emergence and the economic justification of a price for use, in the shape of interest, is founded on the same considerations as those on which the price of material goods is founded." The use is an instrument for the satisfaction of a human need just as truly as material goods are, and is an object that is "economically valuable and economically valued."[46] I should like to add that Knies avoided not only any relapse into the productivity theory, but even the very appearance of such relapse, and that he appended to his theory some very notable criticisms, particularly of the socialist interest theory. That addition will, I trust, serve to signalize the meritorious character of his contribution to the elaboration of Hermann's use theory, and to pay tribute to a thinker no less notable for his keen perception than for his conscientious research.

3. Menger's Maximum Development of the Use Theory

WE ARE now ready to consider a third member of our triumvirate, the writer who put the use theory into the most perfect form of which it was capable. That was Carl Menger, the author of *Grundsätze der Volkswirtschaftslehre*.[47]*

Menger's interest theory is superior to those of his predecessors because he erected it on the foundation of a much more complete theory of value, and especially on one which furnishes a detailed and satisfactory answer to the very difficult question of the relation between the value of products and that of their means of production. Does the value of a product depend on the means by which it is produced, or does the value of the means of production depend on that of their product? The economists before Menger rather groped in the dark for an answer. It is true that a number of writers had occasionally made statements to the general effect that the value of the means of production depends on the value of the prospective product. Such writers include Say, Riedel, Hermann and Roscher.[48] But these statements were never couched in the form of a general law, and still less were they supported by instances to demonstrate their universal applicability. And we have observed furthermore, that their writings contain other statements as well which are open to the opposite interpretation. And the opposite view is espoused in that extensive body of economic literature which recognizes, as a fundamental law, the proposition that the cost of goods determines their value.

As long as there was obscurity among economists with respect to this causal sequence, their treatment of the interest problem could scarcely

* English translation: Carl Menger, *Principles of Economics*, The Free Press, Glencoe, Illinois, 1950.

be more than an uncertain groping. For how is it possible to account for the difference between two quantities of differing magnitude, (that is to say, between expenditure of capital and yield of capital) without knowing which of the two is to be regarded as cause, and which as effect?

It was Menger who performed the highly meritorious service of clearly defining the causal sequence, and thus marking the exact point at which the interest problem had to be attacked, and the direction in which its solution had to proceed. He defines that relationship by saying that the *value of the means of production,* ("goods of higher order" in his terminology) *always and without exception is determined by the value of their products* ("goods of lower order") *and not vice versa.* He arrives at this conclusion by the following course of reasoning.[49]

Value is the importance "which concrete goods, or quantities of goods, acquire for us through the fact that we are conscious of being dependent on having them at our disposal, for the satisfaction of our wants." The magnitude of value that goods possess always depends on the importance of those wants which depend for their satisfaction on our disposal over the goods in question. Since goods of "higher order" (means of production) are of service to us only through the medium of those goods of "lower order" (products or consumption goods) which result from them, it is clear that the means of production can have importance for the satisfaction of our wants only to the extent that such importance is possessed by the consumption goods produced from them. Means of production, the sole use of which consisted in the making of valueless goods, could evidently not acquire value for us at all.

Every group of wants the satisfaction of which depends on a consumption good is identical with any group the satisfaction of which depends upon the means of producing that consumption good. It follows therefore, that the *degree* of importance for the satisfaction of wants which a consumption good possesses, must in the nature of things, be identical with the corresponding degree of importance possessed by the means of producing it. As a consequence, the prospective value of the consumption good is not only an indication of the *existence* of value on the part of the means of production, but also a measure of the *magnitude* of such value. Finally, since the subjective value of goods is also the basis for their *price,* the price, or as some people call it, the "economic value" of goods is regulated by the same principle.

On that basis, the interest problem assumes the following form.

A capital is nothing but a sum of "complementary goods" of higher order. Now if this sum derives its value from the value of its anticipated product, how is it that it never quite reaches that value, but is always less, in definite proportion? Or, if it is true that the anticipated value of the product is the source and the measure of the value of the means of its production, how is it that capital goods are not valued so highly as their product?

Menger has an ingenious answer to this question.[50]

The transformation of means of production into consumption goods, that is to say, the process of production, always requires a certain period of time which varies in length. For the purposes of production it is not sufficient to have disposal of the means of production only for *a single moment* within that period of time. It is necessary to *retain* the disposal of them, and to unite them in the process of production throughout the period. We must, therefore, include among the several conditions of production, one which consists in *the disposal of quantities of means of production during definite periods of time*. It is this disposal which, for Menger, characterizes the essential nature of the use of capital.

This sort of use of capital or disposal of capital, in so far as it is not present or not offered in sufficient quantity, can now attain value or, in other words, it can become an economic good. When this happens, as is usually the case, the number of the usual means of production employed in a concrete production is increased by one. In addition to the obvious ones, such as raw materials, auxiliary materials, labor, and so on, there is an additional contributor to the sum of value contained in the prospective consumption good. That contributor is the *disposal* of the goods that are required for the production. Another name for it is "use of capital." And since the sum of value must include an equivalent for the economic good we called "use of capital," the other means of production cannot account for the full magnitude of value of the prospective consumption good. This is the origin of the difference in value between the means of production thrown into an undertaking and the consumption good. And this, at the same time, is the origin of interest.[51]

In this doctrine of Menger's the use theory finally attained full theoretical clarity and maturity. He completely avoided all relapse into ancient error, or the faintest dubious resemblance to the old productivity theories, and thus definitely transmuted the interest problem from a question of production, which it is not, into a question of value, which it is. At the same time, Menger stated the problem of value so clearly and so sharply and marshalled its elements so felicitously by his exposition of the relationship between value of product and value of the means of production, that he not only surpassed his predecessors in the use theory, but laid a permanent foundation for all subsequent serious research into the problem of interest.

For that reason the critic's assignment with respect to Menger is different from that with respect to any of his predecessors. In considering the latter, I have deliberately ignored the question whether the fundamental principle of the use theory was sound or not. I have treated only the greater or lesser degree of excellence with which they presented its fundamental principle, the greater or lesser degree of intrinsic consistency and clarity they attained. So far I have, so to speak, measured each particular use theory for its correspondence with an ideal use theory. But I have not measured that ideal use theory for its correspondence with the truth. With respect to Menger, only the second measure need be taken. In regard to Menger, we need ask only a single question; but it is, of course, the scientifically all-important one. *Is the use theory, in any event, capable of a satisfactory answer to the problem of interest?*

I shall try to find an answer to this question which will furnish, not merely a specific treatment of Menger's formulation of the theory, but also the basis for an opinion on the whole theoretical movement that reaches its highest development with Menger.

I am aware that, in doing so, I have undertaken one of the most difficult tasks in the field of criticism. It is difficult because of the general nature of the material, which has for so many decades taxed the endeavors of the finest minds. It is especially difficult, because I shall be compelled to contradict opinions advanced after careful consideration, by the best minds of our nation, and supported with admirable ingenuity. Finally, it is most particularly difficult because I shall be compelled to oppose ideas that were vehemently contested in times long past, then were brilliantly victorious over their opponents, and have since been taught and believed as veritable dogma. And so I must entreat the reader to peruse the following pages with an open mind, with patience, and with attentiveness.

B. CRITIQUE OF USE THEORIES

1. The Points of Contention

ALL the use theories are based on the assumption that, leading a companionate existence, as it were, there is beside each capital good a "use" thereof which is an independent economic good, possessing independent value. There is a corollary assumption that this latter value, when added to the capital good itself, constitutes the value of the consumption good.

I deny the validity of those assumptions.

*In the first place, there simply is no such thing as an independent "use of capital," and consequently it cannot have independent value, nor by its participation give rise to the "phenomenon of excess value." To assume such a use is to create an unwarrantable fiction that contravenes all fact.** To guard against a misunderstanding which I should very much deprecate, let me say in so many words that I have no intention of denying the existence of "uses of capital" altogether. What I must deny is the existence of that special something which our theorists call "use of capital," and which they endow with a variety of attributes which, in my opinion, violate the nature of things. I shall go into detail later.

In the second place, even if there existed the kind of use of capital that is postulated by the use theorists, it would still not provide a basis for the satisfactory explanation of the phenomenon of interest, as the latter actually manifests itself. Therefore the use theories are founded on a hypothesis which is neither consonant with reality nor capable of attaining the solution which was its purpose.

The recorded history of economic science places me in a more un-

Translators' note: The remainder of this paragraph was originally a footnote.

favorable position for proving the first of my contentions. For while the discussion of the second opens up virgin soil, undisturbed as yet by the strife of economists, my mention of the first seems to reopen a closed issue, a *res judicata,* a case which has been carried through all the courts, from the lowest to the highest, and in which a final verdict has long since been rendered against me. Essentially it is the same question which was at issue centuries ago between the canonists and the defenders of loan interest. The canonists maintained that property in a thing includes all the uses that can be made of it, and that there can therefore be no separate use which stands outside the article and which can be conveyed with it, when the article is loaned. The defenders of loan interest maintained that there was such an independent use. And Salmasius and his followers managed to urge their views with such effectual arguments that the public opinion of the scientific world soon supported them, and that today we merely smile tolerantly at the "shortsighted pedantry" of these old canonists.

Well, with full awareness that I am laying myself open to the charge of eccentricity, I maintain that the much decried doctrine of the canonists was nevertheless right! Their allegation was, that independent use of capital really does not exist. And I feel confident that I can prove that the verdict handed down in this literary suit even by those high courts, for all their unanimity, was nevertheless wrong.

First Proposition to be Proved:
that there is no "use of capital" of the kind postulated by the use theorists.

The first thing we have to do is, of course, to define the matter in contention. What is this use, the independent existence of which is maintained by the use theorists and denied by me?

As to the nature of the use, there is no agreement among the theorists themselves. Menger, in particular, gives a definition essentially different from that of his precedessors. I am thus constrained to divide my inquiry into at least two parts, the first of which will treat the concept of use according to the Say-Hermann school, while the second will deal with Menger's concept.

A. Critique of the Use Concept of the Say-Hermann School

1. USEFUL NATURAL PROPERTIES OF GOODS EXIST

EVEN within the ranks of the Say-Hermann school no exact agreement prevails in the description and definition of "use." But this want of agreement appears to me traceable, not so much to any real difference of opinion about the thing itself, as to a common lack of a clear idea of its nature. Their definitions differed, not because they had different objects in mind, but because the one object they all had in mind was glimpsed only in hazy outline. One proof of this lies in the fact that the individual use theorists are at loggerheads with their own definitions almost as often as with those of their colleagues. Let us begin by listing the most important of these definitions.

Say speaks of "productive services" of capital, and defines them as a "labor" which capital performs.

Hermann in one place (*p. 109*) defines the use of goods as their "employment."[52] He repeats this on page 111, where he says that the employment of goods of perishable material may be thought of as a good in itself, as a "use." Use is in this passage identical with employment, but not in a passage on page 125, where Hermann says that employment means "expenditure of the use" (*Verwendung der Nutzung*). And finally, on page 287, he explains "the holding together of the technical elements of the product" as the service, the "objective use of liquid capital."

Knies also identifies use and employment.[53]

Schäffle in one place defines use as the "application" (*Anwendung*) of goods (*Das gesellschaftliche System der menschlichen Wirtschaft,* III, *p. 143*); similarly on page 266 as "acquisitive employment." On page 267 he calls it "the functioning of an economic individual by means of wealth, a utilization of wealth for fruitful production." On the same page it is called a "dedication" of wealth to production, which is hardly consistent with his speaking on the next page of a dedication of the "use of capital," or in other words, of a dedication of the "dedication." In his *Bau und Leben,* finally, Schäffle explains the uses in one place (III, *p. 258*) as "functions of goods," and somewhat later (*p. 259*) as "equivalents of useful materials in living labor," while on page 260 use is defined as the "releasing of the utility residing in material goods."

If we examine this somewhat chequered array of definitions and elucidations, we can discern two interpretations of the concept of use, one subjective and one objective. These two interpretations of the concept correspond rather closely to the two senses we attach to the word "use" in ordinary speech. For that word describes, on the one hand, the *subjective* activity of the one who does the using. It signifies a "utilization" or an "employment," if you will, in the subjective sense in which the latter equally ambiguous word can be used. It means the "act of using" (*Gebrauchshandlung*). On the other hand the word "use" also describes the *objective* function of a thing that is used, the purpose which the thing is serving, or the service being rendered *by* the thing. When Hermann writes "use" and "employment" without discrimination, we are vaguely conscious of the subjective meaning, and we are definitely aware of it in the earlier writings of Schäffle. On the other hand, the objective meaning predominates strongly in Say, and almost as much so in other passages by Hermann, who at least once avails himself of the express term "objective use" of capital. And Schäffle too, in his most recent work, reveals the same tendency, for he has reached the point where he interprets use to mean "function of goods."

It is obvious that of these two, only the objective sense of the word "use" fits the requirements of the use theory. It is at once apparent that the uses which the borrower buys from the lender and pays for with loan interest cannot possibly be called subjective uses. They cannot be the lender's "acts of using," for he does not perform any. Nor can they be the borrower's "acts of using" either. For, although he may intend to perform such acts, he naturally does not need to buy his own acts from the lender. And so, to say that a loan represents a conveyance of the uses of capital makes sense only if we understand by "uses" objective elements of use of some kind. Therefore I think I am justified in ignoring the subjective interpretations of "use," as they occur sporadically in the writings of individual use theorists, on the ground that they are inconsistencies which contradict the spirit of their own theory. I shall confine myself exclusively to the objective interpretation, which is the one intended most of the time, and indeed, since Schäffle's change of front, all the time. The Say-Hermann school, then, means by "use" *an objective element of use emanating from goods, which attains independent economic existence and independent economic value.*

Now nothing can be more certain than that there are really certain objective useful services of goods which attain economic independence, and which may quite properly be termed "uses." I have already treated them in detail elsewhere, and have done my utmost to describe their true nature as exactly and thoroughly as possible.[54] Singularly enough, my attempt to do so seems to be the only one of its kind in economic literature. I say "singularly enough" advisedly, because we do seem to face a very strange situation. Here is a science which from beginning to end hinges on the satisfaction of wants by means of goods, and on the relative usefulness of goods to man. And yet this science has not even inquired into the technical nature of the use of goods. Its practitioners have written pages, chapters, and even monographs on many another concept, but not so much as two lines devoted to the definition or elucidation of the fundamental concept, "use of a good"! Instead, the expression is dragged into every scientific research, burdened with all the haziness, confusion and ambiguity which encumber it in the mouth of the layman.

2. THE THEORY OF THE USE OF GOODS

FOR our present purpose nothing is so important as a dependable conception of the useful functions which goods may serve. And so I feel constrained to go into the matter again at this point, and with some exactitude, and I beg the reader not to regard it as a digression, but as strictly germane to the subject.[55]

All material goods are of use to mankind by virtue of the activity of the natural properties inherent in them. They are a part of the material world, and for that reason all their activity, including their useful activity, must bear the character that activity in the material world has generally. It is a functioning of natural properties according to the laws of nature. What distinguishes the functioning of material goods from the functioning of other kinds of natural things, indifferent or hurtful, is the single circumstance that the former can be controlled to man's advantage. Both functioning and control proceed in accordance with the laws of nature. That is to say, all things are endowed with functioning natural properties, but experience shows that this functioning will admit of control toward a definitely useful end only when the matter which possesses these properties has taken on certain forms that favor the exercise of such control. All things on the surface of the earth, for instance, possess the kinetic energy which is imparted by gravity. But while man can do nothing with this form of energy when stored up in a mountain, that same energy is useful when the thing possessing it has assumed a favorable form, such as that of a clock pendulum, or a paper weight, or a hammer. Similarly, the natural properties of carbon are identical for every molecule of it. But we derive direct economic utility from those properties when the carbon has assumed some such form as that of wood or coal, though not when it exists as a component part of the atmosphere. We may therefore say that what characterizes material *goods,* in contrast to material *things* that are not useful, is the fact that they constitute such special forms of matter that their natural properties can be controlled for man's benefit.

From these statements we can draw two inferences, of which one concerns the character of the useful functions of material goods, and the other concerns the character of the employment of goods.

The function of goods can consist only in delivering performances or manifestations of natural properties. Viewed as a natural phenomenon, it affords a perfect parallel to the useful function performed by a manual laborer. A porter or ditchdigger is of use when he exerts the natural properties residing in his body in the form of rendering useful services. Similarly, material goods display *concrete manifestations of such natural properties inherent in them as are subject to control.* Laborer and material goods are "of use" by analogous processes.

The *employment* of a good is effectuated whenever man, at the proper moment, elicits or "releases" performance of the properties peculiar to the good in question, unless it be the sort of good characterized by spontaneous and uninterrupted emanation of its useful properties. Thereupon man establishes appropriate contact between the released properties and the object to which the useful effect is to be applied. For instance, if he wishes to make use of a locomotive, the supplying of water and of heat cause the delivery of motor performance, and that is brought in contact with the cars which hold the persons or things which are to be transported. In the case of a book or a house, the images peculiar to the book, or the sheltering properties peculiar to the house emanate from them uninterruptedly. Man needs but bring them into useful contact with his eye, or his person, respectively, in order to "use" these goods. *But it is impossible to conceive of any use of material goods, which does not consist in receiving useful services rendered by those material goods, by virtue of their inherent properties.*

I think I need not fear that the propositions I have just advanced will encounter any scientific opposition. The concept they convey is no stranger any more to economic literature,[56] and in the present state of the natural sciences its acceptance has become an irrefragable necessity.

If by any chance the objection should be raised that this concept is one that belongs in the field of the natural sciences and not economic science, my answer would be that in these questions economic science must yield the floor to natural science. The principle of the unity of all science demands it. Economics does not explain the facts within its province to the outermost limits, any more than any other science does. It solves the problems of only one portion of the causal connection that binds together a universe of phenomena, and leaves it to other sciences to continue the explanation. The field of inquiry which is the domain of the science of economics is bounded on one side by that of psychology and on another by that of the natural sciences, not to mention additional borders on which other sciences may impinge. Let us cite a concrete example. In the course of an explanation of the circumstance that bread has exchange value, economics will go so far as to point out that bread will satisfy the need for sustenance, and that men will endeavor to ensure the satisfaction of their wants, if need be, at the price of some sacrifice. But the fact of that endeavor, and the reason for it, is not the domain of economics but of psychology. The fact that men need sustenance, and the reason for it, falls within the domain of physiology. The fact that bread fills such a need, and the reason for that, also lies within the field of physiology, but even physiology cannot complete that explanation within its own sphere, but must seek assistance from the more general physical sciences.

Now it is clear that any explanations furnished by economic science have value only on condition that they can be carried on by the contiguous sciences. Economics cannot build on a foundation which a "border science" pronounces untrue or impossible. Otherwise the thread of explanation is severed from the very outset. Therefore, when operating out in its border lands, economics must maintain touch with the neighboring sciences. And the question of the functioning of material goods lies in just such a borderland.

The only thing I may have to fear is that my application of this physical concept to a certain limited class of material goods, especially to the so-called "ideal goods," may at first arouse a feeling of astonishment in some readers. I admit that it may indeed seem strange to claim that a fixed and stationary dwelling house, a volume of poems, or a painting by Raphael should be of use to us because of the activity of its inherent properties. But a little reflection will soon lay at rest objections like these, which have their origin in feeling rather than in reason.

All the things that I have mentioned do actually become "goods" only by virtue of the peculiar natural properties which they possess, and possess, indeed, in peculiar combination. That a house provides shelter and warmth is only a result effected by the forces of gravity, cohesion, and resistance, of impermeability, of poor heat conductivity on the part of building materials. That the thoughts and feelings of the poet are recreated in us, is an out and out physical result of the activity of light, color, and the form of written characters. And this physical part

146

of its instrumentality is the very office of the book. Admittedly there must have been a poetic soul to awaken ideas and feelings and they can be reawakened only in a human spirit and through spiritual forces. But the path from spirit to spirit lies for some little distance in the natural world, and over that distance even the spirit must make use of a natural vehicle. That natural vehicle is the book, the painting, the spoken word. In and of themselves they furnish only a physical stimulus, and nothing more. What there is of the spiritual comes from within us in response to the stimulus. And if we are not prepared to afford it a fruitful reception—if we cannot read, or if, though we can read, we cannot understand or cannot feel—then the physical stimulus is all there is.

I believe that after these explanations I may consider it established beyond question that material goods exert their economic use *by the activity of the natural properties inherent in them.*

I propose, as a designation for the useful activity of inherent properties to be gained from a given material good, the term "rendition of service."[57]* In itself, the name "use" would not be inappropriate, but to adopt it would be to surrender our concept over to all the obscurity which now, unfortunately, clings to that ambiguous term; on the other hand the term "rendition of service" strikes me as very meaningful, for we are speaking literally of performance of a useful service by the inherent properties emanating from material goods.[58]

The concept of rendition of service is, in my opinion, destined to be one of the most important elemental concepts in economic theory. It is no whit less important than the concept of an economic good, but unfortunately it has as yet enjoyed little attention or development. The nature of our task makes it our irremissible duty to repair this neglect to some degree, and set forth some of the most important respects in which rendition of service exercises its function in economic life.

First of all, it is clear that each thing which would lay claim to the name of a "good" must be capable of rendering service or use, and that as soon as it loses that capability, it ceases to have the quality of a good and it drops out of the category of "goods" and reverts to the status of a simple "thing." It must not be supposed that complete consumption of this particular capability signifies the complete loss of any capacity to manifest characteristic properties at all. For what we have called the inherent properties of any matter are as imperishable as the matter itself, and they never cease to manifest themselves or to carry out their functions. But those manifestations may very well cease to be a rendition of service. And that will take place whenever the original good, in the course of rendering its service, has undergone a

---

* Translators' note: *Nutzleistung* is a word coined by Böhm-Bawerk. He seems to use it as a metonymic symbol for a thought to be gathered from the explanations he offers implicitly and explicitly in this chapter. The translators' best definition of *Nutzleistung* or the alternative *Kräfteleistung* would read "the rendition of service by making available to man the useful properties residing in material goods." Using Böhm-Bawerk's own technique of letting two words stand for a long and complicated concept, we shall use "rendition of service" as the translation of *Nutzleistung,* enjoining the reader to associate with it the connotations of the longer definition.

change (through separation, distortion, or combination of some of its component parts with other bodies) provided such change is so extensive that, in its changed form, the manifestation of its properties can no longer be directed to human use. For instance, when the carbon of the wood is burned in the blast furnace, it combines with oxygen in the combustion process. And although it continues to possess and manifest the natural properties of carbon these cannot again be used for smelting ore. The broken pendulum retains as much gravitational force as before, but because it no longer has the form of a pendulum, that force cannot now be directed toward the regulation of a clock. This loss of the capacity for the rendition of service is customarily called consumption of goods.

While all goods necessarily possess in common the ability to render service, they differ basically in the number of such performances at their command. This is the basis for the familiar division of goods into perishable and nonperishable, or better, into perishable and durable.* Even so-called nonperishable goods are perishable, however gradual the process may be. The expression "durable" designates not so much the resistivity of goods to rapid consumption by reason of use, as resistivity to rapid deterioration regardless of use.

Many goods are of such a nature that they render the uses peculiar to them by delivering the entire sum thereof at once, in a single intensive manifestation, so that their first use completely exhausts their capacity for service, and constitutes consumption. This is true of so-called perishable goods, such as food, gunpowder, fuel, and the like. But other goods are by nature capable of delivering many such renditions of service successively, within a shorter or longer period of time, and thus after the first, or even after many of them, they retain a capacity for the rendition of further services, and so preserve their character as goods. This is true of durable goods such as clothing, houses, tools, precious stones, land, and many others.

Where a good successively renders many services the latter are of two kinds. In one kind, successive services are marked by palpable characteristics which permit recognition of them as clearly marked single acts, which can be easily distinguished, differentiated, and counted. An example would be the individual strokes of a triphammer or the operations of the automatic printing press used by a great newspaper. In the second kind the rendition of services emanates from the goods in even and uninterrupted continuity. Such uses would be exemplified by the silent and enduring shelter afforded by a dwelling house. If there is occasion, as often becomes necessary in practice, to separate and divide such a continuous rendition of service, the same expedient is adopted that is used for subdividing all unsegmented magnitudes. Lines of demarcation not naturally present in the magnitude to be subdivided are borrowed from some outside circumstance, such as the expiration of a definite period of time. Thus the lessee of a house acquires the renditions of service which the house delivers *over a period of a year.*

* Translators' note: The remainder of this paragraph was originally a footnote.

Analysis of rendition of service reveals another element which is an essential feature of them. I refer to their ability to attain complete economic independence. This phenomenon is due to the fact that in very many, indeed in most cases, the satisfaction of a concrete human want does not demand the utter depletion of the entire useful content of a good, but only the rendition of a single service. Such rendition thereby acquires independent significance with respect to the satisfaction of wants, and in turn is accorded recognition in actual economic practice. We grant such recognition when we assign independent value to isolated renditions of service. We do so even more strikingly when we conduct independent business transactions which consist exclusively in such renditions, by selling or exchanging a single rendition or numerous renditions of service, apart from the goods from which they proceed. Economic custom and law have created a number of forms in which this is effectuated. Among the most important of these are the relations of "tenancy," of "hire," and of "borrowing in kind" (*commodatum*),[59] or such institutions as "tenancy in fee," "copyhold" and "land rent" (both *emphyteusis* and *superficies*). It is easy to recognize the feature which is common to all these transactions. In all of them some single rendition of service of which a good is capable is segregated and transferred separately, while the greater or lesser number of remaining renditions continue to reside in the ownership of the body of the good, in the hands of its original owner.[60]

In conclusion be it noted that, in point of theory, great importance attaches to the determination of the relation that exists between the rendition of service and the goods from which it emanates. Three cardinal principles may be enunciated, all of which appear to me so obvious that we may dispense here with any detailed proof of them, especially as I have done so in detail elsewhere.[61]

The first of these is that we value and desire goods only for the sake of the renditions of service to be expected of them. The renditions of service constitute the economic kernel, as it were, with which we are concerned, and the goods themselves are only its physical shell. The second and equally axiomatic principle is logically inevitable.

Even when a whole good is acquired and conveyed, the economic substance of the transaction always lies in the acquisition and conveyance of renditions of service, and indeed of the totality of such renditions. The conveyance of the goods themselves constitutes only a form. Admittedly the form is important by reason of the nature of the transaction, but it is still merely a form which accompanies and epitomizes the proceeding. To buy a good can mean nothing, economically speaking, but to buy all its renditions of service.[62] And that leads us to the important third principle.

The value and price of a good is nothing but the value and price of all its renditions of service in a single lump sum. Hence the value and price of each individual rendition of service is contained in the value and price of the good itself.[63]

Before going further let me illustrate these three propositions by means of a concrete example. I think all readers will agree with me when I say, firstly, that a cloth manufacturer values and desires looms only because he expects to get from the looms the useful energies peculiar to them; that, secondly, whether he *hires* a loom, or *buys* it, his purpose is the acquisition of its renditions of service; and thirdly, that the ownership he acquires at the same time in the body of the machine serves only as greater assurance that he will obtain those renditions of service. Even though this ownership in point of law appears to be the *primary* thing, economically it is certainly only *secondary*. Finally, I think it will be granted that the use which the whole machine delivers is nothing but the total of all its renditions of service in one sum. And it must also be conceded that the value and price of the whole machine is likewise, and inevitably, nothing but the value and price of all its renditions of service combined into a single sum.

3. "RENDITIONS OF SERVICE" NOT IDENTICAL WITH "USE" AS POSTULATED BY THE USE THEORISTS

SINCE we have adequately explained the nature and the constitution of the use of goods, let us return to our principal subject, the critical examination of the concept of "use" advanced by the use theorists.

Our first question must be, whether the "uses" of the Say-Hermann school are perhaps identical with these "renditions of service" of ours, which unquestionably do exist. There can be no doubt that they are *not* identical. That something which the use theorist calls "use," is intended to be the basis and the equivalent of *net* interest. Renditions of service, on the contrary, are sometimes (in the case of durable goods) the basis of *gross* interest, which includes net interest and a part of the capital value itself. They are at other times (in the case of perishable goods) the basis of the *entire capital value*. If I buy the renditions of service possessed by a dwelling, I pay a year's rent for the renditions of service which are made available over a period of one year, and that is gross interest. If I buy the renditions of service inherent in a bucket of coal, then even for the rendition of service over a period of but the single hour in which the coal burns to ashes, I pay the whole capital value of the coal. On the other hand, the thing that the use theorists call "use" is paid for quite differently. The "use" that a bucket of coal renders during *a whole year* attains no higher price than, say, a twentieth part of the capital value of the coal. Use and rendition of service must therefore be two entirely different magnitudes. Clearly, the writers who defined what we have called renditions of service, and established their existence, did so under the impression that they were defining and establishing the basis of net interest. Just as clearly, they were under a serious delusion. This criticism applies especially to Say's *services productifs,* and to Schäffle's later definitions of use.

And now we come to the decisive question. *If the "uses" of the use theorists are something other than our "renditions of service" of goods, can they be anything real? Is it conceivable that among, beside, or within these renditions of service is to be found the source of some other useful emanations from goods?*

I can find no other answer to this question than a most emphatic "No!" And I think every one will be compelled to give this answer who admits that material goods are objects of the material world; that material results can be produced only through manifestations of natural properties, and that even the "utility" of a thing is a function. Granted these premises, none of which should encounter opposition, it seems to me simply impossible to conceive that material goods possess any use other than that which consists in the ability to activate the natural properties peculiar to them, that is to say, to make available their renditions of service.

But I need not appeal to the logic of the natural sciences; I appeal simply to the common sense of the reader. An example or two will illustrate what we mean when we say that goods are "of use." A threshing machine, for instance, indubitably derives its economic utility from the help it gives in threshing grain. How does it, how can it, render this use? Only by the functioning of its mechanical properties on one occasion after another, until the worn-out mechanism refuses to function in that way any longer. Or can any reader imagine any guise in which the threshing machine exerts its influence on the separation of the grain from the ear, other than the functioning of mechanical energy? Can he imagine an atom of usefulness in the threshing process that the machine could supply, not by furnishing mechanical power, but through some other kind of use? I doubt it very much. The threshing machine either threshes by exercising its physical properties, or it does not thresh at all.

Nor is there any cogency in positing another kind of use by pointing out all sorts of *mediate* uses that can be derived from the threshing machine. Yes, our grain when threshed is certainly worth more than it was before it was threshed, and the increment in value is a use derived from the machine. But it is easy to see that this is not a use *in addition to* the renditions of service by the machine. It is only a use *by means of* them. It is, in sober fact, the very *use which is peculiar to* the machine. Suppose someone were to give me $5,000, and I were to buy myself a race horse. Can I say that I received two gifts, one of $5,000 and another of a race horse? I have just as little right to consider the mediate use of renditions of service as useful services of goods[64] which exist in addition to and apart from those goods.

What applies to durable goods in that respect is even more obvious in the case of perishable goods. What do I get from a bucket of coal? I get the service rendered by its property of producing heat during combustion, and for which I pay the capital price of the coal, and beyond that, nothing—absolutely nothing! I "use" the coal because its rendition of service, as it emanates from the coal, is brought into connection by me with some object in which I wish to effect a change through heat, and my use lasts as long as that rendition of service continues to be made available to me by the burning coal.

And when I lend a man a bucket of coal for a year, what does my debtor get from it? The same heat-producing properties that emanate from the coal for a few hours, and in addition the same "nothing—absolutely nothing." His use of the coal, like mine, is exhausted in the same short time. "But," you may ask, "can he not, by the terms of the loan agreement, use the coal over a whole year?" The owner, I admit, has no objection, but nature has. She ordains inexorably that the use shall end after a few hours. What is left of the loan agreement is that the debtor is not obliged to replace the coal until a year has elapsed. But it is surely a strange befuddlement that says, "I don't have to replace these ashes with a fresh bucket of coal for a year. That means that I continue to enjoy the objective use of these ashes for the rest of a whole long year!" Neither the world of hard facts, nor the world of logically ordered imagination has any place for a "use of goods" which is anything but their natural "rendition of service."

It may be reasonable to hope that many readers will consider this analysis sufficiently convincing. But the matter is too important, and the opposite views too deeply rooted, for me to rest my case at this point, and so I shall try to adduce still further evidence against the existence of the use postulated by the use theorists. Of course the negative nature of my contention precludes a positive proof. It is not possible to make the reader visualize the nonexistence of a thing. Nevertheless there is no lack of decisive evidence on the point, and indeed it is supplied by my opponents themselves.

There are two criteria of a valid proposition. It must be reached by a correct process of reasoning, and it must lead to correct conclusions. I intend to prove that the proposition of my opponents which maintains the existence of an independent use, will not meet either of those criteria.

I will show, first, *that every syllogism by which the use theorists thought they had proved the existence of the alleged use, contains an error or a misunderstanding.*

I will show, second, *that the assumption of an independent use necessarily leads to untenable conclusions.*

In conjunction with my previous demonstration, that there is no place for any objective use other than rendition of service, the negative proof of these two points should afford the fullest evidence that can be brought forward for my thesis.

4. REFUTATION OF SAY, SCHÄFFLE, HERMANN AND KNIES

OF THE prominent representatives of the use theory, just two took any pains to prove the existence of an independent use, namely, Hermann and Knies. I shall therefore make their argument the chief subject of my critical examination. In addition, the contributions of Say, the Nestor of the use theory, and of Schäffle, deserve our consideration. I shall begin with the two latter authors, since a few words will suffice to show that they were the victims of error.

Say ascribes to capital the performance of productive services, or, as he often expresses it, the performance of "labor," and this labor is supposed to be the foundation of interest. Cavil, if you will, at the expressions "services" and "labor" on the ground that they are better suited to the actions of persons than to those of impersonal goods. But as to the thing, Say is unquestionably right, capital does perform "labor."

However, it is equally unquestionable that the labor which capital actually performs consists in what I have called "renditions of service" on the part of goods, and these either supply the basis of *gross interest,* or constitute the capital value of goods. Say seems to make the tacit assumption that capital performs additional tasks which are distinct from the renditions of service just mentioned, and that the former might furnish a separate basis for net interest, but he does not offer the slightest proof of it. The most likely reason is that he was totally unaware of the iridescent ambiguity of his concept of the *services productifs.*

Very much the same is true of Schäffle. I need not speak of the subjective interpretations of his earlier work, which are inconsistent with the character of the use theory, and which he tacitly retracted in the latest edition of his *Bau und Leben.* In the latter, however, he calls goods "stores of useful energies" (III, *p. 258*), and he calls uses "functions of goods," "equivalents of useful materials in living labor" (III, *pp. 258, 259*), "living energies of impersonal social substance" (*p. 313*). This is all quite correct; but the function of goods, the expenditures from the store of useful energies, are nothing more or less than our renditions of service which, as we have shown, are not the equivalent of net interest, as Schäffle assumes, but of gross interest or, in the case of perishable goods, of capital value. Say and Schäffle, therefore, have misunderstood what it was they had to prove, and their arguments are therefore entirely beside the mark.

The way Hermann arrives at his independent "use" is psychologically interesting. His first introduction of the concept of use occurs when he speaks of the use of *durable* goods. "Land, dwellings, tools, books, money, have durable use value. Their use, while they last, may be conceived of as a good in itself, and may attain exchange value which is called interest."[65] He submits no actual proof of the existence of an independent use possessing independent value, and indeed there is no need of proof, because every one knows that in actual fact the use of a piece of ground, or of a house, can be independently valued and sold. But one thing must be emphasized in this connection. The use that every reader will and must think of here is the *gross* use of durable goods, the basis of the rental of land or of a house, the thing we called the rendition of service on the part of goods. We can envision an existence of this "use" independent of that of the good that renders the use, only because the use in question does not exhaust the good itself. We are forced to admit that the use is something apart from the good itself and independent of it, because the good continues to exist and to retain an unexhausted residue of its use content.

The second step that Hermann takes is to draw an analogy between the use of durable goods and that of perishable goods, and to try to prove in the case of the latter also, the existence of an independent use with independent value apart from the value of the good. He finds[66] that perishable goods, though altered in the course of a technical process, still preserve their usefulness despite the change in form and "can acquire permanence for their use." For instance, when iron ore, coal, and labor are transformed into pig iron, they contribute the chemical and mechanical elements needed for a new usefulness which emerges from the combination. "And if the pig iron possesses the exchange value of the three goods of exchange employed in its making, then the former sum of goods persists, qualitatively bound up in the new usefulness, and added together quantitatively in the exchange value." But if even perishable goods are capable of lasting use, "then," continues Hermann, "what is true of durable goods is also true of goods that change their form qualitatively while retaining their exchange value, and therefore that use can be conceived of as a good in itself, as a use which itself can attain exchange value."

Thus Hermann of course reached his goal, the proof that even perishable goods possess a use apart from the good itself. But let us examine his proofs a bit more closely.

First of all, it should be noticed that the sole prop of his proof is a *conclusion based on analogy.* An independent use of perishable goods, unlike that of durable goods, cannot rely for proof of its existence on the testimony of the senses or on practical economic experience. No one has ever seen an independent use detach itself from a perishable good. Anyone who thinks he has, merely for the reason that a loan is nothing but a transfer of the use of perishable goods, is mistaken. He does not see an independent use, he only infers one. He sees only that the borrower receives $100 at the beginning of the year, and gives back $105 at the end of it. That the $100 is given for the sum that was borrowed, and the $5 for the use of it, is not an immediate sensory perception but his interpretation of what he has observed. And anyhow, if the existence of an independent use on the part of perishable goods is in question, a loan cannot be cited in proof. For as long as the existence of that use is questioned, of course the right to interpret the loan as a transfer of that use must also be questioned. To try to prove the one by the other is obviously begging the question.

If, therefore, the existence of an independent use of perishable goods is to be anything more than an unproven assertion, it can be so only through the force of an argument by analogy that Hermann introduced in substance, if not in form, in the passage just quoted. His syllogism runs as follows. Durable goods are capable, as every one knows, of affording a use independent of the goods themselves; close observation reveals that perishable goods are capable of just as lasting use as are durable goods; it must therefore be concluded that perishable goods are capable of affording a use independent of the goods themselves.

The conclusion thus drawn is false, for, as I shall prove immediately, the analogy fails just at the critical point.

I admit without ado that perishable goods, through technical change of form, really become capable of durable use. I grant that coal and iron ore deliver a first use in the production of iron. I grant that the use which the iron then affords is merely a further functioning of the properties of those first things. It is also true that the latter are used in the shape of iron for the second time, and again in the nail that is made out of the iron, for the third time, and in the house which the nail helps to hold together for the fourth time. In a word, the use is *durable.* But it is very important to note, concerning this durability, that perishable goods are completely different from durable goods, both with respect to the underlying basis of that durability and with respect to its essential nature. Durable goods are used repeatedly, but each act of use exhausts only part of the use content, so that the remainder is left undisturbed for future acts of use. But perishable goods are used repeatedly by exhausting the *whole* of their use content over and over again, that is to say, by exhausting the whole useful content of that form which the goods have at the time. But since this useful content then takes on a new shape, the exhaustive use is repeated once more. The two kinds of use differ from each other in the same way in which the continuous *outpouring* of water from a reservoir differs from a similarly continuous *repouring* of water achieved by emptying water from one vessel into another and back again. If we wish to choose an example from the economic world, we can cite two differing methods of repeated realization of the proceeds of the sale of a tract of land. One method is to sell the tract *in small lots.* The other is to use the proceeds from the sale of the entire tract for *the purchase of a new tract,* then to sell that, and to continue the process.

A few words more will bring out more sharply the halting nature of Hermann's analogy.

Between the "durable use" which Hermann ascribes to perishable goods, and that of durable goods proper, there is really a perfect analogy to be found, but Hermann failed to find it and drew another parallel instead. We have a matter to deal with here which demonstrates how vengeance has been visited upon economic science for the neglect of which it was guilty with respect to the expression "use of goods." If Hermann had examined the concept of "use of goods" more accurately, he would have perceived that the name covers two very distinct things which, for want of a better expression, I shall distinguish as the *immediate* and *mediate* uses of goods. Immediate use (the only one perhaps, which has any claim to the name of "use") consists in receiving renditions of service delivered by a good. The mediate use (which perhaps ought not to be called "use" at all) consists in receiving renditions of service delivered by *those other goods* which do not come into existence until the renditions of service by the first "used" goods make them available. Furthermore, mediate use consists in receiving the services of the goods that proceed from renditions by these latter goods, and so on. In other words, "mediate use" consists in receiving the more distant members of that chain of causes and effects which begins with the first immediate use—members that may possibly go on evolving to the crack of doom. Now I do not maintain that it is downright wrong to call the use of these remote *functionings* of a good a use *of the good itself,* but certainly the two kinds of use have an entirely different character. If any one likes to call my riding on a horse a use of the hay that my horse has eaten, it is at least manifest that this is an entirely different

155

kind of use from the immediate use of the hay, and that it is in some essential respects subject to totally different conditions.

And so, if we wish to draw an analogy, with respect to use, between the two goods, or two classes of good, we must obviously confine ourselves strictly to *identical kinds* of use. We may compare the immediate use of one good with the immediate use of another, or the mediate use of one good with the mediate use of another. But we may not compare the immediate use of one good with the mediate use of another, particularly if we wish to deduce further scientific conclusions from the comparison. That is the error of which Hermann was guilty. Durable goods as well as perishable goods permit of two kinds of use. Coal, a perishable good, has its immediate use in burning; it has its mediate use, as Hermann has quite correctly pointed out, in the use of the iron which is smelted by its aid. But that is the case with every durable good. For instance, every spinning frame, besides its immediate use which consists in the spinning of the yarn, has mediate use in the making of cloth as well as in the use of cloth for making clothing, and beyond that in the use of clothing itself and so on. Now the proper comparison would obviously be between the immediate use of the durable goods and the momentary use of the perishable goods,[67] or between the durable mediate use of the perishable and the similarly durable mediate use of the durable goods. But Hermann chose the wrong parallels. He drew his analogy between nonanalogous elements, the immediate use of durable goods and the mediate use of perishable goods. He was misled by the circumstance that both kinds of use are "durable," and he overlooked the fact that in the two cases this "durableness" is based on highly different considerations.

I trust that the present analysis has at least made it clear that the analogy which Hermann drew between the "durable" use of durable and of perishable goods is not complete. More important, however, is the fact that it is easy to show that the inadequacy of his analogy touches on a critical point. Why is it that we can perceive in durable goods an independent use possessing independent value, and existing independently of the good itself? The answer is not simply because the use is a durable one, but rather because the use of the good that has already been begun, does not exhaust the good, but leaves a residue of the good, and of the value of the good, and because in that portion of the immediately useful content that has been released and in the portion that is not yet released we have two different things which exist side by side and which individually and simultaneously possess economic value. But in the case of perishable goods the exact opposite is true. Each use completely exhausts the useful content of the form which the good had at the moment, and the value of the use is always identical with the entire value of the good itself. At no one moment do we have two things of value side by side, but only one and the same valuable thing twice in succession. When we use coal and iron ore to make iron, we consume them. We pay the entire capital value of these goods for their use, and do not save the tiniest speck of either which might continue to exist and to have independent value beside and after this consumption. And it is just the same when the iron is consumed again for the making of nails. It is consumed, the whole capital value of the iron is paid for it, and not the smallest fragment of it continues to exist. There never is a single moment when we have both the thing *and* its use beside each other. We have only the things "coal and iron ore," or "iron," or "nails," after one another, as a result of their successive use. Since that is so, neither an analogy nor any other device can serve to demonstrate how the "use" of a perishable good can attain an existence and acquire a value independent of the good itself.

In truth, the conclusion Hermann draws from his analogy is no less erroneous than one like the following. I have a great water tank from which, for a period of an hour, I can draw off a gallon of water per second. Each of the 3,600 gallons thus poured out has an independent existence of its own, and is perfectly distinct from the water previously drawn and from the water that remains in the tank. But suppose I have only one gallon of water, and I pour it back and forth from one vessel into another. In that case too, I cause a gallon of water to be poured out every second for a period of an hour. Therefore in this case too, there must be 3,600 independent gallons that are poured out from my vessels!

Finally Hermann attempts a third step. He resolves the use of durable goods into two parts, of which only one deserves the name "use." The other he calls "consumption." I must confess that this last step reminds me very forcibly of a well-known feat of Münchhausen. The baron lets himself down by a rope from the moon by repeatedly cutting off the rope above his head, and tying it on again beneath his feet. Very much in the same way Hermann at first treats the whole gross use of durable goods as "use," up to the time when, by building on it as the basis for a conclusion by analogy, he has demonstrated the possession of use by perishable goods also. No sooner has he gained that objective than he tears his primary conception of use in pieces, quite unconcerned over the fact that with it he destroys the peg to which he attaches his later concept of independent use, and that that concept is now left hanging in the air.

I shall return later to further inconsistencies to which this error led. In the meantime I am content to make the point that Hermann's argument, which looks so persuasive at first glance, proves on closer examination to boast no better support than a false analogy.

There would be an obvious gap in my critique, if I failed to extend it sufficiently to include the thorough and conscientious efforts which Knies applied to the subject. The work of this distinguished thinker has a twofold similarity with Hermann's doctrine. His arguments, like Hermann's, are remarkably convincing at first sight, and they owe this power to the effective employment of analogies. And his analogies, also like Hermann's, I feel bound to declare false.

Knies encounters our subject when discussing the economic nature of the loan. He pays homage to the view that the essence of the loan consists in a transfer of the use of the sum loaned. And when with his wonted care he attempts to substantiate this view, he is compelled to go into the question of the existence or nonexistence of an independent use in perishable goods.

In his introduction he takes as his point of departure the idea that there are economic "transfers" which do not imply the transfer of property rights. Conveyances of only the use of goods seem to be of this sort. He goes on to mention the distinction between perishable and nonperishable goods, and then turns to a detailed consideration of the transfer of the uses of nonperishable goods. This serves him, as it did Hermann, as a bridge by which to arrive at an explanation of the much more delicate phenomenon involved in the use of perishable goods. Here he points out the distinction that must be drawn between a use which is, on the one hand, "the utilization of a good continuing over a period of time, and subject to definitive time limits," and, on the other hand, the good itself as the "bearer of the use." The economic principle of the transfers in question, Knies says, is that the intention is to transfer a use, but not the bearer of a use. But in the nature of things every transfer of the use of goods necessarily involves certain concessions in regard to the bearer of the use. For instance, the owner of a leased piece of ground must turn it over physically to the lessee, if the lessee is to use it. The extent of these concessions, the attendant risk of loss and the ensuing deterioration of the good which bears the use, all vary with the things concerned and with the particular circumstances of the individual case. The renting of a house, for instance, involves a certain amount of depreciation, and the consent of the owner to such depreciation is indispensable.[68]

Then, after explaining the meaning of the legal categories of fungible and nonfungible goods, Knies puts the following question (*p. 71*), "Is it not factually possible, and as the intention of a compact quite readily understandable, that the use of a fungible, and even of a perishable good should be transferred?"

This question of Knies asks by implication, whether there is not an independent use of perishable goods. He answers the question by putting the following case, which I render verbatim.

"A hundredweight of grain is a fungible and perishable good of this kind. There can be circumstances under which the owner does not wish to part with, exchange or sell this hundredweight of grain, perhaps because in six months he will find it necessary or desirable *to consume it* himself. And yet until that time he does not need it. Therefore, he might very well agree to transfer *the use* of the hundredweight of grain to someone else for the next six months, provided he could recover his good at the expiration of that time. Now let us suppose there is another man who desires the grain but cannot acquire it by barter or purchase. He will say he cannot acquire the *use* of the hundredweight of grain, which is a perishable good, except by *consuming the grain itself,* say as seed. But that he is willing to replace it with another hundredweight of grain from the harvest to be obtained by means of *the use* thereof, which will have been transferred to him. The owner may find this arrangement definitely to his economic interest, since the transaction involves a fungible good.

"The situation here depicted does not contain the faintest suggestion of anything at all impossible, far-fetched, or artificial. But such an arrangement taken by itself (that is to say, the transfer of a hundredweight of grain, on condition that the borrower return a hundredweight of grain at the end of six months) undoubtedly belongs to the class of transactions called loans. For that reason loans may be classified with those transfers of a *use* (specifically, the use to be derived from fungible goods) which are conveyances so complete as to extend to the same right of utilization as is possessed by the owner himself, and which are limited only by the requirement that the fungible good be replaced in identical quantity! Naturally, in the case of the loan it is of the greatest consequence to understand clearly that, whatever may be the extent of the concessions with respect to the bearer of the use, it is not the concessions that embody the principle of the transaction. The extent of the concessions is always determined by the exigencies which control attainment of the use at a given time. And in the case of a perishable good these concessions must, for that very reason, be extended to include the same authority as is possessed by the owner himself to consume the goods completely. And even in that extreme case nothing in the entire situation can vitiate the basic principle, that we are concerned with the transfer of a use. In a loan, therefore, the transfer of the property right is unavoidable, but still only as an accompanying circumstance."

I admit readily that these analyses are calculated to make an entirely convincing impression on anyone who does not scrutinize them very closely. Knies has not only shown unusual skill in drawing the analogy used by the old opponents of the canonists between lease and hire on the one hand and loans on the other, but has enriched it with a new and effective feature. For the most serious hindrance to the acceptance of the time-honored analogy between loans and rentals lay in the circumstance that when goods are loaned there is a complete transfer of title. But Knies overcame this difficulty by devising the argument that certain concessions with respect to the bearer of a use inevitably accompany every transfer of such use. And what had seemed to be the greatest *obstacle* in his path he thereby converted into a force for the *advancement* of his cause.

But if we refuse to be carried away by these brilliant analogies, and begin to consider them critically, we can readily recognize that their admissibility, and hence their potency as proof, depends on whether or not an important preliminary question can be answered in the affirmative. That question is whether there is such a thing as an independent use of perishable goods, which can be transferred by a loan. And we shall have to examine more closely the kind of evidence that Knies furnishes specifically in support of his stand on this question, which is the key to his whole loan theory.

At this point we make the astonishing discovery that Knies has not said a word to prove the existence, or even the conceivability of an independent use, but has steered a course to avoid the reef that could wreck his theory, by recourse to a piece of duplicity about the word "use." I shall try to expose his error.

On page 61 he himself assigns the meaning of utilization to the expression "use of a good." He knows besides, (*p. 61 again*) that in the case of perishable goods "use" cannot possibly mean anything but consumption. He must, therefore, also know that the *use* of perishable goods is synonymous with their *consumption*. On the other hand, the word "use," both as it appears in his statement of the problem, and also in his concluding sentence ("For that reason loans may be classified as transfers of a use . . .") evidently has a significance that is not synonymous with consumption, but signifies durable use. And Knies arrives at that concluding sentence after alternating the word "use" in the first sense and in the second. And finally, after a series of statements which are true only of "use" in the first sense he draws a conclusion from them, that there is such a thing as a "use" in the second sense!

His first sentence reads: "There can be circumstances under which the owner does not wish to part with, exchange or sell this hundredweight of grain, perhaps because in six months he will find it necessary or desirable to consume it himself. And yet until that time he does not need it."

In this sentence the kind of use that is meant and, in the nature of things, the only kind that can be meant, is quite correctly indicated as the *consumption of the good*. Then he continues: "Therefore he might very well agree to transfer the *use* of the hundredweight of grain to someone else for the next six months, provided he could recover his good at the expiration of that time."

This is where the equivocation begins. What is the meaning of "use" here? Does it mean consumption? Or does it mean a kind of use that lasts over a period of six months? Obviously the only conceivable use is consumption, but the words "use during the next six months" are calculated to suggest a durable use, and thus the process of substitution begins.

Then the third sentence reads: "Now let us suppose that there is another man who desires the grain but cannot acquire it by barter or purchase. He will say he cannot acquire the *use* of the hundredweight of grain, which is a perishable good, except by *consuming the grain itself*, say as seed. But that he is willing to replace it with another hundredweight of grain from the harvest to be obtained by means of the *use* thereof, which will have been transferred to him. The owner may find this arrangement definitely to his economic interest, since the transaction involves a fungible good."

This sentence contains the decisive act of interchange. Knies has the applicant for the loan say in so many words that a use of perishable goods cannot be anything but a consumption of them. Yet in the same breath, he himself uses and sets down the words "use" and "consumption" in such a way that the two concepts are kept separate from one

another, and appear *not* to be identical. The more unconcealed, the less
noticeable is the prestidigitation by which this victim of dialectic self-
deception thus slips the concept of a durable use into the sequence of
ideas. With his next breath he pronounces the words "harvest to be
obtained by means of the use thereof, which will have been transferred
to him," and it would be only reasonable to suppose that the sole "use"
that can be expected to effect a harvest is the "use" which is synonymous with "consumption" of the grain planted as seed. Now, the sound
of this "use, thereof, which will have been transferred" is strongly
reminiscent of the "transfer of a use" which is still echoing in our ears
from the time when that term signified the opposite of "the transfer of
the *bearer* of a use." The power of that reminiscence suffices to make
us think involuntarily of this consumption as a *durable use,* by force of
analogy with the use of durable goods. Any doubts we might harbor
about the conceivability of such a use tend to be overpowered by the
statement that a harvest is effected by it. And since a harvest is a definitely real result, the reader, beguiled as he is in the meshes of substitution, naturally accepts the proof that *a use* exists, in terms of a "durable
use."

And now Knies gathers the fruits of his deception. He has said "the
situation here depicted does not contain the faintest suggestion of anything at all impossible, far-fetched or artificial." And that is quite true
if we replace the word "use" every time it is equivocally used, with an
expression like "use-consumption," in which case, however, his hypothetical situation yields no results. As it is, he does draw a conclusion,
namely, that loans may be classified as transfers of a simple use.

This conclusion is simply fallacious. The proof that he was to furnish
simply has not been supplied. On the contrary, the thing that was to be
proven is quietly introduced into the conclusions in the guise of a presupposition. "Use," in the sense he claims for the word, is spoken of as
if it were a familiar fact, and nothing is said to substantiate the possibility that such a use exists. But the difficulty of the task of exposing this
fundamental flaw in the argument is very greatly enhanced by two circumstances. The first of these is that the flag of the genuine use flies over
its spurious namesake as well, and we fail to protest against the existence
of the counterfeit "use," because the dialectical skill of the author prevents our distinguishing it from the genuine use, which unquestionably
does exist. The second is the very simplicity with which he enlists the
power of suggestion. For without really devoting a word to the problem
whether or not perishable goods can conceivably possess durable use,
Knies represents the owner and the applicant for the loan as negotiating
the transfer of the "use" with an assurance that implies that the existence
of the use is an established fact. And the reader almost involuntarily
becomes imbued with that assurance.[69]

A comparison in retrospect of the efforts made by the individual
writers of the Say-Hermann school to justify their peculiar use of capital
reveals the fact that, despite variation in matters of detail, they exhibit
a measure of general agreement which is highly enlightening.

All the authors of that school, from Say to Knies, begin their discussion of use of capital with references to the *renditions of service which actually exist.* Under cover of this truth they obtain the reader's admission that the "use of capital" really does exist, that it exists as an independent economic factor, and that it possesses independent economic value. But they suppress the fact that this independence is not the independence of a second whole beside the good itself, but only that of an independent and separable part of the content of the good. They also suppress the corollary, that the delivery of the renditions of service is always attended by a diminution in the value of the good itself, and that the remuneration for this service is *gross interest.*

But no sooner have they thus obtained recognition of the "independent use of capital" than they supplant the genuine renditions of service on the part of capital, under cover of which its recognition was won, with a fictional and imaginary use of their own, which they endow with an independent value *beyond the full value of the good.* And in the end, they spurn the true uses which served as stepping stones to reach the false ones. Say and Schäffle pursue this method only briefly and cursorily, by silently allowing the conversion of gross interest into net interest. But Hermann and Knies follow the method in complete detail and before our very eyes. Blunders like these show us how urgently necessary it is to set a new objective for those "revisions of fundamental concepts" which have become so popular, and to devote some attention to the unpretentious concept of the use of goods. I for my part have attempted to make the first contribution in that direction.

5. INTRINSIC CONTRADICTION NECESSARILY ARISING FROM ASSUMPTION OF AN INDEPENDENT USE

I TRUST that in the foregoing pages I have redeemed my promise to prove that "every syllogism by which the use theorists of the Say-Hermann school thought they had proved the existence of the alleged use, contains an error or a misunderstanding."

But the charge that the assumption of that independent use is completely unproven, is not my only indictment. I charge in addition, that the making of the assumption necessarily leads to intrinsic contradictions and untenable conclusions. I now mean to substantiate this charge as well.

It is customary among the use theorists, and also among others,[70] to make a distinction between a *gross use,* which is the basis of gross interest or rent, and a *net use,* which is the basis of net interest. Strangely enough, we have all acquired the habit of innocently repeating this distinction, without observing that we are propounding an insoluble riddle.

If we are to believe the unanimous assurance of our theorists, use is synonymous with utilization in the objective sense of the word. Now, if there is a net use and a gross use, are we to understand that there are two uses, two utilizations of the same good? This good does not mean, mark you, two successive or two alternative kinds of use, but two *simul-*

taneous cumulative uses that are enjoyed beside or in each other in every transaction, however elementary.

We can readily understand that two uses can emanate successively from a good, or that one good affords two alternative uses, such as wood for building and for burning. It is even quite conceivable that one good is subject to two methods of utilization simultaneously, and in juxtaposition, and that these furnish two distinct uses. For instance, a beautiful grill work bridge can at the same time support vehicular traffic, and provide aesthetic satisfaction.

But when I rent a house or a lodging, and make use of it as a dwelling, am I, in one and the same series of acts of use, receiving and exercising two different uses? Is there a broader use for which I pay the whole rent, and a narrower one for which I pay the net interest contained within the rent? Does every stroke of my pen on paper, every glance I cast at a picture, every cut that I make with my knife; in short, does every use, however simple, that I derive from a good always provide me with two uses, in or beside each other? To think so is to contradict nature and belie common sense. If I look at a picture, or live in a house, I make one use of the picture or the house; and if there are two things present, and I call both of them use, then one is a misnomer. Which one?

On this point, too, a very strange opinion has gained currency. The theorists really seem a bit ill at ease about this matter of two uses beside each other. For although they ordinarily call both things by the same word "use," every once in a while they make a start toward the elimination of one of them. And it is, in fact, gross use which is eliminated and split up into *net use plus partial replacement of capital.* According to Roscher, whom we are justified in quoting as representative of current opinion,[71] "the use of a capital must not be confounded with its partial replacement. House rent, for instance, must include a sum, *over and above the payment for the use of the house,* sufficient for repairs, and even for the gradual accumulation of capital with which to erect a new building." Apparently we are being given to understand that the thing for which we pay net interest is really a use, that the thing for which we pay gross interest is only called a use, and that even to call it so is both erroneous and inaccurate.

I do not believe that it would be possible to make any more embarrassing demand upon the holders of that strange opinion than to challenge them to define what they mean by use. What can it mean other than the acceptance of useful services rendered by a good? Or if it be objected that such personification is not sufficiently objective, let us say that use consists in making available the useful services of which a good is capable. Or, if there is objection to my "renditions of service," let us say "useful services" with Say, or "release of a use from material goods" or "reception of useful effects" with Schäffle, or anything else. But define the word as we will, one thing seems to me beyond dispute. When *A* turns over a house to *B* for temporary habitation, and *B* inhabits it, then *A* has transferred the use of the house to *B,* and *B* makes use of the house. And if *B* pays anything for the use, he does not pay even

163

an infinitesimal part of the rent for anything other than the right to avail himself of the useful qualities and properties of the house. In other words, he is paying only for the use transferred to him.

Hold on! Maybe he does! Has not *B* consumed part of the value of the house itself? And if so, was not a part of the value of the house itself transferred to him in addition to the use of the house? Anyone who thought so would, in rather strange fashion, be mistaking two aspects of one event for two events. The truth of the matter is that the tenant has received only the use of the house, but by using it, he has diminished its value. Out of a "store of energies," some have been made available to him to "release," and he has done nothing but "release" or use them. Of course, the value of the remaining store of energies has been diminished thereby. But it would be an error to construe that as meaning that the lessee has received two distinct and coordinate things, namely, use and partial value of capital. For comparison, let us assume a man buys a fourth horse to match three he owns already. Certainly his purchase could not be considered an acquisition of two separate things, first a horse, and second, the filling out of the team of four. Nor could it be maintained that of the $500 he paid, only a part, say $250, was the price of the horse, while the remaining $250 was for completing the team! Or it might be compared to a situation in which a workman puts up the cross on a church steeple thereby completing the building of the steeple, and then claims that he has performed two acts; first, put up the cross, and second, finished the building of the steeple, and moreover, that since he took an hour to do the whole job, not more than three-quarters of an hour could have been needed for the erection of the cross, since part of the whole time expended, say a quarter of an hour, would have to be charged to the second act, the completion of the building of the steeple!

But if anyone claims, nevertheless, that utilization consists, not in gross use, but in another something which is hard to define, let him say in what the use of a meal consists. In the eating thereof? Impossible, for that is a gross use, which swallows up the whole value of the capital, and of course gross use must not be confused with true use. But in what then does it consist? In an aliquot part of the eating? Or in something entirely different? I am glad it is not I, but the use theorists whose duty it is to answer that question.

If the words "utilization" and "use" are not to have a meaning at variance with that which they have in ordinary speech and everyday life, a significance in defiance of practical as well as scientific requirements, then gross use cannot be denied the quality of a true use. But if there cannot be two uses, and if in any case gross use must be recognized as entitled to convey the concept of use, then the verdict against the net use of the use theorists becomes automatic.

But we can even ignore all that, and consider my next point. Whether the gross use be a genuine use or not, at any rate it is indubitably something. And the use theorists would have it, that net use, likewise, is something. Now these two quantities, if they both actually exist, must certainly stand in some relation to each other. Either net use must be a part of gross use or it is no part of it. There is no third possibility. Now let us examine the situation. When we consider durable goods, it seems plausible that net use is a part of gross use. For since the payment for the former, namely net interest, is included in the payment for the latter, namely gross interest, it follows that the first object of purchase (net use) which is included in the second (gross use) must presumably also be a part thereof. The use theorists themselves maintain just that, when they analyze gross use as the sum of net use plus partial replacement of capital. But now let us consider perishable goods. The net interest I pay in this case is *not* paid for their consumption. For if I replace the perishable goods immediately with their fungible equivalent, I do not need to pay any interest. What I pay interest for is only the delay in replacement with an equivalent, or in other words, for something that is not included in consumption (the most intensive possible gross use) but stands quite apart from it. Are we to conclude then, that net use is at the same time *part* and *no* part of gross use? How can the use theorists explain this contradiction?

The list of riddles and contradictions to which the assumption of a net use must lead, can be greatly extended. For instance, I might ask the use theorists what I am to picture as 10 years' use of a bottle of wine which I consume on the first day of the first year. That use must exist, of course, for I can buy or sell it under a loan contract running for 10 years. I might point out how strange it is, how it verges on the ludicrous, to assume that a good which in actual fact *ceases to be of use* the moment its exhaustion is completed, should choose that moment *to begin* a career of usefulness in perpetuity! Or I might comment on the strangeness of the belief that the borrower who replaces a borrowed bottle at the end of 1 year consumes less than the one who does so at the end of 10 years, since the former has enjoyed only 1 year's use, and the latter has had 10! It is patently clear, of course, that actually both have derived the same use, and that the earlier or later maturing of the obligation to return the second bottle has absolutely nothing to do with the shorter or longer continuance of the objective use of the first bottle. And so on *ad infinitum.* But I have probably already said more than I need to, to be convincing.

I should like to sum up by saying that I believe I have established three points. The *first* of these is that the nature of goods, as material bearers of useful natural properties, precludes the conceivability of any use that does not consist in the functioning of those useful natural properties, or, in other words, of any use that is not identical with what I have called the *renditions of service* on the part of goods. And those renditions of service are the basis not of *net* interest, but of *gross* interest, or in the case of perishable goods, of their entire capital value.

The *second* point I have established is that all attempts on the part of the use theorists to demonstrate the existence or the conceivability of a "net use," apart from the rendition of service, lead to erroneous conclusions.

My *third* point is that the assumption of the net use postulated by the use theorists necessarily leads to absurd and contradictory conclusions.

I think, therefore, that I am entirely justified in maintaining that the net use, on the existence of which the use theorists of the Say-Hermann school base their explanation of interest, does not exist in fact but is only the figment of a misguided imagination.

6. THE HISTORICAL ORIGIN OF THE NET USE FICTION

BUT how did this remarkable creation enter the field of our science? And how came it to be taken for reality? With some brief observations on the history of the problem I hope to dispel any lingering doubts and, in particular, to furnish a basis for an accurate appraisal of such prejudgments as might continue to be entertained on the basis of the erstwhile victory of the Salmasian theory.

Here we are dealing with one of those cases, not altogether uncommon, in which a fiction came into being in the field of jurisprudence, and was turned to practical account in full awareness of its fictive nature. The fiction was then transferred to the field of economics where this consciousness of its character was lost. The law has always had a great need for fictions. In order that a relatively small number of simple principles of law might suffice to order the manifold realities of legal practice, the law is often forced to use a fiction which will produce a parallelism between cases which are not in essence alike, but which can in practice be advantageously treated as if they were. It was in this way that the *formulae fictitiae* of Roman civil procedure arose, such as "legal persons," or *res incorporales* (things incorporeal) and innumerable other fictions of the law.

Now it sometimes happened that a fiction which had grown venerable finally petrified and acquired the credence due the truth. Where for hundreds of years two things had been customarily treated, both in theory and in practice, as if they were essentially the same, it might finally and under favorable circumstances be entirely forgotten that their sameness was a fiction. That is the case, as I have already shown, with the "things incorporeal" of Roman law, and it is also the case with the independent use of perishable and fungible goods. It is still possible to follow, step by step, the course whereby the fiction became petrified into dogma.

There are some goods, the individuality of which is of no importance, goods which are considered only with respect to kind and amount, *quae pondere numero mensura consistunt* (which possess only weight, number or size). These are called in law fungible or replaceable goods. Since no importance attaches to their individuality, any unit of such goods is a perfect substitute for any other unit which it replaces. For certain purposes of practical legal procedure these goods could simply be treated as identical. There was a particularly strong tendency to do so in legal transactions involving the conveyance and recovery of fungible goods, where it was convenient to conceive of the return of an equal amount of fungible goods as a return of the very same goods. In other words, the fiction was created of the identity of the fungible goods returned with those received.

So far as I know, the sources of Roman law do not put this fiction into words. They say quite correctly that, in the case of a loan, *tantundem* (the same amount) or *idem genus* (the same kind) not simply *idem* (the same thing) is given back. But in deed, if not in word, the fiction is there. The so-called *depositum irregulare* (irregular deposit) was a device whereby the depositary was allowed to employ on his own account the sum of money given over to his safe keeping, and to replace the deposit with *other* pieces of money. Its treatment as a *depositum*[72] can be explained only as a reliance on a fiction whereby the pieces of money replaced were considered identical with those given in for safe keeping. Modern jurisprudence has occasionally gone further, and speaks expressly of the "legal identity" of fungible goods.[73]

From this first fiction to a second was but a step. Once the debtor in a loan or similar transaction is deemed to return the same goods he receives, then logical consistency demands that he be deemed also *to have retained them throughout the period of the loan, to have had the uninterrupted possession and use of them during that time,* consequently to have enjoyed a durable use of them, thus becoming liable for the interest for the entire period.

And the lawyers did actually take this second fictive step. They knew quite well, to begin with, that they were dealing only with a fiction. They also knew quite well that the goods returned are not the identical goods received, that the debtor does not hold and possess these goods during the whole period of the loan, that on the contrary, the debtor usually must part with the goods entirely if he is to fulfill the purpose of the loan. Lastly, they knew quite well that, for this very reason, the debtor does not derive any durable use from the goods he borrows. But the fiction serves the practical purposes and requirements of both parties as well as if it were fact, and that is why the lawyers are permitted their fiction. They reveal their position with relation to that fiction by their admission of several expressions into the technical language of the law. Thus they confirm that expression for loan interest which long ago found admittance to the language of the man in the street, the term *usura,* meaning money paid for a use. They still teach that interest is paid for the use of money loaned, and that even *perishable goods* yield a usufruct. To be sure, the lawyers compromise here on a *quasi usufruct,* since they are quite aware that they are dealing with a fiction. On one occasion, in fact, they even emphasized its fictitious nature by correcting a legislative act that had given the fiction too realistic an expression.[74]

7. AN EVALUATION OF THE FEUD
BETWEEN SALMASIUS AND THE CANONISTS

AFTER the world had been taught for centuries that *usura* was money paid for a use, and after the vibrant spirit that once animated classical jurisprudence had largely yielded place to an all the more abject obeisance to tradition and to form, there came a violent attack, conducted by the canonists, upon the institution of loan interest and the considerations advanced to justify it. One of their deadliest weapons was the exposure of this fiction in regard to the uses of perishable goods. The rest of their arguments seemed so convincing that it looked as if loan interest were doomed, once the premise were granted that there is no such thing as an independent use of perishable goods. And so that fiction all at once attained an importance it had never had before. Those who expressed belief in the actual existence of the *usus* thereby expressed approval of interest; those who expressed disbelief seemed committed to its condemnation. In this dilemma there was an inclination to save interest by doing the legal formula more honor than it deserved. And Salmasius and his followers racked their brains to find reasons to justify acceptance of the formula as a fact. The reasons they did find were just good enough to convince people who were eager to be convinced, because the rest of Salmasius's really excellent arguments had persuaded them that, *on the whole,* he was right. On the other hand, his opponents were so obviously wrong on their chief point that they were distrusted, even as to the minor point on which, by exception, they were right. So it happened (not for the first time, and certainly not for the last) that under the pressure of practical exigencies a fallacious theory was born, and the old fiction of the lawyers was proclaimed as fact.

Thus it has remained ever since, at least in political economy. While modern law has largely abandoned the doctrine of Salmasius, modern political economy has clung fondly to the old stock formula from the legal repertoire. In the seventeenth century the formula had provided a practical justification of interest. In the nineteenth it served equally well as the ways from which to launch a theoretical explanation which might otherwise have been embarrassingly difficult to set afloat. That puzzling "surplus value" had to be explained. It seems to hang in the air. Something is needed from which to hang it. What a welcome recourse the old legal fiction is now! As befits a theory now subjected to increased demands, it is decked out with new embellishments of every kind, and so becomes worthy at last, under the name of "use," to be raised to the place of highest honor and become the keystone of a theory of interest as distinctive as it is comprehensive.

Perhaps it may be my privilege in these pages to break the spell which the custom of centuries has cast over our attempts to understand this question. Perhaps the "net use" of capital will be finally returned to that domain from which it never should have migrated, the domain of fiction, of metaphor, which, as Bastiat once only too aptly remarked, has so often led our science astray. With it many a deeply rooted conviction will have to be given up. The use theory, in the proper and narrower sense of the word, which makes use its chief pillar in the explanation of interest, will have to go. And a number of other theories which are commonly accepted outside the ranks of the use theorists, and which employ that concept along with others will be affected. Another favorite which will have to be renounced is the interpretation of a loan as the transfer of uses, and as a phenomenon analogous to rent.

But what is to be put in its place?

To answer that is not, strictly speaking, the function of this critique at this point. It is rather that of the positive statement which I have reserved for the second volume of this work. But since I have assumed the defense of one of the chief tenets of the canonists' doctrine, it may justly be demanded of me, perhaps, that I should at least point out the avenue of escape from their obviously false conclusion. And so I will set down here, in brief, my understanding of the nature of loans, with the reservation that I shall offer a more detailed treatment of it in my next volume. In the meantime I request the reader to postpone a final verdict on my theory till such time as I have stated it in detail, and have indicated its relation to the entire theory of interest.

I believe my best point of departure is the old canonist dispute itself. In my opinion only the canonists were wrong in their conclusions, while both parties were wrong in the reasoning leading to their conclusions. The canonists, oddly enough, were wrong because they made only one mistake in their reasoning. Salmasius made two mistakes, but the second cancelled the harm done by the first, and while the stream of his argument is marked by turbulent headwaters, its lower course finally finds the truth at its mouth. The details are as follows.

Both parties agree in regarding it as an axiom that the capital sum replaced at the expiration of the loan contract is the equivalent and, in fact, the exact and full equivalent of the capital sum borrowed. Now this assumption is so false that we must marvel that it was not long ago exposed as a superstition. Every economist knows that the value of goods does not depend simply on their physical qualities, but to a very great extent on the circumstances under which they become available for the satisfaction of human needs. It is well known that goods of the same kind (grain, for instance) have very different values under different circumstances. Among the most important of the circumstances that influence the value of goods, aside from their physical constitution, are the *time and place* at which they become available. It would be strange, for instance, if 10 cords of wood in the forest had exactly the same value as 10 cords of wood at the railway terminal, and if these again had exactly the same value as 10 cords of wood at the fireside. But it would be just as strange if a sum of $100, which is at my disposal today, were exactly equivalent to $100 which I am to receive a year later, or 10 or 100 years later. On the contrary, it is clear that if one and the same quantity of goods is at the disposal of an economizing subject at different times, it will exercise a varying influence on his economic position, and thus have a varying value. It is impossible to agree with Salmasius and the canonists, and to assume complete equivalence between the present goods given in loan and the goods of like number and kind returned at some distant period. Such equivalence, on the contrary, can only be a very rare and accidental exception.

It is easy to determine the source from which both parties derived their completely unscientific view of the equivalence between the capital sum given and that received in return. It is the old legal fiction of the identity of fungible goods of the same kind and number. If this fiction is taken to mean that the same $100, which the creditor advanced to the debtor, is returned by the debtor to the creditor at the expiration of the period of the loan, then of course this replacement must be looked on as one that is exactly equivalent and just. It was the common mistake of the canonists and of their opponents to fall into the trap laid for them in the first part of the legal fiction. That was the sole mistake of the canonists, but only Salmasius's first. The further development was simple.

The canonists remained in error because this was their only mistake. Once they had made it they acquired a belated keenness of vision, which enabled them to expose the fiction of the alleged independent use of loaned goods. That removed every vestige of support for a justification of the payment of interest, and they were bound, erroneously but logically, to condemn it as unjust. But the first error that Salmasius had made, when he accepted the fiction of the identity of the capital received and the capital paid back, was counterbalanced by a compensating error when he accepted the further implications of that fiction, to the effect that the borrower possesses the "use" of the loaned goods throughout the period of the loan.

Neither construction embodies the truth. *The loan is actually an exchange of present goods against future goods.* For reasons that I shall give in detail in my second volume, present goods invariably possess a greater value than future goods of the same number and kind, and therefore a given sum of present goods can be purchased only with a larger sum of future goods. Present goods command a premium in future goods. *This premium, or agio, is interest.* It is not a separate equivalent for some inconceivable separate durable use of the loaned goods. It is a part of an equivalent of the sum loaned, which is kept separate for practical reasons. But the sum loaned has not been replaced by a full equivalent until the interest has been added to the "return of the capital sum."[75] My aim up to this point has been to prove that there can be no such thing as an independent use of goods in the form in which the use theorists of the Say-Hermann school (and in imitation of their example, almost all present-day economists) assume it to exist. It still remains for me to prove that there can be no independent use, even in that essentially different form envisioned by Menger.

B. Critique of Menger's Use Concept

WHILE the Say-Hermann school represented "net use" as an objective factor of use, emanating from goods, Menger explains it as *command* or power of disposal. In fact, he modifies this by terming it "a power of disposal over quantities of economic goods within a definite period of time."[76] To the extent that this disposal provides an economizing subject with the means to better and more complete satisfaction of his wants, the disposal acquires, says Menger, the character of an independent good, and because of its relative scarcity, it ordinarily will be an *economic* good at the same time.[77]

Now it strikes me as a display of temerity to maintain that the power to dispose of goods, which is after all merely a relation to a good, is itself a good. I have stated elsewhere[78] and at length my reasons for my opinion that it is economically inadmissible to recognize relations as real goods, in the sense that is assigned to that term in the parlance of economic theory. I should like to amplify them here with just a few remarks.

There might be an inclination to say (and in fact I have heard it said) in refutation of my contention, that a clientele, an opportunity for future profits, is not a mere "phantom." In fact, their reality is attested every day by the fact that the "good will" of a business can be sold, that a real price is paid for it. It is my opinion that this argument mistakenly claims the status of a perception of actual fact for something that is merely an interpretation of appearances. The former could admittedly prove something; the latter offers nothing in the way of proof or disproof germane to our problem.

I will begin my attempt to show the nature of the fallacy which has crept in here, by means of a few related examples which make the error more easily recognizable. Ice is worthless at the North Pole, but valuable in New York. Do I not therefore "see" that the "presence" or the "location" of the ice is being paid for? Ore that is mixed with slag is useless, but pure metal is useful. Do I not "see" that the "purity" of the metal is a source of remuneration to the owners of the smelting furnaces which effect that purity? Is it not likewise true that the eye beholds how a woodcarver who makes a figurine out of a worthless piece of wood is paid for "form," and that the dyer who dyes a piece of cotton indigo blue is being paid for "color," that is to say, the color of the cotton? And if we can "see" payment being made for "location," "purity," "form," "color," do we not have tangible proof that all these categories are not mere "phantoms," but must be genuine, actual goods, and independent economic objects?

It is easy to see whither such reasoning leads us, and that it leads us too far. Nor is it difficult to uncover the deceptive element in the reasoning. What we really see in these examples is that a concrete price is paid for a something of some sort. But we do not by any means see that that "something" is the abstract category called location, place, form, color and so on, rather than the concrete good known as ice, metal, figurine, or cotton. We interpret subjectively what our senses perceive, and we do so by means of some more or less metaphorical phraseology. In precisely the same way our earlier examples of clientele and good will are a matter of sensory perception only to the extent that a concrete price is paid for an indefinite something, and one which in this case is not very easy to determine. But that this something—this purchasable and salable something—is actually and literally a "relation" and not, after the fashion of any purchase on speculation, merely the sum of the prospective profits to be derived from the clientele, *that,*

171

dear reader, is not a sight which our eyes perceive, but merely an interpretation which we render of the event that we do perceive. But whether that interpretation is correct and admissible, whether it corresponds to the physical facts or in turn merely represents another metaphorical locution, that is the very question that must be answered on the basis of scientific examination. And the question is not answered, but merely suppressed, if we place our reliance on an alleged perception of our visual sense.

However, if we pursue our analysis to its very limits, we are confronted by a problem of almost metaphysical character. And yet, in spite of that character, the question fortunately admits of a very definite answer, at least with respect to the phase of it with which we are here concerned. There are agencies which produce phenomena. About the true nature of those phenomena we know nothing. We try to approach them from various angles by means of our concepts and our language. Sometimes we give names to *things themselves,* their matter, material, body, substance. At other times we define them by their *capacities,* then again by their *properties,* and at still other times by something closely akin to these, namely their *relations.* But the thing, the capacity and the property certainly do not represent any actual triplicate entity of the thing that is. They mean only that we have three different ways of looking at one and the same existent entity. We must leave open the question as to which of them is the correct one, and even *whether* one of them is the correct one. Neither physical nor metaphysical science is sure of that answer. But one thing is sure—and illuminating. And that is that the existence of several subjective ways of regarding and naming an entity *must* not be considered proof of the objective existence of several species of that entity. The variety of our conceptions cannot be taken as a proof of the actual plurality of things. It is perfectly legitimate to ponder the question whether matter, *or* properties, *or* qualities and relations constitute the truly useful aspect of those things which we call goods. But it is obviously indefensible to convert the stumbling block of our own uncertainty into the cornerstone of a certainty that matter *and* properties *and* qualities and relations exist as genuinely separate realities.[79]

If all this meant merely that, when we inventory our goods or the sources of our welfare, we use different names for the same thing, that would be an evil which would be slight, easily born, and possibly even unavoidable. It would be an inconsistency in nomenclature, but not a statement that in any material respect would distort the truth. It is my opinion that science is often in a position where it is forced to tolerate inconsistencies in nomenclature, or even perpetrate them. This results from the simple circumstance that a science is neither able nor willing to invent a new language of its own "from the ground up," which will meet its needs perfectly and with complete accuracy. And so, if it would use the language of the populace at all, it must perforce accept, for better or for worse, the inaccuracies and inconsistencies to which the vernacular is heir. Science is not always able, nor necessarily required to remove these blemishes in its nomenclature, as we might call them, but is measuring up quite fully to the demands of duty if it puts up a warning signal, as it were, by calling attention to the inaccuracy as such, and by conscientiously refusing to avail itself of it in a pinch. Such a "pinch" would arise, not from the mere need of a convenient name for an object, but out of the temptation to draw objective inferences therefrom as to the true nature of the object so named. It is a problem of that kind which I treated in an inquiry I made some time ago[80] into the question of legal rights and relations, and the allegation that they possess the nature of an economic good. I concluded my inquiry with the admission that I believed we should as a rule continue, both in practical affairs and in scientific theory, to adhere to the linguistic usage, incorrect perhaps, but of long standing, which elevates rights and relations to the level of goods. But I made the proviso that we explain the exact truth concerning their nature once and for all, and then relegate the explanation to the storehouse of settled issues, to be dragged forth only in case accuracy becomes vitally necessary.

Actually, it is a terminological inconsistency to mention and recognize, as I do, as two separate categories, tangible goods and objective renditions of service. It would be more consistent, and perhaps more correct, to have our inventory of goods include, in place of tangible goods, an item called "aggregate of renditions of service." Or, conversely, if we wish to retain the category of tangible goods, we should list renditions of service as "constituents of tangible goods." But both devices present difficulties. On the one hand, our habits of thought and speech make us loath to forego the reality of tangible goods, because the term "goods" has so long and so firmly been associated with *things,* with concrete objects. On the other hand, renditions of service which tangible goods furnish do not correspond at all to any definite and severable parts of the substance of the good. They are smaller economic units than the tangible good, but they are not literally constituent *parts* of the concrete material of which the good consists. Under these circumstances it seems the lesser drawback to avail ourselves of an "opalescent" terminology and to designate the aggregate by a term drawn from a category of concepts different from the one from which we derive the name used for the parts. That entails the duty of establishing the objective relationship between the two categories by an explicit elucidation. That is to say, we must show that tangible goods and renditions of service are not two kinds of causes of our well-being, differing from each other and operating side by side, but rather, identical kinds of causes which function in varying degree, at times as a whole, at other times as a part, or, if preferred, now as an aggregate, and now as a constituent. If, with due regard to this consideration, we apply the term "goods" to both tangible goods and "renditions of service," we are guilty of an inconsistency which is no worse and no more damaging than the one which would result if a merchant, setting up his balance sheet and listing his assets by categories, were to classify his small bank notes, which are used for day-to-day petty transactions, as "cash," but list a bank note of large denomination, such as one for $10,000, under "notes receivable." The objection might be raised that his classification of assets is open to question, but certainly no one could make the charge that his balance sheet is therefore in error.

Of course, it would be an entirely different matter if our merchant, dazzled by the iridescent refulgence of the bank note (which *can* from one point of view be considered as cash, but from another as a note receivable) were to list it twice on his balance sheet, once under "cash" and once more under "notes receivable." That would no longer be a harmless bit of inconsistency, but a definitely falsified balance sheet. Now it is just that kind of objective integrity of the balance sheet which is involved when, for purposes of establishing a use theory, a claim is made for the existence of an independent good in the form of a relationship called "disposal." For the line of argument in this case is that the tangible good itself and the power of disposal over it are two separate goods which are sacrificed side by side, and which must therefore be listed as two separate items in the statement of costs of production. Such an argument strikes me as being a claim that the relation of disposal is genuinely of the nature of a good. Furthermore, that claim is advanced by Menger in all conceivable seriousness and with full acceptance of all its implications. Therefore, I feel it embodies the very principles to which the objections I have just registered are most emphatically applicable.

In order to withstand such serious intrinsic objections, Menger's hypothesis would have to muster the support of highly persuasive extrinsic arguments. I doubt its capacity for doing so in adequate measure. Any direct proof, any concrete demonstration that disposal is really a good, is obviously out of the question from the outset because of the peculiar nature of the theorem to be proven. It can only be a question of whether the hypothesis can be supported by a consensus of testimony on the part of sufficiently numerous and sufficiently relevant *indirect* arguments. I am constrained to believe it cannot.

It appears to me that there is actually only one single indirect argument for his hypothesis, and that is the existence of the otherwise unexplained surplus value. Astronomers who observe otherwise unexplained aberrations from their orbits by known planets, deduce from them the presence of disturbing and hitherto unknown planetary bodies. In similar fashion Menger postulates the existence of a bearer of the otherwise unexplained surplus value. And since the disposal of quantities of goods during definite periods of time seems to stand in some regularly determined relation to the occurrence and magnitude of surplus value, he does not hesitate to advance the hypothesis that this disposal is the bearer he is seeking, and that as such it is an independent good, possessing an independent nature. I am convinced that this distinguished thinker would have refrained from advancing that hypothesis if he had been able to envision the possibility of any other explanation.

Now, is that one and only argument for the independent goods character of "disposal" compellingly persuasive?

I have two reasons for denying that it is. For one thing, I hope to offer proof in my next volume that the phenomenon of surplus value can be perfectly satisfactorily explained, even without recourse to Menger's hypothesis, and as a matter of fact, explained along lines that are indicated by Menger himself in his classic theory of value.* And for another thing, I intend to submit to the reader forthwith a few considerations which, in my opinion, furnish a convincing *refutation* of the independent goods character of his questionable "command."

According to Menger's theory a loan is to be regarded as the conveyance of the disposal of goods. The longer the period for which the loan is to run, the greater, of course, must be the magnitude of the "disposal"—the good that is transferred. Where a loan runs for two years, more disposal is conveyed than where it runs for only one, and a loan for three years transfers still more than one for two years, and so on. Hence a loan for 100 years transfers an almost unlimited magnitude or quantity of disposal. If the return of the capital were not merely postponed to a very remote date but completely dispensed with, there would be a transfer to the recipient of a disposal that would be in literal fact unlimited. Such is the case, for instance, when an aggregate of goods is the object, not of a loan but of a gift.

The question now arises, how much value does the donee in such a case receive? There can be no question that he receives as much as *the capital value of the gift amounts to.* And what of the perpetual disposal that was donated with it? Obviously, it is included in the capital value. Hence I draw a conclusion which I am certain cannot be a nonsequitur. If the "plus," namely the value of the perpetual disposal, is included in the capital value of the good itself, then the lesser quantity contained therein, namely the temporary disposal of the good, must likewise be contained in the value of the good itself. Therefore the temporary disposal cannot possibly be an independent bearer of value, in the manner which Menger assumes, aside from the value of the good itself.

†Or if we put the illustration a bit differently, perhaps we can demonstrate still more trenchantly that the value of the disposal is included within the value of the good. Let us assume that *A* first lends *B* a thing for 20 years without interest, that is to say, that *A* makes *B* the gift of the good "disposal for 20 years." Now let us further assume that a few days later *A* makes *B* a gift of the thing itself. In that case *A* has, by two separate acts, made *B* two gifts—one of the 20-year disposal, and one of the thing itself. If the disposal were a thing of independent value, apart from the thing itself, then the total value of the two gifts would manifestly have to exceed the value of the thing itself, which just as manifestly is not the case. Now if the explanation is offered that the subsequently donated thing, from which the 20-year disposal had

* Translators' note: See American edition, *Principles of Economics,* The Free Press, Glencoe, Illinois, 1950.
† Translators' note: This paragraph was originally a footnote.

already been severed, no longer had its full original value, but only that value diminished by the severed disposal, then that explanation is more than ever an admission that the disposal and its value is not, as Menger postulates, something outside the thing, but at most something within it.

Second Proposition to be Proved:
that even if we accept the hypothesis that an independent net use exists, the use theory cannot lead to a satisfactory explanation of interest.

I believe I have proven that there is no such thing as that use, whose independent existence the use theorists assume to be a fact. But even if it did exist, that would not enable us to formulate a satisfactory explanation of the phenomenon of interest. I hope it will not require many words to prove that thesis.

The use theory employs a method of analysis peculiar unto itself, which calls for a distinction between a value which *goods possess in and of themselves,* and a value which the *use of goods* possesses. Throughout the course of their explanations, the point of departure is ever the tacit assumption that the ordinary appraisal value or purchase price which a capital good attains, represents the value of the good itself, exclusive of the value of its use. For the explanation of surplus value is based on the very circumstance that the value of the use is added as a *new* element to the value of the capital substance, and that only after such addition is the value of the consumer's good complete.

But this assumption is quite at variance with the actual state of affairs in the economic world.

Everyone knows that a bond has its full market value only if all the interest coupons are attached, or in other words (to use the language of the use theorists) if the buyer of the bond acquires with the bond the disposal of all its future "uses." But if one or more coupons should be missing, the purchaser would always make a corresponding deduction in the purchase price. A comparable condition exists with respect to all other goods. If, in selling a landed estate which would otherwise bring a price of $100,000, I reserve the use of it for one or several years (because, let us say, by terms of a bequest it is encumbered with a usufruct of several years' duration in favor of a third party) there is no doubt whatever that the price I shall realize for the estate will be less than the $100,000 by an amount which corresponds to the "uses" reserved, or belonging to the third party. Such facts, which can be multiplied at will, admit of only *one* interpretation, namely, *that the ordinary appraisal or purchase price of goods includes the value, not only of the goods "in and of themselves," but also of their future "uses," if any.*[81]

But that interpretation is tantamount to saying that this "use" fails in that very function of explaining which the use theory had expected it to perform. For that theory claims to explain the fact that the value of a capital of $100, by the time it is represented by the product of the capital, has been augmented to $105. And its explanation is that a new independent element in the amount of $5 has been added. This explanation is vitiated at the moment when the use theory is forced to acknowledge that the capital value of $100 already embraced and took into account all future uses. Even though we may admit the existence of such uses, they still do not explain the riddle of surplus value. They merely alter the form of the question in which it is propounded. The question now reads, "How is it, that the value of the component elements of a capital product, namely *capital substance and capital uses,* which was at the outset $100, is augmented during the process of production to $105?" As a matter of fact, the number of riddles has now increased. For originally we had the problem which is posed for every interest theory by the nature of the phenomena it must consider, and which runs, *"Why does the value of the elements dealt with increase by the amount of the surplus value?"* Now the use theory has added a second riddle of its own making, which reads, *"How do the future uses of a good and the value of the 'good in and of itself' combine to produce the present capital value of the good?"* And that is a problem whose troublesome solution has not even been attempted by any use theorist.

And so the use theory winds up with more riddles than it had at the start.

But even if the use theory did not succeed in reaching its goal, at least it did more than any other theory to smooth the road toward it. While numerous other theories wandered down blind alleys, the use theory managed to uncover many a highly important morsel of knowledge. I should like to compare it with two older theories in the field of the physical sciences, namely, the antiquated combustion theory based on the mystical element "phlogiston," and that still older theory of heat which operated with a "warmth fluid." Phlogiston and the fluid both proved to be fabulous entities, just as "net use" did. But the symbol, temporarily assigned to a space which until then had been filled by a still unknown something, nevertheless was of assistance, much after the manner of the "x" in an algebraic equation, by uncovering laws and relationships that revolve about that unknown something. It did not as yet designate the truth, but it helped the truth on its way.

IX

THE ABSTINENCE THEORY

1. Predecessors of Senior

N. W. SENIOR must be regarded as the founder of the abstinence theory. He first enunciated it in lectures delivered at Oxford University and later again in his *Outlines of the Science of Political Economy*.[1]

If we are to appraise Senior's abstinence theory accurately, we must take a moment to visualize the situation with respect to the doctrine of interest, as it obtained in England during the thirties of the last century.

The two leading spirits of the modern economic school had declared labor to be the sole source of capital value, Smith having been less emphatically decided about it than Ricardo. Any consistent application of this principle would necessarily preclude interest altogether. Nevertheless interest was there as an indisputable fact, and one which exercised an undeniable influence on the relative exchange value of goods. Smith and Ricardo take note of this exception to the "labor principle" without making any serious effort either to reconcile the disturbing exception with the central theory, or to explain it on the basis of some independent principle. Hence it may be said that interest constitutes an unexplained exception which contradicts the Smith-Ricardo labor principle.

The next generation of economists began to be aware of this discord and attempted to restore the harmony between theory and fact along two different lines. One group tried to adapt the facts to their theory, maintaining the principle to be valid, and attempting to establish that interest is the consequence and wage of labor. Naturally that attempt failed dismally. The most important representatives of this group are James Mill and McCulloch.[2]

Another group more wisely evinced a willingness to adapt their theory to the facts. This action, too, proceeded along several lines. Lauderdale maintained that capital is productive, but found little support for his principle among his compatriots because thought processes dating back to Locke had inculcated the conviction that labor is the source of capital itself. And that conviction had become too inveterately habitual for them to be amenable to any recognition of capital as an independent creative force. Then others again had, under the leadership

of Malthus, seized upon the expedient of declaring interest to be another constituent, along with labor, of the costs of production. That was
at least a way of bringing the phenomenon of interest into formal harmony with the prevailing theory of value. Cost, they said, controls value;
one of the items of cost is interest; therefore consumer goods must
have a sufficiently high value to yield an allowance for interest, as well
as for the compensation of labor. In actual fact this explanation was
quite inadequate, because it was only too clear that originary interest is
an *excess over costs,* and not a constituent part of them and that it is
therefore an outcome and not an element contributed and sacrificed.

And so none of the scientific pronouncements which at that time
indicated a stand on the interest principle was truly satisfactory. The
adherents of every theory were less numerous than its opponents, who
welcomed the opportunity for attack offered by the weaknesses of the
respective doctrines, and then made copious use of such opportunity.
One party had to submit to being told, with devastating logic, that an
excess is not an expenditure, while the other had to suffer the barbs of
ridicule directed against their contention that the augment in value which
appears when a barrel of wine lies supinely in the cellar, is attributable
to labor. And while two parties were thus wrangling about the true
reason for interest, a third party began to become audible, though but
faintly at first, and to be heard to say that interest is not reasonable at
all, not justified, but an exploitation of labor.[3]

In the midst of this restless and unproductive turmoil of opinion
Senior appeared upon the scene with a doctrine which proclaimed a
new principle with respect to interest. He called it a *reward for abstinence
on the part of the capitalist.*

Isolated hints of this principle had been repeatedly bruited even
before Senior's day. Faint traces of it can be recognized in frequently
recurring remarks by Smith and Ricardo, to the effect that the capitalist
must receive interest because he would otherwise have no inducement
to amass and preserve capital. And then there is the neat contrast drawn
elsewhere by Smith[4] between "future profit" and "present enjoyment."
And still clearer hints are found in the works of the German Nebenius
and the Englishman Scrope.

Nebenius bases his explanation of the exchange value of the services
of capital on several considerations. These include the one that "capital
can be acquired only *by more or less painful sacrifices* or efforts, to
which the capitalist can be induced to submit only for the sake of a
commensurate advantage." But he does not develop this thought any
further, and reveals himself chiefly as an adherent of a use theory which
borders fairly closely on the productivity theory.[5]

Scrope approximates the idea of abstinence more closely.[6] He first
explains that there must be "some surplus" for the capitalist over and
above the return of the capital itself which has been consumed in the
process of production, because it would not be worthwhile to use capital
productively, unless there were an opportunity of gaining thereby. Then
on page 146 he says, "The profit obtained by the owner of capital from

its productive employment . . . is to be viewed in the light of a compensation to him for *abstaining for a time from the consumption of that portion of his property on his personal gratification."* On subsequent pages, to be sure, he distorts the idea to make it appear that "time" constitutes the thing which the capitalist sacrifices. And he conducts an animated polemic against McCulloch and James Mill because they call time a mere word, an empty sound, which can do nothing, and which is nothing. Scrope even goes so far as to call time a constituent of the costs of production, and to say "The cost of producing any article comprehends the labour, capital and *time* (!) required to create and bring it to market. . . ."[7]

2. *Senior the Real Founder of the Abstinence Theory*

THE predecessors of Senior, whom I have already mentioned, were content to touch cursorily on this idea of abstinence, but Senior made it the central thought of a well-developed interest theory. No matter what opinion one may have concerning the correctness of his conclusions, one cannot withhold respectful recognition of the fact that, amid the confusion prevailing in his day in the realm of economic science, he was outstanding for his unified system of thought, his impressive consistency, and the profound treatment of his material. An excerpt from his exposition of his doctrines will corroborate my statement.

Senior distinguishes two "primary" instruments of production, labor and forces of nature. But these instruments cannot attain complete effectiveness, unless they are supported by a third element. Senior calls this third element "abstinence," by which he understands "the conduct of a person who either abstains from unproductive use of what he can command, or designedly prefers the production of remote to that of immediate results" (*p. 58*).

Senior very keenly and intelligently divulges his reason for departing from the customary practice of naming *capital* as the third productive factor. He tells us that capital is no simple original instrument, but is in most cases the result of cooperation on the part of labor, forces of nature, and abstinence. And so, if one wishes to designate the distinctive element among the productive powers, other than labor and nature, which is effective in capital, and which bears the same relationship to capital that labor does to wages, then that element must be abstinence, and nothing else (*p. 59*).

Senior repeatedly adduces detailed illustrations of the manner in which the element "abstinence" takes part in the accumulation of capital and therefore indirectly in the creation of the results which arise through the process of production. I shall cite one of the shortest of these illustrations verbatim. "In an improved state of society, the commonest tool is the result of the labour of previous years, perhaps of previous centuries. A carpenter's tools are among the simplest that occur to us. But what a sacrifice of present enjoyment must have been undergone by the capitalist who first opened the mine of which the carpenter's nails and hammer are the product! How much labour directed to distant results must have been employed by those who formed the instruments with which that mine was worked! In fact . . . we may conclude that there is not a nail . . . which is not to a certain degree the product of some labour for the purpose of obtaining a distant result, or, in our nomenclature, of some abstinence undergone before the Conquest, or perhaps before the Heptarchy." (*P. 68*.)

The "sacrifice," which lies in the renunciation or the postponement of gratification, demands compensation. That compensation is interest. But how, we ask, is the capitalist in a position to effect compliance in the economic world with his claim to compensation, to which he is certainly morally entitled? The answer to this important question is offered by Senior in his theory of price.

The exchange value of goods, according to Senior, depends in part on the usefulness of the goods, and in part on their "limitation of supply." In the case of the majority of goods, excepting always those which involve any sort of natural monopoly, the limitation of supply consists simply in how difficult it may be to find persons who are ready to expend the costs necessary for the production of those goods. By thus determining the magnitude of the supply, the costs of production govern exchange value. They do so by virtue of the fact that the purchaser's costs of production (that is to say, the sacrifice that would be necessary if the purchaser were to produce or acquire the goods himself) constitute the upper limit of the exchange value, while the seller's costs of production constitute the lower limit. In the case of the majority of goods which are subject to free competition, these two limits approach each other. That is to say, the costs of production of those goods constitute a simple determinant of value.

The costs of production consist of *the sum of the labor and the abstinence* which are required for the production of goods. This statement provides the theoretical connection between the doctrine of interest and the doctrine of price. If the sacrifice called "abstinence" is a constituent of the costs of production, and if the latter govern the value of goods, then that value must always be great enough to leave a sufficiently large remainder to compensate the abstinence. That provides a formal explanation of the surplus value of capital products, and hence of originary interest.

To the exposition of these last principles Senior appends a critique of the interest theory of some of his precedessors which really deserves to be called exemplary. Among his contributions is a striking series of paragraphs in which he points out the blunder committed by Malthus in calling interest an element of the costs of production. He does not confine himself to finding fault with Malthus, but goes on to clarify very cleverly how Malthus was led astray. Malthus had sensed quite correctly, Senior tells us, that in addition to labor there was another element of sacrifice demanded by the process of production. But since he had no expression at his command to designate it, he had called it by the name of that which is its compensation. This is similar to what is done by many who call wages a part of the costs of production. They fail to use the term labor itself for that component of costs, and use the word wages, which designates the compensation for the sacrifice we call labor. On the other hand, Senior tells us, Torrens, who had also previously laid this same error at Malthus's door, had himself committed a sin of omission. He had, quite correctly, eliminated "profit" from cost of production, but had not known what to put in its place.

Since the first formulation of the abstinence theory, the one by Senior is also still the best one, our purpose of forming a critical opinion of the whole school will be best served by an examination of Senior's theory.[8]

I think it is fitting, before I set down my own opinions on the matter, to devote a few words to a few other critiques which have been widely discussed by economists and which, in my estimation, are far too severe in their condemnation of Senior's doctrine.

Of these economists Pierstorff, chronologically among those closest to us, expressed himself most unfavorably on Senior's theory in his *Lehre vom Unternehmergewinn*.[9] He even goes so far as to say that Senior's method of procedure represents a deterioration in comparison with that of his predecessors, and an abandonment of serious scientific research, and even imputes to Senior the substituting of "a social and economic theory tailored to his own requirements for the economic facts underlying the phenomena" which he is examining.

I must confess that I can hardly understand this statement, especially out of the mouth of a historian of economic theory who should be able to appreciate merits, even if they are only relative. Pierstorff to the contrary notwithstanding, Senior is infinitely superior to his predecessors in the study of interest, in point of profundity, systematic organization and scientific seriousness of purpose. It might be appropriate to say of Ricardo or Malthus, of a McCulloch and a James Mill that their procedure denotes an abandonment of serious scientific examination of the interest problem. Some of Senior's predecessors fail to pose the problem at all, some solve it with strange absurdities, and others present a solution which manifestly begs the question. Unfortunately Pierstorff does not discuss Lauderdale at all. Yet even Lauderdale, though he makes an excellent beginning, is balked at the threshold of the interest problem, because a gross misapprehension of its nature seduces him into a completely futile attempt to explain the phenomenon of interest on the basis of his theory of value. But Senior by contrast, recognized with profound insight, not only that there is a problem there, but where the solution is to be sought, and what the obstacles are that lie in its path. Scorning all pseudo-solutions, he goes straight to the heart of the matter, the reason for the surplus value which the consumer good possesses in excess of the capital expended in producing it. If he did not discover the whole truth, it was certainly not for lack of serious scientific purpose. The critical observations alone, keen and profound as they are, which

Senior interpolates at frequent intervals, should have won him immunity from such severe reproaches.

No less excessively censorious are, in my opinion, the words of Lassalle who, in his sweepingly eloquent though exaggeratedly declamaatory style, ridiculed Senior's doctrine in the following words: "Interest is the 'wage of renunciation!' Felicitous word, priceless word! Your European millionaires are ascetics. Like Indian penitents they stand, like stylites on one foot atop a pillar, and pale of mien they lean over to stretch out an arm to the populace, holding forth a plate to receive the wage of their renunciation! In their midst, and towering high above its fellow penitents, playing its rôle of chief penitent and leading renouncer, behold the house of Rothschild! So that is how society is organized! And to think that I've been blind to it all this time!"[10]

In spite of this brilliant attack, I believe that there is a germ of truth in Senior's doctrine. It is undeniable that amassing and preserving a capital always requires abstinence from immediate gratification and demands a postponement of gratification. And it seems to me equally indubitable that, when goods result from a capitalist production process, their price is increased if the gratification of them is subject to longer or shorter postponement. For instance, if two goods require an exactly equal amount of labor for their production, say 100 days, but one is ready for consumption immediately upon completion of the work, while the other, say new wine, must lie in storage for a year, then experience shows that the good which is subject to delayed consumption is higher in price by about the amount of a year's interest. Now I have no doubt that the reason for this increased price is the circumstance that the enjoyment of the work performed must be postponed. For if the immediately consumable good and the one which is subject to delay in consumption were of equal value, everyone would prefer to apply his labor where it would come to immediate fruition. This factor would inevitably bring about an increased supply of the immediately consumable goods, and that in turn a decrease in the price of them, in comparison with the goods subject to delayed consumption. And thus, finally, the producers of the latter would be assured of an excess return above the normal compensation of labor, which of course tends to equalize in all branches of production. In other words, they would be assured of interest.

But it is also undeniable that the existence of interest and its rate do not exhibit the slightest degree of correlation with the existence and the degree of the "sacrifice of abstinence." And that is why the attacks of the embattled Lassalle made such a favorable impression. It is possible to receive interest in exceptional instances, where there is no individual sacrifice of abstinence. There are many cases in which one of Lassalle's millionaires collects high interest, although he makes but a slight sacrifice of abstinence. And there are also many cases where interest is very low, in spite of the great sacrifice which the abstinence entails. The servant girl's hard-earned dollar deposited in the savings bank earns, both relatively and absolutely, lower interest than the easily spared hundred thousand which a millionaire banker loans out on call. These hard facts of everyday life fit badly into a theory which makes the broad assertion that interest is the "wage of abstinence," and in the hands of a skillful controversialist like Lassalle, they were just so many sharp-edged weapons to be turned against that theory.

And yet the crucial weakness of the theory seems to me to lie elsewhere than in the absence of consistent correlation between the degree of sacrifice demanded and the amount of reward obtained. For in any sphere where costs or other sacrifices determine the price of goods, it is well known that, as a rule, when different portions of the supply reach the market at unequal costs, then the highest costs which an adequate supplying of the market will support, are the ones which determine the general, uniform market price. Whenever unequal costs are requited at a uniform price, it is fundamentally impossible that the compensation be in every single case in direct proportion to the extent of the sacrifice that has been made. It is, on the contrary, quite obvious that when producers bring goods to market which have been produced at a cost below the rate of the highest controlling costs of production, then those producers are always rewarded relatively more generously than their less favorably situated competitors. The disparity between the interest received by millionaires and their ridiculously slight "sacrifice of abstinence" may be conspicuously wide in degree. But in kind it is no more incongruous to the mind of the student of economics, than is the fact, so familiar to him, that the same high price which is dictated by the high cost of production necessitated by the least productive land under cultivation, is perforce also paid to the owners of the more fertile land as well, who therefore produce the same crops at lower cost, or even at no cost at all.[11]

The real and definitive shortcomings to which Senior's theory is subject, I believe I can, on mature deliberation, reduce to two. In the first place, I believe Senior has taken a thought which is essentially correct, and has based generalizations on it that are insufficiently discriminating and excessively stereotyped. There can, to my mind, be no doubt that the factor of postponement of gratification, which is given great prominence by Senior, does in actual fact exercise a certain amount of influence on the origin of interest. But I do not think that that influence is so simple, nor so direct, nor so exclusive that we may say, "Interest is the wage of abstinence, and that's that." I cannot offer a more detailed discussion at this point, but must reserve it for my second volume.

In the second place Senior has presented the essentially correct aspect of his theory in a guise which is, as a matter of form, vulnerable to attack. For I consider it an error in logic to present the renunciation of gratification, or abstinence in the abstract, as a second and independent sacrifice, *apart from* the labor that is sacrificed in production.

It will be more to the purpose if I proceed, by means of a concrete example, to develop this somewhat difficult point, and then formulate the principle underlying it.

Let us imagine a man living in the country who is trying to make up his mind how to spend his working day. There are a hundred possibilities open. Just to mention a few, he might go fishing, or hunting or harvesting fruit. All three activities have one thing in common, and that is that they yield their result at once, by the end of that same working day. Let us then suppose further that our rural laborer decides in favor of fishing, and that by evening he brings home three fish. What sacrifice did it cost him to get them?

Disregarding the negligible wear and tear on the fishing tackle, the fish obviously cost him *one day's work,* and nothing else. It is possible that he may count the cost in terms of the gratification which he could have obtained if he had employed his workday differently, and which he must now forego. He may possibly say to himself, "If I had gone hunting today instead of fishing, I should in all likelihood have bagged three hares. What my fish really cost me is three hares, which I am now unable to enjoy."

I think this way of computing the cost of the sacrifice is just as correct. It means that the labor, being considered simply a means to an end, is disregarded because it is merely the first step of the sacrifice, and replaced in the calculation by the end to which it is a means. The same manner of calculation is often encountered in economic life. Let us say I have definitely earmarked a sum of $300 as money I am going to spend, but am hesitating between two things on which to spend it. If I decide on a pleasure trip instead of an oriental rug, I shall probably consider that the sacrifice that the trip cost me is the oriental rug that I now must do without.

In any case it seems obvious that in calculating the sacrifice that is made for an economic purpose, the direct sacrifice in immediate means, and the indirect sacrifice in remote advantages which one might otherwise have obtained, can be used as alternative factors in the calculation, but not as cumulative factors. The sacrifice I make for the sake of the pleasure trip is *either* the $300, which is the direct cost, *or* the oriental rug which is the indirect cost, but not the $300 *and* the rug. Similarly our country dweller can say that the sacrifice which it cost him to catch the three fish is either the directly expended work, or the indirectly renounced three hares (the enjoyment of them, that is). But he cannot say it is the workday *and* the enjoyment of three hares. So much I think is clear.

But in addition to those occupations which yield their compensation at the end of the workday itself, our man-in-the-country has the choice of others which bring results that cannot be enjoyed until later. He might, for instance, sow wheat which could not be harvested for a year, or plant an orchard, which would not bear fruit for ten years. If we assume he chooses the latter, then what has he sacrificed in order to get his fruit trees? (Again let us disregard the negligible wear and tear of tools, and also the matter of land.)

There can, to my mind, be no doubt about the answer. It is again *one day's work* and nothing more. Or, if anyone prefers the indirect method of computation, the gratification of other things can be substituted for the workday, things which could have been obtained if the day had been otherwise employed. In that case the cost is the immediate enjoyment of three fish, or three hares, or a basket of fruit. And again it seems obvious to me that if the gratification which could have been obtained by the work is counted as the sacrifice, then not even the slightest portion of the work itself can be so counted. And if the work is counted as the sacrifice, no slightest portion can be counted of the gratification of other things which are thereby renounced. To do so would mean a duplication which is just as erroneous as charging up as the cost of the pleasure trip in our earlier example, both the $300 which it really did cost, and also the oriental rug that could otherwise have been bought with the $300.

Now Senior is guilty of just such an inadmissible duplication. Not that he goes to such lengths as to compute a total sacrifice comprising the labor and the entire gratification of other things. But he does make the postponement or the renunciation of gratification an item to be computed independently and in addition to the labor. And that oversteps the bounds of the admissible.[12] For it is clear that the sacrifice which consists in the labor comprises the *entire* advantage that might have resulted from applying the labor in another direction. This "entire advantage," to my mind, includes whatever partial or secondary shades of advantage may cling to the chief advantage. If I sacrifice $300 for a pleasure trip, then the sacrifice I am making, not *in addition to* the $300, but *consisting in* the $300, is not only a sacrifice of the oriental rug that I could otherwise have bought, but also of the pleasure that possession of it would have given me, as well as of the long duration of both possession and enjoyment. In exactly the same manner our rural landowner who sacrifices a day's labor in 1914 to plant an orchard which will bear fruit in 1924 is making a sacrifice, *not in addition to* the day's labor but *consisting in* that labor, of other things besides the three fish he could have obtained. Such other things include, let us say, his personal predilection for the flavor of fish, as well as *the advantage that arises from the fact that he can enjoy the fish in 1914, ten years earlier.* And so I say that to charge up the postponement of enjoyment as a component of the sacrifice is a duplication.

It is perhaps not too much to hope that most of my readers will agree with the foregoing arguments. And yet I cannot consider the matter as settled. It cannot be denied that Senior's presentation is uncommonly persuasive, and if we examine the case which was used as an illustration from a certain point of view which is especially favorable to Senior's theory, then the example has all the appearance of a decisive argument against me, and in favor of Senior. That is an argument with which I still have to cope.

Let us draw our parallel as follows. If I use today's workday hours for fishing, my fish have cost me a day's labor. That is clear. But if I spend this working day planting an orchard which will not bear for ten years, then I have not only sweated away a whole day, but in addition I must wait ten years before I can enjoy the fruits of my labor, and perhaps that waiting costs me a great deal of self control and mental anguish. Thus—or so it seems—I actually make a sacrifice that amounts to more than a day's labor, namely a day of arduous labor and besides, the burden of a ten year wait, while my gratification is delayed.

Plausible as the case may sound when it is put that way, it nevertheless stands on treacherous ground. By continuing this same line of reasoning I shall show that it contains a fallacy, and shall go on to expose the source of the fallacy. The exposure will also give me an opportunity to reduce the entire matter to its basic scientific principles.

Let us envisage the following case. I labor all day long planting fruit trees in the expectation that they will bear fruit in ten years. That very night a storm comes up and destroys my planting completely. How great is the sacrifice that I have made in vain? I believe everyone will say, "A day's labor lost and nothing more." And now I ask, "Is my sacrifice any greater because there is no storm, and so without any help from me the trees bear fruit in ten years? Do I sacrifice more when I put in a day's work and have to wait ten years to get results than I do when, on account of a destructive storm, I have to wait through all eternity?" It is certainly impossible to answer in the affirmative! And yet that is what Senior claims. For while my sacrifice in the second case must be scored as a single day's labor, Senior scores that in the first case as a day's labor plus a ten year renunciation of enjoyment, and accordingly something greater than the sacrifice in the second case.

And what a strange course the progression of sacrifice would describe if, according to Senior's principle, the results became increasingly remote! If labor yields results that can be utilized at once, the sacrifice consists of the labor expended only. If they are available in one year, then sacrifice = labor + one year's abstinence. If the labor proves worthwhile after two years, the equation reads: sacrifice = labor + two years' abstinence; if in twenty years, sacrifice increases to labor + twenty years' abstinence. And if it never has results? Does it not follow, that the factor of sacrifice then mounts to the highest conceivable apogee, that when it reaches "infinity" it attains the ultimate in the course of this progression? Not at all! The sacrifice of abstinence then declines to zero, labor alone is counted the entire sacrifice, and the total sacrifice becomes, not the greatest magnitude in the series, but the smallest!

I think all this indicates clearly that in every instance the only real sacrifice is the labor expended, and that any impression that, in addition, a second sacrifice in the form of a postponement of gratification demands recognition, is a false impression created by some element which causes appearances to be deceptive.

But what is this element which leads us into what I admit is a very natural error? It is simply the fact that the time element is actually a significant factor, only its significance lies along a line that Senior and most laymen do not appraise quite accurately. For instead of constituting a second independent sacrifice, the time element exerts its influence by determining the *magnitude* of the *one* sacrifice which really is made. If I am to make this completely clear, I shall have to go a bit further back. Every economic sacrifice that we make is essentially the forfeiture of some well-being that we suffer. This forfeiture may be of two kinds. It can be positive in nature and impose positive hardship, pain, or toil. Or it can be negative in nature and deprive us of joy or satisfaction that would otherwise have been ours. Most economic sacrifices which we make for a definite useful purpose belong in only one of these two categories of forfeiture, and then the calculation of the sacrifice we make is very simple. For instance, if I spend $300 for some useful purpose, then my sacrifice is measured simply by whatever enjoyable things I might have procured for my $300, and must now forego.

But the situation with respect to the sacrifice called "labor" is somewhat different, for it presents two economic aspects. According to one of these it constitutes, in the eyes of the majority of the human race, an expenditure of effort connected with some positive degree of hardship. In its other aspect it is a means for accomplishing many different kinds of useful purpose. And so any one who expends labor for a definite useful purpose is making a positive sacrifice of onerous exertion on the one hand, and on the other hand a negative sacrifice of other gratifications which could have been attained with the same labor. The question then is to hit upon the correct way of measuring the sacrifice that is made to accomplish a specific useful purpose.

The point that must be considered is the position with regard to pleasure and pain which would have resulted, if we had not devoted our work to the attainment of that specific end, but instead to some other rational purpose. The difference is a clear measure of the forfeiture of well-being which our specific purpose has cost us. If we apply this method of measuring difference, we can very soon convince ourselves that the sacrifice we make in the form of an expenditure of labor is sometimes to be measured by the positive burden, and sometimes by the negative deprivation of gratification but never by both at once.

For it is a question of determining *whether or not, by means of the day's labor which we expended, we could otherwise have procured a gratification that is greater than the pain which is caused us by the hardship of the one day's labor.* Let us assume that we feel the burden of a day's labor to be a hardship that can be rated at a relative magnitude of 10. We actually spend the working day fishing, and catch three fish which afford us a satisfaction having a relative intensity which we shall designate as 15. Now when we ask how great a sacrifice it cost us to obtain the fish, we have to decide whether or not, in the event that we had not gone fishing, we should have been able to use the working day to obtain some other satisfaction having an intensity in excess of 10. If such a possibility *did not exist,* then obviously we should have preferred to rest entirely. What our three fish cost us in that case is a *work burden of a magnitude of 10,* which we should otherwise not have assumed. In this instance, there is no question of other gratifications (these were ruled out) because we should not in any event have obtained any. But now let us suppose that, in addition to the fishing task, some possibility *did exist* of using the working day to achieve a satisfaction possessing an intensity in excess of 10. For instance, if to go hunting and shoot three rabbits brought a satisfaction rated at 12, then we should not in any event have remained idle, but should have exhibited the good sense to go hunting instead of fishing. What our fish now really cost us is *not the positive work burden of 10*, since that is what we should have assumed whether we had fished or hunted, *but the negative forfeiture of the gratification of a good rated at 12,* which we should have obtained if we had hunted and not fished. Of course we are not permitted to calculate the forfeiture and the work burden *cumulatively.* It is obviously incorrect to say that if we had not gone fishing, we could have saved ourselves the trouble of fishing and at the same time been able to bag the game which results from hunting. But it is no less incorrect to say that if we go fishing we lose both advantages, namely avoiding the labor burden *and* bagging the game.

What I have just said furnishes the material for a general rule which in practical life is applied with as much facility as assurance, and which can be worded as follows. *When labor is expended for a useful purpose, the sacrifice required is to be measured by the greater of the two forfeitures of well-being which may be in question; it is to be measured by the burden of labor when no other competing satisfaction is under consideration; it is to be measured by a competing satisfaction if such is present; it is never to be measured by the sum of those two.* Furthermore, since modern economic conditions not only offer the possibility, but for most of us impose the necessity of expending our labor, in any case, to some occupational purpose, the first of the aforementioned alternatives occurs rarely and by exception. And therefore our appraisal of the sacrifice that labor entails is predominantly *in terms of forfeited advantages, rather than of burden of labor.*[13]

That brings me at last to the point where it becomes possible to point out the real bearing that the time factor has on the magnitude of sacrifice. For it is a fact, the basis of which it is not yet time to expound, that, other things being equal, we prefer an immediate to a future gratification. And if we have the choice of expending our means of obtaining satisfaction—and our labor is such a means—on filling an immediate need on the one hand, and a future need on the other, the attractiveness of the immediate satisfaction will increase the difficulty of deciding in favor of the future one. *But if we do nevertheless decide in favor of it, we are prone to measure the extent of the sacrifice we have made by the extent of the gratification which we forego. And since the latter is invested with the alluring character of instantaneousness, the scales will tip to that side and make our sacrifice seem even harder than it would otherwise have appeared.* This does not mean that we are making a *second* sacrifice. Whether we choose between two present uses, two future uses, or one present and one future use, we are making *only a single sacrifice, and that sacrifice is labor.* But since, as I have just shown, we generally measure this sacrifice by the magnitude of the use forfeited, our appraisal is colored by our susceptibility to the charm of the earlier satisfaction, and so our estimate of that *single sacrifice* rises

189

above what it otherwise would have been. And that is the true state of the facts of which Senior's theory renders a mistaken interpretation.[14]

I trust my indulgent reader will forgive me for having detained him so long with these abstractions. But they contain the most important theoretical objections to a doctrine which deserves theoretical consideration. It is a doctrine which has so far often been rejected, but, to my mind, never refuted, and it is a less grievous error, so far as I can see, to examine overmeticulously before condemning than to condemn without examining.

3. SUCCESSORS OF SENIOR

SENIOR'S abstinence theory achieved great popularity with economists who believed in interest, not so much because its merits as a theory surpassed those of other theories, but rather because it came along at a time when interest was being subjected to vigorous attack, and this opportune support was welcome indeed. This is to be inferred from the peculiar circumstance that the great majority of its later adherents did not profess the doctrine exclusively, but rather incorporated certain elements of the abstinence theory, in eclectic fashion, into other theories favoring the phenomenon known as "interest." This procedure reveals an ambivalent attitude, as it were. On the one hand, it seems to betray a measure of contempt for the essential principle of the theory, since it evinces no scruples about grossly violating that principle by offering a motley collection of contradictory explanations of it. On the other hand, it seems to offer a welcome to any one bringing grist to the mill of controversy, apparently on the ground that there is merit in a mere numerical swelling of the ranks arrayed in defense of the legitimacy of interest, even though it be at the expense of scientific unity and consistency.

For that reason we shall meet most of the adherents of Senior's abstinence theory later, when we deal with eclectics. It is sufficient at this point to mention the Englishman John Stuart Mill and the perspicacious Jevons, the French authors Rossi, Molinari and Joseph Garnier, and many Germans, but preeminently Roscher and his numerous adherents, and also Schüz and Max Wirth.

Only the more prominent among the economists whose writings preserved the abstinence theory in greater purity need be mentioned here. The Englishman Cairnes wrote a treatise on costs of production,[15] which corresponds in essence to Senior's point of view. The Swiss Cherbuliez belongs in this group, even though his statement that interest is compensation for the "exertion of renunciation" (*les efforts de l' abstinence*) puts him on the borderline between the abstinence theory and a peculiar variation of the remuneration theories which will be discussed in the next chapter.[16] Then there is the Italian Wollemborg, who followed the pattern set by Senior and Cairnes in making a searching inquiry into the nature of costs of production.[17] And finally, there is the German

Karl Dietzel, of whom it must be admitted that he treats the problem only intermittently and cursorily.[18]

Since none of these last named authors has added any important feature to enrich Senior's abstinence theory, we need not enter upon any detailed treatment of their doctrines. But there is one writer whom I must discuss in some detail, one whose theory created a great sensation in his day, and who has exerted considerable influence right down to the present (1884). I mean Frédéric Bastiat.

Bastiat's theory of interest, which has been the subject of a great deal of altercation, can perhaps be described as a copy of Senior's abstinence theory which has been forcibly squeezed into the mold of Bastiat's theory of value, and has been changed, very much for the worse, in the process. The basic idea in both is the same. The postponement of gratification is a sacrifice which demands compensation. Senior uses the French word *abstinence,* Bastiat oscillates between the French words *delai* and *privation.* But the subsequent ramifications follow somewhat divergent paths.

Senior, who derives the value of goods from their cost of production, quite simply calls that sacrifice a component of the cost of production, and thus he has done with it. Bastiat, who insists that the only basis of value is "exchanged services," elevates postponement to the rank of a service. "Deferment," he says, "in and of itself is a specialized service, because it imposes a sacrifice on the one who grants it, and confers an advantage on the one who seeks it."[19] This "service" must be individually compensated, in accordance with the great law of society, "A service for a service." If the capitalist has borrowed his capital, the payment of this compensation takes the form of loan interest (*intérêt*). But even where it is not a matter of a loan, the service must be paid for. For it is a universal and indisputable fact, that anyone who is the recipient of a benefit, must also bear all the charges to which its production is subject. And those include the deferment. The latter is considered a "burdensome circumstance," and therefore is everywhere taken into account in the appraisal of services, and hence in the determination of the value of goods.[20] That, quite briefly, is the substance of Bastiat's doctrine, delivered with rhetorical verbosity and frequent repetition.

I called his doctrine a much debased copy of Senior's theory. If I ignore completely the faults that are inherent in Bastiat's theory of interest, not as such but as elements which belong to his theory of value, this debasement makes itself evident in two respects. (Incidentally, I consider his theory of value quite erroneous.)

In the first place, Bastiat confines his attention and his proofs to a secondary matter, namely the explanation of loan interest, and in doing so neglects the principal matter, which is the explanation of originary interest. Not only his *Harmonies Economiques* but also a monograph called *Capital et Rente*[21] reveal him as indefatigable in expatiating for page upon page on the explanation and justification of loan interest. But he applies his theory to the explanation of originary interest on only a single occasion, and even then he does so just cursorily and in passing. I refer to the passage already quoted from the third edition of his *Harmonies* (*p. 213*), which certainly leaves a great deal to be desired in the way of clarity and completeness.

The consequence of such neglect is that the dominant feature in his explanation of interest, namely the essential nature of the sacrifice represented by postponement, receives far less illuminating treatment at the hands of Bastiat, than it does from Senior. For by basing his expositions on the dealings between the owner of a capital and the *debtor* who borrows that capital, Bastiat merely makes the point that the sacrifice made by the lender consists in foregoing the productive use which could have been derived in the meantime from the capital which, instead, its owner loaned out.[22] That is all very much to the point, provided the purpose does not exceed the one which inspired Salmasius, when he took up arms against the canonists. For Salmasius argued that if a capital will yield originary interest, then it is only just and self-evident that a capital loaned out should also command interest. But this reference to a sacrifice by Bastiat is quite beside the point, if his purpose is to explain originary interest itself, and thus furnish a *final and complete* explanation of the entire phenomenon of interest. For Bastiat's argument presupposes the existence of originary interest as a conceded fact.

The only other sacrifice (other than Bastiat's utilization of capital loaned) which could contribute to a relatively profound explanation of interest, is, quite obviously, the one which is cited by Senior and which is represented by the deferment of the satisfaction of wants. To be sure, Bastiat speaks of that sacrifice, too, but the intrusion of that first sacrifice confuses his doctrine. And it really seems to me that it does so, not only for the reader but also for Bastiat himself. At least, there is no paucity of passages, particularly in his discourse on capital and interest, in which he deserts the abstinence theory and approaches dangerously close to the ground occupied by the naive productivity theorists. That oft cited passage in his *Harmonies* had paved the way to a declaration that the excess value of goods produced under the capitalist system is to be explained by the requirement that the purchaser must pay, not only for the labor which has gone into the products, but also for that "burdensome circumstance" called postponement of enjoyment. But instead, he contends repeatedly that it is self-evident that capital, *because of its inherent productive power,* must produce for its owner an "advantage," a "profit," higher prices, and an improvement in his condition, or in other words, a yield from his capital.[23] But we have already seen that such an argument does not explain interest but merely takes it for granted.

As a matter of fact, the charge has frequently been directed at Bastiat that he completely evaded the main issue, which was the explanation of originary interest. It is a charge which is not quite correct, but after the foregoing statements it is very easy to understand.[24]

That is the first of the two respects in which Bastiat represents a debasement of Senior. The second is a strange supplement. For Bastiat furnishes a second explanation of interest, in addition to the one I have outlined in the foregoing paragraphs. Now this second explanation contains such a miscellany of considerations, and is at the same time so obviously mistaken that I am quite incapable of even a vague surmise as to the relationship which this second explanation bore to his primary one.

Bastiat declares that all production is an aggregate of efforts. But it is necessary to note an essential distinction within that field. One class of efforts contributes to the creation of only a single product, the rendering of a single service. The other class of efforts, however, contributes to the creation of an indefinitely long series of products or services. The first category includes such efforts as those expended daily by the water carrier, which have only the immediate object of transportation of water. In the sphere of agriculture the category would be represented by such labors as sowing, weeding, plowing, harrowing, harvesting, threshing, and so on, all of which are directed to the production of one single crop. To the second category would belong such efforts as the work done by the water carrier in making his wheelbarrow and his water cask, and that done by the farmer in hedging, in preparing soil for cultivation, in reclamation of land under water, in erection of buildings, in short, in any kind of improvement. All these labors are directed toward the creation of what the economist calls "fixed capital," and are of benefit to a whole series of consumers, or of harvests.[25]

Then Bastiat poses the question, "How are these two categories of efforts to be appraised and compensated, in accordance with the great law of 'service for service'?" With respect to the first category, he considers it very simple. The services in that class are to be paid for by those who benefit from them. But that does not apply to the second class of effort leading to the creation of "fixed capital," because the series of persons who benefit from it is indefinite. If the producer of the capital were to have it paid for by the *first* consumers, an injustice would result. Because, in the first place, the first would be paying for benefits enjoyed by the last, and, in the second place, there would inevitably come a time when the producer would still be in possession of his not yet consumed stock of capital and also of the compensation for it.[26] And that, too, would constitute an injustice.

Accordingly, concludes Bastiat, performing a complete logical somersault, the distribution of capital to an indefinite number of consumers can be accomplished only by leaving the capital undisturbed, and charging the consumers with the burden of the interest. Bastiat maintains this is the only conceivable solution of our problem.[27] It is a method which is offered spontaneously by the "ingenious natural mechanism of society," and which relieves us of the burden of substituting an artificial mechanism for it.[28]

That is how Bastiat explains interest as the form in which a capital which has been advanced is recovered by distributing it over the aggregate of the goods produced. "It is in this distribution of a capital advanced throughout the totality of its products that we find the principle of interest and the reason for its existence" (*Chapter* VII, *p. 205*).

I suppose every one of my readers, in the mere perusal of these lines, has observed that Bastiat's explanation reveals the fact that he has been misled into a number of incredibly gross errors. In the first place, it is a palpable blunder to believe that it is impossible to recover a capital investment by distributing the amount among the consumers. Every business man knows that that *is* possible, and he knows, moreover, *that* it is done and *how* it is done in actual practice. It is simply a matter of estimating the probable life of the capital investment, and on the basis of that estimate charging off in each fiscal period, or for each unit of the product, a corresponding depreciation or amortization allowance. Since the consumers are paying a purchase price for the finished product which includes a pro rata charge which amortizes the fixed capital, the "capital itself" is being distributed among them in a very real sense. To be sure, it is not being done in a measure which is absolutely "just," because the estimate of the probable life of the investment is subject to error, and consequently so is the estimate of the periodic charge for wear and tear. But by and large the cumulative payments by the consumers will, for practical purposes, equal the invested capital which is to be amortized.

In the second place, it is a gross error to assume that the producers receive interest *instead of* the undistributable capital itself. Everybody knows that, on the one hand, the capital invested is returned to them in the amortization allowances, and, on the other hand, as long as any part of that capital is still outstanding, that they receive interest *in addition*. Interest therefore has as its basis something utterly apart from amortization of capital. It is really difficult to understand how Bastiat could be guilty of error on matters so simple and so much a matter of common knowledge.

In passing I should like to add one concluding remark. Bastiat enunciates a practical law of interest to the effect that, with the increase of capital, the capitalist's absolute share in the total product increases,[29] while his relative share diminishes. This is something he borrowed from Carey, and his efforts, like Carey's, to prove the validity of this law are, scientifically speaking, utterly valueless, for the simple reason that both men bandy about the concepts of "percentage of total product" and "percentage of capital" (meaning rate of interest) with complete lack of discrimination.

And so on the whole, Bastiat's interest theory seems to me to fall far short of deserving the good reputation which, at least in certain circles, it has so long enjoyed.

X

THE REMUNERATION* THEORIES

I USE this name to embrace a number of theories which have one point in common, and that point is to call interest the remuneration of *labor performed by the capitalist*. Their several views are widely at variance as to the nature of the work which is supposed to constitute the basis of the capitalist's claim to remuneration. And so I have to differentiate among three independent groups within the general category of remuneration theories. Because the adherents of the groups happen to be separated by national lines of demarcation, I will call them the *English*, the *French* and the *German* groups.

1. The English Group

THE first group bases its explanation of interest on the labor which was originally performed in order to create the capital good itself. The chief representatives of the group are James Mill and McCulloch.

It is in his doctrine of the price of goods that James Mill first encounters the problem of interest.[1] On page 93 he enunciates the principle that costs of production regulate the exchange value of goods. The components of the costs of production appear, at first glance, to be capital and labor. But Mill's closer scrutiny reveals that capital itself was created by labor, and that therefore all the costs of production resolve themselves, in the end, into labor alone. Labor then is the sole regulator of the value of goods. (*P. 97.*)

This statement however seems impossible to reconcile with the well-known fact, which Ricardo had already discussed, that the element of postponement also has an influence on the price of goods. If, for instance, a barrel of wine and 20 sacks of flour are produced in the same season and with the expenditure of the same amount of labor, both will admittedly have the same exchange value at the end of the season. But if the owner of the wine puts it in the cellar and stores it for a couple of years, the barrel of wine will be worth more than the 20 sacks

---

* Translators' note: This translation of Böhm-Bawerk's *Arbeitstheorie* is intended to avoid the confusion that lurks in the term "labor theory," and to focus attention where Böhm-Bawerk would direct it, that is to say, on interest as remuneration for services rendered by the capitalist.

of flour. As a matter of fact, the excess in value will be in the amount of two years' interest.

James Mill reconciles this violation of his economic law by saying that interest itself is a wage of labor, that is to say, a compensation for *indirect labor*. He asks, "Why must profits be paid?* To this there is no answer but one, that they are the remuneration for labour, labour not applied immediately to the commodity in question, but applied to it through the medium of other commodities, the produce of labour."

This idea is more fully elucidated by the following analysis. "A man has a machine, the produce of 100 days' labour. In applying it the owner undoubtedly applies labour, though in a secondary sense, by applying that which could not have been had but through the medium of labour. This machine, let us suppose, is calculated to last exactly 10 years. One-tenth of the fruit of 100 days' labour is thus expended every year, which is the same thing in the view of cost and value as saying that 10 days' labour has been expended. The owner is to be paid for the 100 days' labour which the machine costs him at the rate of so much per annum, that is, by an annuity for 10 years equivalent to the original value of the machine.[2] It thus appears (!) that profits are simply remuneration for labour. They may, indeed, without doing any violence to language, hardly even by a metaphor, be denominated wages: the wages of that labour which is applied, not immediately by the hand, but mediately, by the instruments which the hand has produced. And if you measure the amount of immediate labour by the amount of the wages, you may measure the amount of secondary labour by that of the return to the capitalist." (*P. 103.*)

James Mill thinks that he has hereby not only furnished a satisfactory explanation of interest, but also preserved inviolate his law that labor alone determines the value of goods. But it is entirely obvious that he has not succeeded in doing either.

Let us accept his calling capital accumulated labor, and his terming the application of capital the application of mediate secondary labor, and also his regarding the exhaustion of the machine as an expenditure by installments of the accumulated labor. But why is every installment of the accumulated labor paid for with an annuity which contains more than the original value thereof, namely that original value plus the customary rate of interest thereon? Let us grant that remuneration of capital is remuneration of mediate labor. But why is mediate labor compensated at a rate higher than the one for immediate labor, since the latter receives the simple labor wage, while the former receives an annuity which exceeds the labor rate by the amount of interest? Mill does not solve this question. On the contrary, he clings, as to a fixed pole, to the fact

---

* Translators' note: In order to understand James Mill's "profit," the reader must appreciate that for Mill and his contemporaries the word signified a complex concept. Economists of today, some 120 or 130 years later, would resolve this "profit" into its constituent elements and point out that it embraces the remuneration for the entrepreneur's own labor employed in the process of production, the entrepreneur's profit proper, and finally, interest on the capital invested. Our concern here is solely with the last of these three elements. See Böhm-Bawerk's statement in Note 57 on page 469.

that a capital, subject to competitive market conditions, is equivalent in value to a certain annuity *which includes interest.* He seems to lose sight of the fact that he had undertaken to explain interest in general, and therefore also the interest which the annuity must include, in addition to the replacement of capital.

He does, to be sure, say by way of explanation that interest is a wage of labor. But he is very much mistaken as to the potency of this phrase as an explanation. It could serve in a pinch, if Mill were able to show that there is some labor there which has not yet received its normal wage, and is scheduled to receive it only by means of the interest. But it will not serve by any means to explain an increase in wage for labor which has already received a normal wage, in the form of amortization allowances included in the annuity. For the question remains unanswered as to why mediate labor should be more highly paid than immediate labor. And Mill has not given us even the slightest hint on how to answer that question.

At the same time his artificial interpretation does not even afford him the advantage of being consistent with his own theory of value. For his own law, that the price of all goods is determined by the amount of labor expended, is grossly violated if a part of the price depends, not on the *amount* of labor expended, but on the higher *rate of wages* which it receives. In every respect then, Mill's theory falls far short of what it should accomplish.

In the first edition of his *Principles of Political Economy* (1825) McCulloch enunciated a very similar theory, but abandoned it in the later editions. I described it in an earlier chapter, and do not feel that it calls for further comment.[3]

More cursory treatment is accorded the concept by the Englishman Read and the German Gerstner, concerning both of whom I shall have more to say in subsequent pages devoted to the eclectics.

2. The French Group

A SECOND group of remuneration theorists explains interest as the remuneration of that labor which consists in the "saving up" of capital, the *travail d'épargne.* The most detailed treatment which the theory receives is at the hands of Courcelle-Seneuil.[4]

According to Courcelle-Seneuil there are two kinds of labor, the labor of the muscles and the labor of saving (*p. 85*). He elucidates this latter concept as follows. In order to preserve a capital that has once been created, there is need of constant effort in the form of foresight and saving—foresight which takes future needs into account, saving which refrains from present enjoyment of the capital accumulated, in order to use it to meet future wants. This "labor" consists of both an act of intelligence, namely the *prévoir* or foreseeing, and an act of will, namely the saving or "refraining from enjoyment over a given period of time."

It does seem strange, at first blush, to endow saving with the name

197

of *labor*. But this impression is attributable, according to the author's view, solely to the fact that we are ordinarily all too intent upon the material aspect of things. Impartial reflection, however, will convince us that it is just as laborious (*pénible*) to refrain from consuming a good that has been amassed, as to labor with muscle and mind to acquire a desired good. And we shall be likewise convinced that the conservation of capital really requires a special and artificial effort of the mind and the will, and arbitrary action which counteracts the natural bent toward self-indulgence and indolence. After the author has attempted to fortify this course of reasoning by a reference to the customs of savage tribes, he concludes with the following formal statement. "It is a perfectly legitimate statement therefore, and not a mere figure of speech, to say that saving is a form of industrial labor, and hence a productive force. It demands an effort which, it is true, is purely moral in character, but which is nevertheless laborious, and it is therefore as clearly entitled as any muscular effort to be characterized as labor."

The "labor of saving" lays claim to remuneration, just as does the "labor of muscular exertion." While the latter is remunerated in the form of *salaire* (wages), the former accepts its payment in the shape of *intérêt* or interest (*p. 318*). Courcelle explains why this must be the case, and furthermore why the compensation for the labor of saving must be somewhat more enduring. This is his explanation.

"The desire, the temptation to consume is a power which is continuously operative, and it can be arrested only by countering with some other force which is likewise permanently operative. It is apparent that everyone would consume as much as possible, unless he had some interest (*s'il n'avait pas intérêt*) in refraining from consumption. He would cease to refrain, from the very instant when he ceased to have that interest, which must be of continuous duration so that capital may be permanently conserved. That is why we say that interest (*l'intérêt*—note the play on words!) is the wage of the labor of saving and of renunciation, without which capital cannot endure, and which is a necessary condition of industrial life." (*P. 322.*)

The rate of this compensation is governed "by the great law of supply and demand," it depends on the desire and the ability to employ a capital sum reproductively, on the one hand, and on the desire and the ability, on the other hand, to accumulate that sum by saving.

In spite of all the pains the author has taken to represent the labor of saving to be genuine labor, he is unable, in my estimation, to efface the stigma of artificiality which is branded on the brow of this theory. The non-consumption of a fortune is a labor, the effortless collection of interest a suitable wage! What a tempting target for a critic who might, in the manner of Lassalle, choose as his weapon an appeal to the sympathy and impressionability of the reader! However, instead of stating grandiloquently that Courcelle is in error, I prefer to present a rational explanation of *why* he is wrong.

In the first place, it is apparent that Courcelle's theory is merely a thinly disguised variant of Senior's abstinence theory. Wherever Senior says "renunciation" or "sacrifice of renunciation," Courcelle says "labor of renunciation," but essentially both make use of the same basic principle in the same way. For that reason Courcelle's remuneration theory is open to a great many of the objections which can be raised against Senior's abstinence theory, and which have already been advanced as our reasons for adjudging the latter to be without validity.

But in addition, this variant of Courcelle's exhibits weaknesses of its own. It is of course true that foresight and saving do impose a measure of effort. But the mere fact that the performance of labor in a certain set of circumstances is accompanied by the receipt of income is not by any means a justification for maintaining that the income is the wage of that labor. In order to advance such an argument one would have to be able to prove that the income is actually given in return *for the labor* and *only in order to procure the labor.* The best way to prove that would be to show that the receipt of income is present when the labor is performed, and absent when it is not; that the income is high when a great deal of labor has been performed, and is low when little has been performed. But there is hardly a trace to be discerned of any such correlation between the alleged cause of interest and its actual occurrence. The man who unconcernedly clips the coupons from a fortune of millions in securities, or even has a secretary do it for him, gathers in a "wage of labor" amounting to tens or even hundreds of thousands. But the man who undergoes a veritable torment of planning and scrimping to have $50 left over to put into the savings bank, gathers in less than $2. And if another man has undergone just as much hardship to lay aside his $50, but does not dare to lose control of them even momentarily because of the imminence of a pressing need, then this second man gets no "wage of labor" at all.

Why should that be? Why is there such a difference in wages? A difference, moreover, as between the various kinds of persons who labor at saving, as well as a difference in comparison with the wages for muscular labor? Why does "a year's labor" yield a million dollars for the man who possesses twenty millions, while it yields the manual laborer who works hard and can save nothing, only $2,000; and the manual laborer who works hard and does save $50, only something less than $2,002? A theory which explains interest as a wage of labor should certainly undertake to go into a rather detailed explanation of things like that. But instead, Courcelle polishes off the knotty problem of the rate of interest with a generalized reference to the "great law" of supply and demand.

It could really be said—and without any suggestion of irony—that Courcelle would have had just as much theoretical justification for claiming that the physical labor of pocketing interest or of clipping coupons is the reason for drawing interest. It is, after all, a labor which the capitalist performs. And if it were argued that it is strange, in view of the law of supply and demand, that such labor is so extraordinarily highly paid, the answer would be that it is no stranger than that the mental exertions of the man who inherits millions are compensated with so and so many hundred thousand a year. It might perhaps be said, of this latter kind of work, that there are simply so exceedingly few persons who have the "desire and ability" to maintain a capital of millions, that in view of the existing demand for capital, the compensation for it is necessarily that high. But it could with equal justice be said that there are so exceedingly few persons who have the "desire and ability" to pocket hundreds of thousands in interest. Hardly anyone would lack the "desire" in either of these cases. As far as "ability" is concerned, that, in both cases, is principally a question of being lucky enough to possess a capital of millions.

If the foregoing remarks could be so construed as to leave any need for direct refutation of Courcelle's remuneration theory, I should like to submit the following supposititious case. Capitalist *A* lends manufacturer *B* a million dollars for a year at 5%. The manufacturer employs the million productively and earns a total excess of proceeds of $60,000. Fifty thousand of that sum he remits to *A* as loan interest, and he retains the remaining $10,000 as entrepreneur's profit. According to Courcelle, the $50,000 which *A* receives are his wage for having anticipated future wants, and for having resisted all temptation to consume the million immediately, such resistance being an act of will directed toward the renunciation of gratification. But did not *B* perform exactly the same labor, or in fact an even more onerous one? Was not *B* too, once he had the borrowed million in his hands, exposed to the temptation to consume it at once? Could he not, for instance, have spent the million in riotous living, and then gone into bankruptcy? Did not *B*, as well as *A*, resist temptation by an act of will directed to abstinence? Did his achievements in the way of anticipation and advance provision not surpass those of *A*? For he did more than merely think of future wants in general as *A* did. He accorded that specific treatment to the stock of materials in his hands which, by transforming them into products, rendered them in very fact capable of satisfying future wants. Yet *A* receives $50,000 for the labor of conserving his million, whereas *B*, who has done the same kind of mental and moral labor with the same million, but more of it, receives nothing for it. Of course, the $10,000 he does receive in entrepreneur's profit are his compensation for a completely different kind of activity.

Nor is there any validity in the objection that, because the million was not his property, he had no right to consume it, and that therefore there is in his saving no merit worthy of a wage. Under this theory the matter of merit does not enter into the question at all. The wages of saving are great, provided only that the sum which is amassed and conserved is great, and it does not make the slightest difference whether the moral effort required is great or small. But it cannot be denied that the borrower really did conserve the million, and really did resist the temptation to consume it. Why does he receive no "wage of saving?" It seems to me that the real explanation is not open to doubt. The recipient of interest is such, not because he is a worker, but because he is *an owner*. Interest is not income won by labor, but *by ownership*.

A somewhat timid defense of the Courcelle-Seneuil theory appeared subsequently in the pages of Cauwès.[5]

This economist states the theory, to be sure, but not as his only interest theory, nor without certain stipulations and conditions which reveal clearly that he considers Courcelle's interpretation of the labor of saving as somewhat less than unassailable. "Since the conservation of capital presupposes an effort of will, and in many instances also industrial or financial combinations of some difficulty, one might say that it represents genuine labor which could sometimes justly be called labor of saving" (*travail d'épargne, Vol.* I, *p. 183*). In another passage Cauwès seeks to lay at rest any possible doubt as to whether the capitalist should properly receive interest, since lending money does not cost any labor which could form the basis of a claim to interest. His argument runs, "It may be true that it does not demand any labor to make a loan. But it does demand labor to persist in the will to amass capital, and to forebear for a long period of time, to commit any act which constitutes consumption or enjoyment of the value represented by the capital. That may be called, *if the expression does not seem too bizarre,* a labor of saving, of which the wage is interest."[6] At the same time Cauwès presents other explanations of interest, particularly a doctrine of the productivity of capital. For that reason we shall discuss Cauwès again when we come to our treatment of the eclectics.

A few other economists who wrote in French reveal occasional points which they possess in common with Courcelle. There is Cherbuliez[7] who says that interest is a wage for the "efforts of abstinence" (*efforts d'abstinence*). And Joseph Garnier offers a motley explanation of the phenomenon of interest, into which he injects the catchword "labor of saving."[8] But these authors do not pursue the concept to any profound depths.

3. The German Group

THE same basic principle which gave rise in France to a tortured and minutely detailed theory of interest was used, though along less labored lines, by a prominent group of German economists. In deference to a popularly accepted habit of speech I shall call them briefly the "socialists of the chair" (*Katheder-Sozialisten*). But the common possession of the basic idea is responsible for only the most remote resemblance between the remuneration theory of the German socialist professors and its French variant. The German theory originated quite independently of the French theory, and developed along completely independent lines.

Rodbertus-Jagetzow can be regarded as the forerunner of the German remuneration theory, as he touches upon its basic principle in some incidental observations. On one occasion he speaks of the conceivability of a state of society in which, though there may be private property, there is no private property which returns income, so that all existing income is income from labor in the shape of salaries or wages. A state of this sort would exist if, on the one hand, the means of production, land and capital, were socialized, and if, on the other hand, there were recognition of private property rights to goods received as income, such goods being apportioned to each individual in the measure of the labor he performed. Rodbertus adds a footnote concerning this exposition, to the effect that, economically speaking, ownership in the means of production must be defined quite differently from ownership in goods received as income. "Income property performs its economic function when it is consumed in the course of purely domestic economy. Property in land and capital, however, is at the same time an *office,* as it were, implying economic functions on a national scale. These functions consist in administering the national labor supply and the national economic means in accordance with national needs. They consist, in short, in those duties which would be performed by national officials in a state where such conditions of socialized property obtained. The most favorable light in which revenue, viewed from this point of view, can be regarded (whether it be land rent or interest on capital) is to deem it a payment, *in lieu of salary* to the incumbents of these offices, and to consider that it represents a form of salary which engenders a strong pecuniary interest on the part of the official in the correct exercise of his functions."[9]

On another occasion[10] Rodbertus expresses a kindred thought when he makes the comment that, in addition to knowledge, it takes moral strength and honest actions in any given productive process to administer successfully the division and assignment of the various operations performed by a large number of workers. The productive workers themselves are not able to perform this kind of service, but the service is no whit less indispensable to national production. To the extent that useful and necessary services of this kind are performed by capitalists, landowners and entrepreneurs, there will be general agreement that the latter "are as much entitled to demand compensation as any one else who performs any other kind of useful service. They have as much right to do so as, say, a Secretary of Commerce or a Director of Public Works, provided he does his duty."

But Rodbertus had no intention whatsoever of making this thought the basis of a theory of interest, that is to say, of an explanation of that form of the capitalist's income which we observe in actual everyday life. On the contrary, he expressly rejects such an idea by emphasizing repeatedly that what we know as interest today is anything but such compensation for services performed, such wage received in the shape of "indirect participation in the distribution of goods." It is rather, he says, a direct participation in the fruits of national production, which takes place at the time of the "original distribution of goods." And Rodbertus discerns the origin of this participation in entirely different conditions, namely in the coercion that is imposed upon the workers by virtue of the capitalist's ownership of land and of capital.[11]

This same idea, which Rodbertus had touched upon so lightly, but had intentionally failed to make use of for a theory of interest, now bobbed up again a bit later in the work of several prominent "socialists of the chair," and received rather full development as a contribution to their treatment of the interest problem.

The first of these was Schäffle. As early as 1873, in the third edition of his *Gesellschaftliches System der Menschlichen Wirtschaft* he adopts for his formal definition of interest the idea that interest is a remuneration for service performed by the capitalist. "An excess of proceeds" he says "is to be regarded as the compensation which the entrepreneur may justly claim for his services. The latter constitute the *fulfillment of a national function* which consists in the independent economic coordination of the powers of production by means of his speculative utilization of capital."[12]

This view recurs in numerous other passages, and indeed in those passages, as a rule, which treat of interest from a rather general point of view. He also defends it at one point as the only tenable theory in comparison with all other theories of interest, which, without exception, he rejects completely.[13] The more esoteric details of the doctrine of interest, such as the rate of interest, are not worked out by Schäffle, peculiarly enough, in accordance with the basic principle I have just quoted. Instead, he draws his weapons from the technical armory of the use theory, though it must be admitted that the subjective interpretation to which the concept of use must submit at his hands makes his use theory somewhat similar to the remuneration theory.[14]

In his more recent principal work *Bau und Leben des sozialen Körpers* the concept that interest is remuneration granted in recognition of a "functional service" on the part of the capitalist receives greater emphasis. It affords Schäffle the possibility of defending interest, at least in the present era, and for as long a period as society fails to devise a more efficient system which will enable it to dispense with the expensive services which are performed by private capital.[15] But even in this work the details of the phenomena of interest are not elucidated in terms of this newly formulated principle. Remnants of the use theory are still in evidence, and the use concept underlying it has now, moreover, become objective.[16] And so we may say that Schäffle has struck the keynote of a remuneration theory, but no more than that. He did not go on and develop the theory in complete detail, as Courcelle-Seneuil did.

Wagner went a little further, but only a little. He, too, calls the capitalists "functionaries of society for the development and employment of the national fund of means of produciton."[17] And he calls interest an income which they receive *for* or at least *in* the exercise of this function (*p. 594*). But he is more definite than was Schäffle as to the terms in which he characterizes as genuine "labors" (*pp. 111, 592, 630*) the performances by capitalists which consist in the "development and application of private capital" or in the "activities of saving and dispensing." They are labors which constitute an element of the total costs which must be expended on the production of goods, and they are therefore an "essential element in value" (*p. 630*). Just how this element contributes to the creation of the value of goods, how its efficacy determines

203

the ratio of interest to the capital sum, or the rate of interest—these and similar questions were left quite as completely unanswered by Wagner, as they had been by Schäffle. And so he, too, did no more than strike the keynote of the remuneration theory, though he may have done so with somewhat greater definitiveness.

Under these circumstances I do not dare state conclusively whether the "socialists of the chair" intended this course of reasoning as a theoretical explanation of interest, or merely as a justification of it from the point of view of social policy. There are several considerations that argue for the first of these alternatives. For one thing, they have adopted the remuneration motive as part of their formal definition of interest. For another, Wagner at least, has rejected all other theories of interest, and so, if the remuneration theory is not his theoretical explanation of interest, then he has left it entirely unexplained. Finally, Wagner has expressly pronounced the "labor" of the capitalists to be a component of the costs of production and "an essential constituent of value." And it is hardly possible to deny that he means thereby to signify that the phenomenon of "surplus value" has its scientific origin in the expenditure of labor by the capitalist—a labor which demands remuneration.

But there are several points which might indicate that the "socialists of the chair" merely meant to argue that the "services" of the capitalists justify interest, as we know it to exist, without any intention of explaining its existence. One such point is the lack of any scientifically detailed working out of the principle. Another is the fact that Schäffle, to the extent that he goes into detail at all, makes use of an entirely different interest theory. And finally there is the great preponderance of emphasis, throughout the writings of those socialist professors, on the political rather than the theoretical aspects of the question.[18]

Under the circumstances, I consider it appropriate to cast my critical appraisal in the mold of a hypothetical presentation.

If the references by the "socialists of the chair" to the "performances of labor" by the capitalists were intended only to justify interest from the point of view of social policy, their remarks might be termed highly noteworthy. But any searching investigation of this phase of the question lies outside the scope of the task I have set myself for this portion of my book.

But if the "socialists of the chair" meant their statement to *explain* the existence of interest *as a matter of theory,* I should be compelled to render the same verdict of complete inadequacy against the German variant of the remuneration theory as I did in the case of its French counterpart.

In the course of its historical development economic thought has been so often marked by the confusion of the social and political justification of interest with the theoretical explanation of it, that it may well be worth while to make the difference unmistakably clear. To that end I will present a parallel which will, I hope, clarify this difference and at the same time demonstrate the inadequacy of the remuneration theory.

The original acquisition of a piece of land is regularly connected with a certain amount of exertion or labor on the part of the person acquiring it. Either he first had to make the land arable, or in any event he had to put forth a certain amount of effort in connection with his taking possession. Under some circumstances those efforts must have been anything but slight as, for instance, when it was necessary to conduct a long search for a location suitable for settlement. Now the piece of land yields rent to the man who acquired it. Can the existence of that rent be *explained* on the basis of the original expenditure of labor? No one ever dared to make that claim except Carey and a small number of men who shared his eccentric ideas. Nor can any one make the claim who is not blind to logic. It is perfectly clear that if a fertile hollow yields rent, it is not because its occupation cost some labor; and it is equally clear that if a rocky mountain slope bears no rent, the reason is not because its occupation was effortless. It is also undeniable that two pieces of land which are equally fertile and equally well-situated will yield equal rent, even if one of them was by nature fertile and merely needed to be occupied at the cost of but little effort, while the other, with the expenditure of a great deal of labor, first had to be made arable. It is also clear that the reason why 200 acres yield twice as much rent as 100 acres is not because the former were twice as laborious to acquire as the latter. And finally, it is clear that the increase in rent of a given piece of ground which accompanies an increase in population, has not the slightest connection with the original expenditure of labor. In short, the occurrence of land rent, and particularly the amount of it, is so completely unrelated to the occurrence and the amount of the labor which was originally expended on the acquisition of the land, that it is impossible to discover in that labor the principle which can explain the occurrence of land rent.

But it is an entirely different matter to ask whether that expenditure of labor can *justify* land rent. In this respect it is quite reasonable to take the point of view that the person who first made a piece of land arable, or even as a pioneer first occupied it on behalf of civilization, thereby performs a meritorious service which entitles him to compensation which is as lasting as are the advantages that accrue to human society from his action. It is quite possible to contend that it is right and just for the person who has gained a piece of land in perpetuity for the cause of civilization, to receive, also in perpetuity, a portion of the yield of that land, in the form of land rent. I will not contend that this consideration must under all circumstances be conclusive for the institution of private ownership of land, and for the consequent private receipt of land rent. But it certainly *may* be conclusive under some conditions. It is for instance quite conceivable that a colonial government would be well advised to stimulate settlement of its territory by guaranteeing, as a premium for the labor of clearance and first occupation, the ownership of whatever lands are placed under cultivation and hence the right to the perpetual receipt of land rent. It is accordingly quite correct to say that consideration of the labor expended by the original person to take possession of a piece of land can constitute a highly plausible *justifi-*

cation, and a decisive social and political motive for the introduction and retention of land rent. But it is certainly absolutely impossible to say that it constitutes an *explanation* of land rent.

The situation is quite similar with respect to the relationship between interest and the "activities of saving and dispensing" performed by the capitalists. Some will regard these activities as the most effective means of accumulating and efficiently utilizing an adequate capital supply. Those same persons will point out that it is hardly to be expected that these activities will be engaged in by a sufficiently large number of private persons, unless they have a prospect of lasting advantages in return. To the extent that these considerations concerning the capitalists' services are valid, they constitute a most substantial justification and a conclusive legislative motive for the introduction and maintenance of interest. But that is something entirely different from the question whether the existence of interest can be explained in theory, by reference to that "labor." If interest could be so explained it would have to be possible to establish some positive correlation between the alleged result, which is interest, and the ostensible cause, which is the expenditure of labor on the part of the capitalist. But in the realm of reality such correlation will be sought in vain. A million dollars will yield $50,000 interest, no matter whether the saving and the employment of the million cost its owner a great deal of toil, very little toil, or no toil at all. A million will yield 10,000 times as much interest as 100, even if the saving of the 100 involved infinitely more worry and tribulation than the saving of the million. The borrower who conserves and utilizes another's capital receives no interest in spite of his "expenditure of labor," and the owner does receive interest, even if his "labor" amounts to zero. Even Schäffle himself on one occasion is forced to admit, "There is no such thing as a distribution in proportion to the extent and to the meritoriousness of the service, either as between one capitalist and another, or as between the laborer and capital. Such distribution *neither conforms to a principle, nor results as a fortuitous consequence.*"[19]

But if experience shows us that interest does not bear any relationship whatever to the labor performed by the capitalist, how can it be rationally possible for that labor to provide the principle which will explain interest? It is my belief that the truth is too clearly demonstrated by the facts for any long exposition to be necessary. It is an unqualified certainty that there is *no* correlation between interest and expenditure of labor by the capitalist. It is equally certain that there *is* perfect positive correlation between interest and, firstly, the fact that capital is possessed and, secondly, the amount of capital possessed. I repeat what I said earlier, interest is income arising from possession, not from labor.

And so the remuneration theory, in all its variants, proves to be quite incapable of offering any tenable theoretical explanation of interest. Nor could any impartial person expect any other result. Only a person who takes delight in devious ratiocination could doubt for a moment that the economic power of capital is founded on something other than the capitalist's "capacity for labor," and that interest is not only in name, but also in fact, something other than a wage of labor.

The fact that, in spite of all, recourse was taken to all sorts of remuneration theories, can be accounted for by the prevalence of a fashion, persisting since the days of Smith and Ricardo, of attributing all value to labor. Not even the most extravagantly artificial explanations could daunt the theorists in their attempt to force interest to don the strait-jacket of conformity with the labor principle, and to trace its origin to the only family tree which could, allegedly, endow it with legitimacy.[20]

XI

JOHN RAE

1. Belated Recognition of Rae's Highly Original Ideas

JOHN RAE[1] belongs to a group, more numerous than it should be, of excellent economists who failed to attract the notice of their contemporaries, and whose importance was recognized only by later generations, after their forgotten discoveries had in the meantime been rediscovered by others and brought to general notice and discussion in an era more receptive to them.

It was on the subject of the theory of capital, more specifically, that Rae held a number of exceedingly original and remarkable views, and those views exhibit unmistakable similarity to views which were developed about a half century later by Jevons and myself. But it was those very parts of his doctrine which bear the stamp of originality, which his unheeding contemporaries passed by. There was one circumstance that might have been expected to assure his doctrine the widest and most rapid circulation. I am referring to the fact that that most brilliant and widely read author on political economy of his time, John Stuart Mill, quotes from Rae's book so widely and in such detail. But it is a strange fact that in all his numerous quotations John Stuart Mill never included any of the material which constitutes the essence of Rae's original ideas. He quotes, instead, merely ornamental incidentals, and even among those only the sort of thing that could be used to illustrate the traditional doctrines that Mill himself was presenting.[2] And since Rae's book seems to have been read in the original by only extremely few persons,[3] just the most interesting part of its contents remained unknown to his contemporaries. There was little likelihood that they, and even less that subsequent generations would be apprised by Mill's quotations of the importance of the book, or impelled to conduct any research into his quickly forgotten work.

Herein would seem to lie the explanation for the fact that even Jevons, who lived in England and possessed a thorough knowledge of the literature of economics, does not seem ever to have seen the book. At least I could not discover in Jevons's work the slightest indication that he was acquainted with Rae. Considering the close kinship that in many instances marks the opinions of the two authors, and in view of Jevons's unimpeachable integrity, it is impossible to doubt that there would have been such indications, if he had known Rae. At the time that my first edition of *Kapital und Kapitalzins* appeared, his book was completely unknown to me, too. I simply knew Mill's quotations from it, and these did not give me any grounds for believing that it was particularly significant.[4] Not until quite recently was Rae rescued from limbo by his compatriot C. W. Mixter, who wrote an extensive treatise,[5] in which he detailed the essential contents of his work. In it he also expressed the opinion that the main points in the modern theory of capital, which was later advanced by me, had already been anticipated by Rae. Rae, in fact, had presented it in a form that was more complete and less open to contravention.[6]

I welcome the opportunity which is offered me by the appearance of a new edition of my *History and Critique of Interest Theories,*[7] to fill in what is indubitably a gap in my first edition, with a detailed exposition of Rae's doctrine. I should not feel that I were fully meeting the obligations imposed by that task, if I did not go further. I feel that I must do with respect to Rae, just what I have done with respect to every other author whom I have discussed in this work, which is at once a history and a critique. That is to say, I feel compelled to add to my exposition of his views a critical appraisal of them. And I know the latter will not coincide in all respects with that of Mixter.

2. *Exposition of Rae's Interest Theory*

RAE, a Scot who had emigrated to Canada, wrote his book on theory as a basis for accomplishing practical results. On the question of free trade, which played an especially important role in the relations between Canada and the mother country, he was in decided disagreement with Adam Smith. To lend validity to his dissenting argument, he returned to first principles for his very profound theoretical inquiry, in the course of which he expatiates particularly on "the nature of stock and the laws governing its increase and diminution." That is the theme to which the second section of his book is devoted, the section which is the longest (*pp. 78 to 357*) and of primary interest to us. A far shorter section (*pp. 7 to 77*) is devoted to a proof of the proposition that "individual and national interest are not identical," while the even shorter third section (*pp. 358 to 386*) bears the title "Of the Operations of the Legislator on National Stock" and contains the application of theory to practice.[8]

As to the first section, the citing of a few remarks will serve our purpose. Rae first states that ways and means by which individual wealth can be acquired and increased are by no means the same as those which make a nation as a whole wealthy. Individuals enrich themselves by simple acquisition of goods already on hand, nations only through the production of previously nonexistent goods. "The two processes differ in this, that the one is *acquisition,* the other a *creation"* (*p. 12*). Even in his introductory remarks Rae emphasizes the enormous importance of intellectual progress, of inventions and of improvements for the welfare of nations. In a somewhat rhetorical turn of phrase he declares invention to be the sole power on earth which can be termed genuinely creative. Accordingly, the wealth of a nation, in contrast to that of individuals, cannot be augmented without cooperation by the "inventive faculty" (*p. 15*).

In his second section Rae pursues a strictly systematic, well-considered course of investigation which he develops point by point, in his attempt to track down the factors which create national wealth and cause it to increase and diminish.

He begins with the elements of the production of goods. Man has the ability to comprehend "the course of events and the connection of one with another." This faculty, which sets him apart from the lower animals, enables him, on the one hand, to predict his future needs and on the other hand, to provide for their future satisfaction, because by his intervention he can assure the creation of suitable means of meeting those needs. Herein Rae demonstrates his perfectly clear insight into the nature not only of the production, but also of the adaptation of goods. He quite correctly characterizes goods as "arrangements of matter" (*p. 81*) and makes the statement that, while we cannot change the "nature of things," we can change their form, and that we can "so alter the trains of events proceeding from them or depending on them," that they are themselves transformed into satisfactory means of meeting future needs, or that with their assistance such means can be created or brought within our control (*pp. 81-82*).

He introduces as a technical term peculiarly his own, the name "instruments." He uses the word in a much wider sense than is ordinarily associated with it in popular usage. It covers all those products resulting from human labor which serve to meet a future need. In other words, it covers not only durable goods but even consumption goods, provided they are meant to serve future needs. It would accordingly be applied even to consumption goods as quickly consumable as bread, applied, that is, up to the moment of actual consumption (*p. 88*). It would be used for lasting consumption goods also, such as hats (*p. 93*) or saddle horses (*p. 105*) even after use of them has already begun, so long as they are not completely consumed.[9] The pure gifts of nature, which come under consideration as the "materials" for human labor, belong in a category entirely different from that which embraces Rae's "instruments" (*pp. 92, 93, 99*).

All instruments necessarily possess certain characteristics in common. All instruments have come into existence, directly or indirectly, through labor. All of them, furthermore, produce or help to produce events which satisfy human wants and then are "exhausted." Rae's term for their power to produce these events, or for the amount of them is "capacity"[10] (*p. 92*). And finally, all instruments possess in common the characteristic that between their creation and their exhaustion *a period of time must elapse.* "This necessarily occurs because all events take place in time" (*p. 93*). The period of time may be short or long, may encompass years, months, or even shorter periods, but it must always be there.[11]

It now becomes necessary, says Rae, to have a measure by which to compare the capacity or the returns of the instruments with the direct and indirect labor which were required to produce them. Rae accepts labor as the measure. Hence "the events brought to pass by any instrument" are measured by the amount of labor to which they "are esteemed equivalent" in value by the owner of the instrument (*p. 92*). Rae holds the opinion—and we shall see that it is not entirely correct—that putting it this way "has no other effect than that of giving directness to our nomenclature." To justify his opinion he relies on the consideration that frequently the returns of the instruments are in actual fact measured in terms of labor, because they effect a direct saving of labor. Water mains, for instance, save the labor of carrying water and therefore "may be said indifferently, . . . either to supply a certain amount of water, or save a certain portion of labor" (*p. 92*). Rae makes use of this alternative method of expression on frequent occasions in later passages (*for instance, p. 171*).

On a subsequent occasion he finally adds that when we thus use labor as a measure by which to compute the "capacity" of goods, we are not really concerned with the physical and mental exertions of the laborer, but rather with the *wage* he receives. Rae, disregarding wage fluctuations which he is well aware actually do take place, treats that wage, for purposes of his theoretical investigation, as a given and constant quantity (*p. 97*).

In addition to the three characteristics already mentioned, which all instruments possess in common (creation through labor, capacity for useful services, time interval between formation and exhaustion), Rae feels it indispensable for the purposes of his investigation to assume another characteristic to be possessed in common, which it really is not, in the fullest sense. That is to say, if we compare, with respect to their capacity for rendition of service, several instruments which serve the same kind of needs, then we often measure them by the relative physical effects which the instruments produce. If, for instance, a cord of firewood of a certain kind will give exactly twice as much heat as a cord of firewood of another kind, then the "capacity" of the first is twice that of the second. And "if the one be equivalent to four, the other will be equivalent to exactly two days' labor." But there are numerous exceptional cases in which the relative capacity of instruments of the same kind depends on causes other than their purely physical characteristics.[12] Nevertheless, Rae says that it would be exceedingly difficult to treat the subject on any other assumption, and that he is therefore constrained to base the further development of his thesis on the hypothetical assumption that capacity *is* determined solely by the physical characteristics of the instruments. He compares it with such assumptions as that of the existence of purely mathematical lines, or that of the ab-

211

sence of friction, for purposes of a scientific examination of a mechanical problem, and contends that the assumption of presuppositions of that sort is necessary and legitimate (*p. 94*).

This leads Rae to a further and interesting comparison of relative and measurable magnitudes which involves the addition of a third factor when measuring the capacity of instruments in terms of labor required for their formation, or in terms of the cost of their formation. That third factor is the *time* which elapses between formation and exhaustion of the instruments. All three elements can be numerically expressed. And according to the varying relationships among them which are present in the different instruments, one may set up a "series of rankings" to some one of which it must be possible to assign every existing instrument. Rae explains the setting up of such a series (which really amounts to nothing more than ranking goods according to the percentage of return which creation or possession of them yields) in a way that is as unusual as it is abstract. He prefaces his explanation with the remark that "in conformity with a principle to be explained later," only such instruments are deliberately brought into existence as have a capacity which exceeds the amount of their labor cost. Furthermore, he makes the assumption, for the preliminary steps of his explanation, that not only the creation, but also the exhaustion of every instrument takes place at a single definitive point of time with respect to each.

If we make these presuppositions, it must be possible to find for every instrument a place in a series, the members or "orders" of which are governed by the length of time within which the instruments assigned to their respective places in the orders "issue in events equivalent to double the labor expended in forming them, or would issue, if not before exhausted." These members or orders may be represented by the letters *A, B, . . .* on to *Z, a, b, c,* and so on. Class *A* will comprise those instruments which are converted within a year into services of a value double that of the labor expended in creating them, or would be so converted if their exhaustion did not take place earlier. Class *B* then comprises those which, within a period of 2 years "issue in events equivalent to double the labor expended in forming them." In class *C* the time for reaching the doubling of the cost of formation is 3 years, for class *Z* it is 26 years, and so on. In general, Rae calls the classes which entail a shorter doubling time, so to speak, that is to say, class *A* and the ones named by the early letters, as "the more quickly returning orders" and later classes, toward the letter *Z* "the more slowly returning orders."

In actual practice, of course, the procedure seldom fits the neat round numbers of this abstract scheme. For one thing, the periods of time within which the instruments are exhausted are seldom measured in exact years, but rather run over frequently into fractional parts of a year. For another thing, the total capacity of an instrument is not exactly equivalent to double its cost, but rather is greater or smaller than double. Nevertheless the scheme is serviceable, requiring only certain adaptations, with respect to which Rae gives the following directions. If the capacity is exactly equivalent to double the cost, but the time period not an exact number of years, then the instrument belongs in an intermediate class which must be interpolated at a corresponding level of the scheme. Let us say an instrument lasts for 7½ years, then it belongs in a class between class *G* and class *H*. If the capacity of an instrument for service is exhausted before it has returned twice the amount of its cost, then one must make an imaginary prolongation of its duration to determine how long a period would elapse before its "issue" were twice its cost, assuming that the rate at which the return exceeded cost continued the same during the imagined period as it was during the actual period. Let us suppose, for instance, that someone forms an instrument at a cost of 2 days' labor and that this instrument is exhausted at the end of 6 months, after having delivered a return having a value of 2.828 days' labor. In such a case, if the amount by which the capacity exceeds the cost were to continue to augment in the same proportion, then the capacity would attain a magnitude of 4 by the end of a period of 12 months. "For 2.828 is a mean proportional between 2 and 4." Therefore the instrument would belong in class *A,* which attains a return of double the cost in one year (*pp. 102, 103*). It is necessary to follow an analogous procedure in the case of instruments whose total capacity amounts to more than double the amount of capital. In such cases the progress of their capacity must be traced backwards until the point in time be determined which (assuming a uniform rate of progression) would have marked the close of a period which would have been just sufficient for a product of exactly twice the value of the costs. That time period determines the assignment to the correct class in the scheme (*p. 103*).

Finally, there may arise a further complication in that the formation or the exhaustion may not, as was originally presupposed, take place at a single point in time, but that either or both may in actual fact be spread out over a more or less extended period. Indeed, that is usually the case. However, such periods of time always have, as it were, "a chronological center of gravity,"[13] about which the services are so distributed that the premature incidence of one part of them just offsets the retardation of another part. Such "centers" thus represent "the true period," that is to say the actual definitive point of time which marks the end of the formation or of the exhaustion, as the case may be[14] (*pp. 104, 105*). In the end Rae sums up all the factors which influence the classification of instruments within his system of returns in the following principle. The order to which an instrument is assignable ranks the more highly in just such measure as:

A] Its capacity for yielding returns is greater, or
B] Its cost is lower, or
c] The period of time between formation and exhaustion is shorter (*p. 108*).

As the alert reader will readily perceive, this whole matter of division into classes can also be described in other terms—terms in which we are far more accustomed to imagine and to express these phenomena.

In fact, they are terms which Rae himself employs, but not until he has reached a more advanced point in his book (*p. 195*). Quite simply, Rae's class *A* comprises those *goods* which yield an excess of return over cost of production which amounts to 100% per annum, and thus doubles its original value in the space of one year. Instruments in class *B* yield 41% per annum; those in class *C*, 26%; class *G*, 10%; class N, 5%; and so on.[15] And so Rae's system simply amounts to ranking goods in the order of the rate of return which they yield.

Having developed the fundamentals of his doctrine about instruments by means of this preliminary exposition, Rae approaches the problem which constitutes the purpose of his book and therefore engages his main interest. For he inquires into the causes which determine the aggregate of the instruments which a nation amasses and possesses. For it is this very aggregate which reflects the extent of the national wealth.

Rae is of the opinion that four such causes can be recognized. They are:

1] The quantity and quality of the "materials" which the nation possesses, that is to say, the natural resources which are at its command;
2] "The strength of the effective desire of accumulation";
3] The wage rate;
4] The advancement attributable to the inventive faculty (*p. 109*).

Rae does not have very much to say about the first and third of these causes.[16] But all the more detailed and the more original are his remarks anent the "desire of accumulation." But these, too, are preceded by the propounding of a law of economic experience which is very interesting from the standpoint of theory, and which is partly reminiscent of Thünen's doctrine, and partly marked by affinity with modern theories of capital.

If we suppose that the knowledge of man concerning the powers and qualities of materials remains unchanged, then the capacity which is communicated to those materials by their conversion into instruments "cannot be indefinitely increased . . . without moving the instruments formed continually onwards in the series, *A, B, C* etc.," that is to say, into classes of longer and longer "doubling periods." To put it in familiar parlance, the instruments yield a decreasing percentage of return. On the other hand, if the amount of knowledge once becomes quite extensive, then even if that amount remain stationary, the capacity which can be communicated to the materials is capable of indefinite augmentation *without forcing the instruments completely beyond the series A, B, C and so on*. Or in other words, the amount by which their capacity exceeds their cost, or the percentage of return, cannot be reduced to the vanishing point. To put it in Rae's own words, "there is no assignable limit to the extent of the capacity which a people having attained considerable knowledge of the qualities and powers of the materials they possess, can communicate to them without carrying them out of the series *A, B, C* etc., even if that knowledge remain stationary" (*p. 109*).

Rae <u>bases</u> the first half of this law on the following consideration. The capacity of instruments can be increased, through an increase either in their durability, or in their efficiency. Either the period of time during which they render useful services is prolonged, or the quantity of the services which they render within a given time is increased.

The durability of instruments can, as a rule, be augmented only by an increased expenditure of labor. Let us say that we increase the amount of labor which goes into the building of a house and thereby extend its useful life from the 30 years it would have lasted, to 60 years. The procedure would be tantamount to devoting that additional labor to the construction of a second house, good for 30 years' service, which would not begin to be used until after the first had collapsed. But since the additional labor must be performed now, there is a wide disparity, in point of time, between the expenditure of the costs involved and the receipt of the returns from the additional labor. And so those returns, even though they may exceed the cost, will nevertheless attain the "doubling point" only at a remote point in time. The action is therefore tantamount to the formation of an instrument belonging to an "order of slower return." The only conditions under which that would not obtain would arise if the additional labor which results in a definite prolonging of useful life, could be subject to continuous diminution in geometric progression. But that, as Rae very correctly remarks, would lead to an absurdity.[17]

With respect to the possibility of increasing the *efficiency* of materials by modification of the process of manufacture, it must be considered that eventually improvement along that line will inevitably encounter new or increased difficulties which can be overcome only by increased expenditure of labor. For there will be an initial tendency to process such materials first, as possess qualities which can most easily be availed of, and which produce the desired results with the greatest rapidity and in the greatest quantity. But since the supply of materials which a society possesses is limited, the members of that society must eventually deal with that factor. If, on the one hand, their knowledge does not increase, and if they nevertheless harbor a desire constantly to increase the quantity of the instruments which they fashion from those materials, they will eventually have to resort to materials which either offer greater difficulties in processing, or produce the desired results only less abundantly or less expeditiously. In all such cases the effectiveness of the instruments is accomplished at greater cost; in other words, the instruments must undergo a change in classification in the direction of "orders of slower return" (*pp. 112, 113*).

This change will be an early one, whenever the given technical science is in the first stages of development, or when men have not yet learned many ways of utilizing the materials and therefore soon exhaust their known methods of advantageous utilization. But in the advanced stages of technical development, when men have acquired a knowledge

215

of numerous methods and combinations by which a desired goal may be attained, the "tapering off" of efficiency will be a very gradual one. And although some methods will always prove to be more advantageous than others, in general the transition that necessarily ensues from the exhaustion of the most advantageous methods will signify only an adoption of the next most advantageous means of forming an instrument in a category that is only slightly inferior to the one which preceded (*p. 113*).

And when, finally, a knowledge has been acquired of a very large number of forces and qualities in a very large variety of materials, then the number of combinations in which those forces and materials can be caused to interact becomes, for practical purposes, infinite. It is a process analogous to the one by which mathematical quantities are capable of adding more and more digits, and so increasing until the capacity for combination attains infinity. This is the aspect which explains the second half of Rae's law to the effect that, in the case of nations which have attained a highly developed stage of technical advancement, there is no limit to the possibilities in the way of constant augmentation of its supply of instruments. The only exception to this absence of limitation is, as the first half of the law states, that the instruments, as they continue to increase in number, must successively be assigned to less and less advantageous categories (*p. 115*). Rae is of the opinion that this abstractly derived conclusion is confirmed by Great Britain's concrete experience. Her situation is certainly characterized by a development in the working up of her resources to an extent not surpassed by any other nation of our era. And yet there is certainly room for further development in this respect—so much room, that the calculable future offers no prospect of exhaustion (*p. 116*).

When technical development is held stationary, the degree to which the existent room for development is turned to practical account depends on the factor which Rae calls "the strength of the effective desire of accumulation." His discussion of this topic constitutes the subject matter of one of Rae's most interesting chapters (*p. 118 ff.*).

All instruments require for their formation the expenditure of a certain quantity of labor or of its equivalent, and they yield another, and greater, amount of labor or of its equivalent. The formation of every instrument, therefore, involves the sacrifice of a smaller present good. If the opinion is entertained that the creation of the future greater good is worth the sacrifice of the present smaller good, then the instrument is formed; in the absence of such opinion, it will not be formed. Under these conditions any society may well continue for a time to increase the number of instruments. Now such increase involves the relegation of the respective instruments to categories requiring increasingly longer periods before a given instrument returns double its value. The degree of relegation which a society is willing to put up with in the cause of that increase will depend on how long a period its members consider that it is worth while to wait, before the sacrifice of a present good returns to them twice as great a future good. If that willingness to wait extends as long as 1 year, or 2 years, or 3 or 20, then the formation

216

of instruments will multiply up to the point of relegation to class *A,* or *B,* or *C,* or *T* respectively. The point at which the willingness to make the sacrifice ceases, constitutes the point at which formation of the instruments must discontinue. The "determination" to sacrifice a given amount of present goods for the sake of acquiring another greater amount at a future time, is designated by Rae as the "effective desire of accumulation" (*p. 119*).

Rae proceeds to examine the motives which determine man's attitude on this question and the consequent strength of his acquisitive urge. His first conclusion is that two circumstances tend to make "most men place a far higher valuation on present than on future" benefits. One of these is the uncertainty and brevity of life, the other is the decrease in capacity for enjoyment which occurs in old age. Why should we providently amass goods which we shall not be able to enjoy until some future time which we may not live to see (or even one so remote that we surely shall not see it) or until a time when our capacity for enjoying them will be reduced (*pp. 119, 120*)? In addition, there is the fact that the prospect of an *immediate* pleasure engages our attention, stimulates our imagination, whets our desire far more potently than the prospect of *future enjoyment.* "There is no man perhaps, to whom a good to be enjoyed today, would not seem of very different importance, from one exactly similar to be enjoyed 12 years hence, even though the arrival of both were equally certain" (*p. 120*). And so if men, says Rae, consult only their own personal interests, the power of their "effective desire of accumulation" would be but slight, and only instruments with a short "doubling period" would be created (*p. 121*). But man's pleasures are not altogether unselfish. Man gives thought not only to his individual well-being, but also to that of his family, his friends, his country, his race. This causes those future goods which one can obtain by the sacrifice of present enjoyment, to lose the greater part of their "uncertainty and worthlessness." Consideration for those we leave behind us, or to express it in Rae's more general terms, "our social and benevolent affections" tend to strengthen materially our "effective desire of accumulation" (*p. 122*).

The extent to which our mental faculties constitute a further factor in this respect depends upon the potency with which they influence us in opposing the desire of the moment in favor of requirements for the future. Insofar as they stimulate us to awareness of such needs and to a proper recognition of their relative urgency, these faculties lend strong support to the impulse to provide for future wants (*p. 122*).

It is, furthermore, a general truth that the instinct of acquisition will be rendered more potent by any circumstances which enhance the likelihood that some provision we make for the future will benefit ourselves or others. Circumstances that have this effect include such things as a healthful climate, or a healthful, safe occupation. Conversely, sailors, soldiers or inhabitants of unhealthful regions are extravagant. The safety or insecurity of social conditions, or of the administration of law and order has a similar effect (*p. 123*).

For that minority of men which is governed by conscious motives at all, the conditions just mentioned are the principal ones which determine the relative value they place on present and future benefits. And they learn this preference during the period when their life habits are being formed. Those habits, once formed, take over the determination of their subsequent conduct, and assume command, as it were, over their former masters. The great majority of men, incidentally, does not form its habits through choice and deliberate direction, but simply conforms to the pattern furnished by environment, and follows the general course which society pursues in its methods of thought and behavior (*p. 123*). With respect to these there are very important differences between one nation and another which bring about other correspondingly great differences, in proportion to the relative progress the respective nations may have registered in the formation and accumulation of instruments. Rae gives an exposition and an explanation of his principle by means of a series of examples culled from history.

Then by a very strange transition Rae switches to a consideration of the exchange of goods, of the laws which govern it and of its tool, money. He takes as his point of contact the fact that every one makes an effort to exhaust the capacity of his instruments as rapidly as possible, because in that way they yield their return sooner. Insofar as the effort succeeds, they become instruments belonging to categories with short "doubling periods," which supplies a stronger stimulus to the accumulation and increase of instruments. It is from this point of view, says Rae, that we must assess the advantage of the *division of labor*. If everyone were to limit himself to a single branch of production, and hence to the formation of such instruments as are necessary to its operation, then the instruments would never be idle, and hence there would be a shorter time interval between their formation and their exhaustion. They would undergo a transfer to an "order of quicker return," which entails the possibility of increased accumulation and of better provision for the future needs of all society (*pp. 164, 165*). This view of the division of labor, which in the light of our modern concepts is highly prejudiced, appears so important to Rae that he devotes a special appendix (*pp. 352* ff.) to the defense of it. In it he attacks the views of Adam Smith who, as is commonly known, had explained the advantages of the division of labor on entirely different grounds.

But there is no division of labor without exchange, and therefore the latter must be taken into account as well. In this connection Rae develops a short but remarkable theory of price. It is a carefully and skillfully formulated *theory of replacement costs*. Assuming that the only element of cost is labor, things which cost equal amounts of labor are exchangeable on a basis of equality. But it cannot be said that the sole reason for the truth of this statement is that they have cost equal amounts of labor. A further reason lies in the fact that both are instruments for the satisfaction of future needs. And still another lies in the soundness of the assumption that they cannot be obtained for a lesser expenditure of labor. However, should this latter assumption prove false

218

—should the producer, for instance, have expended a given amount of labor only through inefficiency or ineptitude, then the purchaser will not pay a price equal to the labor which has actually been expended. So Rae modifies the formula of his price law by stipulating that, as far as labor is concerned, things are exchanged, not on the basis of the work *which has actually been performed,* but on the basis of the work *which it is necessary to bestow,* in order to produce equally suitable means of satisfying needs. Then Rae very aptly points out that wherever there has been a technical advance in the process of production, articles are no longer sold for the amount of labor they have actually cost, but rather for that smaller amount of labor which is now required for the production of the same article (*pp. 166-169*).

But in addition to labor the *element of time* is also "one of the items to be taken into account." Almost always we have, in addition to labor, instruments, materials, tools and the like which are used up or worn out. These must likewise be compensated for in the price of commodities. Furthermore, it is not sufficient that, in computing the price, consideration be given only to the labor that was expended for their production. Consideration must also be given to the time elapsing between the performance of that labor and its compensation in this price, and that must be done with due regard to the strength of the "effective desire of accumulation" which prevails at the time. Let us take as an example a loom which the weaver wears out in seven years. Let us further suppose the loom cost 100 days of labor. If the effective desire of accumulation in the individual in question has a "strength sufficient to carry him to the order *G*," then the operation of the loom requires compensation which will equal 200 days' labor at the end of a seven-year period, or, if received before that time, a compensation smaller in proportion to the reduction in time, but in any event in excess of 100 days. If the weaver, says Rae, were not morally certain that he could receive that much, he would not have formed the instrument, and if compensation at that rate did not continue, he would not replace the instrument (*pp. 169, 170*).

But even in cases in which apparently nothing but labor is being compensated, the time factor has its effect on the determination of price. For instance, if a laborer undertakes to fell the trees of a given parcel of woodland, and the performance of the task requires three months, the amount of the payment he receives will vary according to whether payment is made at the beginning or at the end of the three months' period. And the difference between the two amounts will be determined, just as it is in other cases, "by the particular orders to which instruments, in that particular situation, are generally wrought up" (*p. 170*).

This thought is accorded very interesting clarification by means of another statement which Rae makes a little later, although in a different connection. All instruments have the capacity to satisfy needs or save labor.[18] But these services lie in the future. And we certainly cannot place the same valuation on equal quantities of needs satisfied, or of labor saved regardless of whether we benefit by them tomorrow, or

219

in 5 years, or in 50. If we did, we should have to appraise as equal in value, 100 full-grown trees which will yield us 100 cords of firewood tomorrow, and 100 saplings which will not yield that much firewood for another 50 years. The natural standard by means of which to compare such goods one with another, or to find common expression for all in terms of quantity of labor, is furnished by the *relative estimate* as between present and future, which is made by the individuals concerned. In other words, that standard is furnished by the *strength of the effective desire of accumulation* which prevails in the society in question. If that desire of accumulation *is sufficiently strong to promote the formation of instruments as far as order E, with a doubling period of 5 years,* then an instrument which at the expiration of 5 years will yield a return equivalent to 2 days' labor, can properly be appraised as having a present value equivalent to 1 day's labor (*pp. 171, 172*).

In a subsequent passage (*p. 300*) he finally sums up his theory of price tersely and succinctly by saying that commodities are exchanged "for equal quantities of labor, reckoned according to the time when applied, and the actual *orders of instruments.*"*

It will perhaps not have escaped my very alert readers that in these various statements Rae has formulated a dual principle. He has alternated between two dissimilar ways of expressing the fact that time exerts an influence in determining price. I have pointed out the two alternatives by my use of italics. In some statements he enunciates the principle that the time factor demands compensation in proportion to the strength of the desire of accumulation which is present, either in the individual or the society concerned. In other words its influence depends on the potency of psychological factors. But again, in accordance with other statements, the measure of compensation is to be deduced from that class or order of return which marks the stage to which the formation of instruments has actually progressed in the society in question. These two principles are by no means identical, and Rae was very well aware of it. For the strength of the desire of accumulation is customarily at a stage more advanced than that which has been reached by the accumulation itself, since the latter is the effect of the former. Not until the desire of accumulation "has had time to operate" can it be fully overtaken by the actual accumulation.[19] However, that overtaking is always delayed by certain circumstances, among the most important of which, Rae says, are new inventions. These circumstances are responsible for an ever-recurring adjustment by which the gap, which threatened to close, is again widened between the stage actually attained by the accumulation process, and the one that the psychological factors represent to be attainable. At this point I am merely calling attention to this twofold character of Rae's formulation of the law of price. I am reserving the right to return to this point later, in my critical appraisal of his theory.

Money is now the medium in which we express all accounting opera-

* Translators' note: Italics by Böhm-Bawerk.

tions dealing with the return yielded by instruments in proportion to the time which elapses before it is received. Introduction of money in that capacity has made it possible to reduce all the operations to simple and uniform terms. Computation is in terms of per cent per annum.[20] The yield from instruments which are loaned out on credit is called "interest," that from instruments which are retained and used is called "profit of stock." By the term "profit" we designate, as a rule, the compensation for physical and mental exertion as well, on the part of the entrepreneur, and also for the risk he assumes. If these elements are eliminated, the customary rate of interest can be regarded as a suitable standard by which to measure the actual average rate of profit in a country. And it can, in logical consequence, be deemed to designate the order of return "at which instruments are there arrived" (*pp. 195, 196*).

Although the effective desire of accumulation varies widely in different individuals of the same nation, it is observable that in one and the same community all instruments belong to the same, or to nearly the same order of return. In more familiar terms it may be said that all capital yields approximately the same rate of interest. Rae offers the following explanation for this. Spendthrifts, or persons who, generally speaking, are possessed of a less potent "desire of accumulation" than is the average, can obtain in exchange for the instruments they own more than they are worth, according to their own appraisal of the relative value of present and future goods. So they sell those instruments, and gradually sink into poverty. Conversely, persons who are possessed of an acquisitive urge exceeding the average would be inclined to form instruments of a lower rate of return than that which is usual. However they find it unnecessary to do so because they can purchase from the spendthrifts the instruments, rejected by the latter, which yield a normal return. "They are the natural recipients of the funds passing from the hands of the prodigal, and their excess of providence balances his defect, and maintains the whole mass of instruments in the society, at nearly the same orders" (*p. 199*). This uniformity of the rate of return which is derived from instruments leads to the result that individual members of the community come to adopt that rate as a standard by which to judge their business enterprises. And so a business which promises to yield the prevailing rate of return is regarded as profitable and is engaged in. A business that does not promise to yield that rate, people will not engage in, and they will term it an unprofitable or a losing business. To be sure, these characterizations, as Rae very aptly adds, are not entirely accurate, and in any event have only very relative validity and are limited in their applicability to a given country and a given era (*pp. 205, 206*).

In addition to the desire of accumulation there is another powerful factor which is operative, and that is the *advancement attributable to the inventive faculty*. Rae's observations on the subject are of great interest, generally as well as historically speaking. However, the limita-

221

tions of our topic lead us to concern ourselves principally with the way in which technical progress influences, first, the extent of a country's wealth and, second, the rate of interest that prevails.

The essence of technical inventions consists for the most part in the discovery of new or more suitable materials, or of useful properties in them, or methods of processing them that were previously unknown. In the last-named field especially, the advances of science play an especially important part (*p. 224 ff.*). The first result of advancement is always to make labor more productive, in that we either achieve a greater result from the same labor, or attain the same result with the expenditure of less labor. At this point we must bear in mind that Rae at the outset postulated what he termed the theoretically indispensable presupposition, that instruments are to be appraised in terms of their physical productiveness.[21] To the extent that this presupposition has validity, there follows a second result, which is that the instruments, in consequence of the improved ratio between capacity and costs, are promoted to "more speedily returning orders" (*pp. 258, 259*). And as a matter of fact this result, though at the beginning it applies only to those instruments which are immediately affected by the invention, very soon extends to all the instruments which the community possesses. For instance, if the bread-baking industry registers some improvement which makes it possible to produce equally good bread with an expenditure of half the former cost in labor, or in fuel, the benefit of this advance would not fall to the bakers exclusively but would be spread throughout the entire community. "The bakers would have a small additional profit, the whole society would have bread for the product of somewhat less labor, and all who consumed bread, that is, every member of the society, would from the same outlay have somewhat larger returns. The whole series of instruments owned by the society would be somewhat more productive, would be carried to an order of quicker return" (*p. 259*).

And thus, by promoting the total mass of instruments to "more productive orders," every invention brings about an increase in what Rae calls that nation's "absolute capital and stock." By that he means capital measured by the ideal yardstick which Rae posited previously for the valuation of all instruments serving future needs (*His p. 172, foregoing p. 219 f.*). Let us suppose that instruments are appraised at a value equal to their future yield, this amount, however, being converted to an amount of present labor computed at the prevailing ratio for present to future values. If an advancement occurs which effects a doubling of the yield, and if there is no change in the "desire of accumulation," the result must be a valuation of the instruments at double their previous figure or, in other words, a doubling of the absolute capital which the instruments represent. But ordinarily people value their instruments by a different measure, since they compare them, one with another, in terms of their reciprocal exchangeability. To do so, they avail themselves of one particular good as a standard by which all instruments are to be compared with each other, namely, money. A valuation according to that measure, that is to say according to exchangeability, leads to the concept of *"relative* capital" or *"relative* wealth" (*p. 172*). This relative capital is not increased directly by inventions. For improvements bring about a direct increase, not in the mass of instruments but only in the capacity of the existing mass. And if the increase affects all instruments uniformly, there would be no apparent reason for any modification of the exchangeability that marked their previous relationship to each other. And even if they should not all be affected equally by the given improvement, the only result will be that some instruments will command a greater number of instruments of other kinds than had previously been the case. But that simply means that the latter have suffered a corresponding decrease in exchange value. The total "relative or exchangeable value" of the national wealth remains unchanged (*p. 260*).

Nevertheless there are three circumstances which demonstrate that the increase in the absolute wealth has real significance.

The first is that the members of the community have a more abundant provision for future needs.

The second is that the state of the economy of the country in question undergoes an improvement in comparison with that of other nations.

The third is that *indirectly* there is an augmentation of the totality of instruments, or of the national wealth. For technical improvements render it possible to utilize in the productive process materials which were previously ignored because they lent themselves less readily or not at all to processing. That results in making more numerous the kinds of thing which are capable of being worked up, and hence in augmenting the totality of instruments which can be gained from the country's resources. That, in the end, brings about an increase in the grand total of exchangeable value which the increased mass of existing instruments represents, or in other words, an increase in the nation's "relative capital." How large this increase is depends entirely on the quantity and quality of "materials of the next lower grades," which are now, because of the improvement, made available for processing. At times even a slight improvement can promote the availability of a large quantity of material to the range of the prevalent desire of accumulation. On other occasions a very considerable advance may result in only a slight augmentation of the existing instruments (*pp. 262, 263*).

Unless opposing forces are operative, the introduction of improvements will result in a high rate of return for the reasons indicated in the foregoing paragraphs. And a high rate of return which is attributable to such cases is indicative of the occurrence of a direct increase in the absolute capital of a nation, and it will lead, in the manner I have just indicated, to a resultant increase in its relative capital. But a high rate of return must be expected, too, in a country in which the effective desire of accumulation is weak. But in that case it must be interpreted quite differently. It is in that case indicative, neither of any growth in the income of the members of the community, nor of an imminent increase in its relative capital (*p. 263*).

Finally Rae devotes some consideration to negative forces which are inimical to an increase in national wealth. Chief among these he rates indulgence in luxuries, and waste. Waste may stem from the actions of individuals or of states (war!). It is of scientific interest to note his segregation of goods into "utilities" and "luxuries." He classifies goods as utilities to the extent that they are valued for those physical properties which render them suitable for the satisfaction of genuine needs. He says goods are luxuries to the extent that they are valued for their suitability for satisfying our vanity (*Table of Contents, p.* xv). It is the luxury articles of which Rae said at the beginning (*p. 94*) that they were not amenable to his theoretical presupposition that goods are mutually comparable and relatively valuable according to their physcial properties. In their casc, valuation is predicated, not on their suitability to the satisfaction of real needs, but on their costliness (*p. 305 et al.*).

A consideration of the combined effect of all the circumstances which influence the nature and the production of goods finally brings Rae to a concise contrast of the methods of operation of the two chief forces, the "inventive principle" and the "accumulative principle." The former extends human power and increases national wealth by promoting the instruments which make up that wealth to orders of quicker return. The "accumulative principle" induces men to widen the range of processes which they include in their operations, and it enhances wealth by raising the capacity of instruments already formed, or by working up new materials. Thus, in direct contrast to the "inventive principle" it moves instruments toward classification in orders of slower return (*pp. 321, 322*).

3. Critique of Rae's Doctrine

IF WE are to form an unbiased judgment of Rae's achievements in our own field, we must, above all, keep in mind that Rae's interests and purposes were concerned with something other than an explanation of interest. His concern is the augmentation of national wealth. He pursues his profound investigations in all fields to the point where they yield something that he can apply to his central theme. It is from that point of view that he treats some questions which are related to interest, and among those questions the most prominent is the one that concerns his classification of instruments on the basis of their varying rate of return. The rate of return of this or that instrument marks a rate of interest, to be sure. But Rae is less interested in the influence exerted on the interest rate, than he is in the fact that the variability of the "returning order" exerts an influence on the total mass of instruments which can be created, and hence on the amount of "national wealth." Rae treats the question of interest only because, and only insofar as it is incidental to the course of his principal inquiry, and this leads to a peculiar lack of uniformity in his treatment of interest. Those premises of the problem which are at the same time premises for his views on the increase of national wealth, are worked out with great thoroughness and attention to detail. Such a premise, for instance, is found in the factors determining "effective desire of accumulation." On the other hand, those premises which concern the question of interest purely as a problem of distribution he disposes of with laconic brevity. Thus the whole matter of determining exchange values and prices is compressed into four pages (*pp. 166-170*). It is also highly characteristic that the matter of the wage rate is deliberately ignored. And yet the undeniable inter-relationship between wage rate and interest rate ought to have constituted a factor indispensable to any treatment of the problem of distribution. But Rae merely accepts it as a given and constant quantity (*pp. 97, 130 f.*). As a further consequence it may be noted that, while Rae displays phenomenal thoroughness and continuity when he marshals his ideas for the treatment of his main theme, those qualities are not always in evidence when he touches on and disposes of something that is for him only incidental. And for Rae the question of interest is just that—an incidental problem of distribution.

Rae's remarks on the problem of interest seem to show two lines of reasoning. The first of these seems to account for interest as a result of the influence of time on the valuation of goods and needs. Although Rae has not made a unified presentation of his line of reasoning but leaves it to be pieced together from statements made from time to time, yet the reasoning itself is completely logical, and its content might be summarized as follows. Since the frailty of man subjects us mortals to the brevity and uncertainty of life, since we may expect to suffer a diminution of our capacity for enjoyment, and since, finally, the present has greater attractiveness for us than has the future—we therefore lay greater store by present joys and needs, and hence also by the means of satisfying present needs, than we do by future joys, future needs and future means of satisfaction. Because we place this higher valuation on the present, we should not consider ourselves adequately compensated for a present sacrifice in labor or goods, if we received, in the course of production, a future compensation merely equal to the present sacrifice. Indeed, we consider our present sacrifice equalized only if the future yield of production exceeds the present sacrifice of production in at least the same proportion as that in which we place higher value on the present than on the future. If the price of a product does not include compensation which is adequate in these terms, the production of any given article would be abandoned (or not undertaken, as the case may be) and so, in the long run, a price rate is of necessity established which will meet two requirements. It must reimburse the entrepreneur for his expenditures, and yield a surplus value which is satisfactory in terms of the prevailing appraisal of the relative value of present and future goods. That surplus value must also satisfy the appraisal prevalent in the society concerned as to the acceptable length of time within which expenditures are to be reimbursed. That surplus value becomes originary interest.[22]

This line of reasoning contains a great and an original step forward, in comparison with several attempts found in earlier writings. As we know, Galiani and Turgot had already coined occasional catch-phrases which hinted at a connection between interest and a difference in the estimation of present and future goods. However, they did not develop the idea nor even adhere to it.[23] This is perhaps the best place at which to inject the remark that the famous utilitarian, Bentham, later expressed the same idea with complete clarity, but also failed to develop it into a theory of interest and to work it out in detail. For in one of his philosophical works he sets up the specifically psychological premise that the "value" of gratification is enhanced or diminished, depending partly on the time interval which intervenes before the gratification is realized.[24] And he establishes a relationship between this psychological fact and the phenomenon of interest by a remark, made in a different connection, to the effect that two equal sums of money are not of the same value if one of them is payable immediately, and the other at the expiration of the tenth year from the same date; and that, at an interest rate of 5%, the value of the second sum is but half that of the first.[25] And in one of his works on economics he has left us a statement that is a veritable gem for clarity and pertinence. He says the lending of money at interest is nothing but the exchange of present for future money.[26] Nevertheless, Bentham has left us in doubt as to whether he meant to derive the principle of interest from the psychological premise mentioned above, or conversely, to derive that premise from the obvious existence of interest.[27] At any rate, he made no attempt to develop any further the intermediate steps between that psychological premise and the phenomenon of interest—especially originary interest—and so Bentham did not contribute in any materially greater degree to the development of the theory of interest than did his predecessors Galiani and Turgot. It may be noted in addition, that the fortuitous course of events prevented Bentham's interesting and stimulating idea from having the slightest effect on subsequent literary contributions to the theme. Marked as was the influence of Bentham's hedonistic philosophy in general on the contemporary British school of economic thought, that detail in his psychological doctrine seems nevertheless to have escaped attention. At least I can discover no unmistakable evidence of his literary influence on any writer earlier than Jevons. With respect to Rae in particular, the lack of any definite evidence forces me to leave completely open the question as to whether Rae knew those statements of Bentham's at all, and whether he was at all influenced thereby.[28]

At any rate, Rae is the first to give the seeds contained in those thoughts the benefit of carefully reasoned and unified development. At the same time that development fills out, in another direction, a framework, the outlines of which had been sketched by Smith, Ricardo and Malthus, but only in inadequate and slogan-like utterances. For these authors had pointed out that the capitalist necessarily has an interest in the growth of capital and in its productive employment, and that the growth of capital must cease and wither if commodity prices do not provide for interest.[29] But it remained for Rae to invest all these superficial observations with a content that permitted the construction of a genuine theory.

I should like to make an observation at this point, anticipatory in nature perhaps, to indicate Rae's position with respect to later developments in the literature on interest. Even if this line of reasoning had been Rae's only contribution, he would have anticipated approximately what Jevons maintained 37 years later, along very general lines, concerning the theme of present and future values. He would have anticipated exactly what Launhardt and Sax taught, another 15 years later, on the subject of originary interest, though their application of the Jevons principle was rather mechanical. And Rae would, finally, have anticipated some ideas that occurred to me in the earliest stages of my research into the causes underlying originary interest—ideas, however, which had failed to satisfy me as a completely adequate solution of the problem.

For I consider it entirely correct to think of interest as having its ultimate roots in a difference in our estimation of present and future goods. I also consider it quite correct to say that the purely psychological reasons that Rae sets forth for this difference in valuation are a very material factor. But I consider it equally unquestionable that these reasons cannot supply an exhaustive explanation of the phenomenon of interest as it in fact exists. And Rae, as well as Jevons, knew that too. Our factual experience leaves no room for doubt that the interest rate and the fluctuations in it are subject to other factors beside our realization of the brevity and insecurity of human life and of our capacity for enjoyment, as well as our greater susceptibility to the joys of the moment. These are the purely psychological factors. But there are also technological methods of production which influence interest. I am referring to those factual experiences which induced one group of interest theorists which we have already discussed to postulate an independent "productivity of capital." The difficulty is—and indeed, I think it is at once the greatest and the most stimulating difficulty of the whole problem of interest—the difficulty is, to explain in what manner, and by the employment of what intermediary processes those heterogenous component elements (they include objective technical factors, and highly subjective psychological motives) combine and cooperate to produce that end result which we know as the homogeneous phenomenon of interest. Perhaps the best thing I can do to clarify Rae's position on this question is to attempt, again by way of anticipation, to sum up in a phrase or two, and so characterize the position of the writers subsequent to Rae, who were impelled to treat the question. And as a matter of fact, I shall reverse the chronological order and begin with my own theory.

I wish to make an effort at this point to expound a conviction concerning the facts of the technique of production. I am considering them in the light of the higher physical productivity which results from roundabout methods of production which consume more time. That conviction is that those facts themselves constitute part of the reason for valuing less highly than present goods the future goods which it becomes possible to acquire through the adoption of just those time-consuming, more productive, roundabout methods of production. According to that conviction then, the technological and the psychological factors combine

227

forces at the very outset to work toward the attainment of a common objective, namely, the higher valuation of present goods than future goods. This objective then stands as an explanatory link between the partial causes which bring it about and interest which eventuates as a further consequence.[30]

Jevons on the other hand seems to have neither perceived nor discovered any possibility that there might be any common characteristic, in the way of explaining interest, possessed by both the factual technological factors of production and the purely psychological factors. Hence he offers a double-barreled eclectic explanation, of which neither barrel is capable of exploding the opinions of the old school. He adduces the technological factors of production along the lines of the old productivity theory. In his exposition the time interval between initiation and termination of the production process is the only factor that is convincingly portrayed as having causal influence on the magnitude of the physical yield. And finally, he exploits the psychological factors only to explain interest under the old shibboleth of "abstinence." Alas! the brilliant and original discoveries concerning the psychological reasons for a higher valuation of present than of future goods are allowed to wither on the vine.[31]

Launhardt and Sax do not seem to have felt that there was any need at all of including the technological facts of production among the requirements for an explanation of the phenomenon of interest as it actually exists. While Jevons prepared but failed to utilize the elements of a partial explanation, these two authors, doubtless quite at variance with the intention of their exemplar, were content to use those elements as the sole basis of an explanation purporting to solve the entire problem of originary interest.[32]

Rae, finally, recognized quite correctly that in addition to psychological considerations operative in the human mind, there are certain objective and factual elements of the methods of production which have something to do with originary interest. He knows, for instance, and specifically states, that even where the status of the psychological factors remains entirely unchanged, the interest rate is apt to rise when an improvement takes place in technological production methods. For that reason Rae set up, in addition to the first line of reasoning based on purely psychological factors, a second line based on *technological* elements. And yet I feel that this is the Achilles heel of his doctrine. In this respect my opinion differs from that of Mixter.[33] Rae did not master the difficulties presented by the problem in this regard. Like so many before him, and like even Jevons after him, Rae took for granted, somewhat offhand and superficially, that a mere physical increase in production is identical with an increased excess in value over the costs of production. By so doing he prematurely interpreted considerations which can explain only an increase in production, as an adequate explanation of the phenomena of surplus and interest. In this part of Rae's work it is especially apparent, as I have noted before, that the explanation of originary interest was not the principal objective of Rae's theo-

retical research. Rae makes light of certain inquiries which are essential
only for the problem of distribution and not for that of production, and
does not furnish his readers nor require of himself an unremitting pursuit of them to a logical conclusion. Thus, gaps in his logic or discrep-
ancies between his stopping place in an interrupted line of reasoning,
and his point of resumption, or finally, out and out contradictions, can
escape detection more easily than would have been the case if Rae had
made the problem of interest his chief theoretical concern, and had
tested and welded, link by link, the chain of reasoning which was to
connect the empirical facts to the explanation of originary interest.

Rae introduces the technological factor into his psychological explanation of interest at two points. The *first* of these involves an explanation, on technological grounds, of the necessity for putting up with
progressively diminishing surplus value, when there is an absence of
new invention. Rae says the explanation lies in the limited scanty supplies of first quality materials, and in the necessity to take recourse to
ever poorer materials for the production of instruments, so that the
same yield of production is possible only at an increase in labor or costs,
and as a result, there is a smaller excess of "capacity" over costs.[34]

The *second* involves an adaptation of a rule encountered in the
psychological line of reasoning. It is the rule which provides that the
rate of interest must correspond to the psychological "strength of the
desire of accumulation." That rule he now modifies, on technological
grounds as before, so that in its altered form it provides that the rate
of interest must correspond to the order of return to which the actual
accumulation so far attained has raised the production of instruments.
Here especially, Rae has the "inventive principle" play its part. Since
the success of inventions lies in their ability to endow instruments with
enhanced capacity from the same amount of labor, therefore the excess
of capacity over costs is augmented, and accordingly the instruments
move up into orders of shorter doubling time, or in other words, of a
higher percentage of return. But as long as there are instruments of a
higher percentage of return to be constructed, even those people whose
"strength of the effective desire of accumulation" would allow them to
descend to the formation of instruments of a lower order, would now
not do so. And as long as that is so, in all business calculations, in
the setting of prices and of the generally acceptable rate of return, the
psychological "desire of accumulation" will not be the determining factor.
The chief consideration will be the enhanced actual yield of whatever
order of instruments has been arrived at under a system of graduated
utilization of the best facilities of production. Accordingly, in most of
the pertinent passages of his book Rae substitutes for "strength of the
effective desire of accumulation," as the factor which determines interest, the "actual order at which instruments are arrived" or "to which
instruments are generally wrought up."[35]

It is readily apparent that Rae is here placing the factual aspects of
the technological methods of production in the forefront of his explanation. And it is no less obvious that he does so in a way that is most

229

strikingly similar to corresponding arguments found in Thünen. Thünen, too, advanced as a technological reason for successive reductions in the interest rate the fact that after the most profitable production facilities are exhausted, "continued creation of capital must devote itself to implements of lesser effectiveness." But this is not the only principle that is enunciated by both authors in almost the same words. Even Thünen's formula that the prevalent rate of interest is determined by the profitableness of the "most recently invested fraction of capital," is obviously only another form of expression for Rae's thought. Rae says the capacity for yield of that particular order of instruments at which one has arrived through the graduated utilization of the most advantageous facilities of production determines the usual rate of interest.[36] It becomes our duty in the case of Rae, as it was in the case of Thünen, to ask whether the premises in the field of technological methods of production were utilized in a manner to attain the purpose for which the premises were originally posited. That purpose was the achievement of a genuine and truly adequate explanation of that which Rae intended to explain. We were constrained to answer that question in the negative with respect to Thünen. We find it just as impossible to render an affirmative decision with regard to Rae.

It is the same old story that was told by the productivity theorists. There is a constant confusing of the production of physical quantities and the production of value. This substitution of one for the other permeates the whole thinking of Rae, and strangely enough, in part consciously and in part unconsciously. The vehicle for this confusion is the concept of "capacity" and the term "return" which is often used as a synonym of "capacity." In the official definition capacity is first defined as a purely technical term. On page 92 he says, "All instruments produce events or contribute to production of events which satisfy human needs. Their power to produce such events, or the amount of them, we shall call capacity." That is to say, capacity is great or small according to whether many or few needs are satisfied or, in the case of producers' goods rather than consumers' goods, whether many or few products result from the use of the instrument. This technical sense of the word capacity is illustrated by examples in numerous passages. A fruit tree bears fruit, a field yields a harvest, an aqueduct gives water (*p. 92*). In the same way the manner in which the capacity of goods may be increased is illustrated on page 109 ff. on a downright technological and physical basis. One may either lengthen the period of time during which the instruments render their services, or one may increase the quantity of the services which the instrument renders within a given time. The greater capacity of macadamized roads is illustrated by the fact that they permit use by 200,000 vehicles. And on page 259 Rae illustrates the principle that the improvement resulting from inventions brings greater returns from the same expenditure by citing the case of the improved plow which makes possible the plowing of a larger piece of land without any increase in labor or draft animals. In short, capacity of an instrument is a technological magnitude to be measured in terms of the quantity of satisfactions or of products resulting from the employment of that instrument.

But in addition, Rae is constantly—and inconstantly—applying the *value* term capacity to the amount of *value* which the products or services yielded by an instrument represent. He introduces this modification by remarking that it is necessary to have a standard for comparing the capacity or the returns of an instrument with labor expended on the creation of the instrument. He accepts labor as such a standard, and labor in terms of its exchange value, that is to say, wages. Therefore the capacity of an instrument is considered by Rae to be greater or smaller, according to whether its services are equivalent to more or less wages or, in other words, represent a larger or smaller amount of value. He does not seem to be aware at first that he is thereby creating a second concept of "capacity," which has an inherently different content. For he adds to this modified definition of "capacity," the statement that he is merely clarifying his terminology (*p. 92*). But later on he makes a remark which may be construed as a conscious justification for identifying physical productivity with productivity of value, and which probably is meant by Rae as such a justification. For he states that his explanations necessarily are based on the assumption that man values his instruments in accordance with their physical qualities, that is to say, on their physical ability to produce; and furthermore that such an assumption is in conformity with reality, the sole exception being luxury goods which serve only man's vanity.[37]

At the same time, however, Rae sets up a contrary rule of value within his own system. For he maintains that the value of goods is determined by their *costs of reproduction.*[38] Rae's laconic and somewhat disjointed utterances do not afford any definite explanation of the relationship in Rae's own mind between these two divergent rules of valuation. It is one of many such points in Rae's work. What I consider most likely is that after the fashion of the day, Rae had before him a twofold concept of value—something akin to a use value (though I have not found the expression "use value" itself anywhere in his book) to which the rule about valuation according to physical qualities was to apply, and an exchange value (and Rae uses that specific name for it) which follows the law of reproduction costs. Be that as it may, it is incontestable that the phenomenon of surplus value, which leads to originary interest, arises from a difference in the *exchange value* of product and costs. It is equally unquestionable that the fluctuations in the exchange value of the product under varying conditions of production will by no means correspond to the changes in its physical quality or its usefulness. But Rae is misled by the double meaning of his term "capacity," which really has the triple meaning of physical capacity, use value and exchange value. Hence, reasoning which could prove a case only for physical capacity is extended by Rae, without benefit of intermediate steps, to conclusions relating to amounts of value and surpluses of exchange value. Presenting data as evidence which are taken entirely from the field of technology, such as the quality of materials worked up, increased knowledge about the properties of materials and natural processes and the like, Rae makes the increase or decrease of physical capacity plausible. But then without ado he interprets this as equivalent to a corresponding increase or decrease of value, to a greater or lesser excess of exchange values over costs, and to a corresponding progression or retrogression of the instruments in Rae's "series of orders." But these "series of orders" are nothing but a classification of goods according to the percentage of excess value which these goods return to their owners over and above the value of their costs.

This reasoning is of course entirely fallacious and can be easily and clearly proven to be so, as was the case with respect to the details of the two aforementioned lines of reasoning by which Rae incorporates the technological element of production in the theory of interest.

Rae claims that the decrease in the rate of interest in the case of increasing accumulation of capital is explicable by virtue of the necessity for taking recourse to materials which are increasingly more fractious and more difficult to work up. The result is that instruments of the same efficiency can be produced only at greater cost. "That means," says Rae "that they have to move into orders of slower return."

However, "that means" in truth something quite different. If people make instruments of more stubborn material—for instance, if they raise herds or grow turnips or grain on less fertile soil, then, in the absence of any change in technological knowledge, there will certainly be an increase in the direct and indirect labor costs of producing an equal quantity of "instruments" or products, such as a bale of wool or a hundredweight of grain. But in that case, according to Rae's own law of the costs of reproduction, the bale of wool or the hundredweight of grain will now acquire a higher value than before, although its "physical efficiency" or "capacity" remains unchanged. And so, if the capacity is valued in accordance with the quantity of labor, or of wages which are its equivalent (and again we are following Rae's own rule),[39] then the increased costs are offset by an increased amount of value represented by the capacity of the instruments. And there is nothing in Rae's doctrine that proves, or even makes it seem probable, that value of the product will rise in a lesser ratio than the costs have risen. Indeed, Rae's law of cost of reproduction would lead us to expect, on the contrary, that the value of the product would necessarily rise in the same proportion as the costs, in which case there would be no understanding why the excess of the value of the product over the costs should be smaller, and so why the rate of return yielded by the instruments in question should fall. But Rae does not enter into any demonstration of this rather delicate question as to why the value of the product may have risen in a smaller proportion than have the costs. And that is because his failure to discriminate between physical capacity and value capacity misleads him into thinking he has arrived at his goal, when he has done nothing but show that the same quantity of product now represents greater costs.

Ricardo had been more perspicacious on this point. It is easy to recognize in Rae's train of thought an affinity with that very "law of diminishing returns" by which Ricardo wants to explain the tendency toward a declining interest rate. Only Rae put the law in somewhat more general and more abstract terms by speaking of a universal necessity for taking recourse to less productive "materials," while Ricardo, sticking to more concrete terms, pointed only to the most important and principal instance, namely, the compulsion to make use of ever less productive *land.* But Ricardo carefully and correctly kept in mind that the increase in the quantity of labor required to effect production of the same quantity by no means, in and of itself reduces interest. He realized that, on the contrary, the value of that quantity of product would necessarily rise, and indeed rise in the same proportion as the quantity of labor rose, which was required for its production. And he kept in mind, further, that only because wages would under the given conditions necessarily rise as well, would there be a decrease in the excess of the value of the product (a value risen in smaller degree) over the costs of production (costs risen in greater degree) and hence a decrease in the rate of interest.[40] This idea (which admittedly does not lead to any solution, as we have seen) was entirely foreign to Rae, who deliberately and expressly states that in his discussions wages are assumed to be a given and constant quantity.[41]

What Rae has to say about the relationship between new inventions and an increase in the rate of interest is hardly any better as an explanation of that problem. Let us suppose that a brilliant invention makes it possible to produce with the same amount of labor as before, 10 times as large a quantity of a given product. Ruling out the possibility of a monopoly, which Rae does not seem to have in mind at any point, it is certainly impossible to maintain that the product would represent 10 times as great an amount of value, and that it would yield 10 times as large an excess over the cost of the instrument itself, whereby the latter would be correspondingly advanced to an order of quick return. Rather is it the case that the value of the product would decline, in accordance with the principle expressly enunciated by Rae on page 168 in his theory of price, and would fall to a point determined by the reduced labor costs. Furthermore, I cannot see that it follows, nor *why* it follows, that where value and costs are thus equally reduced, the difference between them, which is the source of interest, should have become any greater than before.

In the case of inventions the lowering of the value of the consumers' goods affected by the invention is such a conspicuous and notorious phenomenon that Rae could not avoid taking notice of it. The passage in which he does so—a total of 16 lines—is especially worthy of note because it is the only one in which he touches, though but extremely lightly, on the really essential point of the problem of interest. For he makes the statement that although the effects of improvements "directly and initially" extend only to the improved instruments, "they very soon extend to the entire mass of instruments which society possesses." And then follows the example which I cited above (*p. 222*) of the technological progress in bread baking which brings the bakers "only a small increase in returns" but cheaper bread to all members of society, and thus a somewhat larger return for the same expenditure, and which thus promotes all instruments possessed in society to orders of higher return.

What actually takes place, and what Rae has in mind is, quite obviously, that the value of bread, as a result of the reduced cost of production, decreases in accordance with the established law of exchange value. To the extent that this decrease takes place, the two capacities between which Rae failed to discriminate go separate ways. The *physical* capacity of bread, that is to say, its ability to satisfy human needs, remains undiminished, but its capacity in terms of value is reduced. Incidentally, this furnishes convincing evidence of the fact that the introduction of the factor of value into the concept of capacity is, after all, something more than a mere clarification of terminology. In such measure as the law of exchange values becomes operative, there is reciprocal cancellation of the forces on which Rae's explanation relies to bring about a rise in the interest rate. For while the exchange value of bread is falling in proportion to the reduction in its costs, the yield of course provides no greater margin in excess of costs than before, the instruments of bread baking are *not* promoted to a higher order of return, and the rate of interest is *not* raised.

To be sure, Rae adds two remarks which, in his opinion, probably are supposed to indicate an avenue of escape from the dilemma which would otherwise explode his theory. As a matter of fact, they do no such thing. His first claim is that the tendency of invention to bring about a higher interest rate, though it is gradually cancelled with respect to bread by the falling bread prices, is extended in compensatory fashion to all the other instruments which society possesses. Now it is patently erroneous to maintain that the advantage which the public enjoys by reason of cheaper bread assumes the form of higher interest earned by property. In the first place, the advantage is enjoyed not by property owners only but by the workers as well, for whom the cheapening of consumers' goods represents a genuine rise in wages. And in the second place, whether or not that advantage is really the result of an exchange of goods, there is still nothing in Rae's line of reasoning that can explain an increase in the yield of those goods above their cost. Rae has simply become a victim once more of the self-deception that arises from his failure to distinguish between physical productivity and productivity of value. If everyone gets more bread in exchange for his own goods than before, then it is of course possible to maintain, in a certain sense, that the *physical* capacity of all goods has been increased, because by handing them over one can satisfy a greater amount of needs. And one can even maintain further that the *real exchange value* of those goods has increased, inasmuch as the exchange ratio of all classes of goods has improved in relation to *one* class—bread—and has remained unchanged with respect to all other classes, so that their overall exchange value is a trifle improved. But all that is not sufficient grounds for maintaining that improvement of ratio between the yield of the instrument and its cost of production or its own value has been effected to the extent that is required for a promotion to an "order of quicker return." For the same slight improvement in real exchange value which comes to every class of goods other than bread, is applicable to their producers' goods, including the commonest producers' good, labor. And therefore the very same kind and the very same degree of increases in value occur on both sides of the revenue statement, the "cost" side as well as the "income" side, and I simply cannot see how a situation like that can lead to an increase in the excess of yield over costs.

But Rae hints at a second point. He says the bakers would still retain "a small additional profit." In these words for the first time in his whole book, I believe, and then only by way of bare assertion, Rae touches on the point which ought to have constituted the core of any attempts at explanation, if there is to be a clear-sighted theory of interest. If there is a "leveling" law for cost, why does competition stop at a point that is still above cost? That is the question we have had to put one after the other, to all the productivity theorists in the most varied versions, adapting each version to the individual nature of the particular doctrine, beginning with Lauderdale and his labor-saving looms and continuing right down to Strasburger with his compensation for the forces of nature. And now we must put that question to Rae as well. "Why must the bakers, despite the 'leveling' competition, retain permanently their 'small' additional return?"[42]

Rae probably thought that each of these two last suggestions supported the other. If it were true that a fall in the price of bread signified an immediate rise in the rate of return for all other industries, then one could indeed understand that the baking industry would not need to be satisfied with any lower rate of return than are other kinds of enterprises. And it would be understandable that the continued influx of capital which brings about the leveling effect of the law of cost would come to a halt at a point which would leave the baking industry a higher rate of return than previously. In fact it would be the same rate as would now prevail in all other industries as a result of the cheaper bread. But since, as we have seen, this condition is contrary to the facts, it can furnish no support for the former conclusion.

Nor can the other conclusion about the tendency of invention to bring about a higher interest rate for the other instruments find support within itself. It must be admitted that Rae's *complete theory* has one superiority over those of the pure productivists. It does contain one support for the contention that competition will never depress bread prices clear down to the cost basis, that is, to the bare recovery of wages and similar expenditures advanced. That is taken care of by those purely psychological factors and forces which constitute a part of Rae's complete theory by virtue of their inclusion in the "first line of reasoning," as I called it.[43] But this theory fails completely to furnish any support for the maintenance of prices higher than those accounted for by the purely psychological forces. It does not supply a basis for what Rae, in his particular example calls the "little additional profit," that is to say, for what he incorporates in his general theory by means of the substitution of his "actual order of instruments" which indicates a higher actual rate of return, for his purely psychological "strength of effective desire of accumulation."[44] This continued maintenance of price is supposed to be caused and explained by technological influences in the field of methods of production. But Rae's line of reasoning, which follows in the footsteps of the productivity theorists very faithfully, is quite incapable of explaining the continuance.[45] For the quantitative surplus of goods is *not,* once and for all, the surplus of excess values which Rae uses as a point of departure for the continuation of his reasoning. That is blatantly conspicuous in all cases in which the improved instruments themselves, in the ratio of their enhanced physical capacity for production, are promoted by him to "orders of quicker return." It is less conspicuous, but for the careful reader not less characteristically marked, in that one remarkable passage where his observations refer to the depressing influence of competition. For by promoting all instruments, instead of only the improved class of instruments, to "orders of quicker return," Rae causes the augmented quantitative product to be transformed without any intermediary step into an alleged excess value. And this excess is neither dissipated nor even reduced by the depressing force of competition, but is, on the contrary, distributed uniformly over the entire mass of instruments!

But to make the cup overflow, Rae's doctrine contains one more principle which, with a modicum of logical reasoning, would have precluded misinterpreting an increase or decrease in goods which can be created through the medium of an instrument, and calling it a greater or smaller surplus return. For on one occasion he expressly lays down the cardinal principle that the value of instruments is to be estimated in terms of their prospective producing power, giving due consideration to their temporal remoteness. He claims this to be their "natural" criterion of appraisal, and declares his own intention to apply it in his subsequent investigation.[46] If we apply that criterion, then an instrument which, through a fortunate invention, has been made doubly effective would have to be appraised at double its former value. And since it is consumed in the course of production, the doubled product would be charged with double the cost, so that any increase in the difference between product and cost would most surely be impossible to explain!

That leads me to a final observation by which Rae's error can be demonstrated in the most simple and illuminating way of all. Rae attributes all changes in the methods of production to two causes. Favorable ones are to be laid to fortunate inventions; unfavorable ones, which occur in the absence of inventions, proceed from the need of turning to the working up of less favorable materials. In the last analysis all changes proceed from changes in the *productivity of labor*. A given amount of labor is able, in the former case, to achieve a greater physical result; in the latter, a lesser one. In one case then, labor is more productive; in the other case, less productive than before.[47] Rae admits the

236

occurrence of changes in value in all instruments which are affected by
this fluctuation in productivity, whether it be their use value or their
exchange value with the one single exception of labor itself. No matter
whether, on the one hand, that labor is twice as effective as before in
satisfying human wants, because of fortunate inventions, or whether,
on the other hand, because of exhaustion of suitable materials it accomplishes only half so much as formerly, Rae never permits the process
to be termed a change in the value of labor itself. The value and the
wages of labor, by the terms of an explicitly expressed assumption,
stipulated by Rae for the entire compass of his theoretical discussion,
are to be treated as a given constant quantity (*pp. 97, 131; foregoing,
pp. 211 and 214*). That was permissible, when his theoretical aims were
concerned with something other than the explanation of the creation
of values, which affect and are affected by the value of labor. But as to
its methodology it was an irreparable error and a cardinal sin, when
the very development of differences in the values of goods as compared
with that of labor constituted the subject of the explanation. And by
its very nature originary interest is just that. Obviously the increased
productivity of labor, other things being equal, would influence its own
value—be it use value or exchange value—for the same reasons and in
the same direction as the value of the product created is influenced. And
one other thing is obvious, too. We have here a theory which disposes
of the existence of a disparity between two magnitudes which vary in
the same direction, merely by stating that under the theory the one quantity may be assumed to react freely to the varying force, while the other,
subject though it be to the same force, must be assumed to remain
stationary; and this by virtue of nothing more than a hypothesis arbitrarily created and completely unwarranted! What is obvious here is
that the theory is wrong.

Rae, then, failed to understand the basis and the extent of the factors
which exert their influence beyond the field of the technology of production and extend it into the field of originary interest. And he could
not fairly have been expected to understand it, since he did not yet
have at his disposition as a tool, a well-worked-out theory of value.
Such a theory (as for instance the modern theory of marginal utility)
would have enabled him to pursue in detail the interactions and reactions
of variations in the quantities of products, as they affect the use value
and exchange value of the products themselves and those of the means
of production as well. It is the great merit and original contribution
of Rae to have furnished an essentially correct exposition (flaws in
minor details need not be discussed at this point) of that line of reasoning which contains the psychological reasons for man's differing estimation of the value of present and of future goods. Furthermore, in applying that reasoning to the field of originary interest his contribution exceeds even that of Jevons. On the other hand, his reasoning in the field
of the methods of production was anything but felicitous. Even though
Mixter credited him in this regard with complete and accurate understanding,[48] Mixter was probably misled by certain external features which

could indeed, upon cursory examination, easily be responsible for such misappraisal. For Mixter already had in mind certain theories concerning interest which had been worked out in detail and which had resulted from subsequent research, especially by the writer of these lines. It is a remarkable coincidence that the machinery that Rae makes use of shows a vast number of parts that exhibit a striking similarity to the expressions, to the laws and to the methodological devices of which the later interest theories availed themselves. It is, to be sure, a further coincidence that the externally similar component parts of the two theories are for the most part completely different as to content and significance.

Thus my theory operates with a "tendency toward diminishing surpluses";[49] Rae's with a "series of orders" having diminishing percentages of return. But the content of each "series" is completely dissimilar from that of the other. Entirely different things are assigned to the groups, and they function subject to entirely different factors. My material is the gross yield of units of labor; Rae's is the net yield of capital goods; my factor is the length of time during which the process of production is carried on; Rae's is the length of time required for the capital to double its initial value. So of course the conclusions we reach are also completely different.

Further, my theory has a law of "diminishing surpluses"; Rae's theory a law of "diminishing returns"[50]—but again, in content they are totally different. From the fact that natural resources, being limited in quantity, will furnish materials deteriorating in quality, Rae derives the following law. In the absence of new inventions there must be a real decrease in the yield from labor, and hence each successive unit of labor must result in a decreasing quantity of the product. My theory is derived from considerations that have nothing to do with the limitations on natural resources. According to my law the lengthening of the time of production enables a unit of labor to produce an increasingly larger quantity of goods, with the proviso, however, that the progression according to which the quantity of the goods increases will be gradually retarded.[51]

My theory gives rise to the technical expression "intermediary products"; Rae's to the term "instrument" concerning which I have just shown that it denotes a different class of goods, but which Mixter erroneously considers to be the same as my "intermediary products."[52]

Finally, the factor of time plays an outstanding part in the two theories. Insofar as the influence of time is concerned in the valuation of present and future wants—that is to say, with respect to the oft-mentioned "first line of reasoning," there is, in actual fact, complete parallelism in the two theories. But in the field of the technology of production there is a repetition of the intrusion of the long arm of coincidence, with its somewhat similar concepts, and its similar or even practically identical names, which nevertheless have different meanings. My theory is interested in the "period of production" which embraces the time up to the completion of the product. Rae uses, here and there, the almost identical term "period of formation." But it is not this period of time which Rae considers important for his conclusions. For him the important time is that other period between the completion of the product and its exhaustion. In other words, he is not so much interested in the time during which it *becomes* a good, as in the time during which it *is* a good. Accordingly, the time interval that Rae has in mind serves more of a distributive function. The instrument, which exists by grace of the inventive faculty,[53] will bear a yield for the duration of its life. The extent of that life determines whether the yield is to be distributed as a gain over a long or a short period, that is to say, whether it represents a high or a low percentage per year. But the incorporation into Jevons's theory and later into mine, of the technological factors in conjunction with the purely psychological ones represents something foreign to Rae's train of thought. And that is the idea that the duration of the process of production is a *causative* factor which is reflected in the physical magnitude of the product. This is a circumstance which Mixter is careful to mention, at least indirectly, but he is disposed to record it to Rae's credit, rather than otherwise.[54]

And yet these essential differences, or rather contrasts, are discernible only upon close examination. It must be considered that there is complete harmony between Rae's theory and mine in several respects.[55] I have in mind not only Rae's "first line of reasoning" in the psychological field, but also certain fundamental elements of the doctrine of production, particularly the basic characteristics of production and of the services of goods. And it must further be borne in mind that Rae, in any case, expressed himself only very briefly and often obscurely on those phases of the problem of interest which are vital to that problem as such. Therefore it is not difficult to feel and understand how Mixter allowed himself to be somewhat prematurely deluded. He supposed that the use of similar expressions and devices necessarily implied that there were coinciding thoughts concealed in the rest of the structure of my theory. That is why he read into the technological portion of Rae's doctrine, thoughts to which Rae was in actual fact a stranger.[56]

I am afraid that many readers will get the impression that in this chapter I have spoken at undue length and with unseemly anticipation, not only about Rae, but also about my own theory. I should certainly not have done so, had not the very special character of the situation imposed upon me the necessity, and indeed the duty of doing so. Had I been in a position to agree with the entire contents of Mixter's critique, I should have accorded recognition to Rae as an originator with respect to the technological aspect of the interest problem as gladly and readily as I now and here do for his psychological contribution. But—*amicus Plato, sed magis amica veritas!* ("Plato is my friend, but a greater friend is the truth!") And if, in my dual capacity as historian and critic of economic theories, I reached a conclusion different from Mixter's, I considered myself under the obligation to furnish the most scrupulously accurate exposition of the facts. This was especially true because Rae's book has become extremely rare and is unavailable to most readers. For that reason the material on which they are to pass judgment had to be submitted to them in complete form.

All in all, I believe I can say this about Rae. Half of his doctrines are the work of an original thinker and a pioneer. With respect to the other half, he may be classed, despite some original details, with the members of the school of the productivity theory. In this respect he belongs with his peer and contemporary Thünen, whom he resembles closely—in doctrine, in mental attitude and in independence of thought unimpaired by what he has read.

XII

THE EXPLOITATION THEORY

A. HISTORICAL SURVEY
OF THE EXPLOITATION THEORY

1. General Characteristics of the Exploitation Theory

I NOW come to that notable theory the formulation of which may not be one of the pleasantest scientific events of the nineteenth century, but is certainly among its most portentous. It stood at the cradle of modern socialism and grew up with it. And it constitutes today (1884) the focal point about which attack and defense rally in the war in which the issue is the system under which human society shall be organized.[1]

The theory has as yet no short and distinctive name. If I wanted to give it the name of a characteristic displayed by its principle followers, I could call it the *socialist* theory of interest. But if I am to be guided by a principle which I consider more appropriate, and make use of the theoretical content of the doctrine itself as the source of its name, I could find no appellation more suitable, I think, than the *exploitation theory*. Compressed into a few sentences, the essential nature of the doctrine might, for the time being, be described as follows.

All goods that have value are the product of human labor, and indeed, from the economist's point of view, the product of human labor *exclusively*. The workers however do not receive the entire product which they alone have produced. The capitalist exercises the control over the indispensable means of production which the institution of private property guarantees him, and he uses such control to secure for himself a part of the workers' product. His means of doing so is the wage contract which permits him to purchase the labor of the true producers, who are forced by hunger to accept the contract. The price the capitalist pays them is a fraction of what is produced by them, and the rest of the product falls into the lap of the capitalist at the cost of no exertion to himself. *Interest therefore consists in a portion of the product of the labor of others, acquired by exploiting the situation which places the worker under coercion.*

241

2. Origin of the Exploitation Theory

THE genesis of that doctrine had been foreshadowed long before and had in fact become inevitable because of the peculiar turn taken by the economic doctrine of value after Smith and even more after Ricardo. It was generally taught and believed that the value of all goods, or at least of the very great majority of economic goods, is measured by the amount of labor they embody, and that this labor is the origin and the source of the value of goods. Such being the case, it was inevitable that sooner or later the question should arise, why the worker did not receive the entire value to which his work had given rise. And as soon as that question had been raised, it was impossible to find any answer except one which could conform to the spirit of that same theory of value. That answer was that, after the fashion of the drones, one group of society, namely the capitalists, appropriates unto itself part of the value of the product produced solely by the other party in society, namely the workers.

To be sure, the originators of the labor theory of value did not as yet give this answer, as we have seen. Several of their earliest followers likewise avoided giving that answer. They did make the point quite emphatically that labor has the power to create value, but in their general conception of economic life they followed faithfully in the path of their masters. Two such were the German economists, Soden and Lotz. But the answer was nevertheless inherent in their doctrine and followed as its necessary logical consequence. It needed but a suitable motivating incident and a disciple addicted to the lure of the syllogism, to guarantee that it rise to the surface sooner or later. So Smith and Ricardo may be considered the unwilling godfathers of the exploitation theory. And they are regarded as such, even by the followers of the theory. They, and they almost alone, are spoken of by even the most dogmatic of socialists with the sort of respect that is due the discoverers of the "true" law of value. The only fault that is laid at their door is the lack of logical persistence which would have enabled them to crown their theory of value themselves with the exploitation theory.

Anyone fond of conducting research into the genealogies, not only of families but of theories as well, can probably find many a pronouncement of bygone centuries which fits in well with the school of thought behind the exploitation theory. Entirely aside from the canonists, whose conclusions agree with those of the "exploitationists" more by accident than by design, there is Locke, for one. On one occasion[2] he points out with great emphasis that labor is the source of all goods, and on another[3] he calls interest a fruit of the labor of others. Another is James Steuart who reveals a similar line of thought but couches it in terms that do not align him so unmistakably with this school.[4] Sonnenfels belongs to this group too. He occasionally describes capitalists as that class of persons "who do not toil and who feed on the sweat of the working classes."[5] Then there is Büsch who also calls interest (by which, to be sure, he means only loan interest) an "income from property derived by means of the industry of others."[6] These examples could probably be multiplied, if one made an industrious search of the older literature.

Nevertheless, the birth of the exploitation theory as a conscious and integrated doctrine can be ascribed only to a later period. It was preceded by two preparatory developments. The first of these, as I have already mentioned, was the development and the popularization of Ricardo's theory of value, which furnished the theoretical soil in which the exploitation theory found a bed naturally adapted for its thriving growth. The other was the victorious spreading of capitalist mass production which, by creating and exposing a yawning gulf between capital and labor, at the same time moved the question of interest derived without labor into the forefront of the great social problems.

Under the influence of such forces as these our own era seems to have been ready ever since the third decade of the nineteenth century for the systematic development of the exploitation theory. I choose to ignore the "practical communists" whose aspirations naturally stemmed from similar concepts, but who may be disregarded in a history of economic *theory*. Aside from these the earliest theorists to develop the exploitation theory in any considerable detail were William Thompson in England and Sismondi in France.

The cardinal principles of the exploitation theory were developed briefly but with notable clarity and acuity by Thompson.[7] He starts with the theoretical premise that labor is the source of all value and arrives at the practical conclusion that the producer is entitled to the entire proceeds of what he has produced. He makes the statement that the worker, despite this claim to the full produce of his labor, actually is limited to a wage that is barely sufficient for subsistence, while the additional value that can be derived from an equal amount of labor by the use of machines and other capital is taken by the capitalists who have amassed it and advanced it to the workers. Land rent and interest therefore represent deductions from the full produce of labor, to which the worker is entitled.[8]

There is a division of opinion as to how far Thompson influenced subsequent writings. At any rate he has left few discernible traces. In the economic literature of England there has been little tendency to continue the Thompson trend,[9] and the most illustrious socialists in French and German economic literature do not reveal any external resemblance to him. Anton Menger[10] recently defended with great vigor the opinion that Marx and Rodbertus borrowed their most important socialist theories from older English and French models, and especially from Thompson. But it is difficult to determine whether that is so. I for my part consider his argument not at all convincing. When a doctrine is floating in the atmosphere, as it were, the fact that it is taken up by a writer need not necessarily be evidence that he has borrowed it. Nor does it constitute proof or disproof of his originality in such event, to say that he expressed a few years earlier or later a fundamental idea that was in the air. On the contrary, the true test of his creativeness is his ability to make original additions to the idea and so advance the erection of a sound and vital theoretical structure. In the world of science, in any case, the intuitive, groping expression of an idea is often a much easier and less meritorious achievement (I say this despite examples of the opposite) than is the sound proof, corroboration and development of that same idea. Let me remind the reader of the position occupied by Darwin with respect to the vaguely prophetic thoughts of Goethe on the subject of evolution. The same is true of Adam Smith, who seized upon the germ of an idea expressed much earlier by Locke, and successfully developed it into his famous "industrial system." In our present case I feel that the development of the labor theory of value virtually put the word "exploitation" into people's mouths. But it seems to me, furthermore, that Rodbertus and Marx seized upon and developed the idea in such original fashion, that I, for one, should not be willing to characterize them as "borrowers," in their relationship either to each other, or to their predecessors.[11]

On the other hand, it should be pointed out that the influence of Sismondi was indubitably strong and far reaching. If I cite him as a representative of the exploitation theory, it is done with a bit of reservation. For Sismondi outlined a doctrine which has all the essential features of the theory of exploitation with one exception. He refrains from pronouncing an adverse judgment on interest! It is simply a case of his belonging, as a writer, to the period of transition. While he is essentially converted to the cause of the new theory, yet he has not broken with the old one so completely that he can avoid shying away from its novel viewpoint.

The great work of Sismondi which exercised so much influence, insofar as our subject is concerned, bears the title, *Nouveaux principes d'économie politique.*[12] In this work Sismondi's thesis sets out from premises which he shares with Adam Smith. He accepts the latter's principle that work is the sole source of all wealth,[13] and agrees with it warmly (*p. 51*). He is displeased because the three types of income, namely rents, profits and wages are frequently attributed to three different sources, namely land, capital and labor. In actual fact, says Sismondi, all income arises only from labor, and those three categories are merely so many different ways of participating in the fruits of human labor (*p. 85*). For the worker, by whose activity all goods are produced, has "in our stage of civilization" not been able to retain control of the necessary means of production. In the first place, arable land is usually the private property of another, and the owner demands a part of the fruits of the worker's labor, in return for supplying the cooperation of the "productive force" termed land. Such part constitutes land rent. In the second place, the productive worker ordinarily does not possess a sufficient supply of provisions on which to live during the time he is performing his labor. Nor does he own the raw materials and the frequently costly instruments and machines necessary for production. The rich, who own all these things, thus acquire a certain control of the labor of the poor. Without doing any of the work themselves, they take in advance the best part of the fruits of that labor, to compensate themselves for the advantages which they put at the disposal of the poor (*la part la plus importante des fruits de son travail*). This "best part" is interest (*pp. 86 and 87*). Thus, by reason of the organization of society, wealth has achieved the ability to reproduce itself through the labor of others (*p. 82*).

And although the laborer's daily efforts produce far more than his daily needs, there is little left over for him, after he has shared with the landowner and the capitalist, than his bare subsistence, which he receives in the form of wages. The worker needs his subsistence much more than the entrepreneur needs the worker's labor. He needs his subsistence to be able to live, whereas the entrepreneur needs his labor only to make a profit. And so the bargain almost always turns out to the disadvantage of the worker, and he must almost always content himself with the most meager subsistence, while the lion's share of the advantages that accrue from the increased productivity that comes about through division of labor falls to the entrepreneur (*p. 91 f.*).

Anyone who has followed Sismondi's exposition thus far, and has also read the sentence which states the "rich devour the product of the labor of the others" (*p. 81*) will necessarily expect Sismondi to conclude by declaring interest an unjust and extortionate gain that is to be condemned. But that is not the conclusion Sismondi draws. Suddenly shifting ground, he manages to conjure up a few obscure and ambiguous clichés in favor of interest, which finally stands before us robed in righteousness. First he says of the landowner that he earned a *right* to land rent by the original labor of making the land arable, or even by settlement of virgin territory (*p. 110*). Similarly he endows the owner of capital with a right to interest based on the "original labor" to which the capital owes its existence (*p. 111*). These two types of income have one characteristic in common, in that they constitute income derived by virtue of ownership, and they may therefore be contrasted with income which is derived by virtue of the performance of labor. And yet Sismondi manages to establish their good repute by demonstrating that they, too, owe their origin to labor, being different only in that their honorable origin dates back to an earlier era. For the worker, through new labors, acquires every year a new claim to income, while property owners in an earlier period of time and through original labors acquired a permanent claim which makes each year's work more advantageous[14] (*p. 112*). "Everyone," he concludes, "receives his share of the national income only in proportion to what he or his representatives contribute or have contributed to the creation of that income." Of course, Sismondi does not offer any answer to the questions whether and how this last statement can be reconciled with his earlier ones, according to which interest is something taken in advance out of the fruits of other persons' labor.

However, others very soon and very decidedly drew the conclusions which Sismondi himself did not dare to draw from his own theory. He is the connecting link between Smith and Ricardo on the one side, and the subsequent doctrines of socialism and communism on the other. Those two economists, with their theory of value, had supplied the originating impulse of which the exploitation theory was born, but had not themselves formulated any such theory. Sismondi virtually worked out what was in essence a theory of exploitation, without as yet giving it any application to the social and political field. He was followed by that massive force which, under the names "socialism" and "communism," pursued the logical sequence of the old doctrine of value to the very ultimate limit of its theoretical and practical implications, arriving finally at the dictum, "Interest is exploitation, and so it must go."

3. The Socialists

IT WOULD not be of any theoretical interest for me to cull the voluminous socialist writings of the nineteenth century for quotations from all the statements which proclaimed the theory of exploitation. I should be forced to weary the reader with a multitude of parallel passages which hardly vary in wording, and which reveal an extremely uninteresting monotony in content. Moreover, the very large majority of them do not go beyond merely asserting the cardinal principles of the exploitation theory without offering any better proofs than an appeal to the authority of Ricardo and adding a few commonplaces. The simple fact is that the majority of the "scientific" socialists exercised their intellectual power less in proving the fundamental correctness of their own theories than in launching corrosive attacks on those of their opponents. I shall therefore restrict myself to mentioning a few out of the mass of socialistically tinged writers who became especially important for the development or dissemination of our theory.

The author of the *Contradictions économiques,* P. J. Proudhon, is outstanding among such writers for the clarity of his views and the brilliance of his argumentation, and these qualities made him the most effective apostle of the exploitation theory in France. Since we are more concerned with content than with form, I shall forego quoting detailed samples of his style, and restrict myself to summarizing the kernel of Proudhon's doctrine in a few sentences. It will be at once apparent that, except for a few peculiarities of language, Proudhon's doctrine does not differ much from the general outline of the exploitation theory, as we have already given it.

To begin with, Proudhon accepts as established the principle that labor creates all value. Hence the worker has a natural claim to ownership of his entire product. By his wage contract he foregoes that claim in favor of the owner of the capital and in return for a wage which is *smaller* than the product which he foregoes. Herein he is cheated. For he is not aware of his natural right, nor of the magnitude of his concession, nor yet of the significance of the contract which the property owner makes with him. In this transaction the owner takes advantage of error and surprise, not to say deceit and sharp practice (*erreur et surprise, si même on ne doit dire dol et fraude*).

This is the explanation of the fact that the modern worker is not able to buy his own product. His product costs more in the open market than he has received in wages. It costs more by the amount of all sorts of gains which are caused by the existence of the right of property and which, known under most varied terms such as profit, interest, yield, rent, tithes, etc., constitute just so many "tolls" (*aubaines*) which are imposed on labor. For instance, what 20 million workers have produced for a year's wages of 20 billion francs, costs 25 billions because of and inclusive of those gains. But that means "that the workers who, to be able to live, must buy back the same products, are compelled to buy back for five, the things they produced for four, or in other words that they must fast one day out of every five." And so, interest is an additional tax on labor, a pre-emptive reduction (*retenue*) of wages.[15]

The German Rodbertus is fully the peer of Proudhon in the purity of his presentation, by far his superior in the profundity of his thinking and his prudent insight, but admittedly far inferior to the passionate Frenchman in the vividness of his language. For the historian of economic theories he is the most important of the personalities that deserve mention at this point. For a long time his scientific significance went unrecognized and, strangely enough, because of the very fact that his work is so predominantly scientific. Because he did not make his appeal as others did directly to the populace, because he restricted himself primarily to scientific investigation of the social question, because he was moderate and restrained in his practical proposals as they affected the most immediate interests of the great masses, his reputation lagged for a long time behind that of other far lesser men who took over his intellectual wares second hand, and in their own fashion made them palatable for the interested multitude. Only in modern times has full justice been done to Rodbertus, that most charming socialist, and recognition paid to him for what he is, the father of modern scientific socialism. Instead of the passionate attacks and oratorical antithesis in which the great throng of socialists loves to indulge, Rodbertus has bequeathed to us a profoundly and honestly reasoned theory of the distribution of goods. Mistaken as it may be in many respects, it nevertheless contains enough that is valuable to assure its originator lasting pre-eminence among economic theorists.

I wish to reserve the privilege of returning later, and in some detail, to his formulation of the theory of exploitation. In the meantime I should like to go on to a consideration of two theorists who succeeded him in time, and who differed as completely from one another as they did from Rodbertus.

One of these is Ferdinand Lassalle, the most eloquent, but as to content the least original of the socialist leaders. I mention him here only because his brilliant eloquence enabled him to exercise great influence on the spreading of the theory of exploitation. But his contribution to its theoretical development is just about nil. I can therefore dispense with quotations or excerpts from his doctrine, which does not differ in content from that of his predecessors, and restrict myself to commenting in a footnote on one or two of the most striking passages.[16]

While Lassalle is an agitator exclusively, Karl Marx is pre-eminently a theorist, and indeed, after Rodbertus, the most distinguished theorist of socialism. Although his doctrine coincides in many respects with the pioneering research of Rodbertus, he displayed undeniable originality and a high degree of keen logic in developing his doctrine into a distinctive whole with which it will likewise be our duty shortly to become thoroughly acquainted.

4. Acceptance of Exploitation Theory
Not Restricted to Socialists

ALTHOUGH the exploitation theory was developed chiefly by theorists of the socialist "persuasion," the ideas peculiar to it were adopted by writers in other literary circles as well. And these writers were many, and of many kinds.

Some of them declare themselves for the exploitation theory, lock, stock and barrel, or decline to subscribe only to the most extreme practical applications of it. One of that sort is, for example, Guth.[17] He accepts all the essential principles of the socialists and their content in their entirety. For him labor is to be regarded as the sole source of value. Interest comes into being because the unfavorable conditions under which labor competes force its wages to lag behind the value of its product. In fact, Guth does not scruple to introduce the harsh term "exploitation" as the technical term which describes that process. But in the end he recoils from the practical consequences of this principle and takes refuge behind a few hedging provisos. "Far be it from us to imply that the exploitation of the worker, as the source of the original margin of gain, is an act which violates the tenets of justice. Rather, it is based on a voluntary agreement between employer and employee which, to be sure, is entered into under conditions which are usually unfavorable to the latter." The sacrifice which the "exploited" worker makes is rather to be thought of as only an "advance against something to be returned." For the accumulation of capital brings about a progressively greater productivity on the part of labor. As a result, the products of labor become cheaper, the worker can buy more, and hence his real wage rises. At the same time "increased demand brings about a wider sphere of possible employment, whereupon his money wage also rises." Hence "exploitation" resembles an investment of capital which indirectly and in increasing measure brings in returns to the worker.[18]

Dühring is another whose theory of interest stands entirely on socialist ground. *"Interest is in its nature an appropriation of the principal portion of the product of labor. . . .* The increase in productivity and the saving in labor are effects of improved and more extensive means of production. But the fact that the obstacles and difficulties encountered by production become less, and the further fact that *unskilled labor, by the acquisition of technical skill, makes itself more productive, do not justify any claim that an inanimate instrument should absorb even the least bit of a surplus over and above what is required for its replacement.* Therefore interest is not a concept that could be developed on the basis of considerations that apply solely to production, or that would fit into the pattern of a system of economics. It is a form of appropriation and the result of distributional circumstances."[19]

Another group of writers accepts the ideas of the exploitation theory in eclectic fashion, incorporating some of them with their other views on the interest problem. Examples of this group are John Stuart Mill and Schäffle.[20]

Still others were sufficiently impressed by socialist writings to adopt individual features of the doctrine, even though they were unwilling to accept the structure in its entirety. It seems to me that the most important event of this nature was that a renowned group of German university professors, the "socialists of the chair" revived the old principle that *labor is the only source of all value,* that is to say, the only power which can "create value."

5. The Principle that Labor Is the Only Source of All Value

IT IS a strange fate that has befallen this principle, the acceptance or rejection of which is of tremendous import in passing judgment on the most important economic phenomena. It had originated with the English economists, and in the first decades following the publication of Smith's system had shared the widespread acceptance which the latter had enjoyed. Later, under the influence of the teachings of Say, who developed the theory of the three factors of production, nature, labor and capital, and then under the further influence of Hermann and Senior, the principle was discredited among the great majority of economists, even in England. For a time the socialist authors were almost the only group who kept it alive at all. Then, when the German "socialists of the chair" adopted the principle as they took it out of the pages of a Proudhon, a Rodbertus and a Marx, the principle once more acquired strong support among scholarly economists. And now it almost seems as if the reputation enjoyed by the distinguished leaders of that school might enable it, from this point, to embark upon a second triumphal course through the economic writings of all nations.[21]

Whether or not this is a desirable development will be shown by a critical appraisal of the exploitation theory, to which the ensuing pages will be devoted.

B. CRITIQUE OF THE EXPLOITATION THEORY

1. General Outline of This Critique

THERE were several avenues open to me by which to approach the task of a critique of the exploitation theory. One of those would be to appraise all the representatives of the theory individually. And while that would have been the most accurate way, the high degree to which the individual expositions coincide would have resulted in unnecessary and wearisome repetition. Another way would have been to base my critique on the general system which is common to all the individual expositions of it, without taking up a detailed consideration of any one of them individually. That procedure however would have exposed me to two complementary evils. On the one hand I should have been in danger of really failing to do justice to certain individual shades of difference. On the other hand, even if I had escaped the first danger, I should most certainly have been charged with making my task too easy, and with having made an appraisal, not of the actual theory, but of a version of it which I had wilfully distorted. And so I decided to approach the problem by a third avenue, and that was to select from the great multiplicity of individual statements of the theory a very few which I consider the best and the most complete, and to subject these individually to criticism.

For that purpose I selected the exegeses by Rodbertus and Marx. They are the only ones which offer a reasonably profound and coherent foundation. Rodbertus's is, in my opinion, the best presentation of the theory. Marx's however is the most widely recognized, the one that is, so to speak, the official pronouncement of modern socialism. By subjecting both of them to a detailed examination, I am looking at the exploitation theory, I think, "with its best foot forward." I am trying to adhere to a policy which Knies put so well when he said, "He who would be victorious on the field of scientific research, must allow his adversary to advance in all the panoply of his armor and in the fullness of his strength."[22]

One preliminary remark will perhaps prevent misunderstandings. The sole purpose of the pages which immediately follow is to make a critical estimate of the exploitation theory *as a theory,* in other words, to attempt to determine whether the origin of the economic phenomenon called interest really lies in those circumstances to which the exploitation theory ascribes that origin. Conversely, it is not my intention to render any verdict at this point with respect to the *practical* side of the problem of interest or its implications from the point of view of *social legislation.* Nor do I plan to judge its goodness or badness, nor to advocate the retention or abolition of interest itself. To be sure, I do not by any means propose to write a book on interest and take refuge in silence concerning the most important question which is connected with it. But I cannot profitably discuss the "practical" side of the subject until there is complete clarity with respect to the theoretical side, and I must therefore reserve such discussion for my second volume. But at this point—I repeat —it is my intention only to seek to establish whether interest, be it good or bad, exists for the reasons which the exploitation theory alleges.

A. Rodbertus[23]

1. DETAILED PRESENTATION OF RODBERTUS'S DOCTRINE

THE point of origin for Rodbertus's theory of interest is the principle "introduced into the science of economics by Smith and more firmly corroborated by the Ricardo school" to the effect that "all goods, economically considered, are only the product of labor and cost nothing except labor." Rodbertus elucidates this principle, which is habitually expressed in the form "only labor is productive" by stating it as follows. *Firstly,* only those goods belong to the class that may be termed economic goods, which have cost labor, while all other goods, no matter how necessary and useful they may be to man, are *natural* goods which have nothing to do with economics. *Secondly,* all economic goods are *solely* a product of labor, and from the economist's point of view are not to be conceived of as produced by nature or any other power, but only by labor. Any other view belongs in the field of the physical sciences rather than economics. *Thirdly,* all goods are, economically considered, the product of only that labor which performed the material operations which were necessary to their production. But such labor includes not only that labor which produces the good directly, but also such labor as creates the instrument which serves in the production of the good concerned. Grain, for instance, is the product not only of the labor that drove the plow, but also of that which built that plow, etc., etc.[24]

The manual workers who create the entire good have a natural and just claim, at least "according to the idea of pure justice," to acquire title to their entire product.[25] But there are two important reservations. In the first place, the system of division of labor under which a great many cooperate to produce a single product, makes it a technical impossibility that each worker receive his product in kind. Therefore in place of the claim to the whole *product* must be substituted the claim to the entire *value* of the product.[26] Furthermore there must be some provision made out of the sum of all products, for a share for all those who render useful service to their fellow men without participating directly in the making of the product, as for instance, clergymen, physicians, judges, naturalists and also, in Rodbertus's opinion, the entrepreneurs who "know how to employ a large number of workers productively by means of a capital."[27] But such labor, which is only "indirectly economic," will have to urge its claim to be compensated, not out of the "original distribution of goods," in which only producers share, but out of a "secondary derivative distribution of goods." Hence the claim which, under the idea of pure justice, can be advanced by the manual workers, is to be construed as a claim to *the whole value of the*

251

product of their labor in the original distribution, undiminished by reason of the secondary claims to compensation by other useful members of society.

Rodbertus finds that under the present organization of society this natural claim is not realized. For workers today receive only part of the value of their product at the original distribution in the form of wages, while the rest falls to the share of the owners of land and of capital in the form of surplus proceeds (*Rente*). Rodbertus defines surplus proceeds as "all income that is received without work, purely on the basis of ownership of property."[28] It includes two kinds of income, *interest on land* and *interest on capital goods.**

Rodbertus now asks, "Since all income is the product of labor, why do some members of society draw income, and in fact original income, though they have not stirred a finger to produce it?" With those words Rodbertus has framed the general theoretical problem of interest.[29] His answer to the problem is as follows:

Surplus proceeds owe their existence to the combined effect of two facts, the one economic and the other legalistic. *The economic reason* lies in the fact that since the introduction of the division of labor, the workers' labor produces more than they need for their subsistence and for the continued performance of such labor. As a result, others, too, *can* live off that labor. *The legal reason* lies in the existence of private ownership of land and of capital goods. Since the workers are excluded by this institution of private property from control of the conditions indispensable to production, they cannot produce at all except as employees of the proprietors and under the terms of a previously concluded agreement. And the latter, in return for making the conditions of production available, impose upon the workers the obligation to cede a portion of the product of their labor as surplus proceeds. Indeed, the cession takes place under the still more onerous guise of a surrender by the workers of title to the entire product of their labor in favor of the proprietors, who then return to them only a part of its value as wages, limiting such wages to the indispensable minimum required for subsistence and for the continued performance of their labor. The power which compels the workers to accept this contract is hunger. But let us read it in Rodbertus's own words.

"Since there can be no income, except as it is the result of labor, an

---

* Translators' note: Rodbertus's concept of *Rente* corresponds to what economists today would call "surplus of gross proceeds over labor costs." They conceive of this magnitude as a complex which includes four elements: (a) the price of the entrepreneur's own labor employed in the production process; (b) the entrepreneur's profit proper; (c) interest on the entrepreneur's capital; and (d) interest on borrowed capital. In the hope that these connotations will remain more vividly present, the translators will generally render Rodbertus's *Rente* by the more precise modern term "surplus of proceeds over labor costs," or more briefly and simply, "surplus proceeds." Rodbertus's distinctive terms *Kapitalgewinn* and *Grundrente* might be conveyed in modern terminology by rendering them as "interest derived from the utilization of capital goods" and "interest derived from the use of land." We are dealing with but a single economic phenomenon, namely *interest*, but in two manifestations with respect to factors of production. One is interest on capital goods, the other is interest on land.

excess of proceeds over labor costs depends on two indispensable pre-requisites. First, there can be no surplus proceeds unless the labor at least produces more than is required for the continuation of the labor. For it is impossible for anyone to draw an income regularly without himself doing any work unless there is such a margin. Second, there can be no surplus proceeds, unless conditions exist which deprive the workers of this margin in whole or in part, and divert it to others who do not work themselves. For the workers are, in the nature of things, in possession of their product at the outset. That labor does create such a margin is the result of economic factors, in particular such as increase the productivity of labor. That this margin is wrested in whole or in part from the workers and is diverted to others, is the result of legalistic factors. Just as law has from the beginning been in coalition with power, so in this instance this diversion takes place only by the continued exercise of compulsion.

"Originally this compulsion was exercised by the institution of slavery, which came into existence at the same time as tillage of the soil and private ownership of land. The workers who created a margin in the product of their labor were slaves, and the master to whom the slaves and hence their product itself belonged, gave the slaves only just so much as was required for the continuation of their labor, and kept the rest, the margin, for himself. When all the land in a country is privately owned, and when at the same time title to all capital has passed into private hands, then this ownership of land and capital exerts the same compulsion on liberated or free workers. This brings about a twofold effect. The first effect is the same as that produced by slavery, in that the product itself does not belong to the workers, but to the owners of land and of capital. The second effect is that the workers, who own nothing, are glad enough to receive from the masters who own land and capital even a part of their own product to support themselves, that is to say, to allow them to continue their labor. Only now the commands of the slave owner have been replaced by the contract between worker and employer, a contract which is free only in form but not really in substance. Hunger makes almost a perfect substitute for the whip, and what formerly was called fodder is now called wages."[30]

According to this argument all surplus proceeds are the fruit of *exploitation,*[31] or as *Rodbertus* occasionally puts it still more caustically,[32] a *theft* of the product of other men's labor. This description is appropriate to all classes of surplus proceeds in equal degree, whether it be interest on capital or on land, or even the derivatives of these two, namely hire and loan interest. The two latter are as fully justified a charge against the entrepreneurs who pay them, as they are unjustified charges against the workers, at whose expense they are ultimately collected.[33]

The amount of excess proceeds increases with the productivity of labor. For under the system of free competition the worker receives generally, and in the long run, just the amount necessary for subsistence, that is to say, a definite concrete quantity of the product. Now the greater the productivity of labor, the smaller is the percentage of the total value of the product which that concrete quantity of the product represents. And the greater is the percentage of the product and of the value, which is left over as the portion of the owners, that is to say, their interest.[34]

Although the foregoing statements indicate that all interest is basically a unified mass of completely homogenous origin, in practical economic life it is commonly recognized that it takes two different forms, namely interest on capital goods and on land. Now Rodbertus explains the reasons and the laws of this duality in exceedingly individual fashion. Throughout his investigation he proceeds, it must be noted by way of introduction, from the theoretical assumption that the exchange value* of all products is equal to their labor cost.[35] He assumes, in other words, that all products are exchangeable, one for another, on the basis of their relative cost in terms of labor. The remarkable thing about this assumption is that Rodbertus knows that it is not in accordance with fact. But he thinks that the deviation from actuality is only a matter of the "real exchange value sometimes being greater and sometimes being smaller." He feels furthermore that there is always a gravitational tendency in evidence toward the point which is "the natural, and hence also the equitable exchange value."[36] He rejects entirely the idea that it should be a *normal course of events* for goods to be exchanged on the basis of some standard other than the labor that has been expended on them. He excludes the possibility that deviations from that basis might be the result, not of fortuitous and momentary market fluctuations, but of the operation of a definite law which influences value in a different direction.[37] I call attention to this circumstance at this point, for it will be important later.

The production of goods viewed as a whole is divisible, according to Rodbertus, into two parts; *raw production* avails itself of the help of the land to produce raw materials, and *manufacture* works up the raw materials into further products. Before the introduction of the division of labor, the obtaining of raw materials, and the further processing of them were performed in immediate succession and by the same entrepreneurs, who then also received the entire resulting surplus proceeds without differentiation. At that stage of economic development there was as yet no division of interest into that derived from the utilization of capital goods and that derived from the use of land. But once the division of labor had been introduced, the entrepreneurs of raw production and of the subsequent manufacture became different persons. The preliminary question is the determination of the proportion in which to divide surplus of proceeds over labor costs resulting from the entire productive process. What shall be the respective shares of the producers of the raw materials and of the entrepreneurs who do the manufacturing?

The answer to the question lies in the nature of interest. Interest, being a deduction from the value of the product, is a percentage thereof. The amount of interest that can be gained from a given productive pro-

---

* Translators' note: *Exchange value* is the capacity of a good to obtain in exchange a quantity of other goods. *Price* is the exchange ratio between money and that quantity of other goods.

cess is determined by the exchange value of the product. But since the exchange value of the product, again, is determined by the quantity of the labor expended, raw production and manufacture will share the total surplus proceeds in the proportion born to each other by the *respective labor costs* of these two branches of production. Let us consider a concrete example. This example is not in Rodbertus's book, but I insert it to guard against confusion in this difficult line of reasoning.

If 1,000 working days are required to produce a given quantity of raw materials, and the processing of it requires another 2,000 working days, and if the overall surplus proceeds means a deduction of 40% from the exchange value of the product for the benefit of the proprietors, then the proprietors of the raw production will receive the product of 400 days, and the manufacturing entrepreneurs that of 800 days, as interest. The amount of *capital* employed in each of the productive processes is immaterial for purposes of this division. It is true that the rate of interest is computed on the basis of the capital employed, but it is not determined by the amount of that capital but by the quantities of labor that were applied.

The very fact that the magnitude of the capital employed has *no* determining influence on the amount of interest that may be realized from one branch of production, becomes a causative factor in the origination of interest on land. Rodbertus elucidates as follows. Interest, although it is the product of labor, is regarded as the yield of wealth, because it is conditioned by the possession of wealth. Since in manufacture only capital goods, and not land are employed, the entire amount of interest which is derived specifically from manufacturing is regarded as the yield of capital, or as interest on capital. By following the custom of computing the ratio of the amount of yield to the amount of capital which returns that yield, people arrive at a position in which they speak of the definite percentage of return that can be earned by capital employed in manufacture. That rate of yield, which will be approximately uniform in all activities because of the recognized influence of competition, will also become a criterion for the computation of the yield on capital engaged in raw production. That will be true, if for no other reason, because a far greater part of the "national capital" is employed in manufacture than in agriculture. For, as is readily comprehensible, the yield of the vastly predominant portion of capital can dictate the rate of yield which is to be deemed acceptable in the case of the smaller portion. For that reason those engaged in raw production will consider that portion of their total surplus proceeds which represents the customary rate of earnings calculated on their capital employed, to be their interest on capital. The rest of the surplus proceeds over labor costs however will be thought of as the yield of the land, and constitutes the additional residuum of interest on land.

According to Rodbertus the latter *must* always necessarily be left over in the production of raw materials by the terms of that one presupposition that products are exchanged on the basis of the labor incorporated in each. And this is Rodbertus's argument to prove it. The amount of interest that can be derived from *manufacture* depends, as was pointed out earlier, not on the quantity of capital expended, but on the amount of work performed in the process of manufacture. This labor consists of two components, direct manufacturing labor, and that indirect labor "which because of the exhaustion of instruments and tools must be taken into account." Of the various elements of which capital expenditure is composed, only a few have any influence on the amount of surplus proceeds, namely those that consist in wages and in expenditures for machines and tools. Capital expenditure for raw materials, however, does not exert such an influence because this expenditure offers no counterpart corresponding to any labor cost expended in the manufacturing stage of the production process. And yet this part of the expenditure *does* add to the amount of capital which serves as the basis for computing the yield which the surplus proceeds represent. The result is that part of the capital outlay—the expenditure for raw materials—increases the capital devoted to manufacture but does not increase the yield. And the further result ensues that the presence of such a part of the capital obviously and necessarily reduces the ratio which interest, represented by the yield, bears to the increased capital employed in manufacture. In other words, it depresses the rate of interest on manufacturing capital.

Now interest in the field of raw production will also be calculated at this lower rate. But in the case of raw production the situation is more favorable. For since agriculture begins its production *ab ovo*—"from scratch" as it were—and does not process any material which comes to it from a preceding production, its capital outlay does not include the component "raw material." The only thing it might offer as occupying an analogous position would be the land itself. That however is assumed in all theories to cost nothing. Consequently participation in the distribution of surplus proceeds is limited to those parts of capital only which have had some influence on the amount of those proceeds. And as a further consequence it follows that the ratio of the surplus proceeds earned to the capital employed must be more favorable in agriculture than it is in manufacturing. But since the rate of earnings in agriculture must be computed at the lower rate prevailing in and borrowed from the field of manufacturing, there must always be an additional residuum for the landowner, which he receives as interest on land. This, according to Rodbertus, is the origin of interest on land and of its distinction from that on capital.[38]

In order to make my presentation complete, I should like to state briefly that in spite of the severe theoretical condemnation which represents Rodbertus's verdict in judging the predatory character of interest, he does not desire the abolition of either private ownership of capital nor of the income from it. Rather does he ascribe to private ownership, both of land and of capital "an educative power" which we cannot forego, "a sort of domestic power which we should be able to replace only if we had for that purpose a completely different national system of education. But for that we do not as yet have even the necessary conditions."[39] In the meantime he thinks of private title to land and to capital goods as a "species of public office which entails national economic functions—functions which consist in guiding the economic labor and the economic resources of the nation as best befits the national needs." From this favoring point of view interest can be looked upon as a sort of salary which those "public officials" receive for the exercise of their functions.[40]

I have already remarked that this observation of Rodbertus, recorded rather casually and as a mere footnote, constitutes the earliest mention of a thought which some subsequent writers, particularly Schäffle developed into a peculiar variant of the remuneration theory.

2. DEFICIENCIES OF RODBERTUS'S SYSTEM

THAT brings me to my critique of Rodbertus's doctrinal system. Let me say at once and without mincing matters that I consider the interest theory which is a part of it to be completely erroneous. I am convinced that it suffers from a series of grave theoretical defects. In the following pages I shall attempt to set forth those defects as clearly and as impartially as I can.

＊

A] The first stumbling block which my critical appraisal encounters is the cornerstone on which he erects his structure. He lays down the principle that all goods, economically considered, are only the products of labor.

First of all, what does he mean by "economically considered"? Rodbertus clears that up by an antithesis and contrasts the point of view of economic science to the point of view of the physical sciences. He expressly concedes that goods are physically the product, not only of labor but also of the forces of nature. If nevertheless goods are supposed from the economist's point of view to be only the product of labor, he can mean only one thing. He must mean that the cooperation of natural forces in the process of production is a factor to which we may be completely indifferent when we study human economy. On one occasion Rodbertus expresses this point very strongly when he says, "All other goods (other than those which have cost labor), no matter how necessary or useful they may be to man, are natural goods, with which *economics has no concern.*" "Whatever preliminary results nature has achieved may be a cause for human gratitude, for man has been spared just that much work. *But economics takes them into account only insofar* as labor has complemented the work of nature."[41]

That is just downright wrong. Even purely natural goods, whenever they are rare in comparison with the need for them, are the concern of economics. Or does a nugget of pure gold that falls as a meteorite on a landowner's property, or a silver mine which he happens to discover on his land mean nothing to the economist? Will the owner allow the gold or silver which he has received as a gift from nature to lie disregarded, or will he give it away, or squander it, merely for the reason that nature has presented it to him without any exertion on his part? Or will he not take care of it just as carefully, protect it from the greed of others, prudently dispose of it on the market, in short, husband it with the same economy as he would in the case of gold and silver which he had acquired through the labor of his hands? And is it really true that economics concerns itself with those goods which have cost labor, only to the extent to which *labor* has complemented the work of nature? If that were so, the economic behavior of men would treat a barrel of the choicest Rhine wine as the absolute equivalent of one of those local country wines which, though well tended, is by nature a mediocre vintage. For approximately the same amount of human labor has been expended on each. The fact that nevertheless the Rhine wine often has an economic value 10 times as great, is an cloquent refutation which life offers of Rodbertus's theory.

Negations of that kind are so obvious that Rodbertus could really have been expected to intrench his first and most important fundamental principle behind very carefully prepared defenses against them. But such expectations are unfulfilled. Rodbertus has marshalled a few items intended to make his thesis convincing. But they consist partly of some not overly persuasive references to authorities, and some just as unconvincing argumentation which does not touch the point at issue, but evades it.

The former category includes his oft-repeated invoking of Smith and Ricardo as authorities to support that principle "concerning which there is no more dispute among progressive economists," which has acquired full citizenship among English economists and is at least represented in France, and "what is the most important, has been indelibly impressed on the consciousness of the people, so that it is proof against the sophistries of a doctrine freighted with ulterior motives."[42] We shall have occasion a little later to establish the interesting fact that Smith and Ricardo merely allege the axiomatic truth of the principle we are discussing without furnishing any proof of it whatsoever. And furthermore, both of them have themselves failed to adhere consistently to that principle, as has been very nicely demonstrated by Knies.[43] Now it is obvious that in a scientific discussion even authorities furnish proof, not by the weight of their names, but by the cogency of the reasons that they advance. But since in this case the names are not represented by any reasons at all, nor even by a consistently maintained statement, the conclusion is inescapable that all Rodbertus's invoking of authorities effects no actual strengthening of his position; and furthermore that that position is entirely unsupported except for such arguments as he himself is able to advance for his thesis.

In this connection we must give consideration to a rather long argument in the first of five theorems which Rodbertus entitled *Zur Erkenntnis unserer staatswirtschaftlichen Zustände*. And we must deal with his *Zur Erklärung und Abhilfe der heutigen Kreditnot des Grundbesitzes*.

In the former Rodbertus begins by developing with entire correctness the point that we deal in our economy with goods that cost labor, and why we must do so. He is quite right in placing in the foreground

258

the quantitative disparity between "the infinitude and the insatiability of our capacity for desiring," that is to say, of our wants on the one hand, and our limitations on the other hand, as to time and energy. He mentions only secondarily and more by way of intimation, that labor is "toilsome," and a sacrifice of "freedom" and the like.[44] Similarly, he expounds, with reasons, the unimpeachable truth that an expenditure of labor must be considered "costs." "One simply needs," says Rodbertus,[45] "to grasp the concept behind the word 'to cost.' It means more than saying that 'a' is necessary for the production of 'b.' The essential point is not only that an outlay has been made of something which therefore is no longer present to be laid out for something else, but also this outlay has been made by a person who *feels* the irrevocability of it. The latter point constitutes the reason why only man can experience cost."

That is entirely right! Nor is it any less right, as Rodbertus goes on to say, that both criteria of cost are applicable to labor. For the outlay of labor which every good has caused "is no longer there to be expended on another good," and thus the first criterion is satisfied. And the outlay is felt by no one but man, for it is an outlay of his energy and his time, and both of these are a finite quantity, in contrast to the limitless series of goods—all of which satisfies the second criterion.

But now it devolves upon Rodbertus to prove that the phenomenon of "costing" and hence the right to recognition as an economic factor applies to labor alone, and is not applicable to any other element. He has to concede, first of all, "that one thing (in addition to labor) is necessary and is active in the production of a good. And that one thing —barring ideas which are supplied by the mind—is material which is supplied by nature, plus natural forces which "in the service of labor assist in accomplishing a transformation or an adaptation of material." But nature's contribution fails to meet both criteria of cost. For the active forces of nature says Rodbertus are "infinite and indestructible. The force that combines the substances necessary to the production of a kernel of grain, is always at the disposition of those substances. The material that nature supplies for *one* good is concededly not available for the production of a different one. But one would have to personify nature if one wished to argue that therein lay a reason for speaking of 'costing' and one would have to speak of *her*—i.e., Mother Nature's— costs. Material is not an outlay which *man* makes to produce a good. Only those things may be termed costs of a good which are a *cost to man*."[46]

Of the two parts which comprise the foregoing dual conclusion, the first one which denies the applicability of criterion number one is quite obviously fallacious. Yes, the forces of nature *are* perpetual and indestructible. But for purposes of expenditure for production it is not a question of whether those forces continue to exist at all, but a question of whether they continue to exist and to operate in a manner which makes them capable of a repetition of their productive useful functioning. And in this respect—which is the only respect that is pertinent to our discussion—there is of course no such thing as continued existence and indestructibility. When we have burned our coal, the chemical characteristics of carbon, it is true, continue to exist after it has combined with the oxygen in the air to provide us with the desired heat. But the effectiveness of its properties does not now go beyond remaining, as atoms of carbon, in combination with atoms of oxygen to form carbon dioxide. There is no possibility, for the present, of a repetition of the functioning of these forces of nature. The expenditure of chemical forces which we have made by burning coal as an element in the production of a good cannot be repeated toward the production of an additional good.[47] Exactly the same thing is true, of course, of materials used in production. And Rodbertus really admits it. To be sure, he does so only inadequately, when he says they are not "for the time" available for use in another good. As a matter of fact they are unavailable not only "for the time" that they are incorporated in the first good, but regularly continue to be unavailable subsequently for the production of another good. Thus when I use wood for dowel beams, that wood is unusable, not only during the 100 years of its service in the house as a dowel beam and of its gradual decomposition there, but also after it has rotted. And it cannot serve for the production of another good for the reason that its chemical elements, admittedly still in existence, are nevertheless in a condition that makes them no longer adapted for service to man. Somewhat later, while discussing an objection that he raises himself, Rodbertus abandons his first argument, and places his sole reliance on the contention that the second criterion is lacking, the requirement that costs must apply to a person.

But in this respect, too, Rodbertus is at fault. Even the expenditure of rare gifts of nature constitutes an expenditure the irrevocability of which is felt as a loss by the person concerned. It thus meets that requirement of Rodbertus's definition of the meaning of "to cost," and it does so for the same reason which he himself says applies to labor. Now Rodbertus is making an inquiry into the reason for our being compelled to deal economically with labor and its products. The answer that he supplies does not ascribe our sense of compulsion, as one might expect, to the unpleasantness that is associated with labor. Instead he says, and repeatedly emphasizes, that the cause lies in the quantitative limitation of labor in comparison with the infinitude of our wants. And what is the meaning of this thesis? Surely, Rodbertus can mean only that, as it is, we have but an inadequate supply of labor for the complete satisfaction of our wants, and that therefore any waste of labor creates a still larger deficiency. But Rodbertus's reason would be just as valid, even if labor were entirely unconnected with any feeling of pain, annoyance, compulsion or the like. It would be so even if labor afforded the worker pure unalloyed pleasure, provided the amount of labor continued to be inadequate for the production of all desired goods. A person thus feels a loss because of a wasted expenditure of labor—or indeed any expenditure of labor—simply because he thereby loses the satisfaction of a want that would otherwise be obtainable.[48] And exactly the same thing takes place when a rare gift of nature is wastefully consumed, or consumed at all. If I dissipate a valuable deposit of coal or other mineral, either wantonly or by extravagant mining methods, then I am wasting a quantity of facilities for satisfying wants which I could have fulfilled if I had acted economically—satisfactions which I fritter away by my uneconomical behavior.[49]

Rodbertus does not lose sight of this objection, which it is almost impossible to overlook. The objection might be raised, he says, that for the owner of a stand of timber, costs include, in addition to the labor that he expends on felling trees, etc., the cost of the material itself, "since it has been used for one good and hence cannot be used for another, and since it therefore represents an expenditure which the owner feels as a deprivation."[50] But Rodbertus evades this objection with a bit of sophistry. He claims that the objection is based on a "fiction" inasmuch "as it consists in making a provision of statutory law into the basis of an economic action, which should of course be governed only by valid natural law." Only from the point of view of statutory law, says Rodbertus, can it be assumed that natural resources have any "owner" before any labor has been expended on them. The situation would be entirely altered, if private ownership of land were abolished.

But of course that would not alter the case at all, with respect to its decisive feature. If standing lumber is a relatively rare natural resource at all, then it follows from the very nature of things and irrespective of any provision of law, that any wastage of rare natural resources affecting weal or woe, must proceed from persons. The legal provisions are concerned only with the question of which specific persons suffer the deprivation. Under a system of private ownership of land the proprietor is the person interested, and the one who feels the loss; under a system of socialized property in land, the entire circle of society would be the persons concerned; in the absence of any system of law and order it would be the incumbent in actual control, be he the first or the strongest. But it would be unavoidable that the loss or any diminution of rare natural resources, would affect disadvantageously a person or a group of persons in the satisfaction of human wants. One might imagine an exception if the forest had no human inhabitants at all, or if the inhabitants, from some noneconomic motive such as a religious one, refrained on principle from using wood in any way, shape or form. In such case, to be sure, there would be no economic treatment of wood. But it would be not because purely natural resources are incapable, as a matter of principle, of being the subject of a loss involving deprivation to a person. It would be because the factual circumstances applying in the given case were such as to exclude such personal relationships, which in and of themselves might very well have been involved.

In a later work Rodbertus devotes another short bit of argumentation to his thesis, advancing what is apparently the same idea, though it appears, in part, in somewhat different guise. Everything can be called a product, he says, which achieves economic relationship to us by means of labor. All such products are to be credited, economically speaking, solely to human labor, because labor is the only original force and the only original expenditure with the help of which human economy is transacted.[51] This line of reasoning encounters, first of all, the counter argument that it is highly doubtful whether the premise from which he proceeds is itself correct. And certainly Knies's attacks upon its soundness were delivered with great decision, and were backed, in my opinion, with cogent arguments.[52] In the second place, even if his premise were correct, his conclusion from it would not be. Even if labor were the only original force with which man carries on his economic activity, I still cannot see why man should not have grounds for conducting his economy through the instrumentality of additional forces besides the "original forces." Why not through certain achievements of that original force, or the achievements of other original forces? Why not through that meteorite we discussed some pages ago? Why not through that fortuitously discovered jewel? Or the natural coal deposits? The simple fact is that Rodbertus is too narrowly limited in his conception of the nature and the causative forces of human economy. Now, he is quite correct in saying that the reason why we deal economically with the original force called "labor" is "because labor is limited as to time and quantity, because labor, once put to use is used up, and finally, because it represents a sacrifice of our freedom." But those are all only intermediate reasons, not the one ultimate reason for our economic behavior. In the last analysis we carry on our economy with the help of labor, limited and onerous though it be, because if we deported ourselves uneconomically with respect to labor, we should suffer an impairment of our well-being. Exactly the same motive impels us to carry on our economy with respect to any other useful thing which we cannot forego or lose without a sacrifice of enjoyment, because the supply of it is limited. That applies whether or not it be an original force, whether or not it may have cost some original force called "labor."

The position taken by Rodbertus then becomes more untenable than ever, when he adds the further statement that goods are even to be regarded solely as products of *manual labor*. This statement, in addition to other things, excludes from consideration as economically productive activity even the indirect intellectual labor of the supervision of production labor. And it leads to a host of internal inconsistencies and faulty conclusions which exclude any possibility of doubt as to the erroneous character of the statement itself, and which were unearthed by Knies in such striking fashion that it would be superfluous repetition on my part to go into the matter again.[53]

And so Rodbertus finds himself, after the setting up of his very first fundamental principle, at loggerheads with fact. Now to be completely fair I am compelled to make an admission at this point which Knies could not make from his point of view as a representative of the use theory. My admission is that the refutation of his initial fundamental principle is not a refutation of his theory of interest. That principle is erroneous because it misrepresents, not the contribution of capital, but the contribution of nature to the production of goods. I believe with

Rodbertus that if we consider all the successive stages of production as a single process, capital goods cannot be said to occupy an independent position among the costs of production. Capital goods are not as Rodbertus contends, exclusively "labor expended in the past" but they are so in part, and as a matter of fact usually they are so in greater part. As to the rest, capital goods are valuable accumulated natural forces. Let us assume a case where there is an absence of the latter. Let us assume a production process which throughout all its stages employs only free gifts of nature and labor, or uses only such intermediary goods as themselves result from nothing but free gifts of nature and labor. Wherever that condition obtains, we may truly say with Rodbertus that such goods, economically speaking, are products of labor alone. Inasmuch, then, as Rodbertus's fundamental error does not apply to the part played by capital but to the contributions made by nature, the conclusions that he draws from them on the nature of interest need not necessarily be in error. Not until subsequent developments in his doctrine exhibit essential errors shall we be able to reject it as erroneous. Such errors will, to be sure, make their appearance.

In order not to draw undue advantage from Rodbertus's first error, I shall, for all the remaining pages of this investigation, frame all my presuppositions in such a way as to eliminate completely all the consequences of that error. I shall concede that all goods are produced only by the cooperation of labor and *free* forces of nature and with the assistance of only such capital goods as are the result of the cooperation of labor and free forces of nature, without the intervention of natural material resources having exchange value. Within the limitations of this presupposition I can admit the validity of Rodbertus's fundamental principle that all goods, economically speaking, cost only labor. Let us continue.

*

b] Rodbertus's next thesis is that by the laws of nature and according to the "idea of pure justice" the entire product, having been produced by the worker alone, must belong to the worker, or in lieu of it, its full value without deduction. I am fully in accord with this thesis, too, since under the terms of the limiting presupposition which I stipulated before, there can be no question of its correctness and its fairness. But I do think that Rodbertus and all the other socialists have a false conception of the realization of this truly just principle. Misled by that misconception they desire the creation of a condition which is not in accordance with the principle, but directly opposed to it. I consider it remarkable that the numerous attempts that have been made hitherto to refute the exploitation theory have touched on this decisive point only superficially at best, but never presented it in its true light. I shall therefore take the liberty of requesting my readers to devote some measure of attention to the following development of the point. This difficult subject certainly requires it.

The error that I censure I shall first name and then elucidate. The completely just proposition that the worker is to receive the entire value of his product can reasonably be interpreted to mean either that he is to receive the full *present* value of his product *now* or that he is to get the entire *future* value in the *future*. But Rodbertus and the socialists interpret it to mean that the worker is to receive the entire *future* value of his product *now*. At the same time they act as if that were entirely self-evident and the only possible interpretation of that proposition.

Let us illustrate the matter by a concrete example. Let us imagine that the production of a good, for instance a steam engine, costs five years' labor, and that the completed machine commands a price of $5,500. Let us further ignore for the moment that in actual practice the labor is distributed among many workers, and imagine that a single workman produces the machine by five years' continuous labor. Now let us ask what wage is due him in the sense of the proposition that the worker is to receive his whole product, or the full value of his product. There cannot be a moment's doubt that the answer is the whole steam engine or $5,500. But *when*? On that score, too, there can be no slightest doubt. Obviously at the expiration of five years. For by the laws of nature he cannot receive the steam engine before it is in existence, cannot gain possession of a good valued at $5,500 and created by himself, before he has created it. In that case he will have received his compensation according to the formula, "the whole future product, or its whole future value at a future time."

But it often happens that the worker cannot or will not wait until his product has been fully completed. Our worker wishes, for instance, after the expiration of one year to receive a corresponding partial compensation. The question arises, as to how that is to be measured in accordance with the aforementioned principle. I think this, too, can be settled without a moment's hesitation. The worker will get justice if he gets all that he has labored to produce up to this point. If, for instance, he has up to this time produced a pile of unfinished ore, or of iron, or of steel material, then he will be justly treated if he receives the pile of ore, of iron, or of steel, or receives the full exchange value which this pile of material has, and of course has *now*. I do not think any socialist could find fault with that decision.

How large will that value be, in relation to the price of the finished machine? Here is the point at which a superficial thinker can easily go wrong. The worker has up to this time performed a fifth of the technical work which the production of the entire machine demands. Accordingly, a superficial consideration of the problem might tempt us to answer, the present product will possess an exchange value of one-fifth of that of the whole product, that is to say, $1,100. The worker is to receive a year's wage of $1,100.

That is wrong. One thousand one hundred dollars is one-fifth of the price of a completed, present steam engine. But what the worker has produced up to this time is not one-fifth of a machine that is already finished, but only one-fifth of a machine which will not be finished for another four years. And those are two different things. Not different by a sophistical splitting of verbal hairs, but actually different as to the thing itself. The former fifth has a value different from that of the latter fifth, just as surely as a complete present machine has a different value in terms of present valuation from that of a machine that will not be available for another four years. And it will be so, just as surely as it is true in general that present goods have a value different from that of future goods.

That present goods have a higher value, in the esteem of that present in which the economic events take place, than future goods of the same kind and quality, belongs to the most widely known and most important economic facts. The causes to which this fact owes its origin, the multifarious variations in which it is manifested, and the equally multifarious consequences to which it leads in economic life, will be the subject of detailed investigation in the second volume of this work. That investigation will be neither so easy nor so simple as the simplicity of the basic idea might lead us to expect. But even before I have completed that investigation, I think it justifiable to rely on the fact, as a fact, that present goods do have a higher value than identical future goods. The crudest empirical tests of everyday life establish it beyond any question of a doubt. If you ask 1,000 persons to choose between a gift of $1,000 today and $1,000 50 years from today all 1,000 of them will prefer to have it today. Or ask another 1,000 persons who are in need of a car, and who would be willing to pay $2,000 for a good one, how much they would give today for an equally good car to be delivered in 10 or 15 years. All of them would offer a far smaller sum, if indeed they offered anything at all, thus demonstrating that people, when acting economically, universally regard present goods as more valuable than identical future goods.

Accordingly our worker at the end of a year's work on the steam engine that will be finished in another four years has not yet earned the entire value of one-fifth of a completed engine. He has earned some smaller amount. Smaller by how much? I cannot at this point explain that without a lot of awkward anticipation. Let the remark suffice here that the amount of that difference bears an ascertained relationship to the rate of interest prevailing in the locality as well as to the remoteness of the time at which the whole product is scheduled to be completed. If I assume a prevailing interest rate of 5% then the product of the first year's labor will, at the end of the first year, be worth about $1,000.[54] And so, if the principle is valid that the worker is entitled to the full produce of his labor, or to the entire value thereof, then the wage for the first year of labor will amount to $1,000.[55]

If anyone has the impression, in spite of the line of reasoning laid down above, that this is too little, I offer the following for consideration. No one will question the statement that the worker is not being underpaid if at the end of five years he receives the whole steam engine or its whole price of $5,500. Let us for the sake of comparison also compute the price of the anticipated payment of wages in terms of its price at the end of the fifth year. Since the $1,000 that he receives at the end of the first year can be deposited for another four years at interest he can thus earn interest at 5% for four years. That is to say, he can receive an additional $200 (ignoring the compounding of interest) for the possibility of using his money that way is open to the worker when he has received his wage. Obviously then, $1,000 paid at the end of the first year is the equivalent of $1,200 paid at the end of the fifth year. So if the worker gets $1,000 at the end of a year for one-fifth of the technical work, he is clearly being compensated by a standard which is not less favorable than if he had received $5,500 at the expiration of five years.

But how do Rodbertus and the socialists envision the principle that the worker is entitled to receive the entire value of his product? They demand that the entire value which the product is going to have when completed shall be used for payment of wages, but not at the conclusion of the whole process of production, but made available in installments during the course of the work. Let us weigh carefully what that means. That means, in the case of our steam engine, that the entire $5,500 which the engine will be worth at the end of five years, is received by the worker at the end of 2½ years, which is the result attained by averaging the installments received over five years. I must confess I find it absolutely impossible to justify this demand by that premise. How can it be according to the laws of nature and in keeping with the idea of pure justice, for someone to receive at the end of 2½ years a whole which he will not have created until the end of five years? This is so little "in accord with the laws of nature" that it is, quite on the contrary, just naturally impracticable. It is not feasible even if we free the worker from all the bonds of his much maligned wage contract, and put him into the most favorable conceivable position of an entrepreneur entirely "on his own." As a worker and entrepreneur he will of course get the whole $5,500, but not before they are produced, that is to say, not before the end of five years. And how is a thing to be brought to pass, in the name of the idea of pure justice, through the instrumentality of the wage contract, which the nature of things denies to the entrepreneur himself?

What the socialists want is, in plain English, for the workers to get under the wage contract, *more* than their work produces, more than they could get if they were entrepreneurs in business for themselves, and more than they bring in to the entrepreneur with whom they have made the wage contract. What they have created, and what they are justly entitled to is $5,500 at the end of five years. But the $5,500 at the end of 2½ years, which is what is being claimed for them, is more than that; in fact if the interest rate is 5%, it is equivalent to about $6,200 at the end of five years. And this state of relative valuations is not, mind you, the result of social institutions of debatable merit which have created interest and established a rate of 5%. It is a direct result of the fact that we humans live out our lives in a temporal world, that our Today with its needs and cares comes before our Tomorrow, and that our Day-After-Tomorrow may perhaps not be assured us at all. Not only the "profit grasping capitalist," but every worker as well, indeed every human being makes this difference between present value and future value. How the worker would complain of being cheated, if in place of $10 out of his week's wages which are due today he were offered $10 to be paid a year from today! And is something that is not a matter of indifference to the worker supposed to be such to the entrepreneur? Is he to pay $5,500 at the end of 2½ years for $5,500 which he is to receive, in the shape of a finished steam engine, at the end of five? That is neither just nor natural! The thing that is just and natural—I am glad to concede it again—is that the worker should receive the whole $5,500 at the end of five years. If he cannot or will not wait five years, he shall still receive the entire value of what he produces. But of course it must be the *present* value of his *present* product. This value however will necessarily be smaller than the future value of the product which his labor produces, because in the economic world the law obtains that the present value of future goods is less than that of present goods. It is a law which owes its existence to no social or governmental institution, but directly to human nature and to the nature of things.

If there is any excuse for discursiveness anywhere, it might be at this point where it is a question of the confutation of a doctrine as pregnant with possibilities as is the socialist exploitation theory. And so, at the risk of seeming tedious to my readers, I shall submit a second concrete case which will, I hope, afford me an opportunity of proving the socialists' error even more convincingly.

In our first example I ignored the fact that division of labor is an economic actuality. Now I shall change the conditions of the problem in this respect so as to approach the realities of economic life more closely. Let us assume that five different workers participate in the labor of producing a machine, and that each of them contributes one year's work. One worker, perhaps, is a miner who procures the necessary ore, the second prepares the iron from it, the third transforms the iron into steel, the fourth constructs the necessary steel parts, the fifth finally assembles these and, in general, does the finishing. Since each of these successive workers, by the nature of his work, cannot begin his work until the one before him has completed his preparatory stage of the work, the five years' work of our laborers cannot be carried on simultaneously, but only in succession. The completion of the machine, just as in our first example, will likewise take five years. The value of the machine we shall again assume to be $5,500. Now, in conformity with the principle that the worker is to receive the full price of what he produces, what can each of the five who share the labor claim for what he accomplishes?

Let us first solve the problem for a case in which there is no introduction of an outside entrepreneur, and in which therefore the claims to compensation, or the method of dividing the article produced need to be adjusted only among the five workmen. In such a case two things are certain.

The *first* of these is that a distribution of the product itself cannot take place *until the expiration of five years,* because before that time there is nothing there to divide. For if there were any desire, at the end of the second year let us say, to distribute to the individuals as compensation the ore and the iron that had been produced in the first two years, then the raw materials would be lacking for the succeeding stages. On the contrary, it is clear that the intermediary product that is achieved each year must be excluded from any early distribution and retained for the production process until its conclusion.

The *second* thing that is certain is that there will be a total of $5,500 to be distributed among the five workers. But in what proportions?

Certainly not, as one might easily suppose at a first—and superficial —glance, in equal fifths! For that would mean a distribution favoring the worker whose labor is performed in later stages, over those whose work was done early. The worker who puts the finishing touches on the machine would receive $1,100 for his year's work immediately after its conclusion. The one who prepared the individual parts for assembling into the complete machine would receive the same amount, but would have to wait a whole year after he had completed his work to collect his compensation for it. And then there is the extreme case of the worker who mined the ore, and who would not receive his wage until four years after he had completed his work. Since a delay of that sort could not possibly be a matter of indifference to the persons concerned, everyone would want to perform the final labor, which does not suffer any postponment of compensation, and no one would want to assume the work of the preparatory stages. In order to find anyone to assume those jobs, the workers in the late stages would be compelled to consent to an arrangement by which a larger portion of the ultimate exchange value of the product would be accorded to their co-workers in the preparatory stages, to compensate them for the delay. The amount of the difference would depend partly on the length of the postponement, and partly on the degree of difference in the valuation of present and future goods which prevails within our small society, as determined by the economic and cultural conditions which exist there. If the degree of that difference is, for instance, 5% per year, then the shares of the five workers would be graduated as shown below.

The first worker, whose wage is not paid to him until four years after the completion of his year's labor, receives	$1,200
The second, who waits three years	1,150
The third, who waits two years	1,100
The fourth, who waits one year	1,050
The last, who receives his wage immediately upon completion of his labor	1,000
Total	$5,500

It would be inconceivable that each of the workers should receive an equal share of $1,100, except under the hypothesis that the difference in time is a matter of indifference to them. It would be conceivable only if they all considered themselves equally well paid at $1,100, no matter whether they received that sum three or four years later, or immediately after finishing their labors. I hardly need to observe that such a hypothesis never holds, and never can hold. But in the absence of the introduction of a third party it is in any case *completely impossible for each of them to receive $1,100 immediately after completion of his labors.*

It is probably worth while in passing to call special attention to one circumstance. I do not think that anyone could find the distribution plan that I have recorded above an unjust one. And I am especially convinced that, since the workers share their own product only with each other, there can be no contention that there has been an injustice done by a capitalist entrepreneur. And yet the worker who completed the next-to-last fifth does not receive a full fifth of the ultimate price of the product. He gets only $1,050, and the last worker caps the climax by receiving only $1,000!

Now let us make the further assumption, with which reality is ordinarily in agreement, that the workers cannot or will not wait for their wages until the process of producing the machine has been completed. That leads to their entering into an agreement with an entrepreneur whereby they will receive their wage immediately upon completion of their labor, in return for which he is to become the owner of the final product. Now let us make the still further assumption that this entrepreneur is an entirely just and unselfish man, who would be thoroughly incapable of making use of any possible distress to which the workers might be a prey, in order to depress by extortionate measures their claims to wages. Let us ask what the conditions would be of a wage contract drawn up and signed under such circumstances.

The answer is fairly easy to find. Obviously the workers are being treated with complete justice if the entrepreneur offers them as a wage the same as they would have received as their distributive shares, had they been engaged in independent production. This principle gives us a reliable standard for one worker, to begin with, namely, the last of the five. The latter would have received $1,000 immediately after performing his work. So the entrepreneur, to be completely fair, must offer him the same $1,000. But the rest of our table of shares does not give us any direct standard. For since the point of time at which compensation is made is now different from the one that would have applied in the case of their own distribution of shares, the amounts set up for the latter would no longer be directly applicable. However, we have another firm criterion. For since all five workers have contributed the same amount of service toward the genesis of the product, they are in justice entitled to equal wages. And since each one is paid immediately after he has completed his labors, the wages will be equal sums. Justice is served if each worker receives $1,000 at the end of his year's labor.

If anyone should think that that is too little, I refer him to the following easy example in arithmetic. It will prove that the workers now receive exactly the same amount as they would have received through a distribution among themselves—and that amount was shown to be indubitably just. Worker No. 5 receives $1,000 from the distribution, immediately after the end of the year's work, and in the case of the wage contract he receives the same amount at the same time. Worker No. 4 receives $1,050 through the distribution, one year after his work is completed; in the case of the wage contract he receives $1,000 immediately after his work is completed. Now if he puts that out at interest for a year, he achieves exactly the same position that he would have in the case of the distribution, for he then has $1,050 one year after completing his work. Worker No. 3 receives by the distribution $1,100 two years after his work ends, by the wage contract $1,000 immediately which, put out at interest, amounts to the same $1,100 at the same time. In the same way the $1,000 which the first and second workers receive under the wage contract, with the addition of interest are exactly equal to the $1,200 and the $1,150 which, under the distribution, would have been received after four and three years respectively. And if each of the individual wage sums is the equivalent of the corresponding distributional share, then the aggregate of the wage sums must be the equivalent of the aggregate of all the distributional shares. Hence the total of $5,000 which the entrepreneur pays immediately upon performance of the labor to the workers is the exact equivalent of the $5,500 which, in the other case, could have been distributed among the workers at the end of the fifth year.[56]

Any higher wage, such as a yearly wage of $1,100, would be conceivable only under one of two alternatives. Either something to which the workers are not indifferent, namely the difference in time, would have to be a matter of complete indifference to the entrepreneur, or the entrepreneur would have to have the desire to make a gift to the workers of the difference between $1,100 in present funds and $1,100 in future funds. Neither the one alternative nor the other is to be expected of the private entrepreneur, at least not as a rule. Nor could one make it a matter of the slightest reproach, and least of all would it justify a charge of injustice, exploitation, or predacity. There is only one person of whom the workers could expect such behavior as a regular thing, and that is the *state*. For the state is, on the one hand, an entity that exists in perpetuity, and is not therefore compelled to take such strict account of the temporal difference in the giving and receiving of goods. And the state, whose ultimate purpose is the welfare of all its members, can, on the other hand, afford to give instead of to bargain. And so it would concededly be thinkable for the state—but *only* the state in its capacity of giant entrepreneur in the production field—to offer the workers a wage representing the entire future product of their future production and to give it to them *now*, that is to say, immediately after the performance of their labor. Whether the state shall or shall not do so, and thereby afford a practical solution of the social problem in terms of socialist doctrine, is a question of expediency, which it cannot be my purpose to discuss here. But one thing I should like to repeat here and with all possible emphasis, and that is this. If the socialist state pays out now to the workers, as wages, the entire future exchange value of their product, then that is not a *fulfillment but a violation* of the fundamental principle that the worker is entitled to receive as his wage the value of what he produces. And it is a deviation dictated by social and political considerations, rather than the restoration, as the socialists allege, of a situation which of itself is natural or which accords with the idea of pure justice, but has been upset through the avidity of the capitalists for exploitation. On the contrary, it is an artificial interference intended to render possible what in the natural course of things is an impossibility, and to make it possible by means of a veiled and perpetual gift by a generous communal entity known as the state, a gift granted to its more penurious members.

And now a short practical application. It is easily perceived that the stage of distribution which I last described in our example, is the one at which we have actually arrived in our market economy. In this system too, the full value of the product of labor is not distributed as wages, but only a lesser sum, though at an earlier point in time. But the worker suffers no unjust curtailment in his claim to the full amount of what he produces, provided one condition is fulfilled, and that condition provides as follows. The total sum of wages distributed in installments must not fall short of the ultimate price of the final product by a greater amount than is necessary to bridge the gap representing the prevailing difference in the valuation of present and future goods. In other words, the total wages must not be exceeded by the price of the final product to a greater degree than is represented by the prevailing interest rate. The workers in that case receive the full value of their product at a valuation which duly reflects the point in time at which they receive their wage. Only to the extent that the total wage lags behind the ultimate exchange value of the product by a margin in excess of the prevailing interest can that lag, under some circumstances, indicate genuine exploitation of the workers.[57]

Let us return to Rodbertus. The second decisive error with which I charged him in the immediately preceding pages was his interpretation of the statement that the worker is entitled to receive the entire value of his product. I conceded the correctness of the statement but not of his unjustified and illogical interpretation, to the effect that the worker is entitled to receive *now* the entire exchange value which his completed product *will some day have.*

●

c]   If we institute a search to discover what led Rodbertus into this error, we find that the source of it was still another error, and the *third* important one which I hereby charge he made in his exploitation theory. For he proceeds on the assumption that the exchange value of goods is determined exclusively by the quantity of labor which their production has cost. If that were a correct assumption, then the intermediary product, which in our example represents one year's labor, would indeed at that stage already be invested with a full fifth of the value which the

271

completed product, with its five years of labor behind it, will one day possess. And in that case there would be justice in the claim that the worker is already entitled to a full fifth of that value as his wage.

But in the form in which Rodbertus presents it, his assumption is unquestionably wrong. Now, if challenged to prove this, I am not even under the necessity of discrediting Ricardo's famous law of value, that labor is the source and the measure of all value. I merely need to call attention to the existence of a highly important exception to that law. It is an exception which Ricardo himself conscientiously registered, and which he discussed in detail in a special chapter. But Rodbertus, strange to say, takes no note of it whatever. That exception concerns the fact that, if two goods have been produced at the cost of equal amounts of labor, then a higher exchange value will attach to the one which requires for its completion either a longer period of time, or the prior performance of a greater amount of preliminary work. Ricardo accords notice to that fact in strange fashion. In Section IV of the first chapter of his *Principles* he makes the following statement: "The principle that the quantity of labor expended on the production of goods determines their relative value, *is subject to considerable modification* by reason of the use of machines and of other fixed and durable capital." In Section V he adds, "also by reason of the unequal duration of capital and the unequal rapidity with which it is returned to its owner." Sometimes the production of goods requires the use of fixed capital of great magnitude or of long duration; sometimes production is of such a nature that a long turnover period is required for the entrepreneur to recover his liquid capital. Goods so produced have a higher exchange value than goods to which these considerations apply in lesser degree or not at all, despite the fact that the latter may have cost the same amount of labor as the former. And the degree of difference in such exchange value is the amount of interest charged by the capitalist.

Even the most partisan defenders of his labor theory of value could hardly harbor any doubt that there really is such an exception to it as is here observed by Ricardo. They may be equally certain that under certain circumstances the factor of temporal remoteness may have even greater influence on the price of goods than the factor of magnitude of labor costs. I remind my readers, as examples, of the price of a wine which has been seasoned for decades, or of a 100-year-old tree in a timber forest.

But there is another very special point in connection with this exception. For it does not require any unusual keenness of perception to notice that the exception really contains the essence of originary interest. For the margin in exchange value which is acquired by those goods that require for their production an advance expenditure of capital, is the very thing that sticks to the fingers of the entrepreneur capitalist in the guise of interest, when the time comes for the distribution of the yield of the product.[58] If that difference in value did not exist, then originary interest would not exist either. The former makes possible the latter, encompasses it, is identical with it. There is nothing easier than to illus-strate this, if indeed any one demands proof of such a patently obvious fact. Let us assume that three consumers' goods require for their production one year's labor each, but that they differ from each other in the length of the period for which this labor must be advanced. Let the first require that the year's labor be performed only one year prior to completion, the second ten years previously, the third twenty years previously. Under these circumstances the exchange value of the first good will and must be sufficient to cover the wage for one year of labor and in addition the interest for one year on the amount of the labor "advanced." It is perfectly obvious that the same exchange value is not sufficient to meet the wage for one year's labor and in addition either the ten years' interest or the twenty years' interest on an "advance" of the same amount of labor. The payment of such interest can be met only when and because the exchange value of the second and third consumers' good is correspondingly higher than that of the first, even though all three have equal labor costs. And the difference in exchange value is clearly the source from which the ten years' and twenty years' interest can and does flow.

And so that exception to the labor theory of value has no lesser significance than that it is identical with the principal instance of originary interest. Whoever wants to explain the originary interest must explain Ricardo's exception. Without an explanation of the exception, there is no explanation of the interest problem. If a treatise makes it a point to deal with originary interest, and yet ignores this exception, not to say denies its existence, then that must be characterized as a blunder so gross that its equal cannot be imagined. For Rodbertus to ignore that exception is nothing short of an utter disregard of the main topic of the subject he was supposed to explain.

Nor can it be urged as an excuse for his blunder, that Rodbertus had not intended to establish a rule that was valid for real life, but merely to set up a hypothesis of which he availed himself, in order to conduct his abstract investigation with greater ease and accuracy. He does, to be sure, on occasion advance, in the guise of a mere presupposition, his dictum that the value of every good is determined by its labor costs.[59] However there is no dearth of passages in which Rodbertus reveals his conviction that his law of value also has validity in real economic life.[60] And in addition it must be urged against Rodbertus that it is not permissible to assume by way of presupposition anything one wishes! Even in the case of a merely hypothetical presupposition, it is permissible to eliminate from consideration only such factual elements as are irrelevant to the question under examination. But what can be said of a scientific inquiry into interest which begins by presupposing that one of the main instances of interest does not exist? What of an explanation in which the best part of that which is to be explained is conjured away "by hypothesis"!

Rodbertus of course is right in one thing he says. If you want to discover a principle, such as that underlying interest, you cannot, says he, "have value dancing up and down";[61] you must assume the validity of a stable rule of value. But we have recorded the following fact. If goods show a greater time interval between expenditure of labor and completion of production, they will also, other things being equal, have greater value. Is not that a stable rule of value? And does not that rule of value have fundamental significance for the phenomenon of interest? And is it to be eliminated as a factor, in the same manner in which we disregard fortuitous and coincidental market conditions?[62]

The consequences of this strange kind of negative presupposition made themselves apparent in due course. I have already touched upon one. Rodbertus overlooked the influence of time on the valuation of a good, and so he easily could and inevitably did commit the blunder of confusing the claim of the worker to the entire present value of his product with his claim to its future value. We shall encounter without delay a few other consequences.

*

D] A *fourth* charge which I level against Rodbertus is that his doctrine contradicts itself in important respects.

Rodbertus's whole theory of interest on land is based on the often and emphatically repeated pronouncement, that the absolute quantity of "interest" to be gained in a production process depends, not on the quantity of capital employed, but entirely on the quantity of labor applied in the course of the production in question. Let us assume that in a given industrial production process, for instance a shoe manufacturing business, there are 10 men employed; that each worker produces a product in one year having an exchange value of $1,000; that the necessary sustenance which he receives as wages amounts to a deduction from that amount of $500. In that case, no matter whether the capital employed is large or small, the entrepreneur has a year's excess of proceeds amounting *in toto* to $5,000. If the capital employed amounts to $10,000 ($5,000 for wages and $5,000 for materials) then the surplus proceeds amount to 50% on a base of the capital of $10,000. Now let us suppose that another productive enterprise, say a jewelry factory, also employs 10 men. Under the assumption that the value of products is determined by the amount of labor they represent, these 10 men, too, will produce a yearly product of $1,000 each, of which half belongs to them as wages, and the other half as surplus proceeds to the entrepreneur. But since gold, the material in the second case, represents a markedly higher capital value than the shoemaker's leather, the total surplus of $5,000 in the second example will be computed percentage-wise on a far larger business capital as a base. Assuming that the latter amounts to $200,000, consisting of $5,000 for wages and $195,000 for materials, then the surplus proceeds will be computed as 2½% computed on the base of the business capital of $200,000. These two examples of mine are conceived entirely in the spirit of Rodbertus's theory.

In almost every manufacturing enterprise the ratio of the number of workers employed, directly and indirectly, to the magnitude of the business capital employed will vary from the ratio obtaining in others. If consistency were to be preserved, that would mean that in almost every enterprise the rate of earnings for the business capital employed would have to vary correspondingly and within extremely wide limits. Now Rodbertus himself does not dare to maintain that such is the case in real life. Instead, we find a remarkable passage in his exposition of his theory of interest on land. The assumption is there set down that, by reason of the competition between capitals throughout the manufacturing field, a uniform rate of surplus proceeds will be established. I will submit the passage in Rodbertus's own words. He makes the observation that in the manufacturing field the only factor of production in use is *capital* goods, and that therefore all surplus proceeds earned in that field are looked upon as income on capital. Then he continues as follows.

"Furthermore, the resulting rate of return will exert an influence tending toward equalization of all incomes on capital, and so will furnish a certain rate of surplus proceeds which will be the standard for the surplus proceeds from raw materials also, and for its calculation on the basis of the capital employed in raw production. For if, as a result of the generally accepted exchange value, there arises a uniformly designated criterion to express the ratio of yield to capital, then that will serve also in the case of surplus proceeds derived from a manufacturing process. In other words, it will be possible to say that the surplus in a given industry amounts to such and such a percentage of the capital employed. That percentage of surplus proceeds will then furnish a standard by which to equalize all surplus proceeds. *Wherever an industry shows proceeds at a rate exceeding the general rate, competition will cause additional capital to be attracted, and will thus cause a general tendency toward the equalization of all proceeds.* For that reason no one will invest capital, unless he can expect an income at that rate."[63]

It will be worth while to examine this passage more closely.

Rodbertus calls competition the factor which will bring about the adoption of a uniform rate of surplus proceeds in the field of manufacturing. He hints only very vaguely how that will take place. He makes the assumption that every time the rate of proceeds in an industry exceeds the uniform rate, an influx of additional capital investment will depress the rate to the uniform level. Conversely, we are presumably entitled to add, every instance of lower-than-normal rate will cause a withdrawal of capital so that the income rate will rise to the average.

Let us carry our consideration of these events a little beyond the early point at which Rodbertus breaks it off. In what way can an increase in capital investment depress an abnormally high rate of surplus proceeds to the general level? Obviously the only means will be as follows. With the increased capital the production of the particular good will be increased, and the increased supply will depress the price to the point where, after deduction of wages, the reduced surplus yield amounts to no more than its normal rate. In the example we gave of the shoe industry, we should have to imagine the procedure by which the abnormally high return of 50% would be reduced to the normal rate of 5% to be apparently as follows. Attracted by the high yield rate of 50% a great many persons will take up shoe manufacture as a new business, and in addition, those already in the shoe industry will increase their production. That increases the supply of shoes, and the price and the exchange value of shoes goes down. This process goes on until the point is reached where 10 workers in the shoe industry produce a year's product which has an exchange value, not of $10,000 but of $5,500. Now after deduction of the necessary wages of $5,000 the entrepreneur has only $500 left as his surplus proceeds. Computed on the basis of the same $10,000 capital investment as before, this represents the prevailing rate of 5%. The exchange value of shoes must remain permanently at the point which has now been reached, if the earnings in the shoe business are not to become abnormal again, in which case there would be a repetition of the entire levelling process we have just described.

In similar fashion the lower-than-normal rate of surplus proceeds in the jewelry manufacturing business of 2½% is raised to 5%. Because of the inadequate rate of earnings, participation in the jewelry business is restricted; as a result the supply of jewelry is reduced; then its exchange value rises to the point where the amount of jewelry turned out in a year by 10 workers in the industry attains an exchange ratio of $15,000. Now after deducting the same wages of $5,000, the entrepreneur has surplus proceeds of $10,000. This amount, computed on the same base of $200,000 as before, represents an interest rate of 5%. Thus the point of stabilization is reached at which the exchange value of jewelry like that of shoes in the first example, can be regarded as permanently established.

Now the equalization of abnormal rates of surplus proceeds cannot be effected without permanent changes in the exchange value of the goods concerned. That is an important point, and before I proceed any further I should like to discuss it from another aspect and remove all possible doubt. For if the exchange value of the products remained unchanged, the only way to raise an inadequate rate of earnings to the normal rate would be to supply the deficiency at the expense of the necessary wages of the workers. If, for instance, the product of 10 workers in the manufacture of jewelry retained unchanged the exchange value of $10,000 which is equal to the quantity of labor expended, then leveling of the rate of yield upwards to 5% would require an increase in the amount of yield from $5,000 to $10,000. Obviously no other method is conceivable than to eliminate entirely the wages of the 10 workers at $500 each. That would mean that the entire product is acquired by the capitalist as his return. Without even considering the point that this assumption involves a sheer impossibility, I wish merely to point out that it is equally at variance with experience and with Rodbertus's own theory. It flies in the face of experience because our experience demonstrates to us that the leveling reduction of supply in a given industry is regularly reflected in an increase in the price of the product and not in a reduction of workers' wages. Nor does experience furnish any evidence that wages are essentially lower in those industries which demand heavy investment of capital, than in the others. And yet that would have to be the case if the requirement of a greater quantitative surplus were met by a reduced wage rather than by an increased price of the product. However, the assumption also violates Rodbertus's own theory. For that theory presupposes that in the long run the workers always receive the necessary cost of subsistence as a wage. And the method of leveling which I have just described would, to say the least, be a grave infraction of Rodbertus's rule.

It would be no more difficult to prove the converse proposition. To reduce returns *in excess* of the average without a change in the exchange value of the product could be effected only by *increasing* the wages of the workers above the normal. And that, too, is counter to experience and to the theory of Rodbertus itself. I believe I may claim that I have described the process of the leveling of returns in the foregoing paragraphs in entire conformity to reality and to Rodbertus's own presuppositions. In doing so I assume, be it noted, that the leveling of abnormal returns is brought about by a permanent change, be it upward or downward, in the exchange value of the products in question.

But if the year's product of 10 workers in the shoe industry has an exchange value of $5,500 and that of 10 workers in the manufacture of jewelry has an exchange value of $15,000—and they must have those exchange values, if there is to be a permanent leveling of surplus proceeds as Rodbertus presupposes—then what becomes of his other presupposition that products are exchanged on the basis of the labor they represent? And if the employment of the same quantity of labor results in surplus proceeds of $500 in one industry and of $10,000 in another, what becomes of the principle that the amount of surplus proceeds over labor costs to be gained in a production process, is not in proportion to the magnitude of the capital employed but to the labor performed? The contradiction in which Rodbertus has involved himself is as patent as it is irreconcilable. There are two possible alternatives. The first alternative is that a permanent system of exchange is really established whereby goods are exchanged at values which are in proportion to the labor that the respective goods represent, and whereby, furthermore, the magnitude of the surplus proceeds to be derived from production is really determind by the quantity of labor expended. If that alternative obtains, then any equalization of the ratio of surplus proceeds to capital is an impossibility. The second alternative is that such an equalization does take place. If that alternative obtains, then products cannot possibly continue to be exchanged at values which are in proportion to the labor they represent, nor is it possible that the quantity of labor expended shall be the only determinant of the magnitude of the surplus proceeds to be derived. Rodbertus would have been compelled to observe this manifest contradiction if he had devoted to this process of the leveling of surplus proceeds even a modicum of genuine reflection, instead of tossing off a fine phrase about the equalizing effect of competition and so contenting himself with an utter superficiality.

But actually the situation is worse than that. The whole explanation of interest derived from the use of land, which in Rodbertus's theory is so intimately bound up with the explanation of interest on capital goods, is based on an inconsistency so conspicuous that it required almost incredibly gross negligence for him to overlook it.

He offers two alternatives of which only one is possible. A leveling process in the earnings on capital either is or is not brought about through competition. Let us assume it is. In that case, what justifies the assumption by Rodbertus that leveling takes place throughout the entire field of manufacture, but ceases at the borders of the field of raw production as if spellbound? If agriculture promises a temptingly higher return, why should not more capital be attracted to it? Why should not more land be placed under cultivation, more intensive methods be applied, cultivation be improved, all to the point at which the exchange value of raw products achieves harmony with the newly increased capital engaged in agriculture, so that the latter yields only the prevalent rate of return? Rodbertus's "law" says the quantity of surplus proceeds over labor costs is not in proportion to the outlay of capital, but only in proportion to the amount of labor expended. But if that law did not prevent leveling in manufacture, how will it do so in raw production? But in that case what has become of the constant excess over the prevailing rate of interest, that is to say, the additional residuum of interest on the use of land?

Or, to examine the other alternative, let us assume that leveling does not take place at all. Then there simply is no general prevalent rate of earnings; then, just as for production in general, so for agriculture in particular, there is no definite norm by which to compute what proportion of "interest" is to be counted as interest on capital goods; and finally, there is then no line of demarcation between interest on capital goods and interest on land. And so, no matter whether the leveling of surplus proceeds takes place or not, in either case Rodbertus's theory of residual interest on land dangles in mid-air. And so we find contradiction upon contradiction, and not, indeed, in the matter of trifles, but in the very fundamentals of his theory!

✻

E] Up to this point I have made detailed features the target of my criticism. I will conclude by putting the theory as a whole to the test. If the theory is sound, it must be able to supply a satisfactory explanation for the phenomenon of originary interest as we encounter it in real economic life, and in all the important manifestations of its existence. If it is not able to do that, the verdict is rendered—the theory is false.

I now maintain and shall at once prove that Rodbertus's exploitation theory might, in a pinch, serve to make intelligible the earning of interest by those portions of a capital which are invested in wages, but that it is absolutely impossible by means of his theory to explain the earning of interest by those portions which are invested in materials used in the process of manufacture. I call on the reader to judge.

A jeweler engaged principally in making pearl necklaces employs five workers who make up genuine pearls into necklaces which have a price of a million dollars yearly, and which he disposes of, on the average, in one year. He will therefore have a capital of a million dollars constantly invested in pearls, and this capital must yield an annual income, at the prevailing interest rate, of $50,000. The question now is, how this earning of interest by the jeweler is to be explained.

Rodbertus's reply is that it is a predatory income, gained by pinching it off from the natural and just compensation of labor. But from the wages of which laborers? The five who sort the pearls and assemble them into necklaces? That can hardly be, for if one is supposed to be able to nibble off $50,000 from the just wages of five workers, that just compensation would have to be something in excess of $50,000, or of $10,000 each. That is an amount of just payment that surely can hardly be taken seriously, especially in view of the fact that the occupation of sorting and assembling pearls is not very far exalted above the level of unskilled labor.

Let us examine the problem a little more closely. Is it perhaps the workers of an earlier stage of production whose labor gave rise to the product which the jeweler is exploiting? Might it be the pearl divers? But the jeweler had no contact at all with those workers. He bought his pearls directly from the entrepreneur of the pearl fishery, or even from a middleman. And so he had no opportunity to make any deduction from the product, or from the exchange value of the product of the pearl divers. But maybe it was the entrepreneur of the pearl fishery who did so, instead of the jeweler, so that the latter's gain arises from a deduction from wages of which the former mulcted his workers? That, too, is impossible. For the jeweler would obviously still make his gain, even if the pearler had made no deduction whatsoever from his workers' wages. And even if the pearler distributes the whole million dollars which the pearls are worth, and which he received from the jeweler as the purchase price, among his pearl divers as wages, the only thing he accomplishes is that he himself receives no income. Certainly the jeweler would not sacrifice any of his earnings. For to the jeweler it is certainly a matter of complete indifference how the purchase price he pays is distributed, provided it involves no increase in that price. And so, strain your imagination as you will, you will search in vain for the workers from whose just wages the jeweler's $50,000 gain could conceivably have been withheld.

But possibly this example of mine may leave some of my readers with unresolved doubts. Some may perhaps consider it somewhat strange that the labor of the five pearlsetters should be the source from which the jeweler can derive so considerable a gain as $50,000, yet they may find it not entirely inconceivable. And so I will present a still more striking example. It is a good old example, one by which in the course of time many a theory of interest has already been tried and found wanting.

The owner of a vineyard has harvested a cask of good young wine. Immediately after the harvest this cask of wine has an exchange value of $100. He leaves the wine to lie undisturbed in the cellar, and after 12 years the wine, which has aged, now has an exchange value of $200. The difference of $100 constitutes an increment for the owner of the wine as interest on the capital represented by that wine. What laborers, pray, were predaciously mulcted of that interest on capital?

Since there was not a stroke of work done to the wine during the period of maturation, the only conceivable victims of exploitation are the workers who produced the new wine. The owner of the vineyard paid them too little as their wage. But then my question is, "How much should he 'in all justice' have paid them?" Even if he paid them the whole $100 that the new wine was worth at the time it was harvested, the increment, which Rodbertus brands as a gain through exploitation, would still belong to him. Yes, even if he had paid them $120 or $150 in wages, he still would be branded with the stigma of exploitation. He could not be purified short of having paid them the whole $200.

Now can it be the subject of a serious demand to ask that the "fair labor wage" for a product *worth no more than $100 shall be $200?* Does the owner know in advance whether the product will ever be worth $200 anyhow? Is it not possible that he will be forced, contrary to his original intentions, to use or to sell the wine before the expiration of 12 years? And would he not in that case have paid $200 for a product that never was worth more than $100 or $120? And how is he to recompense those other workers who produce the new wine which he sells immediately for $100? Shall he pay them $200, too? That means ruin. Or only $100? Then different workers get a different wage for completely identical work. And that certainly is an injustice, not to mention the practical difficulty that comes from not knowing beforehand whose product is going to be sold immediately, and whose is going to lie in storage for 12 years.

But there is more to come. Even a wage of $200 for a cask of new wine would not be an amount of compensation that would guarantee immunity from the charge of exploitation. For the proprietor of the vineyard can let the wine mature, not merely 12 years, but 24 years. And then the wine will be worth, not $200, but $400. Is he for that reason to be obliged "in all justice" to pay in place of $100 the sum of $400 to the workers who produced the wine for him 24 years earlier? The thought is too absurd! But if he pays $100 or even $200, he earns his interest on capital, and Rodbertus will say that by withholding a part of the exchange value of his product he has cheated the worker of some of the wage justly due him for his labor.

*

F] I do not think anyone would have the temerity to maintain that the instances of the receipt of interest which have been presented here, or the numerous analogous cases that might be, have been explained by Rodbertus's theory. Now a theory which fails to explain a significant proportion of the phenomena it is meant to explain, cannot be the correct one. And so this concluding investigation and summary yields just about the result which might have been expected from the critique of some of its detailed features which I submitted in my earlier comments. That result is: Rodbertus's exploitation theory is unsound in its foundations, and false in its conclusions, and it contradicts both itself and the realities of our world.

In the foregoing pages it has been my aim to render a critical appraisal of that theory. The very nature of my task required me to forego any semblance of impartiality and to select for discussion only the errors of which Rodbertus was guilty. However, I believe I am performing an equally binding duty, when I pay tribute to the memory of this prominent figure and to his outstanding services in the development of economics. Unfortunately, the description of those services is something that lies outside the scope of my present task.

B. Marx[64]

3. PRESENTATION OF MARX'S THEORY OF VALUE AND INTEREST

MARX'S life work on economic theory is his large three volume work on capital. The fundamentals of his exploitation theory are laid down in the first volume, which was published in 1867 and was the only one to appear during his lifetime. The second volume, published posthumously by Engels as early as 1885, is in content closely akin to the first. It is common knowledge that there is less homogeneity between these two and the third which was published in 1894, and thus followed the preceding volume, as had the second, only after an interval of several years. Many persons, including the writer of these lines, are of the opinion that the content of the third volume is incompatible with that of the first volume, and vice versa. But Marx himself refused to admit this irreconcilability. On the contrary, he insisted in his third volume on the continued and complete validity of the doctrines he had enunciated in the first volume. Therefore a critic has both the right and the duty to regard the first volume as the true and continuing opinion of Marx, despite the existence of the third volume. And of course he commands the same right and must acknowledge the same duty to cite the third volume by way of illustration and criticism, at the proper juncture.

Marx takes as his point of departure the principle that the value of all commodities is controlled exclusively by the amount of labor which their production costs. He places greater emphasis on this principle than does Rodbertus. While the latter mentions it more or less incidentally in the casual course of his analyses and, in fact, frequently pronounces it only in the form of a theoretical presupposition, without ever wasting a word anywhere to prove it,[65] Marx places the proposition in the very forefront of his entire doctrine, and devotes to it detailed proof and elucidation.

The research area that Marx undertakes to examine in order to "get on the trail of value" (*Vol.* I, *p. 23*)[66] is originally limited by him to *commodities,* by which we must understand that he means, not all economic goods, but only those that are produced by labor for disposition on the market.[67] He begins with an "analysis of commodities" (*Vol.* I, *p. 9*). A commodity, regarded from one point of view, is a useful thing possessing properties which make it capable of satisfying human needs of some sort and therefore possessing use value. Regarded from another point of view, it constitutes a material carrier of exchange value. Then his analysis takes up the latter aspect. "Exchange value first appears as the quantitative relation, the ratio, in which use values of one kind are exchanged for use values of another kind. This relation varies constantly with time and place." It seems therefore to be something fortuitous. And yet behind this variation there must be a constant, and that is the object of Marx's search. He pursues that search in his well-known dialectical fashion. "Let us take two commodities, such as wheat and iron. Whatever the exchange relation may be between them, it is always possible to express that relation in an equation, of which the members are a given quantity of wheat and some quantity of iron, that is to say one bushel wheat $= x$ hundredweight iron. What is the significance of this equation? It signifies that there is something, identical in magnitude, possessed in common by two different things, namely by one bushel of wheat and x hundredweight of iron. Both things therefore are equal to a third thing which, in and of itself, is neither the one nor the other. Each of them then, insofar as it has exchange value, must be reducible to this third something."

"This common element" continues Marx "cannot be any quality—geometric, physical, chemical or otherwise natural quality of commodities. Their physical properties in any event are deserving of consideration only insofar as such properties make them useful, or in other words enable them to qualify as use values. On the other hand, however, the exchange relation of commodities is apparently characterized by a disregard of their use values. Within that relation one use value is worth just as much as any other, provided only it is present in the proper proportion. Or, as old Barbon says 'one kind of commodity is as good as another, if the exchange value of both is equally great. There is no difference and no differentiating between things having equal exchange value.' In their capacity as use values, commodities are primarily of differing quality; in their capacity as exchange values they can differ only in quantity, and as such do not possess an atom of use value.

"If we disregard the use value of objects that can be classified as commodities, then they retain only a single quality, that of being products of labor. And yet the product of labor is transformed as soon as we have it in hand. If we eliminate its use value from consideration, we likewise eliminate the physical component parts and the form which render it a use value. It is no longer table or house or yarn or any other useful thing. We obliterate all the qualities it possesses which are registered by sensory perception. It is also no longer the product of carpentering labor, of building labor, of spinning labor, or of any other specific productive labor. As the useful character of the products of labor is eliminated, so also the useful character of the labors they represent is eliminated; the differing concrete manifestations of those labors also vanish; they no longer differ from each other, but are all reduced to identical human labor, human labor in the abstract.

"Let us consider this residuum of the products of labor. There is nothing left of them but that aforementioned spectral objectivity, a mere coagulation of undifferentiated human labor, of an expenditure of human energy without regard to the form in which it was expended. These things are now merely symbols of an expending of human energy, an accumulating of human labor. As the crystallization of that social substantiality which they all have in common, they are—values."

Thus the concept of value is discovered and determined. It is, in the terms in which Marx's dialecticism presents it, not identical with exchange value but it stands in most intimate and indissoluble relation to it. It is a sort of conceptual distillate of exchange value. To put it in Marx's own words, value is "that common possession which asserts itself in exchange ratio or in exchange value." Conversely too, "exchange value of necessity comprises the manner in which value expresses itself, or the form in which it manifests itself" (*Vol.* I, *p. 13*).

Marx goes on from the determination of the concept "value" to the exposition of its measure and its magnitude. Since labor constitutes the substance of value, the magnitude of the value of all goods is, quite consistently, measured by the quantity of labor they contain, or more specifically, by the labor time. But that does not mean the individual length of time that this or that person who may have fashioned the commodity happened to need for it. It means the "socially necessary labor time." Marx explains this as meaning "the time required to produce any use value when operating under the conditions of production normally prevailing in a given society, and when utilizing the degree of skill and application normally available there" (*Vol.* I, *p. 14*). "It is only the quantity of socially necessary labor, or the labor time socially necessary for the production of a use value, which determines the magnitude of its value. Any single given commodity is considered the average example of its kind. Commodities or goods which contain equal quantities of labor, or which can be produced in the same labor time, have therefore the same amount of value. The value of one commodity bears the same relation to the value of every other commodity, as the labor time necessary for the production of the one bears to the labor time necessary for the production of the other. As values, all commodities are only definite measures of crystallized labor time."

From these statements we can deduce the content of the great "law of value" which is "inherent in the exchange of commodities" (*Vol.* I, *pp. 141, 150*) and which controls exchange conditions. This law provides, and in the light of the preceding remarks can provide only, that commodities are exchanged on the basis of the average amount of socially necessary labor which they embody (*e.g., Vol.* I, *p. 52*). The same law is expressed in other terms, such as the statement that commodities *are exchanged at their values* (*Vol.* I, *pp. 142, 183; Vol.* III, *p. 167*) or that *one equivalent is exchanged for another* (*Vol.* I, *pp. 150, 183*). Of course, under the influence of transient fluctuations in supply and demand, prices appear that are higher or lower than those values. But these "constant oscillations of market prices are self-compensatory, they cancel each other out, and finally resolve themselves into the average price which is their essential rule" (*Vol.* I, *p. 151, Note 37*). "In the fortuitous and constantly fluctuating conditions of exchange," however, it will in the long run always be true that "the socially necessary labor time will find enforcement as the controlling natural law" (*Vol.* I, *p. 52*). Marx terms this law the "eternal law of the exchange of commodities" (*Vol.* I, *p. 182*), the "law of ratio," the "natural law of equilibrium" (*Vol.* III, *p. 167*). Those instances in which commodities are exchanged at prices which are at variance with their values—and such cases admittedly do occur—are to be regarded as "accidental" deviations from the rule (*Vol.* I, *p. 150, Note 37*) and the deviations themselves as "violations of the law of the exchange of commodities" (*Vol.* I, *p. 142*).

On this foundation of the theory of value Marx then erects the superstructure of his doctrinal edifice, his famous *principle of surplus value*. He probes into the source of the gain which the capitalists derive from their capital. The capitalists put in a certain sum of money, transform it into commodities and then, with or without an intervening productional process, they convert them, by means of a sale, back into more money. Whence does this increment come, this excess of the sum of money drawn out over the sum originally advanced, or as Marx calls it, this "surplus value?"

Using a dialectic method peculiar to himself, Marx begins by defining the conditions of his problem by exclusion. His first point is that this surplus value cannot arise out of the fact that the capitalist regularly purchases commodities for less than their value, nor can it be that he regularly sells them for more than their value. The problem therefore may be put in the following words, "Our . . . possessor of money must buy commodities at their value, and sell them at their value, and yet at the end of the transaction he must take more value out than he put in . . . Those are the conditions of our problem. Here lies Rhodes, here is the gap to be spanned!" (*Vol.* I, *p. 150 ff.*).

Marx finds the solution to this problem in the fact that there is one commodity, the use value of which possesses the peculiar faculty of being the source of exchange value. That commodity is the ability to labor, or labor power. The latter is offered for sale on the market under two conditions. The first of these is that the worker be personally free. For otherwise it would not be his power that were for sale, but his whole person, that is to say, he would be a slave. The second condition is that the worker be without "all those things that are necessary to the activation of his labor power." Otherwise he would prefer to act as an independent producer, and to offer his products for sale, rather than his labor power. By trading in this commodity the capitalist acquires his surplus value. And he does so in the following manner.

The value of the commodity "labor power" is regulated, as is that of any other commodity, by the labor time necessary to reproduce it. In this case that means the labor time required to produce as much of the materials needed for human sustenance as is necessary to preserve the existence of the worker. If a social labor time of six hours, let us say for example, is required to produce what is necessary for one day's sustenance, and if at the same time we may assume that those six hours are embodied in $9, then the labor power of one day is purchasable for $9. If the capitalist has completed such a purchase, the use value of the labor power is his, and he realizes it by having the worker work for him. If he had him work only just so many hours a day as are embodied in the labor power itself, and just so many as he had been compelled to pay for when he made the purchase, then no surplus value would arise. For six labor hours cannot, by our hypothesis, add to the product in which they become embodied any greater value than $9, and that is what the capitalist paid in wages. But that is not the way the capitalists do business. Even if they have purchased the labor power for a price that corresponds to six hours of labor power, they have the worker work the whole day for them. Now there are more work hours embodied in the product that is produced during that day than the capitalist had to pay for, and the product therefore has a greater value than the wages paid. And the difference is the "surplus value" which the capitalist receives.

Let the following serve as an example. Let us assume that a worker, spinning for 6 hours, converts 10 pounds of cotton into yarn. Assume that the cotton itself required 20 hours' labor for its own production, and accordingly has a value of $30. Let us assume further that during the 6 hours of spinning labor the cotton spinner causes wear and tear of the loom corresponding to 4 hours' labor, in other words representing a value of $6. Thus the total value of the means of production consumed in the spinning process will amount to $36, the equivalent of 24 work hours. During the spinning process the cotton "absorbs" an additional 6 work hours, and so the completed yarn is the product, *in toto,* of 30 work hours and consequently will have a value of $45. On the assumption that the capitalist has the employed worker labor no more than 6 hours a day, the production of the yarn has really cost the capitalist a full $45, namely $30 for cotton, $6 for wear and tear of equipment, $9 for wages. There is no surplus value.

It is an entirely different story if the capitalist has the worker work 12 hours a day. In 12 hours the worker converts 20 pounds of cotton, already representing 40 work hours and hence worth $60. Furthermore the wear and tear of machinery represents 8 work hours with a value of $12. But the worker has added in the course of a day a value of 12 work hours, that is to say a new or additional value of 6 hours. The statement now reads:

Exchange value of yarn spun in one day and represent-
    ing a cost of 60 work hours $90.00
Outlay by the capitalist   81.00
    (Cotton $60, Wear and Tear $12, Labor $9)
Remaining surplus value $ 9.00

According to Marx, then, surplus value is a result of the capitalist's having the worker labor for him for part of the day without paying for it. The work day of the worker thus comprises two distinguishable parts. In the first part, that of the "necessary labor time," the worker produces his own sustenance, or the value thereof, and for that part of his work he receives an equivalent in wages. During the second part, the "surplus work time," he is "exploited"; he produces the "surplus" without receiving any equivalent of any kind for it (*Vol.* i, *pp. 205 ff.*). "Capital is therefore not only, as Adam Smith says, control over labor. It is essentially control over unpaid labor. All surplus value, in no matter what specialized form it is later crystallized, whether profit, interest, rent or the like, is by its nature something which has materialized out of unpaid labor time. The secret of capital's ability to create values out of itself resolves itself into its control over a certain amount of unpaid work performed by others" (*Vol.* i, *p. 554*).

4. MARX'S INNOVATIONS AS COMPARED WITH RODBERTUS

THAT is the essence of Marx's exploitation theory, as it is set down in the first volume of *Das Kapital,* and, as we shall later see, contradicted in the third volume. He may possibly contradict it involuntarily, but at any rate he does not in any way repudiate it. In this exposition the attentive reader will recognize once more all the essential features of Rodbertus's doctrine. Even though some of them appear in somewhat altered garb, we find the elements from which Rodbertus assembled his theory of interest. Thus the principle that the value of goods is determined by quantities of labor; that only labor creates all value; that the worker under a wage contract receives a lesser value than he creates, and is forced by necessity to consent to this arrangement; that the capitalist appropriates the excess, and that the excess he thus gains bears the characteristics of the predacious fruit of the labor of others.

Because of the duplication in content of both theories—perhaps it would be more correct to say of both formulations of the same theory —everything that I said in refutation of Rodbertus's theory applies with entire validity in contravention of Marx as well. I can therefore restrict myself to a few supplementary arguments. I consider these necessary, partly in order to adapt my critique in a few matters to the peculiar formulation Marx employs, and partly to discuss a few genuine innovations by him.

Among these innovations the one that is by far the most important is his attempt to go beyond mere statement and to adduce proof for the proposition that all value is founded on labor. My refutation of that principle in Rodbertus's work was casual, as was Rodbertus's own statement of it. I did not go beyond raising such objection as consisted merely in the mention of a few indubitable exceptions to the principle. But I never really went to the root of the matter. But that is something I cannot and will not neglect in the case of Marx. To be sure, I am entering a field which has been plowed up frequently, and by excellent scholars, in the course of literary altercation, and so I can scarcely hope to unearth much that is new for presentation here. But I believe it would ill become me, in writing a book on the critical presentation of theories of interest, to evade the detailed examination of a principle which has been regarded as fundamental to one of the most important of those theories and placed in the vanguard of its forces. It is also unfortunate as well as true, that economic science is at a stage today where renewed efforts at critical examination can by no means be regarded as superfluous exertion. For in our time, more than ever, it is true that that proposition threatens to achieve adoption in ever widening circles, like a profession of faith. In sober truth it is nothing but a fable, once told by a great man and ever since repeated by a credulous multitude.

5. WEAKNESS OF MARX'S PROOF BY AUTHORITY, BASED AS USUAL ON SMITH AND RICARDO

THE two proud names of Adam Smith and Ricardo are generally regarded as indicating the originators of the principle that the value of all goods is founded on labor. And they are just as generally regarded as the august authorities to whom all witnesses take recourse. This general practice is not without justification, but neither is it completely correct. The proposition is indeed found in the writings of both men. But Smith contradicts it every once in a while.[68] And Ricardo places such restrictions on the field in which it has validity, and so interlards his comments with exceptions to the principle that one is hardly justified in maintaining that he held forth labor as the general and exclusive factor on which the value of goods is based.[69] He begins his *Principles* with the express statement that the exchange value of goods rises from *two* sources— their *rarity* and the *quantity of work* that it cost to obtain them. Certain goods, he points out, such as rare statues and paintings, derive their value exclusively from the first source. The value of only such goods as can be reproduced, by means of labor, in any desired quantity, is determined by the quantity of labor costs. Ricardo admits that the very great majority of all goods belong to this class. But even with respect to these Ricardo feels constrained to make a further reservation. For he is forced to admit that the exchange value of even these goods is not determined by labor exclusively. On the contrary, considerable influence is exerted by the *time* which elapses between the outlay in work advanced, and the realization of the ultimate product.[70]

And so neither Smith nor Ricardo accepted the principle we are discussing as unreservedly as is popularly believed. And yet they did establish it within certain limitations. Let us examine a little further to determine to what extent this is so.

And here we make a strange discovery! Smith and Ricardo *did not furnish any proof of the principle at all,* but merely stated its validity as something quite self-evident. The famous words in which Smith expressed himself on this topic, and which Ricardo adopted word for word as part of his own doctrine, read as follows: "The real price of every article, what every article really costs him who wishes to acquire it, is the effort and difficulty of acquisition. What every article is really worth to the man who acquired it and wishes to sell it or to exchange it for something else, is *the effort and difficulty which it enables him to avoid and to unload on others.*"[71]

Let us pause here a moment. Smith speaks these words in a "tone of voice" as if their truth were immediately and convincingly obvious. But is it really obvious? Are *value* and *effort* concepts so indissolubly connected that the conviction is immediately forced upon us that effort is the reason for value? I do not believe that any unprejudiced person can so maintain. That I have slaved to acquire a thing is *one* fact; that the thing is worth slaving for is a second and different fact. And that both facts do not always go hand in hand is far too well corroborated by experience to admit of any possible doubt. Every one of the countless unsuccessful efforts which are wasted every day on valueless results bears witness to this, quite regardless of whether the cause be technical ineptitude, misguided speculation, or merely bad luck. No less convincing is each of the many instances in which slight effort is rewarded with high value. Examples are the settlement of a tract of land, the finding of a jewel, the discovery of a gold mine. But even if we disregard cases like these, on the ground that they are exceptions to the normal course of events, we know it to be a fact, indubitable as it is completely normal, that the same amount of effort expended by different persons has a widely differing value. The results of one month's effort by an outstanding artist is quite regularly worth 100 times as much as the results of a similar month's effort on the part of an ordinary house painter. How could that be, if effort were really the basis of value? How could it be possible if some direct psychological connection compelled our judgment of value to rely on effort and difficulty, and on nothing else? Surely no one will maintain that nature is so aristocratic as to compel our psyche, by her psychological laws, to prize the efforts of an artist as 100 times more precious than the more modest efforts of a house painter![72] I think that a little cogitation, in place of blind acceptance, will lead to the conviction that there really can be no such thing as the direct and compelling appreciation of an inner connection between effort and value, such as Smith seems to take for granted in that passage.

But does the passage really apply only to exchange value, as has been silently and fondly taken for granted? I do not believe that this can be maintained either, by anyone reading the passage with unbiased eye. It does not apply to either the exchange value, or the use value or any "value" in the strictly scientific sense. As his very use of the word "worth" rather than "value" indicates, Smith has been dealing with value in that very wide and vague sense that the word has in the mouth of the general populace. That is a very significant feature! Smith has the involuntary feeling that he could not gain approval for his principle before the forum of strictly scientific consideration, so he employs the medium of everyday language and turns his attention to the less accurately formulated concepts of everyday life. Experience shows that he did so with some success, which in the interest of economic science is much to be deplored.

The whole passage can in any event lay little claim to scientific accuracy. This is evident from the fact that its words, few though they be, contain even one more contradiction. For Smith, in one and the same breath, attributes with equal confidence to two different entities the quality of being the basis of "real" value. They are the effort which one can save oneself through ownership of a good, and the effort which one can impose upon another. But those are two quantities which, as everyone knows, are by no means identical. At the present stage of the division of labor, the effort that I should have had to expend, personally, to acquire ownership of a desired article is ordinarily very much greater than the effort it costs a technically trained worker to produce it. Which effort is it, the one which I have been "spared," or the one which I have "imposed" on someone else, that is immediately recognizable as the effort that determines the real value?

In short, the famous passage in which Adam Smith, the Old Master, introduces the labor principle into the doctrine of value, is as far removed as it well can be from what it is ordinarily claimed to be. For the claim is usually made that it must be recognized as a great and well-supported scientific fundamental proposition. But it is not compellingly self-evident; it is not supported by a single word of substantiating argument; it is clothed in the careless language, has the neglectful character of untutored speech; finally it contradicts itself. That it should have nevertheless enjoyed general credence is due, in my estimation, to the combination of two circumstances. In the first place, it was spoken by an Adam Smith; in the second place it was spoken with no vestige of substantiation. Had Adam Smith addressed himself with a single word to the intellect, instead of directly to the emotions, the intellect would not have permitted any invasion of its right to examine the evidence behind the statement in the cold light of reason. In that case its threadbare character could not have failed to be revealed. Doctrines like that can score a victory only when people are taken by surprise.

But let us listen to what Smith continues to say, and after him Ricardo. "Labor was the first price, the original purchase money that was paid for all commodities." That sentence is rather unobjectionable, but at the same time proves nothing with regard to the principle of value.

"In that early and rude state of society which precedes both the accumulation of stock and the appropriation of land, the proportion between the quantities of labour necessary for acquiring different objects *seems* to be the only circumstance which can afford any rule for exchanging them for one another. If among a nation of hunters, for example, it usually costs twice the labour to kill a beaver which it does to kill a deer, one beaver *should naturally* exchange for or be worth two deer. *It is natural* that what is usually the produce of two days' or two hours' labour, should be worth double what is usually the produce of one day's or one hour's labour."

We search in vain for any assignment of reason, any motivation in this statement. Smith simply says *"seems* to be the only circumstance," *"should naturally," "it is natural,"* and so on. But he leaves it to the reader entirely, to convince himself of the "naturalness" of these dicta. Incidentally, that is a task which the critical reader will not find it easy to accomplish. For if it were really "natural" that products should be exchangeable solely on the basis of the relative labor time that their acquisition costs, then it would perforce be natural for a rare, gaily colored butterfly or a rare edible frog to be worth 10 times as much among the savages as is a stag. For ordinarily it takes a 10 days' search to find such a butterfly, whereas it is usually possible to get a stag with a single day's labor. That is a matter of relative values that would hardly seem so "natural" as to appear self-evident to anyone.

The upshot of the immediately preceding remarks is, I believe, this: Smith and Ricardo stated the proposition that labor is the principle of the value of goods, without any supporting argument, and as if it were completely axiomatic. But it is not an axiom. Consequently, if the proposition is to be maintained at all, Smith and Ricardo must be ignored entirely as authorities, and corroboration sought elsewhere, and independently.

Now it is a very curious fact that almost no one among their successors has done so. The same men who otherwise probed thoroughly into traditionally accepted doctrines with the scalpel of their devastating criticism, the same men who seemed to consider no time-honored doctrine so firmly entrenched as to be secure against being questioned anew, and against being required to prove itself sound, these same men have failed to show even a trace of incredulity with respect to this very principle of fundamental import, borrowed from the old doctrine. From Ricardo to Rodbertus, from Sismondi to Lassalle, no one has deemed it necessary to bolster the principle with any further support than the name of Adam Smith alone. Anything original contributed by any of them consisted of nothing but repeated assurances that the proposition is true, irrefutable, indubitable. But no one made any attempt really to prove the truth of it, really to refute objections, really to resolve any doubts. Those who look with scorn upon proof by authority are themselves content to invoke authority; the foes of statements that are mere presumptions without benefit of proof, are themselves content to make statements without proof. Only very few of the advocates of the labor theory of value are an exception to that charge, and one of those few is Marx.

6. EXAMINATION AND REFUTATION
OF MARX'S BASIC PROPOSITION

TO ANYONE seeking a genuine proof of that thesis, two methods offer obvious avenues of approach that afford a natural way to seek and find such proof. Either the empirical method or the psychological method might conceivably serve. For one might, on the one hand, simply examine the conditions under which experience tells us exchanges are made, and observe whether there is any actual harmony in evidence between the magnitude of the exchange value and the expenditure of labor. Or one might, on the other hand, avail oneself of a mixture of inductive and deductive reasoning such as is common usage in our science, and analyze psychological motives. One might, then, ask what motives actuate people when they carry out exchange transactions, or when they determine exchange prices. Or again, we might inquire into the motives at work when they participate in production. From the nature of these motives we might draw inferences as to typical human behavior patterns. In so doing we might conceivably discover, among other things, some relation between the prices that are regularly demanded and paid for commodities, and the amount of labor necessary for their production. And yet Marx did not adopt either of these two natural courses of investigation. It is interesting to discover from his third volume that Marx himself was well aware that no result favorable to his thesis could be achieved either through an examination of the facts, or through an analysis of the motives that are operative during "competition." Instead of that he adopts a third course, one that is certainly rather strange when applied to material of that sort. It is the course of purely logical proof, of dialectic deduction based on the essential nature of exchange.

Marx found the idea ready to hand in old Aristotle, who said, "There can be no exchange without equality, there can be no equality without commensurability" (*Vol.* I, *p. 35*). He uses this idea as his point of departure. He symbolizes the exchange of two commodities by an equation, continues the logical thought process by inferring the existence of a "common element of the same magnitude" in the two things that have been exchanged and which therefore have been rendered equal. He concludes by making it his problem to discover the common element to which the equal things are "reducible" as exchange values (*Vol.* I, *p. 11; see foregoing page 281 ff.*).

I should like to make one comment at this point, by way of interpolation. Even the original presupposition that in any exchange of two things an "equality" manifests itself, seems to me open to two objections. Marx is thinking along lines that are not only out of date (which in the last analysis might not be material) but also very unrealistic. And that, in plain English, means fallacious. Wherever equality and exact equilibrium prevail, there is customarily no change in the state of quiescence previously existing. And so, since any case of an exchange brings about the result that the commodities change owners, it is rather to be taken as evidence of a previously existing inequality or lack of equilibrium, the very effect of which was to compel a change. This situation is analogous to that which results when two chemical compounds are so joined that they may interact. New compounds are created if the chemical "affinity" of an element of the first compound with an element of the second compound is of a strength which is not just equal to, but greater than its affinity with any other element or elements of the first compound. Modern economists are, as a matter of fact, unanimous in their opinion that the old views propounded by the scholasticists and theologians are untenable in their espousal of an "equivalence" of the values that are exchanged. But it is not my purpose to ascribe any further importance to that point. I prefer to turn my attention to a critical examination of the logical and methodological procedures by which Marx's quest for the "common element" yields him labor as the desired distillate.

Marx's procedure in his search for the "common element" that characterizes exchanges is as follows. Whatever qualities are possessed by the objects which are balanced against each other in the exchange are allowed to pass in review. Then all those which cannot meet the test are excluded under the Marxian elimination method, until at last only one quality is left. This one—the quality of being a product of labor—must then be the object of our search, the quality that is possessed in common.

This procedure is somewhat strange but not in and of itself to be condemned. But it is odd to refrain from applying positive tests to the presumptive characteristic quality. I admit that to do so would have meant to adopt one of the two methods we discussed previously, and which Marx deliberately avoided. The strangeness consists in Marx's attempt to convince himself by a purely negative procedure that that presumptive quality is just the very one he is looking for. The reason he gives is that no other qualities are what he is seeking, and there must be one such quality. Still, that method can lead to the desired result, if it is applied with the necessary care and all-inclusiveness. That is to say, if meticulous care is exercised to put into the logical sieve everything that belongs there, and to make absolutely certain that by no possible inadvertence can any single thing slip through the meshes of the sieve, which should not do so.

But how does Marx proceed?

From the outset he places in the sieve only those things possessing exchange value, which also possess the quality which in the end he means to sift out as the "common" one, and he excludes all others. His procedure is like that of one who has a strong desire to demonstrate that a white ball can be drawn out of an urn, and takes the precaution to insure that result by placing nothing but white balls in the urn. For from the outset he restricts the scope of his search for the essence of exchange value to "commodities." While in so doing he does not exactly define this concept "commodities" with meticulous care, he does nevertheless set limits that are narrower than those which define "economic goods," and he restricts the field to products of labor and excludes gifts of nature. Now it is certainly obvious that if exchange means an equivalence, which presupposes the existence of a "common element of equal magnitude," then such common element should necessarily be sought and found in all categories of goods that are made the subject of exchange. It should be present, not exclusively in products of labor, but also in such natural resources as land, timber, water power, coal deposits, stone quarries, oil wells, mineral waters, gold mines and the like.[73] Under these circumstances it is really nothing short of methodological high crime to exclude, in a search for the common element that belongs to all exchange values, all goods possessing exchange value without being products of labor. It would be exactly comparable to the procedure followed by a physicist conducting a hypothetical investigation as follows. He wishes, let us say, to determine the reason for a quality possessed in common by all bodies, such as weight. His method is to sift the qualities of a single category of bodies, let us say, transparent ones. He passes in review all the qualities that are common to transparent bodies, he demonstrates with respect to all their *other* qualities that these cannot be the reason for weight. And on the basis of that proof he proclaims that transparency is the reason for weight.

It would certainly never have occurred to Aristotle, the father of the idea of equivalence in exchange, to exclude natural resources. It is all the less justifiable since some gifts of nature, such as land, belong among the most vitally important objects of wealth and commerce, and since, furthermore, it can by no means be maintained that the exchange values of natural resources are always only fortuitously and haphazardly determined. On the one hand products of labor, too, show at times fortuitous prices. And on the other hand the prices of natural products often exhibit very distinct relationship to firmly established reasons or determining factors. It is very well known, for instance, that the purchase price of real estate is frequently determined as a multiple of the income it yields at the prevailing interest rate. It is equally certain that standing timber and coal in the mine vary in price, and not out of pure coincidence but because of differences in quality, or location, or transportation conditions.

And Marx takes every precaution to avoid being caught up in the necessity of accounting for the fact that his investigation from its inception excluded one class of goods possessing exchange value. With equal care he avoids giving any reason for doing so. In this instance, as in so many others, he exhibits the necessary skill to escape, with the slipperiness of an eel and by sheer dint of his dialectic cleverness, from the tight places into which his argument has led him. To begin with, he avoids calling to his readers' attention the fact that his concept of "commodities" is narrower than that of all goods with exchange value. With exceptional cleverness he paves the way for his subsequent restricting of the investigation to his "commodities." The very natural paving stones he uses are the words of a generalization which appears as an apparently harmless bit of verbiage at the beginning of his book. "The riches," he says, "of those societies in which capitalistic methods of production prevail, appear as a monstrously large *collection of commodities.*" This statement is completely erroneous if the expression "commodities" is accepted in the sense in which Marx uses it later of "products of labor." For nature's gifts, including land, comprise a very considerable and by no means negligible portion of personal wealth. But the insouciant reader can easily overlook this inaccuracy, because he does not know that at a later time Marx is going to assign a much narrower significance to the term "commodities."

Nor does Marx clarify this matter as he goes on. On the contrary, the first few paragraphs show him wavering in his choice from among the terms "thing," "use value," "good" and "commodity" without making any sharp distinction between the last of these and the other three. On page 10 he says, "the usefulness of a thing makes it a *use value.*" And again, "an object classifiable as a commodity . . . is a *use value or good.*" On page 11 we find, "Exchange value . . . manifests itself . . . as the quantitative proportion in which *use values* of one kind are exchanged for *use values* of another kind." Be it noted that here the one Marx has cast in the rôle of the hero of the exchange value phenomenon is use value, alias good. Then Marx continues after the words, "Let us consider the matter more closely." Surely those words are not intended to announce a transition to a different and more restricted field of investigation! Yet Marx goes on to say, "A single *commodity,* a bushel of wheat, is exchanged in the most varied proportions for other *articles.*" He also says, "Let us take two further *commodities,*" etc. In the same paragraph the expression "things" even occurs again. In fact, it appears as part of a statement that is very important for our problem, to the effect that "a common element of identical magnitude exists in two different *things*" (i.e., two things which are being treated as equivalents in an exchange).

But on page 12, the page immediately following, Marx prosecutes his search for the "common element" only with respect to the "exchange value of *commodities,*" without breathing the slightest word to put us upon notice that he intends to limit the field of his investigation to only a part of the things which have exchange value.[74] And on the very next page the limitation is immediately abandoned, and the conclusion that he has just established for the limited field of commodities is extended as if it had validity for the wider field of the use values of goods. "A *use value, or good,* has value only because it represents human labor in the abstract which has materialized and been rendered objective!"

If Marx had not at the crucial point restricted his investigation to products of labor, if he had looked for his common element in natural resources as well, it would have been patently manifest that labor cannot be that common element. If he had made his delimitation explicitly and avowedly, he would himself inevitably have stumbled upon his methodological blunder. And his readers too! And they would have been forced to smile at the naive artifice by which he seeks to prove his point. The end product of his process of distillation is indeed the quality of being a product of labor, as one element possessed in common by the class of things he has distilled. But Marx himself excluded beforehand from the materials he placed in his retort all things which are not products of labor, even though they deserved to be included because they are by nature things possessing exchange value. The trick was impossible to perform, except in just the way Marx performed it—surreptitiously and by employing a dialectician's device that consisted in skimming over a ticklish point with celerity and facility. I must express my sincere admiration of the cleverness with which Marx was able to make an acceptable presentation of such a fallacious procedure. But I am of course also compelled to report its complete fallaciousness.

But suppose we go a bit further. After all, the end achieved by this trick of Marx's that we have just described, was no more than to admit labor into the circle of aspirants. The artificial delimitation of the field simply made it *one* quality that was possessed "in common." There was the possibility that other qualities, also held in common, might compel consideration. How was he to oust these competitors?

That end he achieved by two thought processes, each of which contains only a few words, but one of the most grievous errors in logic.

The first of these is Marx's exclusion of all "geometrical, physical, chemical or other natural properties of goods." For "their physical properties in any event are deserving of consideration only insofar as such properties make them useful, or in other words enable them to qualify as use values. *On the other hand, however, the exchange relation of commodities is apparently characterized by a disregard of their use values.*" For "within that relation (the exchange relationship) *one use value is worth just as much as any other, provided only it is present in the proper proportion*" (*Vol.* I, *p. 12*).

What would Marx have said to the following argument? In an opera company there are three excellent singers, a tenor, a bass, and a baritone who receive a salary of $20,000 a year each. The question is, "What is the element possessed in common which causes them all to be paid the same salary?" My answer is, that in the matter of salaries one good voice is worth as much as any other, a good tenor voice is worth the same as a good bass voice or a good baritone, provided only it is available in the proper proportion. Consequently there is "apparently" an elimination, in the matter of salary, of the factor of good voice, and consequently the good voice cannot be the common cause of the high salaries. It is obvious that this line of reasoning is fallacious. It is equally obvious that the Marxian logical sequence, of which it is an exact copy, is no whit more correct. Both contain the same error. They confuse elimination *of a factor generally,* with elimination *of the special phases* the factor exhibits in special instances. The factor which can be disregarded in our problem is the special phase in which the factor "good voice" manifests itself. It may be immaterial whether we are paying for a tenor, a bass, or a baritone. But rest assured it is not so as to "any good voice." In the same way, consideration of the exchange relation of commodities may disregard the special phase in which their use value manifests itself, for instance whether the commodity serves to provide food or clothing or shelter, but it certainly may not disregard the use value itself. The utter impropriety of summarily dismissing use value from consideration could have been deduced by Marx from the very fact that there can be no exchange value where there is no use value. Indeed, that is a fact which Marx himself is repeatedly compelled to admit.[75]

Marx is in still worse case when it comes to the next link in his chain of argumentation. "If we disregard the use value of objects that can be classified as commodities, then they retain only a single quality," Marx says, to quote him literally, "that of being products of labor." Really? Only *one* quality? Do not goods possessing exchange value have other qualities in common? For example, are they not *rare* in relation to the demand for them? Or are they not the object of supply and demand? Or are they not privately owned? Or are they not "products of nature"? For no one states more clearly than Marx himself, that they are as much products of nature as they are of labor, when he declares, "Objects classifiable as commodities are combinations of two elements, natural materials and labor," or when he quotes approvingly from Petty, "Labor is the father of it (material wealth), and the earth its mother."[76]

Now my question is, why the principle of value cannot just as well be contained in one of *these* common qualities, as in the quality of being a product of labor. For Marx has not offered a ghost of a positive reason to support the latter. His only reason is the negative one that the successfully eliminated use value is *not* the principle of exchange value. But does not this same negative reason apply with equal force to all the other qualities which commodities possess in common but which Marx overlooked?

But there is more to come. Let us look at page 12 on which Marx conjured away the influence of use value on exchange value with the argument that one use value is worth as much as any other, provided only it is present in proper proportion. There he says, with respect to products of labor, the following. "And yet the product of labor is transformed as soon as we have it in hand. If we eliminate its use value from consideration, we likewise eliminate the physical component parts and the form which render it a use value. It is no longer table or house or yarn or any other useful thing. We obliterate all the qualities it possesses which are registered by sensory perception. *It is also no longer the product of carpentering labor, of building labor, of spinning labor, or of any other specific productive labor.* As the useful character of the products of labor is eliminated, so also the useful character of the labors they represent is eliminated; the differing concrete manifestations of those labors also vanish, *they no longer differ from each other, but are all reduced to identical human labor, human labor in the abstract.*"

Is it possible to say more distinctly or more explicitly that for the exchange relation not only one use value, but also one kind of labor and labor products "is worth just as much as any other, provided only it is present in proper proportion"; in other words, that the very same circumstances which serve as the grounds on which Marx pronounces his verdict of elimination against use value, can be made to apply to labor? Labor and use value have a qualitative and a quantitative side. As surely as the use values of table, house and yarn differ from one another qualitatively, just so surely is there such a difference in the case of the labor done in carpentering, building or spinning. And as surely as labor of different kinds is comparable on the basis of its quantity, just so surely are use values of different kinds comparable on the basis of their magnitude. It is absolutely incomprehensible why the identical set of facts can lead to the elimination of the one competitor, and to the crown of olive leaves for the other! If Marx had happened to reverse the order of his inquiry, he could have eliminated labor by the very same logical succession which led him to the elimination of use value. And by the same procedure which led to the coronation of labor, he would have come to proclaim use value to be the sole surviving and thus the desired common quality, and value to be a "coagulation of use value." I think it could be maintained, not facetiously but in all seriousness, that the two paragraphs on page 12 could be interchanged. I mean that in the first paragraph in which the influence of use value is eliminated, and in the second in which labor is proved to be the desired common element, the subjects could be interchanged, without the necessity for any change in external logical correctness. That is to say, without any change in the sentence structure of the first paragraph one could in every instance replace the word "use value" with "labor and labor products," and similarly, one could replace the word "labor" throughout the second paragraph with "use value"!

Such is the logic and the methodology of Marx's procedure in introducing into his system the fundamental proposition that labor is the sole basis of value. As I stated recently elsewhere,[77] I consider it utterly out of the question to suppose that this dialectical hocus pocus furnished the source and justification of his convictions for Marx himself. I cannot believe that this represents the procedure by which he originally attained conviction or sought to examine the facts and freely and impartially to determine their inter-relationship. I consider Marx an intellect of the very first order, and I believe it would have been impossible for a thinker of his caliber to seek the truth by paths that are in their very nature so devious and unnatural. Nor could a mind of such stature have blundered through sheer mischance or adverse fortune into all those errors of logic and of method I have just described. Had his line of research been in truth so mistaken, it could not possibly have yielded as its result, achieved without prescience or premeditation, the thesis that labor is the sole source of value.

I believe the true situation was quite otherwise. I do not doubt that Marx was really and sincerely convinced of his thesis. But the reasons for his conviction are not the ones he wrote into his system. He believed in his thesis, as a fanatic believes in his dogma. He doubtless embraced it because it stood under the aegis of those celebrated authorities, Adam Smith and Ricardo. And he was certainly imbued with it on the strength of the same vague and casual impressions, accepted without searching intellectual scrutiny, that had misled those illustrious intellects into the expression of similar ideas. And it is improbable that he ever reached the point where he entertained the faintest doubt of its correctness. And so for Marx himself his proposition stood firm as an axiom. But for his readers he had to furnish proof. The principle could not have been demonstrated empirically, nor along the lines of the psychology which underlies economic phenomena. And so he took recourse to rationalization of a dialectical character, a procedure, incidentally, that accorded with the bent of his mind. With an adeptness most admirable of its kind, he tinkered and puttered around, manipulating the compliant concepts and premises of his thesis, until at long last the predetermined and premeditated result was finally produced in a form that was to all outward appearances reputable and conclusive.

This attempt of Marx's to play the dialectician in order to furnish his thesis with such props as would make it convincing, collapses completely, as we have just seen. But could not some support have been found for it by following either the empirical or the psychological method which Marx avoided?

In the second volume of this work, its positive phase, I shall show that the psychological method, for one, would not. An analysis of the psychological forces that are operative in the matter of exchange values leads to results quite at variance with Marx's thesis. And as a matter of fact, Marx's posthumously published third volume really contains an admission to that effect.[78] There still remains to be considered the attempt along empirical lines, the test of factual experience. What does that show?

Experience shows that the exchange ratio of goods is in proportion to the quantity of labor necessary for production in the case of only some goods, and then it is only incidental. That this statement sums up the situation as it exists in hard fact ought to be well known, because the data which support it are a matter of common knowledge. And yet its truth is seldom acknowledged. It is true that the whole world, including the socialist authors, is unanimous in admitting that experience does not bear out the labor principle in all cases. But the opinion is very frequently encountered that the cases in which actuality coincides with the labor principle constitute a very large majority, and that the cases which are at variance with the labor principle are exceptions to the rule and relatively rare. That opinion is a very badly mistaken one. I should like to correct that opinion once and for all. To that end I will devote the succeeding pages to grouping together the "exceptions" which experience tells us exist in our economic world, in violation of the labor principle. It will become apparent that the "exceptions" preponderate so vastly, that there is hardly any room left for the "rule."

1] In the first place, all "rare goods" are exempt from the labor principle. That means all goods which, because of some factual or legal obstacle, cannot be reproduced at all, or at least not in unlimited quantity. Ricardo lists a few examples, and these include statues and paintings, rare books and coins, vintage wines and the like. He adds the remark that these goods "constitute only a very small part of the goods which are exchanged in the open market every day." If it be considered that this class of goods also includes all real estate, plus the myriad goods involving patents, copyrights and trade secrets, the extent of these "exceptions" will be found to be by no means inconsiderable.[79]

2] In the second place, all goods which are produced by skilled rather than unskilled labor constitute exceptions. The product of a day's work performed by a sculptor, an expert cabinet maker, a maker of violins, a mechanical engineer, etc. does not embody more labor than the product resulting from the work done by a common laborer or a factory hand. And yet the former product has an exchange value greater than that of the latter, and often it will be many times as great. Naturally, the adherents of the labor theory of value could not overlook this exception. Strangely enough, they pretend that this is no true exception, but only a little variant, which really still falls within the rule. Marx, for instance, hits upon the device of calling skilled labor a multiple of ordinary labor. He says (*on p. 19*), "More complicated labor counts as simple labor raised to a higher power, or rather, simple labor multiplied. Thus a smaller quantity of complicated labor is equal to a greater quantity of simple labor. Experience shows that this reduction process goes on constantly. A commodity may be the product of the most complicated kind of labor, but its value places it on a par with the product of simple labor, and the commodity therefore represents merely a certain quantity of simple labor."

There, forsooth, is a bit of legerdemain in the theorizing line that is astounding in its naiveté! We can concede that it is quite possible to rate a sculptor's working day as equivalent to a ditchdigger's five in some respects—for instance as to emolument. But certainly no one will care to maintain that the sculptor's 12 working hours actually *are* 60 hours of ordinary labor. Now in matters of theory, such as the inquiry into the principle of value, it is not a question of the fictions that men may choose to deal with, but a question of that which really is. As a matter of theory the product that the sculptor brings into being in a day is the product of *one* day's work and that is final. And if the product of one day's work is worth as much as another good which is the product of *five* day's work, then the case presents an exception to the ostensible rule that the exchange value of goods is determined by the amount of human labor they represent. And it remains an exception, no matter what fictions man may create to deal with it. Suppose a railroad sets up a tariff schedule which, generally speaking, scales the charges in accordance with the distance that passengers and freight are transported. But suppose, further, that the schedule provides that distances over a certain stretch where conditions make operation especially costly, shall be computed as two miles for each mile of the road elsewhere. In such case can anyone maintain that the distance traveled is *really* the sole principle employed by the railroad in fixing its tariffs? Of course not. A *fiction* is employed, making distance the ostensible principle. In effect, however, the principle is modified by taking into consideration the *nature of the terrain* which comprises the distance. The situation is the same with respect to the theoretical consistency of the labor principle, and no amount of prestidigitation can save it.[80]

I trust it requires no further details to establish that a considerable proportion of commercial products falls into this class of exceptions. In fact almost all goods, strictly speaking, fall into this category. For almost every commodity will require, somewhere in the course of its production, specialized labor of some kind—that of an inventor, a manager, a foreman and the like. And that—in terms of the labor theory of value—raises the value of that commodity somewhat above the level that it would have attained on the basis of the quantity of labor alone.

3] There is a third class of exceptions to add to the foregoing. But if the theorist is content to account for this limited influence of labor on exchange value, he is spared the necessity of seeking a motivation sufficiently basic to make labor the key to that earlier and more inclusive proposition. It is an embarrassing necessity because no such motivation exists. I refer to such things as handwork done by women, embroidery, needlework, knitting and such. The products of such labor then also have an abnormally low exchange value. It is not unusual, for instance, that the product of three days' work by a plain seamstress will have an exchange ratio that is not equal even to that of the product of two days' labor by a factory girl.

All the exceptions that I have mentioned so far tend to exempt certain groups of goods entirely from the operation of the labor value law. That is to say, they restrict the domain in which that law obtains. Really, they leave subject to that law only those goods which encounter no obstacles of any kind to reproduction in any desired volume, and at the same time require only unspecialized labor in their production. But even this restricted domain is not subject to the sway of the labor law of value without exception. Rather is it the case that even here exceptions bring about a further easing of the strictness with which the law may be applied.

4] A fourth exception to the labor principle is offered by one phenomenon that is universally known and admitted. Even those goods the exchange value of which, by and large, is in harmony with the quantity of their labor costs, still do not exhibit that harmony at all times. Fluctuations in supply and demand often cause the exchange value to rise above or fall below an amount which would correspond to the quantity of labor these goods embody. That quantity represents a center of gravity toward which the exchange value is drawn, rather than a fixed point at which it rests. To my way of thinking the socialist adherents of the labor principle are far too ready to shrug off this exception nonchalantly. Yes, they do confirm its existence, but they treat it as an ephemeral little irregularity, the existence of which by no means impairs the great "law" of exchange value. But it cannot be denied that all these irregularities constitute just that many examples of exchange values which are the result of factors other than the quantity of labor costs. At the least, this should have started an investigation into the question as to whether there might not be some other principle of exchange value. Might there not be a more general principle which would account simultaneously not only for the "regular" manifestations of exchange value, but also for those which, from the point of view of the labor theory, appear as irregular? But you may look in vain for an investigation of that sort by the theorists of the school we are discussing here.

5] Finally, there is a fifth deviation from the law. Aside from the aforementioned momentary fluctuations, the exchange value of some goods fails to correspond to the quantity of labor they embody, in a way which is *enduring* and to a degree which is not inconsiderable. Of two goods, the production of which costs the same amount of labor in terms of the average prevailing in a given society, that one will command a higher exchange value which requires the greater advance outlay of "preliminary" labor. As we know, Ricardo discussed in detail this departure from the labor principle in two sections of the first chapter of his *Principles.* Rodbertus and Marx, in the course of deriving their theories,[81] ignore it without expressly denying it—a thing they could not legitimately do. An oak tree that is 100 years old has a higher price than can correspond to the half minute it takes to plant the acorn. That is a fact too well known to be successfully denied.

Let us summarize. The alleged "law" provides that the exchange value of goods is determined by the quantity of labor embodied in them. It is a law which a considerable proportion of goods *does not obey at all,* and the rest *not always,* and *never exactly.* Such is the empirical material with which he must deal who would formulate a theory of value.

What conclusions can the impartial theorist draw from such material? Surely not that the origin and determinant of all value is to be found solely in labor. A conclusion like that would be no whit better than to conclude, let us say, as follows: Electricity, experience tells me, often results from rubbing, and also often, to be sure, in other ways. Therefore there is a law, "All electricity is the result of friction."

On the other hand one can fairly conclude that expenditure of labor is a circumstance which has a far-reaching influence on the exchange value of many goods. It should be carefully noted, however, that this applies to labor, not as an ultimate cause, but as a specific intermediate factor. Any ultimate cause of value would have to be possessed in common by all value phenoma. However, in accounting only for this more limited influence of labor on exchange value, the theorist would be relieved of the embarrassing necessity of discovering as basic a motivation as was sought—necessarily in vain, of course—in the attempt to prove labor to be the key to that earlier and more inclusive proposition. It might be quite interesting and quite important to pursue further the question of the influence of labor on the exchange value of goods, and to formulate the results in the shape of laws. Only it would be imperative never to lose sight of the fact that those would then only be specific laws of value, which do not affect the general nature of value.[82] I might make use here of an analogy. The laws which formulate the influence of labor on the exchange value of goods stand in the same relation to the general law of value, as that in which the law "East wind brings rain" stands to a general theory of rain. East winds are a widespread intermediate cause of rain, just as expenditure of labor is a widespread intermediate cause of the value of goods. But the essential nature of rain is no more attributable to the east wind than that of value is to labor expended.

Ricardo himself overstepped the legitimate bounds only by very little. As I have already shown, he knows very well that his labor law of value is only a specific one. He knows, for instance, that the value of "rare goods" has an entirely different basis. His only error is that he greatly overestimates the extent to which his law is valid and practically ascribes to it almost universal applicability. A related phase of the same error consists in his tendency in the later stages to forget entirely the lightly regarded exceptions to his law which he had very correctly mentioned himself toward the beginning of his work. In consequence he comes to speak—quite incorrectly—of his law in phrases that imply that his law really is a universal law of value.

It was only his successors who, exercising less foresightedness than he, committed the almost incomprehensible error of positing labor, with complete and conscious assurance, as the universal principle of value. I say "almost incomprehensible error" because it is really difficult to understand how scientifically trained men after mature deliberation can maintain a doctrine for which they can simply not find a shred of logical support. There is none in the nature of the problem, for that shows absolutely no necessary connection between value and labor. There is none in experience, for that, quite on the contrary, shows that value for the most part does *not* harmonize with the expenditure of labor. Nor, finally, is there any even in authority, for the authorities on whom they rely never maintained the proposition in that pretentious all-inclusiveness with which their successors were fond of endowing it.

And the socialist adherents of the exploitation theory seek to maintain such a proposition, built on sand as it is! Nor do they employ it just incidentally, and to shore up some inconsequential angle of the structure of their theory. Indeed, they make of it a keystone to support the very façade of their most vital and practical claims. They uphold the law that the value of all goods consists in the labor time they represent. Then the next moment they attack any creation of wealth that is in conflict with this "law," such as the differences in exchange value which accrue to the capitalist as a surplus value. They call it "contrary to the law," "unnatural," "unjust," and recommend that it be abolished. That is to say, first they ignore the exception, in order to be able to proclaim their law of value as having universal validity. And after their furtive theft of that quality of universal validity, they revive their memories of the exceptions, to brand them as violations of the law. This method of argumentation is truly just as bad as that which would be followed by one who, observing that there are many foolish men, ignores the fact that there are also some wise men, in order to derive the "universally valid law," that "all men are foolish," and then demands the extirpation of the "unlawfully" existent wise men!

7. THE POSTHUMOUS VOLUMES OF THE MARXIAN SYSTEM

THE foregoing is substantially the verdict that I rendered many years ago, on the subject of the labor theory of value in general, and of

Marx's arguments in its favor in particular. That was in the first edition of this book. In the meantime the posthumously published third volume of Marx's *Kapital* appeared. Its publication had been awaited with a certain eager curiosity among economists of all persuasions. They were eager to learn how Marx would solve a certain difficulty which was the inevitable consequence of the doctrine he had laid down in the first volume. It was a difficulty which he had not only failed to solve in the first volume, but had hitherto left completely unmentioned.

In discussing Rodbertus I have already called attention to the absolute incompatibility of two of his assumptions. The first of these is that goods are exchanged on the basis of the relative quantities of labor with which they are indued. The other, and incidentally one which is indubitably corroborated empirically, is that earnings on capital are subject to an averaging process.[83] Naturally Marx in *his* presentation was beset by the same difficulty, and in fact he was more drastically vulnerable still, because just that part of the doctrine which contains the bone of contention is formulated by him with such special emphasis that it virtually invites objection.

For Marx distinguishes, within the capital which serves the capitalist as his means of acquiring a surplus, two component parts. The first is the part which is the source of labor's compensation, and which Marx calls the "variable capital"; the second is the part that constitutes the outlay for concrete materials of production such as raw materials, instruments, machines and such, and which Marx calls the "constant capital." Since only the labor of living persons can really create new additional values, only that part of capital which has been converted into labor power can change and increase in value during the process of production. That is why Marx calls it the "variable" capital. That part alone reproduces its own value and something in excess of it, the surplus value. The value of the consumed means of production, on the other hand, is merely preserved intact, since it reappears in the value of the product, altered in form, unaltered in magnitude. That is why Marx calls it the "constant" capital. It is not capable of "putting on surplus value." From this it necessarily follows (nor does Marx neglect to point out the syllogism with all possible emphasis) that the amount of surplus which can be produced with a capital can be in direct proportion to *the variable part* of the capital, but not to *the total capital*.[84] And it follows further, that equal capitals must produce unequal quantities of surplus value, if they differ as to their composition, with respect to relative amounts of constant and variable capital. This is what Marx calls their "organic composition." Let us accept, for a bit longer, Marx's terms and call the ratio of surplus value to that portion of the variable capital which is paid for wages the "rate of surplus value." And for its ratio to the total capital employed by the capitalist—what the latter in practice ordinarily uses as the base on which to compute the surplus value he has gained—let us use the term "profit rate" or "rate of return." Marx would now say, if the degree of exploitation is equal or the rate of surplus value is equal, then capitals of varying organic composition must yield unequal "rates of return." Capitals which are of such composition that the variable portion predominates, must bear a higher "rate of return" than those in the composition of which the constant capital predominates. But experience says that because of the operation of the law of the leveling of returns, capitals will in the long run bear equal "rates of return" without regard to their composition. Accordingly there is a manifest conflict between that which is, and that which, according to the Marxian doctrine, ought to be.

Marx himself was not unaware of the existence of this conflict. In his first volume he had already made laconic mention of it as "merely apparent," and referred his readers for his solution to the parts of his system which were to come later.[85] The long suspense in which the world had waited interminably to learn how Marx would try to extricate himself from this awkward dilemma was finally relieved through the appearance of his third volume. It contains a detailed discussion of the problem, but of course no solution. He merely corroborates the irreconcilable contradiction (nor could anything else have been expected) in what proved to be an abandonment of the doctrine in his first volume—veiled, unacknowledged, glossed over, to be sure—but still an abandonment.

For now Marx develops the following doctrine. He admits explicitly that in reality, and because of competition, the rate of return on capitals, quite irrespective of their organic composition, is leveled off, and necessarily must be leveled off to a uniform average rate.[86] In addition he admits explicitly that a uniform return rate, in the case of varying organic composition of capitals, is possible only if the individual commodities are interexchanged in a proportion other than that which reflects their value as determined by the labor they contain. Indeed, the exchange will be such that commodities produced with capital that is predominantly constant will be exchanged at more than their value, and those produced with predominantly variable capital at less than their value. Here he adds the term "capital of higher composition" for capital with a higher percentage of constant capital; conversely "lower composition" designates capital with a lower percentage of constant capital and a higher percentage of variable capital.[87] And finally Marx admits explicitly that the determination of prices in practical life really takes place in this way. On page 136 of the third volume he defines the "price of production" of a commodity as containing three things. In addition to repayment of wages paid plus means of production consumed (the "cost price") it also contains the average return for the capital employed in production. This price of production "is actually the same thing that Adam Smith calls 'natural price,' Ricardo calls 'price of production,' the physiocrats *'prix nécessaire,'* because in the long run it is the condition on which the supply, the reproduction of commodities in each particular sphere of production depends" (*Vol. III, p. 178*). In real life then, goods are no longer exchanged according to their values, but according to their prices of production. Or as Marx is fond of saying euphemistically (*for instance, Vol. III, p. 176*) "values are transformed into prices of production."

No one can fail to realize that these concessions and affirmations in the third volume are a striking contradiction of the fundamental principles laid down in the first volume. In the latter the reader was presented with a logical thesis to the effect that out of the essential nature of exchange arises the necessity that two commodities that have been accorded equivalence by virtue of the exchange must contain a common element in equal magnitude, and that this common element of equal magnitude is labor. In the third volume the reader is informed that when commodities are rated as equivalents in an exchange, they actually and regularly contain, and necessarily must contain, unequal amounts of labor. In the first volume (*p. 142*) we had read, "It is true that commodities may be sold at prices that are at variance with their values, but this variation constitutes a violation of the law of the exchange of commodities." And now we read that the law of the exchange of commodities provides that they are sold at their prices of production, and that the latter, as a matter of principle, cannot coincide with their values! I do not imagine there ever was a system of which the end repudiated the beginning so conclusively, so scathingly!

Of course Marx will not admit there is any contradiction. Even in this third volume he still claims that the law of value, as it is stated in the first volume, governs the actual conditions of the exchange of goods. And he expends many an effort, resorts to many a subterfuge, in his attempt to prove that in some degree, in some way or other, it still continues so to govern. I have discussed all these subterfuges elsewhere and in detail,[88] and exposed their futility. At this point I should like to comment expressly on just one of them. This is partly because it might really, at first blush, appear to have something alluring about it, and partly because Marx is not the only one to employ it. For I find its counterpart in the writings of one of the most capable among the theorists of the socialist school in the present generation. In 1889, which means before the publication of Marx's third volume, an attempt was made by Konrad Schmidt to carry to completion the part of Marx's system that was then still lacking. It was to be an independent creation, but presumably in the Marxian spirit.[89] And so he was led to a construction of the problem which likewise modified its provisions to the effect that individual commodities cannot, as the letter of the law—the Marxian law of value—demands, be exchanged in the ratio of the quantities of labor they represent. And so of course he found himself face to face with the question how far he could maintain the validity of the Marxian law of value if indeed he could maintain it at all, after such an admission. And Schmidt, as early as that, attempted to rescue the validity of the law by means of the same dialectician's argument that crops up again in Marx's own third volume.

The course which that argument takes is as follows. Individual commodities admittedly are exchanged in part above, and in part below their values. But these deviations compensate each other or cancel out, so that, for all the exchanged commodities taken together, the total of the prices paid is equal to the total of the values. Hence the law of value, applied to the totality of all branches of production, does after all find enforcement "as the governing trend."[90]

The dialectical web of this pseudo argument however, can be very easily torn asunder, and that, too, I have already demonstrated on another occasion.[91]

For what is the purpose of the law of value, anyhow? Certainly it can only be to explain the ratio of exchange as we observe it in real life. We want to know, for instance, why a coat is the equivalent of 20 yards of linen cloth, why 10 pounds of tea is considered to have the same value as half a ton of iron, and so on. And that is the way Marx himself conceived the task of explaining the law of value. Obviously one can speak of an exchange *ratio* only in the sense of the relation of two individual and dissimilar goods *to each other*. But as soon as we consider all goods *taken together* and add up the prices of them, we necessarily and deliberately ignore whatever internal relations may exist within that totality. The relative differences in price as between members within the group are compensated out of existence in the total. The amount by which tea is worth more than iron is the amount by which iron is worth less than tea, and vice versa. In any case, we get no answer to our question as to the exchange ratio of goods in an economic system, when we are told the total price that all goods combined will command. We might just as well ask by how many minutes or seconds did the winner of a foot race better his competitors' time for the distance, and then be told, "All the men in the race, taken together, took 25 minutes and 13 seconds"!

Now the situation is this. In answering the question of the problem of value, the Marxists begin with their law of value, that commodities are exchanged in the ratio of the labor time they embody. Then they make a disavowal—disguised or undisguised—of their first answer, so far as it concerns the exchange of individual commodities. But of course the question has no significance at all, except insofar as it does concern these. And then the Marxists claim complete validity for their answer only so far as it concerns the entire sum of the "national production." And that of course is a field in which the question has no point at all. They are thus forced to admit that the facts belie the "law of value" as an answer to the real question of the problem of value. And the only application which does not belie the law is then no longer an answer to the problem to which we really require a solution, but could at best be an answer only to some other question.

But it is not even an answer to another question. It is no answer at all, it is rank tautology. For every economist knows that if we pierce through the veil of money transactions, we perceive that commodities are really exchanged for other commodities. Every commodity that is the subject of exchange is at one and the same time a commodity and the price of what is received in exchange. Accordingly the total of the commodities is identical with the total of the prices paid for them. Or it can be put this way. The price of the total national product taken together is nothing more nor less than the total national product itself! Under these circumstances it is, to be sure, quite correct to say that the total price which is paid for the whole national product combined, is equal to the total exchange value that is "crystallized" in that national product. But this tautological dictum does not represent any genuine addition to our knowledge. Neither is it of any particular use as a test of the correctness of the alleged law which provides that goods are exchanged in the proportion of the labor they embody. By use of that method it is possible to supply just as good a proof—or rather just as bad a proof—of any "law" you wish to name. Let us imagine a law providing that goods are exchanged in the proportion of their *specific gravity!* For even though it be true that as an "individual commodity" a pound of gold can be exchanged, not for one pound of iron, but for 50,000 pounds of it, nevertheless the *total* price that is paid for a pound of gold plus 50,000 pounds of iron *combined* is not more and not less than 50,000 pounds of iron and one pound of gold. Accordingly the total weight of the total price, 50,001 pounds, is exactly equal to the total weight embodied in the total commodities, namely likewise 50,001 pounds. Consequently *weight* is the true standard by which the exchange relationship of goods is governed!

C. THE MARXIAN DOCTRINE AS INTERPRETED BY HIS SUCCESSORS

1. Attempts at New Interpretations by Sombart and K. Schmidt

UNLESS I am mistaken, the appearance of Marx's third volume signified the beginning of the end of the labor theory of value. That was the rock on which Marxian dialecticism foundered so manifestly, that blind faith inevitably began to weaken, even in the ranks of the most devout believers. Literary signs are already noticeable. For the time being these consist in attempts to rescue the doctrine, now no longer tenable in the exact words in which Marx set it down, by subjecting it to new interpretations.

In very recent times several serious theorists have proclaimed such interpretations. Werner Sombart openly admitted that the Marxian law of value is not tenable if it is put forward with a claim that it is in accordance with empiric reality. His idea is to interpret the Marxian doctrine as only an attempt to provide us with a "device for assisting our thinking," that device being Marx's concept of value. Value, as Marx defines it, does not appear in the exchange relation as it concerns the objects of capitalist production. Nor does it play any part as a factor in the distribution of the annual "national product." Consumers' goods, because of their qualitatively heterogeneous character are otherwise not commensurable. But by means of this auxiliary concept our minds are enabled to conceive of them as quantitative entities and they are thus rendered commensurable for our thinking. The Marxian concept of value becomes defensible when it functions in this capacity.[92]

In my opinion this proposition bears all the earmarks of a compromise that is quite unacceptable to both sides, and I have already expressed that opinion elswhere.[93] It cannot satisfy the Marxians because it is in direct contradiction to the most unequivocal pronouncements of Marx himself, and because it contains a complete surrender of the very essence of the Marxian doctrine. For it is self-evident that a theory which by its own admission is not in accordance with reality cannot have any significance for the explanation and evaluation of real conditions. And as a matter of fact voices have already been raised in disavowal in the camp of the Marxists.[94]

On the other hand, neither can the impartial theorist be satisfied with this compromise from the point of view of purely scientific requirements. For even auxiliary concepts, while they may be assumptions made in neutral disregard of reality, must not be a contradiction of it. So I consider Sombart's attempt at a new interpretation to be a pronouncement which will hardly win many friends and impel them to take up their pens and champion its cause.

Konrad Schmidt recently announced a pending fresh attempt at a reinterpretation of Marx which may be expected to provide more material for discussion than Sombart's. He commented on my previously mentioned *Zum Abschluss des Marxschen Systems* and conducted his discussion with commendable objectivity and impartiality. He comes to the conclusion that Marx's law of value, in the light of the facts recorded in the third volume, does actually lose the meaning "which, according to its presentation in the first volume, it seemed to have," and against which my criticism was leveled. But, says Schmidt, by that very fact it gains "a new and deeper significance, which only needs to be worked out more clearly in its contrast to the original version of the law of value." By a "revised thinking out" of the law of value "along lines that Marx concededly has not clearly laid down" it will be possible "at least in principle" to reconcile the contradictions that I pointed out. And Schmidt does give a hint of the basic lines along which his revised thinking will proceed.

He says price and labor time are both measurable quantities. A twofold relationship between them is thinkable. "Either the magnitude of the price is in direct proportion to the labor time contained in the commodity, or there are variations from this direct relation which follow certain rules that can be formulated, at least in a general way." Since the latter alternative is as readily conceivable as the former, it would not be permissible to do more than consider as a hypothesis the law of value which is based on the former of the two alternatives and it is "the task of further concrete investigation, either to confirm that hypothesis or further to modify it." Marx's first two volumes "pursue the original simple hypothesis to its remote conclusions" and thus are able to compose "a detailed picture of the capitalist economy, under a system of exploitation, as it would appear if price and labor time coincided exactly." But even though this picture "reflects the fundamental features of the capitalist reality," it contradicts that reality in certain respects. Therefore the hypothesis must be modified in order "to reconcile the partial contradiction between it and reality." And that is what takes place in the third volume. "The simple rule according to which the two factors coincide, which was absolutely necessary for a preliminary orientation, must now be modified. It must now be said that in reality prices deviate from the assumed norm in accordance with a rule which can be formulated in general terms." By this circuitous route, and only by this circuitous route, is it possible to arrive at recognition and detailed understanding of the actual relationship between prices and labor time. And that means an understanding of the real method of exploitation.[95]

I cannot prophesy any brighter future for this attempt at reinterpretation than I did for the original by Marx. Konrad Schmidt is a keen dialectician, and it may well be that when he proceeds to the detailed delineation of the doctrine he has sketched out, he will attempt to present it agreeably, with many a clever turn of phrase and many an alluring argument. But with all his artistry of presentation and argumentation, he will not be able to avoid foundering on two objective rocks which, judging by the sketch he has submitted of his program, are certain to lie athwart his course. That program already reveals two methodological sins, one of commission, one of omission. The first is a self-contradictory question-begging assumption, the second is the inherent untenability of his point of departure.

I spoke of a self-contradictory begging of the question (*petitio principii*). Let us occupy the point of view that Schmidt invites us to take. Let us for the present regard as a mere hypothesis the "law of value" according to which the exchange ratio of commodities is determined solely by the labor embodied in them. It is a hypothesis of which the correctness is not yet established, but is only to be put to the test by a more searching examination of the facts. What is the outcome of that test?

It is frankly conceded by its protagonists that the test does not completely and fully confirm the hypothesis. Quite on the contrary, it must be admitted that the quantity of the embodied labor does not constitute the sole determinant of the prices which the owner of commodities receives for them. Now, it must be remembered that the really distinctive and characteristic feature of Marx's law of value is its claim that labor is the *exclusive* determining factor. That it is a contributing influence is admitted under any theory of value. It now appears that the "less than full and complete confirmation" in this case, really signifies a *refutation* of the hypothesis with regard to its one essential feature.

My next query is, "What right has Schmidt to postulate that this hypothesis, which is unconfirmed as to its principal point, nevertheless 'reflects the fundamental features of capitalist reality'; and more specifically, that it does so in depicting the receiving of interest by the capitalists as based, in principle, on a 'genuine exploitation' of the workers?" If Schmidt advanced any other considerations which could prove the exploitative character of interest, we should of course have to make an independent examination of those considerations. But Schmidt does not establish any such additional independent reasons in his program, nor can he supply any, as we shall see in a moment. His only argument to prove the exploitative character of interest lies in the hypothetical law of value. However, the hypothesis bases its conclusion as to the exploitative character of interest on the premise—and exclusively on the premise—that in the labor that is incorporated in the commodity is to be found the sole cause of exchange value, and of the magnitude of that value. Schmidt must demonstrate that not an atom of exchange value can arise from any other cause than labor, in order to establish that any share of the value which a nonworker receives out of the product, is received only at the expense of the worker, and therefore is the fruit of exploitation. But as soon as it must be admitted that the exchange value of commodities is not exactly equal to the quantity of labor they embody, then it is clear that in addition to labor some other causative factor influences the creation of exchange value. And as soon as that happens, there is no longer any certainty that the capitalist's share arises from exploitation of the workers. For it could quite conceivably, and even quite probably, arise from that other cause of exchange value which competes with labor, and concerning the nature of which nothing is as yet established. In other words, the justification for using the hypothetical "law of value" as a reason for regarding originary interest as an exploitative gain stands or falls with a *full and complete* verification of the hypothesis. To discredit it even in part is to dig the ground right out from under the feet of the thesis, because the latter took its stand upon just that unconfirmed part of the hypothesis, namely the assumption that labor is the *exclusive* determinant of exchange value. Thus Schmidt presents an assumption, suspended in mid-air, to the effect that the exploitation hypothesis "reflects the fundamental features of capitalist reality." But he treats that suspended hypothesis as an ostensibly verified proposition which follows logically from the corroborated portion of the law of value, and in so doing he is guilty of an obvious *petitio principii,* assuming as true exactly what needed to be proven to be true.

And that blunder is made even more vicious by the presence of a contradiction. The mere presumption without proof of the exploitative character of interest would still not get Schmidt to his goal. In the course of the logical argument which is supposed to lead to an explanation of the phenomenon of interest as it actually exists, he is forced into that contradiction. Again it pertains to that ill-starred proposition, that the magnitude of the value is determined exclusively by the amount of labor it represents. Schmidt is forced to treat it in two ways, first as having validity in actual practice, then as not having validity in actual practice. That is because he is required to explain not only the cause of interest, but its amount as well. In doing so he takes the same position as the Marx of the third volume. He explains the determination of the interest rate as follows. The total surplus predatorily acquired by the capitalists is distributed uniformly and in accordance with the "law of the equalization" of profits, over all capitals employed, in proportion to their amounts and to the length of time for which they are invested. In order to make this portion of his explanation hold good, Schmidt has to concede expressly that the tentative hypothesis of the law of value is not in accord with actual practice, that is to say, that the exchange of commodities is *not* exactly in proportion to the labor incorporated in them—in short, that the hypothesis does not have validity.

But that is not yet quite enough to explain the interest rate. There still has to be an assumption and an explanation on the subject of how large that divisible quantity is, which is to be uniformly distributed, in other words that total of the capitalists' predaciously acquired surplus value. For this portion of his explanation Schmidt joins forces with the Marx of all three volumes. He assumes that the capitalists are able, in disposing of the commodities that they have their workers produce, to realize a price for them which is in complete accord with the hypothesis of the law of value—a price which corresponds in magnitude exactly to the number of labor hours which are embodied in the commodities. And so at two stages of a single explanatory line of reasoning he treats the law of value, first as empirically valid, then as empirically invalid. Even that possibility might be entertained if the two stages in his explanatory line of reasoning corresponded to two distinct stages in the empirical course of events. That is to say, if the creation of the surplus value were *one* separate and independent process, and the distribution of the surplus value, after its creation, were another independent and subsequent process. That would correspond to the business experience of a corporation. There the gaining of surplus proceeds and the amount of them are determined by the business transactions of the year. But the distribution of them does not take place until later, and by action completely independent of the business activity that brought about the surplus, namely by the declaration of a dividend in accordance with a resolution of the board of directors. But that is not the situation with respect to the "surplus" of the capitalists. The very contention of the Marx-Schmidt doctrine is that the creation and the distribution of the surplus are not divisible into distinct actions, but that they result from one and the same action, namely, the creation of the exchange value of commodities. The surplus value is created in the manner and to the extent that Marx claims, because the exchange value of commodities which is realized by the entrepreneur capitalists is determined entirely and solely by the number of labor hours embodied in them. And the surplus value is distributed in the manner that Marx declares because *the same* exchange value of commodities which is realized by the entrepreneur capitalists is *not* determined entirely and solely by the number of labor hours embodied in them! And so it is literally true that with respect to one and the same fact, namely the determination of the exchange value of commodities, Schmidt maintains that the law of value is a complete empirical reality, and that it is *not* a valid hypothesis!

In the Marxian camp there is a fondness for pronouncements that are analogous to the laws and the hypotheses in the natural sciences. And comfort is derived from the fact that the empirical effectiveness of those laws is subject to certain modifications by reason of disturbing factors, without causing those laws for that reason to be considered any less valid. If the law of gravity, for instance, governed in strict conformity with its terms, falling bodies would behave distinctly differently

311

from the way they actually do when their actions are affected by disturbing factors such as air resistance and the like. Nevertheless the law of gravity is not questioned as a genuine, valid and scientific law. The same is true, they say, of the "law of value." The law is correct, only in practice its application is distorted because of the existence of the institution of private capital which demands a uniform rate of return. Just as air resistance prevents falling bodies from moving at the exact speed assigned to them under the law of gravity, so the influence of the institution of private capital, with its claim to uniform interest rates, prevents the exchange value of commodities from conforming completely to the quantities of labor incorporated in them.

It is a lame analogy. The Marxian syllogism exhibits a deformity that does not and cannot find its counterpart in the impeccable syllogism of the physicist. The latter is quite clear on the principle that in a vacuum gravity is the only determinant of the velocity of falling bodies. He is equally clear as to the fact that in atmospheric space the velocity of falling bodies is essentially a result of the interaction of a number of causes. He is therefore careful to avoid making a statement with respect to atmospheric space that is valid only where gravity may be assumed to be the only force at work. Not so the Marxists. Even after they have introduced the existence of the institution of private capital into their hypothesis (as analogous to air resistance) they still maintain, as we have seen, that exchange value is determined solely by embodied quantities of labor. It is not until they explain the distribution of the total value over the individual parts of capital that they begin to remember the existence of a competing cause. That is just as if the physicist were to say that the total velocity of a falling body is the same in atmosphere as it is in a vacuum, only the velocity is distributed differently over the successive stages traversed in atmosphere, from the way it is distributed in a vacuum!

Moreover, the physicist has a very good reason for his assumption that at least in a vacuum falling bodies would conform exactly to his law of gravitation. But the Marxist does not occupy the same position with respect to his analogous assumption. To do so he would have to be justified in assuming that in an economy without the institution of private capital the exchange value of commodities would follow exactly the law of value which he claims to be in force. But for such an assumption the Marxist has neither a good nor a bad reason, he simply has no reason at all. And that brings me to the second cardinal sin of Schmidt's program, namely the literal untenability of his point of departure.

It is my opinion that the Marxists make it somewhat too easy for themselves in positing the "hypothesis" of the value of labor. The hypothesis certainly contains nothing which is basically and *a priori* unthinkable or impossible. But even that is not enough to justify setting up a hypothesis as the basis of a theory that is to be taken seriously. It is not *a priori* unthinkable, either, that exchange value might be determined by specific gravity! Now you cannot defend the contention that a hypothesis is entitled to be considered valid until its literal, palpable refutation has been achieved. I might, for instance, set up the hypothesis that the universe is filled with an infinitude of large and small sprites which push and pull bodies about, and by means of these pushings and pullings bring about those phenomena which the physicists, following another hypothesis, term gravitational attraction. Any theorist will grant me that an unimpeachable refutation of that fantastic hypothesis, extravagant though it be, is impossible with the knowledge available to us. It will never be possible to prove that the pushing and pulling sprites do not exist. The best that could be done would be to show that their existence is extremely improbable. And yet I should deservedly be the object of ridicule, were I to claim that my hypothesis were entitled to consideration in preference to any other until such time as it had been absolutely refuted. It has been held since time immemorial in all scientific research that only those hypotheses can lay claim to serious scientific consideration which offer some positive reason for considering them to be good hypotheses, or at least to be relatively the best.

But in the present stage of economic knowledge there is just no support at all for the hypothesis that the value of commodities is based on their embodied labor alone. We have already seen that it is certainly not an axiom, carrying direct conviction and capable of dispensing entirely with proof. The only attempt to furnish logical proof of it is Marx's, and that was a failure. And apparently Schmidt has abandoned it as a failure. For it is obviously asking too much of us to believe that we necessarily must conceive of every exchange as an exchange of equal amounts of labor. How can we, when Marx himself in his third volume proves to us that under certain circumstances it is an economic necessity that *unequal* amounts of labor be considered equivalents? Nor do we have that strict coincidence of hypothesis and empiric reality which, under some circumstances, can replace proof and indeed must replace it in all cases in which we are dealing with ultimate facts incapable of any further analysis. We know the very reverse to be true, for, as has been sufficiently emphasized, experience shows numerous flagrant exceptions, and throughout the whole investigation no exact coincidence of "hypothesis" and reality. A final possibility, which also would require internal proof, is an analysis of the forces in operation when exchanges take place. The object would be to prove thereby, or to make understandable, a tendency inherent in values toward agreement with the quantities of labor—a tendency which is blocked only by external obstacles. Nothing along this line was ever attempted by the Marxists since any such attempt would have been foredoomed to failure. I feel, on the contrary, that everything experience reveals to us and teaches us concerning the motivating forces that actuate exchanges, compels us to assume that value and amounts of labor never could be in harmony. That is no less true of a real world marked by the existence of private capital than it would be of a noncapitalist society. In any form of society, in any distribution of wealth, man is swayed by considerations of usefulness and cost. Those considerations indubitably include that of the amount of labor expended, but just as indubitably do not consist of that exclusively.

313

And especially would the length of time required for goods to deliver their usefulness play a part. And for that part the unrealistic hypothesis of the labor value of goods has no room.

2. Bernstein's Interpretation

IN MOST recent times a remarkable publication has issued from the camp of the socialists. It withdraws a short but important distance behind even the line that Konrad Schmidt defended, and no longer makes any claim at all that the law of value lends proof and support for the socialists' exploitation theory. It is true that the author, Edward Bernstein[96] does devote to the law of value a sort of lukewarm apology, that contains a line of reasoning about midway between Sombart's and Schmidt's. The unrealistic character of the law of value is freely admitted, insofar as it is supposed to apply to the conditions under which single commodities are exchanged. Labor value is declared to be a "purely intellectual creation," "a purely intellectual fact built up on an abstraction"; he calls it "absolutely nothing but a key, a symbol, like the animated atom." With his "imputation" that single commodities are sold at their value, Marx had wanted only to use a "hypothetical individual case" in order to make it possible to "visualize" the process that, in his opinion, total production did in fact go through. The fact that he has in mind is "surplus labor." However Bernstein has no intention of proving "surplus labor" on the basis of the law of value. He probably has the feeling that the law of value is itself far too unsound to be used as a foundation for anything else. At any rate he says, "Whether Marx's theory of value is correct or not, is a matter of complete indifference, so far as the proof of surplus labor is concerned. The theory is in this respect not a corroborative thesis, but a means of analysis and visualization."[97]

And it is significant that to this concession Bernstein adds the following further admissions. The value of labor, even as a key, "fails to serve its purpose after a certain point has been reached and so has brought disaster upon almost every student of Marx." In any event "the doctrine of value is no more a criterion by which to judge the justice or injustice of the distribution of the product of labor, than the theory of the atom is a criterion by which to judge the beauty or ugliness of a statue." "The marginal utility of the Gossen-Jevons-Böhm school" which, just like the Marxian labor value, does have "some relation to reality" as a basis but is built on abstractions, bears still further resemblance to it in that "for certain purposes" and "within certain limitations" it can lay "claim to validity." In view of the fact that Marx, too, had emphasized the significance of use value, it is impossible "to dismiss the Gossen-Böhm theory with a few supercilious phrases."[98]

Now what will be Bernstein's replacement for the supporting proof which the older Marxian school had sought in the theory of value, and which Bernstein has renounced? There must be such a replacement if he is to continue, as he does, to support the exploitation theory. He takes refuge in an extraordinarily simple premise, but one that is, to be sure, also extraordinarily questionable as to its conclusiveness. He simply points out the fact that "the production and distribution of commodities is achieved by the active participation of only a part of the entire population. Another part consists of persons who either receive an income for services that have no direct bearing on production, or who receive income without doing any labor. The total labor that is contained in production therefore supports a considerably greater number of human beings than those who actively participate in it. And over and above that, statistics on income show that the share appropriated by the ranks of those not active in production is a far larger fraction of the total product than would correspond to their numerical relation to the productive workers. The surplus labor contributed by the latter is an empirical fact, demonstrable through actual experience, which needs no deductive proof."[99]

Of course Bernstein thinks of "surplus labor" in pronouncedly Marxian vein as exploited work. Therefore he states, in effect, the following. It is a simple fact that something less than the entire national product is paid out in wages to the productive workers, and that there are other forms of income. That simple fact, Bernstein would have us understand, constitutes *empirical* proof of the exploitation of the workers, so that there is no need for any further enlightenment by deductive reasoning on the correctness of that conclusion. But I say the conclusion is on the contrary, so obviously premature, shows so patently that he takes for granted what he intends to prove, that there really is no need to make a proper refutation. Using the same method of argumentation it would be possible to outdo even the physiocrats and prove that all humanity lives by an exploitation of the agricultural population. For it is a fact, after all, that the products of the soil which the workers on the farms produce provide sustenance for a great many other people!

But the problem is really not that simple. Experience shows most clearly that production arises from the cooperation of human labor and material means of production. The latter are in part natural (land) and in part man-made in origin (capital goods). The natural product is then distributed, by some formula or other, among those who contribute the cooperating forces. Now a person might entertain the very debatable opinion that of all those who actually participate in that distribution only one has any right to do so, so that participation of any others is, from the outset, an exploitation of the one. But the holder of that opinion would certainly be under the duty of casting a clear light on the relations between the contributing forces and of presenting grounds from which the whys and wherefores can be deduced. He would have to explain why, despite the multiplicity of cooperators, one of them means everything—everything in general, or at least everything in respect to distribution specifically, and why therefore the one is entitled to claim everything for himself, and why the others have no claim at all. And Marx did conceive the problem in those terms. Goods have significance in economic life in accordance with their value, and therefore Marx was entirely logical. In order to prove that the worker had the sole right to the entire value of his product, he attempted to show that value is specifically the creation of labor alone. His law of value was to him a means of proof by which the landowner's and the capitalist's claim to participation were to be deduced out of existence.

I do not suppose Bernstein himself expects that he can get along without any deducing at all. Evidently his proof, purely empirical though he alleges it to be, does nevertheless contain an unspoken deductive factor, namely the proposition out of Rodbertus that from the economist's point of view all goods are purely the product of labor. Once the Marxian law of value has been expressly excluded from the premise which is to serve as the basis of a process of proof, Bernstein must avail himself of Rodbertus's proposition at least, in order to set up his chain, otherwise his syllogism would lack formal completeness. But this deductive premise to which Bernstein is forced to retreat, is not capable of lending support to the exploitation theory any more effectively than is the Marxian law of value. The Rodbertian proposition, as we know, is absolutely erroneous, insofar as it fails to recognize and to admit the significance for man's economy and production of the rare gifts of nature.[100] And what is more important for our question of interest is the fact that, even to the extent that it is correct, it does not furnish any support for that concept and those conclusions which the exploitation theorists would have it support. For, be it remembered, the exploitation theory does not restrict itself to claiming for the workers all that they create, but in addition claims it at an earlier date than that at which they create it; and this artificial prematurity has neither any natural title, nor any title naturally derived, the disregard of which could on principle be branded as "exploitation." The adherents of the exploitation theory do not provide themselves or their readers with any very clear idea of this interpolated factor, unnatural as it is, if indeed it should not be said that it flies in the face of nature. It represents an element intruded into their set of postulates which are alleged to be derived from self-evident natural principles; and while its nature is not clear, its existence is not to be denied. I made my point in this respect in discussing Rodbertus, and illustrated with an example, in miniature, as it were.[101] Now, in refutation of Bernstein I shall make the point again but on a large scale. For it seems, now that the episode of the remarkable Marxian law of value is at last approaching final disposition, that the battle over the exploitation theory is about to resume and to achieve ultimate decision in the same positions in which Rodbertus marshalled his theorems.

Bernstein summarizes the thought content of the point at issue in a concept of disconcerting simplicity by pointing out that other people beside the productive workers live off the natural production. I intend to oppose to that a few facts no less simple and elementary.

It is a fact that the production methods customarily practiced today involve long range preparatory measures calling for "indirect labor" on materials, tools, machines, auxiliary materials, means of transportation and so on. And it is also a fact that these methods are far more productive than those which do not include such long-range preparations.

It is likewise a fact that if we consider as one whole process all the labor that has been expended, directly and indirectly, on a finished consumers' good, we must be aware that we cannot get possession of the end product, ready for our use and enjoyment, before the expiration of a long period of time covering several or even many years, all filled with labor. And it is a fact that the socialists lay claim to this whole product, or to its exchange value, exclusively for the workers engaged in producing it, as the "full product of their labor"; that they are however by no means disposed to tolerate postponing the distribution of this entire value among the workers until such time as the product they have created is completed and ready for distribution; that they demand, on the contrary, that each worker, immediately upon performance of his quota of the labor, shall receive the full value equivalent of that which will not eventuate from the cooperative labors of all of them until several years have passed.

And at this point a second series of facts joins forces with the first. It is a fact, that if any distribution at all is to be made to the workers before the completion of their work, it must be made from goods which are ready for use and service, and are on hand before the workers' labor is concluded. That can be possible only when the goods to be distributed are derived from some other source. It is a further fact that only under such conditions is it possible to direct labor to objectives representing temporally remote enjoyment of the product. That is another way of saying that only under such conditions is it possible to adopt roundabout methods of greater productivity. Failing that, it becomes necessary to put up with the smaller returns from labor to which we are restricted when we employ production methods characterized by less efficient preparation and less roundabout processes. Such supplies of goods are at present in the hands of the capitalists, being handed on and increased from generation to generation. Let us ignore for the time being the question as to whether the acquisition of those supplies may have been partly legitimate and partly illegitimate. The fact remains however that the creation and preservation of this supply of goods must be credited to individuals other than the ones who are to be maintained and paid during the course of the production process already begun.

And so it is not even to be credited entirely to the workers active today, to *their* industry and *their* skill alone, that a certain more abundant product will one day come into existence, after the passing of so and so many years. Part of the origination and part of the credit is due to some group of people who did advance work, who provided for the creation and preservation of the stored up supplies of goods. And are we then being told that the services of these workers of today confer on them an unquestionable claim, not merely to be the recipients of that larger more abundant product to the full extent of its value, but over and above that, to receive it in full before the product itself has achieved existence?

That is what the exploitation theory would have us believe, but even the warmest friend of labor could never be convinced of it if he looked

317

all the facts straight in the face. But of course the exploitation theory does not do that. Until now that theory, in whatever terms it may have been formulated, has evaded the salient point at issue, that of the time difference. This is a twofold evasion, for it concerns not only the interval between the payment of wages and the completion of the product, but also the significance of the time element for the technological production process and for the evaluation of goods. Either it leaves this subject untouched, or it touches upon it in a misleading and mistaken fashion. And Marx has his share of sins to answer for in this particular, too. On one occasion he says that for the creation of the value of goods it is "a matter of complete indifference" that part of the labor necessary for the producing of a finished product had to be expended in an earlier period, that "it is in the pluperfect tense."[102] In another place he even reverses the argument, and by a bit of maddening casuistry contrives to show that the custom of distributing wages on periodic "pay days" is not an anticipation but a delay in the payment of wages, which is to the workers' disadvantage. He maintains that since the workers are not in the habit of receiving their wages until the *end* of the day, or week, or month during which they have already been working for the entrepreneur, it is not he who advances their wages, but on the contrary the workers who advance their labor![103]

Of course that statement would be entirely correct if it were made by someone who takes the position that the worker's claim to compensation has no further concern with the product that results from his labor. Such a position would also mean maintaining that the entrepreneur does not buy the future product that will result from the labor, but merely the present physical performance of labor by the worker. It would also mean contending that, once the wage contract has been performed, neither the worker nor his claim to wages is in the least affected by the degree of usefulness, if any, to which the product may attain, that question being one which concerns the entrepreneur alone. One who takes that position could of course say with full justification that whenever wages are paid upon completion of the performance of labor, it is not the entrepreneur who advances the wage, but the worker who advances the labor. But Marx and the socialists consider the claim to wages a direct claim to the product itself which will result from the labor, and maybe that claim is not without justification. They therefore base their criticism and their decisions concerning the payment of wages on the very relation that exists between those payments and the end product of the labor. But if that is so, then they must not overlook and deny that the payments, even though they may follow the performance of the individual installments of labor by a negligible period of time, do precede by a considerable interval the completion of a good that is ready for use or service. That entails recognizing further than when the entrepreneur pays wages which are actually a claim to the product itself, he is really satisfying the claim before it is due. And finally it means recognizing that since there is a difference in value between present goods and future goods, the anticipation in satisfying the claim must receive some compensation, which it does through the adjustment of the wages paid.

I have always expressed myself reservedly and rather negatively whenever in the foregoing pages it devolved upon me to discuss the rest of the participants in production. It befitted the nature of my present task to do so. The correctness or incorrectness of the exploitation theory does not depend on whether or not those parts of the national product which are not expended as wages are dispensed on an accurately graded scale which is in accordance with the true deserts of the participating parties. It depends solely and only on whether it can be proved that what the workers have earned constitutes an unqualified claim to an artificially premature payment to them of the total product. If that cannot be proved, then the exploitation theory is wrong. Then part of the product remains, and other claimants may then urge their legal or just pretensions to it. In the absence of such claims let an enlightened system of law dispose of it in accordance with such considerations of expediency as give due regard to the permanent advancement of the common good. Such might be quite possible, and indeed there seems to be a strong tendency in that direction in the development of our system of jurisprudence as evidenced by modern social security, graduated income taxes, increasing government ownership and controls and so on. Yes, it is quite possible, I say, that the share of the workers, based on naturally justified claims, will be increased temporarily by our laws through artificial measures based on considerations of expediency in the best sense of the word. And the increase would come out of that part of the national product still available after wages. And so, directly or indirectly, there would be a limitation of the income that is derived solely by virtue of possession. But the consideration and decision of these matters involve reasons which are completely disparate from those to which the exploitation theory appeals, and which it considers to have determining force. The significance of the exploitation theory, in the last analysis, can be summed up as follows. It first advances a specious claim to imagined rights, and aims thereby to cut off discussion; then when it comes to a settlement concerning that part of the national product not covered by a valid and just claim of the workers, the exploitation theory refuses to allow the genuinely pertinent considerations and reasons to be heard.

3. Conclusion

I HAVE devoted an exceptionally and disproportionately large amount of space to the discussion of the exploitation theory. I have done so advisedly. Certainly none of the other doctrines has approached it in the influence it exercised on the thoughts and the emotions of whole generations. And just our era has seen it at its apogee. And unless I am mistaken, its descent has already begun. But it is to be expected that there will still be attempts at stubborn defense or at revivification by metamorphosis. And so I thought I should be serving the good cause if I avoided restricting myself to a purely retrospective critique of the developmental stages of the doctrine, now definitely terminated. I thought it would be well to look forward, and even now cast some critical illumination on the intellectual theatre of operations to which, according to definitely discernible signs, its adherents are intending to transfer the renewed controversy.

So far as that old socialist theory of exploitation is concerned, which has been presented here in the person of its two most distinguished protagonists, Rodbertus and Marx, I cannot render a verdict any less severe than the one I handed down in the first edition of this book. It is not only fallacious but, considered from the point of view of theoretical soundness, it occupies one of the lowest places among all theories of interest. Grievous as may be the errors in logic made by the representatives of other theories, I hardly think that anywhere else are the worst errors concentrated in such abundance—frivolous, premature assumptions, specious dialecticism, inner contradictions and blindness to the facts of reality. The socialists are excellent critics, they are exceptionally weak theorists. The world would have been convinced of that long since, if the positions of the two parties had happened to be reversed, and if a Marx or a Lassalle had mustered for an attack against the socialist theories the same brilliant rhetoric and the same accurately aimed, mordant irony, which they directed against the "bourgeois economists."

The wide extent to which faith was—and is—placed in the exploitation theory, despite its essential weakness is attributable, in my opinion, to the influence of two circumstances. The first of these is the fact that it drew up the line of battle on a field where the heart, as well as the head is wont to speak. What people wish to believe, they believe very readily. The situation of the working classes is indeed wretched, for the most part, and every philanthropist must desire to see it improve. Many capital earnings are indeed fished up from turbid waters, and every philanthropist must hope those streams will run dry. When the implications of a theory point toward raising the claims of the poor and lowering those of the rich, many a man who finds himself faced with that theory will be biased in its favor from the outset. And so he will in large measure neglect to apply the critical acuity which he ordinarily would devote to an examination of its scientific justification. Naturally it goes without saying that the great masses will become devotees of such doctrines. Critical deliberation is of course no concern of theirs, nor can it be; they simply follow the bent of their wishes. They believe in the exploitation theory because of its conformity to their preferences, and despite its fallaciousness. And they would still believe in it, if its scientific foundations were even less stable than they actually are.

A second circumstance that redounded to the benefit of the exploitation theory and to its wide dissemination was the weakness of its opponents. As long as the scientific controversy was conducted on the basis of such equally vulnerable theories as those of productivity, abstinence or remuneration, and in the manner of a Bastiat or a McCulloch, of a Roscher or a Strasburger, the battle could not have an outcome unfavorable to the socialists. Their enemies could not attack their true weaknesses from such ill-chosen positions; their opponents' weak attacks could be repulsed without any great difficulty, and the enemy victoriously pursued into his own camp. And the socialists managed to do so with a felicity that equalled their skill. That fact, and that fact almost alone, accounted for the support that socialism furnished to the cause of the theory. If some socialist writers have achieved lasting significance in the history of economic theory, they owe it to the energy and adroitness with which they succeed in destroying many an old and deep-rooted fallacious doctrine. To be sure, the socialists were not able themselves to replace error with truth—less able, even, than many of the opponents whom they so deeply despised.

XIII

THE ECLECTICS

1. General Character of Eclecticism

PROBABLY nothing indicates more clearly what difficulties were encountered by economic science in its attempts to solve the problem of interest, than the fact that most of the nineteenth-century writers on political economy never did form any settled opinion on the problem.[1]

From about the 1830s on there was a change apparent in the way this lack of a firm conviction took form. Before that time there had always been numerous writers enmeshed in the toils of uncertainty, and they evinced their indecision by simply declining to treat the interest problem at all. Thus they comprised that category of economists whom I have already dubbed the "colorless" group. When in later years the problem of interest became the subject of sustained scientific discussion, such tactics could no longer pass muster. It became impossible for an author to avoid showing his colors. And so the undecided ones became eclectics. There had been a plethora of interest theories put forward. Any economist unable to make one of his own, or equally unable or unwilling to align himself completely with one of the available theories, selected from two or three or even a greater number of heterogeneous theories such features as appealed to him, and wove them together into a whole that was for the most part lacking in unity. Another method of procedure was to abandon any attempt to erect a structure possessing external unity, and to introduce into the course of his observations one theory after the other in turn, selecting what best fitted his purpose of the moment.

It goes without saying that the attainment of a position of any eminence at all was out of the question for an eclecticism of this sort, since it displayed such frivolous disregard of the cardinal duty of the theorist—consistency. Nevertheless this group, like the earlier "colorless" one, included a few intellects of the first order, as well as numerous writers of mediocre ability. Nor should that be cause for astonishment. The theory had developed in such peculiar fashion, as to expose the capable thinkers, even more than the others, to a well-nigh irresistible temptation to become eclectics. There was such an abundance of heterogeneous theories that it was easy to believe that the number of possibilities was exhausted. A truly critical judgment could not pronounce any one of them entirely satisfactory. But it was also undeniable that many of them contained at least the proverbial grain of truth. The productivity theory, for instance, was certainly not satisfactory in its entirety. And yet no unprejudiced mind could be impervious to the impression that there had to be some connection between the existence of interest and the greater yield of the capitalist system of production, or the productivity of capital, as it was called. Then again, the "capitalist's abstinence" was likewise incapable of furnishing a complete explanation of interest, and yet it was hardly possible to deny that sacrifice, which is the usual price of saving, cannot fail to exert an effect on the existence and on the rate of interest. Under these circumstances nothing could be more natural than to attempt to glean bits of truth from all the different theories presented. This was especially true at that time because not only the economic nature of the problem of interest, but also its social aspect was the order of the day. As a result, the zeal to justify interest induced many a theorist to renounce the unity of his theory in favor of a multiplicity of arguments in justification of interest itself. To be sure, the fragments of the truth remained but fragments in the hands of the eclectics, and their sharp edges grated harshly, stubbornly resisting attempts to fit them together into a harmonious and unified mosaic.

2. Combinations of Productivity and Abstinence Theories

ECLECTICISM presents us with a variegated sample card showing combinations of all the various single theories. The most frequent combination brings together the two theories which are generally understood—or misunderstood—as having obvious relation to reality. Those two are the *productivity theory* and the *abstinence theory*. I should like to make special mention of Rossi and I single him out from among those who use this combination, both because his version of the productivity theory has some marks of originality, and because his methods may be regarded as typical of the inconsistency so usual among the eclectics.

In his *Cours d'Économie Politique*[2] he makes use of the productivity theory and the abstinence theory alternately, without making the slightest effort to fuse them into a unified theory. He seems, on the whole, to prefer the abstinence theory whenever he is dealing with wider aspects of the phenomenon of interest and its origin. When it is a matter of detail, and particularly when he is examining the question of the amount of interest, he prefers to rely on the productivity theory. I propose to record the most important instances of this procedure in simple sequence. I shall spare myself the effort of bringing them into accord with each other, since the author himself made no such effort.

Rossi registers the traditional recognition of capital as one of the three factors of production, the two others being labor and land (*Vol.*

I, *p. 92*). In return for its contribution to the entire process capital requires remuneration in the form of a gain for which Rossi uses the French word, profit. Why? That question is temporarily answered only in the mystic words, to be interpreted no doubt in the spirit of the productivity theory, "For the same reason, and by virtue of the same title as labor" (*p. 93*). He speaks more clearly, and certainly in the spirit of the abstinence theory, when he summarizes the third lesson of the third volume in the words, "The capitalist demands the compensation to which the *privation* is entitled, which he imposed upon himself" (*Vol.* III, *p. 32*). In the course of the subsequent lesson he develops this idea in more detail. He begins by reproaching Malthus for including in the cost of production the element of interest on capital. Rossi makes the point that this is no expenditure by the capitalist, but on the contrary, income. Incidentally, he should have directed this same reproach against himself. In the sixth lesson of the first volume he expressly and with all formality included interest among the components of the cost of production.[3] But at this point he registers as a legitimate element of cost the "capitalized saving" (*l'épargne capitalisée*) by which he means the acts of refraining from consuming, and of productively using available goods. On later pages there are frequent references (*Vol.* III, *p. 261 and 291 are examples*) to the capitalist's foregoing of consumption of a good as a moving force in the origin of gain.

Although Rossi has up to this point shown himself to be predominantly an adherent of the abstinence theory, there are passages, beginning with the second half of the third volume, which constitute at first sporadic and then increasingly frequent evidences of the fact that he was also influenced by the widely circulated productivity theory. At first he states in rather vague terms that there is a connection between interest and the fact that "capital contributes to production" (*Vol.* III, *p. 258*). But a little later (*p. 340*) he says quite definitely, "Interest is the compensation justly due to the *productive force* . . ." He no longer says "to privation." Finally the amount of interest is explained as being measurable, in the broadest sense, by the productivity of the particular capital. For Rossi regards it as "natural" that the capitalist receive as his share of the product such proportion of it as his capital has produced. Such share will be large if the productive power of his capital is great, and will be small if its productive power is scant. And so Rossi arrives at the point where he formulates a law. The amount of interest is by nature in direct proportion to the degree of productive power possessed by a capital. His first development of this law is by means of a hypothesis which assumes a production which requires for its execution *only* capital, so that the factor of labor may be disregarded as negligible. In this connection his computation is entirely in terms of the use value of the product. Under the assumed conditions he envisions, for instance, a hypothetical piece of land which will yield, say 20 bushels of grain in excess of the capital laid out, when it is worked with only a spade. If a more effective capital is used, say a plow, it is quite obvious, says Rossi, that after complete recovery of the capital laid out the same piece of land will yield more, say 60 bushels of grain. The reason is, "that a capital of greater productive force has been used." And the same natural fundamental law is likewise valid under the complicated conditions of our actual economic life. Here too it is "natural" that the capitalist should share with the workers in the total product, in the proportion which the productive force of his capital bears to the productive force of the workers. If, for instance, a production process has hitherto been carried on by 100 workers, and a machine is introduced which replaces the labor of 50 of those workers, then the capitalist has a claim to one-half of the total product, that is to say, to the wages of 50 workers.

There is only one disturbing element to upset this natural relation, and that is that the capitalist plays a double role. He not only contributes his capital to the common undertaking, but he combines with that a second undertaking, the purchase of labor. By virtue of the former his receipts would always be limited to the natural return which corresponds to the productivity of his capital. But since he purchases labor sometimes at low prices and sometimes at high, he may either increase his own natural return at the expense of the natural wages of labor, or he may suffer a partial diminution of it in favor of the workers. It may, for instance, happen that the 50 displaced workers, by increasing the supply of labor, will depress wages. In that case the capitalist may purchase the labor of the 50 workers retained for a smaller share of the total product than corresponds to the proportion that their productive force bears to the productive force of the capital. Thus he may purchase their labor for 40% instead of 50% of the total product. In that case he receives, in addition to the natural gain on capital, an additional gain of 10%. But in its nature this is something entirely foreign to the gain on capital, with which it is ordinarily and erroneously lumped together. It is rather to be regarded as a gain arising from the purchase of labor. And it is not the natural return on capital that causes antagonism between capital and labor, but this extraneous addition. Moreover, it is only with reference to this addition that it can be said with any degree of correctness that the capitalist's excess of proceeds rises when wages fall, and vice versa. The natural genuine return on capital does not affect wages and depends only on the productive force of capital (*Vol.* III, *lessons 21 and 22*).

After all that has been said in a previous chapter about the various productivity theories, I believe it well to dispense with a detailed critique of the particulars in Rossi's theory. I wish to point out just one monstrous inconsistency. If Rossi were correct, then all surplus production resulting from the introduction and improvement of machines, or from the development of capital in general, would have to pour into the pockets of the capitalists, in full measure and undiminished, and in all eternity, without any portion of the blessings of such progress ever being of benefit to the workers. For those surpluses are attributable to the increased productive force of capital, and their fruits constitute the "natural" share of the capitalists![4]

Closely akin to the line of thought followed by Rossi were those of Molinari[5] and Leroy-Beaulieu[6] among the French writers, and of Roscher among the Germans as well as of Roscher's disciples, Schüz and Max Wirth.[7]

Among the Italian writers of this same school the one I should emphasize is L. Cossa. Unfortunately this highly able author of a monograph[8] investigating the nature of capital did not extend its scope to include the question of originary interest. And so we are restricted in this connection to his very fragmentary allusions to the subject which are to be found in his well-known *Elementi di Economia Politica*.[9] Judging by its contents Cossa is another of the eclectics. And yet his manner of performing his task as self-appointed interpreter of the prevailing doctrines seems to me to betray very clearly that he is not without his doubts concerning them. And so, although he grants that interest is to be regarded as a compensation for the "productive service" rendered by capital (*p. 119*), he refuses to acknowledge that capital is a primary factor of production, and admits it has validity only as a "secondary instrument" of production.[10] Furthermore, although he follows the lead of the adherents of the abstinence theory in listing the factor of deprivations (*privazioni*) among the elements of the cost of production (*p. 65*), yet he seems to utilize this point in presenting the doctrine of interest in a manner that would indicate he is not so much expressing his own convictions, as transmitting the teachings of others.[11]

But in my estimation the most interesting of the eclectic theories which combine the abstinence theory and the productivity theory is the one advanced by the Englishman, Jevons. I shall conclude my presentation of this group with his theory.

Jevons's initial effort[12] is devoted to an exposition of the economic function of capital, and his exposition is very lucid and quite free of the mysticism of a special "productive force." That function he conceives very simply as consisting in the power of capital to permit us to expend labor in the form of an advance. It assists us over the difficulty that lies in the time interval which must occur between the beginning and the ending of the production process. There is an infinite number of improvements in the production of goods, which can be introduced only under conditions that make inevitable a concomitant lengthening of the period between the moment when labor is first expended, and the time when the product is finally completed. All those improvements are dependent on the use of capital; and in the fact that capital makes the improvements possible lies the great, and almost the only usefulness of capital.[13]

On that basis Jevons explains originary interest as follows. He makes the assumption that every extension of the time interval between labor outlay and enjoyment of the end product makes possible the production of an increased product with the same quantity of labor. The difference between the product which could have been produced with a shorter interval, and the greater product that is produced with a lengthened interval of time constitutes the gain of that capital, the investment of which made possible the extension of the interval. Let us call the shorter interval *t,* and let $t + T$ represent the interval extended by means of the investment of additional capital. Furthermore let *pt* be the product that is possible with a given quantity of labor in the shorter period. Then by the terms of our assumption the product of the longer period will be correspondingly greater, that is to say, $p(t + T)$. The difference between these two quantities, expressed by $p(t + T) - pt$, is the gain of capital.

In order to determine the interest rate which this amount of gain represents, the latter must be computed as a percentage of the capital investment which made the extension of the period possible. The quantity *pt* must be regarded as invested capital because that is the quantity of product which could have been procured without the additional capital, and at the expiration of the shorter time interval. The length of the period during which the additional capital is invested is *T*. The whole quantity of the additional investment is therefore represented by the product $pt \times T$. If the previously mentioned difference is divided by this last quantity, the result is the interest rate. This interest rate then is equal to

$$\frac{p(t + T) - pt}{T} \times \frac{1}{pt} .^{14}$$

The more completely a country is saturated with capital, the greater is the product *pt* which can be achieved without additional investment of capital. It follows that the greater also will be the capital that serves as the base for computing the percentage of the gain that results from the further lengthening of the interval. In other words, the lower is the interest rate which expresses that gain. This explains the tendency toward a decreasing interest rate with increasing prosperity. Furthermore, since all capitals tend to command the same interest rate, all of them have to be content with the rate commanded by the most recently invested capital. Hence the degree of advantage which accrues to production through the most recent addition of capital, becomes the determining measure of the general interest rate throughout the nation.

It is easy to recognize the similarity between the foregoing process of reasoning and the line taken by the German, Thünen. But it is also vulnerable to criticism in similar respects. For Jevons is too ready to identify a physical "excess in quantity of product" with a surplus value, just as Thünen does. What his exposition does in actual fact prove is that there is an "increment of product" as he calls it, in comparison with what would have resulted if the production process had been compelled to operate without benefit of the most recent addition to capital. But at no point has Jevons made it acceptably clear that this increase in the physical quantity of output at the same time represents an increased surplus value over the capital consumed in the process of investment. Let us illustrate this point by means of a concrete example. It is readily understandable that by using an imperfect but readily constructible machine one may produce in a year 1,000 pieces of a given class of goods, whereas the use of a more nearly perfect machine, which however takes a long time to construct, makes it possible within that same year to produce 1,200 pieces of the same kind of goods. But that does not by

327

any means prove that the 200 pieces represent a net additional value. It might be possible that the very capacity of the machine to produce the 200 additional pieces would cause such a high valuation to be placed on the machine that the entire additional quantity of 200 pieces is needed to cover the increased amortization of the machine. It is also conceivable that the new and successful method of production finds such wide application that the increase in supply depresses the exchange value of the 1,200 pieces to the price of the former 1,000 pieces. In either event there is no creation of a surplus value. And so Jevons has here fallen a prey to the same old error made by the adherents of the productivity theory in that he mechanically interprets the readily demonstrable increase in quantity of product as an increase in value.

To be sure, there are undeniable incipient attempts to analyze this very difference in *value*. But Jevons never incorporated them into his productivity theory. They do not complete his theory; they are merely concomitants of it.

One of these incipient efforts consists in his adoption of some elements of the abstinence theory. Jevons cites Senior approvingly, and explains the latter's "abstinence" as that "temporary forgoing of enjoyment which is an essential feature of capital." Or he calls it the "endurance of want" which the capitalist assumes, and he devises formulas by which to compute the magnitude of the sacrifice termed "abstinence" (*p. 253 ff.*). He counts it as an element in the cost of production; at other times by an ambiguous use of terminology he even calls it *interest;* and in one instance he specifically calls the capitalist's receipts compensation for his "abstinence and risk" (*p. 295 toward the end*).

It is also very interesting to note a series of observations made by Jevons, most certainly under the influence of Bentham,[15] concerning the bearing of *time* on the evaluation of needs and satisfactions. He remarks that we anticipate future joys and sorrows, and that the prospect of future joys is felt to be a prevenient experiencing in the present of an "anticipated" joy. But the intensity of the anticipation is always less than that of the joy itself, and is dependent on two factors. These are the intensity of the future joy which is being anticipated, and the length of the period of time which still separates us from the actual realization of the joy (*p. 36 f.*). Strangely enough, Jevons finds no justification for the difference which we make between the immediate evaluation of a present satisfaction and that of a future gratification. Jevons says this difference is founded on a shortcoming in our intellectual and emotional disposition, and claims that time should have no bearing upon the case at all. Nevertheless, Jevons admits that as a result of our human imperfections a future sensation does in actual fact always exert a less potent influence on us than does a present impression (*p. 78*).

Jevons is entirely correct in his judgment that our ability to anticipate future sensations is bound to exert a strong influence in economic matters, for it is one of the motives underlying all accumulation of capital (*p. 37*). Unfortunately he restricts himself to hints of the most general nature, and to a few quite fragmentary applications of them.[16] But he never attains to a truly constructive development of the idea or to a comprehensive utilization of it to advance the theory of value and income. His failure to do so is all the more to be wondered at, because some features of his theory of interest seemed to contain a strong invitation to exploit the time factor very assiduously for the explanation of interest. For one thing, he had emphasized more strongly than anyone before him[17] the part that is played by time in the functioning of capital. It certainly would have been closely germane to his thought to inquire whether consideration of the difference in time might not exercise such a direct influence on the evaluation of the product of capital as to form the basis for an explanation of the difference in value that lies at the root of originary interest. Instead, Jevons persists, as we have noted, in the old habit of explaining interest simply on the basis of a difference in the *physical quantity* of the product. It might have seemed even less remote to seek to establish a connection between "abstinence" (a concept that Jevons likewise treated) and the difference we make in our evaluation of present and future enjoyments. This might have led to making the point that the sacrifice which the postponement of gratification is supposed to entail consists in that very reduction in value that attaches to a use which lies in the future. But Jevons not only fails to put such a thought into express words, he even deliberately excludes its possibility. For he says, as we pointed out above, that this lower estimation of value is merely an *error* attributable to our human weakness. But he declares that "abstinence" on the other hand, is a *real and true sacrifice,* which consists in the continuation of a passive condition of want.

And so, although Jevons expresses quite a few interesting and perspicacious thoughts, they do not fuse in any creative union with respect to our theme. Jevons remains a brilliant eclectic, but after all only an eclectic.

3. Combinations Involving the Remuneration Theory

A SECOND group of eclectics draws on the remuneration theory in one or another of its variations as an ingredient in their combination. The first one of these whom I should like to discuss briefly is Read. It is true that his work[18] belongs to a period when the English writings on interest were in their most confused stage, and that his contribution to it reveals a particularly heterogeneous hodgepodge of opinions.

Read at the outset put his greatest emphasis on the independent productivity of capital, of which he is firmly convinced. "How absurd" he exclaims at one point (*p. 83*), "the assertion must appear that labor produces everything and is the sole origin of all wealth! As if capital produced nothing and were not also a real and distinct source of wealth!"* Somewhat later he concludes an elucidation of what capital accomplishes in certain industries with the statement, entirely in the spirit of the productivity theory, that everything that is left over after payment of

---

* Translators' note: Translated from the German. The original by Read in English was not available to us.

the workers engaged in the production process "may fairly be claimed *as the product and reward of capital.*"*

Subsequently however he regards the matter in an essentially different light. For he now places special emphasis on the fact that capital itself has arisen through labor and saving, and on that basis constructs an exegesis of interest which invokes in nearly equal measure the spirit of James Mill's remuneration theory and that of Senior's abstinence theory. He now says (*p. 310*), "The person who worked in the past and did not consume the product of his labor but husbanded it, and now uses it to support another worker engaged in the process of production, is entitled to his gain or interest (*which is the reward for past labor and for storing up of the fruits of that labor*) just as truly as the worker of today is entitled to his wage, which is the compensation of his more recent labor."*

It goes without saying that an eclectic "about face" of this sort cannot be executed without contradictions of all kinds. And so Read himself now resolves capital into previously performed labor, against which he protested vehemently at an earlier stage.[19] And now Read himself explains interest as the wages of previous labor, whereas on a previous occasion[20] he took McCulloch most harshly to task for obliterating the line that separates the concepts of "profit" and "wages."

Perhaps the closest German parallel to Read is furnished by Gerstner. He gives an affirmative answer to the "well-known question" whether capital produces, independently and apart from the other two sources of goods. He believes that it is possible to determine with mathematical exactness the degree of participation of the production tool "capital" in the creation of the end product, and he concludes without further ado that this share in the product is "the interest that capital is justly entitled to derive from the total gain."[21] However, Gerstner injects into this very sketchy productivity theory elements somewhat reminiscent of Mill's remuneration theory. Thus on page 20 he alludes to the instruments of production as "a sort of anticipation of labor," and on that basis continues by declaring that "the interest derived by capital which is attributable to the instruments of production constitutes a delayed wage for labor previously performed" (*p. 23*). There is a very closely related question as to whether this previously performed labor has not received a previous wage in the capital value of the capital itself; and in that case the further question presents itself as to why there should be additional wages in perpetuity in the form of interest. But those are questions which do not occur to Gerstner any more than they do to Read.

This group of eclectics should also embrace the Frenchmen, Cauwès[22] and Joseph Garnier. I have already shown[23] that Cauwès acknowledges himself, with some reservations, to be an adherent of the remuneration theories of Courcelle-Seneuil. But in addition he develops a wide variety

* Translators' note: Translated from the German. The original by Read in English was not available to us.

of views which have their roots in the productivity theory. In a polemic against the socialists he claims for capital an independent "active role" in production, which it performs side by side with labor (*Vol.* I, *p. 235 f.*). He regards the "productivity of capital" as the factor which determines the rate of loan interest[24] that may prevail at any given time. And in general he derives the existence of an "excess value" from the productivity of capital, inasmuch as he bases his explanation of interest on the fact that "a certain excess value is to be attributed" to the productive employment of capital.[25]

In the theories of Joseph Garnier[26] we actually find the elements of three different theories eclectically combined. The basis of his views is obviously derived from Say's productivity theory. He even carries over from it a feature long since rejected by economists generally, namely the inclusion of *originary interest* in the cost of production.[27] Side by side with the foregoing theory he cites the "renunciation" (he uses the French word *privation*) which the lender of capital imposes upon himself, by reason of the fact that he parts with that capital, as a justification of interest. His reasoning here seems to follow along lines laid down by Bastiat. And finally he declares that interest gives rise to, and serves as a compensation for the "labor of saving"[28] (*travail d'épargne*).

4. Combinations of Theories Favorable and Hostile to Interest

ALL the eclectics mentioned up to this point combine a multiplicity of theories which, though they may not coincide in their essential motivation, are at least in harmony as to their practical results. That is to say, they all combine theories that favor interest. Strange to relate however, there are several writers who combine elements from the exploitation theory, which is hostile to interest, with one or with several theories that are more or less favorably disposed toward it.

J. G. Hoffmann, for example, evolves on the one hand a peculiar theory favorable to interest, which declares interest to be a compensation for certain labors to be performed by the capitalist for the common benefit.[29] On the other hand he rejects in no uncertain terms the productivity theory which had already gained currency in his day. Indeed, he characterizes as the veriest delusion the idea "that creative forces inhabit the dead mass of capital or of land."[30] He states quite bluntly that when he collects his interest, the capitalist is garnering the fruits of other men's labor. "Capital," he says,[31] "can as readily be employed to advance one's own labors, as those of others. In the latter event, there accrues to the owner a rental which *can be paid only out of the fruit of labor.* This rental, called interest, has one feature which is equally characteristic of land rent, in that both *flow into the reservoirs of the recipient as a result of tapping the fruits of other men's labor.*"

The combining of conflicting opinions is still more striking in the case of John Stuart Mill.[32] It has frequently been remarked that Mill takes a dual stand, as it were, with respect to two very strongly divergent lines of economic thought, namely the so-called Manchester trend on the one hand, and socialism on the other. It is readily understandable that such a dual position could not in any case be favorable to the development of a strictly unified theory. But least of all could such hopes be entertained in a field which constituted the very lists for the joust between "capitalism" and "socialism," that is to say, the field of the interest theory. And it is a fact that Mill's doctrine of interest is so confused that it would be a grave injustice to that brilliant intellect to base an estimate of his significance to economics on this least successful portion of his work.

By and large Mill's work was a further development of the economic views of Ricardo, and it was therefore natural that his heritage included the Ricardian principle that labor is the chief source of all value. But that principle runs afoul of the factual existence of originary interest. And therefore Mill modifies the principle, out of deference to interest, by casting it in more general terms and designating cost of production as the factor which determines the value of goods. And though he says that labor is the "principal, indeed almost the sole" element comprising the cost of production, he nevertheless concedes an independent place in the cost of production to the element of interest. He calls it the second constant element comprising cost of production.[33] The very fact that he follows the pattern of Malthus, and calls an excess quantity of production a cost of production, lays him wide open to attack. And that is all the more puzzling since this very error had long before been the subject of stricture in English economic literature, and had especially been the target of sharp and apt reproach by Torrens and Senior.

But whence does interest arise? Mill gives us, in place of one explanation, three conflicting ones.

The productivity theory is the one on which Mill levies most lightly for his explanation, and he calls upon it only sporadically and with all sorts of reservations. He begins by stating somewhat guardedly that capital is the third constant independent factor in production. To be sure, it is itself the result of labor, and hence its functioning in production is therefore the functioning of labor in an indirect form. Nevertheless Mill believes that capital requires to be specified separately.[34] He "beats about the bush" in similar fashion when it comes to the closely related question as to whether capital possesses independent productive power. "We often speak of the productive powers of capital. This expression is not literally correct. The only productive powers are those of labour and natural agents; or if any portion of capital can by a stretch of language be said to have productive power of its own, it is only tools and machinery which, like wind or water, may be said to cooperate with labour. The food of labourers and the materials of production have no productive power . . ."[35] Well! Instruments are truly productive, but raw materials are not! A distinction that is as strange as it is untenable!

Mill is much more definite in subscribing to Senior's abstinence theory. It constitutes his official doctrinal position, so to speak; it is set down explicitly and at length in the chapter devoted to interest, and in addition is often referred to in the course of his work generally. In Chapter 15 of the second book of his *Principles of Political Economy,* Mill says "As the wages of the labourer are the remuneration of labour, so the profits of the capitalist are properly, according to Senior's well-chosen expression, the remuneration of abstinence. They are what he gains by forbearing to consume his capital for his own uses, and allowing it to be consumed by productive labourers for their uses. For this forbearance he requires a recompense" (*p. 495*). Equally definite is the following statement at another point.[36] "In our analysis we found that there is another element besides labour. There is also capital; and this being the result of abstinence, the produce or its value, must be sufficient to remunerate, not only all the labour required but the abstinence of all the persons by whom the remuneration of the different classes of labourers was advanced. The return from abstinence is Profit."

But at the same time, and in fact in that same Chapter 15 of the second book, dealing with "profit," he presents still another—a third—theory. In Section five of that chapter he says the following. "The cause of profit is *that labour produces more than is required for its support.* The reason why agricultural capital yields a profit is because human beings can grow more food than is necessary to feed them while it is being grown, including the time occupied in constructing the tools, and making all other needful preparations; from which it is a consequence that if a capitalist undertakes to feed the labourers on condition of receiving the produce, he has some of it remaining for himself after replacing his advances. To vary the form of the theorem: the reason why capital yields a profit is because food, clothing, materials, and tools last longer than the time which was required to produce them; so that if a capitalist supplies a party of labourers with these things, on condition of receiving all they produce, they will, in addition to reproducing their own necessaries and instruments, have a portion of their time remaining *to work for the capitalist*" (*Book* II, *Chap.* XV, *p. 509*). Here the "real cause of interest" is to be found, not in any productive force of capital, nor in the necessity for compensating for a special sacrifice on the part of the capitalist in the way of abstinence, but in the simple circumstance, "that labour produces more than is required for its support," that "labourers have a portion of their time remaining to work for the capitalist." In a word, interest is declared to be an appropriation by the capitalist of the surplus value produced by labor—a declaration that reflects the spirit of the exploitation theory.

The German "socialists of the chair" occupy a similar dual position astride the fence separating "capitalism" from "socialism." The result of this straddling is in their case, too, not infrequently an eclecticism that brings them still closer to the exploitationist position than was the case with Mill. I shall restrict myself to the mention of just one of the leading figures among these "socialists of the chair," one whom we have met repeatedly in the course of this book. I am referring to Schäffle.

With respect to our particular topic Schäffle's works reveal three readily distinguishable lines of argument. His *first* line parallels Hermann's use theory. Although that theory deteriorates in Schäffle's hands by reason of a subjective tinge imparted to the concept of use, by the same token it adapts itself the better to Schäffle's second line of argument. This line holds the dominant position in *Das gesellschaftliche System der menschlichen Wirtschaft,* but there are definite traces of it still discernible in his *Bau und Leben des sozialen Körpers.*[37] His *second* line of argument contends that interest is to be regarded in the light of a professional fee that is charged for certain services rendered by the capitalist. He had already suggested this concept in *Das gesellschaftliche System* and lent it explicit corroboration in his *Bau und Leben.*[38] But along with it we find that in the latter book we can detect numerous passages that convey the beginnings of an exploitation theory quite in the socialist vein. The Schäffle of *Das gesellschaftliche System* had recognized the uses of accumulated wealth as an independent and elemental factor in the cost of production, on an equal footing with labor.[39] But hear the later Schäffle! "Cost is comprised of two component parts, the expenditure of personal goods through performance of labor, and the expenditure of capital. But the latter can also be reduced to labor, for the expenditure in production of concrete goods is reducible to a sum total of many small amounts of labor expended in previous periods. *Accordingly, one may regard all cost as labor cost.*"[40]

If then, among the sacrifices that the production of goods entails, labor is the only one that the economist is required to take into account, it is no longer a far remove to claim the result of production *in toto* on behalf of those who have made that sacrifice. And Schäffle says just that in numerous passages of which his Volume III, page 313 ff. may serve as an example. There he sets up as the ideal of the economic distribution of goods a system whereby the latter could be distributed among the members of society in such measure as they perform labor. He concedes that the realization of such an ideal today encounters all sorts of obstacles. One of them is that capital wealth serves as a means of acquiring wealth. It is used partly in illegal and immoral ways, partly in legal and morally unobjectionable ways of acquiring the product of labor.[41] This "appropriation of surplus value" on the part of the capitalists is not condemned out of hand by Schäffle, but he only tolerates it as an expedient device acceptable only until such time as it "becomes possible to replace private capital, in whatever economic function it serves, with a governmental agency that is demonstrably efficient, more nearly perfect and less 'voracious of surplus value.' "[42]

In contrast to this sort of toleration in the name of expediency Schäffle often proclaims the dogma of exploitation in very plain language, and says that interest is the booty wrung from the produce of other men's labor. Thus he continues, in immediate succession to the words quoted above, as follows. "It must be admitted that the organization of business in the form of speculative private economic enterprise is not the *ne plus ultra* of economic history. It merely serves indirectly the attainment of a social purpose. *It is oriented* directly, not toward the highest immediate service to society as a whole, *but toward the maximum profit for the private owners of the means of production and toward the fullest enjoyment of life on the part of the families of the capitalists.* The possession of the fixed and the movable means of production is made use of *to appropriate the very maximum that can be derived from the product of the national labor.* Even so early an economist as Proudhon furnished complete critical evidence of the fact that *capital employs hundreds of methods of exacting its toll in advance.* The wage earner is a two-legged beast of burden, and yet one endowed with reason, and hence one who cannot be relegated to the level of mere brutish needs. This beast of burden can be assured only such portion of the produce of his labor as is absolutely necessary, if he is to maintain himself at the pitch which history has shown to be requisite if the entrepreneur himself is to meet competition."

XIV

TWO MORE RECENT ATTEMPTS

1. Introduction

I INTERPRET the wide prevalence of eclecticism as a symptom of the dissatisfaction which obtains with respect to the economic doctrine of interest. Whenever no single one of all the theories on a subject is in itself considered to be satisfactory, the effect is to encourage combinations of elements from several theories.

A second symptom pointing in the same direction is the fact that the impulse to add to the literature on the subject of interest continues unabated, despite the large number of theories already in circulation. Ever since "scientific socialism" stirred up a spirit of skepticism with respect to the interest doctrines of the old schools, not a half decade has gone by, and very recently not a year has passed, which failed to witness a new theory of interest greeting the light of day.[1] Insofar as these retained at least some fundamental features of the older explanations, and merely added original nuances with respect to detailed application of them, I have attempted to fit them into the categories marked by the principal schools. And in connection with my treatment of the latter in the foregoing chapters I have dealt with the variants as well.

But a few recent efforts have struck off along uncharted trails. Two of them I consider sufficiently noteworthy to warrant a rather detailed presentation of them. One of them, which bears some resemblance in its basic concepts to Turgot's fructification theory, and which I shall therefore call the "modern fructification theory" comes to us from the American, Henry George. The other, a modified abstinence theory, was fathered by the German, Robert Schellwien.

A. HENRY GEORGE'S MODERN FRUCTIFICATION THEORY

1. EXPOSITION OF GEORGE'S THEORY

GEORGE[2] develops his theory of interest in the course of a diatribe which he directs against Bastiat and the latter's well-known example of the lending of a carpenter's plane. James, a carpenter, has made himself a plane which he lends to William, another carpenter, for a year. But he is not satisfied with the return to him of an equally good plane, because he would in that case not be indemnified for the loss of the advantage which the use of the plane would give him during the year. Hence he demands that William return the plane and a board in addition, as interest. Bastiat had explained and justified the payment of the board on the ground that William "had acquired the power, inherent in the instrument, to increase the productivity of his labor."[3] George denies the validity of this explanation, based on the productivity of capital. He does so for various intrinsic and extrinsic reasons which need not concern us here. He then continues as follows.

"And I am inclined to think that if all wealth consisted of such things as planes, and all production was such as that of carpenters—that is to say, if wealth consisted but of the inert matter of the universe, and production of working up this inert matter into different shapes, that *interest would be but the robbery of industry, and could not long exist . . . But all wealth is not of the nature of planes, or planks, or money,* which has no reproductive power; nor is all production merely the turning into other forms of this inert matter of the universe. It is true that if I put away money, it will not increase. But suppose, instead, I put away wine. At the end of a year I will have an increased value, for the wine will have improved in quality. Or suppose that in a country adapted to them, I set out bees; at the end of a year I will have more swarms of bees, and the honey which they have made. Or supposing, where there is a range, I turn out sheep, or hogs, or cattle; at the end of the year I will, upon the average, also have an increase.

"Now what gives the increase in these cases is something which, though it generally requires labor to utilize it, is yet distinct and separable from labor—*the active power of nature; the principle of growth, or reproduction, which everywhere characterizes all the forms of that mysterious thing or condition which we call life. And it seems to me that it is this which is the cause of interest, or the increase of capital over and above that due to labor."*

The circumstance that labor is necessary for the utilization of the reproductive force of nature, and that therefore even agricultural products are in a sense a product of labor, cannot nullify the essential difference which, according to George, exists between one form of production and another. In those types of production, namely, "which consist merely of changing the form or place of matter, as planing boards or mining coal," labor *alone* is the active cause. "When labor stops, production stops. When the carpenter drops his plane as the sun sets, the increase of value, which he with his plane is producing, ceases until he begins his labor again the following morning . . . The intervening time, so far as regards production, might as well be blotted out. The lapse of days, the change of seasons, *is no element in the production* that depends solely upon the amount of labor expended. But in the other modes of production to which I have referred, . . . time *is* an element. The seed in the ground germinates, and grows while the farmer sleeps or plows new fields."[4]

Up to this point George has furnished an explanation of the fact that naturally fruitful types of capital bear interest. It is well known, however, that all types of capital, including those by nature barren, bear interest. George explains this very simply as the effect of the law of equalization of returns. "Now the interchangeability of wealth necessarily involves an average between all the species of wealth of any special advantage which accrues from the possession of any particular species, for no one would keep capital in one form when it could be changed into a more advantageous form . . . And so, in any circle of exchange, the power of increase which the reproductive or vital force of nature gives to some species of capital must average with all; and he who lends, or uses in exchange, money, or planes, or bricks, or clothing, is not deprived of the power to obtain an increase, any more than if he had lent or put to a reproductive use so much capital in a form capable of increase" (*p.182*).

Now let us apply all that to Bastiat's example. The reason why, at the end of a year, William must return to James more than an equally good plane does not lie in the enhanced power which the plane confers, "for that is not an element." The reason arises from the element of time, the difference of a year between the time when the plane is loaned and the time when it is returned. To be sure, if we restrict our consideration of the problem to this single example of it, "there is nothing to suggest how this element should operate, for a plane at the end of the year has no greater value than a plane at the beginning. But if we substitute for the plane a calf, it is clearly to be seen that to put James in as good a position as if he had not lent, William at the end of a year must return, not a calf, but a cow. Or, if we suppose that the 10 days' labor had been devoted to planting corn, it is evident that James would not have been fully recompensed if at the end of the year he had received simply so much planted corn, for during the year the planted corn would have germinated and grown and multiplied; and so if the plane had been devoted to exchange, it might during the year have been turned over several times, each exchange yielding an increase to James . . . And *in the last analysis, the advantage which is given by the lapse of time springs from the generative force of nature* and the varying powers of nature and of man" (*p. 185*).

2. Objections to George's Theory

THIS doctrine shows obvious similarity to Turgot's fructification theory. Both take as their point of departure the fact that certain classes of goods possess an inherent capacity to produce an increment in value, being endowed by nature with that ability as a gift. And both show that that gift is subjected to two influences. One of them is our system of conducting exchanges, and the other is the universal endeavor of human beings engaged in economic activity to derive from their possessions the most advantageous fructification possible. Under these influences the gift becomes artificially extended, so that it becomes characteristic of all classes of goods. The only point in which these two economists differ is that Turgot removes the point of origin of the increment in value entirely outside the field of capital, and relegates it to "rent-bearing" land and soil, while George seeks it within the field of capital, in certain naturally fruitful classes of goods.

By the variation George escapes the criticism that we levelled at Turgot. The latter had not explained why parcels of land, which bring in their respective amounts of return in infinite succession, can be bought at a relatively low capital cost, and thereby confer on unfruitful capital the advantage of perpetual fructification. Under George's theory it becomes self-evident that unfruitful goods are exchanged on a basis of equality with fruitful ones. For since the latter, by the process of production, can be brought into existence in any desired quantity, the possibility of increasing the supply of them indefinitely prohibits their attaining a higher price than unfruitful goods having an equal cost of production.

On the other hand George's theory is open to two other objections which in my estimation are conclusive.

In the first place, it is impossible to support his distinction of the branches of production into two classes, in one of which the vital forces of nature are supposed to constitute a special element which functions side by side with labor, and in the other of which this is not true. This is a repetition, in somewhat altered form, of the old error of the physiocrats who were willing to admit the auxiliary function of nature in the process of production with respect to only a single field of production, namely agriculture. The natural sciences have long since proved to us that the cooperation of nature is universal. All our production is based on the fact that by utilizing the forces of nature we succeed in converting her imperishable materials into useful forms. Whether the force of nature that we make use of is vegetative, or on the other hand, an inorganic one —mechanical or chemical—does not alter the relation between the force of nature and our labor in the slightest degree. It is entirely unscientific to say that in a process of production by means of a plane "labor alone is the effective cause." The muscular movements of the person using the plane would be of little use, if they did not have the assistance of the natural forces and properties of the plane iron. And can it even be truthfully said, because the task of planing boards is of such a nature that it must be classed as purely "an alteration in the form or location of material," that nature can here accomplish nothing without the help of labor? Can the plane not be harnessed to an automatic driving mechanism, operated by the power of a running stream, which enables it to continue its work unwearied, even while the carpenter sleeps? What more does nature do in the raising of grain? And yet the cooperation of nature is supposed to be an element in the latter case, and not in the former!

In the second place, George himself has not explained the original phenomenon of interest by which he claims to explain all subsequent instances of it. He says all classes of goods must bear interest because they can be exchanged for seed-corn, cattle or wine, and these bear interest. But why *do* these bear interest?

Perhaps at first blush many a reader will think, as George himself obviously thought, that it is self-evident. It is self-evident, he says, that the 10 grains of wheat into which the single planted grain has multiplied are worth more than the single planted grain, and that the grown cow is worth more than the calf from which it grew. But it must be born in mind that the 10 grains of wheat did not grow out of that one grain alone. There was also the service performed by the soil and a certain expenditure of labor. And it is quite clearly not self-evident that the 10 grains are worth more than *one grain plus the service rendered by the soil plus the labor* expended. Nor is it a bit more self-evident that the cow is worth more than *the calf plus the feed* it consumed while it grew up, *plus the labor* which its care entailed. And yet only if it *is* true can there be such a thing as surplus of interest left over, apportionable to the single grain of wheat or to the calf.

Yes, even in the case of the wine which improves while it stands in storage, it is not self-evident, without further ado, that the stored wine is worth more than the inferior immature wine. For in our method of valuing the goods we possess, we unquestionably follow the principle of the anticipation of *future* utility.[5] We do not value our goods according to the use they give us in the immediate present, or at least not exclusively so, but also in accordance with the useful purpose they will serve in the future. We value the field which at the moment lies fallow, with a view to the harvests it will some day yield. A scattered mass of bricks, beams, nails and staples, which in that condition is of no use whatsoever, is already accorded a value in consideration of the use it *will* serve at some future time when those things have been combined into a house. We value the fermenting grape juice which we cannot use in that condition, because we know that some day it will be useful wine. And so we might place a value on an immature wine which we know will be an excellent wine after it matures, more in the light of the future use it will render as a matured wine. But if we accord it a value right now in accordance with that future use, then there is no room for an increase in value and for interest. And why should we not do so?

And if we do not do so, or do not do so completely, the reason can certainly not be, as George says, any consideration of the productive forces of nature. For we may be willing to concede that in the fermenting grape juice which in itself is harmful, or in the immature wine which in itself is as yet of but little use, there nevertheless are natural forces at work which will lead to the creation of precious goods. But if we do, that can only be a reason, in the very nature of the case, for placing on these carriers of those precious forces a value that is *high* rather than *low*. If we nevertheless place a low value on them then that must be not *because* but *in spite* of their being the bearers of useful forces of nature. And so we can be certain that the surplus value ascribed by George to the products of nature is not the simple matter of course that he calls it.

At this point George does, to be sure, make a feeble attempt to explain this excess value by saying that in producing them, time, as well as labor, constitutes an independent element. But is that really an explanation? Is it not rather an evasion of the explanation? What right has the person who places a grain of seed-corn in the earth to demand that the exchange value of the product shall include compensation to him, not only for his labor but for the "time" during which the seed has been lying in the soil and growing? Is time the subject of a monopoly? The temptation lies very near, to counter such an argument with the naive words of the canonist of old, and to proclaim that time is the common property of all, of the debtors as well as of the creditors, of the producers as well as of the consumers!

And so we may suppose that George did not really mean time, but rather the vegetative forces of nature that are performing useful work during that time. But in that case the question arises, "How does the producer get the right to be paid for these vegetative forces of nature in the form of a special surplus value? Does he possess a monopoly of those forces? Must it not rather be said that they are available to anyone who owns a grain of seed-corn? And cannot anyone make himself the owner of one? Since seed-corn can be produced by labor in any desired quantity, would not the amount of it in existence be constantly increased, as long as a monopoly of the natural powers inherent in it continued to make possession of it seem desirable? And would not the supply of it therefore continue to increase until all surplus gain to which it would lead, were nullified, and the production of seed-corn were no more remunerative?"

The alert reader will observe that we have arrived at a line of argument that is identical with that into which we found ourselves drawn when we were appraising Strasburger's productivity theory.[6] At this point in his theory George has underestimated the interest problem in much the same manner as Strasburger did, only to a greater degree, and even more naively. Both are premature in their acceptance of the forces of nature as the origin of interest. But Strasburger is at least making an effort toward an exhaustive explanation of the alleged cause-and-effect relationship of the two factors, and toward fitting every detail into place. George on the other hand offers us nothing more than the presumptuous assertion that in certain processes of production time is an "element." The victory over the mighty problem of interest was not, forsooth, so cheaply to be won!

B. SCHELLWIEN'S MODIFIED ABSTINENCE THEORY

1. Exposition of Schellwien's Theory

THE views of Schellwien[7] parallel Marx's socialist theory for some part of the way. The value of goods is reflected in their price, of which it is the "essence" or the "substance." The factors of price are supply and demand, in other words, production and consumption respectively, which really underlie supply and demand. But production and consumption are factors which influence value in dissimilar fashion. It is of course true that consumption is a factor of value insofar as no good is valued at all which is not consumable or usable. It is in this sense a necessary *condition* to value. But since want and acceptability are in themselves not a matter of rationality, and since usefulness is consequently not measurable, usefulness cannot become the yardstick by which to measure value. That yardstick can be found only in the field of the other factor, that of production or of labor, and as a matter of fact in labor time. A rational basis for the appraisal of individual values can be discovered only in the length of time during which labor had to be expended to produce those values. Moreover the measure must be in units of simple work to which all more complicated work must be reduced.[8]

From this point on Marx and Schellwien go separate ways. It is Schellwien's opinion that Marx failed to give proper weight to one peculiar modification of the result of labor, and it is that modification which gives rise to interest. For, says he, it is not only the consumability or usefulness of a good, but also the actual consumption of it which exercises determining influence on its value. The value at which all goods aim, is *realized* only upon consumption. Not until then, as the word *realize* aptly conveys, is its value *real*. If the good is never, or only belatedly consumed, it is *devalued*. This devaluing nonconsumption sometimes bears a pathological character that is highly destructive of values. On the other hand, it also plays an entirely systematic part in economic life, "where it does not destroy, but enhances value." That takes place in two kinds of case.

The first of these occurs where a temporary nonconsumption of goods is necessary to enable them to enter into consumption at all, or to enter it, possessed of a certain quality. Thus, fruit must be allowed a certain period of time for ripening, wine must have several years in storage to mature. Insofar as such a time interval is necessary between the completion of a product and its consumption, that interval necessarily brings about an enhancement in value. For the temporary nonconsumption implies a "diminution of the result of labor," and that, so far as the price is concerned, is tantamount to an increase in the required labor time. Accordingly, any "necessary period of nonconsumption" is just as much a part of the "socially requisite production time" which determines value, as is the actual labor time.[9]

The second kind of case involves those instances in which the production of an article requires that *other* commodities be not consumed. That applies in any case in which capital is required for production. In other words, it is the general rule. This is what then takes place.

"The capital is not consumed, at least not as such. The individual parts of the capital are of course consumed in the process of production and thus enter into the value of the commodity, for the very reason that they are consumed. The commodity guarantees the replacement of this capital that is consumed, in that its value reappears in the value of the commodity. But the 'consumed' capital must really be replaced, the economically necessary capital must continue to be preserved as capital, it must not be consumed. Since therefore the capital that is being used in production is, to put it simply, withheld from consumption, the commodity must guarantee compensation for such nonconsumption, and that necessitates a corresponding increase in the value of the commodity. If the value of a commodity contained only the equivalent of the value of that capital which was consumed to create the commodity, plus the equivalent of the labor required for its production, then the capital would not be indemnified for its nonconsumption. Economically speaking, that is unthinkable. Planned nonconsumption is a conceivable economic phenomenon only in the sense that, where goods are 'nonconsumed,' and hence rendered valueless as such, they must be realized indirectly, by means of a realization of new commodities."[10] That portion of the value which constitutes the indemnification for nonconsumption is interest.

2. *Critique of Schellwien's Theory*

IT TAKES less effort to snarl up a ball of yarn, than it does to untangle the snarl again. And so I am afraid I shall need more words to straighten out the confused network of errors and contradictions contained in the words above, than it took Schellwien to put it together.

The principal error of which he is guilty is, that he subjects the concept "consumption of capital" to a twofold interpretation that borders on the comical, and thus he perpetrates a duplication in his computation of the compensation for consumed and nonconsumed capital which no less narrowly escapes the charge of laughableness.

Schellwien's initial assumption is that even a merely temporary nonconsumption makes goods "as such, valueless," and that, if the nonconsumption was necessary for the production of other goods, it must be paid for by the purchaser. Even this presupposition is vulnerable to attack. In the absence of natural deterioration or style changes, a good does *not* tend to lose value through temporary nonconsumption. But nevertheless let us allow this presupposition to stand.

In the process of production, units of capital goods are consumed. For instance, wool is consumed in the production of cloth. But in order to be able to continue the process regularly, the entrepreneur replaces the consumed goods immediately with new ones of the same kind. The manufacturer of cloth purchases new wool to replace the wool consumed. But Schellwien looks at this very simple fact from two angles simultaneously. On the one hand, he fixes his gaze on the concrete capital goods, and inasmuch as these are actually used up, he says *the capital is consumed.* On the other hand, ignoring the specific objects, he then looks only upon the generic capital, and since that has been replaced with more of its kind, he says *the capital is "nonconsumed."* The latter point of view is again, in my estimation, open to suspicion, and seems to be more of a play on words than an attempt to depict the real essence of what transpires. But I shall let that, too, stand without raising any objection. But now comes the decisive blow.

Instead of deciding definitely in favor of one point of view or the other, Schellwien emulates the legerdemain artist, alternately taking one stand and then the other, finally to *take both positions simultaneously,* and on that basis to claim indemnification for the capitalist. First he regards the capital as consumed, so that the commodity must provide compensation "for this consumed capital," which means that the purchaser must pay its full value. And the next moment he regards the same capital as "to put it simply, withheld from consumption," so that the commodity must also provide compensation for "this nonconsumption," meaning that the purchaser must pay an addition to the price as a premium for nonconsumption!

I wonder what Schellwien would say to the following example. I have a faithful servant who, however, has a weakness for the bottle. I want to break him of drinking, and make the following agreement with him. If he continues to drink, I will pay for what he actually drinks, but not beyond a maximum of one quart of wine a day. However, if he refrains from drinking, he is to receive the price of two quarts as a premium for each day of abstinence. The contract is sealed. My servant drinks a quart of wine, then buys a second quart, but refrains from drinking it. He then claims from me, in accordance with the terms of our agreement, the price of *three* quarts. He claims one because I promised to pay for the wine he actually drank—and by the tally of "concrete goods," he has really drunk one quart. And he claims two more because, by replacing at once the quart he did consume with a new one which he did not consume, he has not, generically speaking, consumed the wine. Hence he is justly entitled to the compensation for nonconsumption! I am very much afraid that Schellwien will not be able to deny the complete analogy between my example and his theory!

In order to avoid disposing of so important a question by means of mere analogies, and to devote thorough consideration to the problem itself, I will present a concrete case in terms of the Schellwien theory. Let us assume a cloth manufacturer works up $100,000 worth of wool into cloth, and that the process requires one year. Let us ignore the other elements in the costs of production, such as wear and tear of machinery, workmen's wages and so forth, while we concentrate our attention on the question, "How much must the cloth be worth in order properly to compensate the entrepreneur for the cooperation of his wool capital?"

Schellwien says that, specifically speaking, the wool is consumed, but generally speaking it is not. Only one of two possibilities can eventuate. Either the wool loses its value due to the circumstance that it is subjected to temporary nonconsumption, or it does not. Let us assume, with Schellwien, that the devaluation really takes place, and let us put the extent of the devaluation at 5% or $5,000. I concede without more ado that under these circumstances the commodity value must yield indemnification for this devaluation. There really must be an addition in value of $5,000. But an addition to what? To the value of the specifically consumed wool. But if the latter, "because of temporary nonconsumption" has been devalued in the sum of $5,000, then it is obviously worth only $95,000, and the total indemnity which the value of the commodity must furnish amounts to just $100,000 even with the addition included. It is quite clear that no increase in capital has been registered as compared with the initial capital of $100,000.

Or we have the other possibility, that the temporary nonconsumption does *not* have the power to devalue the wool. In that case, of course, the wool passes over into the value of the commodity at its full $100,000.

But then there is no reason why that amount should be increased by reason of nonconsumption, because the only reason why Schellwien demands an addition is because nonconsumption entails a "devaluation," a "diminution of the result of labor."[11]

And so you may twist his presupposition as you will, under no circumstances can you find any explanation of a surplus value over and above the initial value of the capital consumed. Nor can any such be rightly expected, in view of the general direction along which Schellwien's line of reasoning progresses. For according to Schellwien the indemnification for nonconsumption is supposed to be purely the recovery of a loss which the product of labor suffers because of devaluation. It is a recovery "without which the account would not balance." *But how can the recovery of a loss ever become a surplus?* If out of 100 apples, I lose five, and to recover my loss add just as many apples as were lost, then my equation must read $100 - 5 + 5 = 100$, and never 105!!

It is a matter of course that such a muddled theory could never be clearly presented. If Schellwien had framed it precisely, its contradictions would have "stuck out like a sore thumb." Yes, Schellwien goes into detail, in fact into extreme detail. But when he goes into detail, he does not expound his thought with all its particulars, he merely expresses it with frequent repetitions, all characterized by the same confusion and ambiguity. In doing so he falls into a peculiar self-deception with respect to his own relationship to the labor theory of value. Although he declares that not only the actually expended labor time, but also nonconsumption constitutes an independent element of the value of goods, he nevertheless believes he has given us a theory "which springs from the essential nature of labor and of value," one "which follows inexorably from the value theory which is founded on labor."

It is the very errors of Schellwien's theory that make it uncommonly instructive. In most drastic manner it adds the finishing touches to the conviction, how useless the labor theory of value is as a key to the explanation of originary interest. Rodbertus and Marx had attempted to retain an unrelenting grip on the fundamental concept that the amount of labor constitutes the sole principle on which to base a set of laws governing the value of all goods. But they had been able to do so only so long as they were willing to pay the price of simply ignoring the most important field of interest. That was the surplus value possessed by those goods which require a longer period of time for their production while the expenditure of labor is equal. Schellwien had the intellectual honesty to realize that ignoring the factor was no help, and he made a sincere effort to extract an explanation of those facts from the labor theory of value. But what God hath put asunder man cannot join together. With all his twisting and turning from consumed capital that is at the same time unconsumed, to "nonconsumption time" which is part of the production time, and on to an "equalization" that is a surplus, he accomplished nothing beyond a final betrayal of the principle which was his point of departure. He had wanted, instead, to construct a bridge that would close the gap between his theory and that fact which is interest. But the labor theory of value, basically false as it is, must inevitably and always be given the lie by the facts of economic life.

3. DANGERS OF SPECIOUS IDEALIZATION OF THE NATURAL BASES OF ECONOMIC PHENOMENA

I SHOULD like to draw one more lesson from Schellwien's theory. We economists are very fond of divorcing our scientific categories from the universally material basis which gives rise to them, and of exalting them to the rank of freer independent abstractions. For instance, the "value" of goods seems to us to be something too aristocratic to be everlastingly yoked to the material good which is its bearer. We liberate it from this unworthy union, we make it a sovereign being that goes its own ways, independent of—nay, even contrary to—the fate of its base carrier. We allow the "value" to be sold without the owner's parting with the good itself, or we sell the good without depriving ourselves of its "value." We cause goods to be destroyed, but their "value" persists, and we have "values" vanish, while their carriers remain unscathed. Similarly we feel that it is far too simple to bestow the appellation "capital" upon a heap of material goods. We sever them. Capital is something that hovers above the goods and lives on, even if the concrete parts which comprise it suffer anihilation. "Above all," says Hermann, "it is necessary to distinguish the object by which a capital is represented, from the capital itself."[12] And MacLeod says we are using a "metaphor" when we apply the name "capital" to goods.[13]

Honor where honor is due! It is well indeed for a science to avoid confining within the limits of the Procrustean bed of a mechanically and materialistically fettered outlook those truly supernal forces which affect our lives. But one must know, too, where to draw the line. Our material goods and their services, our material capitals and their productive effectiveness really do belong to the sphere of material things, even though that sphere does not exhaust all their implications. To idealize them is not to increase our understanding of them, but to corrupt it. He commits a dangerous act who issues to himself a self-dispensation, whereby he assumes the right to say, "Though I am explaining things that occur in the material world and in accordance with material laws, yet I am free to withhold consideration of those laws, and even to act in contravention of them."

Nor does anyone issue this dispensation, unless he intends to take advantage of it. Anyone who simply and faithfully interprets natural things naturally, is not aided by sublimating phraseology, but is hindered by it. But anyone who, in his explanation of natural things, intends to be untrue to nature, finds such sublimation an excellent pretext. Anything that he cannot explain *in accordance* with nature he first exalts into the realm of the *super*natural, and then offers an explanation of it that is *contrary* to nature.

I have long been accustomed to consider any specious idealizations I may encounter as a warning signal. And I have seldom been mistaken. Our science deals with many simple plain concepts, such as good, wealth, capital, yield, use, product and the like, which have their roots deep in straightforward sensory perception. And when I find that some idealizing interpretation seeks to separate one of these from its sensuous foundation, and even to give it a significance diametrically opposite, then I rarely have to go far to seek the meretricious conclusion for which that interpretation is meant to serve as a base. It is not my intention to delay concluding our observations by supporting this contention, as I very well could, with a long catalogue of such sins garnered from the literature of economic science. The reader who is sensitive to that sort of thing will find corroboration without my help. I wish to mention specifically only the one example which supplied the immediate incentive for this digression, this example of Schellwien's. No sooner has he made the distinction between "capital" and the "concrete goods" of which it consists, no sooner does he divorce them in his thoughts and set them up in conflict with each other, than the game begins with the capital which is simultaneously consumed and not consumed, which is at one and the same time realized at its full value and at its diminished value, and the devaluation of which, by means of an equalization, finally turns into a surplus!

XV

OUR attention has been fixed for all too long on details, and we should now turn it to the field as a whole. We have watched a motley mass of theories of interest come into being. We have considered them with care and tested them with deliberation. Not one of them encompassed the whole truth. Were they for that reason entirely futile? Do they offer us, in the aggregate, nought but a chaotic maze of contradiction and error, from which we emerge only to find ourselves no closer to the truth than we were at the outset? Or is there not, after all, a line of development discernible, which runs through the labyrinth of conflicting doctrines? And even if that line has not led to the very truth, does it at least point the direction in which the truth lies? And what is the direction in which that line runs?

1. The Three Basic Concepts of the Phenomenon of Interest

THERE is no better way to introduce the solution of this final problem than to ask my readers once more to envision clearly the terms of our problem. What is the intention that animates, what is the goal that attracts the solvers of the interest problem? *Their object is to discover and to expose the factors that divert into the hands of the capitalists one branch of the stream of goods which gushes forth each year from the headwaters of a nation's production.* Accordingly it is, beyond the shadow of a doubt, a problem of the *distribution of goods.*

But what determines the point in the course of the stream at which that branch is diverted? The history of economic theory reveals the development of three essentially divergent lines of reasoning which led to three equally dissimilar basic conceptions of the interest problem.

But let us adhere a moment longer to the metaphor of the stream, for it serves well to clarify the situation. The source of the river symbolizes the production of goods; its mouth is the final participation in the income for the satisfaction of consumers' wants; and the intervening course of the stream represents the stage which interposes between production and final distribution of goods, the interval during which the latter pass from hand to hand by way of economic exchange and acquire value as a result of man's valuation of them.

348

The three lines of reasoning are as follows.

One opinion considers that the share of the capitalists is already segregated at the river's source. By virtue of the productive power inherent in them, three distinct sources produce each its own definite quantity of goods with a definite exchange value. And the same value that flowed out of each source will at the mouth of the river pour into the income of those persons who own the property at the source. It is not so much *one* stream as *three* streams which, in the river's middle course, flow along for a time in the same stream-bed without becoming commingled, and which, at the mouth, again become distinctive streams of which the respective volumes retain the relative ratios they had at the separate sources. This conception localizes the whole explanation at the source, in the production of goods. It treats the interest problem as a *problem of production.* That is the conception mirrored by the naive productivity theories.

A second conception is diametrically opposed to the first. It does not look to find any separation until the mouth is reached, and seeks it there exclusively. There is but one source from which the whole stream of goods pours forth undivided. That source is labor. Even the intermediate reaches of the watercourse are single, undivided; there is nothing in the value of goods which would call for a sharing of them by the various participants, for all value is determined exclusively by labor. Only a short distance before the river's mouth, just as the stream of goods is about to be duly poured into the income of the workers who created it, from either bank the weir of monopoly is thrust out into the stream, one by the landowners, one by the capitalists, and part of the water is forcibly shunted to their fields. That is the conception which finds expression in the socialist exploitation theory. It denies to interest any place in the primitive history and early stages of the destiny of goods; it regards interest exclusively as the result of an extraneous, fortuitous, forcible seizure; it treats the interest problem as purely a *problem of distribution, in the harshest sense of the word.*

The third conception takes the middle of the road. It conceives of goods as emanating from two, or as some would have it, three different headwaters, and then running on, united very soon into a single stream. But now goods come under the influence of man's valuation, a force that reticulates the current of the stream and transforms it into a veritable network of ever newborn streamlets. For man begins to observe, for one thing, the intensity of his wants, and, for another, the quantity of the means available for the satisfaction of those wants. With respect to these two factors he then evaluates the interest it behooves him to take in the various goods and classes of goods, in terms of their subjective use value, and of their resultant objective exchange value. And so he comes to discriminate between this portion and that portion of the mass of goods. He exalts one part and depreciates another. Preferences and differences in valuation come into being, and intricate tensions and attractions come to life. And under the influence of these the mass of all goods is gradually differentiated so that it flows in three branches each of which has its own outlet. One empties into the income of the landowners, a second into that of the workers, and the third into that of the capitalists. But those three branches are neither identical with, nor proportionate in their volume to the two or the three springs that formed the headwaters. It is not the relative volume of the spring at the source which determines how great the volume of the stream shall be at the outlet, but rather how great a proportion of the united stream has been pushed into the channel of each branch through the operation of the laws of value. All the remaining interest theories meet on the common ground of this conception of the problem. Since they regard the ultimate distribution as already foreshadowed in the stage at which value is ascribed to goods, they consider it their duty to evolve a theory which goes backward far enough to cover the field of the establishment of value. In other words, the distribution problem which interest presents must be complemented and extended so that it constitutes a *problem of value*.

2. Interest Is Not a Problem of Production, Nor of Distribution, but of Value

WHICH of these three basic conceptions was the correct one? No dispassionate and unbiased observer could hesitate in rendering his decision.

Certainly the first version was not correct. Nor does the only reason lie in the fact that capital cannot be an originary source of goods, since it is itself the fruit of nature and of labor. But there is an added reason of which we have had ample opportunity to convince ourselves. It is the following. There exists no power possessed by any production factor whatsoever, which of itself can endow its physical products with its own specific sort of value. Neither value in general, nor surplus value in particular, nor yet originary interest, is born full grown into the world in the course of the production of goods. The interest problem is not purely a problem of production.

Nor was it possible that the second version should be the correct one. It is in contravention of the facts. It is not true that no foreign element, other than labor, intrudes at an earlier stage than that of distribution. For such an intrusion already takes place in the valuation of goods. A 100-year-old oak tree, which during the long years of its growth required a single day of labor expended on its care, has an exchange value 100 times greater than does a chair which likewise required but a single day's labor to fashion it out of a few bits of wood. But the oak tree, which is the product of a single day's labor, did not, all in a flash, attain an exchange value 100 times that of the piece of furniture which cost a single day's labor. But day by day, year by year, the increasing bole of the tree widened the margin by which it exceeded the exchange value of the chair. And the same thing that is true of the exchange value of the oak tree is also true of that of all products which require not only labor, but also time.

Those same silently and unremittingly operative forces which, bit by bit, elevated the price of the oak tree further and further above the price of the chair, have by the same token been giving rise to interest. At work long before the time for distribution of goods has arrived, they have foreshadowed the future line that would mark the distinction between wages and interest. For the only possible basis for the compensation of labor is "equal pay for equal work." But if the exchange value of goods which have been produced by equal labor has become unequal because of the operation of those silent forces, then equal wages will not always coincide with unequal exchange values. Only the exchange value of goods unfavored by those silent forces will agree and is fully satisfied by the universal wage rate which it sets. All favored goods exceed that ratio to the extent to which they are favored in the valuation of goods, and they cannot be fully satisfied by the universal wage rate. When they reach ultimate distribution, they must inevitably and automatically leave a surplus value, after all workers have received their equal pay for equal work. And that surplus the capitalist can and will appropriate. The reason why they leave this surplus is not that at the eleventh hour the capitalist suddenly extends a predacious fist and artificially depresses wages. The reason must be sought farther back. For a long time previously, the laws of value have exerted their influence on those goods which require for their production both labor and time. And it is those laws which have augmented the exchange value of such goods above that of goods which are produced at the cost of only immediately compensatory wages. Since the exchange value of goods of this kind must completely satisfy the labor which produces them, it is at the same time the determinant of the universal rate of wages.

So much for the facts. The implications to be drawn from them are clear. The interest problem is a distribution problem. But distribution has its antecedent history and must be explained on the basis of it. The exchange values of goods do not come up to the point of distribution and then explosively disperse. Quite on the contrary, the lines of diffusion which are to separate them were already slowly and gradually sketched in lightly in earlier periods in the destiny of goods. Anyone who intends really to understand and truly to explain distribution must trace down the beginnings of these faint but distinct scratchings which are to mark later differentiation. That procedure leads into the field of the value of goods, where the principal part of the task of explaining interest is to be performed. Whoever treats the interest problem as a production problem exclusively, breaks off his explanation before he has reached the crucial point; he who treats it as a distribution problem and nothing more, does not begin his explanation until that point has been passed. Only the searcher who undertakes to shed light upon the remarkable rise and fall in the exchange values of goods, the extent of which constitutes the "surplus value," can hope to have gathered from them a genuinely scientific explanation of interest. The problem of interest is, in the last analysis, a *problem of value.*

3. *The Rank of the Various Theories of Interest*

IF WE keep that firmly in mind, it becomes an easy matter to indicate the order in which the various groups of theories deserve to be ranked, and the location of the line which reveals the ascending development.

Two theories failed utterly to recognize the true character of the interest problem. And although they are antithetical in nature, they occupy jointly the most abased position in the scale of development. These two theories arc the naive productivity theory and the socialist exploitation theory. The reader may find this alignment surprising. How vastly superior the adherents of the exploitation theory deem themselves to the naive presuppositions advanced by the theorists who proclaim the doctrine of productivity! How proudly they declare themselves to be representative of a progressive critical tendency!

And yet making theoretical bed-fellows of these two is fully justified. In the first place, both theories coincide in their negativity, for neither one comes to grips with the actual problem, and neither one wastes a word on the peculiar heaving which constitutes the rising and falling of the exchange value of goods from which surplus value arises. The productivity theory is content to say, of the fluctuations in prices, simply that they have been brought about. But the exploitation theory does what is almost worse, for it takes no notice of them at all. For the exploitationist the fluctuations simply do not exist; for him, no matter how violently the facts of economic life may belie his contention, the value of goods and the expenditure of labor are absolutely and completely on a par.[1]

However, not only the element of negation, but the positive aspect of the two theories as well, makes them more closely akin than might be thought. In truth, they are fruits of one and the same branch, offspring of one and the same naive prejudice, namely that value grows out of production, as a blade of grass grows out of the ground.

That prejudice has loomed large in the history of economics. In ever-changing form it has controlled our science for the last 130 years, and since it thrust the explanation of the basic phenomenon askew, it cast an obstacle in the path of the progress of economic science. First it bobbed up in the doctrine of the physiocrats, that the earth, through its fruitfulness, produces all surplus value. Smith blunted the edge of its weapon, Ricardo disarmed it completely. But before the prejudice had been entirely dispelled in the form in which it first appeared, Say reintroduced it into economic science in a new and broader form. Then instead of the single productive force of the physiocrats we had three which create values and surplus values in exactly the same way that the physiocrats had accounted for their *produit net*. In this new form the old prejudice exerted its spell upon our science for many long decades. Finally it was once more unmasked, principally through the impassioned yet meritorious criticism of the socialist theorists. But even now it gave new proof of its stubborn will to live. By sacrificing its form but not its essential nature, it managed to preserve its existence in a new mold. By a whimsical quirk of fate it found refuge and a new home among the writings of the very writers who had attacked it most bitterly in the next to last guise in which it had appeared. It found asylum with socialist writers! The *forces* that create value were no more! The *force* that creates value—labor—remained! But so did the old fault of making no effort to account for the marvelously delicate inter-relations in the development of exchange value. *There* was a puzzle that it should have been the economist's plain duty to attack and his proud achievement to unravel! But he brought to the task only a brazen presupposition, and where that failed to apply, a still more brazen denial.

And so the naive theory of the productivity of capital and the sophisticated doctrine of the socialists are in very truth twin brothers. Let us not deny the claim of the latter to be termed a critical doctrine, for it is that. But it is at the same time, we discover, a naive doctrine. It is critical of one naive extreme, only to adopt the no less naive opposite extreme. It is nothing but the belated converse of the naive productivity theory.

In comparison with these the remaining interest theories may lay claim to commendation on the ground that they stand one step higher in the scale. They are seeking the solution of the problem in the field where it is really to be found, the field of the value of goods. To be sure, their efforts are not all equally meritorious.

The theories that attempt to explain interest by dint of those purely external factors which are dealt with by the cost theories, are dragging along a heavy load of ballast in the form of the prejudice which insists that all value arises from production. Their explanation does not provide an exhaustive solution. It is incontestable that the basic force which sets in motion all economic efforts of man, be they selfish or altruistic, is his interest in his own welfare. It is equally unquestionable that no line of explanation for economic phenomena can be satisfactory which fails to reach back in uninterrupted continuity to that indubitably basic force. And there lies the besetting sin of the cost theories. It would seem reasonable for them to seek in its relation to human welfare the significance of the principle of value—that "mariner's compass" of the economist and universal connecting link that motivates all of man's economic activities. But the cost theories seek it, rather, in one of the dry facts of the external genesis of goods, and in the physical conditions of production. By so doing they sidetrack the progress of the entire solution into a blind alley from which there is no thoroughfare to the motive of human action, at which any satisfactory solution must eventually arrive. For all their diversity in details, the great majority of the interest theories we have examined is open to condemnation on this score.

Finally, we must accord a position still another step higher to those theories which have completely renounced the superstition that the value of goods arises from their past, rather than their future. Those theories know what they want to explain, and the direction in which the explanation lies. If, for all that, they still have not discovered the complete truth, their failure is primarily fortuitous, while their predecessors failed to find the truth because their view was cut off by a wall of prejudice which prevented their looking in the right direction. This higher stage of development is characterized by several formulations of the abstinence theory, but especially the later use theory. And in that category Menger's theory is, to my mind, the highest point attained in the course of the development thus far. That is not so much because he furnished the best *solution,* but because his *framing* of the problem was the most nearly perfect. Of these two the latter, in this case as in many others, may indeed be more important and more difficult than the former.

4. The Direction in which the Final Solution of the Problem of Interest Lies

ON GROUND thus prepared I shall now attempt to find for this much discussed problem a solution which employs no fictions and presuppositions, but strives simply and honestly to trace the phenomenon of interest back to beginnings which are among the simplest natural and psychological fundamentals of our economic system, and then to proceed onward through the phenomena of value. The one element which seems to me to constitute the key to the truth deserves to be briefly mentioned once more at this point. That element is the influence of *time* on the value that man places upon goods. To furnish a genuine content to stand behind that catchword shall be the mission of the second, the positive part of my work.

Appendix

1. General Survey

SINCE the publication of the first edition of this book the interest problem has been the subject of unremitting as well as animated and widespread discussion. No earlier period of the same duration can compare with the last three decades in the abundance of its literature on interest. The period has not, to be sure, brought forth any detached and dispassionate solution of the great problem. I was about to say that it is self-evident that such could not be the case. And yet there is a re-alignment of the contending forces discernible upon the field of literary battle, and I suspect that I can detect some indications that we may be progressing toward a settlement of the feud. At least the battle is less desultory than it was a generation ago. New opinions have, to be sure, entered the lists. On the other hand, some of the older ones have been mustered out of the ranks completely, or nearly so. As a result, the action is concentrated today about a few strongly defended positions, and the gaining or losing of those few will be decisive. And with respect to those few the decision appears to me to be materially closer at hand. There is no more light skirmishing, no engaging of the enemy at a distance. Rather may we say that the preliminary actions have fulfilled their purpose, at least to the point where the premises and conclusions of the belligerent theories, the positions which they occupy in strength, as it were, have been felt out and are clearly recognized. There is thus little possibility of straying off into struggles over inconsequentialities, and the issue will have to be joined in a struggle over the truly essential theme.

For well-known reasons it is a hapless task to chronicle the events of the present. He who stands in the midst of the forest, cannot easily survey the woods as a whole. And in my own case, there are two special circumstances that render it even more difficult to be a good historian of the state of affairs as it exists today in the matter of the literature on interest. The first of these is that I am myself the author of one of the competing interest theories, and that nullifies my very best intentions

355

as to impartiality and inevitably makes me a prejudiced party. The second circumstance is as easily appreciated. There is always difficulty in measuring distances and differences accurately when the observer stands close to the object of his observation. Such difficulty is doubled when the observer's personal predilections also come into play. Still further difficulty is provided by the fact that the current generation of economists is undoubtedly in the process of revising its views concerning the interest problem. No matter which theory may eventually achieve victory, one thing is certain. And that is that the concept which is handed on to posterity as ours will be materially different from what *we* found set forth in *our* textbooks and what we absorbed from them, when we were young. All of us transform those views that were handed down to us, even the most confirmed conservatives among us. And to render judgment on a body of literature that is undergoing such transformation, and to fit it into its appropriate historical niche is a task of peculiar and exceptional difficulty. There is a host of transitional views to be encountered. These include, or indeed consist principally of meaningless variations of moribund theories. But there are also a few hopeful forward-looking views, aiming to constitute connecting links in the chain of progress. Often it would require the prophetic gifts of a veritable seer to decide whether a given theoretical structure fits into the first of these categories or the second.

Nevertheless I feel I should be leaving a conspicuous gap in the completion of my task, if I allowed such considerations to deter me from at least attempting a critical orientation for my readers with respect to the present status of the writings on the subject of interest. Surely it is the prime function of the critical historian of theory to illumine the path of subsequent research; and it would constitute an egregious disservice on his part, were he willfully to withhold light from the very stretch of road that has most recently been traversed, and from the very point at which further progress must begin. On the other hand, I feel it my duty to preface this portion of my task with the very explicit reservation that it does not pretend to infallibility or complete adequacy.

With respect to the vast majority of modern literature on interest I shall of necessity restrict myself to a condensed survey. In particular I expect to forego, as a rule, the presentation or the detailed discussion of doctrines which represent mere variants of a basic doctrine. However, I should not wish to have the omission interpreted as an indication that I consider the variant insignificant or the basic doctrine unimportant. I shall indulge in somewhat detailed presentation and critique in the case of only a very few of the newest theories. Even then it will be for one of two reasons. One would be that they are so obviously individual in character as to differ in some essential features from all the types of theory we have discussed up to this point. The other would be that, though mere variations or combinations, they are so definitely formulated and so exhaustively worked out, that the full implications of the variation can be perceived to their full extent and with complete certainty.

2. The Agio Theory and Some Other Attempts at Explanation of Interest

I MENTIONED previously that in very recent times the ranks of the old rival theories have been swelled by new doctrines. The most influential of these recruits is probably that theory which explains interest as arising from a *difference in value between present and future goods.*

At an early stage vague hints of that idea had been dropped by Petty and Vaughan, and somewhat later by Galiani and Turgot.[1] Bentham is the first to consider it from the psychological point of view. A half century later the idea receives very remarkable development at the hands of Rae, who was not destined, however, to exercise any influence on its subsequent course in economic literature. Another 40 years later Jevons appeared on the scene. He based his work on Bentham's theory, and developed the premises on which it is founded, in exemplary and masterly fashion. But he failed to supply the fabric he wove with those fine intermediary threads that would bind his premises to the phenomenon of interest. In this respect his work failed to equal that of his forgotten precursor Rae. But in the working out of the psychological aspects of his premises he is about on a par with Rae, while in his appreciation of the premises based on the techniques of production he is unquestionably superior.

Mention of Jevons necessitates immediate reference to Launhardt[2] and Emil Sax.[3] The only respect in which these two represent any advance beyond Jevons is that they stated in so many words a thought for which the contents of Jevons's writings had prepared the way, but which he never formulated in express terms. Incidentally, it is a thought which in the meantime I had myself announced in 1884 as part of my own interest theory. I am referring to the idea that interest has its roots in the psychological motives underlying the difference in value between present and future goods.[4] Yes, Launhardt and Sax expressed the thought explicitly, but they failed to develop it to a consummation. The absence of any detailed elaboration precluded any conclusive test by these two writers of one point in particular. And that is the question whether the psychological motives for the lower estimation of the value of future goods can in any event offer a sufficiently broad basis for a complete explanation of the phenomenon of interest; or whether, on the other hand, there might not rather be certain technological factors—factors which they ignored—that ought to play their part in that explanation.

Chronologically, the writings of Launhardt and Sax take their place between the time of the publication of the first volume of my *Capital and Interest,* entitled the *History and Critique of Interest Theories* (1884) and that of the second volume. The *Positive Theory of Capital* (1889), as I expounded it in my second volume, was an attempt to explain all the different forms of the phenomenon of interest as arising from a difference in value between present and future goods, but to derive this difference itself from the interaction of a number of factors, some of

357

them psychological and some technological. That attempt encountered a good deal of opposition, but it also met with a great deal of agreement and support. Similar concepts had appeared elsewhere, although less exhaustively worked out, and at first without being consciously divorced from the line of reasoning employed by the older abstinence theory. I am thinking of a number of almost simultaneous pronouncements, especially among American economists such as Simon N. Patten,[5] S. M. MacVane,[6] and J. B. Clark.[7] No less influential were the continued impulses emanating from Jevons's brilliant writing, which was gaining ever more respectful recognition among theorists in widely scattered countries. That theory of the difference in value between present and future goods I should like to designate as the *agio* theory,[8] if I am to give it a short slogan-like name. The fact is, in any event, that whether due to one or to another of the aforementioned inspirations, the agio theory has struck firm roots in the economic literature of all civilized nations, and in some has even attained a dominating position.

Without making the slightest claim to completeness, I should like to list a number of names appearing on the roster of English and American writers of the 1890s who represented more or less comparable views. Such a list would have to include James Bonar (*Quarterly Journal of Economics,* April and October 1889, April 1890); William Smart (*Introduction to the Theory of Value,* London, 1891 and "The New Theory of Interest," *Economic Journal,* 1891); F. Y. Edgeworth (*Economic Journal,* June 1892); E. B. Andrews (*Institutes of Economics,* Boston, 1889); Lowrey (*Annals of the American Academy,* March 1892); Ely (*Outlines of Economics,* New York, 1893); Carver (*Quarterly Journal of Economics,* October 1893); Taussig (*Wages and Capital,* New York, 1896); Irving Fisher (*Economic Journal,* December 1896, June and December 1897); Mixter ("A Forerunner of Böhm-Bawerk," *Quarterly Journal of Economics,* January 1897); Macfarlane (*Value and Distribution,* Philadelphia, 1899). Substantially in the same vein are the writings of Hobson (*Evolution of Modern Capitalism,* London, 1894) and of Hadley (*Economics,* New York, 1896, and *Annals of the American Academy,* November 1893). Partial agreement is registered also by Giddings. The latter, however, believes it necessary in the interests of completeness and profundity to add another feature to the theory. That feature consists in an explanation which he offers for the constant insufficiency of the supply of present goods or of capital. He ascribes it to the circumstance that, where the formation of capital is concerned, we devote to that task, as a matter of principle, only the last hours of our labor, the hours that are freighted with an ever-increasing burden of disutility and vexation. This excess in the onerousness of our labor, he says, constitutes an extra cost in the formation of capital—an excess of cost as compared with the cost of producing goods designed for immediate consumption. Now that extra cost must be compensated for by interest. However, Giddings fails to convince me of either of two considerations. The first is that all the factual conditions he assumes for his theory are in reality present. The second is, that even if they did in actual fact obtain, they would be capable of bringing into existence the phenomenon of interest.[9]

In most recent times the discussion of this related group of ideas has been reanimated and supplied with fresh material by the English and American economists. Particularly J. B. Clark and Irving Fisher have made well-known contributions which are as meritorious as they are persuasive. I am referring to the former's *Distribution of Wealth* (1899) and the latter's *The Rate of Interest* (1907). It is true that Clark is influenced by his widely discussed concept of "true capital" and under that influence presents his ideas concerning the origin of interest in a garb that compels us to class him, as to form, with the protagonists of the productivity theories and, more specifically, the motivated productivity theories. And yet a substantial portion of his factual explanation is so closely akin to the ideas of the agio theory, that perhaps we differ, as to essentials, more in form than in substance. Clark himself once made reference to a considerable mass of ideas that we hold in common. In this connection he remarked that "every complete theory of distribution will in future have to incorporate a substantial part of his (Böhm-Bawerk's) doctrine of time as an economic element."[10] Other theorists closely related to Clark seem to hold similar views with respect to the doctrines for which Clark and I stand.[11] But Fisher's position is to so large an extent taken on ground that is occupied by the agio theory, that he gives the appearance of attempting to improve rather than disprove it. His own theory, upon which he himself has conferred the title of the "impatience theory," he describes as another "form" or a "modification" of my agio theory, differing from it in just a few details.[12] I have gone into such detail elsewhere in my description of Clark's theory of interest as well as Fisher's, and have pointed out our points of agreement and disagreement by so clear a critical treatment,[13] that I can content myself here with this simple mention of those two important works. The things said and written by English economists who share my point of view have by this time become so numerous that I believe I can dispense entirely with listing any more individual names. I should like to limit myself to quoting a single opponent who complains of the wide dissemination of the agio theory, saying that it "has met with wider acceptance than any other explanation of the facts with which it deals," despite the fact that it has also encountered numerous critics who oppose it, and the further fact that the theory has fallen far short of attaining a position where it may be regarded as the final solution of the problem.[14]

In Italian economic literature we find early traces of the adoption of the same trend of thought. The following authors deserve mention. Ricca-Salerno, *Teoria del Valore,* Rome, 1894; Montemartini, *Il risparmio nell' economia pura,* Milan, 1896; Crocini, *Di alcune questioni relative all' utilità finale,* Turin, 1896; Graziani, *Studi sulla teoria dell'interesse,* Turin, 1898. Essentially similar views may be ascribed to Barone as evidenced by his *Sopra un libro di Wicksell* which appeared in the *Giornale degli Economisti* of November 1895, as well as his *Studi sulla distribuzione* in the same periodical, February and March 1896. Benini, in his *Il valore e la sua attribuzione ai beni strumentali,* Bari, 1893, indicates at least partial agreement.

Pareto, whom I myself should prefer to classify with the use theorists, has nevertheless adopted so many ideas closely akin to the agio theory, that his compatriot Graziani felt impelled to remark that Pareto's motivation of interest betrayed that he had adopted the principles of that theory completely.[15] Then there is the case of Natoli. Obviously he is strongly influenced by Ricca-Salerno and Graziani, and like those two outstanding writers he considers the agio theory essentially correct, but in need of some emendation. In very recent times he made a peculiar attempt to present such an improved version of an interest theory in his *Il principio del valore e la misura quantitativa del lavoro* which appeared in 1906. The most prominent characteristic of his theory is the attempt —vigorous, but to my mind unavailing—to demonstrate an affinity between the agio theory and the labor theory of value. For that reason the changes proposed by Natoli do not in my estimation by any means represent an improvement.[16]

Among French publications, otherwise predominantly quite conservative, the one which calls for special emphasis, perhaps, is the important monograph by Landry entitled *l'Intérêt du capital* published in 1904. Despite very considerable divagations from the agio theory, several of the basic ideas of that theory appear in his monograph. Indeed, they appear so pervasively, that his work may well be termed an attempt to improve on the formulation and organization of those ideas. The degree of divergence and of coincidence are the subject of the detailed critical appraisal of Landry's theory which I have added as Essay XIII to the third volume of this work which has the title, *Further Essays on Capital and Interest.* Close as Landry stands to our own way of thinking, he is surpassed in this respect by Aftalion.[17]

The literary figure pre-eminently deserving of mention among the Dutch is N. G. Pierson. He is the author of a classic which is still exerting great influence as an economics textbook. Its title is *Leerboek der Staathuishoudkunde*; it went through three editions, the third edited by Professor Verryn Stuart, and published in Haarlem, 1912-1913. Similar ideas were expressed in an earlier article by him appearing in *The Economist (March 1899, p. 193 ff.).*

The views we have been discussing here have also been extensively expressed in Scandinavian economic literature. The most detailed and independent treatment of interest is found in Knut Wicksell.[18] Swedish scholars who may be regarded as representatives of similar views include Count Hamilton, Davidsohn, Leffler and Brock.[19] Norway's contribution is from the pens of Aschehoug, Morgenstierne, Jaeger, Aarum and Einarsen. Danes who may be inscribed in this category are Westergaard, Falbe-Hansen and Birck, as well as Scharling,[20] who was originally hostile but changed his views in his later works.

In Germany the spirit of the "Historical School" was antagonistic to all pure theory, and so delayed for a long time the modern development of economic theory in that country. And it inspired particularly stubborn resistance to any innovations in theory emanating from the Austrian school. It thus reflects a correspondingly meager participation in this most recent phase of the development of the theory of interest.

But I do feel impelled to make special mention of two earlier original works of German economists which move along a line of reasoning similar to my own. These are Effertz's *Arbeit und Boden,* Berlin, 1889, which appeared almost contemporaneously with my own *Positive Theory of Capital,* and the Swiss Georg Sulzer's profound *Die wirtschaftlichen Grundgesetze in der Gegenwartsphase ihrer Entwicklung,* which was published in Zürich in 1895. Effertz expresses the thought that interest owes its existence to a time difference, and employs for the purpose an original turn of phrase. He says that the "age" or the "seniority" of labor and of land also constitute "an element of exchange value," and that interest is a "remuneration for the quality of seniority possessed by labor and by land" (*p. 190 ff., p. 198 f., p. 278*). The necessity for a "premium" for the "seniority" of the elements of production is the subject of an explanation which, while not inappropriate, is certainly not adequately extensive. For his only argument is that old labor and old land are "rarer" than present labor and present land (*pp. 190, 195, 198; cf. also pp. 218, 221, 354*). Since Effertz seems to avoid, on principle, any bibliographical references whatever, it is impossible to determine to what degree, if any, his book, which appeared in 1889, was influenced by the numerous earlier expressions of the same basic thought. Sulzer's treatment of his material, it seems to me, places him on a "line of operation" lying midway between Jevons's and my own.

I have already[21] spoken of that Nestor of the German school of thought, Adolf Wagner, and have commented on his substantial though not uniformly maintained agreement. Philippovich, author of what was in its time the most widely used and most influential textbook in German economic literature, the *Grundriss,*[22] in the most recent editions seems to occupy a position which cannot, perhaps, be termed complete agreement with the agio theory, but which certainly goes a long way toward adoption of its objective assumptions and the basic ideas of its explanation of interest.

Among the younger generation there is manifest dissatisfaction with the lack of a definite theory which was characteristic of the era just past and of its addiction to styles and fads. At any rate, the concepts of the agio theory are at the moment a powerful ferment among that generation. Its reawakened efforts to develop a theory of its own find the agio theory obstructing its path, and it feels the necessity of coming to terms with it. The fruits of that necessity comprise a host of writings. For the most part these are short articles and polemic essays which bear unmistakable marks of being papers written for seminars in economic theory. But there is also evidence that the ferment has engendered some positive stimulation for the development of theory. It is not necessary to cite individual works as evidence, for the most eloquent testimony is borne by that large compilation which was recently assembled in honor of Gustav Schmoller, and which had for its purpose "a description of the development of the German science of economics during the nineteenth century."[23]

Two economists in particular occupy a position apart from others by virtue of their having developed theories in full detail. The theories presented by Oswalt[24] and Schumpeter[25] maintain substantially the same basic position, with reference to the explanation of interest, as is occupied by the agio theory. Nevertheless they contain essential variations which represent an effort to go further along similar lines. Oswalt's theory contains certain interpolations which he himself regards merely as finely shaded differences in the formulation of the problem. But because I regard them as making his theory a peculiar variant of the use theory, I shall discuss it a bit later when I discuss a number of theories falling in that category. Schumpeter is in other respects largely in agreement with the objective aspects of my theory, but departs from my own concept principally in that he does not see interest as a static phenomenon, as I do, but claims it is of dynamic nature and arises solely as the result of economic progress. I take the liberty of referring the reader to a recent article of mine in which I set down a rather full description of his theory, as well as a statement of the reasons why I cannot subscribe to it.[26]

*

A few other attempts at an explanation of interest have emerged in very recent times, which have been far less influential than the agio theory. They, too, cannot be readily classified in the traditional categories, and for that reason I am compelled to list them among the "new" interest theories, even though I shall not devote any great amount of space to them.

There is one theory, that of Georgievsky, which strikes me as highly unique, but not at all convincing in its explanation. It explains interest and, in fact, all varieties of "net income" as compensation that must be paid for the "general overhead costs of an economic system" in contradistinction to the specific costs of direct production.[27] The arguments that can be raised against such a view of the problem are so very obvious, that an appraisal of it in detail can certainly be dispensed with readily.

Emilio Cossa is another who has devised a highly individual explanation of interest, which is likewise not readily classifiable with any of the large groups of theories. By putting to work a "given combination of producers' goods" the capitalist (?) brings about a certain result. That result is that those goods, being "less useful" for satisfying the immediate wants of consumers and hence possessing inferior value, assume "other previously determined forms." In those forms they are of greater use for the satisfaction of such wants, and thus the capitalist achieves a "surplus value" which becomes for him a net yield (*profitto*).[28] It is perhaps a sufficient commentary to ask a pair of related questions. The first is whether it is really the *capitalist* and not rather the *entrepreneur* who sets the production combinations to work. The second question is which theory of the value of producers' goods Cossa really wants to support. For if he intends, as it seems he does, to derive that value from the usefulness—even the reduced usefulness—of producers' goods for satisfying the "immediate wants" of the consumers, then the remark is in order that producers' goods in their original condition ordinarily possess not merely reduced usefulness, but no usefulness at all. A plowshare will not satisfy anyone's hunger! And we may therefore remark further that the difference in value between the unusable production tool and the usable consumers' good, if it were supposed to originate from that source, would indeed have to be much greater than the percentage of interest. On the other hand, Cossa is an adherent of the doctrine of marginal utility (*see his p. 15*). As such it would be quite natural for him to derive the value of producers' goods from their *indirect* usefulness for the satisfaction of wants. But in that case his theory fails to reveal any feature which would explain why the usefulness of producers' goods is exceeded by the usefulness—and the value—of the product. The very crux of the whole problem remains unexplained.

One theory, advanced by Otto Conrad, makes pretensions to an explanation of interest on the basis of the existence of a "monopoly" in favor of the capitalists.[29] This theory, it seems to me as well as to others,[30] ascribes interest to the old factor of "scarcity of capital." This factor plays a part in almost every theory of interest, and accounts for interest only through an excessively persuasible process of reasoning which leaves the actual difficulties of the problem quite untouched.

And probably Liefmann will also register a claim that, within the framework of his efforts directed toward a revivification of all economic theory, he has advanced a new theory of interest also, that must compel respect. His theory resembles that of Cossa in that it seeks to establish its center of gravity in the consumers' estimation of value.[31] I believe it is my duty to avoid going into extended detail, and my belief rests on two considerations. In the first place I am unfortunately quite unable to share the author's own opinion as to the epoch-making importance of his interpretations of economic theory. In the second place, to peruse the welter of a theoretical exegesis which, to my mind, calls for correction at almost every turn, and to extract from it his specific comments on the interest problem seems to me a task so egregiously ungrateful that I am unwilling to impose it either on myself or on my readers.

Nor should I have any greater desire to go into detail concerning the views of Silvio Gesell, who is the author of numerous polemics aimed at the promotion of neo-physiocratic doctrines. In these he sets forth a sort of naive exploitation theory in which interest is represented as a bit of extortion practiced upon the possessors of goods by the possessors of money. Nor is his position materially at variance with that of Bilgram, who likewise seems to hark back to concepts which could fairly have been regarded as discredited, once and for all, ever since the days of Hume. And Bilgram, in the book he has just published (1914) on *The Cause of Business Depressions* speaks of a "monopoly theory of interest," which draws a sharp contrast between capital and money, makes the claim, with respect to real capital, that it is present to the point of superfluity, but places upon a virtually monopolistic scarcity of circulating moneys the responsibility for the fact that the possessors of money, and thus indirectly, the possessors of capital can constantly draw unearned income (*pp. 236 ff., especially 261 and 266*).

While this edition was in print there came into my hands a copy of Hoag's *Theory of Interest* (New York, 1914).* Hoag is of the opinion that he, too, is promulgating a new theory of interest, and he suggests for it the name of "nominal value theory" (*Preface, pp.* IX *and* X). In my opinion his theory is, as to content, very closely related to the theories of Carver and Fisher. His exposition differs from earlier examples of its kind principally by virtue of the definition, peculiar to this theory, of the nature of "principal," and further by virtue of the consequent introduction of Hoag's concept of "nominal value." He defines principal as two quantities of goods which are equal in some given respect and which are existent at two different points in time. But this equality, Hoag maintains, is not an equality in *kind and magnitude,* as I had erroneously averred, but an equality in *value.* Furthermore, this equality is not one in value on a single market at one and the same point in time but, on the contrary, an equality in value manifested by these two quantities of goods on the fluctuating markets of their own respective points in time. It is to this value on a *fluctuating* market that Hoag assigns the term "nominal value." That is to say, a present and a future quantity of goods, in order to constitute a principal, must have equal value on the markets of their respective points of time—they must have equal "nominal value" (*p. 7 f. and p. 17 ff.*). Hoag regards this concept as the key to a correct understanding of interest. I, for my part, fear that it merely invites the perils of a confusion twice confounded.

For surely the factual conditions which give rise to interest admittedly consist in that very real *inequality* in value which is manifested by present and future goods in that market in which they are mutually exchanged. When the very inequality in value which is indispensable to the origination of interest suffers a distortion into an allegedly necessary equality in value, I am compelled to regard the process as an obfuscation rather than a clarification of the basic principle. Nor can it be urged in its defense that it is introduced "for argument's sake" and for the creation of a new system of nomenclature. And it is, incidentally, not at all true that the two amounts of goods designated for exchange as principal would necessarily possess equal value in the markets of their respective times. One need but consider loans involving fungible goods other than money. I mean such goods as grain, cotton, securities, or even sums of a currency that fluctuates in terms of a standard currency, such as money of a different monetary system, or paper money. In such cases the principal which is replaced at a later time may possess, in terms of the market of its own time, a value utterly at variance with that possessed by the principal originally conveyed, in terms of its own earlier market.

I should like to point out in addition, though briefly, that Hoag's theory of interest is embodied in a theory of price and value based on

---

* Translators' note: The paragraphs on Hoag with which Böhm-Bawerk concluded this section in the fourth edition appeared there as a footnote.

the principle of "final disutility." Interest, for Hoag, is the price of a thing which he designates "advance" (*p. 49*) and which consists in the "exchange of earlier for later services" (*p. 82*) and is the equivalent of "investment" (*p. 104*) or of "waiting" (*p. 157*). This "advancing," Hoag would have us understand gives rise to "costs," which consist in the sacrifice of present enjoyment of the goods or services advanced for the sake of the ones to be subsequently received in their place (*p. 69*); and the point at which the "costs" intersect the "value" of the advances to him to whom they are offered, determines the price to be paid for this thing known as "advance," that is to say, the rate of interest.

These ideas seem to me to be most closely related to the variant which was developed by Carver of the abstinence theory, or as it may be more aptly designated, the waiting theory, to which I shall revert later. But they do not, as I have indicated, make any contribution to either clarity or accuracy by their use of a new nomenclature. I regret, for my part, that Hoag dealt at such length with my *Positive Theory of Capital* without making himself acquainted with my later edition of that book or with my *Further Essays on Capital and Interest* which that edition contained. And yet these had been available for several years. Had he been at all familiar with them, I believe he could not possibly have written certain portions of his book as he did. This applies particularly to his discussion of the role assigned in my theory of interest to the higher physical productivity of roundabout methods of production. Since my more recent commentaries on this subject were precisely tailored to meet his objections, I must conclude that he was unacquainted with them. Indeed, this very topic, it seems to me, furnishes particularly clear evidence that his new concept of "nominal value" did not fail to expose the author to the danger of becoming himself bewildered. For under its baleful influence he passes under review even the purely technological conditions of the various productivities of longer or shorter processes of production, and judges them, in anticipation, in terms of value. In the course of that review he comes to the conclusion that the "true reason" for the greater physical productivity of more time-consuming processes of production lies in the circumstance that present labor invested in longer processes can create a "premium" consisting in a surplus of nominal value (*pp. 126, 129, 145-148*). But if Hoag can reason thus, then his whole reasoning seems to me to resolve itself into an attempt to derive technological productivity from value productivity. Very few persons, certainly, would be inclined to doubt that a logically tenable exposition would have to proceed in exactly the opposite direction. But I suppose Hoag, from his point of view, would call that "arguing in a circle" (*p. 129*)!

3. Use Theories; Especially the Theory of Oswalt

OF THE many schools of thought which were arrayed against each other in the period preceding 1884, some have enlisted no new recruits at all in the interim, and others have gained proselytes in only isolated instances. The theories which have been entirely unsuccessful in this regard may trace their failure to one of two causes. Either they have attacked their problem with all too great simplicity, or they have gone to the opposite extreme of marked and obviously labored subtlety. The former cause explains why the "colorless theories,"[32] such as the "naive productivity theory" and the "fructification theory" of Turgot and Henry George gained no new disciples; the latter would apply to theories like Schellwien's.

The interesting use theory belonged for a considerable length of time to those theories which seemed destined to attract only isolated partisans. Its most prominent representative, Carl Menger, made no new pronouncements on our subject. It is true that during this period he wrote an exceedingly valuable contribution to the theory of capital, "Zur Theorie des Kapitales"[33] in which he devoted a detailed and productive analysis to the concept of capital. But he did not extend his treatment to the debatable question of interest. Walras, who had previously recorded a formulation of the use theory closely akin to that of J. B. Say, continued to occupy the same ground.[34] But while we hear occasional echoes of the use theory in the camp of the eclectics from time to time,[35] the only one in the relatively long period between 1884 and 1900 of whom I should care to say that he has clearly and definitely aligned himself as a newcomer with the use theorists is Ladislas Zaleski, whose *Theory of Capital* made its appearance in Russian.[36] Since my knowledge of this work is limited to a few excerpts which have been furnished to me by persons familiar with Russian, I am not in a position to do more than state that Zaleski expressly espouses the use theory, and seeks to establish its fundamental soundness through reliance on the principle, borrowed from the natural sciences, "of the unity of matter and the conservation of energy." I am not qualified to judge the extent to which this addition by Zaleski causes him to diverge from Menger's use theory and possibly to approach the motivated productivity theory.

But since about 1900 there seems to have been some indication of an increase in the number of authors whose requirements in the matter of an interest theory are satisfied by the tenets of the use theory, or possibly by no more than its phraseology. Perhaps these new converts share the sentiments of one of their spokesmen who says, "the concept that interest is a payment for the use of capital is so *natural*." At any rate, of their number let me enumerate a few, merely as examples. Their writings include Cassel's *Nature and Necessity of Interest,* 1903, Margolin's *Kapital und Kapitalzins,* 1904, Berolzheimer's "Das Vermögen" in the *Annalen des deutschen Reiches,* 1904, Section 11, p. 595 ff., Brentano's *Theorie der Bedürfnisse,* 1908, p. 11, and Oswalt's *Vorträge über wirtschaftliche Grundbegriffe,* 1905, and more particularly his "Beiträge zur Theorie des Kapitalzinses" in the *Zeitschrift für Sozialwissenschaft,* New Series, Volume I, 1910. It may even be proper to include in this group Komorzynski with his somewhat nebulous theory of *Vermögensnutzung* which he expounds in *Die national-ökonomische Lehre vom Kredit* 1903, p. 26 ff.

The majority of these professions of faith in the use theory are so modest in their line of reasoning (despite the assumption of a rather pretentious tone by one or two), that a detailed treatment of them would hardly yield scientific results that would justify the effort. The variants which seem to offer the greatest theoretical interest are those by Cassel and Oswalt. I have expressed myself elsewhere[37] in this work on Cassel and have pointed out that his theory, which attempts to combine the principles of the use and the abstinence theories, is as unsatisfactory as it is individual. It might be in order to set down at this point a few critical remarks concerning Oswalt's presentation of the use theory.[38]

To begin with, the interest problem, according to Oswalt, is quite "casy" (*p. 103*) and "simple" (*p. 2*) and was solved long ago, anyhow (*p. 445*). Oswalt only wants to warn us against allowing doubts and difficulties which are "needlessly trumped up" and "artificially imposed" by the "scholastically minded" (*p. 2*) to deter us from accepting "the very natural view" that interest is something paid for the use of capital (*p. 26*). It is obvious that the doubts which I have cast upon the existence and the reality of any such thing as an independent use of capital loom very large among those unnecessary difficulties imposed by the scholastically minded. And yet those doubts did not fail to make some impression on Oswalt. For one thing, he admits he is compelled to subscribe to some of the arguments I raised against the tenets of the use theory. On page 98, for instance, we find the express admission that "a use, in the sense of a physical or corporeal entity outside the good itself, does not exist." But the most convincing evidence of the effectiveness of my arguments is to be found in the extraordinary caution and diffidence with which Oswalt goes about introducing his concept of use of capital. He disarms all criticism in advance, as it were, by the sheer innocuousness and unpretentiousness of the theoretical premises which he makes his point of departure. The "use" of which he is about to speak is by no means to be taken to mean a "fact which is being invoked in order to explain interest," nor as a "cause" of interest. It is a mere "name" which he is using as a "designation" for certain processes which constitute factual occurrences. The name, moreover, is submitted without prejudice. It has nothing to do with the solution of the problem, but only with its formulation. The problem, says Oswalt, is *why* a certain something, be its name what it may, must be paid for at a price called interest. The formulation, he says further, is equally without prejudice, whether that something be labeled use of capital, as Oswalt does, or surplus value of present goods as compared with future goods, as Böhm-Bawerk does (*p. 15*).

At a later stage of his exposition Oswalt emphasizes still more strongly, if that be possible, the utterly unassuming character of his concept of use. On page 88 ff. he draws a contrast between two possessors of capital, their different methods of using their capital and the different practical results which ensue. Now the possession of a supply of goods "on hand to begin with," that is to say of a capital, is something which Oswalt's theory and my own are in complete agreement upon as an indispensable presupposition. It is the *sine qua non* of the physically more highly productive time-consuming methods—in a word, of the capitalist production method. That supply must necessarily and in the nature of things be consumed in the course of the capitalist production process. But it can be consumed in two ways. It can be consumed without being replaced and in that event the whilom owner is without capital at the conclusion of the production process and is not in a position to effect a constant continuation of the productive capitalist process, because he lacks the required initial supply of goods. Or on the other hand, it is possible, during the time in which the capital goods are being consumed through use, to replace those goods and thus to preserve their quantitative amount throughout their turnover. In that event of course, after the expiration of the first production period, the capitalist method, with all its inherent advantages of greater productivity, can be resumed and indefinitely continued.

Now at this point Oswalt very carefully opens the door for his use of capital to slip in. "It is customary" he says, "to describe" this second method of procedure by saying that the capital is not being "consumed" but only being "used." Both words are placed in quotation marks by Oswalt himself. But Oswalt does not neglect to annotate this "description" quite promptly with all manner of still more cautious reservations. It must be admitted without further ado, he says, that we are only using a "metaphorical phrase" when we speak of merely using capital. Metaphors of that sort, however, are quite permissible "in the interests of facility of expression" with one proviso. There must be previous agreement on "what is the thing one has in mind, when speaking *without benefit of metaphor.*" And at this point Oswalt confirms with all the exactitude and correctness one could desire that the two persons, of whom one "consumes" and the other "only uses" his capital are in reality both acting *in identical fashion.* "The capital of each one has, in the same manner but in a longer or shorter time, as determined by its physical nature, been *used up,* or in other words *destroyed.* The difference between the two procedures relates rather to other goods which they might have consumed." Or rather, as Oswalt takes the trouble to expound with still more exactitude, it relates to the component constituents of which these other goods are composed. And he goes on to say of this difference, that "it consists in the fact that the first capitalist really consumes those other goods, whereas the second leaves them unconsumed for a time." The practical difference lies in the fact that when the original capital is gone, one has no capital any more, but the other has a capital equal in value to the one that is gone. And in accordance with that practical result, says Oswalt, a *metaphorical* expression was coined by saying the second capitalist had "only used" his capital (the italics are Oswalt's!). It is a matter of individual taste, he goes on to say, whether the metaphor be considered apt or not. But no one will be able to deny the factual difference between the two situations.

Up to this point the reasoning is apparently unexceptionable. I am of course completely in accord with the statement that there is a vast real difference between the two situations. Oswalt has stated quite correctly wherein that difference consists "without recourse to metaphor." He has said that in both cases capital is "used up, that is to say, consumed," that the difference extends only to their position with respect to entirely different goods or materials. Hence Oswalt expressly concedes that the figure of speech "mere use" of the capital does not express the essential nature of the matter correctly, but merely furnishes a "metaphor" which serves to "facilitate expression." And certainly it is not my province as an economic theorist to pass judgment on his "individual taste," even though I do not share it.

But after this impeccable introduction Oswalt's demands on behalf of his use of capital furtively begin to become more importunate. The reader with a sense of humor, if he scans the appropriate passages in juxtaposition, will derive amusement from observing how the quotation marks, which in the beginning always conscientiously mark the metaphoric "mere use" of capital, gradually become rarer and finally disappear altogether. And he will perceive how the "symbol" or "name" (*once, on p. 26, Oswalt calls it an "auxiliary image"*) bit by bit takes on reality and acquires being. And soon he learns that "we have seen" (*p. 90*) or that "it has been established" (*p. 103*) that the use of capital is something useful. Thereupon we read, too, that such use of capital, because of its usefulness and its relative scarcity, has value. Whereupon the reader involuntarily succumbs to an analogy with Descartes' *Cogito ergo sum* and is prone to yield to the kindred suggestion that a thing which is useful and valuable must, above all things, *be,* hence that it must exhibit the traits of existence and reality.

Furthermore the thing which was once a metaphorical "auxiliary image" has now taken on the concrete attributes of a "means of production" (*p. 10*); in fact, Oswalt is now able to state quite precisely that it is a *fundamental* means of production, a third material (*p. 10, p. 151*) or an "elementary good" (*p. 244, p. 439*) which enjoys independent existence on a par with labor and land.

This last statement, set down with such assurance, sounds especially strange coming out of Oswalt's mouth. For elsewhere he agrees with a statement of mine which is completely at variance with this one of his. I set down, as one of my views, that there are only two elementary goods, namely labor and land, capital being merely an intermediary product of labor and land. Now Oswalt explicitly states that he considers this view "certainly correct," and hence acknowledges it to be an established principle "that all the proceeds of our economy are, in the last analysis, the product of these *two* factors" (*p. 91*). To be sure, Oswalt attempts to keep open an avenue of escape which will enable him to disregard this "acknowledgment." He does so by calling it "practically, as well as theoretically barren." Even if that were true, could one ever justify the teaching of that which is the reverse of the truth—even of a "barren" truth? Furthermore, I suspect the very zeal Oswalt displays in picking his way around that acknowledgment and veering away from it. Is that not an indication that he finds it an obstacle in tracing the pattern of his theory? Does he not betray that it is anything but unimportant for the theoretical consideration of our problem—in other words that it cannot possibly lack that very quality which must be termed theoretical fruitfulness?

There is presumably no need of further comment concerning the case that Oswalt then goes on to plead for the practical barrenness of the principle. For he argues that it would be vain to rely on it in practical life as a means of avoiding the payment of interest. This bears all too obviously the earmarks of a *petitio principii,* an attempt to utilize the existence of interest itself as a proof of the particular interest theory that he favors.[39]

Now that use of capital has been granted advanced standing as an independent elementary good, it can finally be presented as a third "factor in costs," something very industriously sought for by the use theory. As such it is reflected, on a par with the two factors of cost (labor and land) in the value and price of the product (*pp. 103 and 291*). In that capacity it can of course demand compensation, and what it receives as such is, naturally, interest. And thus Oswalt, beginning with no more than a "name" submitted entirely without prejudice, and with a mere "symbol," has brought use of capital to the point where it has inched its way into all the same entirely real positions which it has traditionally occupied in every other use theory. There remained only one step to be taken. It was necessary for Oswalt somehow or other to clarify the relationship of his "use" to the products themselves. That is accomplished by incorporating the use in the products. Of course it is not, as he says on one occasion (*p. 98*) "anything corporeal or material existing *outside* the good itself." However, the uses, according to his dictum on page 103, are "part and parcel of" the goods concerned. Now here is a point to note. On page 90 Oswalt stated explicitly that the processes which give rise to the figure of speech "mere use," in contrast to the word "consume" in its general sense, do not affect those goods whose "mere use" is the subject of the metaphor, but apply to other goods or elementary goods entirely. But now he asks us to accept the conclusion that a thing which, by his own admission, has nothing to do with those first mentioned goods nevertheless is included or is inherent in them—God alone knows how!—as a true elementary good!

And Oswalt takes this matter of "being inherent" so seriously that he charges me on countless occasions with mal-observation as my chief and decisive error. He claims that I overlooked the presence of the uses which are likewise incorporated or inherent in consumers' goods![40] And the final upshot of all this? The same Oswalt who on page 15 explicitly excluded use from the facts which are to be adduced for the *explanation* of interest sounds his final note in these summarizing words on page 443: "My *explanation* of interest is that it is the price of the *use of capital*"; that this price develops in the course of exchange and expresses the value of the *use of capital*; and that this value, on its part, arises from the conjunction of the usefulness and the relative scarcity of that very use of capital.

Now let us be honest about this! Is the use of capital, as it figures in this chain of explanatory reasoning, still intended to be regarded as nothing more than an empty name, submitted without prejudice and not purporting to explain anything at all? Or is it not fairer to say that Oswalt asserts the existence of a real and independent "elementary good" and then bestows on it that name? And is it not more accurate to say also, that its existence constitutes an indispensable material link in the chain of his explanation? And when and where has Oswalt uttered one single word in proof of the real existence of such an elementary good?

Let us not deceive ourselves. Oswalt is of course absolutely correct in his contention that interest is paid for something, and that this "something" must be useful and relatively scarce if there is to be any possibility of its having value and price. But certainly our problem consists in a correct determination of the nature of this "something." And as long as Oswalt remains sincere in professing that he is not prejudging the question or stealing a march toward his objective by using the *name* "use of capital," just so long has he failed to utter a word concerning that nature. He might just as well (to borrow Knies's illustration) have bestowed on it the name "Hoho!" or "Sasa!" Or he could have used the conventional "x" employed by the mathematician to designate any quantity still unknown.

It is evident in particular that the act of giving to that something an independent name does not in the slightest degree constitute either statement or evidence that that something must necessarily, or in any respect, be an *independent* something. Or let me put it more concretely. The opposite possibility is, at the very least, still open. It is quite possible that the present goods which have been given out on loan may themselves possess greater value because of superior utility and relative scarcity. In that case interest is not a price for a particular independent something. On the contrary, it completes what is otherwise only a partial equivalent in the form of the less valuable future goods. It must be added to the latter, so as to enhance their value sufficiently for them to attain equality with the more valuable present goods alone, which were received from the lender. This conception of the matter (and it is *my* conception) is one that Oswalt feels constrained to acknowledge on several occasions. He admits in so many words that it is a "description,"[41] or a "formulation" which also "does justice to the actual facts" (*pp. 15 and 100*). I might say besides, that it has the indubitable advantage of requiring the invention of no fictions. It depicts quite literally the facts which Oswalt describes in those passages which he fashions "without benefit of metaphor" (*pp. 90 and 98*). For it deals with the receipt of a good, with the "destruction" in the course of its use, of that which has been received, and finally with the replacement of it with *another* good.

Under these circumstances we may at any rate count the following points as established. First, we can accept it as indubitable that the possession of a supply of present goods—of a capital—entails for the possessor a gain or advantage. Further, we must reject the argument that the mere existence of the advantage justifies the conclusion on our part that any portion thereof is attributable to the operation of a distinct element, a particular "elementary good" other than labor or land. Then, too, we are even more surely obliged to deny the thesis that such a conclusion follows from the introduction of a special *name* (and, above all, a name submitted without prejudice!) by which we are to designate the still undiscovered complete or partial cause of the advantage. Finally, we must recognize that we are facing what is clearly and unequivocally an assertion of a hitherto undemonstrated fact, which therefore ought somehow to have been specially and factually proven to us. But I fail to find in Oswalt's work even the slightest trace of any attempt at such proof!

Oswalt, then, failed to furnish any sounder foundation on which to erect a use theory than did his predecessors. Rather the reverse is true, and his structure is put together, even more conspicuously than theirs, out of empty phrases. In contrast to all previous adherents of the use theory, Oswalt imparts his distinctive personal touch in the form of the candid admission which he makes at the very outset—the admission that "use" is a mere phrase, nothing but a "name," a "metaphorical expression" which by no means describes the thing it designates. By his own frank announcement of the purely rhetorical character of his fundamental concept he exempts it immediately from all the critical requirements which would have to be met by an objective designation seriously advanced. But of course no one would expect a purely ethereal figure of speech to measure up to standards of that sort. And after he has thus benumbed our critical conscience—and his own as well—he still uses this mere name as a veil of concealment behind which to conjure up again a figure which presents, one after another, features and attributes that are neither unexacting nor unsubstantial. And he accomplishes this without fulfilling any single one of the duties which would have been imposed upon him by an outright assertion of the reality of that figure.

Of course under these circumstances all the objections I raised in Chapter VIII of this book to the use theory in general remain in full force with respect to Oswalt's presentation of it. I do not believe I need to weary the reader with a repetition specifically directed against Oswalt. But I should like to add just one remark. The argument which I directed against the use theory created a dilemma from which an attempt at rescue was made by Margolin and approved and supported by Oswalt. It lay in the futile reliance on the presence in every exchange, and in equal degree for both parties, of a use in perpetuity of the good bought and the good sold.[42] I say "futile" because if we follow such artifices to their logical conclusions we find ourselves involved in another welter of contradictions and the remedy proves to be as vain as it is artificial. In addition, we are dealing with a palpable *petitio principii*. For while the question is, whether such "uses" can and do exist at all as a real and independent entity, this newest reference to uses existing on both sides of the exchange constitutes a presupposition that the still-to-be-demonstrated existence of these uses has already been demonstrated!

On the question of what part, if any, use of capital has to play in the explanation of interest, Oswalt's views and mine are as far apart as is well conceivable, and beyond all possibility of reconciliation. On many other questions however, which also concern the explanation of the phenomenon of interest, we are a great deal closer together. And particularly in the matter of our conception of the nature and the consequences of the time-consuming capitalist production methods, our differences are hardly more than a matter of wording.[43]

Oswalt is far less concerned with his presentation of the idea of capital use, which he had treated as a mere matter of formula, than he is with his organization of those material facts which seem to him to supply the basis for the price and value of that use. Since that is so, he would probably consider my presentation of his theory unduly fragmentary if I failed to conclude with at least a brief treatment of that portion of it which appears to him the most important.

Oswalt lists three facts which he regards as "the causes of interest."

Fact number one, a "technological fact," is the higher productivity of the more time-consuming capitalist methods of production and consumption.

Fact number two, a "subjective fact," bears the further terse designation of "the requirements of current consumption" and constitutes a possible obstacle to the full utilization of the advantages of the first, or technological fact.

Fact number three, a "historic fact," is the presence or absence of human success in so limiting the requirements of current consumption that they can no longer constitute an obstacle to the general adoption of that method of production which, in the sense of fact number one, is technologically the most productive, meaning the cheapest.

In this succession the technological fact determines the *usefulness* of the elementary good, use of capital; the subjective fact, by keeping the existing quantity of capital and of capital use scarce, can determine the *value* of the latter; and it depends on the third, the historical fact, whether this relative scarcity and the value of capital uses to which it gives rise *really takes place,* in which case the phenomenon of interest occurs. Hence, according to Oswalt, the occurrence of interest always presupposes the simultaneous and concurrent operation of all three causes. This pronouncement by Oswalt is accompanied by a vigorous polemic against my theory, because I had said upon occasion, with respect to my own three causes of the occurrence of interest (they are of course *not* the same as Oswalt's three!) that each one by itself, though only in lesser degree, was capable of giving rise to the phenomenon of interest.[44]

Despite that polemic there seems to me to be very little difference between our two theories, if we disregard the interpolation of his alleged elementary good, use of capital. The differences, for the most part, affect only the external organization, and it will facilitate a correct estimate if I set down a few observations in advance.

Oswalt's "technological fact" is essentially the same thing as my "third cause." But his "requirements of current consumption" would seem to resemble a large-mesh seine, a catch-all that gathers in a number of rather heterogeneous groups of facts without very accurate differentiation. For the "requirements of current consumption" are so broadly inclusive that they cover the following:

1] My entire "first cause," that is to say, those cases in which the enhanced importance of present wants is based on completely objective conditions which cause a scarcity in present supply;

2] My "second cause" which envisions causes and cases where present wants of a given objective intensity obtain precedence over future wants possessing an equal degree of intensity;

3] One fact of a completely general nature, one which does not put a name to any specific reason for preferring present goods. Indeed, it is concerned with nothing more profound than one of the most elementary presuppositions which underlie the conduct of every rational economy—the assumption, namely, that behavior is to be governed by economic principles. For in the origin of interest Oswalt assigns to the "requirements of current consumption" the function of preventing the originary productive forces from exhausting all opportunities for investment in those methods of production which attain the maximum in physical achievement and in time-consuming character. Granted! But many other facts take part in that function, including one exceedingly simple one, and one, indeed, which performs by far the greatest share of it. That is the fact that when we satisfy our wants we do so, in the regular course of things, according to the economic principle of satisfying wants in the order of their importance. Now if one part of our wants belongs in the future but another part to the present, it is self-evident that the latter must be satisfied first. There is no need of invoking any principle of the precedence of present wants. Insofar as the latter are, in and of themselves, more important, they will take precedence over less important future wants. And this simple fact leads us on to that "prevention" which Oswalt quite correctly asserts is operative; and it does so in the following way, which is the same way I traced quite explicitly in Book IV, Chapter I, third cause of my *Positive Theory of Capital*. If there were unlimited saving and amassing of capital, and if at the same time the originary means of production of the present were directed exclusively or by preference through the channels of maximum technological achievement toward production goals of a remote future, what would the resulting situation be? Clearly, the wants of the distant future would be provided far to excess, and those of the present and of the immediate future would be disproportionately and inadequately met. In other words, wants of greater importance in the more immediate future would fail to be satisfied, and that failure would be preceded by the satisfaction of less important wants of a more remote period. All of which would quite simply constitute a violation of the elementary principle of any rational economy which demands that the order in which wants are satisfied be in conformity with the rank they occupy in respect to importance.

Oswalt and I are thus in complete accord on the issue that those simple and general facts play an indirect part in the origination of interest by bringing about a "scarcity of capital." And there can be no question of my committing an "oversight."[45] The difference between us is merely that Oswalt deemed it his duty to extend assiduously the scope of his "subjective fact" and so to have it embrace among the special "causes of the origination of interest" even such facts as belong to the commonest presuppositions of any human economy. I, on the other hand, was and still am of the contrary opinion, namely, that there should be designated as special reasons for the origination of interest only *special* reasons for the precedence of present goods. It follows that I believe the universal and fundamental facts of any rational economy should be introduced into the theorist's presentation only in the proper place and at a point where they are required in order to demonstrate how he traces the phenomenon of interest to the specific causes which he designates as the reason for its coming into existence.

Or let me put it as follows. I grant that I am completely convinced there could be no such thing as a phenomenon of interest (nor, to be sure, a human economy) if there were no wants, or if the failure to satisfy them did not cause man to experience discomfort. And yet I do not consider it either necessary or appropriate to extend my list beyond three reasons for the rise of interest in order to have it include, as special reasons, something like:

4] The existence of human wants;

5] The disadvantageous consequences of not satisfying them. If I did, I should just as properly be compelled to add:

6] The existence of goods;

7] Specifically, the existence of *economic goods;*

8] Adherence to sound economic principle;

9] The appraisal of goods according to their marginal utility. And I should have to enumerate many similar ones as specific "causes of interest" since no single one of all these general facts can be omitted if there is to be a complete explanation of the phenomenon of interest. What Oswalt includes in his "subjective fact," above and beyond what is conveyed by my first two causes, does not really mean anything more nor less than what I have covered in the axiomatic generalities which I have listed above after the numbers four and five. Pointing out that there are current present wants to be satisfied only *seems* to be a more significant statement than the very general truism that there is such a thing as human wants. For if they exist at all, then it stands to reason that they are not going to remain suspended in an everlasting future, but must exist at a time that sooner or later becomes the present. When Oswalt says, on page 85, that an attempt to "postpone" the satisfaction of these wants beyond a certain point will have as its consequence the "physical extinction of mankind" or at least "an impairment of his material well-being," he is merely putting into different words his statement concerning the disadvantageous consequences of any failure to satisfy wants. For a "want *not yet* satisfied" after all marks a *failure* to satisfy wants that are felt as present ones. Dress up an unsatisfied want as you will with the intention of performing the act of satisfying it at some future time, it still represents the *omission* of satisfaction at the present time. The intention can of course neither alter nor mitigate the hardship represented by the consequences of the omission. Nor can it ever produce the effect of having the future fulfillment, provided it ever does take place, serve as a satisfaction of the *present* want or an assuagement of the presently experienced wants or sufferings. If it quiets the stirrings of any want at all, it will at best be a want other than the definitely unsatisfied want of the present. If I "postpone" until tomorrow the satisfaction of my hunger for today's breakfast, then I have unquestionably gone hungry today. And that is just exactly as true (not more and not less) as it would be, if I had resolved from the outset to skip breakfast this morning. And then if I eat breakfast tomorrow, that will merely prevent other and new pangs which would otherwise have had to be endured tomorrow by way of repetition.

It is true that the dire consequences of a failure to satisfy present wants can exert a real and even a direct influence in the precedence of present over future wants. But if they do, then their influence is exerted by virtue of the motives and facts of either my "first cause" or my "second cause." In terms of my first cause, a pressing want in the present makes a present sum of goods preferable to an equal sum of goods at a future period when, presumably, the want will be less pressing. In terms of my second cause, and where the situation is one which involves needs that are a matter of life and death, then even if no difference, as between present and future needs, were to be anticipated in their pressing character, the provision for the immediate need of the means of subsistence would take priority over provision for future needs of that kind. This would belong in the category of reactions to the "brevity and insecurity of human life." For if the necessaries for the immediate support of life cannot be provided, then continuance of life obviously succumbs to that uncertainty. Life comes to an end and so does the benefit that can be derived from a sum of goods which will not be available until sometime in the future. Both life and the benefit are the victims of an uncertainty which has destroyed the value of the future sum of goods.

What is left after we have eliminated those special combinations of Oswalt's "requirements of current consumption" which have been taken care of by my first two causes? For Oswalt was careful to say that it was his claim that his "requirements" included more than is covered by my two "causes." It seems to me that the only thing that is left after the foregoing discussion is reducible to a single and trivial point. That point is that there is such a thing as human wants—not always, of course, wants in the future only, but in the present as well; and that these present wants must naturally urge their claim to satisfaction, if the untoward consequences of nonsatisfaction are to be avoided. It is certainly entirely correct and accurate to say that because of the competing claims of present wants, the means of satisfying future wants become scarcer than they would otherwise have been. But to set them down in a formula as a separate category of factors in the origination of interest seems to me trivial. It would be comparable to an argument like the following. Suppose I am accounting for the value of a certain kind of good and in the course of it I strive to prove the presence of a "factor in creating value" or a "factor in enhancing value" which operates in favor of just this one kind of good. The argument I advance is the fact that the want which my kind of good serves is not the only human want there is. Hence the claims which other sorts of want urge in favor of their satisfaction make it impossible that *all* our labor and *all* our land be devoted exclusively to the production of my one kind of good. If they could be so devoted, then goods of my kind could be made available in much greater quantity, would therefore have a much lower value, and might even conceivably become a free good and thus completely valueless! There are occasions, of course, when one is forced to invoke that sort of general and trivial truth. One example is the argument which I cited previously from Book IV, Chapter I of my *Positive Theory of Capital* and which was intended to show the range of applicability of my "third cause." Another, and one which I employed on an even more extensive scale, is my whole theory of saving and the creation of capital.[46] But for the reasons given above I considered it neither necessary nor appropriate to list the latter among the *special* facts which explain a *preference* for present as compared with future goods.

I suppose similar things may fairly be said of Oswalt's third "historical" cause. As to his fact, I am in complete agreement with him in the matter of the necessary part played by "relative scarcity." Of course, I do not mean the scarcity of his imaginary uses of capital, but that of present goods. And I have often used the point in my theory—explicitly and with emphasis.[47] But I am of the opinion that it is redundant to assign to it an independent and equal rank when listing the reasons for placing a higher value on present goods; because "scarcity of capital," wherever it occurs, is an intermediate consequence arising from the other "causes" of the origination of interest, and not a special cause in addition to them. As a matter of fact, this state of affairs is recognized quite clearly by Oswalt himself, and is even clearly stated (*p. 82*) when he attributes interest to the combined influence of only *two* facts—his "technological" and his "subjective" facts. And while he feels that the "historic" fact, which he lists as a third item, converts into a "reality" the "possibility" which received its initial impulse toward existence from the two first facts (*p. 86*), he still feels that a "more accurate" way of defining it is to call it the "degree of effectiveness of the aforementioned two factors."

Let that suffice by way of a judgment as to whether Oswalt's different organization of the general and specific facts which give rise to interest —facts which we both recognize—is an improved organization or not. I should like to add a few words anent an opinion which he aired in the course of his violent polemic against me. I mean his rejection of my statement that each one of my three causes of the rise of interest could, in and of itself, bring about the phenomenon of interest. Oswalt maintains that only the technological and the subjective causes, working in conjunction, can bring about the result. I think his polemic stems in part from a misunderstanding, and in equal part from a factual error. Oswalt seems to me to be in error as to his facts when he asserts that interest could not exist at all without the contributing activity of his first (my third) cause. In other words, there is no interest in the absence of the greater physical productivity of capitalist methods. I, on the contrary, have no doubt at all that a tribe living entirely, let us say, on the harvesting of fruit by still unmechanized agricultural methods, might very well institute consumers' loans. There, without the operation in the slightest degree of his first cause, would be a situation in which "consumers' interest" might well be born.

After what has gone before, it should be easy to recognize as a misunderstanding Oswalt's disputatious contention that my third cause could never, "all by itself," give rise to interest, but only if it were operating in conjunction with Oswalt's "subjective fact." Of course it cannot without a part of such fact. The part I mean is that which, in contrast to my first two causes, is a mere distention that serves as a catch-all for much that is axiomatic. For instance, it could not do so if there were no present wants, nor if the latter, in defiance of economic principle, were systematically denied preference. But it can do so very well "all by itself" in the sense in which I had claimed it could, namely, without any cooperation on the part of *my* first two causes.[48]

I should not like to terminate this discussion of Oswalt without expressly repeating a remark which I have felt it incumbent on me to make with respect to several authors. I must express my regret that my task as a critic imposes upon me the obligation of pointing out, from a necessarily restricted viewpoint, nothing but the errors and shortcomings of a theory. And yet the theory, in all respects except those on which I take issue, reveals a wealth of brilliant examples of profound theoretical insight, combined with eminent artistry in scientific presentation.

4. Abstinence Theories

DURING the last 30 years the abstinence theory has been the subject of animated discussion, and I might almost say this animation has exceeded what might have been anticipated.

If I may be allowed to preface my treatment of this theory with a few details, I should like to point to an interesting effort which a few writers have made to fortify it. They have put forward an effective plea in its defense—at least with respect to the chief criticism so vociferously leveled at it by agitators in general and by socialists in particular. That criticism had been that the richest capitalists are just the individuals who have the least occasion to practice "abstinence." There is thus a manifest lack of correlation between the magnitude of the alleged cause, namely the abstinence practiced, and the supposed effect, namely the amount of interest obtained.

By applying a principle common to both the Ricardian and the marginal utility theories several writers have urged, not without logic, that such lack of correlation, duly weighed, does not constitute a compelling

378

reason for believing the theory unsound. For it is necessary to bear in mind one principle. The market price of a product represents compensation for the sacrifices required in order to produce it. But there may be differences in the amount of sacrifice required. Where such differences exist, this compensation tends to be an equivalent for the greatest amount of such required sacrifice. Hence it is not remarkable that a uniform rate of interest which is just adequate to compensate for the greatest sacrifice in the form of abstinence, may provide excessive remuneration for those persons from whom accumulation and maintenance of capital requires a relatively smaller sacrifice of that nature. Marshall calls this "saver's surplus."[49] But this argument meets only one objection—and indeed the most superficial objection—to the abstinence theory. It does not offer the slightest refutation of that more fundamental objection, which I had based on essential and logical grounds, and on which I had founded my rejection of the abstinence theory.[50]

And then MacVane proposed a change in terminology, and one of real importance. He replaced the expression "abstinence," which was open to objection on several counts, with the name "waiting," which may be weaker but is certainly more accurate.[51] It conveys a certain approach to the point of view of that theory which, in explaining interest, places its main reliance on the influence of the time difference on the evaluation of present and future gratification and present and future goods. And it is significant that since then many of the most recent adherents of the abstinence theory consider the content of their theory to be identical with that of the *agio* theory.[52] But there was and still is one very important consideration which prevents a complete identification of these two theories. The obstacle lies in the fact that abstinence, even in the pale guise of "waiting," is still claimed by MacVane and his successors to enjoy the position of an independent entity and to be a sacrifice which must count in addition to and distinct from labor.

The earlier adherents of the abstinence theory evinced a fondness for the eclectic's maneuver of incorporating into their own exposition of the interest problem arguments which belong to other schools of thought. The same fondness is manifest today. Their frequent admixture of elements from the *agio* theory is an obvious example of this, and a procedure which is easy to explain, in the light of the paragraph immediately preceding. But there are other eclectic combinations which may be observed, such as Loria's interpolation of some elements of the exploitation theory.[53]

There is a goodly number of coherent and positive expositions which belong in this category of the abstinence theories, but I feel it is my duty to single out two of them for special discussion. The first of these is, as it were, a model exposition of an abstinence theory which does justice to current developments and which enjoys the weight of authority bestowed upon it by a pre-eminent scholar. Its spokesman stands in the full flower of his powers of research and presentation, and it is manifest that his exposition is conscientiously fashioned, both to achieve finality and cohesiveness and also to be all-inclusive in its consideration of every recent pertinent fact. The second of these two theories compels notice because of the originality which marks its attempt to supply an entirely new interpretation of the "sacrifice termed abstinence."

The first of these two theories is that of Alfred Marshall.

Marshall recognizes two things as the fundamental causative factors in the origination of interest, and he gives us two catchwords by which to designate them. He speaks of the "prospectiveness" and the "productiveness" of capital. Its "prospectiveness" is the quality which manifests itself in the fact that capital yields its advantages only in the future. In order to accumulate capital, "men must act prospectively," they must "wait" and "save," they must "sacrifice the present to the future."[54] Its "productiveness" is the quality which is responsible for the advantages which the help of capital makes available, in that it makes production easier and more productive.[55] Thus its productivity makes capital the object of demand. But because of the sacrifice which its "prospectiveness" entails, the supply of capital remains sufficiently scarce for the use of capital to command a price and become a source of income.[56]

All further ramifications follow from the universal law of exchange of which Marshall considers the interest problem to be simply one specific case. According to that universal law the "normal" value of goods will stabilize at the level at which demand and cost of production are in equilibrium. In this connection Marshall makes it a point to emphasize the co-ordinate rank of these two factors and their reciprocal influence. The true costs of production are represented by nothing less than the sum total of all the "exertions and sacrifices" which are required for the production of a good. These include, in addition to the necessary labor, the sacrifice[57] which accompanies the "waiting," the "postponement of gratification" which is the inevitable concomitant of every accumulation, every use of capital. Marshall points out that to follow the example of numerous earlier economists and call this sacrifice "abstinence," is to employ a less suitable term and to invite error. For the greatest accumulations of capital are achieved by exceedingly rich men, who most assuredly do not practice "abstinence" in the sense of abstemiousness. Rather, says Marshall, is it correct to follow the lead of MacVane and to describe the nature of the sacrifice by calling it merely a "postponement of gratification," or a "waiting." Nevertheless that constitutes a genuine sacrifice, and one that is to be taken into account as something quite apart from the labor performed (*p. 668*).

Just like labor, this sacrifice must find its compensation in the average price of goods, and must do so, in fact, at its "marginal rate" (*p. 607*). That is to be understood as follows. Of the sacrifice necessary for creation of the supply of capital there must be an ultimate or marginal part which was suffered with the greatest degree of reluctance and unwillingness; the compensation must be high enough to be just adequate as remuneration for that part (*p. 217*). That compensation is interest and it may therefore aptly be described as the "reward of the sacrifice involved in the waiting" (*p. 314*). Many people would save, to be sure, even without such reward, just as many would work without reward of any kind. And many accumulations of capital would take place in any event, even if the interest rate were lower than the one which actually obtains. The significance of this is not that we have a violation of the principle that the price must just compensate adequately for that part of the supply which involves the maximum sacrifice; it means rather that those particular savers receive compensation in excess of the value of their smaller sacrifice. They receive what Marshall calls a "saver's surplus" or a "waiter's surplus." But since few would do any considerable accumulating of savings if there were no reward in the form of interest, we are nevertheless justified in stating that interest is a "reward of waiting" (*p. 314*). Now the socialists make the claim that the value of goods is derived solely from the quantity of labor which is expended in producing them. Marshall's reply to them (delivered most emphatically, too) is that their contention would be correct, if—and only if—the service which is performed by capital were offered as a "free good" and involved no sacrifice (*p. 669*). But it is false, he says, if—and because—"the postponement of gratifications involves *in general* a sacrifice on the part of him who postpones" (*p. 668*).

I believe it would not be erroneous to characterize this view advanced by Marshall as essentially another abstinence theory, although one that is carefully formulated and couched in improved terminology. Its basic thoughts coincide completely with Senior's doctrine. The accumulation of capital makes a demand upon the capitalist of a genuine sacrifice which consists in the postponement of gratification and constitutes an independent element in the cost of production, over and above labor. Hence that sacrifice must be compensated for by an independent element in the price of goods and must do so after the fashion and according to the laws under which, in general, costs govern the price of goods. Be it said, incidentally, that Marshall formulated those laws with greater care than Senior did.[58]

It is readily understandable that my views on Marshall's interest theory cannot differ widely from my views on the abstinence theory in general; and those I have already expressed in an earlier chapter of this book. It is true that I am in complete accord with Marshall's thesis that both the "prospectiveness" and the "productiveness" of capital have something to do with the explanation of interest. I think, on the other hand, that the connecting link in his explanation reveals the same flaw as does that of other proponents of the abstinence theory. Both he and they cast it in a mold which necessitates a contradiction of the facts, for one thing, and even a violation of the laws of logic, for another.

To begin with, when we deal with "putting off consumption" such as is inseparable from the devoting of labor to the attainment of a future gratification, it is, in my opinion, erroneous to regard the postponement as a separate sacrifice which must be taken into account over and above that labor. In a previous chapter[59] I set forth in detail my reasons for that opinion. But they were apparently not sufficiently convincing for Marshall, since, despite his being fully cognizant of them, he still holds to his theory, which is substantially identical with the abstinence theory. And so I want to make an attempt to support my opinion with a few additional explanatory statements, and for these I find I am offered a welcome point of contact in a few remarks taken from Marshall's own theory.

For Marshall, like Jevons,[60] interjected into his theory some considerations touching the psychology which underlies man's appraisal of future joys and sorrows. Human nature being what it is, most men esteem a future gratification—even one whose attainment is absolutely assured—less highly than they do a present gratification of like kind. They "discount" its magnitude, as it were, making a deduction which varies in amount, as between one person and another, according to the degree of patience and self-control of which the particular individual is capable.[61] The present value of a future pleasure and hence "the present marginal utility of a distant source of pleasure" is lower than the value of an equal present pleasure, or lower, even, than that which the same future pleasure will possess at the time when it is actually realized. If, for instance, the temperament of a given individual is such that he discounts future pleasures at 10%, then in the case of a pleasure which one year hence will possess an actual magnitude of 11, he will value it today at 10, in round numbers.[62] Now we can gather from numerous statements of Marshall's that he does not distinguish between two psychological facts that are present here—one, that the great majority of men accord precedence to present satisfactions over future ones, and the other, the one on which Marshall bases his assumption that waiting involves a sacrifice.[63] To say that in general mankind prefers present pleasures to equal future pleasures, and to say that mankind feels waiting for future pleasures to constitute, in general, a sacrifice which increases the expenditure made to obtain them—those two statements are, for the purpose of Marshall's theory, only two different ways of expressing the identical psychological fact.

But as a matter of fact they are not two different expressions, but on the contrary, two distinct concepts. And indeed they are two conflicting and irreconcilable concepts, and that has very real bearing on our problem. Moreover, one of them is correct, and one of them is wrong, but in any event it is a sheer impossibility to argue in favor of both concepts at the same time. The truth of the matter is as follows.

The problem we are dealing with concerns the correct interpretation of a psychological fact which manifests itself in human experience too commonly for anyone to disbelieve. That experience consists in our willingness to make sacrifices in labor or in money which are of unequal magnitude, in order to attain gratifications which, though equal in other respects, vary in their temporal remoteness. If, for instance, the objective magnitude of a gratification is 10, then we are willing, provided the attainment of the gratification is immediate, to assume a labor sacrifice amounting to 10, or an equivalent sacrifice in money—say $10—for its acquisition. But suppose that same gratification of a magnitude of 10 were attainable only one year hence. Now if that psychological fact manifests itself in our particular case to such a degree that we require a discount rate of 10%, then we shall be willing to expend for its acquisition a present amount of labor having a magnitude, at the most, of a little more than 9 (9.09 to be exact), or we shall be willing to sacrifice money to the amount, at most, of somewhat more than $9 ($9.09 to be exact). And if that same gratification should be five years distant, then the limit of our willingness to acquire it in exchange for a present sacrifice of labor or money, would be fixed at labor in a magnitude of about 6 (or exactly 6.21) or at a money sacrifice of $6.21.[64]

This fact—and Marshall and I are in complete agreement,[65] as I have already said, that it *is* a fact—could, in and of itself, admit of two interpretations. One possibility as an interpretation would be to conclude that the temporal *remoteness causes the magnitude of the gratification to diminish* in our eyes, and we place a lower valuation on a future advantage than on a present one, simply because it is a future one. That is the explanation which must be gathered from those remarks of a psychological nature to which I referred above as being interjected by Marshall in connection with the valuation of future gratification. The present value of a future gratification is less than 10; if the temporal interval is one year, it is about 9; if the interval is five years, the value is only about 6. And because the gratification is not worth more to us than 9 and 6 respectively, we will not make any greater sacrifice to acquire it than is indicated by the figures 9 and 6.

It must now be obvious that by the terms of this concept the figures 9 and 6 do not designate merely the magnitude of *that part of the sacrifice* which consists of labor or money, but that they must indicate and limit the magnitude of the *whole sacrifice* that we are willing to make in order to attain the future gratification. In other words, it must be obvious that this interpretation leaves no room for any additional sacrifice in the form of "waiting"—a sacrifice that is made in addition to the sacrifice of labor or of money. For it is equally obvious that we should be violating every principle of economics if, in order to acquire a gratification which we value at 9 or 6, we should undertake a conglomerate of sacrifices which would be composed of labor and waiting or of money and waiting, and which would exceed the value of the gratification itself, and amount, let us say, to a magnitude of 10.

Conversely, the second of the two conceivable interpretations leads to the very opposite conclusion, namely, to the acceptance of a sacrifice of just such greater magnitude. It is this interpretation which is conveyed by Marshall's statements concerning the existence of an independent sacrifice, over and above labor—a sacrifice of "waiting." And it formulates the matter for the theorist as follows. A future gratification will, at the end of one year or of five years, have a value of 10. The prospect of that gratification induces us to assume the burden of a conglomerate sacrifice, composed of labor and waiting. When we take into account the degree of onerousness which the waiting imposes upon us, as well as the presumable duration of that waiting, we arrive at an estimate of 10 as the value of the combination of sacrifices.

Again the obvious confronts us. For this second interpretation of the situation presupposes that the prospect of the future gratification owes the influence which it exerts on our present decision to the fact that the full and undiminished magnitude of that gratification is operative. Unless we estimate the value of the future gratification at its undiminished magnitude of 10, then a decision to acquire it through a sacrifice which totals 10 in magnitude becomes both rationally and economically impossible. Now the abstinence theory makes express provision for including this thought and even places emphasis upon it. It makes the assertion that the very reason why the price of a future production good or consumption good cannot sink below a given point (in our example that point is 10) is that the addition of the sacrifice of waiting raises the amount of the total cost to that sum. The producer would not consider himself adequately compensated for that magnitude of sacrifice if the price of the good were any less. This line of reasoning includes the absolutely express presupposition that in the producer's calculations the price of the future good is figured at the undiminished magnitude of 10.

In other words, what is obvious is that we can embrace the second interpretation only if we turn our backs upon the first. We may assume one of two things; of these the first is that temporal remoteness diminishes the value of a future good in our estimation; and the second is that such remoteness increases, in our estimation, the amount of sacrifice that must be taken into account—increases it by the amount of "sacrifice of waiting." But the one thing of which we may be entirely certain is that it is impossible to make both these assumptions at once. Such a double-barreled assumption would be nonsense, economically as well as mathematically speaking. For it would mean maintaining, in the first place, that in the producer's calculation the future value is reduced from 10 to 6, and in the second place that the sacrifice, by virtue of the adding of a sacrifice of waiting is increased from 6 to 10! And in spite of all that, the production supposedly is considered profitable!

In order to preclude at the very outset any possibility of our going off on the wrong track, I want to meet at once a certain conceivable counterclaim. A superficial examination could result in exposure to the temptation to explain the matter somewhat as follows. The utility of a good which will, at the expiration of five years have a value of 10, really suffers a diminution only in perspective, as it were, and is estimated at a present value of 6.21. But this present value of the future good is in balance with a present sacrifice of likewise only 6.21, whether in labor or in money. The sacrifice of waiting however lies only in the future, and it will be compensated for *at that time* out of the full future value of a magnitude of 10, which the good will eventually possess. Hence the present value and present sacrifice, on the one hand, and the future value, on the other, are susceptible to perfectly satisfactory reconciliation with the magnitude of the total sacrifice, which includes the future sacrifice as well.

The trouble is that this reasoning overlooks the fact that any economically rational calculation must take into account not only the sacrifices that are due, but also those (even if in installments) which are not yet due. And indeed, this accounting must be performed *at the very beginning*. If I am considering the purchase of a dwelling that has been offered me for $20,000 to be paid in 20 annual installments of $1,000, then it is not enough for me to compare the present value of the house with the value of that installment of the sacrfice which is due in the present. That is to say, I cannot compare it with the immediate "down payment" of $1,000. It stands to reason that I must measure the value of the house against the value of all the installments of the purchase price, and I must do so at once. In doing so, I must compute the installments not yet due at a certain discount which will reduce them to their present value.

The reasoning by the adherents of the abstinence theory presents a relatively close analogy. For them the entire sacrifice that is to be expended for a temporally remote gratification represents the sum of one first installment of the sacrifice, consisting of labor or money, plus a series of additional installments of "waiting sacrifices" which are spread out over the entire intervening interval of time. These waiting sacrifices may be taken into account, just as in the case of the purchase of the dwelling are the installments which are not yet due. That is to say, they may be discounted at a rate which corresponds to their temporal remoteness. But they must be taken into consideration without fail— the more especially so because, as we know, the abstinence theory holds that it is the consideration of these very "waiting sacrifices" which is supposed to deter producers from directing their production toward less valuable future goods. If we apply this reasoning to our own example, we shall find it results in the following mathematical alignment. The immediate sacrifice (in labor or money) amounts to 6.21. Hence the cumulative total of the sacrifices of waiting over the five-year period, which will make the total of all sacrifices amount to 10, must be 3.79. But since these sacrifices are all still in the future, their present value must be set at a lower figure. And as the average time throughout which these sacrifices must be "endured" amounts to 2½ years, the application of our previous discount rate of 10% would reduce the 3.79 to a present value of approximately 2.96. Accordingly the present value of all the sacrifices which must be taken into consideration will equal 6.21 plus 2.96, or a total of 9.17. However, the present value of the desired gratification was only 6.21. That is very clearly a pair of magnitudes having a relationship which cannot provide a basis for economically rational behavior.

Frankly, I am astonished, in view of Marshall's mathematical treatment of the whole question, at his failure to be disturbed by disparities of this kind, since his own computations ought surely to have made them inescapably patent. I confess that I am not enough of a mathematician to pass judgment on the details of his computations. Marshall supplies involved mathematical formulae for determining the discount which represents the reduced present value of future marginal utility, as well as for figuring the agglomerating sacrifices of waiting by means of geometrical progressions. That is all the more reason why I am unable to explain how or why it was possible for such a palpable and unmistakable error to escape his attention (*see Notes* XIII *and* XIV *of his mathematical appendix*).*

I rather suspect—and let mathematicians verify my suspicion—that Marshall evaded a clear and mathematical issue by presenting alternative formulae in his mathematical Note XIII, rather than a single one. We are given to understand that these two formulae differ from each other only with respect to the temporal "point of departure" which is chosen for each. Actually, however, the difference between the formulae is that between diametrically opposed conceptions of the problem itself. And each formula is an application of the conception which is directly opposed to that on which the other formula is based.

The first formula chooses as its starting point that instant at which construction of the house is begun, and then progresses, unless I am quite mistaken, by steps that constitute an accurate and faithful adherence to the agio theory. That is to say, the value of the future gratification is taken into account as an amount which reflects a diminution or discount, but no account whatever is taken of any sacrifice of waiting. The second formula takes as its starting point that instant at which the construction of the house has been completed. Then, conversely, it takes the production goal (the finished house) into account at full value and, by way of equalization, takes into account not only the sacrifice of labor but in addition the sacrifice of waiting, as components of the cost of production. This mutation in the principle underlying Marshall's calculations becomes less conspicuous because of a complication inherent in his choosing just the illustration he did—namely, the construction of a house.

For a house is a durable object of gratification and it obliges us therefore to deal with two goals—the goal of production, which is to say, the completion of the house, and the goal of gratification, namely the occupation of that house. But these two goals are not achieved simultaneously. Hence we must deal with two waiting periods as well. The first of these extends from the beginning of the process of construction to the completion of the building. The second is a graduated waiting period which extends from the termination of the building process to the end of a span of many years throughout which the durable good called "dwelling house" is actually received in installments of service.

But the second waiting period receives the same mathematical treatment from Marshall in formula II as it does in formula I. That is to say, he computes the present value of the finished house from the discounted value of the future use services, and for that he declines to include in his calculation of the sacrifices anything for those sacrifices of waiting which follow the completion of the house. In the midst, as it were, of his formula II he reverses himself with respect to his conception of the problem. Up to the time the house is completed his calculations are in accord with the abstinence theory, but from that point forward they follow the agio

---

* Translators' note: The next nine paragraphs concerning Marshall's formula appear as a footnote in the German original.

theory. But because the calculations of formula II correspond for part of the way to those of formula I, the false impression is created that the same principle has been followed without change throughout the calculations of both formulae, and that the difference in the latter stages of the calculation is really attributable to nothing more than the choice of a different temporal point of departure.

But actually there has been a breach of principle. For even though the instant at which the house is completed may mark the *beginning* of the period during which gratification is derived from it, it would obviously be preposterous to say that with the first hour's use of the house the *entire sum* of labor expended in its production has received its compensation. The reverse is true, for it will be a very long time before the vastly greater part of the labor of construction is compensated for by the gratification which is to be the remuneration for that labor. Now in his Note 1 to Book V, Chapter 4, Section 1, Marshall, speaking in the spirit of his abstinence theory, says explicitly that "the *evil or discommodity*" of the exertions of production *increases,* by reason of the waiting for future gratifications, in geometric proportion with the waiting time. If that is true, it would have to continue to be true even after the house has been completed, and that same increase in geometric proportion must necessarily continue to apply to the sacrifices represented by that portion of the labor of production which has not yet been requited by the gratification which occupancy bestows. Hence I call it an inconsistency and a repudiation of part of his own theory, for Marshall to fail to include this geometrically proportionate increase in working out the second part of his formula II.

Indeed, the same inconsistency and repudiation are present in the entire formula I because of Marshall's failure to include it at that earlier time. It would concededly have been necessary to include it only by computing a graduated series of discounts, as I indicated in the main body of the earlier text. But it would have been indispensable to take it into account in *some* measure, and that Marshall failed to do. For what he discounts in that first formula under the heading of sacrifices is not the sacrifices of *waiting,* but the "value" of the sacrifices of *labor.* And the latter are quite properly his concrete (and, alas, very tedious!) example of the construction of a house. But let us suppose that Marshall had chosen, instead of the building of a house, some example in which the expenditure of labor, on the one hand, and the gratification derived from the good, on the other, had been instantaneous and simultaneous. And of course I mean respectively different moments! In that case the whole calculation would have been much simpler, much more lucid; and the two horns of the final dilemma would have become more apparent —one, the inconsistency in using different points of departure, the other the fallacy in the calculation.

I wish to make two concluding remarks concerning Marshall's mathematical formulae.

The first of these touches Marshall's contention that his point of departure in formula II is "the more natural from the point of view of ordinary business." In my estimation it is not at all adapted to promoting visualization of the thing Marshall would have us visualize, judging by the content of the accompanying paragraph of his text, and by the whole thought process of the abstinence theory. I am referring to that weighing of utility against sacrifice as the action which *guides and determines the decision whether or not to produce at all.* That action must, in the very nature of things, take into account advantage and sacrifice as they appear to the prospective producer, not after the process of production concludes, but before it begins. And yet the latter is Marshall's point of arrival rather than his point of departure in his formula ı!

My second concluding remark concerns the footnote that Marshall added in the fifth edition of his book, his Note 3 on page 352, in which he expressly denies the charge which he thinks he discerns in the arguments I advanced in my book. It is the charge that he made a "double calculation" of interest. Now as I have just pointed out, the truth of the situation seems to be that Marshall did not, in actual fact, make any such double calculation—a calculation that would inevitably have become immediately patent by reason of a mathematically incorrect result. Nevertheless, if he had adhered to the theoretical premise which he himself set up, he would have *had to* make such a double calculation. He escaped the necessity of doing so only by his inconsistency and his tergiversation between his two irreconcilable premises. And the commentary which Marshall has added to his most recent utterance on the subject, and which supposedly furnishes a clarification of his procedure, has the very effect of confirming me in my original conviction.

But if it be once conceded that there is no escaping the necessity of a choice between the two conceptions which Marshall has conjoined in his doctrine, then there cannot be a moment's hesitation as to which way that choice must fall. I am convinced that such would be the case even for that outstanding scholar himself, whose opinion I am here constrained to contradict. On the one hand everyday experience leaves us all with the impression, stamped deep beyond all possible denial, that men, and in especial thoughtless men, will place a lower valuation on the prospect of remote gratifications, than on gratifications in the present, though these be in magnitude identical. On the other hand, those doubts which argue against the existence of an independent sacrifice, either of abstinence or of waiting, those objections, that is to say, which I set forth in such detail in the ninth chapter of this book will in all likelihood, if a choice of alternatives becomes inescapable, be given greater weight by those who previously had been able to elude their impact. I believe that renewed and attentive examination will make it impossible to escape for long the conviction, let us say, that nongratification still does not merit designation as suffering, or the firm belief that fruitless work cannot be termed a sacrifice of infinite magnitude, that is to say, a sacrifice composed of a limited quantity of the sacrifice of labor and an unlimited quantity of eternal and everlasting waiting. It would not be difficult to add similar examples to the two just cited. To provide for the remote possibility that some exceptionally skeptical readers may still harbor some trace of doubt, I should like to conclude by submitting the following additional considerations.

Anyone who concurs with the thought processes peculiar to adherents of the abstinence theory by maintaining that waiting is an independent sacrifice, must reconcile himself to the conclusion that follows from it. And that is that careless people, with never a thought for the future, are perfectly willing to make exactly equal sacrifices for a gratification decked out with every temptation of immediacy, and for the attainment of one in the future, be it never so remote. This equal sum of sacrifice would simply be of varying composition in each case. For the present gratification, it would consist of labor alone, whereas in the case of the future gratification, it would consist of somewhat less labor but would attain the same level of total sacrifice by supplying whatever might be lacking in "waiting"!

One more thing! There can be no doubt (especially since Marshall himself agrees) that the psychological phenomenon under discussion is applicable not only to the valuation of future joys, but also to that of future pains.[66] Let us assume that some person is threatened by an ill which will materialize one year hence, unless provision is made against it now, and which will at that time possess a potency of 10. If that person discounts future events at a rate of 10%, he will be willing to assume a present burden in order to ward off the ill, but that burden must not exceed a present labor sacrifice of nine. Now it might be possible for me, if really hard pressed, to imagine that in dealing with the preparation of some positive enjoyment, I might feel the waiting for its realization to be a sacrifice, and that that sacrifice would ultimately raise the total sacrifice to a magnitude of 10. But I confess it to be quite beyond my power to imagine what possible sacrifice I am making during the interim in which I do *not yet* suffer the ill that threatens me, by not being, as yet, in a position to avert it, either. What painful suffering do I supposedly endure, in the form of "continuation of the state of want,"[67] simply because in midsummer I do not yet possess next winter's overcoat because that garment has its situs, for the nonce, on the spindles and looms where it is in the process of fabrication? Or consider the case of the man of 30 who is going to be so presbyopic at 50 that he will need corrective lenses. Pray tell me the nature of the suffering that is his, because he must do 20 years of "waiting" for the glasses to be finished, not forgetting that the miners, the builders of machinery and many others have already begun preparations for the remote completion of his eyeglasses.

I think the impartial observer will recognize the truth with complete clarity. The false picture we are asked to envision is that of the scale pan of sacrifice which is originally weighted only with the sacrifice of labor. But on this scale pan there is then placed a continuously increasing weight of painful waiting for a nonexistent ill to be averted. Finally the combined weight grows great enough to counterbalance the full magnitude of 10 which the prospective advantage (or disadvantage) will possess. But the true picture is quite different. It shows the two scale pans in perfect balance at the very outset. That balance was achieved at the single instant which was decisive for the whole phenomenon, the instant at which economic calculation and decision became final. The method of establishing balance was to place a smaller valuation on the threatening ill by regarding it in the attenuated perspective of its temporal remoteness, and consequently considering avoidance of it to be a correspondingly lesser advantage. And in further consequence, a labor sacrifice of correspondingly lesser magnitude was considered to be sufficiently heavy to balance the scales.*

There might be those who would interpose an objection at this point and argue that the labor which is expended on providing assuagement of future pain could also have been used for obtaining some other gratification, and indeed, a present and positive gratification. Their contention would then be that the forfeiture of this other gratification constitutes the content of the sacrifice of waiting. My reply would be, first, that such playing battledore and shuttlecock with the fundamental question is to evade it rather than solve it. Furthermore, I should like to point out that difficulties of that sort can be nipped in the bud by the choice of a concrete situation which shuts off any avenue of evasion.

Let us assume, for instance, that our illustration concerns a prisoner who has no winter clothing and knows that he will be released one year hence, which will be when the winter cold is most severe. According to the regulations of that particular prison he is permitted, but not required to perform convict labor by which he will earn a sum sufficient to purchase winter clothing. But for the duration of his imprisonment he is not permitted to devote his earnings to any other purpose, and consequently not for the attainment of any other, earlier gratification. Here is a situation which provides no conceivable material out of which may be fashioned a sacrifice of waiting—nothing, that is, which may be construed as a burden imposed upon the prisoner, over and above the labor sacrifice itself, by virtue of the fact that his labor must be devoted to the acquisition of warm winter clothes.

I doubt if any of our objectors are prepared to deny entirely the obvious fact that even a man in the position of our prisoner is less influenced by considerations of the future than by inducements of the present. And yet unless they are so prepared, they must admit that there is but one conclusion to be drawn from this and so many other pertinent situations. And that is, that temporal remoteness causes us to lower our present valuation of future joys and sorrows.

Herein, then, lies the fundamental error of the abstinence theory. It deals with differences in value which exert an unfavorable influence on the balance sheet of our welfare, and which are unquestionably attributable to differences in time. But the abstinence theory enters these differences on the wrong side of the balance sheet and records as an increase in sacrifice an item which is actually a decrease in enjoyment. That is to say, the theory when confronted with two conceivably correct interpretations of the facts, makes the wrong choice. Now it was the time of Rae and

* Translators' note: The next three paragraphs appear as a footnote in the German original.

Jevons which witnessed the introduction into economic science of the psychological fact that future joys and sorrows suffer a reduction in our estimation of their value. The attempt to incorporate that fact into the abstinence theory is an error committed by Marshall and other economists.[68] But it is not their only one. For in addition he—and they—failed to realize that the situation demands not reconciliation of two alternatives but elimination of one of them, for the simple reason that survival of one requires extinction of the other.

Those are the most important, though not the only reasons why I am unable to regard Marshall's treatment of the interest problem as a satisfactory solution. As has been pointed out elsewhere,[69] Marshall is inclined to attach very little significance to mere differences or inadequacies in the manner of expressing an idea. At the same time he is prone to attach wide significance to a concept which is a mere variant of an earlier expression of a given thought. But in this case we have, beyond any possibility of doubt, something more to deal with than a shortcoming in the manner of expressing a correct thought. It is a question here of an essential and characteristic link in the chain of logic which is to lead us to the explanation of interest. That Marshall himself considers this critical link to be highly essential, is apparent from the way he draws the issue between himself and the socialists. And I say this even though I think that here, too, he is in error. But he does believe that the verdict on the correctness of his conception, as opposed to that of the socialists, depends on whether or not we may ascribe to the sacrifice of waiting the nature of an independent sacrifice over and above that inherent in labor.[70]

That his conception at any rate differs markedly from my own is also clearly apparent. Let us consider the situation that would result upon cessation of that psychological fact which manifests itself in the preference accorded to present over future gratification. By the terms of Marshall's theory the consequence would inevitably be the disappearance of interest as well. By the terms of mine, the consequence would at most be that, so to speak, only one of the wellsprings of the phenomenon of interest would be rendered parched and arid. Interest itself would still flow on, though the tide might ebb. For even without any biased underestimation of the future, the fact that roundabout methods are more highly productive is still operative. And its effect would be to guarantee to the present stores of goods, which make possible the adoption of these methods, a superiority in value over future stores of goods.[71] Indeed, such superiority would be not for the moment only, but for periods of time so extended that, measured by even the most exacting standards, they would deserve to be classed with the longest of "secular" or agelong periods.[72]*

Marshall himself thinks such a change in the familiar arrangements of our physical and moral world by no means inconceivable. Adhering strictly to the logic of his own explanation, that interest is a "reward of the sacrifice involved in waiting," he reveals clearly his opinion that in a case of that kind "interest would be negative all along the line." Indeed,

* Translators' note: The following four paragraphs appear as a footnote in the German original.

he does not stipulate the complete cessation of all preference for present gratifications of equal magnitude. Even without that he expects this same result to occur if so many people experience such an intensification of the impulse to provide effectively for old age and for their families, that the sums laid aside as savings for this purpose exceed the requirements for "new openings for the advantageous use of accumulated wealth" (*p. 485, Note 3*).

I should like to interject a warning here to the reader who is fond of tracking down subtleties, lest his attention be arrested by this last phrase referring to advantageous opportunities for production. I extend the assurance that it should not be construed as an indication that the opinions of Marshall and myself are by any means in full agreement intrinsically. In the first place, it is my opinion that even in a completely stationary economy, that is to say, one marked by a complete absence of "new" ways of employing capital, interest nevertheless would be maintained—and maintained for an indefinite time and entirely without assistance—by one single factor. That factor is the higher physical productivity of the more time-consuming roundabout methods of production (on this point see my treatise, *Einige strittige Fragen der Kapitalstheorie,* Vienna, 1900). In the second place, Marshall, in the passage cited, apparently stipulates one condition. Only on that condition, it seems, does he consider the presence of numerous new opportunities for investment to constitute an obstacle to the complete disappearance of interest. That condition is that there still remains a difference in the estimation of the value of present and future gratifications which are otherwise equal.

For, as Marshall has himself set forth with such incomparable clarity in his Note 1 to page 197, it is necessary to distinguish between two acts of differentiation. There is, on the one hand, an estimation at different values of present and future *gratifications* of equal magnitude. On the other hand we have an estimation at different values of present and future *amounts of goods* of equal magnitude. In the second instance it is possible that an influential factor is the circumstance that the same good possesses at different times differing degrees of objective marginal utility. Hence, a person who would normally accord preference to a present gratification over a future one of like magnitude may nevertheless make up his mind to practice a species of extortion on himself and lay by some savings. And he would do so even without the prospect of any interest on the amount saved, provided that amount, used at a future time, possessed a sufficiently greater degree of marginal utility at that time than it would have, if it had been expended immediately. An example might be the postponement of such use to an impecunious old age. Obviously Marshall's argument has reference to a consideration of this nature. For a time the need for new investments of capital will be adequately covered by the savings of those whose lower valuation of equal future gratifications is counterbalanced by the increase in the degree of marginal utility possessed by amounts of goods whose use is postponed. For that same length of time there is no sacrifice of abstinence to be reckoned, and to demand compensation. And for that long the absence of interest will be tolerated.

Now if that is really Marshall's opinion—and I have no doubt that it is—then his theory demands the continued existence of a difference in the valuation of present and future *gratifications* as a *conditio sine qua non*. It becomes such an indispensable factor because he makes it a necessary basis for the sacrifice of abstinence which is compensated by interest. But such is not my opinion. I do not consider the presence of a difference in valuation of gratifications to be indispensable. The reason is that the difference in valuation of *goods*—which I do admit is a necessary condition for the existence of interest—could and would be brought about by the unaided activity of the higher physical productivity of the more time-consuming roundabout methods of production (*see the passage in my* Positive Theory of Capital, *pp. 276-278, cited in Note 71, page 479*).

In conclusion let me say that Marshall's book contains in addition numerous utterances which emphasize, in rather pointed fashion, a special relationship of interest to the *employment* of capital. In fact, if they were his only words on the subject of interest, they might very well furnish some foundation for the supposition that Marshall had adopted the methods and ideology peculiar to adherents of the use theory.[73] And yet Marshall seems to be skeptical as to whether even the most confirmed partisans of the use theory would have wanted to maintain complete and strict orthodoxy in preaching the tenets peculiar to that doctrine.[74]. In view of his doubts I feel all the less entitled to assume that Marshall wanted to do so himself. Rather am I compelled to surmise that his use of phrases and idioms characteristic of the use theory has its origin in a certain freedom and insouciance in choice of expression which Marshall apparently claims as a prerogative for himself and others in the domain of inquiry into the theory of interest. This betokens a disregard for the obscurities and ambiguities in wording which have been responsible for so many errors and misapprehensions in this field. And it violates a principle which this same pre-eminent scholar has otherwise applied—and with all propriety, surely—by emphasizing the importance of incisive clarity and accurate formulation of ideas.

I have already remarked that we need to record another and very recent attempt to supply a new interpretation of the old abstinence theory. This attempt was made by an American named Carver.[75] It reveals great acuity in reasoning and remarkable facility in synthesis. But Carver goes astray because of a misconception, as I understand him, concerning the basic point of his problem.

The somewhat subtle sequence of his cerebration, which he has rendered easier to visualize by means of a number of geometrical diagrams, might be rather freely and briefly described as follows.[76]

Carver takes as his starting point the perfectly correct opinion that great amounts of present goods would be laid by as savings for the future, even if the owners received no interest, nay more, even if they had to pay for the expense of keeping their savings in custody. Carver is also entirely correct in drawing the line of demarcation where saving without receiving interest will cease. A reasoning and economically minded man will save for future use such a portion of his present supply of goods that the degree of marginal utility which will be yielded in the future by the last increment (let us say, the last dollar saved), is just equal to the degree of utility yielded by the last dollar marked for expenditure in the present. Even if there were no such thing as interest, a person who had a fortune of $100,000 and a modicum of prudence in its management would certainly not expend the whole amount, or even any considerable portion of it, on immediate consumption. His reason would tell him that such a course would secure him present satisfaction of quite unimportant and extravagant wants, but at the cost of his being deprived of the means of satisfying wants in the future, including even important ones. In fact, he would first give due consideration to other supplies of goods which could be expected to become available in the future, and would then end his present consumption after just so many thousand dollars that the marginal utility of the last dollar he spent would be of the same degree as the future marginal utility of the last dollar he saved.

The principle established in the foregoing paragraph is subject to one very important proviso, and one which Carver has also recorded with complete precision in his diagrams. Most men are wont to undervalue future joys and sorrows, the degree varying for each according to the bent of his mind and his temperament. Consequently they undervalue future goods in the same way. Thus a careless or an extravagant man may be asked to appraise a gratification or a good which will not come into existence until one year hence, but which will, at the moment it achieves reality, have a magnitude which we will designate by the number 15. Perhaps this man will not be inclined to accord it a present valuation of more than, say, 10. Now present economic decisions naturally are influenced only by present valuations of those satisfactions among which we are free to choose. Therefore some modification is required in the first criterion by which to determine the limit at which non-interest-earning saving will stop. That modification is to the effect that saving will be continued only to such a point that the marginal utility of the last present dollar to be spent equals the *present valuation* of the future marginal utility of the last dollar saved. In our example that point will be reached when the marginal utility of the last dollar spent amounts to 10, but the future marginal utility of the last dollar saved amounts to 15. For that future marginal utility of 15, in terms of present valuation, is simply the equivalent of a present utility of 10.

In order to cast more light on the modification fathered by Carver, I should like to inject at this point and without delay one point that I consider definitely established. All previous representatives of the abstinence theory had—explicitly or implicitly—shown a connection between the sacrifice of abstinence and precisely this last difference.[77] For them the preference accorded to present gratifications constitutes the principal reason why the foregoing of present gratifications or the waiting for them until the future is a "sacrifice" at all. The intensity of the preference varies widely from person to person, as is attested by that famous scale which ranges from the American Indian who will sell the ancestral hunting grounds for a dram of "firewater" to the sober, provident and educated scion of Europe's cultured peoples. The more intense the preference is, the greater is the resistance which that very preference opposes to the act of saving or to the accumulation of capital. And that resistance can be conquered only if and to the extent that the "sacrifice" which the conquest entails is appropriately rewarded by interest. And that establishes a relationship between the intensity of the preference and the rate of interest. To express it in terms of the older abstinence theory, let us say then that the actual driving force is that differential which is represented in our example by the relationship "15 minus 10." While I deliberately chose figures that are in themselves excessive, the point is that they represent true magnitude of a future utility minus present discounted undervaluation of that same utility.

At this point Carver begins to blaze an entirely different trail. As I mentioned before, the existence of that psychological fact is likewise recognized by him and expressly noted. But the abstinence which demands remuneration is not to be found, Carver reasons, in that fact, but elsewhere. Saving admittedly means that present goods are transferred to the future and will yield utility then. But as long as that utility enjoys even a present valuation which exceeds that which the savings could have yielded if they had been consumed immediately, just so long is it impossible to claim that saving has entailed any true sacrifice. In other words, up to that point accumulation of capital has taken place "at no cost" and therefore requires no interest as compensation for any sacrifice.[78] No real sacrifice begins until there is an obligation or a compulsion to continue the saving beyond that limit. For if, in our example, still more goods are to be withheld from present enjoyment and turned over to the future, then it can only be at a price. Indeed, the price is twofold. In the first place, the satisfying of wants in the present must end with wants which possess an importance which still just attains the magnitude denoted by our number 10. In the second place, the stratum of wants which register between 10 and 11 in importance must be denied satisfaction. But now let us suppose that these very goods, the last to be withdrawn from service in the present, are then "pieced on," as it were, to the most recent supply constituting provision for the future. Furthermore, it must be recalled that it was by virtue of the saving "at no cost" that this supply was just adequate for the satisfaction of wants presently valued at 10. It thereupon becomes clear that this new increment can be applied only to the satisfaction of still less important wants, such as those of the stratum which has an importance between 10 and 9. Thus, the continuation of the process of saving carries with it the consequence that a quantity of goods which would have yielded a marginal utility, in present consumption, of 10 to 11 will now yield a utility in the future corresponding to a present valuation between 10 and 9. That is to say, they will yield a smaller utility. And that difference represents a net loss resulting from the saving process, and is a genuine sacrifice caused by abstaining from present enjoyment. A sacrifice of this nature cannot and will not be made unless it is appropriately compensated for. And that compensation is interest. In Carver's own words, "The loss in the subjective valuation of this last increment must be compensated for by an increase in objective goods or interest."[79]

If the requirements of production could be met by no more than the small amount of capital which can be accumulated through that part alone of savings which demands no sacrifice, then there would be no interest at all (*p. 49*). But if more capital is needed, then interest must make its appearance. This "if" clause should be amplified to read "if a graduated system of utilizing all opportunities for profitable investment will permit the accommodation of more capital than that which is accumulated 'at no cost' without reducing the return on capital to zero." Carver's own words put it more briefly thus: "if more can be used and still afford profit at the margin." Interest must then appear because then someone, in order to provide those additional savings, must assume the sacrifice described above, the sacrifice of the subjective valuation of his savings. And that sacrifice demands compensation. And as a matter of fact the rate of interest is determined by "the marginal sacrifice of saving." The latter may perhaps be defined as that magnitude of sacrifice necessary to provide the last, the costliest part of the saving—a part which is required to satisfy the demands of production and the part which involves the greatest loss of subjective value.[80]

It is probably easy to see that Carver's explanation of the nature of the sacrifice of abstinence which requires compensation in the form of interest is quite different from that offered by the other abstinence theorists. The latter emphasize the fact that man, being what he is, finds waiting for gratification an irksome business. For Carver, on the other hand, the sacrifice stems not from the postponement of the gratification in and of itself, but from the further circumstance which is conditionally bound up with it, namely, the circumstance that the relation of demand to supply is so distorted by the situation with respect to savings, that a given quantity of goods may have a lower degree of marginal utility and a lower value in the future than it has in the present. Carver sees the nature of the sacrifice as consisting, not in the fact that the future gratification *is attained later* than is the competing present gratification, but that it *is smaller*. This difference in nature may be visualized by once more using the figures of our former illustration. The intensity of the earlier force, as has been remarked, would be expressed by the relation 15 minus 10, that is, by the difference between the true magnitude of a future gratification and the present valuation thereof. The magnitude of Carver's sacrifice of abstinence is measured by the relation 11 minus 9, which is entirely different from the first, and which arises from completely different causes. Carver's measure is supplied by the difference between the last use realized in the present and the present valuation of the last use realized in the future.

But there is another thing which can also be seen easily, and that is that Carver has mistakenly regarded as the *cause* of interest one circumstance which is purely an *effect* of it. All the facts that Carver advances are quite in order, and that even includes the matter of the diminution of marginal utility[81] which occurs in the event that a future time is more richly endowed with funds than is the present. But Carver makes the error of transposing cause and effect. It is not correct to say that because the future is more richly endowed, interest comes into being; nor to say that in such degree as that endowment is enhanced, the rate of interest becomes progressively higher. The correct statement reads just the other way round. We must already know of the factual existence of interest before we can be attracted by any economic inducement into endowing the future with more of our present goods. And the higher the interest rate, the greater are the lengths to which we can go and shall go in increasing that endowment of the future. In the event that and for the reason that the interest rate is 5%, we shall have a sound motive for increasing the endowment to such a point that it will require 105 units of next year's goods to yield the same degree of utility as do 100 units of present goods. If and also because the interest rate is 20%, it will be permissible to increase still further our endowment of the future, up to the point where it requires 120 units of next year's goods to give a utility equal to that of 100 units of present goods. And so on. But it is understood that we are speaking throughout in terms of present valuation.

As for the *origination* of interest, on the other hand, it is obvious and indubitable that some contribution has been made to it by the psychological factor which the other abstinence theorists considered to be the essence of the sacrifice of abstinence. Let us continue to assume that people have so strong a preference for immediate gratification over future satisfactions that in their present valuation they rate a future gratification of an effective magnitude of 15 as no more than equal to a present gratification possessing a magnitude of 10. If that is so, then the situation is certainly well adapted to furnish the real *cause* which effects the result, that goods produced for the future attain and maintain a value in excess of their cost. For under these conditions the producers cannot be willing to assume costs amounting to any greater magnitude than 10, in order to acquire a product which, though it will some day have a value of 15, is rated in the present valuation of the producers at a value no higher than 10. The performance of the process of production results, after the expiration of one year, in a product which then has a value of 15. Since the producer needs to offset against that value a cost of production amounting to only 10, the automatic result is a surplus value—that is to say, interest—in the amount of 5. Now that surplus, be it well noted, ensues even in the complete absence of any collaboration on the part of Carver's sacrifice of abstinence. And it must ensue, provided no greater quantity of goods is transferred to the future than will permit the unit of goods, *in terms of present valuation,* to be employed both in the present and in the future at the same marginal utility of 10.

And not even competition would effect the cancellation of that surplus, for under the given conditions such a result would be prevented by the very forces responsible for the occurrence of the surplus. There would be no necessity for any intervention by Carver's sacrifice of abstinence. Let us suppose, by way of illustration, that a temporary increase in production depressed the objective value of the product in question from 15 to 14. Now, providing the same ratio of undervaluation of future goods were maintained, this figure 14 would be considered the equivalent, in present value, of an amount somewhat lower than 10, or about 9.3. Since we must continue our previous assumption that provision for present consumption is undertaken only down to a marginal utility of 10, we see it is obvious that to expend means on producing gratifications which are valued at only 9.3 is uneconomical behavior. Preference would first be accorded to an additional stratum of present wants, namely all those the importance of which registered below 10 but exceeded 9.3. Since these would receive preference over the less remunerative employment for the future, the consequence would be that a lesser quantity of means would be employed for future wants, and as a result of that, in turn, the production of temporally distant goods would be curtailed and hence, finally, the value of the latter would again be enhanced. This phenomenon would continue until the previous relationship were restored, namely the equivalence of an objective future value of 15 and a present marginal utility of 10. And the restoration of that relationship would mean the restoration of the surplus value in the amount of 5.

Once interest has been brought into existence by these truly creative forces, the phenomenon which is its logical consequence will also make its appearance, and people will endow the future more copiously than they would have done, had there been no interest. And that, again, provokes the diminution, which Carver observed, in the future marginal utility, in terms of present valuation—a diminution to a point below present marginal utility of the unit of the good. Which is of course not the same thing as saying a diminution of the real marginal utility which is, in the present, subject to normal *discount*. But it is a phenomenon which is the necessary sequel to the interest phenomenon itself. Possibly it may give rise to a secondary reaction which will have an effect on the rate of interest itself. But it must be well noted that such reaction will work toward a *reduction* of interest. And the medium through which it will operate to achieve that end will unquestionably be the increase in savings, and not by any means Carver's sacrifice of abstinence. Indeed, that sacrifice would necessarily follow exactly the opposite course, and *rise* as a result of an increase in savings—an increase which really means a very rich endowment of the future, and of which the consequence must be a very sharp reduction in the marginal utility of those very savings.

This brings up a point which permits me perhaps to throw as revealing a light as is possible on the error Carver committed. There is no denying the principle that the cause of interest is *scarcity* of capital, which is another way of saying that of the materials needed for the satisfaction of wants there is only a small quantity available for devotion to the future. But Carver, quite on the contrary, ascribes interest to an *abundance* of those means of satisfaction, to a sort of plethora of savings. Now Carver has been completely accurate with respect to the facts he has observed, but not with respect to their proper place in the sequence of cause and effect. The following analogy may serve to show that place most accurately. A rise in the value of gold currency due to a money stringency ordinarily tends to be checked by a secondary current which the rise itself sets in motion. For, as is well known, when money has high purchasing power, quantities of precious metals previously used for jewelry, tableware and the like, are attracted to the mint. This then brings about an increase in the supply of currency. Similarly, interest due to a scarcity of capital by its very existence sets in motion a secondary current which tends to limit the dimensions which the tide of interest will itself attain. The existence of interest carries with it a temptation to extend the act of saving beyond the limits at which, in the absence of interest, it would have ceased. But we cannot and may not say that the increase in the reminting of gold and silver objects is the driving force behind the rise in the value of money. No more can we or may we say that the increase in savings, caused by the existence of interest, or that the lowering of marginal utility suffered by savings as a mere concomitant of that existence, constitutes the prime force which causes interest and determines its rate.[82]

Insofar as the subject of "abstinence" enters into the explanation of interest at all, I feel compelled to say that in choosing between the older conception of the abstinence theory and this newer interpretation of Carver's, I must rate the older one as being at least relatively better. For the latter was at least an examination of the correct basic phenomenon, the one which is actually active as a primary factor in the origination of interest, even though the abstinence theory did represent an erroneous conception and presentation of the nature of that activity. But Carver, led astray as he was by an ingenious but erroneous combination of ideas, picked up the scent of a completely false trail, and so kept tracking down a purely concomitant and subsequent phenomenon, instead of the real cause of interest.*

It is interesting to note that Carver, like Macfarlane, considers my own theory of interest to be essentially an abstinence theory, but with an admixture of some features of the productivity theory. He merely thinks he is presenting my theory, amended to some extent in the interest of correctness, but primarily in a version that is easier to understand. His own words concerning my theory read, "With certain corrections, which will be noticed later, his theory may be regarded as correct; but it is to be hoped that the interest problem can be explained upon principles more easily understood by the average reader" (*op. cit., p. 44*). I find Carver's and Macfarlane's arguments, added to the brilliantly discriminating but for all that unconvincing commentaries of Jevons and Marshall to be highly instructive. They demonstrate the multiplicity of variations possible on a theme apparently so simple as the relationship of present and future. They also furnish support for my

---

* Translator's note: The following paragraph appeared as a footnote in the German original.

own conviction that it is not a display of needless pedantry on my part for me to decline, both in my critical presentation and in my positive theory to be content with vague and casual hints concerning the "prospectiveness" and "productiveness" of capital. They may explain why I insist that these ideas bear the stamp of utter definitiveness and that they have the clarity and precision of outline which alone will enable us to fit them into the structure of a truly cohesive, and factually and logically unassailable explanation of our phenomenon.

5. *Remuneration Theories*

IN CHAPTER X of this treatise I had pointed out three variants of the remuneration theory which differed from one another in essential features. The first of these, represented in the earlier period by James Mill and McCulloch, has not, as far as I know, enlisted any new followers in recent times, and may therefore fairly be considered an exploded theory.[83]

The second or "French" variant, which regards interest as compensation for the morally commendable "labor of saving" has, so far as I have been able to perceive, recruited no new adherents, though it may not have lost any of the old ones in the narrow circle where it commanded any allegiance at all.

The third variant is the one which claims that the explanation of interest lies in regarding it as a sort of "emolument of office" which is paid to capitalists to whom society entrusts the office of accumulating capital and directing production. With respect to this variant there is at least one notable event of recent times which deserves to be recorded. It concerns Adolf Wagner, whom I had provisionally assigned to this group. After some initial vacillation he seems to have decided to support the tenets of the remuneration theory, inasmuch as they furnish a justification of interest. But he goes beyond that and espouses them as a theoretical explanation of interest, even citing them in support of my own theory. They contain the ideas, he says, from which may be derived the material necessary for the consummation of the explanation offered by my theory. That theory he pronounces to be "on the whole successful" although "in need of being perfected."[84]

In the meantime this same variant of the remuneration theory was adopted by Stolzmann[85] who prepared a detailed substantiation of it. Since Stolzmann's theory contains some original features, and at the same time presents what is certainly the most careful and coherent elaboration this principle has yet enjoyed, it might be in order to devote to it a reasonably thorough presentation and evaluation.

Stolzmann's point of departure is the theory of value. He advocates a peculiarly modified version of it, to which he himself gives the name "labor cost theory."[86] The exchange value of goods is determined, by and large, by their labor costs. This does not mean, as Ricardo and the socialists teach us, by the labor expended on the products, in and of itself. Nor does it mean, as some other theorists used to teach—and still do—by the magnitude of the disutility or trouble connected with the labor. On the contrary, labor determines exchange value "because it demands compensation and to the extent it demands it," and the determinant is "therefore not really labor itself" but the wages of labor (*p. 335*). There is however a second fundamental premise to Stolzmann's system. And that is that wages, like any sort of distribution at all, are determined by the balance of power held by the respective groups of our society. The worker must live. For each temporal interval of his existence he requires a certain quantum of the means of subsistence. Now Stolzmann uses that term in its very widest possible sense, and bestows upon it the name "unit of subsistence." He considers this concept to be of extraordinary importance, and looks upon it as an indispensable constituent element in the formation of goods and the determination of their value. Proceeding from an acceptance of the generally widespread opinion that the wants of different individuals are incommensurable,[87] he goes on to reason that the value of goods cannot therefore be derived from, or determined by those wants; but rather that "here, as throughout all science, the whole human being and the integral mass of his wants must be regarded as the one immediate comprehensible unit of value" (*p. 264*). The process of determining values proceeds as follows. The first step is that the relative command of social power determines the magnitude of the unit of subsistence that the worker can obtain for himself. That magnitude conforms to no physiological or other naturally established law, but is the result of a social struggle. In that conflict no purely economic condition, but rather the amount of power possessed, determines what standard of living the worker can establish for himself, and decides how large an allotment of the means of subsistence he can wrest for himself. Then from the magnitude of the unit of subsistence which is to be received as wages, is derived the exchange value of the individual products in accordance with the following simple rule. A product is always worth as many units of subsistence as its production has cost in corresponding units of labor or aliquot parts thereof. Stolzmann suggests the working day as one conceivable unit of labor.

Stolzmann first develops this law of labor cost for a hypothetical primitive prototypical society. He imagines a social group of 10 persons who obtain the means of satisfying their 10 collective human wants, in other words their 10 units of subsistence, through division of labor and in accordance with a common economic plan. The members are all equally industrious and equally skillful, and each one devotes himself to the production of one of the 10 kinds of good which comprise a complete communal unit of subsistence. Each one pursues the necessary steps of production from beginning to end, each one works for the same length of time, and each one completes 10 pieces of the product. Under these conditions, says Stolzmann, distribution can and will take place according to just one pattern. The total product will necessarily be distributed among the 10 individual associates in such a way that each one will receive for the complete labor unit he has contributed to the production, one full and equal unit of subsistence. And that unit will consist of 10 pieces of the communal product, each set of 10 comprising one example each of the 10 different kinds of good produced. And these individual pieces of the product, being created by equal quotas of labor units, also represent equal quotas of units of subsistence. Therefore they would be exchanged on a basis of exact equality, if any formal exchange took place at all. Why so, do you ask? Why, because under the conditions depicted, all 10 associates possess equal power, and none of them is in a position where he must submit to compulsion. Instead, each of them would have at his command an effective countermove in the possible event that his associates attempted to restrict him to a smaller unit of subsistence or to compensate him on a more unfavorable scale for the products he had completed. He could simply threaten to "desert."[88]

Stolzmann's law of labor costs, being thus rendered plausible for a "prototypical society," is then by transference made applicable to a fully developed national economy, after making allowances for some modifications which now become necessary. Distribution becomes a far more complicated problem. One reason is that the unit of subsistence cannot be "assembled" from its component elements with quite the same ease of simplicity. It must first be arrived at via complicated processes of exchange. Another reason is that the workers are no longer the sole participants, but find beside them the capitalists and landowners competing to become participants. But the nature of the process of distribution remains the same. Stolzmann repeatedly, and with all the emphasis at his command, rejects the idea that each of the factors in production is remunerated with a share of the total product proportionate to its contribution to the creation of that product. It must follow, then, that he denies the possibility that technological or economic factors may determine how the shares are apportioned in the distribution process. Nor could anything else be expected in a work upon which the author has so advisedly bestowed the title of *Die soziale Kategorie*. For he devotes his entire book to a proof of the thesis that it is *not* purely economic forces but rather the condition that prevails with respect to the balance of social power, which governs decisively the question of present day distribution of goods.

On page 41 we read, *"Power alone* and the laws of distribution prescribe how large or small shall be the share received." And on page 341 f., "Computing what technical contribution nature makes as a factor in distribution *leads to results totally different* from those derived by reckoning her social influence and her effect on income." On page 338 we read, "It matters relatively little what a factor in the physical manufacture of a product contributes. What the owner of that factor can and must receive as his remunerative share of the proceeds in return for allowing it to be used—that is the thing that decides how great his share in the distribution shall be." The value of the total product is not distributed in accordance with a mathematical computation of the fractions which the various factors in production have contributed to the fabrication of that total product. No, it is distributed among the owners of the three factors "in accordance with *an entirely different* principle, namely, that of the balance of social power" (*p. 61*).

That distribution takes place as follows. The worker wants and needs his "worker's unit of subsistence." Whether it is large or small does not depend, as other economists teach us, on the productive effect of his labor, but on the "prevailing relationship among the social categories; the worker's previous mode of living, his power, the urgency of his demands, and the respect which in his day and age is accorded him as a fellow human being, the prevailing conception of human dignity and the current respect for the mandates of ethics and of religion"—all these determine the amount of wages that shall be his prize of battle (*p. 334*). But the capitalist, too, wants to live. He, too, needs and wants a "capitalist's unit of subsistence." And the magnitude of that, just as in the case of the worker's unit, is determined by conditions of social and educational power. Stolzmann cites as examples thereof the cultural standard set for his class, the compass of wants dictated by fashion, educational preparation for membership in the capitalist group, the degree of cooperation among capitalists through associations, coalitions and syndicates, and even the application of pressure to bring about governmental action (*p. 371 ff.*). And indeed, the rate of capital earnings is determined by the minimal necessaries which fill the framework of these social considerations for the "last," that is to say, the least important capitalist. Or let us put it into other words. Given the prevailing ratio of borrowed to fully owned capital, it is then necessary that capital return such a percentage as will provide the smallest capitalist with the unit of subsistence appropriate to his station. In this connection "smallest" means the marginal member of the stratum of entrepreneur capitalists who is only just able to meet competition under prevailing conditions of ownership and production, and yet is indispensable to the providing of society's productional requirements.

Thus are determined the elements out of which a fully developed national economy constructs the exchange value of its products. The exchange value of goods becomes stabilized at such a level as is requisite to compensate for the labor expended in their production, in accordance with the scale of wages which the workers have succeeded in putting into effect. That level must also provide, as remuneration for the participating capital, the rate of return necessary to cover the capitalist's unit of subsistence. But the landowner's position is that of "residual claimant." He receives as his land rent "that portion of the yield which still remains after deduction of the first two fixed contractual charges from the total value of the product, and which is payable to the landowner in accordance with the validity of his claim to ownership of the land" (*p. 411*).

The theory of value that Stolzmann presents here considers the source of value to lie in elements, one being labor and its wages, the other being the *services of capital,* which require compensation. How then can he still call it a *labor* cost theory? The answer is, by declaring the activity of the capitalists, which receives its remuneration in the form of interest, to be a kind of labor. And that is what Stolzmann does. At the very end of his systematic presentation he refers to his conception of interest as a "socially necessary reward for the socially necessary functions of accumulating capital and employing capital." He characterizes it as a view which is "not new" and in its essence one that coincides with that conception which I previously described as the German variant of the remuneration theory. Stolzmann puts his stamp of approval on a statement he cites from Adolph Wagner, according to which the "labor" which represents the cost of production also includes the necessary services of the private capitalist and the private entrepreneur. And Stolzmann adds the explicit statement that, whereas Wagner bases on that thought merely a social justification of interest, he himself makes it the foundation of an actual theory of interest.[89] This final statement is a logically indispensable conclusion of the entire system by which he builds up his theory. But it is also something which he apparently did not succeed in keeping constantly in mind throughout the entire course of his book. Statements do appear which convey the idea that the labor costs which determine value consist of nothing but the quotas of labor which the workers—in the narrower sense of that term—are obligated to perform in return for their "worker's units of subsistence."[90] However, it seems to me that his real opinion finds expression, not in statements like these, which contradict his basic principle, but rather in his elevation of the services of the capitalist to the status of labor—which, since it *is* labor, needs to be remunerated.

I believe that Stolzmann's doctrine is open throughout to numerous objections. The strictures which, at points that I deemed appropriate, I have already levelled at remuneration theories in general, and which naturally are aimed no less at the Stolzmann version, I have no wish to repeat here once more at great length. I shall therefore confine myself to indicating a few of the most glaring weaknesses which afflict Stolzmann's formulation of the remuneration theory in particular.

To begin with, the fundamental basis of his whole theory of value, his law of labor cost, is completely untenable. It is Stolzmann's purpose to endow his fundamental theory with plausibility, and his attempt to do so consists in an illustration which depicts a "prototype" of society, designed by himself with the expectation that it will furnish what must strike us as an absolutely obvious and, so to speak, as the one and only possible basis of the creation of value. But in doing so he commits an error which becomes interesting in the sidelight cast on it by another event. It so happens that he had just previously—and quite justifiably —taken Ricardo to task in connection with the latter's labor theory of value. Ricardo had derived his law from the same sort of arbitrarily constructed example of a prototypical society. Stolzmann criticized his oversight in failing to recognize that the coinciding of value with quantity of labor employed was brought about only by the fortuitous circumstances prevailing in the arbitrarily chosen illustration (*p. 34 f.*). Yet in the same breath Stolzmann perpetrates the very same blunder. For he sets up a threefold hypothesis; he assumes, first, that all the associates in that primitive society are equally industrious, second, that they are all equally skillful, and third, that they devote themselves to production for equally long periods of time.[91] By so doing he has eliminated from the conditions present in the example all factors which could have caused the values of the products to lose their correspondence, not only to the Ricardian "quantities of labor," but also to the labor costs of Stolzmann. Likewise, he removed all possibility that his factors might evince any tendency to conform to a "standard" differing from his own.

And for this very reason Stolzmann's key to the problem of distribution, like Ricardo's is only a "fortuitous peculiarity of this special hypothesis," but not a generally valid theoretical discovery. If Stolzmann had introduced some unequally skillful or unequally industrious associates into his hypothesis, he could have convinced himself with celerity and certainty that even in the absence of any factor of compulsion, it is not always possible to attain completely equal worker's units of subsistence. And he would have seen that at least a very considerable part of what Stolzmann disposed of by tossing it into the maws of his "power," is really derived from nothing less than the economic efficiency of the particular production factor concerned. The truth about the threat of desertion is easy to penetrate as is also the reason for it. Obviously there is far less "compulsion" in the threat of a lazy or a clumsy worker to "desert" if his associates do not grant him a generous unit of subsistence than there is in the same threat on the part of a worker who is skillful and industrious!

The same situation obtains with respect to the varying length of the time interval which extends from the time work begins until its matured fruits may be garnered. Someone has to "wait out" that stretch of time. Of course, in Stolzmann's primitive society labor cost is the key to his riddle, and there is no necessity for giving consideration to this time interval—a consideration which might have made it very difficult to turn the key. The very simple reason is that for all types of labor and for all categories of product the period of time is assumed to be equal. It therefore is no factor, being an automatic and reciprocal offset. It is quite evident, however, that Stolzmann cannot assume, and does not claim to assume, that such equality of time intervals occurs in real life. It is particularly out of the question to assume, without ado, that it could occur to a degree so nearly complete that it might be regarded as typical of the normal case, and as a foundation for universally valid laws. Nor is it any more permissible for Stolzmann to assume without proof that a difference in the time interval, when it does actually occur, has no bearing on the question of the imputation of value. And yet that is the very thing that Stolzmann does assume.

He discusses the question on page 303 of his book, where he expresses the opinion that labor "previously performed" and labor "subsequently performed" are "of the same nature," that the difference is "only" a temporal one, and that such difference (in his primitive society) does not "exercise any perceptible influence on value and distribution." The labor "invested" is in both cases the same, and hence, for purposes of distribution, labor previously performed must be put on the same footing as labor subsequently performed. The only part that time can play at all in the *imputation* of value and in distribution is as *labor* time, inasmuch as "the values distributable to the individual workers must be quantities of units of subsistence which are expressible in terms of multiples or aliquot parts of the time *occupied with performance of the individual tasks or labors.*" And it makes no difference whether these tasks are performed as previous labor or as subsequent labor.

In my opinion all that is sheer presumption, and presumption that flies in the face of the facts. It reminds one of the similar and unproven statements by which Marx denies the thesis that waiting time is capable of exercising any influence at all.[92] And in the cases of both writers it constitutes, in identical fashion, a *petitio principii* in favor of the principle of value which they themselves invoke.[93]

To my mind Stolzmann perpetrated a violation of the essential nature of things by distorting what is undeniably income based on ownership into remuneration of labor. But after all the deficiencies of that kind which I have already laid at the door of the remuneration theories in general, it is hardly necessary for me to repeat myself here.

Stolzmann's one final, obvious and unqualified blunder seems to me to be his attempt to assign to his "capitalist's unit of subsistence" a determinative or causative rôle in the process of ascribing and distributing value. If there is any one thing in this entire subject under discussion which is not a cause, but rather an effect of the existence of interest and of its rate, then that one thing is the capitalists' standard of living. There is no such thing as a minimum property standard with respect to which one can say there is a technological or other socio-economic requirement that it provide its owner with an *income from capital* sufficient to maintain him in accordance with a certain standard of living. An economy needs capital—yes! If, and as long as the accumulation of capital is accomplished principally through the activity of private individuals, that economy needs capitalists—agreed! But by no manner of means does it require that any person or persons be maintained in accordance with some particular standard of living, *exclusively on income derived from capital earnings!* If a person has too little capital of his own to live on the income from it in the manner demanded by his station in life, there is no urgent necessity for him to withdraw from that station. If that were true, then we should designate the position of the unemployed "gentleman of independent means" as a special "station"! Certainly no claim can be advanced that there is an inexorable economic need of such a station! Nor is the collector of insufficient dividends condemned to termination of his economic existence. He can always eke out what is inadequate for meeting his claims in full by making demands— or increased demands—on his personal industriousness. That is what the owner of a small capital does, who looks for a "sideline" or supplementary occupation—be it as a physician, or in civil service, or even in domestic service. And the same thing is done by an employer who does not limit himself to being the armchair executive of his establishment, but takes an active hand in the very work itself, performing the duties of a manager, a foreman or a simple journeyman and thus he acts as his own employee, earning a salary or, if you prefer, wages.

Stolzmann did not fail to keep in mind a veritable profusion of difficulties which beset the path of one who would advance his doctrine of the determinative unit of subsistence payable to the last capitalist. Among the considerations arrayed against him he had to contemplate the following:

That capitalists—and indeed especially the smallest capitalists—are at the same time people who do not necessarily have to live solely on the income from their capital, since they may also be mechanics, laborers, civil servants and the like;

That the term capitalist and the term employer do not necessarily coincide;

That the inactive investor is not a social necessity;

That one may regard not the capitalist, but rather the entrepreneur who employs capital productively as the determining individual; in which case the entrepreneur does not by any means confine his employment of capital to that which he himself owns; the result of all of which is, that the amount of capital owned by the last (or least) entrepreneurs is not at all identical with the amount of capital employed in the last enterprise;

That there are many other similar stumbling blocks.

And in fact, he not only passes these difficulties in review, after having himself summoned them before us, but he accompanies that action with a very lively recognition of their seriousness. The confession is wrested from him that when he contemplates his problem in the full glare of reality, he finds his theory "opposed by quite insuperable difficulties." He admits, too, there is an especially stubborn obstacle that threatens one principle which forms a cornerstone of his theory. He is referring to the relation of his objective factor to his subjective factor, the relationship between the factor of production, capital, and the personal possessor of it, the capitalist. And of this relationship he concedes that it "either is not present at all, or is only very incidental and highly tenuous."

In treating this theme more in detail he expresses the opinion that one of the difficulties lying in his way "is quite serious," in fact that at first blush it appears "almost annihilating." Still another one causes him "almost to despair" of the correctness of his theory, and yet another puts his theory in an "absurd" light. And thus he continues. But in spite of all that, Stolzmann thinks himself capable of picking his way through this multitude of towering obstructions by means of a chart depicting a system of devious explanations and hazardous inferences. But they are explanations which make me sense that Stolzmann is defending a concept which could hope to meet approval only in the eyes of one whose predilection for it were as intense as that of the author himself. And so I feel that a running and detailed critique of Stolzmann's explanations is not indispensable. But I should like to single out one point and comment in some detail upon it, because of some rather recent remarks by Stolzmann on the topic.

In the second edition of this book I had expressed an assumption which proved to be erroneous. That assumption concerned the person Stolzmann had in mind when he spoke of the last, that is to say, the "least" of the entrepreneur capitalists, the one still just able to meet competition. I thought he was assigning this rôle to, say, artisans or persons whose livelihood is derived not solely from income on their capital, but from a combination of income on capital and earnings by their own labors. And out of the materials of that supposition I had fashioned the barbs of controversy which I aimed at Stolzmann. His reply was an authentic interpretation in which he makes it plain that artisans and all people "who *also* work with capital" are to be unequivocally excluded from his concept of the "last capitalist." He went on to say that "capitalists," in his sense of the word, means only those entrepreneur capitalists in whose enterprises the employment of capital constitutes its "essential foundation." They are the persons who, as proprietors of "purely capitalist enterprises," can so perform their function in the market that they must be looked upon as "powerful" and "determinative." Such capitalists, moreover, would at the most "in exceptional cases, and when bad times have forced them to dismiss their managers, themselves take over the executive function." But ordinarily they would perform no actual labor in their own enterprises. For a "capitalist" does not "work" and does not draw "wages." The idea of anyone's receiving wages from the business he himself owns is a contradiction in terms, and an "absurdity."[94]

I trust I may be permitted to designate this marginal capitalist by an expression that Stolzmann did *not* use, but which expresses the matter clearly, if somewhat oddly. If I am correct in my understanding of Stolzmann's authentic interpretation, this capitalist could be defined as "the least among the very great" and the capitalist who, by his standard of living, dictates the rate of interest. Capital must yield such and such a percentage, so that the "least" among the entrepreneur capitalists, as defined above, may live on a scale befitting his station and *"on interest exclusively."*[95] There is to be no additional income for him by virtue of any labor he performs, because for a capitalist, by definition, wages are strictly barred.

It is difficult to imagine how any opponent of Stolzmann's, whose desire it might be to reduce his theory to an absurdity, could have presented it in a manner better calculated to accomplish just that, than the one Stolzmann himself adopted for these emphatically couched elucidations. He certainly sounds as if he were making ironical allusions to the theory of marginal utility, and were borrowing a concept out of the system of thought contrived by its adherents. There is just such a ring to the phrase he fashioned—his "least and smallest capitalist," and an ironic sound to the invitation to seek him in the ranks of the "big men" among capitalists! But the main thing is that his epigrammatic summary makes it so very clear, how justly he deserved my disapprobation when I charged him with mistaking cause for effect, and effect for cause. Even the idea that forms the basis of Stolzmann's theory of distribution, that is, his "socially necessary unit of subsistence" seems to me a violation of the very nature of things and an instance, from start to finish, of placing the cart before the horse. The fact that people maintain a certain standard of living is the *result* of the process of distribution and not its elucidating *cause*. It is not correct to say that because people are under the "social necessity" of living on a certain scale, therefore the factors of production which they possess yield enough for them to maintain that standard. Quite on the contrary, there is a cause inherent in the fact that their production factors obtain compensation for them at a given level in accordance with certain laws. The effect consists in the ability of the people behind those factors to achieve a certain standard of living, and to become accustomed to it as the one suitable to their station. As for the laws I mentioned, enlightenment concerning them constitutes the very essence of the problem of distribution.

And this relationship of cause and effect is applicable even to the wages of labor. That is something which is becoming ever clearer to us, although wages are the very thing which might most readily have appeared in just the opposite light. Yet it is generally recognized that even with respect to the wages of labor modern economic science is no longer willing to accept Ricardo's laws of the "natural" wages of labor, sanctioned as necessary in accord with considerations of station and custom. The reason is that the experiences which we have since accumulated have furnished increasingly convincing evidence that Ricardo's law, insofar as it is exemplified at all in our factual environment, reverses the relationship of cause and effect. Wages do not rise if and because workers become accustomed to an improved standard of living. On the contrary, they become accustomed to a higher standard of living if and because wages—for quite different reasons—have been high for a considerable period. And the task of discovering the reasons which account for the rise is the very problem the wage theory has to solve.[96]

This error of transposition is strikingly apparent in the case of income from capital. Probably no effort could be more completely futile than an attempt to persuade us that capital bears interest, and especially some particular rate of interest, for the reason that Stolzmann offers. That reason is, I repeat, that there is a social necessity for the existence of people who, as owners of business enterprises, retain salaried managers and nevertheless are able to live on interest alone, in a manner befitting the station of an exalted capitalist. To anyone not completely prejudiced it is clear that the opposite is true. There can be people of that kind solely because capital has yielded an income for which the activity of certain factors has been responsible. It is the task of economic theory to discover the reasons why that is so. In the process of investigating those reasons it will probably be necessary to discuss certain facts, the quality of which is partly natural, partly technological. Now Stolzmann makes every possible effort to relegate those facts to the back-

409

ground—such facts as the higher physical productivity of methods which employ larger amounts of capital, and the like. But it will prove to be necessary to discuss those questions much more thoroughly than the one about the highly dubious "social necessity" which requires the existence of certain "least" ones among the independent entrepreneurs who nevertheless can live without any personal participation in labor, and solely on their interest.

I am loath to conclude without mentioning that some of Stolzmann's individual observations often make a certain appeal because of their refreshingly original features, and because they bear such manifest testimony to his zealous bent for research. But, as the foregoing pages indicate, I am compelled to the conclusion that the positive results which his findings contribute to the field of economic theory are of such questionable adequacy that they hardly seem destined to exert any far-reaching influence on the history of interest theories.

6. *Motivated Productivity Theories,* *with Particular Reference to Wieser*

AMONG economic theorists of recent—yes, even most recent—times there is no inconsiderable number who are adherents of a *motivated productivity theory*. Some are its forthright champions, others accept it on eclectic grounds. Without making any pretensions to completeness I submit here a number of names that belong in this category. There is a group of writers using Romance languages of whom I should like to mention Maurice Block,[97] Pantaleoni[98] and Landry;[99] another group consists of such Anglo-Americans as Francis Walker,[100] J. B. Clark[101] and Seager;[102] and of writers of German we may list Philippovich,[103] Diehl,[104] Julius Wolf,[105] Wieser,[106] Gebauer,[107] Engländer,[108] Bundsmann,[109] and Karl Adler.[110] Then there is Dietzel,[111] who employs a peculiar method of eclecticism by which he hopes to use the exploitation theory for his explanation of some of the manifestations of the interest phenomenon, but nevertheless holds in reserve the productivity theory to take care of the rest.

This class includes a number who, to my way of thinking, should be grouped together and given a special listing of their own. For while they do more or less expressly designate theirs as a "productivity theory," they derive interest from the productivity of capital via channels so closely akin to the more modern lines of thought laid down by the agio theory that, so far as subject matter goes, their doctrines are closer to that theory than they are to the productivity theories of the old order. Nor should we wonder at the occurrence of that variant of the productivity theories. For the fundamental fact that ordinarily goes under the name of the "productivity of capital" is really the higher physical productivity of capitalist methods of production. And it is a matter of general knowledge that the agio theory avails itself of that feature too, and in fact does so to such an extent that it has frequently been described, by protagonists as well as antagonists, as one kind of productivity theory.[112]

The tendency so to describe the agio theory seems to be more mark-edly evident among those writers named in the foregoing list whose books bear the imprint of more recent dates of publication. This may certainly be said of the theories of Clark, Seager, Landry, Bundsmann and Karl Adler. Perhaps we might also include Philippovich who, at least in the most recent editions of his well-known and widely distributed textbook, has exhibited a perceptible tendency to be drawn into the orbit of the agio theorists' system of thought.

Most of the other offerings keep within the bounds respected by any typical productivity theory or else overstep them to so slight a degree that a detailed presentation and critique of them would be impossible without subjecting my readers to wearisome repetitions of thought processes already quite familiar.[113] I think the only one which merits special investigation is a theory by Wieser which is notable for its marked individuality.

Wieser has earned the lasting gratitude of economic science by his penetrative research into the broader outlines of the relation between the value of capital goods and that of their products.[114] We are also indebted to him for his incomparably pellucid presentation of one particular point. When we are required, says Wieser, to ascribe to each of several factors collaborating in the making of a common product their appropriate shares, it is one problem to give the answer in physical terms, but an entirely different one to present a solution in economic terms. But, adds Wieser, it cannot be said one or the other problem is insoluble, either in practice or in theory.[115] He plies a somewhat less felicitous hand, it seems, in his development of the positive phase of the solution he essays, particularly in the application of his imputation (*Zurechnung*) theory to the explanation of interest. I believe the main reason for this is his failure, in this particular instance, to remain completely faithful to his own theoretical assumptions. Wieser allowed the course of his inquiry to veer over to an idea which does not parallel his own solution but cuts obliquely and obstructively athwart the other premises of his imputation theory.

In drawing up his exemplary pattern of the problem of imputation Wieser chooses a twofold point of departure. The first is that the share of the economic burden which is assumed by each of the collaborating factors, and which Wieser entitles its "productive contribution" can be ascertained and segregated. The second is that the value of capital goods is derived from the magnitude of this "contributed" share of the proceeds. This derivation takes place in such manner that the aggregate value of the product is distributed over the aggregate of the capital goods collaborating in its production. It may be remarked parenthetically that this aggregate value is determined in accordance with the "marginal law."[116] It is further to be noted that, while the share of each single factor is based on the magnitude of its own "productive contribution," the sum total of all productive contributions must be exactly equal to the value of the product.[117]

There is no need for a discussion at this point of the ways and means by which, according to Wieser's views, the magnitude of each individual factor is to be ascertained.[118] Important as that question may be in the case of other problems, it is quite irrelevant to the solution which Wieser is attempting to find for the problem of interest specifically. Suffice it to remember that the solution Wieser offers is organized on the basis that products arise, as a general thing, through the collaboration of land, capital and labor, and that to each of these three factors—and hence to capital also—a certain part of the product is to be attributed as its productive contribution. Does the shell of that contribution conceal the kernel of net interest? In Wieser's opinion, which I think is certainly correct in this particular, the answer to that question does not depend at all on whether or not the productive contribution of capital, as compared with that of land or of labor, is estimated to be larger or smaller. It depends entirely on processes which take place within the confines, as it were, of that share of the final product which may be ascribed to capital. The manner of that proceeding is as follows.

Every capital produces an immediate and direct yield called *gross return,* that is, a return which is secured at the cost of a diminution of the substance of the capital.[119] Wieser defines the conditions under which such a gross return may become the source of a net return by stipulating that all parts of the capital which have been consumed must be renewed and replaced. If there is then a surplus still remaining, that surplus may be called net return. Moreover, with respect to that surplus and to the "productivity of capital" which has been directed towards its creation, it is necessary to discriminate nicely between two groups of entities. The first of these is composed of the *physical* surplus and a *physical productivity* on the part of capital. The other comprises the *surplus value* and a *productivity of value* on the part of capital. Anyone who makes any pretensions to a solution of the problem of interest must in the last analysis prove and explain that capital possesses *productivity of value.* The necessary entering wedge for arriving at that proof is furnished by an antecedent proof that capital possesses *physical* productivity.[120] Accordingly Wieser proceeds with his explanation in two stages. During the first stage it is his aim to prove and explain that capital has physical productivity, by which is meant that "the quantity of goods yielded as a gross return exceeds the quantity of capital goods consumed in production." During the second stage he faces the problem of explaining why "the *value* of the gross return exceeds the *value* of the capital consumed."

He devotes the following exposition to a proof of the thesis which marks the first stage:

"The total return from all three factors of production, land, capital and labor, is undoubtedly large enough to replace the capital consumed and yield a net return. That is an economic fact which is a matter of common knowledge and does not require proof, any more than do such facts as the existence of goods or of production. It must be conceded that now and then an enterprise undertakes production and fails to recover the amount of its outlay; and it is even true that many an enterprise fails to turn out any useful product at all. But these are exceptions. The general rule is that net returns are registered; in fact, net returns attain such inordinately large volume, that they not only sustain the earth's population of well over a billion human beings, but in addition provide surpluses from which increases in capital are constantly being made. Hence there can be only one question, and that is whether a portion of this indubitable net return is to be imputed to the factor capital. But even that cannot be seriously regarded as disputable. Why should capital be singled out as the one not entitled to such a portion? Once it has been understood and admitted that capital is an economic factor of production which is included among the factors to which the result of production is imputed, then it is also understood and admitted that capital is entitled to a portion of the net return; for the result of production becomes apparent only as the embodiment of net return. Could it be possible for capital always to be capable of producing only a result that is somewhat less than a replacement of itself? Such an assumption would be patently arbitrary. Could it be possible for capital always to be capable of producing only a result that is just equal to a replacement of itself, no matter how variable the success which attended the processes of production? That assumption would patently be no less arbitrary. Anyone who denies capital a net return, can do so only if he denies it any return whatsoever."[121]

This is the point, I believe, at which Wieser started to go astray. For he allows himself the presupposition that it is possible to impute a net return or a portion of a net return directly to any one factor, and in so doing he has endowed the process of imputation with a power which, by its very nature, it cannot possibly possess. Let us close our ears to all beguiling words and stick to dry and sober facts. According to Wieser himself, what is the substance and the function of the imputation process?

It is the apportionment of the *total result of production* among the several factors contributing to the producing of it. In other words, it is the ascertainment of the portions contributed by the various factors to the attainment of a *gross product*. That is how Wieser repeatedly and unequivocally formulated the problem of imputation; that is how he clarified it by means of practical illustrations; and that is the understanding of it which we must perforce accept, if we are to apply the method he prescribes for ascertaining the imputed shares.[122] Consider his examples. In the case of a tin vessel he imputes the value of it to the labor of the artisan and the material of which it is fashioned;[123] in ascertaining the share of the farmer's produce which should be credited to the factor land, the total value of the produce is his starting point.[124] Furthermore, he lays down two principles. One is that the sum total of all contributions to production must be exactly equal to the value of the total product;[125] the other is that each factor derives its value from its respective productive contribution. All this makes it absolutely clear that what he distributes by his imputation process is—and can be—only the gross product, and more particularly that the productive contribution of the factor capital is not—and cannot be—anything except an aliquot part of that gross product.

Let us suppose that a farmer employs the services of "farmhands" and also of a capital consisting of seed, agricultural implements, fertilizer, livestock, and so on; let us further suppose he raises on his land a total crop (or product) of 330 bushels of grain. Here it is the function of the attributive process to determine what proportion of the 330 bushels the farmer owes to the farmhands who helped him, and what proportion to the agricultural capital which cooperated and which was partly consumed in the process. If, perchance, the considerations which determine that question should result in the assignment of an equal part in the raising of the produce to each of the three factors, then the productive contribution of each would be fixed at 110 bushels each. And in that case it would be quite clear that the 110 bushels imputed to capital represent an aliquot share of the gross product. Whether or not this share of the gross product contains within it any share of a net product, and whether, in similar fashion, the proportions of gross product imputed to land and to labor can, from any point of view at all, be considered to represent a net product—all those questions lie beyond the province of the imputation problem. They are problems in the solution of which the magnitude of the imputed shares of the gross product may perhaps be a relevant element—nay, even a supremely important element, but after all, only just one element. There are different and additional facts and considerations which influence the result without having anything at all to do with imputation. In our example imputation ends as soon as it has pronounced its decision that the farmer owes 110 bushels each to the collaboration of land, of labor, and of capital. Further than this, imputation has no say in the matter at all.

But Wieser, in spite of all that, thinks he can make it appear plausible that, by the process of imputation one can assign to capital even a share of the *net return*. It is as interesting as it is significant that his only way of establishing a point of contact for his exposition of this thesis is to use the term "net return" in a sense that is utterly misleading because Wieser was unconsciously practicing equivocation. "Undoubtedly" he says categorically in the passage already quoted, "the total return from all three factors of production, land, capital and labor, is large enough to *replace the capital consumed and yield a net return.*" That is certainly true, and for reasons quite easily understood. For the word "net return" as he uses it in this statement is the amount by which the total product derived from land, capital and labor exceeds the value of just the capital consumed alone. In other words, it is the amount by which the value of the product of *three* factors exceeds the value of *one* of those factors. But that three factors combined can produce more than the value of one of them is not only a very plausible matter, in and of itself, but is actually a self-evident matter, when viewed within the framework of such a theory as Wieser's. One of the principles on which he founds his theory is that the value of the product must equal the sum of the values of its factors. Under the conditions of such a theory the presence of that "net return" is axiomatic for the same reason and to the same degree as it is axiomatic for the whole to be greater than any of its parts. A full container must have not only a "gross weight" but also a "net weight" in addition to the weight of the empty container.

In general, it is customary to compute the net return from production by deducting from the gross return the value of the capital consumed. But this does not mean that an amount is similarly deducted for the consumption represented by use of land and by performance of labor. And the reasons for such difference in procedure are obvious. Moreover, it is well known that those reasons depend solely on the point of view which is taken by the observer who is appraising the results which attend the process of production. If the point of view changes, then the procedure will change with respect to including or omitting a deduction for the value of those two remaining factors of production. The entrepreneur, for instance, who purchases and pays for the labor of other persons will certainly take the position that it is, economically speaking, required of him to deduct the value of labor consumed from the gross return.[126] On the other hand, we may take the point of view of the so-called "national economist," as Wieser does when he refers to those "net returns of inordinately large volume" which sustain a population of well over a billion. If that is done, then the deduction has not been made. At the same time it must be entirely patent that the question of imputation has not the remotest connection with either the choice among the different possible points of view, or with the various corresponding methods of computing net return. How much of the gross return is attributable to the factor labor—that is one question and it is admittedly a question of imputation. Whether or not we must then deduct from the gross return the value of labor that is based on that imputation—that is a second question and one that is completely independent of the first and disparate from it.

Thus, then, we can describe the antecedents and the nature of Wieser's net return. Nonetheless he intends to use its existence as an entering wedge to open the way for his contention that capital, too, is entitled to have a specific net return imputed to it. His expression for it, in the passage cited above, is that the only question there can be is whether a part of that unquestionable net return is to be imputed to the factor capital. But even that, he says, cannot be seriously questioned. For "why should capital be singled out as the one not entitled to such a portion?"

The answer to this question is very simply this. What is called net return of capital just is not "that kind of" net return, but on the contrary a magnitude which must be quite differently defined, and which is dependent on completely different and, indeed, much more stringent conditions. It is true that a *net return of production,* from the point of view indicated above, is concededly present when the total gross return yielded by all three collaborating factors exceeds the value of the capital consumed. But a *net return of capital* is not present until the individual *aliquot share* which is attributed to capital out of the gross return exceeds the capital consumed. And the existence of the first condition, by very reason of the radical difference in the presuppositions, leaves absolutely no ground for inferring the existence of the second. Indeed, it fails to justify even the faintest suspicion that either by analogy or by the laws of probability the second condition must or will obtain. It may be thoroughly understood and understandable that three men together are capable of lifting a load weighing more than does one of them. But the fact that three men together are capable of raising an "excess weight" exceeding the weight of one, does not give us the slightest reason to conclude that this one man alone would also be capable of lifting a weight exceeding his own. Perhaps he can. But anyone who makes that assertion, and particularly anyone who professes to explain it, will have to present some special reason, applicable to *that one person*. But it is absolutely impossible to discover or even to corroborate any such reason by means of citing the fact that three men together are capable of lifting more than the weight of one member of the trio!

Wieser has erected a precarious bridge of explanation by which he means to span the gap between net return in one sense and net return in the other sense. Should anything cause that bridge to collapse, then there is nothing left to his argument, no basis for an explanation of net return on capital. To the question, "Could it be possible for capital always to be capable of producing only a result that is somewhat less than a replacement of itself?" he answers, "Such an assumption would be patently arbitrary." And herein he is entirely correct. But then he goes on to ask, "Could it be possible for capital always to be capable of producing only a result that is just equal to a replacement of itself, no matter how variable the success which attended the processes of production?" And again he answers, "That assumption would patently be no less arbitrary." But now his position is no longer completely unassailable. For we might very well have such a situation as the following. The fortuitous variation in the degree of success attained might concededly result in such fluctuation in the amount of the yield from capital and the amount of capital consumed, that either might exceed the other by turns. And yet there could be a consistent and prevailing tendency for the two, *on the average,* to equal each other. Be it remembered, too, that the conditions of a theory like Wieser's make it a basic principle that the value of the factors of production is derived from the value of the product. Under those conditions the assumption could hardly be termed completely arbitrary.

But even granting that it were so, still the arbitrary character of the first two assumptions does not justify his conclusion. For he asserts that because of their arbitrariness, the third assumption must be true, and that capital therefore regularly produces more than its own replacement. But these are valid grounds neither for looking on his assertion as correct, nor for considering it justified nor, above all, for accepting it as an explanation. Though it were certainly arbitrary to assume that a man is always capable of lifting only *less* than his own weight; and though it be just as arbitrary to assume that he should be capable of lifting *just exactly* his own weight, no more and no less; yet it is certainly, in itself and until some additional positive reason is supplied, not one whit less arbitrary to assume that every man should be capable of lifting *more* than his own weight. If of three possible rules two are not capable of proof, it still does not follow by any means that the third rule must apply. It may very well be that the absence of any regularity at all still remains as an unexplored possibility. But let us even suppose that in the case before us we have recourse to something other than syllogisms of this kind. That is to say, suppose we know as a fact within our experience that the portion of the gross return attributable to capital exceeds the amount of capital consumed. Even in that case these syllogisms, in themselves quite inconclusive, certainly fail to cast a single ray of enlightening illumination on that fact, in the manner that it behooves and befits a theory of interest to shed light on our problem.

Nor is such light to be discovered in the pages that follow. Wieser hopes to present his general principle with complete persuasiveness by means of a concrete example, and he chooses for the purposes a machine which supplants manual labor. "In every instance in which labor is replaced by capital—for example, the case of a machine which performs a function previously carried out by human hands—there must be imputed to capital, that is to say, to the machine, at least the same proportion of the return as was previously imputed to labor. *But the latter was a net return, and therefore a net return must be deemed attributable to capital also.*"[127]

The reader, having already been put upon notice, will hardly need to be told again that here is a syllogism which rests upon the same weak foundation as its predecessor, namely on the equivocation which I have already censured and which is latent in Wieser's use of the term "net return." Indeed, the fallacy in this instance is even more blatant. The net return in Wieser's first sense, be it remembered, is derived *without* deducting the value of labor itself from that of what it produces. That kind of net return would be yielded even by an employment of labor which is unprofitable, uneconomic, incapable of covering labor costs and which consequently involves a loss for the entrepreneur. Such an employment of labor would be one, let us say, in which labor is consumed that has a value of $100 and yet adds a value of only $50 to the raw material processed. But who would accept the conclusion at which we arrive by the Wieser method of reasoning? He argues that even where *this sort of labor* is replaced by a capital which is equally or slightly more productive, there is attributable to such capital not only a gross return, but a net return as well. The reason Wieser offers is that at least the same return must be imputed to it as was imputed to the labor it replaces, and that was a "net return"!

Subsequently Wieser expounds at length and in a manner reminiscent of Thünen, the considerations[128] by which he hopes to lend plausibility to his contention that a capital must be instrumental in the formation of a product which exceeds the substance of the capital itself. In making the attempt he finds in his path the same stumbling block which barred the way for Thünen in *his* day. For a capital does not literally produce its own replacement plus something in addition. On the contrary, it gives rise to products of several kinds differing from its own kind, and these products are incommensurable with capital except in terms of value. Bows and arrows do not deliver what they produce in the form of bows and arrows, but in the form of the huntsman's quarry. But even when we know it to be true that this quarry is more valuable than the bows and arrows consumed in the chase, we are still not in possession of a technical fact which could explain the net return on capital—explain, that is to say, the substance of the interest problem. We simply know what substance it is that constitutes the problem; we know the fact itself which has to be explained.[129] Wieser recognizes the stumbling block quite clearly, and says very explicitly that the return yielded by bows and arrows "is a gross return in the form of other kinds of goods which do not replace them, but which may be compared with them in value even though they are not quantitatively commensurable with them."[130] But he imagines he can circumvent the obstacle by means of rather vague disclosures concerning an *"indirect* productivity of capital." "Although the possession of bows, arrows and nets does not contribute to the actual replacement of them, it facilitates the creation of conditions favorable to such replacement. That facilitation is effected by means of extraordinary augmentation of the gross return in the form of game and fish, and it has as its consequence a great increase in the quantity of labor that is liberated for the production of capital. That is why these capital goods must ultimately be credited with a net return incorporated in the total product, just as surely as if they were directly responsible for producing their own replacement and a surplus in addition."

It is my own opinion that it would be quite possible to be in doubt as to whether this "indirect" connection is sufficiently firm and uninterrupted to serve as the basis for an exact imputation. More specifically, I believe doubts could well be entertained concerning the commensurability of goods the worker consumes with goods he produces. Does the interpolation of a mediating factor called "person of the worker" not tend more to destroy than to preserve such commensurability? For—barring the case of slave labor regarded from the crassest point of view of the slaveholder—the worker, viewed as an economic entity and in his capacity as a factor of production, is unquestionably an originary productive power. On the other hand, in his capacity as a consumer he represents the ultimate and destined recipient, the goal and terminus toward which all the efforts of the antecedent production are directed. Hence any interpolated factor seems to represent not a carrying forward of one single process of production, but rather a discontinuity in the technical process of production, a termination of the previously conducted process of production directed toward consumption, and an inception of a new process of production.

However, I intend to disregard entirely this question which is as delicate as it is difficult. Even if it were possible to refrain from taking exception to the many and heterogeneous uncertainties to which this question gives rise, still the solution that Wieser is attempting would founder on the rocks that lie in the second part of the course which the question must pursue. I refer to that part of the problem which contains the difficult task of deriving a productivity of value from capital's physical productivity. Let us suppose Wieser had really succeeded in proving that there must be imputed to capital a physical quantity of the product which exceeds the quantity represented by the consumed capital itself. There still remains the task of proving and explaining that this greater quantity of product has a higher value than the capital from which it sprang. Here again is something which not only is not axiomatic, but which actually conflicts with the broad presuppositions of Wieser's theory of imputation. The very fundament of his whole theory of value and imputation is the idea that the value of goods arises from the (marginal) utility that is to be attributed to them. That is true of producers' goods as well as consumers' goods. Now producers' goods deliver their utility only through their products, and therefore the utility which a producers' good affords must, as a matter of basic principle, be exactly equal to the utility afforded by its products. And since value is derived from utility, it just as necessarily follows that the producers' good must be of exactly the same value as the product which arises from it. Ergo, in the absence of any additional factor which exercises a new and special influence, a surplus value of the product in comparison with its corresponding producers' good is a sheer impossibility. In other words there simply can be no such thing as a productivity of value on the part of capital.

Wieser is fully aware of this obstacle too. It is the same one which I had pointed out in my discussion of the older productivity theory as well.[131] And Wieser is no less explicit in making its outlines clearly visible both for his own eyes and for those of his readers. He says, "Capital receives its value from its fruits. And so, if the value of the capital consumed is deducted from the value of its fruits, then the remainder must always be zero. For it will always be necessary to deduct just so much as the value of those fruits amounts to, because it is that very value which furnishes the measure of the deduction that must be made. Consequently this method of computing values leaves a remainder of zero to represent the net return, and interest not only remains unexplained, but is demonstrated to be a *non esse*."[132] But Wieser is of the opinion that these "uncertainties" can be "resolved" through the assistance provided by the results of his research into the matter of imputation. His theory of imputation entitles him, he says, to impute to capital not only a gross return but also a physical net return. "In its gross return capital reproduces itself and produces a physical surplus in addition, which is the net return. It follows then that the value of the capital *cannot* be assessed at an amount equal to the entire value of the gross return. When the reproduction process is completed, capital represents only a part of its own gross return, consequently it can absorb only a part of the value of that gross return." If the gross return has a value of 105, Wieser goes on to say, and if 5 represents the amount deductible as representing fruits which can be consumed without impairing the complete restoration of the capital, "then only the remaining 100 can be counted as the value of the capital."[133]

In my opinion this line of reasoning is open to two objections. The first is one I took pains to present above, namely, the debatable character of Wieser's very premise that procedure in conformity with his rules of

419

imputation has as its consequence the imputation to capital of a physical net return.[134] My second objection is that even if his premise were correct, the conclusion drawn from it would not be. Let us assume a capital consisting of 100 units, and let us further assume that a gross return of 105 like units were really attributable to that capital, in other words, that there were a "physical net return" of 5 units. Such an alignment of facts would permit just one correct conclusion which would conform to the general principle of the equality of value as between means of production and their products. That conclusion would be that the value of the individual unit simply cannot be the same for both generations of capital. The 100 units of the earlier generation must necessarily have a value equal to that of 105 units of the next generation, let us say the generation of the following year. In that case the principle of the equality of value as between capital and its total gross return would have been preserved inviolate.

How, then, did Wieser arrive at the opposite conclusion, namely, that the value of a capital can be assessed only at an amount smaller than that of its gross product? He could do so only by committing a further violation of logical reasoning, though one that must be laid at the door of a delusive dialectical twist. For Wieser repeats an error now notorious in the history of the interest theory, one committed long ago by the canonists as well as by their opponents of that era,[135] and then repeated in very recent times by Knies.[136] In exactly the same way Wieser hypothesizes the identity of an original capital with a like number of like pieces of goods in a subsequent period. He introduces this fiction as a mere dialectical hypothesis. So he assumes—rightly or wrongly—a factual situation in which there is attributable to a capital a greater number of units of its products than the number of which the capital itself consists. He expresses this supposititious situation in the following seductive words. "In its gross product capital reproduces *itself* and a physical surplus in addition." With that as a basis he reasons onward, step by step. "In the process of its own regeneration capital appears as only a part of its own gross product," and consequently "it" (meaning capital) can absorb only a part of the value of its gross product. To be correct Wieser would have had to limit his first sentence to the statement that "in its gross product capital produces a *like number of like units* of goods available at a different period of time, and it produces in addition a surplus of such units." In that case his second sentence would have been correct if it had read, "The *aforementioned like number* appears as only a part of the gross product." And his concluding sentence could then properly have gone so far as to state that *the aforementioned like number* can absorb only a part of the value of the gross product. In short, what Wieser has done is to present vividly and to prove conclusively that 100 units of the *second generation of capital* are less valuable than 105 units of that selfsame second generation. But since the original capital of 100 units is not by any means identical with 100 units of the second generation, there is absolutely no vestige of justification for concluding that the relationship between value of gross product and capital of the second generation also obtains with respect to the original capital.

The truth is rather, that capital preserves a parity in value with its total gross product, even though the latter may possibly consist of a greater number of units. Indeed, the general fundamentals of Wieser's theory postulate this very truth, but the author of the theory has not remained entirely true to its fundamentals. We are still faced by the question how, despite the initial parity of value, an increment in value can be generated which furnishes the material for interest. And that, of course, is the very heart of the problem of interest. It is my opinion that the one explanation which touches that heart is to be found in the influence of temporal remoteness on the estimation of the value of goods and in the maturing of future goods which are initially discounted, but which with time rise in value to the point where they achieve the full value of present goods.[137] But it does not constitute a satisfactory explanation to fabricate a supposition which violates all basic principles, and to make the assumption that capital goods, unlike all other goods, derive their value from only a part of the utility which owes its origin to those capital goods!

Strange to relate, in the later course of his research Wieser arrives at the point where he accords recognition to the basic pronouncement which forms the core of my own interest theory. I refer to the observation that present goods are as a rule worth more than future goods. Only, instead of making it his point of departure, Wieser offers it as a conclusion to be drawn from the relationships he has demonstrated; he sees it, not as the cause of the phenomenon of interest, but as a result of it.[138]

And yet, unless I am completely mistaken, Wieser's views are such that they could never serve as a basis from which that pronouncement could be drawn as a conclusion. Quite on the contrary, they are entirely irreconcilable with it. If we can believe that a capital of 100 units can in one year yield a gross return of 105 units, then certainly we cannot at the same time believe that the capital consisting of 100 present units has a value 5% *smaller* than its gross product consisting of 105 units, and that nevertheless those 100 present units are *exactly equal in value* to 105 of next year's units. Wieser was able to arrive at the latter assertion[139] (which is, incidentally, perfectly correct) only by abandoning his completely illogical fiction of the identity of a present capital with a like number of units of its product. To be sure, he ought never to have hypothesized that fiction in his preliminary argument!

Wieser presents his theory of interest with great eloquence and considerable ingenuity. It attracts particular interest because it represents an odd attempt at what might be termed reverse renovation. He takes a structure consisting of a thoroughly modern system of thought and seeks to install in it an old-fashioned interior consisting of two antiquated ideas. These are the "productivity of capital" which has appeared upon

421

the stage in so many different guises, and the time-honored fiction of the identity of original capital with the "principal sum" which is to be repaid at a future time as its "replacement." His attempt has not, in my estimation, been successful. The old and the new ideas are in conflict with each other. It is only because of the author's dialectical complaisance that it was possible to draw a curtain barely adequate for the concealment at critical stages of the quarrel between the old and the new. The injection of the latter must be recorded to Wieser's lasting and well-deserved credit. But the conflicting elements resemble contestants who find it impossible to effect a reconciliation of their bickering spirits. The failure, despite the availability of such great theoretical resources and energy, of an attempt to revive the productivity theory seems to me the best proof that the lines of thought peculiar to the productivists will never in the world lead to a solution of the problem of interest.[140]

7. The Exploitation Theory and Its Common Offshoot

DURING the entire period we are reviewing in this appendix the exploitation theory was the subject of very extended discussion among writers in the field of economics. Such discussion was rendered especially lively and turbulent because of a peculiarly personal aspect it assumed, and even by virtue of a sort of dramatic suspense. For of all the socialist authors, Karl Marx had exercised by far the greatest influence on the adherents of the socialist school. Perhaps this ascendancy was accorded him at the cost of unmerited disparagement of other authors, particularly of Rodbertus who deserved his eminence as a scientist among economists. But it was Marx's *magnum opus* which was looked upon as the official creed of the socialism of that day. As a result it constituted the focal point for attack and the rallying point for defense. The controversial writing of the era was pro-Marx and anti-Marx writing.

And this situation obtained under especially thrilling circumstances. Marx had died before he had completed his book on capital. But his estate included in manuscript form virtually all the missing portions. It was supposed that the latter would include one matter of especial importance—one that had borne the brunt of the attacks on the exploitation theory, one which, according to the expectations of both parties of disputants would supply the touchstone to reveal the soundness (as the pro-Marxians expected) or the unsoundness (as the anti-Marxians anticipated) of his system. That one matter was the reconciliation of the empirically familiar uniformity of interest rates both with the law of value which Marx had developed in his first volume and with his theory of exploitation.[141] And it had to be just this third volume, just the volume in which this topic was to be treated, that was delayed for eleven long years after Marx's death and was not published until 1894. Suspense marked the general speculation on what Marx himself was going to say concerning this, the most ticklish point in his doctrine. The tension found release in a sort of prophetic writing, the object of which was to work out from the premises set down by Marx in his first volume, what opinion he was likely to deliver on the subject of the "average rate of profit." The decade from 1885 to 1894 is replete with this prognostic writing and it has bequeathed to us a goodly array of publications, some brief and some rather lengthy.[142] Then the second act of our play and the climactic point in the dramatic development was Engel's publication of the posthumous third volume in 1894. That was followed by a third act consisting of a most highly animated discussion carried on by a host of writers. Their purpose was to offer a critical evaluation of that third volume, then to determine what position it occupies with relation to the original point of departure of the Marxian system, and finally to appraise the future prospects confronting Marxian socialism. That discussion does not promise, even now, to reach an early conclusion.[143]

I believe I may confine myself at this point to the mere enumeration of these events because I have already recorded their scientific significance on preceding pages of this volume, and have also set down my own critical comments respecting them. And I have not been reticent in expressing my opinion that in the great test the verdict that was returned was decidedly against the Marxian theories of value and surplus value. Nor have I concealed my belief that this verdict seems to portend the beginning of the end of Marxism.

But the period we now have under observation presents an additional and a very peculiar theoretical fabrication which I feel constrained to mention in connection with this topic. It is one that might be described in the terms I used elsewhere[144] to characterize this common offshoot from the socialists' exploitation theory. For there is presented for our examination a most peculiar phenomenon. We see several prominent theorists who are not adherents of the socialist school and who do not accept those premises of the exploitation theory which deal with the theory of value. And yet they entertain views on the subject of interest in general which really do not differ essentially from the tenets of the exploitation theory, although they are marked by far greater moderation and reserve in expression or by less consistency in form.

The most striking utterances of this nature come to us from the pens of Dietzel and Lexis. Dietzel professes his faith in the belief that "there is no denying the essential correctness of the exploitation theory." And he affirms unalterable adherence to a conviction which he words as follows. "The exacting of interest is a categorical phenomenon developed in the course of man's history and permeating the entire body of the law that controls his actions in the economic relationships of the present day. It is, in fact, one of those kinds of income the nature of which may justly be termed a 'reproach' to a social organization like our present one, since they are necessarily in conflict with the rule of *suum cuique* —'to each his own.' "[145]

And then Lexis proclaims the opinion that the average return on capital "is connected with" the economic balance of power that depends on the possession or nonpossession of capital. The source of the slaveholder's income is unmistakable, and the same is true of that of the proprietor of a "sweatshop." In the normal relationship between entrepreneur and worker there is, Lexis admits, no "exploitation of that kind," but the worker's position is, after all, one of economic dependence, and that fact undoubtedly exercises an influence on the distribution of the product of his labor. The worker's share of the yield from production depends on a circumstance which places him at a disadvantage, namely on the impossibility of his exploiting his own labor power independently. He is forced to forgo the product of his labor and instead, to sell that labor for a more or less adequate subsistence.[146] On another occasion Lexis elucidates these views of his concerning the origin of interest in more detailed fashion. He says, "The capitalist seller, the producer of raw materials, the manufacturer, the wholesaler, the retailer, all make a profit in their businesses because each one sells more dearly than he buys, each one adding to his cost a certain percentage as a "markup." Only the worker is unable to make that sort of price increase. Because of the unfavorable position he occupies in relation to the capitalist, he is compelled to sell his labor for exactly what it costs him, namely the necessary means of subsistence. The capitalists, to the extent that they buy goods at increased prices, surrender part of what they gained in their capacity as sellers through their price increases. But those increases are visited without offset of any kind upon the wage earner in his capacity as a buyer, and they thus become the instrument by which he transfers a part of the value of the total product to the capitalist class.[147]

In all these utterances one thought finds unmistakable expression. The source of interest is the pressure which the property-owning classes can exert on those who possess no property, by exploiting the stronger position they occupy in the battle of prices. And this, be it noted, does not mean any excessive portion of that interest, seized under abnormally burdensome conditions, but just the usual "normal" return as such. Essentially, then, we have here the same idea as the one which furnishes the chief content of the socialists' exploitation theory.

To complete an objective picture of these statements it is necessary to point out two circumstances which in all likelihood are interconnected to a certain extent. In the first place, these statements have so far been made merely as occasional declarations. And the occasions, while they were such as to demand an acknowledgment of faith with respect to the problem of interest, did not impose upon these authors any necessity for supplying a coherent justification of their views. For the occasions were all critical discussions of interest theories advanced by outside parties. Marx and I were those outside parties. In the second place, these statements were, purely and simply, expressions of opinion. They were avowals of faith on the part of their authors for which no cohesive and scientifically sound substantiation was achieved, or even attempted. Dietzel does not supply a single word to support the statements he makes on the subject. Even the meager remarks which accompany Lexis's expression of opinion are so vague, and they also so manifestly leave the real pith of the problem untouched[148] that their author himself would hardly advance the claim that they contain a genuine explanation which meets the requirements of scientific procedure, or even the sketchiest outlines of such an explanation.

The regular protagonists of the exploitation theory rely on the socialist theories of value and of surplus value in their attempts to substantiate their exploitation theory. But the authors now under discussion neither depend on those theories to corroborate their kindred theory of interest, nor have they offered any other valid verification. In view of these circumstances it becomes my province as a historian of theory to do no more than record the fact that these opinions actually are entertained, though for the time being they are but undemonstrated assertions and "without benefit of theory," so to speak. It remains to be seen whether a serious attempt may still be made to elevate those confessions of faith to the status of genuine theories that attempt to build on a solid foundation. Or will they be no more than the voices of a mood that responds to the spirit of our time, destined to be hushed into silence, mere fancies incapable of being bound down to the premises of solid scientific research?[149]

There seems to be a strong and close kinship between the views just discussed and the theories of distribution very recently published by Oppenheimer[150] and Tugan-Baranowsky.[151] Both of them lay stress upon the exploitation idea and indeed, both display considerably greater acrimony in doing so than did Dietzel or Lexis. Both explicitly renounce the Marxian theory of value as a support of the exploitation theory. Oppenheimer owns allegiance to a combination of the marginal utility theory and the cost theory; Tugan-Baranowsky is a confirmed devotee of the marginal utility theory. Quite naturally their abandonment of the old intermediate motivation leaves the same hiatus in the sequence of their explanations as Dietzel and Lexis had left unfilled. Nor have even their attempts at closure succeeded in sealing it. Tugan-Baranowsky regards the "economic power" or the "social power" of the property-owning classes as an adequate basis for his immediate imputation to them of the exploitative appropriation of the product of other men's labor. He does not avail himself of any intermediate details, such as determination of value and price, in order to arrive at his charge. His overleaping of this step in his logical sequence is an evasion of the real difficulties of the problem, but he tries to justify it. Others generally and quite properly, I think, assume the problem of distribution to be merely a matter of applying the general considerations of value and price to the specific instance of goods which play their part as "factors of production." But not so Tugan-Baranowsky! He maintains that the question of distribution lies entirely *without* the pale of the question of value and price and is a problem *sui generis*.[152] Oppenheimer however believes he can bridge the chasm that yawns in the path of his explanation by means of the catchword "monopoly" and by arguing that it is the property owners who possess such a monopoly. I think one particularly unsatisfying detail in Oppenheimer's exposition is his attempt to place the responsibility for the origination of interest, in the last analysis, on monopoly in land.[153]

425

8. Eclectic Theories; a Defense
of Eclectic Principles by Dietzel

AND finally there is a group of theorists in most recent times, neither small in number nor inconsiderable in importance, who, in seeking support for their explanation of interest, rely in eclectic fashion on elements found in a number of different theories. Nor need this be looked upon as any cause for wonderment, as I have already had occasion to remark.[154] We can hardly fail to recognize what the most recent research efforts, and particularly in our field, have made increasingly clear and vivid. That is, that more than one group of facts may be said to have a causative bearing on the phenomenon of interest. This applies most especially to the higher productivity of capitalist production, to mention one, and to the postponement of gratification, to name another, which attends every investment of capital. Each of these two aspects has served as a foundation for independent theories. No ready solution presented itself, or was recognized as such, which permitted the interoperation of these heterogeneous contributing causes to be viewed from a single and comprehensive point of view. So long as that situation existed, the temptation was strong—and it still is—for authors to pick and choose and combine. And this is pre-eminently true of those circumspect writers who are resolved not to shut their minds to any factual human experience.

I have already spoken of Loria[155] who combines some elements of the abstinence theory with some from the exploitation theory. Diehl links a sort of motivated productivity theory to certain concepts of the use theory and to some of its terminology.[156] Expressions which likewise are usually characteristic of the use theory can be found in Sidgwick, as well as discussions which teach and defend the abstinence theory.[157] It is my opinion, incidentally, that it is quite possible that his employment of expressions which reflect the spirit of the use theory are merely fortuitous, whereas the true opinions of this excellent author are represented only by the abstinence theory. Neurath's somewhat nebulous utterances do not afford an opportunity to recognize any clearly defined core of theory, but they do seem to indicate partial agreement with a whole series of traditional theories or at least some fondness for them all.[158]

And I do not believe I am giving offense by including among the eclectics Maurice Block, the learned and brilliant author of *Progrès de la Science Économique depuis Adam Smith*. Confirmed believer that he was in the complete justifiability of interest, he could not bring himself to turn his back upon any one of several views which all seemed to him similarly plausible and favorable to interest. In his richly charged discussions of our theme I find passages representative of the productivity theory, the abstinence theory and also the use theory.[159] There can have been nothing repugnant to this outstanding scholar himself in the idea of being considered one of the eclectics. The proof of that is to be found in an address expressly prepared by him as a defense of eclecticism, and which he delivered on one occasion, presumably with the intention that it be regarded at the same time as an *oratio pro domo*.[160]

Charles Gide's opinions seem to indicate leanings partly toward the use theory and partly toward the agio theory,[161] while the expositions of Nicholson and of Valenti likewise show some partiality for the agio theory, but in other respects bear some marks of the abstinence theory.[162] And anyhow, the latter combination seems to make its appearance rather frequently in recent times, as I have already had occasion to point out in Sections 2 and 4 of this Appendix.

It may be noted in conclusion that among the writers who incline toward eclecticism Dietzel occupies a thoroughly unique position. Though always ingenious, he is not at all times calmly deliberate. He published a detailed discussion of my own theory of interest and that afforded him an opportunity to avow his own faith as an eclectic with respect to interest theories. And he defined his eclecticism as an exclusion of all the various current interest theories except the exploitation and productivity theories to which he accords equal rank, declaring each of them to be accurate and applicable to some of the manifestations of the interest phenomenon. He says, "In the field of research into the theory of interest it becomes necessary to formulate *different* explanations applicable to the different categories of phenomena possessing social and economic aspects, depending on the difference in economic position and inter-relationship of the individuals concerned."

Let us suppose, for instance, that the hirer of a piano or the renter of a house possesses a capital sufficient for the purchase of the piano or the house, but prefers to invest it in a productive enterprise, or to leave it so invested. In such a case the income received as interest by the owner of the piano or of the house may properly be explained as arising from the productivity of his capital. If, on the other hand, the hirer or the tenant does not possess the capital needed for the purchase of the good he hires or rents, then the only way the income received in the form of interest can be accounted for is to recognize it as an exploitation of the hirer or renter. "The exploitation theory" ("no denying its essential correctness"), says Dietzel, "must intervene to supply the explanation of interest."[163] At the same time Dietzel defends the use theory[164] and finally, if I understand him correctly, concedes a measure of correctness to my interest theory too, at least with regard to one certain group of interest phenomena, namely, the explanation of interest received as a result of extending consumer credit.[165]

I have worked out in detail and submitted elsewhere[166] my opinion that Dietzel's methodological position is utterly hapless and completely untenable. It is true, of course, that any eclectic procedure is open to some objection. But there is an enormous difference between methods. It is one thing to follow the path usually trodden by eclectics and, in order to explain a phenomenon, *to devise a theory* in which elements of various theories are commingled—elements which do not achieve gen-

427

uine inner coherence, perhaps, but which do present the outward appearance of unity. It is quite another thing to attempt, as Dietzel does, to work out or to acknowledge for every group of instances of one and the same phenomenon what is basically an entirely different theory and indeed a radically disparate one. There is a form of income which economists differentiate from rent, from wages, and from profit, and which they designate in all its manifestations by the comprehensive name of "interest." Now if those examples possess any common characteristic at all, anything that unites all examples of the class to each other and sunders them from the other types of income, then certainly that characteristic feature cannot be some different thing for each new case, and especially not something completely dissimilar and even irreconcilable one with another.

Anyone who, nevertheless, tries to join Dietzel in attempting to explain instances of the same basic phenomenon on the basis of principles borrowed from divers antagonistic theories will be unable to escape twofold embarrassment. There is, first, inevitable entanglement in absurd syllogistic sequences. For instance, a houseowner rents out the same de luxe apartment in two successive years at the same rental of $3,000. But since his first tenant is a bank president on an annual salary of $25,000 and the second a factory owner with an income of $25,000 derived entirely from his capital, the first year's income is attributable to a bit of exploitation practiced by the houseowner, the second year's income to the productivity of his capital! Now who would be willing to go on record as endorsing a reasoning sequence like that?

The second source of embarrassment is inevitable entanglement in the most palpable contradictions. For clearly, each one of the contradictory theories contains premises that must be accepted by those who want to explain even a single case in terms of that theory. But the premises of the first theory conflict with those of all the others to the point where they are mutually exclusive. And yet all those other premises also must be accepted, if there is to be any explaining of the remaining cases according to the methods prescribed by Dietzel. Could anyone declare himself for the essential correctness of the exploitation theory and at the same time explain any instance of interest income in terms of the productivity theory? Or vice versa?

It was possible for Dietzel to evade these blatant contradictions, I think, because he was regaling his public with a rather nonchalantly publicized rule for methodological procedure, delivered in his rôle as a critic rather than that of a theorist. He was therefore under no compulsion to submit the efficacy of his methods to any practical test.

9. The Present State of Opinion

THE opinions arrayed in hostile alignment today are numerous and varied. The final outcome of their battle has certainly not yet been determined. But the contest has at least not continued to be carried on in the same spot. Over the wide expanse of the battlefield there have been some indubitable successes and just as many undeniable reverses. Certain views are in the ascendancy and are pushing forward, others are in retreat or are hard pressed in their defense of the unfavorable positions to which they have been forced back, and of which the strongest outer ramparts have already fallen. If I may display the hardihood required for an attempt to depict the situation of the moment on the field of battle as my eyes behold it, I should like to trace the lines as follows.

On one main front of the highly ramified battleline, the issue was joined between the exploitation theory on the one side and the various theories friendly to interest on the other. I really believe the outcome there to be no longer in doubt, and the defeat of the exploitation theory to be an impending certainty. The enforced forfeiture of the vital base in the form of its "theory of value" led to a retreat under pressure to a position now no longer tenable. Of course, its troops will prolong the fight for some little time and it is hardly to be expected that the tenet of exploitation will very soon disappear from the propaganda paragraphs introduced into the proclamations addressed to the party membership. But economic science will soon consign it for all eternity to the limbo of fallacies that have been permanently confuted. And even that offshoot from the exploitation theory which I called a variety cultivated by "dilettante theorists" and to which we recently devoted some attention, could hardly be expected to have enough vegetative vigor to revive and rejuvenate the main bole of the plant and inspire any hope of further and fruitful development.

A rivalry flourished simultaneously among the theories "friendly to interest," if I may be allowed to use this term which, though commendably brief, is not entirely suitable for nonpartisan theories. And the conflict in which they engaged among themselves and against one another was not without certain lasting results. I think it may be regarded as fairly well established and quite widely recognized, that there are two ultimate causes concerned in the phenomenon of interest. One of these is to be found in certain facts relating to the technique of production, the other in the postponement of gratification. These correspond, perhaps not perfectly but certainly approximately to what Marshall meant to convey by his popular catchwords "productivity of capital" and "prospectiveness of capital." Some theories constitute ramifications to which the recognition of that thought has not penetrated or which show themselves to be unaffected by it. Such theories, it seems to me, no longer have any prospect that a retrogressive movement could ever turn back the course of development in economic science, and direct it once more into the backwaters where those theories are now stagnating. This applies, on the one hand, to several individual subspecies of the remuneration theories and, on the other hand, to the genuine and professed productivity theories. The latter particularly, which once occupied so prominent a position in economic theory, betray what from our modern point of view must be accounted to be two cardinal deficiencies. In the first place, it seems impossible for them to proceed from their self-chosen premises and by a logical progression to arrive at the positive goal of their explana-

429

tion without turning a logical somersault on the way. In the second place, they completely ignore a full half of the factual causes of the phenomenon of interest. One significant symptom of the hopeless situation of those genuine productivity theories is furnished by a certain manifestation which, to my mind, constitutes both a repudiation of the state of affairs as it actually exists, and a breach of fidelity to historical truth. I have in mind the incipient tendency to deny completely the very existence of such genuine productivity theories and to imply that their representatives in reality entertain views which resemble more closely the conception of the problem which prevails today.[167]

But those participants in economic development in whom the vital spark still glows, are advancing with one accord toward a goal which few today will hesitate to pronounce the correct objective toward which our search for enlightenment should strive. And though there may at present still be some indecision and vacillation as to the choice of the path most certain to lead unerringly to that goal, there is complete assurance that sooner or later the goal itself will be attained. The aim is to find an explanation which will do justice to both groups of causes, that is to say, both to the technological factors of production and to the psychological facts connected with the postponement of gratification. And this end must be so achieved that not only each part of the explanation is, in and of itself, empirically and logically incontrovertible, but also that both halves of the explanation will fit together and become a unified whole without factual or syllogistical blemish.

Of the divers theories that are rivals in striving to attain this end, let us consider first the use theory. Once it is correctly and fully understood, we can readily concede that this theory does establish contact with both groups of causes and is therefore adequately comprehensive. But in completing the full course of its explanatory mission this theory encounters serious factual and logical obstacles; and it seems that in wider and wider circles economists are coming to feel and to appreciate that these obstacles are just that—obstacles!

The abstinence theory likewise finds the path it has chosen to follow toward an explanation to be beset with difficulties of both a factual and a logical nature, and I was at some pains in the immediately preceding pages to point out those difficulties with even greater clarity than I had already done previously. Moreover, it seems to me that the manner in which it seeks to do justice to "productiveness" as well as to the "prospectiveness," which impresses on its explanation the imprint characteristic of the theory itself, fails to bring about a felicitous fusion of both elements into one truly unified theory.

The eclectics naturally have to contend not only with the specific weaknesses that are inherent in each separate theory which is made a member of the eclectic combination, but also with the refractoriness with which the disparate elements resist fusion into a harmonious whole.

Since the time of Rae the element postponement of gratification had become such an important factor in moulding the point of view of the theorists that they were able to avoid any questionable interpretative admixture of elements from the abstinence theory. But on the other hand, in the matter of solving the second knotty problem in his explanation Rae had been held enthralled by the bonds of the faulty thinking and halting imagination peculiar to the productivity theorists. Then again, Jevons does somewhat better with this second knotty point, but is correspondingly less successful in his treatment of "prospectiveness" and is thus beguiled into the ways trodden by the abstinence theorists. In any event we sense that Jevons has not satisfied the requirement of a resolution of the various explicatory notes into a logically harmonious coda.

In contrast to its predecessors the newest addition to the ranks of competing interest theories, the agio theory, has registered an attempt at a solution which may or may not be adjudged successful. But no one can deny that it has at least kept its eyes clearly and consciously fixed on the goal to be attained. And that goal has been the derivation, by means of a comprehensive examination of all motivating ultimate causes, of a self-contained and unified explanation of the phenomenon of interest.

It is hardly likely that any party to the controversy will harbor any doubt that the agio theory has faithfully carried out the first part of its program. Some of the individual friends of the theory, in communicating their agreement with it, remarked at the same time that they were in accord with it because it was really a productivity theory. Others acted the same way, but on the ground that it was really an abstinence theory. All of which is certainly significant testimony to the comprehensive character of its examination into both "productiveness" and "prospectiveness."[168] And perhaps the light of even more significant recognition shines forth from under the bushel of a certain measure of reproach on the part of one of my most illustrious opponents. Marshall accuses me of exaggerating the differences of opinion, with respect to the theory of interest, between me and my predecessors. In support of his accusation he cites the fact that even the opinions of my predecessors already gave equal consideration to "productiveness" and "prospectiveness." Now if Marshall says that, then he obviously considers this equal consideration to be a component element that is common to his theory and to mine. Hence he cannot deny that it is a feature of my agio theory.

Whether the agio theory was as successful in the second part of its program, or at least more successful than its rivals, will be revealed by continued discussion. The more closely research and criticism have heretofore defined the limits within which the paths leading to our goal must be sought and charted, the more painstaking will be the searching and testing that can and will be undertaken in the future within those narrower limits. We know the approximate direction in which we must go. Or, as J. B. Clark once said in a scholarly survey of *The Future of Economic Theory,* "Explanations of interest that cannot be far from the truth have been offered."[169] He may have been a bit optimistic, he could hardly have been entirely wrong. From now on it will be a matter of confining ourselves to those narrower limits and there examining the paths on which the still contentious theories invite us to walk, and testing them step by step, to determine whether the footing is firm, and to make certain they will afford us uninterrupted and undeviating progress toward our goal. Because our approximate orientation has been sufficiently well established, we can now afford to be more urgent, more exacting, more discriminating than before. We can no longer advance our progress by guideposts pretending to no more than approximate correctness; they must meet our requirements with pinpoint accuracy. No matter what the final outcome may be of the future development of theory and criticism, one thing already appears certain. The spirit of critical meticulousness having once been awakened, no solution will be accepted which is incapable of satisfying the most exacting scientific criteria. The danger is over—and over forever—that we shall ever complacently accept one of those superficial and specious solutions which are so easy to couch in a sluggard's catchwords, but which cannot be carried on in orderly thinking to a logical conclusion.

FROM THE PREFACE

TO THE FIRST EDITION

THE status accorded in the field of economics today to the subject of "capital and interest" relieves me of the necessity for advancing any special justification for undertaking to write on this theme. No one will question the statement that the material concerned is hardly outranked in importance by any which it is incumbent upon economic science to explore. Nor is it open to question that it also belongs to the most difficult topics in economics. And it is also unfortunately beyond question that it is one of those topics which that science has so far coped with in a most unsatisfactory manner. I could not mention one important concept, beginning with that of capital itself, and hardly any one tenet of the theory of capital which can be considered to have been definitely removed from the realm of controversy. Opinions on the most important questions are so widely divergent that our surprise at the number of doctrines is exceeded only by our amazement over the width of the chasm that yawns between them. The quest for that truth which alone can reconcile such differences appealed to me as being at one and the same time the performance of a duty and the satisfaction of a desire.

Considerations of expediency prompted a division of my work into two independent parts. The first volume, which is now in the hands of my readers, contains the *History and Critique of Interest Theories*. The second, which I hope to complete in the near future, will present the *Positive Theory of Capital*.

The decision so to divide the work was neither welcome nor easily reached. A history of theory belongs by nature to the most refractory material with which scientific inquiry has to deal. The burdensomeness of this handicap increases in direct proportion to the growth of the tome in volume, and to the number of individual theories it treats. For the reader is confronted with the weary task of familiarizing himself with the point of view of each new author, only to abandon it the next moment, and to trace out the thought processes of still another theorist. Finally, the historian's labor becomes more difficult in just such measure as he is conscientious and painstaking in his endeavor to present each of these individual worlds of thought. What is true in these respects of the history of theory in general, applies with even more validity to a history of interest in particular.

And yet I feel it to be my duty to write a unified critical history of the theory of interest. There might have been sufficient inducement to such an undertaking in the purely extrinsic circumstance that the literature of economics, though it is so abundantly supplied with histories of other theories, is strangely deficient with respect to the interest theory, being utterly innocent of even a single such history. However, other intrinsic considerations sufficed to determine my action.

Among the questions touching on the theory of capital no single one is more important and at the same time more confused than the problem of interest. Anyone who will take the trouble to enumerate interest theories can easily account for a dozen, perhaps two dozen different theories. Was I, then, simply to add another to the score or more already in existence? This probably would have resulted only in confusion further confounded. What the situation seemed to me to demand most urgently was an extensive and intensive sifting of the voluminous existing material. Until now, such sifting had been done only in most inadequate measure. I do not mean to say that there was a complete lack of critical works, but rather that those in existence served to embitter the conflict, not to settle it. Why this was so, it is not my intention to discuss here in detail. Suffice it to say that two reasons appear to me pre-eminent among the many which prevented a fruitful settlement of the controversy. The first is the circumstance that the planted field of purely theoretical investigation was choked and overgrown with the rank vegetation of passionately biased concern with interest in terms of social policy. The second is the fact that the predominantly historical viewpoint of the contemporary economist tended not only to minimize his interest in strictly theoretical problems, but also to lower his capacity to solve them.

Once I had with good reason decided to devote special care to a critique of the interest theories, it was clear that this could be done only in an independent volume. Now the avowed purpose could not be accomplished by any superficial and fragmentary appraisal. For if my critique were to be even reasonably detailed and complete, it would deal with a literature so vast in extent as to preclude the possibility of interpolating that critique appropriately within the confines of my exposition of the theoretical material. It thus followed automatically that my comprehensive critique had to be expanded into a *History and Critique of Interest Theories*. It would be inevitable that the small increase in my expenditure of labor would be generously compensated for by that improved understanding of my evaluation of the theories which the reader would gain from a fuller acquaintance with their history.

There is not much I can add concerning my own conception of my task. After what has been said it is self-evident that the critical phase of that task was my main objective. Nevertheless I trust that the verdict of my readers will pronounce me innocent of any neglect of its historical aspect. It would of course be too much to expect that I have presented the historical material without any gaps whatever, particularly in view of the almost total absence of any help which might have been gleaned from the preliminary work of earlier writers. The excellent work by Endemann on the canonical doctrine of interest was, comparatively speaking, of the greatest help, but of course it covers only a very limited field. Pierstorff's theory of entrepreneurial profit was highly useful, though his historical material in the field of economic theory coincides to only a small extent with the subject of my inquiry. By far the largest part of my subject matter was therefore virgin territory through which I had to blaze new trails. But I hope that such gaps as I have left are no more than details and do not mar the general picture of the development. While it is likely that I have omitted many an author, it is highly improbable that that is true of any theoretical school, or even of any truly characteristic representative of it.

It is true that I have deliberately and advisedly gone into exact detail both in the historical presentation and in the critical discussion of many theories. And I am quite keenly conscious that I have thus added in no inconsiderable degree to the difficulties which would at best be presented by the exposition of such refractory material. And yet I hardly need defend my procedure before those who are expert in this field. For they know that it is very often the minutest features which constitute the characteristic elements in the visage which a theory presents to the world. And they are well aware that a critic cannot hope to convince an adversary unless the very manner of his criticism conveys absolute assurance that the critic is thoroughly conversant with the theory he attacks and that he has understood it and duly appraised it. And they know full well that the critic can commit no more heinous sin than to indulge in shallow generalities and deliver them as his considered judgment of a theory he has inaccurately portrayed.

E. BÖHM-BAWERK

Innsbruck, May, 1884

FROM THE PREFACE

TO THE SECOND EDITION

THE second edition of the *History and Critique of Interest Theories* contains numerous modifications and additions. The modifications are not extensive and are limited to a few improvements in wording and the correction of occasional slips. On the other hand I have felt the need for the inclusion of supplementary material which has increased the size of the book by more than a third.

It has been necessary, in the first place, to fill in sporadic gaps in the listing and description of the earlier literature. The most notable addition of this sort concerns the Canadian John Rae. I hope that the devotees of economic theory will welcome the enrichment of the material offered in my volume by the detailed exposition of Rae's ideas. Despite the striking originality of his thinking he has by some strange mischance remained so far virtually unknown. It became my duty, in the second place, to bring up to date the *History and Critique of Interest Theories* which of necessity terminated with 1884, the year in which the first edition appeared. In this respect I was faced with a veritable superabundance of material, because the last 15 years have been a period of particularly active research in the field of capital. And so, even if I had been willing to restrict myself, in general, to a cursory survey, and, in particular, to a critical analysis of only a very few especially striking treatises of the most recent years, I should still not have been able to avoid extensive additions.

As to the manner in which this new and additional material was to be incorporated, I was faced with two alternatives. It would be possible to segregate the recently formulated doctrines according to their kinship with one or another of the groups of economic theories, and then fit the treatment of each into the appropriate chapter of my own book dealing with that group. Or it would be possible to leave my old volume as nearly unchanged as possible, and add an integrated survey of recent research in the form of an independent supplement. After mature consideration I decided in favor of the latter alternative. Moreover, my previous volume—whatever might be the general judgment as to its value—did indubitably expound all the problems of capital more extensively than any previous work and did so from the historical, the critical and the doctrinal viewpoint. It was therefore inevitable that its very existence should call forth some reaction on the part of subsequent writers on the same subject. This was especially true because the book had the good fortune to meet with unexpectedly rapid and wide distribution. Now in many cases there actually did prove to be essential kinship between the analysis of capital I had set forth in my first edition, and some of the most recent statements and formulations of the theory of capital. In such cases any attempt to merge my treatment of those newest formulations with the historical presentation on which I had based my earlier analytical judgment would have led to a rather confusing species of anachronisms. I believe, too, that those who are interested in the historical development of our ideas concerning the problems of capital will find it considerably easier to orient themselves and also to evaluate the individual doctrines without prejudice, by reason of the sheer physical segregation of all that material which preceded my first comprehensive analysis of capital, from that which followed. I have been forced to deviate from this principle with respect to only a single exception. That exception is the theory of exploitation. A peculiar chronological abnormality arose with respect to this point, in that the later volumes of Marx's *Kapital* were already in existence in manuscript form at the time of the appearance of the first edition of my work, but did not actually achieve publication until many years later.

If I have found little reason to change details in my historical and critical presentation, I have found still less ground for deviating from the principles underlying my approach. It might be argued that this could be taken for granted, since my book enjoyed such a predominantly friendly reception, and since I might justifiably derive therefrom the assurance that my conception of the task of the analytical historian of economic doctrine had not been inaccurate, or certainly not basically misguided. And yet I feel constrained to discuss this matter in some detail. For among the voices which have been raised in dissent, I hear those of a few scholars whose good opinion I value too highly for me to treat their objections with indifference or to disregard them. And their objections, moreover, have been raised on grounds which are to me at once most unexpected and most unwelcome.

For Francis Walker and Alfred Marshall accuse me, quite bluntly, of excessively harsh criticism of my predecessors in the field of the theory of capital. Walker does so in rather sharp terms, Marshall uses far milder words, though stinted neither as to number nor gravity.

Instead of seeking out with tolerance and charity, says Walker, the things the individual authors actually meant and said, I have noted to their discredit mere imperfections of exposition and "blunders of expression";[1] and Marshall conveys the impression that I not infrequently and quite unjustly assumed the existence of differing and quite biased opinions, when in actuality there was nothing but a mere lack of uniformity in their presentation, or a disproportionate increase or decrease in emphasis upon this or that element in the explanation. Such variation in emphasis, incidentally, might be intentional on the part of the author, or merely the result of a procedure not completely systematic. And so Marshall considers himself justified in the opinion that "the presentation which I gave of the 'naive productivity theories, the use theories' etc., would hardly have been accepted by the older writers themselves as well balanced and complete presentations of their several systems."[2]

If these recriminations were actually, as they at first glance appear, merely a question of differing interpretations of the true meaning of the writings of third parties, or in other words mere technical details on which historians of doctrine differ, it would not be fitting, nor worth the pains, to mention them in this preface. I could—and should—confidently rely on the contents of the following pages to speak for themselves. For I certainly set up my own analyses before the reader's eyes, as it were, basing them predominantly on a literal transcription of the opinions of the cited authors on the subjects in question. Nor do I believe that opponents will deny that the transcription is a painstaking and faithful one.

Actually, the point at issue is quite different. These contrary opinions as to the content and value of the writings of other authors really reflect only our own basically divergent conceptions of the problems of capital which confront us, and of the requirements for a true solution of them. The question as to whether I have criticized my predecessors in kindly or in unkindly fashion is only the apparent issue between my opponents and me. The true issue is whether they (Walker and Marshall) or I perceive more clearly wherein the kernel of the problem of interest lies, and what a true solution of it demands. This question, however, can properly and easily be answered right here. For my opponents' strictures are accompanied by comments which reveal why they arrive at an interpretation of the history of economic doctrine which is so at variance with my own. And I trust that a brief examination of their reasons will suffice at the very outset, to make it evident why I could not have been willing to share their interpretation.

This is crystal clear in the case of Walker. He is an adherent of the theory of productivity, no less convinced of its correctness than he is complacent as to its adequacy. He is so thoroughly imbued with the simplicity of the problem of interest and with the adequacy for its solution of the ideational system underlying the productivity theory, that he cannot entertain the thought that some other more gifted mind may have sought the solution of the problem of interest along another path. Therefore he maintains, in all seriousness, that the use theory and the abstinence theory never existed independently of the productivity theories, and that I am quite in error and completely unjustified in having so regarded and so declared them. "No economist of rank, who devoted more than a passing thought to interest" ever held the use theory stated by me in any other sense, "than that the use of capital is productive, as the productivitists employ that term."[3] As for the completely heterogeneous system of thought underlying the abstinence theory, Walker proposes to dispose of it by stating that these thoughts were intended in the minds of the originators only as a social justification of interest, which "no one of them probably ever mistook for a scientific ascertainment of the cause of interest,"[4] and hence a theory advanced for a solution thereof.

According to Walker, then, it is merely "blunders of expression" which create the impression that Hermann and Carl Menger were attempting in their writings to advance an original theory quite apart from the productivity theories! And it is, of course, by a perverse and misleading turn of phrase on the part of Senior that the impression could be created that this eminent theorist meant to contribute to the solution of the problem of interest by pointing out that abstinence constitutes a price-determining factor of the cost of production! However, my exploitation of such "errors of expression" must be termed an "ungenerous" attempt to attribute to these and other scholars original and carefully devised theories! I believe it hardly necessary to state that it would, on the contrary, have been a most "ungenerous" distortion of the facts, and one impossible for a sincere historian, if I had attempted simply to erase the use and abstinence theories from the history of the theory of interest, and instead to offer an interpretation of several ever so heterogeneous explanations by adjudging them to be one perpetual sameness of productivity theories. That would not have been interpreting them at all, but rather laying violent hands upon them to *mis*interpret them.[5]

The criticism of Marshall seems to differ from that of Walker in degree, rather than in kind. Marshall, too, has a predilection for one definite theoretical formula. And by virtue of displaying a most estimable trait of generosity in his interpretation, he reveals a desire to ascribe to as many as possible of the older writers an adherence to this same formula, presumably the best of all possible formulas. But he, no less than Walker, is a victim of a twofold delusion, though Walker is a prey to less subtle error. Marshall is deceived as to the capacity of his favored formula to furnish solutions to the problems presented, and he is in error with respect to the actual relationship of the various theories to the formula which he imputes to them.

For Marshall bases his own explanation of interest on two factors which are jointly operative—on the productivity of capital, which determines the demand for capital, and on its "prospectiveness," i.e., the temporal remoteness of its results, which influences and limits the supply of capital. Both these ideas, Marshall maintains, have been long familiar. It is only that different writers have from time to time laid greater weight on one or the other aspect—now on demand, now on supply. But even those who emphasized the productivity aspect were quite well aware that people are disinclined to save and to sacrifice the present to the future; conversely, those who had by preference emphasized this latter aspect of prospectiveness, had looked upon the productive advantages of a supply of capital as a matter of course. Marshall obviously took offense at my supposed refusal to credit the older writers under discussion, in every instance, with both halves of this one thought. And so he finds fault with my presentation of the naive productivity theory, of the use theory, and of other groups, as biased and inconclusive. I do not know how many nor which groups of theories Marshall includes in the "etc." with which he concludes.

Marshall is, of course, entirely correct when he asserts that the appreciation of the fact that the question of interest is connected with both phases is obvious and one which forces itself upon almost any observer. He could have found a statement in my own book to corroborate his own, or rather, to anticipate it. In my chapter which treats of the "eclectics" I said—and still say—"No unprejudiced mind could be impervious to the impression that there had to be some connection between the existence of interest and the greater yield of the capitalist system of production, or, the productivity of capital, as it was called." But neither can it be "denied that sacrifice, which is the usual price of saving, cannot fail to exert an effect on the existence and on the rate of interest." But this two-way recognition which has admittedly been present in the mind of man, is by no means an adequate explanation of interest. Just as little as it is an adequate scientific explanation of the rainbow (I used this analogy once before with respect to Walker[6]) for me to know and to say that the ultimate causes of a rainbow are sunshine and a precipitating cloud on which the sun falls at a certain angle. The thing that engages sciences is not the determination of the fact that the interesting seven-colored phenomenon called a rainbow has some connection with rays of sunlight falling on a raincloud, but rather the specific explanation of the manner in which, and of the chain of circumstances through which, those obvious and empirical causes bring about that precise result. Such an explanation, if couched in terms of the earlier theory of emission of light, would sound entirely different from an explanation in terms of the modern theory of undulation, in spite of the fact that both theories are certainly in complete agreement with respect to the fact that the rainbow is connected with sunshine and rainfall.

It may similarly be stated that interest owes its existence to the yield of capitalist production and to the temporal remoteness of its fruits. But while this general knowledge may serve to frame the picture, it does not by any means furnish the picture itself, does not portray the conquest of the multitudinous difficulties, nor is it a well-organized attack on those difficulties which lie in the way of a scientific explanation of interest. In fact, the very agreement in acknowledging that both aspects play their part in causing the phenomenon of interest necessitates an explanation of the steps which lead from those causes to that effect. There arises the possibility, not of a single explanation or theory, but rather of a whole series of them. Nor would those theories be mere mutations of the identical thought, varying from one another only in mode of expression. They would, on the contrary, present a thought content essentially different, each from the others, for they would connect those ultimate causes to the effect called "interest" by differing chains of circumstances, and would assert the presence and effectiveness of intermediate causes which are by nature dissimilar.

I find it difficult to assume that Marshall did not recognize this with respect to some of the groups of theories, at least, with which we are concerned. He must, for instance, be ready to admit that the use theory of Menger, the abstinence theory of Senior and the various remuneration theories of German and French authors are theories of essentially divergent content, although they have all incorporated in their system, in some form or other, both the potency of "prospectiveness" and that of the greater yield of capitalist production, just as I have given them a place and a function in my own theory of interest. Insofar as Marshall expresses a dissenting opinion with respect to this relationship, (and he makes it clear that he does hold a dissenting opinion with respect to many groups) he seems to have allowed himself to be deceived by an overestimate of the efficacy of the aforementioned frame as an explanation. This erroneous opinion that the assumptions made in common by the several groups contain within themselves the essentials of the solution, inevitably led him into the further error of concluding that the elements which they did *not* share, namely the points of difference, could be relegated to the domain of the merely incidental, the domain of mere form, expression or style.

In one particular Marshall's criticism is especially pointed. He makes the accusation that in the case of the theories which particularly emphasized the "supply" side or "prospectiveness," I failed to credit them with corresponding consideration of the productivity of capital; and that in the case of those theories which laid especial stress on that very productivity I had failed to credit them with paying any regard to "prospectiveness." In referring to my treatment of the use, abstinence and remuneration theories, Marshall mentions the first specifically, and clearly intends his "etc." to blanket the others as the victims of the mistreatment with which he reproaches me. He says in so many words that I failed in their case to give due weight to their use of the productivity of capital. Conversely he charges that my presentation of the naive productivity theory, which he names expressly, failed to give fitting recognition to its use of "prospectiveness."

This accusation is based, in respect to the first half, on a misunderstanding and has, in respect to the second half, no basis in fact whatever.

A misunderstanding lies at the root of Marshall's statement that in treating those groups of theories which develop the "supply" aspect in especially characteristic fashion (the former of the groups mentioned above) I had denied that they gave any consideration to the productivity of capital. On the contrary, I have never doubted that all those theories presupposed a technical or physical productivity of capital, similar to that which Marshall

440

himself envisions; that, indeed, they were under the necessity of doing so. With respect, for instance, to the use theory, which Marshall singles out expressly as an example of my biased presentation, I was so clearly aware of this that I made frequent statements which may have escaped Marshall's attention, to the effect that the use theory was actually a mere offshoot of the productivity theories, which only gradually attained a certain independence.[7] In my presentation of the several formulations of the use theory I then devoted the same relative amount of space to this particular phase of the matter as had the authors themselves. When discussing the teachings of Say and of Hermann, for instance, I spoke quite at length about the productivity of capital, but very briefly in discussing Schäffle and Menger. Then again, in expounding the characteristic essence of the use theory I spoke very little about it, because although the technical productivity of capital belongs to the inevitable theoretical background of the use theory, that theory is in its essence, oriented in a different direction. I think that if I had taken all the words which Marshall in his extremely careful and meticulously detailed way has said about the technical productivity of capital and its influence on the "demand" aspect, and laid those words in, let us say, Menger's mouth (a totally indefensible procedure, of course, since Menger himself did not say those things) my presentation would in that case have been more prolix and more laden with detail. But there would not have been the slightest alteration in the theoretical substance of the doctrine itself. A succinct recapitulation of it would not have had to contain any more words, nor any different words from those which I actually did use in my exposition of that theory.

The same is true, and in similar fashion, with respect to the abstinence theory. I shall have occasion later on to furnish a striking example along this line and, as a matter of fact, in connection with the theory which is Marshall's very own. For I shall, in the course of this book, take the theory of Marshall, embellished as it was with all its detailed references to the productivity theory, and nevertheless align it with that very type of doctrine to which the abstinence theory belongs. And my analysis will list just as many objections to his theory as I felt constrained to raise with respect to the abstinence theory of the older authors. Yet Marshall accuses me of having presented an incomplete and biased picture of them!

And so Marshall is in error when he maintains that I imply the existence of a hiatus in the reasoning of those theories of interest which emphasize the "supply" side, in that they pay insufficient heed to the "demand" side; and he is mistaken when he says that my analysis thereby places them in an unfavorable light.

But Marshall makes the accusation that I have, conversely, discussed certain theories which emphasize the productivity of capital exclusively, without conceding that they took the "supply side" into consideration. Moreover, he singles out the "naive productivity theories" as the specific grounds for the accusation. My answer to that is as follows. The majority of the authors, including the most important ones, whom I mentioned in this category (such as Say, Roscher, Rossi, Leroy-Beaulieu, Cauwés and others) did, as a matter of actual fact, treat the "supply" aspect expressly. No less expressly, however, was that circumstance recorded by me. Now and then, indeed, I did so in considerable detail, as in the case of J. B. Say's important theory. Even where a propounder of a productivity theory gave only the slightest intimation of a conflicting motive of sacrifice, I was at some pains to set it down faithfully in each instance. I cite Malthus as an example. The clearer the references were to a conflicting sacrifice of the use of capital, of "abstinence," of the labor of saving, the more impossible did it become to reconcile those allusions with the ordinarily very definite reference to a productivity of capital which is "independent," which "creates values" and which is not merely a derivative of the labor which produces capital. Since these divergent elements could not be harmonized, nor even combined into an integral unit, I found it necessary to class most of those writers with the eclectics, at the same time expressly noting their utterances on the subject of "supply."

But others among the adherents of the naive productivity theory have placed great emphasis on capital's capacity for independent productivity without adorning their statements with the faintest hint of the influence of "prospectiveness" or of any kind of motive of sacrifice. Was it either obligatory or permissible for me to construe a conscious theoretical reference to these factors into their doctrines? I do not refer, be it noted, merely to commonplace knowledge, familiar even to Adam Smith, that capitalist production bears only deferred fruits, or that capital can be built up and increased only by saving. I am speaking of the deliberate statement that only with the entrance of this factor do we have a situation which gives rise to interest, and that this factor is operative in addition to and in spite of the productivity of capital. And if my rhetorical question above receives an affirmative answer, then I ask further, "Should I have credited them with the thought, as a nebulous generality, that 'prospectiveness' must have something to do with the origination of interest?" Or ought I rather to have given them credit for having fully formulated a reference to a definite essence of sacrifice as something inherent in "prospectiveness," a reference to a sacrifice of distinct uses, of abstinence, of the burden of saving?

And if the answer to the last of these questions is again in the affirmative, then to which of these quite disparate essences am I to acknowledge they were making reference?

I believe that, no matter what I had done, other than what I actually did do, I should of necessity have been remiss as a historian and at the same time unjust to those authors. Remiss as a historian, because I think there was once a trend of thought which held that the postulation of an independent power on the part of capital to create values furnished a scientific explanation of interest. It is true that this line of thought, though formerly rather widespread, is today thoroughly outmoded. And this line bears an essential relationship to two schools, and in point of time it occupies a middle ground between them. One is represented by the older principle of the physiocrats which asserted the privileged, creative character of land, the other, by the prejudice of the socialists in favor of the privileged, creative character of labor. I regard it as a prepossession which, though of more recent origin, is already on the decline.

But I should have been unjust to the writers themselves if I had hinted at unexpressed thoughts. For I should in that case have had to find fault with them for things which they did not say at all, and most probably did not think at all. If I had ascribed to them that very general consideration of prospectiveness—what I alluded to above as the frame in lieu of the picture—I should have had to raise the objection that not even an attempt had been made at a genuine explanation. I should then not have granted, as I did, that they were promulgating a genuine, though erroneous, theory conceived in the spirit of their time and possessing a character of its own. Instead, I should have laid at their door a nebulous belief which failed to recognize the difficulties and the focal point of the problem—in short, a mere opinion which, so to speak, embodied no theory at all. And I doubt whether that would have been looked upon by my critic as placing them at a more exalted level in the scale of recognition. To have supposed that those reticent authors were intending to offer, within the bounds of that limited frame, a genuine and completely thought out theory of use, or of abstinence or of labor, would have been sheer presumption on my part. That would have meant, not merely that I was filling up with my own imaginings a page which the authors had left completely blank, but, over and beyond that, that I was interpolating the product of my own imagination at a point at which the authors themselves had not wanted to leave even a blank page. Even if the use or remuneration or abstinence theory which my imagination would thus have fathered upon them had been an exact and complete copy of Marshall's own well-conceived and well-knit theory, I should more than ever have been under obligation to take the authors to task, because I cannot consider any of those explanations correct. It is utterly patent that such a procedure on my part would have been deserving in all justice and in full measure of the strictures which Walker and Marshall now seem to level at me without justification. If there is any one thing which brands the chronicler of doctrines as neither faithful nor charitable, it is the bad habit of charging a writer with an error, of which his writings fail to contain even the flimsiest evidence.

All in all, I do not believe that Marshall would ordinarily have imputed such behavior to me. His economic theories are otherwise marked by extraordinary clarity and keenness both in original conception and in subsequent execution. But unfortunately in the very part of his work which is devoted to the problem of capital, these qualities have deserted him entirely. As I have intimated above, the source of his divergent and, in my estimation, erroneous judgment in the field of the history of economic theory is his own insufficiently clear and inadequately profound grasp of the problem. He underestimates the difficulties, he is not aware of all sorts of factual and logical reefs which obstruct his course toward a satisfactory solution. This will be shown with respect to Marshall's own positive theory of interest, which the present volume will permit the reader to evaluate. He is therefore inclined to disdain as superfluous subtleties any efforts which aim to reveal those reefs and to sail wide of them. In the case of the analytical economic historian he is even inclined to take offense at them. Greatly as I appreciate, therefore, being in agreement in other things with the highly esteemed author of *Principles of Economics,* I can see no possibility of finding a correct solution of the problems which are here under discussion, unless I render a judgment completely at variance with that of Walker and Marshall.

E. BÖHM-BAWERK

Vienna, August, 1900

FROM THE PREFACE

TO THE THIRD EDITION

IN THE preparation of the present third edition I have again subjected the text of my *History and Critique of Interest Theories* to thorough and careful examination, and have made improvements and emendations where they seemed necessary. But this time I have limited the extent of further additions as strictly as possible in order to prevent the size of the volume, which had already increased materially at the time of the second edition, from becoming excessive. And so I have attempted to do justice to the great mass of material which has been added to the literature on capital since 1900 by means of brief notices for the most part, even relegating them, where possible, to the footnotes. I have made more extensive interpolations in the text only in rare instances. One such instance is Oswalt's theory of interest. For I should not like to see the historian suffocate here under the burdens of the cataloguer. The center of gravity of my book lies, it still seems to me, in its historical function. It was as such that I first published it some 30 years ago. The continuation of it as a chronicle of day-to-day occurrences is a different matter. Possibly the exceptional circumstance that 30 years after the original appearance of the book not only the author, but the book, too, is still alive has perhaps made it inevitable that this edition should exhibit such character in some degree. But it still remains the prime purpose of this book to present the large outlines of an integrated history, rather than a chronicle whose lines are obscured by masses of detail.

E. BÖHM-BAWERK

Vienna, June, 1914

444

NOTES

NOTES TO CHAPTER I

1. Second edition, p. 111.
2. On this whole question, consult among others, Pierstorff, *Die Lehre vom Unter-* *nehmergewinn*, Berlin, 1875.
3. Of course, only so far as it is *net* interest.

NOTES TO CHAPTER II

1. Of the abundant literature that treats of interest and usury in ancient times note particularly: Böhmer, *Jus ecclesiasticum Protestantium*, Halle, 1736, Vol. v, tit. 19; Rizy, *Über Zinstaxen und Wuchergesetze*, Vienna, 1859; Wiskemann, *Darstellung der in Deutschland zur Zeit der Reformation herrschenden nationalökonomischen Ansichten* (Prize Essays of the fürstliche Jablonowskische Gesellschaft, Vol. x, Leipzig, 1861); Laspeyres, *Geschichte der volkswirtschaftlichen Ansichten der Niederländer* (Prize Essays, Vol. xi, Leipzig, 1863); Neumann, *Geschichte des Wuchers in Deutschland*, Halle, 1865); Funk, *Zins und Wucher*, Tübingen, 1868; Knies, *Der Credit*, Part i, Berlin, 1876, p. 328 ff.; above all, the works of Endemann on the canon doctrine of economics, *Die nationalökonomischen Grundsätze der kanonistischen Lehre*, Jena, 1863, and his *Studien in der romanisch-kanonistischen Wirtschafts- und Rechtslehre*, Vol. i, Berlin, 1874; Vol. ii, 1883.

2. E.g., the prohibition of interest by the *Mosaic Code*, which, however, only forbade lending at interest between Jews, not lending by Jews to strangers, Exodus 22:25; Leviticus 25:35-37; Deuteronomy 23:19, 20. In Rome, after the Twelve Tables had permitted an *unciarium foenus*, the taking of interest between Roman citizens was entirely forbidden by the Lex Genucia, 322 B.C. Later, by the Lex Sempronia and the Lex Gabinia, the prohibition was extended to *socii* and to those doing business with provincials. Cf. Knies, *Der Credit*, Part i, p. 328 ff. and the writers quoted there.

3. I submit some of the passages oftenest referred to. Plato in the *Laws*, Book v, p. 742, says: "No one shall deposit money with another whom he does not trust as a friend, nor shall he lend money upon interest." Aristotle, in *Nicomachean Ethics*, iv, No. 1: ". . . such are all they who ply illiberal trades; as those, for instance, who keep houses of ill-fame, and all persons of that class; and *usurers who lend out small sums at exorbitant rates;* for all these take from improper sources, and take more than they ought." Cato the Elder, according to Cicero, *De officiis*, ii, at end: "Ex quo genere comparationis illud est Catonis senis: a quo cum quaereretur, quid maxime in re familiari expediret, respondit, Bene pascere. Quid secundum? Satis bene pascere. Quid tertium? Male pascere. Quid quartum? Arare. Et cum ille, qui quaesierat, dixisset, *Quid foenerari? Tum Cato, Quid hominem, inquit, occidere?"* Cato the Younger, *De re rustica:* "Majores nostri sic habuerunt et ita in legibus posuerunt, *furem dupli condemnare, foeneratorem quadrupli.* Quanto pejorem civem existimarunt foeneratorem quam furem, hinc licet existimari." Plautus, *Mostellaria*, Act iii, Scene 1: "Videturne obsecro hercle idoneus, Danista qui sit? *genus quod improbissimum est . . .* Nullum edepol hodie genus est hominum tetrius, nec minus bono cum jure quam Danisticum." Seneca, *De beneficiis*, vii, 10: ". . . quid enim ista sunt, quid fenus et calendarium et usura, nisi humanae cupiditatis extra naturam quaesita nomina? . . . quid sunt istae tabellae, quid computationes, et venale tempus et sanguinolentae centesimae? voluntaria mala ex constitutione nostra pendentia, in quibus nihil est, quod subici oculis, quod teneri manu possit, inanis avaritiae somnia."

4. See also Knies, *Der Credit*, i, p. 330 f.

5. Luke 6:35; but see Knies, *Der Credit*, p. 333 ff., on correct meaning of this passage.

6. On the spread of the prohibition of interest, see Endemann, *Nationalökonomische Grundsätze*, p. 8 ff., and *Studien*, p. 10 ff.

7. See Endemann, *Studien*, pp. 11-13, 15 f.

8. To give the reader some idea of the tone which the fathers of the church adopted in dealing with the subject, I append some of their most quoted passages. Lactantius, Book VI *Divin. Inst.,* Chap. XVIII says of a just man: "Pecuniae, si quam credideri's, non accipiet usuram: ut et beneficium sit incolume quod succurrat necessitati, et abstineat se prorsus alieno; in hoc enim genere officii debet suo esse contentus, quem oporteat alias ne proprio quidem parcere, ut bonum faciat: *plus autem accipere, quam dederit, injustum est.* Quod qui facit, insidiatur quodam modo, ut ex alterius necessitate praedetur." Ambrosius, *De bono mortis,* Chap. XII: *"Si quis usuram acceperit, rapinam facit,* vita non vivit." The same *De tobia,* Chap. III: "Talia sunt vestra, divites! beneficia. Minus datis, et plus exigitis. Talis humanitas, ut spolietis etiam dum subvenitis. Foecundus vobis etiam pauper est ad quaestum. Usurarius est egenus, cogentibus nobis, habet quod reddat: quod impendat, non habet." So also Chap. XIV: ". . . Ideo audiant quid lex dicat: *Neque usuram,* inquit, *escarum accipies, neque omnium rerum."* Chrysostom on Matthew 17, *Homily* 56: "Noli mihi dicere, quaeso, quia gaudet et gratiam habet, quod sibi foenore pecuniam colloces: id enim crudelitate tua coactus fecit . . ." Augustine on Psalm 128: "Audent etiam foeneratores dicere, non habeo aliud unde vivam. Hoc mihi et latro diceret, deprehensus in fauce: hoc et effractor diceret . . . et leno . . . et maleficus." The same (quoted in the *Decret. Grat.,* Chap. I, Causa XIV, quaest. 3): ". . . si plus quam dedisti exspectas accipere foenerator es, et in hoc improbandus, non laudandus."

9. Molinaeus, in a work that appeared in 1546, mentions a writer who had shortly before collected no fewer than 25 (!) arguments against interest (*Tractatus contractuum,* No. 528).

10. See Endemann, *Nationalökonomische Grundsätze,* p. 12, 18.

11. *Commentaria perpetua in singulos textus quinque librorum Decretalium Gregorii* IX, V, Chap. III; *De usuris,* V, Chap. XIX, No. 7.

12. *Variarum resolutionum,* III, Chap. I, No. 5.

13. *Summa totius theologiae,* II, Chap. II, quaest. 78, art. 1. Similarly Covarruvias: *(op. cit.)* ". . . accipere lucrum aliquod pro usu ipsius rei, et demum rem ipsam, iniquum est et prava commutatio, *cum id quod non est pretio vendatur* . . . aut enim creditor capit lucrum istud pro sorte, ergo

bis capit ejus aestimationem, vel capit injustum sortis valorem. Si pro usu rei, is non potest seorsum a sorte aestimari, et sic bis sors ipsa venditur."

14. Lib. I, *Nov. Declar., Jus. Civ.,* Chap. XIV, quoted in Böhmer's *Jus ecclesiasticum Protestantium,* Halle, 1736, p. 340.

15. Thomas Aquinas, in a little work *De usuris,* Part I, Chap. 4. Incidentally, the authenticity of this work has recently been questioned. I should like to add here an excerpt from a very interesting note by the Viennese theologian, the prelate Dr. Franz M. Schindler. It occurs in an essay of his which appeared in *Die Kultur,* Vol. for 1903, No. 8, p. 594 ff. He claims that this argument of St. Thomas's caused a great deal of discussion within the ranks of canonistic-theological writers of the sixteenth and seventeenth centuries; that it was, indeed, widely attacked, and that opponents (including the illustrious Archbishop Caramuel, who died in 1682) even then voiced the formula that present money is worth more than future money. According to Schindler (*op. cit.,* p. 604) the defenders of this statement pointed out "that one can derive gain from a present sum in the current year as well as in the following year, but from next year's future sum a gain is possible only next year; and that, furthermore, money claims are in greater jeopardy than cash in hand." This last additional argument seems to me to reduce materially the value of the formula for the theory of interest. For the risk can admittedly justify an insurance premium, but cannot form a basis for genuine interest. And the reference to the greater interim gain which one can derive from a sum available at an earlier date presupposes the possibility of such an interim gain, that is to say, it presupposes originary interest as a fact, without offering any explanation of it. It seems to me, therefore, that this incident in the canonistic controversy about interest is much more closely related to the views of Salmasius and his adherents (which will be discussed in the next chapter) than it is to the *Agio* theory, with which Schindler connects it.

16. "Secundo (usura est prohibita) ex fame, nam laborantes rustici praedia colentes libentius ponerent pecuniam ad usuras, quam in laboratione, cum sit *tutius lucrum,* et sic non curarent homines seminare seu metere." See Endemann, *Nationalökonomische Grundsätze,* p. 20.

17. Endemann, *Studien,* I, p. 361.

18. *De usuris,* II, Chap. IV, Qu. 1.

NOTES TO CHAPTER III

1. *Clem. c. un. de usuris,* 5,5.

2. See Endemann, *Nationalökonomische Grundsätze,* pp. 9 ff., 21 ff.

3. The opinion very commonly held, that the Jews were generally exempted from the

Church's prohibition of interest, is pronounced erroneous in the latest detailed work of Endemann (*Studien,* II, p. 383 ff.).

4. Endemann, *Studien,* II, pp. 243 ff., 366 ff.

5. Wiskemann, *Darstellung der in Deutschland zur Zeit der Reformation herrschenden nationalökonomischen Ansichten* (Prize Essays of the Jablonowskischen Gesellschaft, Vol. x, p. 71).

6. Wiskemann, p. 54-56. Neumann, *Geschichte des Wuchers*, p. 480 ff.

7. Wiskemann, p. 65.

8. Ep. 383, in the collection of his letters and answers, Hanover, 1597.

9. "Ac primum nullo testimonio Scripturae mihi constat usuras omnino damnatas esse. Illa enim Christi sententia, quae maxime obvia et aperta haberi solet: Mutuum date nihil inde sperantes, *male huc detorta est* . . . Lex vero Mosis *politica* cum sit, *non tenemur illa* ultra quam aequitas ferat atque humanitas. Nostra conjunctio hodie per omnia non respondet . . ."

10. Previous to this, in the same year, there had been published the *Extricatio labyrinthi de eo quod interest*, in which the question of *interesse* had been freely discussed, but the author had not openly taken sides on the interest question. Cf. Endemann, *Studien*, p. 63.

11. *Tractatus*, No. 10.

12. "Ea taxatio (the establishment under Justinian law of a maximum rate in connection with the sanctioning in principle of the taking of interest) nunquam in se fuit iniqua. Sed ut tempore suo summa et absoluta, ita processu temporis propter abusum hominum nimis in quibusdam dissoluta et vaga inventa est, et omnino super foenore negociativo forma juris civilis incommoda et perniciosa debitoribus apparuit. *Unde merito abrogata fuit,* et alia tutior et commodior forma inventa, videlicet per abalienationem sortis, servata debitori libera facultate luendi. Et haec forma nova, ut mitior et civilior, ita minus habet de ratione foenoris propter alienationem sortis, quam forma juris civilis. *Est tamen foenus large sumptum, et vera species negociationis foenoratoriae* . . ." (No. 536).

13. Endemann, *Studien*, i, p. 64 f. Endemann, however, underrates the influence that Molinaeus had on the later development.

14. In his notes on Aristotle's *Politics;* see Roscher, *Geschichte der Nationalökonomik in Deutschland*, p. 54.

15. Roscher, *ibid.*, p. 188.

16. Besold resumed the discussion later, in an enlarged and improved form, as he says, in another work, *Vitae et mortis Consideratio politica* (1623), in which it occupies the fifth chapter of the first book. I had only this latter work at my disposal, and the quotations in the text are taken from it.

17. There is a long quotation in the very first chapter of the first book (p. 6). In the fifth chapter the quotations are numerous.

18. I think Roscher (*Geschichte*, p. 201) does Besold too much honor when, in comparing him with Salmasius and Hugo Grotius, he gives him the honorable position of

a forerunner on whom Salmasius has scarcely improved, and to whom Grotius is even inferior. Instead of Besold, who drew at second hand, Roscher should have named Molinaeus. Besold is not more original than Salmasius, and certainly less adroit and ingenius.

19. *Sermones fideles*, Chap. xxxix, (1597).

20. See Grotius, *De jure belli ac pacis*, Book ii, Chap. xii, p. 22

21. *De jure belli ac pacis*, Book ii, Chap. xii, pp. 20, 21.

22. Thus it is not possible to regard Grotius as a pioneer of the new theory in favor of interest. This view, held by many, including Neumann, *Geschichte des Wuchers in Deutschland*, p. 499, and Laspeyres, *Geschichte*, pp. 10 and 257, is authoritatively corrected by Endemann, *Studien*, i, p. 66 f.

23. The list of writings in which our extremely prolific author expatiates on the subject of interest is by no means exhausted by the works mentioned in the text. There is, e.g., a *Disquisitio de mutuo, qua probatur non esse alienationem*, of the year 1645, whose author signs only the initials S. D. B., a signature which points, as does the whole style of writing, to Salmasius (Dijonicus Burgundus). There is besides in the same year an anonymous writing, also undoubtedly traceable to Salmasius, *Confutatio diatribae de mutuo tribus disputationibus, ventilatae Auctore et praeside Jo. Jacobo Vissembachio*, etc. Those names in the foregoing, however, were the pioneers.

24. "Que res facit ex commodato locatum, eadem praestat in pro mutuo sit foenus, nempe merces. Qui eam in commodato probant, cur in mutuo improbent, nescio, nec ullam hujus diversitatis rationem video. Locatio aedium, vestis, animalis, servi, agri, operae, operis, licita erit: non erit foeneratio quae proprie locatio est pecuniae, tritici, hordei, vini, et aliarum hujusmodi specierum, frugumque tam arentium quam humidarum?"

25. To prove the relation in which Salmasius stands to Molinaeus, it may not be superfluous, considering the explicit statement of Endemann (*Studien*, i, p. 65) that Salmasius does not quote Molinaeus, to establish the fact that such quotations do exist in considerable number. The list of authors appended to the works of Salmasius shows three quotations from Molinaeus in Salmasius's *De usuris*, twelve in his *De modo usurarum*, and one in his *De foenore trapezitico*. These quotations are taken principally from Molinaeus's chief work on the subject, his *Tractatus contractuum et usurarum*. One of them (*De usuris*, p. 221) refers directly to a passage which stands in the midst of his most convincing arguments. (*Tractatus*, No. 529; Nos. 528 ff. contain the statement and the refutation of the arguments of the philosophers of classical antiquity, and of the canonists against interest). There can, therefore, be no doubt that Salmasius knew the writings of Molinaeus intimately. And it is almost certain

—as indeed his substantial agreement would lead us to suspect—that he has drawn from them. In the *Confutatio diatribae* mentioned in footnote 23, the statement is made (p. 290) that he was not acquainted with the arguments of Molinaeus, identical with those in his own *De usuris*, at the time when he, Salmasius, writing under the pseudonym of Alexius a Massalia, composed the *Confutatio Diatribae*. But this statement must relate only to his ignorance of those particular passages in which Molinaeus denies that a loan is by nature an alienation. Unless, of course, the statement is merely incorrect.

26. Salmasius begins with the argument concerning the impropriety of a demand for double payment for the same commodity. His opponents had contended that whatever was taken over and above the principal sum lent could only be taken either for the use of a thing which was already consumed—that is, for nothing at all—or for the principal sum itself, in which case the same thing was sold twice. To this Salmasius replies: "Quae ridicula sunt, et nullo negotio difflari possunt. Non enim pro sorte usura exigitur, sed pro usu sortis. Usus autem ille non est nihilum nec pro nihilo datur. Quod haberet rationem, si alicui pecuniam mutuam darem, ea lege ut statim in flumen eam projiceret aut alio modo perderet sibi non profuturam. Sed qui pecuniam ab alio mutuam desiderat, ad necessarios sibi usus illam expetit. Aut enim aedes inde comparat, quas ipse habitet, ne in conducto diutius maneat, vel quas alii cum fructu et compendio locet: aut fundum ex ea pecunia emit salubri pretio, unde fructus et reditus magnos percipiat: aut servum, ex cujus operis locatis multum quaestus faciat; aut ut denique alias merces praestinet, quas vili emptas pluris vendat" (p. 195). At this point he sets forth that there is no more need for the creditor to investigate whether the debtor is really making advantageous use of the borrowed money, than there is in the case of the owner who rents out a house. Then he goes on to say: "Hoc non est sortem bis vendere, nec pro nihilo aliquid percipere. An pro nihilo computandum, quod tu dum meis nummis uteris, sive ad ea quae tuae postulant necessitates, sive ad tua compendia, ego interim his careo cum meo interdum damno et jactura? Et cum mutuum non in sola sit pecunia numerata, sed etiam in aliis rebus quae pondere et mensura continentur, ut in frugibus humidis vel aridis, an, qui indigenti mutuum vinum aut triticum dederit, quod usurae nomine pro usu eorum consequetur, pro nihilo id capere existimabitur? Qui fruges meas in egestate sua consumpserit, quas care emere ad victum coactus esset, aut qui eas aliis care vendiderit, praeter ipsam mensuram quam accepit, si aliquid vice mercedis propter usum admensus fuerit, an id injustum habebitur? Atque poteram, si eas servassem, carius fortasse in foro vendere, et plus lucri ex illis venditis efficere, quam quan-

tum possim percipere ex usuris quas mihi reddent" (p. 196 f.). His refutation of the argument concerning the barrenness of money is particularly trenchant. He replies, "Facilis responsio. Nihil non sterile est, quod tibi sterile esse volueris. Ut contra nihil non fructuosum, quod cultura exercere, ut fructum ferat, institueris. Nec de agrorum fertilitate regeram, qui non essent feraces nisi humana industria redderet tales . . . Magis mirum de aëre, et hunc quaestuosum imperio factum. Qui ἀερικόν imposuerunt vectigal singulis domibus Constantinopolitani imperatores, aërem sterilem esse pati non potuerunt. Sed haec minus cum foenore conveniunt. Nec mare hic sollicitandum, quod piscatoribus, urinatoribus ac nautis ad quaestum patet, ceteris sterilitate occlusum est. Quid sterilius aegroto? Nec ferre se, nec movere interdum potest. Hunc tamen in reditu habet medicus. Una res est aegroto sterilior, nempe mortuus . . . Hic tamen sterilis non est pollinctoribus, neque sardapilonibus, neque vespillonibus, neque fossariis. Immo nec praeficis olim, nec nunc sacerdotibus, qui eum ad sepulcrum cantando deducunt. Quae corpus alit corpore, etiamsi liberos non pariat, non tamen sibi infecunda est. Nec artem hic cogites; natura potius victum quaerit. Meretricem me dicere nemo non sentit . . . De pecunia quod ajunt, nihil ex se producere natura, cur non idem de ceteris rebus, et frugibus omne genus, quae mutuo dantur, asserunt? Sed triticum duplici modo frugiferum est, et cum in terram jacitur, et cum in foenus locatur. Utrobique foenus est. Nam et terra id reddit cum foenore. Cur natura aedium, quas mercede pacta locavero, magis potest videri foecunda, quam nummorum quos foenore dedero? Si gratis eas commodavero, aeque ac si hos gratis mutuo dedero, tum steriles tam hi quam illae mihi evadent. Vis scire igitur, quae pecunia proprie sterilis sit dicenda, immo et dicta sit? illa certe, quae foenore non erit occupata, quaeque nihil mihi pariet usurarum, quas et propterea Graeci *tókov* nomine appellarunt" (p. 198 f.). And Salmasius points "the finger of ridicule" at his opponents' third chief argument as well, namely, their contention that a loan should not be subject to interest, because the things loaned become the property of the debtor. "At injustum est, ajunt, me tibi vendere quod tuum est, videlicet usum aeris tui. Potens sane argumentum. Atque non fit tuum, nisi hac lege, ut pro eo, quod accepisti utendum, certam mihi praestes mercedem, usurae nomine, absque qua frustra tuum id esse cuperes. Non igitur tibi, quod tuum est, vendo, sed, quod meum est, ea conditione ad te transfero, ut pro usu ejus, quamdiu te uti patiar, mihi, quod pactum inter nos est, persolvas."

27. Laspeyres, *Geschichte*, p. 257.

28. Very fully described by Laspeyres, p. 258 ff.

29. Noodt is very much quoted as an authority in the learned literature of the

eighteenth century; e.g., by Böhmer, *Protestantisches Kirchenrecht*, Vol. v, p. 19 *passim*. Barbeyrac, the editor of several editions of Hugo Grotius, says that, on the matter of interest, there is an "opus absolutissimum et plenissimum summi jurisconsulti et non minus judicio, quam eruditione insignis, Clarissimi Noodtii. (*De Jure Belli ac Pacis* by Grotius, Amsterdam edition 1720, p. 384.)

30. Laspeyres, *Geschichte*, p. 269.

31. Neumann, *Geschichte des Wuchers in Deutschland*, p. 546, mentions instances where local laws allowed contract interest about the years 1520-1530. Endemann, it is true, (*Studien*, II, pp. 316 f., and 365 f.) would interpret these as applying only to stipulated *interesse*, which, theoretically at least, was different from interest proper (*usurae*). In any case the taking of interest had thus as a matter of practice won official sufferance.

32. In the last *Reichsabschied*. On the disputed interpretation of the passages referred to, see Neumann, p. 559 ff.

33. Roscher, *Geschichte*, p. 205.

34. *Ibid.*, p. 312 f.

35. *Ibid.*, p. 338 f.

36. Second edition, 1758.

37. Second edition, Vienna, 1771.

38. Second edition, Vienna, 1771, pp. 419, 425 f.

39. *Ibid.*, p. 427.

40. *Ibid.*, p. 430.

41. *Ibid.*, p. 426 f.

42. *Ibid.*, p. 432 ff.

43. Fifth edition, p. 497.

44. See Schanz, *Englische Handelspolitik*, Leipzig, 1881, Vol. I, p. 552 ff.

45. See foregoing, p. 22.

46. *Tract Against the High Rate of Usury*, (1621). I had available only a French translation of this tract (Amsterdam and Berlin, 1754). The passage quoted above is on p. 441 of that translation.

47. For instance, on p. 447, where Culpeper levels the accusation of injustice only against the interest which "ronge et détruit" (consumes and destroys), that is to say, excessively high interest.

48. Unfortunately I was unable to procure this work. The above remark by Child is in the introduction to his *Discourse of Trade* on p. 9 of a French translation which appeared in 1754.

49. *New Discourse of Trade* (1690). The same French translation of 1754 was once more the only thing available to me, the same that was used by Roscher in his essay "Zur Geschichte der englischen Volkswirtschaftslehre" (*Abhandlungen der königl. sächs. Ges. der Wissenchaften*, Vol. III, 1857). See Roscher, p. 59 ff.

50. Roscher, p. 89 f.

51. On the subject of Petty and Vaughan, as on the English literature about interest in general, see the copious and interesting bibliography in Cassel's *Nature and Necessity of Interest*, (1903), pp. 9-16, especially p. 14 f. I cannot, however, fully subscribe

to Cassel's evaluation of the contributions of this period as factors in the development of the theory of interest.

52. *Considerations of the Consequences of the Lowering of Interest and Raising the Value of Money*, 1691, p. 24. I quote from the collected edition of Locke's works, London, 1777, Vol. II.

53. In other places (e.g., p. 4) Locke calls interest a price for the "hire of money."

54. *Of Civil Government*, Vol. II, Chap. v, No. 40. See also Roscher, p. 95 f.

55. See following Chap. XII.

56. *Inquiry into the Principles of Political Economy*, 1767, Vol. II, Book IV, Part I, Chap. VIII, p. 137.

57. *Ibid.*, Chap. IV, p. 117.

58. *Of Interest; Essays and Treatises on Several Subjects*, Basil, 1793, II, p. 60.

59. *Ibid.*, *passim*. Even before the days of Hume, a noteworthy predecessor of his, Nicholas Barbon, furnished one half of this observation when he declared interest to be "rent of stock" and added the remark that interest is ordinarily regarded as being paid for money. But, he goes on to say, this is in error, for interest is paid rather for capital (he called it "stock") since the borrowed money is expended in the purchase of commodities. (*A Discourse of Trade*, 1690, p. 31 f.; see Stephan Bauer's essay on Barbon in Conrad's *Jahrbücher*, New Series, Vol. XXI (1890), p. 561 ff., especially p. 573.)

60. Bentham, who actually belongs to a later age than that under discussion, will receive further mention.

61. See the historical works of Vasco, *L'usura libera* (*Scrittori Classici Italiani*, Parte moderna, Vol. XXXIV), p. 182 ff., particularly pp. 195, 198 ff., 210 ff.

62. Galiani, *Della moneta* (*Scrittori Classici Italiani*, Parte moderna, Vol. IV), p. 240 f.

63. *Impiego del danaro*, 1744. I did not have access to the book itself. But the late Prof. Luigi Cossa kindly informed me that its contents are largely taken from the book by the Dutch theologian Broedersen, written in favor of interest and published in the previous year (*De usuris licitis et illicitis*, 1743).

64. *Della moneta*, Book v, Chap. I.

65. *Lezioni di economia civile*, 1769 (*Scrittori Classici Italiani*, Parte Moderna, Vol. IX, Part II, Chap. XIII).

66. *Elementi di economia pubblica*, written 1769-1771; first printed, 1804, in the collection of the *Scrittori*, Vols. XI and XII, particularly part IV, Chaps. VI and VII.

67. *Usura libera*, Vol. XXXIV of collection mentioned in foregoing.

68. Vasco, p. 209.

69. *De republica*, 2nd ed., 1591, Vol. II, p. 799 ff.

70. E.g., II, *Mémoire sur les Banques; Economistes financiers du XVIII siècle*, edition Daire, Paris, 1851, p. 571.

71. *Essai politique sur le commerce*, *Ibid.*, p. 742.

72. *Esprit des lois XXII.*

73. The passage has already been quoted by Rizy, in his *Über Zinstaxen und Wuchergesetze* and also by Knies in *Der Credit*, Part I, p. 347. It runs as follows: "It is but fair to demand that the values given in the case of a contract which is not gratuitous should be equal on either side, and that neither party should give more than he has received, nor receive more than he has given. Anything that a lender demands from the borrower, over and above what he has given him, therefore constitutes an unjust demand. For by the repayment of the original sum he has already received the exact equivalent of what he gave. In the case of things which can be used without being destroyed, a rental may legitimately be demanded because, this use being always separable (in thought at least) from the things themselves, it can be valued and a price put upon it. It has a price which is separable and separate from the thing. So that, if I have given a thing of this sort to any one for his use only, there is no good reason why I should not demand a rental (which is the price of the use I have allowed him) in addition to the restitution of the thing itself which has never ceased to be my property.

"It is an entirely different matter, however, with those objects which are known to lawyers as 'fungible goods'—things that are consumed in the using. For since in the using they are necessarily destroyed, it is impossible to imagine a use of the thing which is distinct from the thing itself, and which has a value which is distinct from the value represented by the thing itself. From this it follows that one cannot convey title to the use of a fungible thing without conveying title to the thing itself. If I lend you a sum of money for your use, on condition that you pay me back the same sum after a stated period of time, then you receive from me simply that sum of money and nothing more. The use that you make of the money is included in the exercise of the property rights you acquire in the coins I lend you. There is no thing apart, nothing that you have received, outside of the sum of money. I have given you only this sum, and nothing but this sum. I cannot therefore justly ask you to give me back anything but the sum lent. For justice demands that only that which was given be returned."

74. Amsterdam, 1764.

75. *Op. cit.*, p. 269 ff.

76. Pp. 257-262.

77. P. 267.

78. P. 284.

79. See particularly pp. 276, 290, 292 f., 298 f.

80. Written in 1769; published 20 years later, 1789. I quote from the collected edition of Turgot's work by Daire, Paris, 1844, Vol. I, pp. 106-152.

81. Funk, *Zins und Wucher*, Tübingen, 1868, p. 116. On the reception that this liberal decision of Rome, August 18, 1830, met from a portion of the French clergy, see Molinari, *Cours d'economie politique*, 2nd ed., Vol. I, p. 333.

82. *Wealth of Nations,* Book II, Chap. IV.

83. For instance Sonnenfels, *Handlung,* 5th ed., pp. 488, 497. Steuart, Book IV, Part I, p. 24; Hume, *Of Interest*, p. 60; see foregoing, pp. 26 and 30.

84. Some historians of theory, who are at the same time adherents of the productivity theory (which we shall examine later), such as Roscher, Funk, and Endemann, are fond of ascribing to the writers of this period "presentiments" of the "productivity of capital," or even "insight" into it; and of claiming them as forerunners of that theory. I think this is a misunderstanding. These writers do speak of the "fruitfulness" of money, and of all sorts of other things, but this expression with them serves rather *to name* the fact that certain things bring forth a return than *to explain* it. They simply call everything "fruitful" that yields a return or a "fruit," and are not even remotely suggesting that they claim to be thereby offering any normal theoretical explanation of the origin of these returns. This is very plain from the writings of Salmasius on the subject. When Salmasius calls air, disease, death, prostitution, "fruitful" (see note 26 on p. 448), it is evidently only a strong way of putting the fact that the state which lays taxes on the air, that the physician, the gravedigger, the prostitute, all gain from the things just named. But it is just as evident that Salmasius did not in the least seriously think of deriving the sexton's fee from a productive power that resides in death. And the fruitfulness of money, which Salmasius tried to illustrate by comparing it with these, is not to be taken any more seriously.

NOTES TO CHAPTER IV

1. "Les intérêts des avances de l'établissement des cultivateurs doivent donc être compris dans leurs reprises annuelles. *Ils servent à faire face à ces grands accidents et à l'entretien journalier des richesses d'exploitation, qui demandent à être réparées sans cesse.*" (*Analyse du Tableau économique*, edition Daire, p. 62.) Cf. also the more detailed exposition directly preceding the passage quoted.

2. *L'Ordre naturel*, edition Daire, p. 459.

3. On his attitude towards loan interest see foregoing p. 34. With respect to originary interest his position may be summed up as follows: He approves of interest derived from capital invested in agriculture without offering any very profound explanation of it. (*Philosophie rurale*, p. 83 f. and

also p. 295). But his opinion of gain derived from commerce and industry is couched in hesitant terms, and he seems to regard it as a fruit of activity, *"de la profession,"* rather than of capital (p. 278).

4. Written in 1766, published in 1769 in *Ephémérides du citoyen.* I am quoting from Daire's collected edition of Turgot's works, Paris, 1844, Vol. I.

5. The informality of Turgot's explanation of interest has misled an otherwise exact investigator of his works to maintain that Turgot does not explain interest at all. (Sivers, Turgot's *Stellung in der Geschichte der Nationalökonomie,* in Hildebrand's *Jahrbücher,* Vol. XXII, pp. 175, 183 ff.). This is a mistake. Only his explanation, as will become apparent, is not particularly profound.

6. Cassel, *Nature and Necessity of Interest,* p. 24. Cassel feels it incumbent upon him to defend Turgot with unusual vigor against the charge that he, Turgot, had intended to offer an explanation of interest in the series of thoughts which I have summarized in my text. I think Cassel is in error. The "fructification theory" credited to Turgot is outlined in his writings with complete clarity. This is apparent from the citations given and their unmistakable inner consistency. That should be enough in itself, but there is also the additional fact that they are entirely in the spirit of the physiocratic doctrine. For land rent, that effortless income characterized by Turgot himself in his Sec. 14 as Nature's "pur don" (pure gift), is virtually the Archimedean fulcrum of the physiocratic doctrine of distribution. And now Turgot seeks and finds in this Archimedean leverage point, his point of contact with the subject of interest. His path goes by way of his own Secs. 31 and 59. For in the first he speaks of interest as a second kind of effortless income, the source of which should be the subject of research and be connected with the system of distribution sketched by him. And his second, his Sec. 59, places the purchase of rent-producing land *at the head* of the list of uses of capital (*premier emploi des capitaux*). Then, as I have described earlier all the various ways of obtaining interest are, by means of this connecting link, and in completely parallel and symmetrical ranking, brought into logical relationship to that primary category of effortless income, namely, land rent. Cassel, however, seems to be blind to these points of affinity. But then, I have been forced to the conclusion in other particulars too, that Cassel's judgment on matters of history of economic theory is often subject to being clouded by a strong subjectivism.

7. See Chap. XIV on Henry George's "Modern Fructification Theory."

8. Usually the rent of land is somewhat less than interest on the price paid. But this circumstance, fully explained by Turgot (*Réflexions,* Sec. 84 ff.), has no influence at all on the principle, and may here simply be ignored.

9. "If four bushels of wheat, the net product of an arpent [.84 acre] of land, be worth six sheep, the arpent which produced them could have been sold for a certain amount—a greater amount of course, but one always easy to determine *in the same manner as the price of all other commodities, i.e. first by discussion between the two contracting parties, and afterwards by the current price established by the competition* of those who wish to sell cattle to get lands and vice versa (Sec. 57). It is evident, again, that this price, or this number of years' purchase, must vary as there are more or fewer persons who wish to sell or buy land, just as the price of all other commodities varies by reason of the different proportion between supply and demand" (Sec. 58).

NOTES TO CHAPTER V

1. "In exchanging the complete manufacture either for money, for labour, or for other goods, over and above what may be sufficient to pay the price of the materials and the wages of the workmen, something must be given for the profits of the undertaker of the work who hazards his stock in the adventure . . . He could have no interest to employ them unless he expected from the sale of their work something more than what was sufficient to replace his stock to him; and he could have no interest to employ a great stock rather than a small one unless his profits were to bear some proportion to the extent of his stock" (McCulloch's edition of 1863, p. 22). The second passage runs: "And who would have no interest to employ him unless he was to share in the produce of his labor, or unless his stock was to be replaced to him with a profit" (p. 30).

2. See also Pierstorff, *Lehre vom Unternehmergewinn,* Berlin, 1875, p. 6; and Platter, *Der Kapitalgewinn bei Adam Smith* (Hildebrand's *Jahrbücher,* Vol. XXV, p. 317 f.)

3. Book II, Chap. I, p. 123, in McCulloch's edition.

4. If Platter, in the essay mentioned in the foregoing, comes to the conclusion that, "if Smith's system be taken strictly, profit on capital appears unjustifiable," it could only be by ascribing importance to but one-half of Smith's utterances, and ignoring the other as contradictory to his other principles. Cannan in his meritorious *History of the Theories of Production and Distribution,* (London, 1894, p. 202), draws a similar conclusion, but the subjective nature of his judgment leaves me unconvinced.

5. Book II, Chap. III.
6. Book I, Chap. VI, p. 23. The sentence was written primarily about landowners, but throughout the chapter, interest on capital and rent of land are treated as parallel antitheses to wages of labor.

NOTES TO CHAPTER VI

1. *Handbuch der Staatswirtschaft*, Berlin, 1796, particularly Sec. 8 and 23. Even his later *Abhandlungen die Elemente des Nationalreichthums und die Staatswirtschaft betreffend*, Göttingen, 1806, do not take a more independent view of our subject.

2. *Über Nationalindustrie und Staatswirtschaft*, 1800-1804, particularly pp. 82, 142.

3. *Staatswirtschaft*, Auerswald's edition, 1807-1811, particularly Vol. I, pp. 24, 150 f.; and the very naive expressions, Vol. III, p. 126 f.

4. *Neue Grundlegung*, Vienna, 1815, p. 221.

5. *Die Nationalökonomie*, Ulm, 1823, p. 145. See also p. 164, where the causal connection is reversed and originary interest is deduced from loan interest.

6. *Staatswissenschaften im Lichte unserer Zeit*, Part II, Leipzig, 1823, p. 90. Here Pölitz confines his efforts to proving that interest, assumed to be an established fact, must inevitably accrue to the owner of capital.

7. *Theorie des Handels*, Göttingen, 1831.

8. *Handbuch der Staatswirtschaft*, Berlin, 1808, Sec. 110 and 120. See also Sec. 129, where even contract interest is not explained, but simply discussed as a fact. Schmalz's other writings are no more instructive.

9. *Die Ökonomie der menschlichen Gesellschaften und das Finanzwesen*, Stuttgart, 1845, p. 19.

10. *Die Nationalökonomie*, Leipzig, 1805-1808. I quote from a reprint published in Vienna, 1815.

11. In Lotz's former work, the *Revision der Grundbegriffe*, (1811-1814) there are some rather interesting remarks on our subject, although they are full of inconsistencies. These include a vigorous refutation of the productivity theories (Vol. III, p. 190 f.), an explanation of interest as "an arbitrary addition to the necessary costs of production," and as a "tax which the selfishness of the capitalist extorts from the consumer" (p. 338). This tax is considered not necessary, to be sure, but "very fair" (p. 339). But in another place Lotz characterizes it as direct cheating of the capitalist by the laborer, if the former does not receive as much as "he may be justified in claiming as the effect of those tools used by the worker on his activity and on his gross return," (p. 323). It is very striking that in the next to last passage quoted, Lotz argues that interest is gained at the expense of the *consumer*, while in the last it is gained at the expense of the *laborer*. And so he vacillates on this point in exactly the same way as Adam Smith.

12. *Grundsätze der Nationalökonomie*, Halle, 1805; 3rd ed., Halle, 1825. I quote from the latter.

13. Sec. 211, 711, 765, particularly marked in Sec. 769.

14. *Grundsätze der ökonomisch-politischen oder Kameralwissenschaften*, 2nd ed., Tübingen, 1820.

15. *Die Lehre von der Volkswirtschaft*, Halle, 1843.

16. *Volkswirtschaftslehre*, Vol. I, Sec. 222. Similarly, but more generally, Vol. I, Sec. 138.

17. London, 1817, 3rd ed., 1821. I quote from the reprint of the 3rd ed. in the complete edition of Ricardo's writings, London, 1871.

18. The most complete of these runs thus: ". . . For no one accumulates but with a view to make his accumulation productive, and it is only when so employed that it operates on profits. *Without a motive there could be no accumulation, and consequently such a state of prices* (as show no profit to the capitalist) *could never take place. The farmer and manufacturer can no more live without profit than the laborer without wages. Their motive for accumulation will diminish with every diminution of profit, and will cease altogether when their profits are so low as not to afford them an adequate compensation for their trouble, and the risk which they must necessarily encounter in employing their capital productively"* (Chap. VI, p. 68; similarly p. 67; Chap. XXI, p. 175, and elsewhere).

19. Chap. I, Sec. V, p. 25.

20. Ricardo puts the same causal relation very strongly in Chap. I, Sec. 4, when he gives the magnitude of the "value of labor" as a secondary cause of the value of goods, in addition to the quantity of labor expended in their production, having in mind the influence exerted on the value of goods by the capitalists' claims to interest. The rate of interest is to him only a secondary and intermediate cause, in place of which he prefers to put the ultimate cause of the whole relation. He regards the varying rate of wages as that ultimate cause.

21. As for instance Pierstorff in *Lehre vom Unternehmergewinn*, p. 12 ff.

22. Chap. VI, p. 67 and elsewhere.

23. Chap. VI, toward end (p. 70).

24. Chap. I, Sec. 1.

25. Chap. I, Sec. 4, 5.

26. See also Bernhardi, *Kritik der Gründe*, 1849, p. 310 ff. On the other hand compare Verryn Stuart, *Ricardo en Marx*, The Hague, 1890, and my analysis of this work in Conrad's *Jahrbücher*, Series III, Vol. I (1891) p. 877 ff.

27. Natoli, in his thorough and painstaking *Il principio del valore*, Palermo, 1906, seems to express a higher opinion of Ricardo's contribution to the problem of interest. But perhaps Natoli reads into the great old classicist a little too much of our more recently acquired knowledge. This would be comparable to Natoli's readiness to believe that Ricardo's theory of value, suitably edited, is capable of embracing the modern theory of marginal utility.

28. *An Essay on the Production of Wealth*, London, 1821.

29. "A new creation brought into existence in consequence of this expense" (p. 51); "they create it . . . It is essentially a surplus, a new creation" (p. 54).

30. *Principles of Political Economy*, 1st ed., Edinburgh, 1825; 5th ed., 1864.

31. Pp. 61, 205, 289 f. of 1st ed.; 5th ed., pp. 6 and 276.

32. "The cost of producing commodities is, as will be afterwards shown, *identical with the quantity of labour* required to produce them and bring them to market" (1st ed., p. 250). Almost in the same words in the 5th ed., p. 250: "The cost or real value of commodities is, as already seen, determined by the quantity of labour," etc.

33. "But it is quite obvious that if any commodity were brought to market and exchanged for a greater amount, either of other commodities or of money, than was required to defray the cost of its production, *including, in that cost, the common and average rate of net profit* at the time . . ." etc. (1st ed., p. 249; essentially the same wording in the 5th ed., p. 250).

34. First edition, p. 298 ff.; 5th ed., p. 283 ff.

35. First edition, p. 313.

36. First edition, p. 314.

37. First edition, p. 317.

38. It would be possible to be a bit more lenient in our judgment of McCulloch if we could assume in the above argument that he was using the word "labor" in the same vague and confused sense which appears later (in his note 1 to his edition of Adam Smith, Edinburgh, 1863, p. 435 f.). There he means by it "every kind of activity," that is to say, not only that of man, but also that of animals, machines, or natural powers. To be sure, by such a watering down of its fundamental concepts his theory of value is stripped of every vestige of individuality, and reduced to a mere toying

with words. But at least we should not have to reproach him with talking what, by all the rules of logic, must be called nonsense. And yet even this slight show of clemency is impossible. For McCulloch has said too often, and too unequivocally, that interest is to be attributed to the *human labor* employed in the production of capital. Thus, for instance, in his note 1 on p. 22 of his edition of Adam Smith, McCulloch declares interest to be the wage of that labor which was originally expended in the formation of capital. Here, obviously, the "labor" of the machine itself cannot possibly be meant. And note particularly the passage in his *Principles* (5th ed., pp. 292-294) in which he states expressly, with regard to the illustration of the wine, that its surplus value is *not* produced by the powers of nature, since these work gratuitously.

39. I had access to the 5th ed. only. But I gather from Cannan's excellent *History of the Theories of Production and Distribution* (London, 1894, p. 212, note 2) that the same change was made as early as the second edition of 1830.

40. First edition, p. 221, footnote; likewise 5th ed., p. 240 at end.

41. First edition, p. 319; 5th ed., pp. 294 and 295.

42. *Elements of Political Economy*, London, 1858; *Principles of Economical Philosophy*, 2nd ed., London, 1872.

43. *Elements*, pp. 76, 77, 81, 202, 226, et al.

44. *Ibid.*, p. 62 f.

45. *Ibid.*, p. 216.

46. *Economical Philosophy*, I, p. 638.

47. *Elements*, p. 145.

48. *Principles of Economical Philosophy*, I, p. 634; II, p. 62.

49. *Elements*, p. 66, then 69 f.

50. *Principles of Economical Philosophy*, II, p. 66.

51. *Abrégé élémentaire des principes de l'Économie Politique*, Paris, 1796.

52. *Principes d'Économie Politique*, Paris, 1801.

53. "The earth has been cultivated only *because its product was able*, not only to compensate for the annual labor of cultivation, but also to recompense the advances of labor which its original cultivation cost. It is this superfluity which gives rise to land rent." (P. 5).

54. *Économie Politique*, Paris, 1829.

NOTES TO CHAPTER VII

1. Roscher, *Grundlagen der National-ökonomie*, 10th ed., Sec. 189.

2. It would be easy for me to extend the foregoing list. In the category of "physical productivity," for instance, two shades of meaning can be distinguished. The only one considered in my text is applicable to the situation in which the entire capitalist process has led to the production of more

goods. By the "entire process" we mean *both* the preparatory creation of the capital itself *and* continued production with the help of that capital. But it is also possible that the first phase of the entire process, the creation of the capital, may register such a large deficit that the capitalist process *in toto* fails to show a surplus. This could be true, even though the second phase, the

453

production with the help of capital, may, in and of itself, result in a surplus in goods. Let us suppose that the boat and net, having a useful life of 100 days, had required 2,000 days for their construction. In that case the use of boat and net for 100 days (representing a total of 2,100 days) results in a catch of 3,000 fish. But the catch with bare hands would have been three times 2,100, or 6,300 fish. However, considering the second phase by itself, the capital, once present, shows itself to be productive, because with its help the catch is 3,000 fish, and without it only 300. If for that reason we speak, even in this situation, of a surplus production and of a productivity of capital, (which, in fact, we do) there is some justification for it. Only, these expressions today have an entirely different and much weaker significance. Furthermore, the recognition of the productivity of capital often carries the connotation that capital is an *independently* productive power. It is not merely an intermediate factor in a productive process, which is to be ascribed, in the last analysis, to the labor which created the capital, but a completely independent element, unconnected with labor.—I have carefully avoided discussion of these niceties of discrimination, for the reason that I do not wish to burden the reader with them since, for the present at least, I have no intention of making use of them.

3. In regard to the manner of posing the problem, see my *Rechte und Verhältnisse,* Innsbruck, 1881, p. 107 ff.

4. Published in 1803; I quote from the 7th ed., Paris, Guillaumin et Cie, 1861.

5. Paris, 1828 and 1829.

6. *Cours,* I, p. 234 ff.

7. *Traité,* p. 68 f.

8. Book I, Chap. III, p. 67 toward the end.

9. Book I, Chap. X.

10. *Traité,* pp. 72, 343 f.

11. *Cours,* IV, p. 64.

12. In this illustration I have limited expenditures to those for labor and use of land, and have not introduced, in addition, any consideration of expenditure of capital *substance* consumed. The reason for this is that, according to Say, the latter expenditure is included in the expenditure for elementary productive services.

13. Book II, Chap. VIII, Sec. 2, p. 395, note 1.

14. "Deviennent des fonds productifs de valeur" Book I, Chap. IV, at end.

15. Book II, Chap. I, p. 315 f.

16. *Traité,* p. 71, note 2.

17. *Traité,* p. 395.

18. *Traité,* p. 338.

19. Cassel, whose judgments in the field of the history of theory are usually diametrically opposed to mine, differs with respect to Say as well, and with respect to what I call Say's inconsistency and the contradiction and vacillation which characterize his explanations. Cassel considers these, on the contrary, a laudable completeness of explanation and the mark of a genius in

their grasp of the idea of "reciprocal dependence" of economic phenomena. (*Nature and Necessity of Interest,* p. 26 f., p. 55 ff. and especially p. 60). Some time ago I gave clear and detailed expression to my views on the latter topic in my essay on "Value, Costs and Marginal Utility" in Conrad's *Jahrbücher,* Series III, Vol. 3 (1892), p. 359 f., and more recently in No. VIII of my *Further Essays on Capital and Interest.* And in any case, two contradictory halves do not, in my estimation, constitute a whole. And it is, within certain limits, perhaps natural that Cassel should be influenced in his historical and theoretical judgment by the extent to which a theory he is judging agrees, or seems to agree, with his own theories. He is therefore not shocked by errors which, in my opinion at least, are identical with errors in his own theories. On this last point see *Further Essays on Capital and Interest,* No. XIII.

20. *Neue Untersuchung der National-ökonomie,* Stuttgart and Tübingen, 1835.

21. *Nationalökonomie oder Volkswirtschaft,* Berlin, 1838.

22. *Grundlagen der Nationalökonomie,* 10th ed., Stuttgart, 1873.

23. These include Schulze Delitzsch. For his views which, like Roscher's, are somewhat eclectic and not free from contradictions, see his *Kapitel zu einem deutschen Arbeiterkatechismus,* Leipzig, 1863, p. 24 ff.

24. In the German editions of Böhm-Bawerk appearing in 1884, 1900, 1914 and 1921, there are three pages of criticism on Kleinwächter, which, at the request of the author, were omitted from the English edition of 1890. This wish is here accorded the same respect.

25. Written in 1884.

26. *Essai sur la répartition des richesses,* 2nd ed., Paris, 1883, pp. 234 and 239.

27. *Principi della Economia sociale,* Naples, 1840.

28. Kleinwächter's attempt to demonstrate in detail the power of capital to create value does not call for discussion here, because in Kleinwächter's particular nomenclature the term is limited to the creation of useful goods.

29. This view is widely accepted even outside the ranks of the socialists proper. See, for instance, Pierstorff, *Lehre vom Unternehmergewinn,* p. 22 f.

30. I purposely forego at this point any inquiry as to whether the physical productivity of capital thus conceded is an original power of capital, or whether the productive results attained with the help of capital should not rather be credited to those productive powers through which capital itself originates; particularly to the account of the labor which made the capital. I do so to avoid diverting the discussion from that sphere where alone, in my opinion, the interest problem can be adequately solved—that of the theory of value.

31. See also on this point my *Rechte und Verhältnisse vom Standpunkte der volks-*

wirtschaftlichen Güterlehre, Innsbruck, 1881, p. 104 ff., and particularly pp. 107-109.

32. *An Inquiry into the Nature and Origin of Public Wealth,* Edinburgh, 1804.

33. "By what means capital or stock contributes towards wealth is not so apparent (as with land and labor). *What is the nature of the profit of stock? and how does it originate?* are questions the answers to which do not immediately suggest themselves. They are indeed questions that have seldom been discussed by those who have treated on political economy, and *important as they are, they seem nowhere to have received a satisfactory solution*" (p. 155).

I wish to note here that Lauderdale, like Adam Smith and Ricardo, does not distinguish between interest proper and entrepreneur's profit, but includes both in the term "profit."

34. *Inquiry,* pp. 172, 177, 205.

35. Lauderdale applies his theory with great patience and thoroughness to all the possible ways of employing capital. He distinguishes five classes of such employment—building and use of machinery, home trade, foreign trade, agriculture, and "conducting circulation." The illustration quoted in the text is from the first of these five divisions. I have chosen it because it most clearly illustrates the way in which Lauderdale envisions the connection between interest and the power of capital to replace labor.

36. *Principles of Political Economy,* London, 1820.

37. *Principles,* p. 80 f.

38. *Principles,* p. 84, and many other places; *Definitions in Political Economy,* Nos. 40 and 43.

39. A note in Ricardo's *Principles* at the end of Sec. VI, Chap. I, (p. 30, ed. of 1871) has sometimes given the impression that Ricardo had previously stated this proposition explicitly. That, however, is not the case. He is merely attributing the opinion to Malthus, who had actually put it into words. See Wollemborg, *Intorno al costo relativo di produzione,* Bologna, 1882, p. 26 f.

40. See above, Chap. VI.

41. *Lehre vom Unternehmergewinn,* p. 24.

42. *Principles,* p. 303; similarly p. 299 and elsewhere.

43. ". . . the latter case . . . shows at once *how much profits depend upon the prices of commodities,* and upon the cause which determines these prices, namely, the *supply compared with the demand*" (p. 334).

44. I think I may pass over Malthus's wearisome and barren controversy with Ricardo about the latter's interest theory. It offers many weak points. Those who wish to read an accurate appraisal of it will find it in Pierstorff's *Lehre vom Unternehmergewinn,* p. 23 ff.

45. *An Inquiry into the Natural Grounds of Right to Vendible Property or Wealth,* Edinburgh, 1829.

46. His chief work is the *Principles of Social Science,* 1858.

47. III, p. 109, similarly I, p. 149.

48. III, pp. 50, 74 and often.

49. III, p. 111. Similarly in other passages.

50. III, p. 111. Similarly Vol. I, Chap. VI and in other passages.

51. III, pp. 111-113.

52. III, p. 114.

53. E.g., III, p. 115: "The proportion of the capitalist (i.e., excess of proceeds or interest as the following lines show) declines . . . *because of the great saving of labor.*" P. 143 towards the end: "Decrease of the costs of reproduction and *reduction* of the rate of interest consequent on that," etc.

54. *Handbuch der politischen Ökonomie,* by E. Peshine Smith, German translation by Stöpel, Berlin, 1878. My statements are based on this translation.

55. See use of the term "profit" by the older English economists, p. 30, Translators' Note.

56. *Der isolierte Staat.,* 2nd ed., Rostock, 1842–1863. The page numbers quoted in the text refer to the first Section of the second part (1850).

57. "But how can the borrowed object be maintained and returned unimpaired as to condition and value? his, I admit, is not possible in the case of individual objects, but it certainly is for the totality of objects within a nation. If, for instance, 100 buildings which last 100 years are rented out on condition that the lessee erect one new building a year, the 100 buildings will be maintained in value in spite of the annual wear and tear. In this inquiry we must necessarily direct our attention to the whole. and although only two persons are represented as dealing with one another, that is simply a symbol by which we mean to represent the movement that goes on simultaneously over the whole nation." (Note by Thünen).

58. P. 195, and in greater detail, p. 93 ff.

59. To avoid misunderstanding I should emphasize that Thünen assumes that the excess production of the capital last applied sets the standard for the total amount of capital.

60. I have been loath to slow down the presentation in my text proper with an even greater number of fine points than I felt compelled to include. I am therefore relegating a few supplementary remarks to this footnote. Thünen makes two assertions which can possibly be interpreted as attempts to justify his assumption, and thus as the beginnings of a real explanation of interest. The first is the frequently repeated remark (pp. 111, 149), that capital obtains its highest rate of interest when a certain amount of it is invested, and that the rate of interest sinks when that amount is exceeded, *so that the producers of capital have no interest in pushing their production beyond that point.* It is possible to read this proposition as explanatory of the

fact that the supply of capital *can* never be so great as to reduce net interest to zero. But this consideration of the *general advantage of all capitalists* exerts no compulsion, indeed, perhaps no influence at all on the action of the *individual* capitalist and so cannot prevent the further growth of capital. Each one of us (quite rightly) thinks of the increase of capital funds which his individual savings cause as having but an infinitesimal effect on the prevailing interest rate, but a very perceptible effect on the increase in his personal income in the shape of interest. Therefore, every one who has the inclination and who has the opportunity, will go on saving, undismayed. He does so, just as every landowner improves his land and perfects his methods of cultivation, even though he knows, as a matter of theory, that if all owners were to do the same, and if the size of the population remained unchanged, there would be a reduction in the price of products, and notwithstanding reduced costs, a reduction in rent.

We might rate as Thünen's second attempt, his note (No. 60) on VII, 36, which speaks of the renewal of the capital by the borrower. Thünen points out that "in this inquiry we must necessarily direct our attention to the whole." One could conceivably interpret this warning as an attempt to prove an implication of his argument. It will be recalled that his text described a primitive state with respect to which certain assumptions were made. By the terms of one such assumption, the work done by an individual user of a capital good enabled him to replace it, and in addition to have an excess product left over. Now, what Thünen may have started to prove is, that this assumption will be valid under all economic conditions, if only one substitutes the whole people for the individual. For even if the personal efforts of the single individual do not suffice to replace the capital he used, *one* principle would still be valid for the people as a whole. That principle is, that it is always possible for men, through the use of capital, to produce an excess of products and *in addition* restore the capital consumed with part of the labor saved. This line of thought might be considered a refutation of the stricture I expressed in the text, to the effect that Thünen's assumptions are applicable only to simple conditions, and inadmissible for complicated ones. I do not think that this warning, to "direct our attention to the whole," was meant by Thünen in the sense I have just indicated. But even if it was, it does not invalidate my objection. For in questions of distribution (and the question of interest *is* a question of distribution) one may not in every respect "direct one's attention to the whole." The fact that society as a whole is able, with the help of capital, to renew this capital itself, and over and above that, to produce more products, by no means proves the existence of interest on capital. Since the laborer is just as indispensable to the process as is capital, this plus in products might just as well accrue to the laborer in the form of

excess wages, as to the capitalist in the shape of interest. Actually, interest, as excess value of individual return over individual expenditure of capital, depends on the fact that the *individual* always obtains producers' goods at a price which is less than the value of the additional consumers' goods. But the fact that it is true for society as a whole will not by itself guarantee it for the individual. At any rate it is not self-evident that it will do so. If it were, surely there would not be so many theories concerning a self-evident thing!

61. *Die allgemeine Wirtschaftslehre oder Nationalökonomie*, Berlin, 1858.

62. *Kritik der Lehre vom Arbeitslohn*, 1861. *Grundsätze der Volkswirtschaftslehre* 1864. *Vorlesungen über Volkswirtschaft*, 1878.

63. *Zur Kritik der Lehre Marx vom Kapitale* and *Kritik der Lehre vom Arbeitslohn*, Vols. XVI, p. 93 ff.; XVII, p. 298 ff.

64. Vol. XVII, p. 325, toward the end.

65. See Knies, *Der Credit*, second half, p. 34 f., then 77 f. See also Chap. VIII of this volume.

66. Many a reader may wonder why a writer who is so decidedly opposed to the productivity theory as I, does not avail himself at all of the abundant and powerful support of socialist criticism. In other words, why do I not dismiss the theory with the argument that capital itself is the product of labor, and that hence its productivity, whatever else it be, is not an originary power? The reason is simply that I attribute to that argument only secondary importance in the theoretical explanation of interest. The case seems to me to be as follows. No one will question that capital, once made, manifests a certain productive effect. A steam engine, for instance, is admittedly the cause of a certain productive result. The primary theoretical question suggested by this state of matters now would read, "Is that productive capacity of capital—of capital made and ready—the completely sufficient cause of interest?" If this question could be answered in the affirmative, then it would, to be sure, have to be followed by the question whether the productive power of capital is an independent power of capital, or whether it is, on the contrary, only derived from the labor which produced the capital. In other words, "Does (manual) *labor*, penetrating the medium of capital, operate as the true cause of interest?" But since I had already answered the first question in the negative, I had no occasion to concern myself with the secondary question, as to whether the productive power of capital is an originary power or not.—Incidentally, I shall have occasion to take a stand on that question in a subsequent chapter (XII).

Since the first edition of this book appeared, several additional attempts have been made to defend the productivity theory in one version or another. The most noteworthy of these attempts will be discussed in the appendix on "Recent Literature on Interest."

NOTES TO CHAPTER VIII

1. See note 2, Chap. VII.

2. Indecisiveness of expression on the part of many use theorists is largely responsible for the fact that so little attention has hitherto been paid to the independent character of these theories. Their representatives were usually classed with the adherents of the productivity theories proper, and a confutation of the latter was considered a confutation of the use theorists as well. My statements prove that this is quite erroneous and that the two groups of theories are based on essentially distinct principles.

3. See Chap. VII, Sec. B.

4. See my *Rechte und Verhältnisse*, p. 57 ff. Further details follow.

5. *Cours d'Economie Politique*, Vol. I, Paris, 1823.

6. These last words are a quotation from Say.

7. In discussing the question of the rate of interest, too, this inversion of the relation of originary and loan interest reappears. On p. 285 Storch contends that interest is determined by the relationship between the supply of capital available for loans by capitalists and the amount required by entrepreneurs wishing to borrow it. Yet on p. 286 he says that the rate of income of those persons who employ their productive powers themselves adapts itself to that rate which is determined by the demand and supply of *loaned* productive powers.

8. *Öffentlicher Kredit.* I quote from the 2nd ed., 1829.

9. See for instance pp. 19 and 20.

10. "Two factors constitute the basis for the exchange value acquired by the productive services of capital. The first of these is the necessity and usefulness of capital for the business of production in all its highly diverse manifestations. The other is the hardship of the privations by which capital is amassed. The compensation for these factors consists in the share in the value of consumers' goods in the production of which they have collaborated" (p. 19). "The services of *capital* and of industry *necessarily* have exchange value; the former because capital is acquired only by more or less painful privations or exertions, which people can be induced to undergo only by the prospect of an appropriate benefit . . ." (p. 22).

11. Cassel, 1850-1857.

12. Vol. I, Sec. II, p. 246 ff., and elsewhere.

13. Vol. II, p. 214, and elsewhere.

14. Vol. II, p. 255.

15. Vol. III, pp. 633, 660.

16. See first edition, p. 270 footnote.

17. The second edition appeared in 1870, another unchanged edition in 1874. I quote from the latter.

18. P. 109 ff.

19. Hermann is not uniformly loyal to this concept of capital. In this passage he speaks of the goods which form the basis of a durable use as constituting capital. But later on he is fond of representing capital as something different from the goods, something hovering over them as it were. Thus he says on p. 605, "*Above all, we must distinguish the object in which a capital appears from that capital itself.* Capital is the basis of a durable use which has definite exchange value and it continues to exist undiminished as long as the use retains that value. It makes no difference whether the goods which constitute the capital are useful simply as capital or in other ways as well, or in what form they appear." If the question be put, "What then is capital if it is not the substance of the goods which 'represents' that capital?" it might be difficult enough to give a straight-forward answer, and one that would not be simply playing with words. (Page 111.)

20. Hermann evidently considers the exchange value of uses too obvious to need any formal explanation from him. Even the exceedingly brief explanation which I have set down here, is usually given by him only by indirection, although with sufficient clarity. Thus, on p. 507, he says, "The grower of grain can obtain no compensation for the use of land in the price of his grain, so long as such use is available as a free good in whatever quantity may be desired."

21. Pp. 312 ff., 412 ff.

22. P. 286 f.

23. See what follows in the text.

24. See foregoing, p. 81 f.

25. See also p. 560: "The uses of capital are therefore a factor in the determination of prices."

26. For instance Roscher, Sec. 183. Roesler, who accepts Hermann's results although he ascribes them to somewhat different causes, is the only exception. See Translators' Note, foregoing p. 116.

27. A note which occurs here in the German editions is omitted in accordance with the author's instruction for the English editions. Translators.

28. P. 541; p. 212 of 1st ed.

29. *Versuch einer Kritik der Gründe die für grosses und kleines Grundeigentum angeführt werden*, Leningrad, 1849.

30. For instance, p. 236 f.

31. P. 306 ff.

32. *Volkswirtschaftslehre*, Stuttgart, 1868, particularly pp. 121 f., 137, 333, then 445 and elsewhere.

33. Pp. 122, 432.

34. *Schönbergs Handbuch*, 1st ed., Vol. I, pp. 437 f., 484 ff.

35. *Das Gesellschaftliche System der menschlichen Wirtschaft*, 3rd ed., Tübingen, 1873.

36. *Das Gesellschaftliche System der*

menschlichen Wirtschaft, 3rd ed., Vol. I, pp. 266 ff., Vol. II, p. 458.

37. *Bau und Leben des sozialen Körpers*, 2nd ed., Tübingen, 1881.

38. Knies, *Geld und Credit*, Vol. II, Part II, p. 35. Compare Nasse's *Rezension* in Vol. XXXV of the *Jahrbücher für Nationalökonomie und Statistik*, 1880, p. 94.

39. In *Zeitschrift für die gesamte Staatswissenschaft*, Vol. XV, p. 559 ff.

40. See foregoing p. 31 f.

41. *Der Credit*, Part I, p. 11.

42. *Der Credit*, Part II, p. 38 ff. I trust it is not immodest on my part to conjecture that this respected authority may have been moved to write his polemic by the contents of a paper which I had written as a member of his seminar in economics a few years before, and in which I had expressed the views which he attacked.

43. *Das Geld*, Berlin, 1873, Vol. I; *Der Credit*, Vol. II, Part I, 1876; Part II, 1879.

44. *Das Geld*, pp. 61 ff., 71 ff. I shall return to the details of this inquiry later on, when treating the use theory as a whole.

45. See foregoing, p. 129 f.

46. *Der Credit*, Part II, p. 33 f., and other places.

47. *Grundsätze der Volkswirtschaftslehre*, Vienna, 1871; American edition: *Principles of Economics*, The Free Press, Glencoe, Illinois, 1950.

48. See pp. 94 and 130 f.

49. I regret that I must deny myself the pleasure of introducing more than the barest outlines of Menger's theory of value at this point. Holding, as I do, that his theory is one of the most splendid and most reliable achievements of modern economic science, I feel that under these circumstances it cannot be properly appreciated. In my second volume I shall have the opportunity of going into the subject more thoroughly. Meanwhile, for further details concerning the propositions cited only in highly fragmentary form in the text, I refer the reader to Menger's own very brilliant and convincing exposition in the *Grundsätze*, and especially to the portion beginning on p. 149 of the American edition.

50. Pp. 157-161 of American edition.

51. Mataja in his creditable *Unternehmergewinn*, Vienna, 1884, is in substantial agreement with Menger. See particularly pp. 124, 127, 129 f., 168 par. 2, 186 f., 192 ff., 196 ff.

52. Translators' Note: Hermann uses the words "Nutzung" and "Gebrauch," both of which mean "use" or "employment."

53. *Das Geld*, p. 61. "Use equals the *utilization* of a good lasting over a period of time, subject to definite limitation."

54. See my *Rechte und Verhältnisse vom Standpunkte der volkswirtschaftlichen Güterlehre*, Innsbruck, 1881, p. 51 ff.

55. I take the liberty of repeating, partly verbatim, the argument of my *Rechte und Verhältnisse*, which was written some time ago with a view to the present work.

56. Schäffle, in particular, in the third volume of his *Bau und Leben*, adroitly takes the same point of view. Schäffle, I may say, forms a commendable exception to the economists whom I charged with the objectionable habit of not taking any trouble to formulate the principles that govern the functions of goods. John Rae (see Chap. XI) and Irving Fisher also deserve mention in this respect.

57. "Nutzleistung." I introduced this term before in my *Rechte und Verhältnisse*. Even before that I used it in a work written in 1876 which, however, was not published. Knies uses it a few times in Part II of his *Credit*, but unfortunately with the same ambiguity that applies to his word "use" (*Nutzung*).

58. Say's concept of *services productifs* was attacked because it required the use of a metaphor as scientific nomenclature. Only a person, not a thing, it was said, could render services. I hope that, after all the explanation I have given, I do not have to fear that this same fault will be found with my "rendition of service."

59. This does *not* mean contract loans. (See following text.)

60. See also my *Rechte und Verhältnisse*, p. 70 ff.

61. In my *Rechte und Verhältnisse*, p. 60 ff., where the character of renditions of service as *primary* factors in our economic transactions is emphasized and the value of goods is shown to be derived from the value of these renditions of service.

62. This same idea, in somewhat different terms, is explicitly recognized in Knies's *Der Credit*, Part II, pp. 34 f., 77, 78. He expressly calls the *selling price* of a house the price of the *permanent use* of a house in contrast to the rental, which is the price of the *temporary use* of the same good. See also his *Geld*, p. 86 ff. Schäffle too, in his *Bau und Leben*, 2nd ed., III, describes goods as "stores of useful energies" (p. 285).

63. For further details see my *Rechte und Verhältnisse*, p. 64 ff.

64. A hair-splitting critic might perhaps point out that the possession of good machines helps the manufacturer achieve say, good credit, a good reputation, good clientele. The alert reader will have no difficulty in meeting such objections. "Use through exchange" belongs in the same category.

65. *Staatswirtschaftliche Untersuchungen*, 2nd ed., p. 109.

66. P. 110 f. See quotation above, p. 128.

67. To be convinced of the appropriateness of this analogy we need only visualize the gradation from durable to perishable goods. We should begin at one extreme with goods such as land or precious stones, and proceed through ever less durable goods, such as tools, furniture, clothing, linen, candles, paper collars, and so on, till we reached entirely perishable goods such as matches, food, drink, etc.

68. *Geld*, p. 59 ff.

69. In later editions Knies attempted to defend his interpretation against the excep-

tions I have taken here. I have chosen a suitable occasion in the second, and positive part of this work to comment on that attempt. See my *Positive Theory of Capital*, p. 289 f.

70. I feel it necessary to state clearly that my controversy on the subject of use places me in opposition, not only to the use theorists proper, but to almost the entire literature of political economy. The concept of the use of capital which I dispute is the one that has been commonly accepted since the days of Salmasius. Even writers who explain the origin of interest by quite different theories, such as Roscher, with his productivity theory, Senior with his abstinence theory, and Courcelle-Seneuil or Wagner, with their remuneration theory, always conceive of loan interest as a remuneration for a transferred use or usage of capital, and occasionally they even construe *originary* interest as a result of the same use or usage. There is but one difference between the use theorists proper and the others. The latter employ these locutions naively, using terms that have become popular, and do not trouble themselves as to the premises and conclusions of the use concept, even though it now and again will contradict the rest of their interest theory. But the use theorists erect the structure of their distinctive theory on a foundation which consists in the conclusions drawn from that concept. The almost world-wide dissemination of the error I am opposing may well justify the extensive treatment I accord it.

71. *Grundlagen*, 10th ed., p. 401 f.

72. Sec. 1. 31 Dig. loc. 19, 2, and 1. 25, Sec. 1, Dig. dep. 16, 3.

73. Goldschmidt, *Handbuch des Handelsrechtes*, 2nd ed., Stuttgart, 1883, Vol. II, Part I, footnote to p. 26.

74. Ulpian's passage in Dig. VII, 5, is well known. *De usufructu earum rerum quae usu consumuntur vel minuuntur* (On the Use of Things which are Consumed or Depreciated through Use), quotes a decree of the senate which established the right to bequeath a usufruct in perishable goods. On this subject Gaius remarks: "Quo senatus consulto non id effectum est, ut pecuniae usufructus proprie esset; *nec enim naturalis ratio acutoritate senatus commutari potuit:* sed, remedio introducto, coepit quasi usufructus haberi." (This decree of the senate did not make a usufruct of one's own property possible, for not even by the authority of the senate can a natural truth be altered. But, the legal step having once been taken, a quasi usufruct began to exist.)

I do not agree with the contention of Knies (*Geld*, p. 75) that Gaius was objecting only on technical grounds because there can be a regular usufruct only in *goods belonging to another*, whereas a legatee holds the perishable goods left him as his own property (*res suae*). He would certainly not have invoked the *naturalis ratio* if he had merely intended to level his

criticism at a technically bad definition of usufruct. It is infinitely more probable that he was exercised over the more serious violation of a truth of nature.

75. The rudiments of this interpretation, which I consider the only correct one, are to be found in writings as early as those of Galiani (see p. 31 f.) and Turgot (see p. 35 f.). At a later period, they recur in the works of Bentham and John Rae, treated in Chap. XI, as well as those of Knies, who subsequently and explicitly retracted it as erroneous.

76. *Grundsätze*, p. 132 ff.

77. *Ibid.*, p. 132.

78. See my *Rechte und Verhältnisse*, especially pp. 124 ff.

79. See my *Rechte und Verhältnisse*, p. 34, note 23.

80. *Rechte und Verhältnisse*, p. 148 f.

81. Margolin, in his *Kapital und Kapitalzins*, Berlin, 1904, says on p. 104, that this argument of mine had very "strangely" failed to take one element into account which marks every reciprocal transfer of goods. That element is the fact that the good taken in exchange, as well as the one so given, is capable of further use as a capital good, and that therefore neither of the contracting parties to a purchase is under any obligation to make a separate payment for the use, as a capital good, of the good received. My answer is that I did visualize this counterargument as conceivable, even when I was preparing the manuscript of the first edition of this book. But I rejected the idea of refuting it in advance, as unnecessary, because it seemed to me altogether improbable that anyone would seriously raise that objection. For on the one hand, it fails completely to relieve the use theory of the embarrassing inadequacies I pointed out above, and on the other hand it subjects the simplest business transactions to interpretations that are highly artificial, not to say abstruse in the extreme. Let a single observation suffice. To begin with, Margolin's contention would force us to see in every purchase a "double-barreled" transaction, one half of which is an exchange of goods for goods, and the other half an exchange of perpetual uses for perpetual uses. Only in the event that one set of perpetual uses is incomplete or "short," must there be compensation in the form of an extra payment. This would apply to a missing interest coupon or the reserved usufruct above. But that is only the beginning! Since this payment is an exchange of *uses* for goods, the latter also have attached to them perpetual uses of their own, and these are not being paid for. Unless, of course, Margolin has the temerity to continue postulating, and this time to the effect that the *uses* which were paid for with goods, also and in turn have a similar chain of perpetual uses attached to *them*, which are given in payment for the uses attached to the goods which were given in payment for the uses that were short. But of course

in that case, the same would have to be true of the uses of these uses, and so on, *ad infinitum*. In other words, we should be forced to assume that every link in the unending chain of uses had its own secondary unending chain of uses, every link of which again had a tertiary chain, and so on and on and on. And thus we should have to represent and interpret every exchange, even of the simplest kind, as the mutual transfer of two universes of perpetual uses, comparable to those well-known toys which consist of a series of boxes, each containing a smaller box—the series in this case being extended to infinity. And remember that all this takes place against a background of unresolved practical doubts as to whether these "uses" have a real existence! For that reason I was somewhat astonished to learn that a modern economist like Oswalt should subscribe to Margolin's argument. Nay, more! Oswalt even calls a theory operating with concepts like these, "simple" and "natural," and maintains that it occupies a position far removed from that of the scholasticists!

NOTES TO CHAPTER IX

1. Reprint from the *Encyclopaedia Metropolitana*, London, 1836. I quote from the 5th ed., London, 1863.

2. See foregoing pp. 66 ff. and also 195 ff.

3. Since the advent of Godwin, Thompson and others. See Chap. XII.

4. See foregoing p. 47 f.

5. See foregoing p. 126 f.

6. *Principles of Political Economy*, London, 1833.

7. *Ibid.*, p. 188.

8. Not until very recent times have any refinements been added, which might be termed an improvement in the formulation. But Marshall's contributions in this respect apply not so much to the characteristic essence of the interest theory, as to the *price theory* which is woven in with the interest theory. Further details on this subject will be found in the appendix to this volume dealing with the most recent literature on the subject of interest.

9. Berlin, 1875, p. 47 f.

10. *Kapital und Arbeit*, Berlin, 1864, p. 110.

11. The thought on which this objection is based was, in its essence, set forth by Loria in *La Rendita fondiaria*, Milan, 1880, pp. 610-624. Marshall organized and utilized it, and based on it his interesting concepts of "producer's surplus" and "saver's surplus," both of which are referred to in the appendix to this book, which treats of recent literature on interest. It has also been expressly formulated by Macfarlane in his *Value and Distribution*, Philadelphia, 1899, pp. 175-177. In my first edition, although I based my objection to the abstinence theory on entirely different considerations, I had accorded a measure of correctness to Lassalle's objection as well. Nevertheless, I feel that, with respect to this point, I must subscribe to the views of the aforementioned authors.

12. This passage appeared word for word in my first edition, and yet Landry, in his *L'intérêt du capital*, 1904, p. 181 f. and in his footnote to p. 189, made what is to me an incomprehensible charge. He accuses me of interpreting Senior "inaccurately" and too "narrowly and literally" when I lay at Senior's door the error of calculating sacrifice as consisting of expended labor plus the *entire* gratification of other things, which are thereby lost. His words are *peine dépensée + jouissances perdues.*

13. On this point compare my essay on "The Ultimate Standard of Value" in the *Annals of the American Academy of Political and Social Science*, Vol. v, No. 2, a translation of *Der letzte Masstab des Güterwertes*, which appeared in *Zeitschrift für Volkswirtschaft, Sozialpolitik und Verwaltung*, Vol. III, p. 185 ff., particularly p. 201 ff. See also Book III, Part A, on "Value," especially Chap. VIII in my 2nd vol. of this work, *Positive Theory of Capital*.

14. Even in that minority of cases where the sacrifice of labor is measured by the *pain or burden of labor*, the temporal factor of postponement of gratification cannot constitute the basis of a second and independent sacrifice. For appraisal by measure of the labor burden, as we have seen, governs only when that burden exceeds the intensity of any other result to be attained through the labor, including all enhancement by reason of whatever attraction of immediacy it may possess, and when the only reasonable choice is between the specific future useful purpose to which the labor is directed, on the one hand, and complete inactivity on the other. Since no earlier gratification of a good was ever an alternative, time can naturally not be a factor, in any way, shape, or manner, in an estimation of the extent of sacrifice. Macfarlane, in his *Value and Distribution* (p. 179), expresses a contrary opinion. While he calls the labor burden the basic element in calculating the sacrifice, he feels he is entitled, and indeed constrained, to make "an additional allowance" as well, for the postponement. This contention seems to me just downright untenable. A similar contention is discussed in the appendix to this volume in the course of my treatment of Marshall's interest theory. In the first edition of this book I had based a further objection to Senior's abstinence theory on the fact that Senior's interest theory was a mere interpolation in a cost-value theory, notorious as being valid only for goods producible in

unlimited quantity. I contended that it could for that reason not be accounted a universally valid interest theory, but at best one with only particular applicability. In consideration of the fact that the world of business enterprises, which are open to mutually levelling tendencies, constitutes the very field where the prevailing interest rate is set, I came to the conclusion that it was no longer incumbent on me to maintain that obligation. Incidentally, in this action I was following a suggestion of Macfarlane's (*op. cit.,* p. 181). That objection, too, by the way, had not constituted my "most serious objection," as Macfarlane called it (*op. cit.,* p. 224) but only a rather minor one. What I considered at that time, and still consider the most compellingly destructive argument against the abstinence theory is the factually as well as logically indefensible duplication of a factor which is already contained and accounted for in another element of cost. It is an error akin, in its logical inadequacy, to that which characterizes the use theory when, it seems to me, it lists as a separate factor a use of goods which is already included in their value!

15. *Some Leading Principles of Political Economy,* 1874, (reprinted London, 1883), Chap. III.

16. *Précis de la Science Economique,* Paris, 1862. Especially Vol. I, p. 161 and p. 402 ff.

17. *Intorno al costo relativo di produzione,* etc., Bologna, 1882.

18. *System der Staatsanleihen,* Heidelberg, 1885, p. 48. "The lender of capital bases his claim to compensation for the use of it which he has transferred, on the fact that he has foregone the opportunity to use it to implement his own labor power, on the one hand, and/or, on the other hand, that he has refrained from consuming it, or the value thereof, for immediate enjoyment. This is the basis of interest, which does not, however, concern us here."

19. *Harmonies Économiques,* Vol. VI of his complete works, ed. III, Paris, 1855, p. 210. Compare also his immediately preceding explanations on pp. 207-209, and, in general, his entire Chap. VII.

20. Chap. VII, p. 213.

21. Published in 1849. *Oeuvres complètes,* ed. IV, Vol. V, p. 22 ff.

22. "If our examination penetrates to the bottom of the situation, we find that the lender renounces in favor of the borrower either an *immediate satisfaction* which he postpones for several years, or a *working implement* by means of which he would have increased his powers, or caused the powers of nature to assist him, or he *would have increased, to his advantage, the ratio between his reward and the effort needed to attain it"* (VII, p. 209). "It postpones the *possibility of production . . .*" "I shall use it for a period of 10 years in some *productive form"* (XV, p. 445 f.). He makes frequent similar statements in his *Capital et Rente* as for instance on p. 44 where he tells us how James, who has made a plane and loaned it to William for a year, urges, as his reason for demanding interest, the fact that "I was expecting to *gain something* from that plane, perhaps a more highly perfected piece of work, or a better paid one, or some other improvement in my situation. I cannot give all that up in your favor without compensation."

23. Thus, for instance, Bastiat in his *Capital et Rente,* on p. 40, presupposes that the bag of seed grain borrowed by the debtor enables him to produce an *enhanced value.* On p. 43 he calls the reader's attention, in express terms, to the fact that "the basis of the solution" of the interest problem is the *power possessed by tools to increase the productivity of labor.* He continues, on p. 46, "we may conclude that it is in the nature of capital to *make a profit."* And the introduction to his brochure *Capital et Rente* indicates that his pamphlet is a partisan effort to defend the "productivity of capital" against the attacks of the socialists.

24. Compare Rodbertus *Zur Beleuchtung der sozialen Frage,* Vol. I, p. 116 f., and Pierstorff, *op. cit.,* p. 202 f.

25. Chap. VII, p. 214 ff.

26. Chap. VII, p. 216.

27. ". . . and I defy any one to imagine such a distribution by any mechanism other than interest." Chap. VII, p. 217.

28. "Let us acknowledge that the natural social mechanism is sufficiently ingenious to allow us to relieve ourselves of the duty of substituting for it an artificial mechanism" (p. 216 at end).

29. *Op. cit.,* p. 223.

NOTES TO CHAPTER X

1. *Elements of Political Economy.* My references are to the 1844 reprint of the third edition which appeared in 1826. The first two editions of 1821 and 1824 were unfortunately not available to me.

2. The author (as is evident from a parallel passage on p. 100) means an annuity which replaces the original value of the machine in 10 years, and at the same time pays interest thereon at the prevailing market rate.

3. See p. 66 ff. On the subject of chronological precedence as between James Mill and McCulloch, the following conclusions may be drawn from Edwin Cannan's *History of the Theories of Production and Distribution,* which was published in 1894, 10 years after the appearance of my first edition. The earliest mention of the basic concept of the theory they profess in common appears in an article by McCulloch entitled *Political Economy* in the 1823 Sup-

plement to the *Encyclopaedia Britannica*. Then James Mill adopts the same idea but treats it at greater length in the second edition (1824) of his *Elements of Political Economy*. The version I have cited at this point is from the third edition of 1826, and presents numerous changes in wording as compared with the second edition.

4. *Traité théorique et pratique d'Economie Politique* I, Paris, 1858.

5. *Précis du Cours d'Economie Politique*, 2nd ed., Paris, 1881 and 1882.

6. Vol. II, p. 189; compare also Vol. I, p. 236.

7. See foregoing p. 190 and Note 16 on p. 461.

8. *Traité d'Économique Politique*, 8th ed., Paris, 1880, p. 522: le loyer "rémunère et provoque *les efforts ou le travail d'épargne et de conservation.*" (Rent inspires and requites the *efforts or the labor of saving and conserving.*)

9. *Zur Erklärung und Abhilfe der heutigen Kreditnot des Grundbesitzes*, 2nd ed., 1876, Vol. II, p. 273 f.

10. *Soziale Frage*, p. 146.

11. *Soziale Frage*, pp. 75 and 146. See also Chap. XII of this volume.

12. *Ibid.*, Vol. II, p. 458.

13. *Ibid.*, p. 459 f.

14. See foregoing p. 135 f.

15. I submit the following excerpts from Schäffle. "Accordingly, I cannot subscribe to the complete condemnation of capital and interest as 'mere expropriation of surplus value.' Private capital under present conditions performs a function of cardinal importance by taking upon itself the conduct of what would otherwise conform to Rodbertus's expression 'business which is left to its own devices'" (2nd ed., Vol. III, p. 386). "Historically considered, capitalism has every right to respected existence, and interest is completely justified. To abolish the latter without first having found a better way to organize production, is sheer nonsense." "One may not, as a practical matter, convict interest on the charge of 'expropriation of surplus value' until and unless one can replace the economic services performed by private capital with a public system which is definitely proven to be more efficient as well as less 'voracious of surplus value.'" (Vol. III, p. 422 f.)

16. See foregoing p. 136 f.

17. *Allgemeine oder theoretische Volkswirtschaftslehre*, Part I, *Grundlegung*, 2nd ed., Leipzig and Heidelberg 1879, pp. 40 and 594.

18. Since I wrote those lines in 1884, the doubts expressed have been resolved, as far as he was concerned, by one of these authors through an explicit statement. A. Wagner makes the statement in the third edition of his *Grundlegung* (Part II, 1894, p. 289 ff., Sec. 134), that it had not been his intention, when he made the statements which I questioned, to offer a theoretical "explanation" of interest, but rather a "reason" for it in the sense of a "social justification" of it. As far as the theoretical problem is concerned, Wagner expresses the belief that the explanation of interest which I advanced in the meantime, and which was based on "the influence of the time factor on human valuation of goods," might be regarded as "in the main correct." But he does emphasize the point that my theory still did not include any direct "justification or reason for private capital, as an institution, forming an integral part of our legal system." For that reason, he says, it is necessary to supplement my "explanation" with the views he represents, if interest is to be afforded social and economic justification in the latter sense. However, in his most recent work on the subject, set forth in his *Theoretische Sozialökonomik*, Part I, 1907, p. 322 ff. Wagner has again modified his stand. This time he says that "he urges somewhat more strongly than before the necessity of supplementing" my theory, and that "regarding the social and economic aspects of the interest problem, he still adheres to the remuneration theory." "Because that theory," he claims, "offers the requisite complement" to my theory, and furnishes not only the justification, but also the "explanation and the reason for interest as a purely economic phenomenon." In the meantime Stolzmann, author of *Die Soziale Kategorie*, Berlin 1896, p. 421 f. has taken his stand quite unequivocally, and is an out-and-out advocate of the remuneration theory. See my later treatment in the Appendix.

19. *Bau und Leben*, Vol. III, p. 451.

20. In a final footnote to this chapter, I should like to devote a few words to J. G. Hoffmann. He, too, calls interest a wage for certain labors. "This income too" he says, having in mind interest on capital investments, "is only a *wage for labors*, and as a matter of fact labors very much for the public benefit. For the acceptance of such income implies, essentially and preeminently, an obligation to engage in independent activity in the cause of public welfare, of science and of art, indeed of everything which adds to human existence any elements of ease, nobility and beauty." (*Über die wahre Natur und Bestimmung der Renten aus Boden- und Kapitaleigentum* in the *Sammlung kleiner Schriften staatswirtschaftlichen Inhalts*, Berlin, 1843, p. 566). It is probably safe to say that Hoffmann gives us even greater cause than the "socialists of the chair" to be in doubt as to whether his words, here quoted, were intended as a theoretical explanation of interest. If they were, then his theory is unquestionably even more inadequate than all the other remuneration theories. If they were not, then it does not lie within the scope of my problem to question their correctness in some other connection.

NOTES TO CHAPTER XI

1. *Statement of Some New Principles on the Subject of Political Economy*, exposing the fallacies of the system of free trade, and of some other doctrines maintained in the *Wealth of Nations*, Boston, 1834.
2. See the Essay by Mixter, p. 165, referred to later in this chapter.
3. This is indicated by the great rarity of this book. I tried in vain to unearth a copy that might be for sale, and was not able to examine the work until shortly before the publication of the second edition of my own book. And then it was possible for me to do so only through the kindness of Professor Carl Menger who had succeeded in acquiring a copy for his own library, which is famous for its completeness. Subsequently (1905) Professor Mixter published a reprint of this posthumously famous work under the altered title *The Sociological Theory of Capital*. In doing so he also made extensive changes in the order in which parts of the book appear, but has otherwise given the text word for word (1905 edition by Macmillan Co., New York). Strange to relate, Rae's book remained unnoticed at home, but was translated into Italian 20 years later, and included in the *Bibliotheca dell'Economista*, Vol. XI, (Turin, 1856). However, that does not seem to have caused any wide circulation of it in Italian literature, either. In his *Introduzione allo Studio dell' Economia Politica* (Milan, 1892) on p. 483 Luigi Cossa devotes five lines to Rae, to the effect that he made some apt remarks, adopted by John Stuart Mill, on the subject of the acquisition of capital. This remark of Cossa's would seem to indicate that even he took no note of Rae beyond the quotations from him that appear in Mill. And that, in spite of the existence of the Italian translation!
4. I gave a brief survey in the first edition of my *Positive Theory* (p. 249, note 1) of the treatment that writers up to that time had accorded to the time factor in political economy. There I merely stated that "Rae, who was extensively quoted by John Stuart Mill" had made some "apt remarks" on the subject, but that I considered Jevons to be the first one to have treated the subject avowedly and professedly. I did not mention Rae at all in the first edition of my *History and Critique of Interest Theories*, since I was simply unaware of any interest theory of Rae's, because none could be deduced from Mill's quotation from Rae.
5. "A Forerunner of Böhm-Bawerk" in the *Quarterly Journal of Economics*, Vol. XI, January 1897, pp. 161-190.
6. *Ibid.*, p. 190 ". . . he anticipated Böhm-Bawerk's theory of interest, in the substance of its leading features and in many of its details, and even to a great extent in the exact form of its expression. He did more; he expanded that theory on some sides in

which it was lacking, he avoided its greatest errors."
7. Written in the year 1900 on the occasion of the appearance of the *second* edition of this book.
8. My references are to the original edition of 1834. Owners of the Mixter reprint will find a "Readers' Guide" on p. 484 which indicates the numbering of corresponding pages in the two versions. This "guide" is necessitated by the change in order of sequence of the several parts!
9. Compare also his p. 171, where Rae takes the word "stock" which includes "instruments" of all kinds, and subdivides the concept into "stock for immediate consumption" and "capital." He cites as examples of "instruments" belonging to the first class such things as clothing, dwelling houses, furniture, gardens and playgrounds. His definition of capital, as well as his division of it into fixed and circulating capital, is quite in keeping with what was then current in England, and is as infelicitous as it is unoriginal. In conformity with the custom of the time, his definition lays its principal emphasis on the requirement that goods must be intended for exchange, if they are to fall within the definition of goods which constitute capital, or which require the assistance of capital for their production. Or to quote verbatim, "the instruments to which this term (capital) applies, supply the future wants of the individuals owning them indirectly, either from being themselves commodities *that may be exchanged* for articles directly suited to their needs, or by their capacity of producing commodities *which may be so exchanged*" (p. 171). But such a definition, literally construed, would exclude from classification as capital the production goods of the individual independent producer, such as the plow, the team and the threshing machine of the farmer whose product is consumed within his own establishment! However, as Mixter very aptly points out (p. 169 of his previously cited work), Rae makes practically no application of this narrower concept of capital throughout the course of his book. On the contrary, he avails himself constantly of his broader concept of "stock" as including all classes of "instrument." As a result, his ill-advised definition of capital does not lead to any damaging consequences. On the other hand, I cannot see how Mixter thinks he is obliged to identify this broader concept of "stock" or "instrument" with my own concept of "intermediary products." The fact that both Rae and I include "warehouse goods" in our respective schemes, does not by any means establish their identity. For my concept of "intermediary products" *excludes*, as a matter of principle, consumption goods that are *ready for consumption* (since my understanding of ware-

house goods specifically stipulates that they be *not yet quite ready* for consumption). But Rae, equally as a matter of principle, *includes* warehouse goods among his "instruments," even if they are already in the hands of the consumer, provided only that they are not yet fully consumed. Contrary to the opinion of Mixter, even foodstuffs would undoubtedly be "instruments" according to Rae's definition and his accompanying explanation. That concept of instruments, the distinguishing characteristic of which is the intention of meeting a future need, seems to me to be most closely akin to the idea of capital as defined by Turgot and by Knies. Since then Mixter has himself admitted the not inconsiderable number of instances of his misunderstanding of Rae. I wish to point, in this connection, to a subsequent article by him, which I have quoted at the close of this chapter, entitled "Böhm-Bawerk on Rae."

10. I agree with Mixter (see his p. 168) when he expresses the opinion that Rae's concept and interpretation of useful "events" coincide exactly with my own objective *Nutzleistungen* (renditions of service) as the term was used in Chap. VIII.

11. This is the first occurrence of the time element in Rae. Here again, I must confess, I cannot quite understand how Mixter could identify Rae's time interval with mine. That is to say, I cannot see how Mixter can call Rae's time interval between the formation and the exhaustion of instruments the same as the one on which I based my concept of capitalist roundabout ways of production. Rae says, "Between the formation and the exhaustion of instruments a space of time intervenes," and Mixter says, that is "the same thing as saying that the capitalistic process is a roundabout process." (See his page 169.) That is clearly in error. For I am referring to the interval of time which occurs in the capitalist production process between the first application of productive powers and the final completion of the product, or in Rae's parlance, the period of time which precedes the "formation of the instruments." But Rae is referring to an entirely different interval of time, the one which intervenes between the "formation" and the "exhaustion" of the instruments. If Robinson Crusoe fashions a bench out of some flat stones through the expenditure of a few hours of labor, the bench may last 20 or even 100 years, and there will thus be a very considerable "period between formation and exhaustion," in Rae's sense of "period," but there would be an extremely short period of production in my sense. See also the concluding words of foregoing footnote 9.

12. The exceptions at which Rae hints in this passage and in a later one on p. 259, are enlarged upon in his Chap. XI on "Luxury." They concern instances of a tendency which people often exhibit out of vanity. This tendency leads them to place a much higher value on an expensive article

which serves their real needs no better, or very little better than a cheaper article which would serve the same or very nearly the same purpose. If vanity did not more or less influence people's spending, says Rae, we should find that things would be valued entirely in accordance with their physical properties (p. 283, but compare also the table of contents for his chapter on "Luxury" on p. XV).

13. The term is my own, and does not occur in Rae.

14. Apparently that extended period of time over which the labors are spread in expending them for the formation of an instrument, is the same thing that I called "period of production" in my theory of capital. It therefore coincides with what Rae terms "period of formation." However, Rae is not much concerned with this concept, but only with the interval between the "period of formation" and the "period of exhaustion." And incidentally, when he uses the word "period" in these expressions, he is quite often using it (p. 104, for example) to denote, not an actual *extended space* in time, but rather a *single point* in time. See also preceding note 11.

15. When computing the "doubling period" at these rates, Rae is obviously using the geometric progression as his basis. In other words, he is dealing with compound interest.

16. The quality and quantity of resources are regarded by Rae as an "important but ultimate fact" which does not constitute an object of his investigation (p. 130). The same is true of wage conditions which he likewise states to be an "existing circumstance" which he is disposed to accept. He merely states briefly, that a low wage rate operates in a manner similar to that of an improvement in the quality of the materials to be worked on, or of an advance in technical invention. For all these factors tend in identical fashion to provide the possibility of gaining the same return at smaller cost. But Rae does not neglect to say that in other respects the factors in question are operative along essentially different lines.

17. "If, therefore, continual additions be made to the durability of an instrument, it cannot be preserved at an order of equally quick return unless the several augmentations be communicated to it by an expenditure diminishing in a geometrical ratio; that is, in a ratio becoming indefinitely less, as it is continued. This, however, cannot happen, for it would imply an absurdity" (p. 112).

18. See foregoing p. 211.

19. Rae expressly draws the distinction (for instance, beginning on p. 172 f.) between such cases, on the one hand, "where the effective desire of accumulation of a community has had opportunity to work up the materials possessed by it into instruments of an order *correspondent to its own strength*" and such cases, on the other hand "where the accumulative prin-

ciple has not yet had time fully to operate." There are similar passages on pp. 194 and 264.

20. See foregoing p. 219.

21. See foregoing p. 211 f.

22. This line of reasoning is specifically discernible when we consider, in conjunction with each other, Rae's remarks on pp. 118 ff., 172 and 169 f. It is most tersely set forth in the frequent passages in which Rae establishes the connection between the purely psychological factor of the "strength of the effective desire of accumulation," and the establishment of price and of interest. On the other hand, we shall observe that his introduction of the "actual order of instruments" in place of the "strength of desire" as a regulator of price and interest, has its place in a completely different line of reasoning.

23. See foregoing pp. 32 and 35 f.

24. *Principles of Morals and Legislation*, Chap. IV.

25. *Works*, Vol. IV, p. 540 (Codification Proposal); as quoted by Čuhel, *Theory of Needs*, Sec. 404. A passage at the close of the aforementioned Chap. IV of his *Principles* is similar and only somewhat more general: "The value of a property increases and decreases, *as is generally accepted*, . . . according to the proximity or remoteness of the time at which . . . it is to come into our possession."

26. *Defense of Usury*, Letter II.

27. See Essay XI in my *Further Essays on Capital and Interest*, Volume III of this work.

28. Nothing in economic literature known to me at the time of the first two editions of this book constituted the least trace of any theory of interest held by Bentham. Even Jevons quoted him merely as an authority in the field of philosophy for a general psychological thesis, and not as the author of a theory of interest! For that reason I referred at that time to Bentham only quite cursorily as an opponent of the canonistic prohibition of interest. It was not until Oskar Kraus published his treatise in 1901 entitled *On the Theory of Value, A Study of Bentham* that I became aware of Bentham's interesting position with respect to the theory of interest.

29. See foregoing pp. 47 f., 59, 103.

30. For further details I refer the reader to the second volume of this work containing my *Positive Theory* (Book IV, Chapter I).

31. For further details see Chap. XIII.

32. For further details see Appendix to this volume.

33. See foregoing p. 209.

34. See foregoing p. 215 f. The complementary proof, that the durability of goods cannot be indefinitely increased without a diminution of the rate of return (p. 215 above), is factually correct, but does not go to the bottom of the phenomenon.

35. Instances thereof are his pp. 170, 196, 300 and others. The sequence I have constructed here is likewise constructed out of scattered utterances of Rae's. The most important of these are 258 ff. (inventions), 170 (prices), 205 f. (average rate of profit); as well as 194 and 172 which contain remarks on the question of whether the "desire of accumulation" has had time to become operative.

36. See foregoing p. 112 f. I do not believe there can be the slightest doubt that these two authors arrived at such similar conclusions entirely independently. Their researches, though not their publications, were approximately contemporaneous. And both were solitary thinkers, rather than voluminous readers, and their doctrines are thoroughly stamped with the imprint of original reflection.

37. See Rae's pp. 93 f., 259, 283, Contents XV. When Rae first mentions this law (p. 94) he adds the remark that instruments "which serve the same kind of needs" are to be compared with each other on the basis of their "physical effects." But it should be noted that this does not constitute a limitation of the field in which his law has validity, but merely an expression of the self-evident consideration that like must be compared with like. Where he makes subsequent mention of the law, he does not again expressly mention this subsidiary clause. The language itself and the context in which it appears clearly indicate that valuation on the basis of physical effects is meant to be a general principle for the valuation of all "utilities," whereas the corresponding principle that applies to luxuries is that of costliness, of difficulty of acquisition (see pp. 269, 283, 305 f., and XV of the Contents).

38. See foregoing p. 218 ff.

39. See foregoing pp. 211 and 231 f.

40. See foregoing p. 60 ff.

41. See foregoing p. 224 f.

42. That is, even after completion of the levelling process which was set in motion by the initial abnormal excess of returns of the baking industry. Rae envisions a cessation of the additional return only at that very remote and in any case uncertain point in time at which the accumulation of capital will have caught up completely with the "desire of accumulation."

43. See foregoing p. 224 ff.

44. See foregoing pp. 219 f. and 228 f.

45. See foregoing footnote 42.

46. *Op. cit.*, p. 172; see foregoing p. 219 f.

47. Rae himself puts it into the words, "the inventive faculty must render the labor of the members of society more effective" (p. 258).

48. See foregoing p. 209.

49. *Positive Theory*, Book IV, Chap. III, Tables in Sec. I and Sec. III.

50. Rae himself does not use this term. But Mixter does when he compares the two theories.

51. Mixter also points out explicitly that these two apparently comparable features of the two theories are essentially disparate.

52. See foregoing footnote 9.

53. See foregoing p. 210 ff.

54. For he makes the remark that Rae does *not* cite the effect of time in bringing about an increased amount of the product, as a supporting argument for the preference for present as compared with future goods (*op cit.,* p. 173). On another occasion, with reference to my principle that our experience indicates that time consuming methods of production give a greater yield, Mixter says that "Rae might agree" (p. 188). Rae therefore obviously did not state explicitly that he did agree. At the same time he praises Rae for assigning the right place in the whole question to *invention*—as I did not!

55. See foregoing footnote 9.

56. After the appearance of the 2nd ed. of this book, and with particular reference to the foregoing statements in my text,

Professor Mixter admitted with commendable candor that in his earlier writing he had done a considerable amount of "reading Böhm-Bawerk into Rae," and that he had assumed a great deal more similarity between our two theories than in fact exists. See his "Böhm-Bawerk on Rae" in the *Quarterly Journal of Economics,* Vol. xvi, No. 3 (May 1902), p. 385, footnote. Mixter felt impelled for that reason to make a second critical comparison of the two theories, without however achieving a marked difference in the results. But even now that Mixter has been constrained to abandon part of his assumptions as erroneous, I cannot see that his opinion is any better founded than before. I think therefore that I must maintain unchanged the carefully considered appraisal of Rae that appears in my text above.

NOTES TO CHAPTER XII

1. This was written in 1884, and was retained in the editions of 1900, 1914 and 1921.

2. *Civil Government,* Book ii, Chap. v, Sec. 40. I should like to quote from his essay "On the History of England's Political Economy" a connected passage which reads as follows. "Nor is it so strange, as perhaps before consideration it may appear, that the property of labour should be able to overbalance the community of land. For it is labour indeed that puts the difference of value on everything; and let any one consider what the difference is between an acre of land planted with tobacco or sugar, sown with wheat or barley, and an acre of the same land lying in common without any husbandry upon it, and he will find that the improvement of labour makes the far greater part of the value. I think it will be but a very modest computation to say that of the products of the earth useful to the life of man 9/10 are the effects of labour; nay, if we will rightly estimate things as they come to our use, and cast up the several expenses about them—what in them is purely owing to nature, and what to labour—we shall find that in most of them 99/100 are wholly to be put on the account of labour."

3. *Consideration of the Consequences of the Lowering of Interest,* 1691, p. 24; cf. foregoing p. 28 f.

4. See foregoing p. 29 f.

5. *Handlungswissenschaft,* 2nd ed., p. 430.

6. *Geldumlauf,* Chap. iii, Sec. 26.

7. *An Inquiry into the Principles of the Distribution of Wealth most Conducive to Human Happiness,* 1824. For a treatment of Thompson and his immediate predecessors Godwin and Hall, see Anton Menger, *Das Recht auf den vollen Arbeitsertrag,* Stuttgart, 1886, Secs. 3-5; also Held, *Zwei*

Bücher zur sozialen Geschichte Englands, Leipzig, 1881, p. 89 ff. and p. 378 ff.

8. See Anton Menger, *op. cit.,* Sec. 5.

9. Two works of Hodgskin belong to this period and to this trend; one is his little known *Popular Political Economy* and the other is his anonymously published treatise under the significant title *Labour Defended against the Claims of Capital.* I was not able to see the books themselves, and was made aware of them only through quotations from them in the writings of some of his English contemporaries. Particularly Read and Scrope often quote from them, voicing sharp opposition to their content. The complete title of the anonymous work is, *Labour Defended against the Claims of Capital; or the Unproductiveness of Capital Proved,* by a labourer, London 1825. I deduce that Hodgskin is its author from a remark by Scrope on p. 150 of his *Principles of Political Economy,* London 1833. I submit a few characteristic passages, as quoted by Read. "All the benefits attributed to capital arise from co-existing and skilled labor" (from the introduction). Later the admission is made that more and better products can result from working with instruments and machines than without, but to that is added the following remark. "But the question then occurs what produces instruments and machines, and in what degree do they aid production independent of the labourer, so that the owners of them are entitled to by far the greater part of the whole produce of the country? *Are they or are they not the produce of labour?* Do they or do they not constitute an efficient means of production separate from labour? *Are they or are they not so much inert, decaying, and dead matter, of no utility whatever, possessing no productive power whatever,* but as they

466

are guided, directed and applied by skillful hands?" (p. 14).

10. See Anton Menger, *op. cit.*, preface, p. v, then pp. 53, 79 ff., 97 and many others.

11. A. Wagner said somewhat the same thing in *Grundlegung*, 3rd ed., Part ɪ, p. 37, footnote 1, and Part ɪɪ, p. 281.

12. First ed., 1819; 2nd ed., Paris, 1827. I quote from the latter. In an earlier work by Sismondi, (1803), entitled *De la richesse commerciale*, which occupied ground much closer to the classical viewpoint, there is included an interesting remark. It is to the effect that the employing of every productive worker involves an exchange of present for future goods. The present goods are the wages of the worker, the future goods are the product of his labor that will be received in the future (*op. cit.*, p. 53). A quotation found in Salz's *Beiträge zur Geschichte und Kritik der Lohnfondstheorie*, 1905, p. 65, was responsible for drawing my attention to the foregoing early mention of a thought which I used extensively many decades later in my theory of interest (cf., for instance, my *Positive Theory*, Chap. ɪɪ, p. 297 ff. and p. 310).

13. A principle which Smith, incidentally, by no means adhered to with unfailing consistency. In addition to "labor" he not infrequently cites "land" and "capital" as the sources of goods.

14. Those who wish to, may regard these words as a highly compressed statement of James Mill's remuneration theory. See foregoing p. 195 f.

15. See various passages in Proudhon's numerous writings. Particularly *Qu'est ce que la propriété*, 1840; in the Paris ed. of 1849, p. 162; *Philosophie der Not*, a German translation by William Jordan, 2nd ed., p. 62, p. 287 f.; *Verteidigungsrede vor den Assisen von Besançon*, delivered February 3, 1842 (Edition of Complete Works, 1868, Vol. ɪɪ). Particular attention is directed to Diehl's comprehensive work *P. J. Proudhon, seine Lehre und sein Leben*, in three sections, Jena 1888-1896.

16. The one work of Lassalle's which contains the fullest exposition of his opinions on the interest problem, and which at the same time represents the most brilliant display of his genius for agitation, is his *Herr Bastiat-Schulze von Delitzsch, der ökonomische Julian, oder Kapital und Arbeit* (Berlin, 1864). Chief passages to be noted are the following. Labor is "the source and creator of all values" (pp. 83, 122, 147). But the worker does not receive the entire value, but only the market value of labor, considered as merchandise, which is the equivalent of its cost of production, that is to say, bare subsistence (p. 186 ff.). All surplus falls to the share of capital (p. 194). Interest is therefore a deduction from the product of the labor belonging to the laborer (p. 125, and in very drastic form on p. 97). Opposition to the doctrine of the productivity of capital is found on

p. 21 ff. The abstinence theory is opposed on p. 82 ff. and especially on p. 110 ff. Compare also the other works of Lassalle.

17. *Die Lehre vom Einkommen in dessen Gesamtzweigen*, 1869. I quote from the 2nd ed. of 1878.

18. *Op. cit.*, 109 ff., 122 ff. Cf. also p. 202 ff., foregoing.

19. *Kursus der National- und Sozialökonomie*, Berlin, 1873, p. 183. A bit later (p. 185), in a statement patently reminiscent of Proudhon's *droit d'aubaine* (toll right) he declares *interest* to be a "toll" that is levied for the relinquishment of economic power. The rate of interest represents the toll or tax rate.

20. See Chap. xɪɪɪ.

21. Written in 1884. Since that time there has, I think, been a reversal of this tendency. For a few years the labor value theory, in conjunction with the dissemination of socialist ideas, rather gained currency than otherwise. But in most recent times, among theorists in all countries, the principle has lost ground, chiefly to the theory of marginal utility, which has been gaining more and more headway.

22. *Der Credit*, Part ɪɪ, Berlin, 1879, p. vɪɪ.

23. A rather complete list of the numerous works of Dr. Karl Rodbertus-Jagetzow is available in Kozak's *Rodbertus' sozialökonomische Ansichten*, Jena, 1882, p. 7 ff. By preference I used the second and third letters to von Kirchmann in the somewhat revised reprint which Rodbertus published in 1875 under the title *Zur Beleuchtung der sozialen Frage*. I have also used his *Zur Erklärung und Abhilfe der heutigen Kreditnot des Grundbesitzes*, 2nd ed., Jena 1876, as well as Rodbertus's work, posthumously published by Adolf Wagner and Kozak under the title *Das Kapital*, which was originally his fourth *Social Letter* to von Kirchmann (Berlin, 1884). Rodbertus's theory of interest was at one time made the subject of an exceedingly searching and conscientious investigation by Knies in his *Der Credit*, Part ɪɪ, Berlin, 1879, p. 47 ff. In the main I agree with Knies's estimate. Nevertheless I cannot forego instituting a new and independent critical examination, since my theoretical views diverge sufficiently widely from Knies's, for me to have essentially different opinions on several points. On the subject of Rodbertus see A. Wagner's *Grundlegung*, 3rd ed., Part ɪ, Sec. 13 and Part ɪɪ, Sec. 132; likewise, H. Dietzel's *C. Rodbertus*, Jena 1886-1888.

24. *Zur Beleuchtung der sozialen Frage*, pp. 68, 69.

25. *Soziale Frage*, p. 56; *Erklärung und Abhilfe*, p. 112.

26. *Soziale Frage*, pp. 87 and 90; *Erklärung und Abhilfe*, p. 111; *Kapital*, p. 116.

27. *Soziale Frage*, p. 146; *Erklärung und Abhilfe*, Part ɪɪ, p. 109 ff.

28. *Soziale Frage*, p. 32.

29. *Soziale Frage*, p. 74 f.

30. *Soziale Frage*, p. 33. Similarly and in greater detail on pp. 77 to 94.

31. *Soziale Frage*, p. 115 and frequent other instances.

32. *Op. cit.*, p. 150; *Kapital*, p. 202.

33. *Soziale Frage*, pp. 115, 148 f.; cf. also his *Herr Bastiat-Schulze von Delitzsch, ibid.*, pp. 115-119.

34. *Soziale Frage*, p. 123 ff.

35. *Op. cit.*, p. 106.

36. *Soziale Frage*, p. 107; similarly pp. 113, 147; also *Erklärung und Abhilfe*, p. 123.

37. *Soziale Frage*, p. 148.

38. *Soziale Frage*, p. 94 ff., especially pp. 109-111; *Erklärung und Abhilfe*, Part I, p. 123.

39. *Erklärung und Abhilfe*, p. 303.

40. *Erklärung und Abhilfe*, p. 273 f. In Rodbertus's posthumously published *Kapital* his verdict against private ownership of capital is more severe. And though he does not advocate its abolition, he wishes to see it replaced (p. 116 ff.).

41. *Soziale Frage*, p. 69.

42. *Soziale Frage*, p. 71.

43. *Credit*, Part II, p. 60 ff.

44. *Zur Erkenntnis unserer staatswirtschaftlichen Zustände*, 1842. See First Theorem, pp. 5 and 6.

45. *Op. cit.*, p. 7.

46. *Op. cit.*, p. 8.

47. It is readily understandable that if Rodbertus had been consistent he would have had to maintain that labor (the force "labor," as it were) is also eternal and indestructible since the chemical and physical forces residing in the human organism, like all others, do not disappear from the universe!

48. Who would deny, for instance, that even one who controls the labor of others —be he employer, patriarch or slaveowner —also has a rational motive for dealing economically with the labor *of others*? In such case it is of course no longer a question of the labor involving a loss of *his* time, an expenditure of *his* energy, a sacrifice of *his* personal freedom. Patently the significant factor, as I pointed out in the text, is the satisfaction of wants—his wants or his family's.

49. The provisions found in all legislation prohibiting wasteful methods of operating mines, supply a palpable refutation of Rodbertus, since they make the economical management of rare natural resources an out and out duty—and for very well-founded reasons.

50. *Op. cit.*, p. 9.

51. *Erklärung und Abhilfe*, Part II, p. 160; similarly *Soziale Frage*, p. 69.

52. *Credit*, Part II, p. 69; Rodbertus's statement that "labor is the only original force and the only original expenditure with the help of which human economy is transacted," which is the sole reason he advances in support of his own argument, is purely and simply a factual error. What an astonishing delusion, especially on the part of a landowner, to maintain that it is impossible for the generative power active in our limited parcels of land to be left "lying dead," or to be "dissipated on the growth of weeds," etc., etc.! Such absurd reasoning would in the end justify the statement that the loss of X acres to the owner of Y square miles of land "does not signify any economic loss" in an economy.

53. See Knies's *Der Credit*, Part II, p. 64 ff.; for instance: Any one who would "produce" coal must not only dig, but must dig in the right place. He can perform the same manual labor of digging at thousands of places, without the slightest success. But the difficult and necessary service of correctly locating the place for digging has to be taken on by some special person—say a geologist. And without a further exercise of "intellectual power," it is impossible to sink a shaft. Now, if those things and others are necessary, how can the digging be the only "economic" service?—If in the making of pills, the choice of ingredients, the determination of their relative amounts and the like, are taken care of by a person other than the one who does the actual rolling of the pills, can we then say that the economic value of those objects, of this manufactured medicament, is a product of the manual labor expended?

54. Nothing could be further from my thoughts than to intimate that the rate of interest *causes* the lower valuation of future goods. I know perfectly well that interest and interest rate are only a result of that primary phenomenon. My intention here, anyhow, is not to explain, but to depict facts.

55. At first glance these figures may appear strange, but their correctness will soon be demonstrated.

56. Stolzmann in his *Soziale Kategorie*, p. 305 ff. registered a few objections to this illustrative example of mine. They are, to my mind, rather inconsequential as well as mistaken. He takes as his point of departure his own erroneous impression that I had intended to have my group of workers represent a sort of archetype (or that I ought to have done so)—a little state with its own complete self-sufficient economic system. And then he raises the objection that even the last worker "could not do anything with his completed machine, could not derive a single day's livelihood from it" (p. 307). He makes the further objection that the hypothetical $1,200 that I set up as compensation for the first worker at the end of the fifth year was an inadequate substitute for his five-year-long wait. The worker would moreover have to receive five full years' wages of $5,000, "if he is not to starve during the long period in which he is forced to fold his useless and idle hands in his lap" (p. 308). I hardly need to say in refutation that it was by no means my intention to furnish an example of a self-contained archetype, but that I merely wanted to—and did—depict a little group of five persons, active in the midst of our modern economic life, and organized for the execution of a single project of production, namely, the construction of *one*

machine. I refer Stolzmann to the clear wording of the conditions of my example outlined on p. 264. In addition to other points I made the one there of an "exchange value" of the machine and stated that the only factor I was ignoring was that of the division of labor. Even then I made the stipulation only for the time being and only with respect to the construction of the one machine. Hence there can also be no question of enforced idleness on the part of the participants in the production operation during the time when they were not occupied with it. Later (p. 313) Stolzmann charges me with being guilty of flagrant innuendo, when I state the hypothetical possibility that one of the workers could put out at interest the wage he had received earlier until the expiration of the fifth year. In doing so, says he, I "brand the wage earner as a capitalist." My answer to that is, that not a single word in my example excluded the possibility that one or the other of the participants might not himself possess the means which would permit him to do the waiting. On the contrary, I expressly offered on p. 264 as well as p. 269 the alternative that the workers "cannot *or will not*" wait. Stolzmann, on his pp. 307 and 309 through obvious error misquotes me by saying "cannot *and* will not." Besides all that, I expressly indicated in my Note 54 on p. 468, which also appears in my first edition, that my example was not intended to explain the phenomenon of interest itself, but merely to illustrate a certain line of reasoning with the help of some given facts. Dr. Robert Meyer in his excellent book *Das Wesen des Einkommens*, Berlin, 1887, pp. 270 ff., raises an interesting and much more profound objection. But since it requires anticipating numerous details of my *Positive Theory of Capital* to clear up his likewise mistaken exception, the discussion of it must be reserved for the third volume of this work, *Further Essays on Capital and Interest*. See Essay VI.

57. I shall defer more detailed elaboration of this topic to my second volume. But I wish to protect myself against misunderstanding, and especially against any presumption that I regard any entrepreneur's profit which exceeds the prevailing interest rate as spoliative profit. To that end I should like to insert the following brief remark. There is the possibility that the total difference between the proceeds of the product and wages paid, which difference accrues to the entrepreneur, may consist of four essentially different components. (1) Risk premium to cover the risk of production failure. Correctly estimated, this will, on the average and over the course of the years, be consumed to reimburse the entrepreneur for actual losses and of course involves no deprivation for the worker. (2) A wage for the entrepreneur's own work, which of course is also quite unobjectionable. In fact, under certain circumstances such as the utilization of a new invention by the entrepreneur it can fairly

be computed at a high rate without any injustice being done the workers thereby. (3) The compensation discussed in the text for the time difference between payment of wages and realization of the final product, as measured by the prevailing interest rate. (4) Finally, it is possible for the entrepreneur to increase his income still more by exploiting the distress of the workers to effect an extortionate depression of their wage. Of these four constituent elements only the last violates the principle that the worker is to receive the full value of his product.

58. My opinion is not shared by Natoli who subjoins a polemic footnote to these words of my text. See his *Il principio del valore e la misura quantitativa del valore*, 1906, p. 114, Note 2. In other passages, too, he repeatedly and emphatically insists that the "Ricardian differences" in the exchange value of goods requiring production periods of different length are an entirely different matter. They are by no means identical, says Natoli, with the differences in value between present and future goods. The latter occur in the "capitalist exchange" between capitalists and workers and are the source of interest (see his p. 224 ff.). My error, says Natoli, lies in my confusing these two different phenomena (see pp. 279, 314). Yet I think I can adhere to the view I developed in my text above. And I am the more confident because Natoli himself is compelled to admit that the two phenomena, which he accuses me of "confusing," "are attributable to a similar and even identical cause" (p. 221). In fact, he admits that we are concerned with phenomena which are themselves of downright "identical nature" (p. 241). Natoli's attempt to draw a line of demarcation where, in the nature of things, no such line exists, seems to me merely the counterpart of another equally futile undertaking of his. I am referring to his endeavors to take up predominantly sound ideas, garnered from the theory of marginal utility, or from the agio theory, and to stretch them on the Procrustean bed of the labor theory of value.

59. E.g., *Soziale Frage*, pp. 44, 107.

60. *Soziale Frage*, p. 113 and 147; *Erklärung und Abhilfe*, Part I, p. 123. In the last mentioned instance Rodbertus says, ". . . if the value of agricultural and of manufactured products is regulated by the labor which inheres in them, *which, by and large, always takes place in real exchange* . . ." etc.

61. *Soziale Frage*, p. 111, Note.

62. The foregoing observations had been set down before Rodbertus's posthumous work, *Kapital*, was published in 1884. In it he takes a very strange position with respect to our question, and as a result I now feel inclined to be more censorious rather than more lenient in the verdict rendered in the text. It is true that he now emphasizes vigorously that his labor law of value is not an exact one but rather a mere ap-

proximation, which gives expression to a gravitational tendency (p. 6 ff.). And he does make the express admission that, because of the insistence on an excess of proceeds on the part of the entrepreneurs, a steady deviation takes place in the actual exchange value of goods, as compared with their exchange ratio as measured by the amount of labor (p. 11 ff.). But he grants far too restricted applicability to this concession. For he assumes that this divergence occurs only in the conditions that apply to individual stages in the production of a single good, and not "in general to all production stages." In some cases the production process of a good is broken down into several stages, each of which develops into a separate industry. In such case, according to Rodbertus, the value of the "separate product" that is made at each separate stage cannot maintain a ratio corresponding to the labor expended in it. The reason for this, he maintains, is that the entrepreneurs of the later stages of production are obliged to make a greater outlay for their raw materials, and hence a greater expenditure of capital, and therefore must calculate a higher interest. And that interest can be provided only out of a relatively higher value of the particular product. Correct as this concept may be, it is equally clear that it does not go far enough. The subject is inadequately covered by saying that the variation in the actual exchange value of goods from that of the labor expended thereon, is confined to the preliminary products in the process of producing a good. Nor is the problem completely met by saying that in the course of the successive stages in production these divergences compensate for each other and cancel out, so that the ultimate consumers' goods once more conform to his law of value. For the influence of the factors represented by the amount of capital advanced, and the length of time during which it is advanced, is such that the value of *all* goods is *finally and definitively* at variance with their labor costs. But my severest condemnation is reserved for his stubborn refusal to be ruled by his own admissions. He still insists on the law that all goods are distributed either in the form of wages or of interest. He bases this insistence on the theoretical assumption that all goods possess a "normal" value, by which he means a value corresponding to their labor costs. Rodbertus justifies this attitude by claiming that his "normal" value, whether in its relationship to the deriving of interest in general, or of interest on land and on capital goods in particular, is the most *impartial*. It is the only one, he says, *which does not seize by stealth any part of the thing it is supposed to explain*, which is a fair characterization of the course of any value which, from the outset, is presumed to be so compounded as to include an element which shall be the source of interest (p. 23). Now in this contention Rodbertus is flagrantly in error. He is fully as guilty of the impro-

priety of "seizing by stealth," as any of his opponents can possibly be. Only Rodbertus does it in the opposite direction. While his opponents have practiced their furtiveness by presupposing the *existence* of interest, he postulates its *non-existence*. For he ignores that persistent deviation from "normal value" which constitutes the well-spring and the sustenance of originary interest. And by so doing he simply presupposes the principal manifestation of the phenomenon of interest itself right out of existence.

63. *Soziale Frage*, p. 107 f.

64. *Zur Kritik der politischen Ökonomie,* Berlin, 1859; *Das Kapital, Kritik der politischen Ökonomie,* 3 vols., 1867-1894. Re Marx compare the article "Marx" by Engels in the *Handwörterbuch der Staatswissenschaften,* which includes a complete list of Marx's writings, continued and supplemented in the 3rd ed. of the manual by K. Diehl; then among others, Knies, *Das Geld,* 2nd ed., 1885, p. 153 ff.; A. Wagner in his *Grundlegung der politischen Ökonomie,* 3rd ed. *passim,* especially Vol. II, p. 285 ff.; Lexis in Conrad's *Jahrbücher,* 1885, new series, No. XI, pp. 452 ff.; Gross, *K. Marx,* Leipzig, 1885; Adler, *Grundlagen der Marxschen Kritik der bestehenden Volkswirtschaft,* Tübingen, 1887; Komorzynski, on the 3rd vol. of Karl Marx's *Das Kapital* in the *Zeitschrift für Volkswirtschaft, Sozialpolitik und Verwaltung,* Vol. VI, p. 242 ff.; Wenckstern, *Marx,* Leipzig, 1896; Sombart, "Zur Kritik des ökonomischen Systems von Karl Marx," *Archiv für soz. Gesetzgebung u. Statistik,* Vol. VII, No. 4, pp. 555 ff.; my own essay "Zum Abschluss des Marxschen Systems" in the *Festgaben für Karl Knies,* Berlin, 1896; published in book form in Russian at St. Petersburg, 1897, and in English at London, 1898; Diehl, "Über das Verhältnis von Wert und Preis im ökonomischen System von Karl Marx," reprint from the *Festschrift zur Feier des 25 jährigen Bestehens des staatswissenschaftlichen Seminars zu Halle a. S.,* Jena, 1898; Masaryk, *Die philosophischen und soziologischen Grundlagen des Marxismus,* Vienna, 1899; Tugan-Baranowski, *Theoretische Grundlagen des Marxismus,* Leipzig, 1905; von Bortkiewicz, "Wertrechnung und Preisrechnung im Marxschen System," in *Archiv für Sozialwissenschaft und Sozialpolitik,* Vols. 23 and 25; and many other writings of the voluminous and ever growing literature on Marx.

65. Lifschitz in his *Zur Kritik der Böhm-Bawerkschen Werttheorie,* Leipzig, 1908, on p. 16, claims to have caught me contradicting myself. He cites this remark and also an early passage in this book, p. 257 ff. where I spoke of Rodbertus's "serious attempt to prove his case." But Lifschitz has either read so superficially, or thought so superficially, that he confuses two quite distinct theses. In actual fact Rodbertus did defend the thesis that all goods, economically speaking, can cost only labor. I am speaking here of the totally different

thesis that the *value* of all goods is regulated solely by the *quantity* of labor cost. Lifschitz might certainly have devoted some attention to the very essential difference between these two theses, if for no other reason, then by all means on account of the completely different positions I took with respect to them on p. 262 f. and on p. 271 ff.

66. My quotations from the 1st vol. of Marx's *Das Kapital* are always taken from the 2nd ed., published in 1872, and those from the 2nd vol. are from the 1885 ed. References to the 3rd vol. concern the ed. of 1894 and, be it further noted, the first part of that volume, unless specifically stated to be otherwise.

67. Vol. I, pp. 15, 17, 49, 87 and other passages. Compare also Adler, *Grundlagen der Karl Marxschen Kritik,* Tübingen, 1887, pp. 210 and 213.

68. One instance is found in Chap. V of his Book II, where he says: "Not only the tenant farmer's serving-men and serving-maids are productive workers, so are his beasts of burden, too." Another is his statement: "In agriculture nature works with man; and although its work costs nothing, its products have their value, just as truly as do the products of the most highly paid workmen." Compare Knies, *Der Credit,* 2nd half, p. 62.

69. On this point compare C. A. Verryn Stuart's fine study, *Ricardo and Marx,* and my discussion of it in Conrad's *Jahrbücher* Series III, Vol. I (1891) p. 877 ff.

70. See p. 272 and Knies, *Der Credit,* p. 66 f.

71. *Wealth of Nations,* Book I, Chap. V (p. 13 of the McCulloch ed.); Ricardo, *Principles,* Chap. I.

72. Smith seems to reconcile himself to the phenomenon I describe here as follows: "If the one species of labour requires an uncommon degree of dexterity and ingenuity, *the esteem which men have for such talents* will naturally give a value to their produce, superior to what would be due to time employed about it. Such talents can seldom be acquired but in consequence of long application and the superior value of their produce may *frequently* be no more than a reasonable compensation for the time and labour which must be spent in acquiring them" (Book I, Chap. VI). The inadequacy of this explanation is obvious. In the first place it is clear that the higher value of things produced by especially skillful persons is not based on the "esteem which men have for such talents." How many poets and scholars have been allowed to starve, despite the high esteem which the public accorded their talents? How many unscrupulous speculators has the public rewarded with hundreds of thousands, although it did not esteem their "talents" at all? But even if we admitted that esteem were the basis of value, then we should not be citing an instance of the applicability of the law that value is based on *effort,* but on the contrary, we should be citing a violation of the law.—And when Smith attempts in the second case to attribute the higher value to the effort expended in acquiring skill, he himself admits, through the insertion of the word "frequently," that it is not possible in all cases. The contradiction therefore is still there.

73. There is cogency to the objection that Knies raises to Marx's argument when he says, "It is impossible to perceive from anything contained in Marx's exposition any reason why we may not have, beside the equation: one bushel wheat $= x$ cwt. of wood felled in the forest, the equally valid equation: one bushel wheat $= x$ cwt. uncut timber, $= y$ acres of virgin land, $= z$ acres of pasture on natural meadowland." (*Das Geld,* 1st ed., p. 121, 2nd ed., p. 157.)

74. In this very paragraph he quotes a passage from Barbon which again obliterates the distinction between goods and things. "One kind of commodity is as good as another, if the exchange value of both is equally great. There is no difference and no differentiating between things having equal exchange value!"

75. He says, for instance, at the bottom of p. 15: "A thing cannot have value, if it is not a useful article. If it is not useful, then the labor it contains is also useless, does not count as labor (sic!) and hence does not create value."—Knies has already directed attention to the error I have censured above. See his *Das Geld,* Berlin, 1873, p. 123 f. (2nd ed., p. 160 ff.). Adler, in his *Grundlagen der Karl Marxschen Kritik,* Tübingen, 1887, p. 211 f. reveals that he has strangely misunderstood my argument, when he urges in refutation that good voices are not commodities in the Marxian sense. I was not concerned at all with the question whether or not "good voices" can be classed as economic goods under the Marxian law of value. I was concerned solely with drawing up a sample of a syllogism that embodies the same error that Marx makes. I could just as well have chosen an example that had no relationship whatever to the economic field. I could, for instance, just as well have proved that the one element common to variegated bodies is heaven knows what, but not the combination of several colors. For one combination of colors, say white, blue, yellow, black and violet, is worth just as much as a claim to classification under "variegated," as is any other combination of colors, say green, red, orange, sky-blue, etc., provided only it is present "in proper proportion." Consequently, we eliminate color and color combinations as factors!

76. *Das Kapital,* p. 17 f.

77. "Zum Abschluss des Marxschen Systems," p. 77 ff.

78. This topic will receive further treatment later.

79. Cf. Knies, *Der Credit,* Part II, p. 61.

80. I have repeatedly referred to my essay "Zum Abschluss des Marxschen Systems," where I have treated this point, too,

in greater detail. See my p. 80 ff.

81. Marx does not make express mention of it until his third and posthumous volume. The result is—and it could not have been expected to be otherwise—that he now finds himself in conflict with the laws in the first volume, which had been formulated in disregard of the exception.

82. For that reason I think Natoli in his *Principio del valore,* recently published, goes much too far. He is keenly aware that labor exercises neither a primary nor a universal influence on the value of goods. He is, in fact, well cognizant of the fact that such value depends, without exception, on the *grado di utilità* (marginal utility). And he also knows, finally, that in Ricardo's labor theory of value, cause and effect are interchanged (*op. cit.,* p. 191). Yet in spite of all this, Natoli alleges that ultimately an *equazione utilitaria* (equation of utility) between value and labor can always be established. And by way of that equation he detours to the point where he declares the coinciding of value and labor to be the fundamental law of value. Indeed, he calls it the basic "cardinal law of all economy" (*op. cit.,* pp. 191, 244, 277 and 391).

83. See foregoing p. 277 f.

84. "At a given rate of surplus value and with a given value of labor power the amounts of the surplus value are in direct proportion to the amounts of the advanced variable capitals." "The amounts of value and surplus value produced from different capitals, are, in the case of a given value and of equal rates of exploitation of labor power, in direct proportion to the magnitudes of the variable components of these capitals, that is to say, of so much of their component parts as have been converted into live labor power" (Marx, Vol. I, p. 311 f.).

85. Vol. I, p. 312 and p. 542.

86. "Aside from unimportant, fortuitous and mutually compensating variations, there can be no doubt that in reality a difference in average profit rates as between different branches of industry does not exist, nor could it exist without destroying the whole system of capitalistic production" (Vol. III, p. 132). "As a result of the varying organic composition of the capitals invested in various branches of production . . . the profit rates prevailing in different branches of production are originally widely different. These differing profit rates are levelled off by competition to a general profit rate, which is the average of all these different profit rates" (Vol. III, p. 136).

87. Marx develops this principle by giving an example in schematic form which embraces five classes of commodity and five productive industries with capital of varying organic composition. He supplies a comment on the results revealed by his schematic arrangement in the following words: "Together the commodities are sold at $2 + 7 + 17 = 26$ above their value, and at $8 + 18 = 26$ below their value. Thus the price deviations cancel out reciprocally.

This takes place through an equalizing distribution of the surplus or by addition of the average 22% profit to the cost prices of the respective commodities I to V. Some of the commodities are sold above their value in the same proportion as the rest are sold below their value. And only their sale at such prices makes it possible for the profit rate to be a uniform 22% for commodities I to V, irrespective of the differing organic composition of capitals I to V." The same thought is then discussed in detail on the succeeding pp. 135-144.

88. In my "Zum Abschluss des Marxschen Systems," pp. 25-62. Since that time Hilferding has published an apologia by way of refutation, which appeared in Vol. I (1904) of the *Marx-Studien,* but nothing in it has caused me to change my opinion in any respect. More specifically, I wish to insist at this point on bringing up the matter of some observations by Heimann in his "Methodologisches zu den Problemen des Wertes," excerpt reprinted from the *Archiv für Sozialwissenschaft,* Vol. XXXVII, p. 19. I cannot forego remarking that the schedules I presented (*op. cit.,* p. 53) are entirely correct and appropriate. Hilferding's "corrected versions" of them are as arbitrary as they are irrelevant.

89. *Die Durchschnittsprofitrate auf Grund des Marxschen Wertgesetzes,* Stuttgart, 1889.

90. "In the same proportion in which one part of the commodities is exchanged above its value, another part is exchanged below its value" (Vol. III, p. 135). "The total price of commodities I to V" (i.e., in the schematic example used by Marx) "would therefore equal their total value . . . And thus, taking the totality of all branches of production into account, in society itself the sum of the prices of production of the commodities produced equals the sum of their values" (Vol. III, p. 138). The divergence of the prices of production from values balances out "in that the excessive amount that is diverted to surplus value in the case of one commodity is offset by a corresponding deficiency in another, and in that the deviations from value which are lodged in the prices of production offset each other" (Vol. III, p. 140). Similarly, K. Schmidt (*op. cit.,* p. 51) says: "The necessary divergence of the actual price from the value in the case of particular commodities vanishes . . . as soon as one takes into account the sum of all the individual commodities, that is to say, the annual national production."

91. The first was in a discussion of the aforementioned article by Schmidt which I published in the *Tübinger Zeitschrift,* 1890, p. 590 ff.

92. "Zur Kritik des ökonomischen Systems von Karl Marx," from the *Archiv für soziale Gesetzgebung,* Vol. VII, No. 4, p. 573 ff.

93. "Zum Abschluss des Marxschen Systems," p. 103 ff.

94. For instance, Engels in his most recent work appearing in the *Neue Zeit,* Nos.

1 and 2 of the 14th annual vol. (1895-1896) entitled, "Ergänzung und Nachtrag zum dritten Buch des Kapitals."

95. Supplement to the issue of *Vorwärts* of April 10, 1897.

96. *Die Voraussetzungen des Sozialismus und die Aufgaben der Sozialdemokratie,* Stuttgart, 1899.

97. *Op. cit.,* pp. 38, 41, 42, 44.
98. *Op. cit.,* pp. 45, 41, 42.
99. *Op. cit.,* p. 42.
100. See foregoing p. 257 f.
101. See foregoing p. 263 ff.
102. Vol. I, p. 175.
103. Vol. II, p. 197 ff.

NOTES TO CHAPTER XIII

1. Written in 1884. See the Appendix included in this volume for a treatment of recent literature on the subject.

2. Fourth ed., Paris 1865.

3. Vol. I, p. 93, "Les frais de production se composent: 1. de la rétribution due aux travailleurs, 2. *des profits du capitaliste"* etc.

4. Cf. the sharp but for the most part justified criticism of Pierstorff (*op. cit.,* p. 93 ff.).

5. *Cours d'Economie Politique,* 2nd ed., Paris 1863. His productivity theory is after the Say pattern, that is to say, interest is a compensation for the *service productif* of capital, as appears, for instance, in Vol. I, p. 302. His abstinence theory (cf. Vol. I, pp. 289, 293 f., 300 f.) is rendered especially unsatisfying by the peculiar signification that he gives the concept which he describes by the French *privation.* For Molinari the term covers those deprivations which the capitalists may have to suffer by reason of the fact that his capital is tied up in production and therefore is not available for the satisfaction of pressing needs which possibly might arise in the interim. Certainly an inappropriate basis for a general theory of interest!

6. *Essai sur la Répartition des richesses,* 2nd ed., Paris, 1883. See particularly his p. 236 (abstinence theory), then p. 233 ff., and 238 ff. (productivity theory). See also foregoing p. 87 f.

7. Concerning Roscher consult text, p. 86 f.; Schüz, *Grundsätze der National-Ökonomie,* Tübingen, 1843, especially pp. 70, 285, 296 f.; Max Wirth *Grundzüge der National-Ökonomie,* 3rd ed., Vol. I, p. 324, 5th ed., Vol. I, p. 327 f.—Furthermore, cf. Huhn, *Allgemeine Volkswirtschaftslehre,* Leipzig, 1862, p. 204; H. Bischof, *Grundzüge eines Systems der National-Ökonomik,* Graz, 1876, p. 459 ff., and especially p. 465, note 2; Schulze-Delitzsch, *Kapitel zu einem deutschen Arbeiterkatechismus,* p. 23 f., p. 27, p. 28 etc.

8. "La nozione del Capitale." It appears in the *Saggi di Economia Politica,* Milan, 1878, p. 155 ff.

9. Sixth edition, 1883.

10. P. 34, and in greater detail in the *Saggi.*

11. "Due sono gli elementi dell' interesse, cioè: 1. la retribuzione pel non uso del capitale, o, come altri dice, per la sua formazione, e pel suo servizio produttivo" etc. (p. 119). The foregoing quotation is to be found almost unchanged in the 10th edition of Cossa's *Elementi,* the last edition to appear during the author's lifetime.

12. *Theory of Political Economy,* 2nd ed., London, 1879.

13. P. 243 ff.

14. P. 266 ff. Jevons gives this formula in several other versions which I think may quite properly be omitted here.

15. See foregoing p. 225 ff.

16. Thus in one instance Jevons makes the point that a distribution of a supply of goods, as between present and future, will give recognition to this factor by assigning a smaller portion of the goods to a future time, and smaller in proportion to the remoteness of the time.

17. Written in 1884. Since that time we have discovered the closely related research of his illustrious predecessor Rae, which was presumably unknown to Jevons. See Chap. XI of this edition.

18. *An Inquiry into the Natural Grounds of Right to Vendible Property or Wealth,* Edinburgh, 1829.

19. *Op. cit.,* p. 131, and generally, throughout his polemic against Godwin and the latter's anonymously published *Labour Defended.*

20. *Op. cit.* Footnote to p. 247.

21. *Beitrag zur Lehre vom Kapital,* Erlangen, 1857, p. 16, p. 22 f.

22. *Précis d'Economie Politique,* 2nd ed., Paris, 1881.

23. See foregoing p. 201.

24. *Le principe est donc que le taux de l'intérêt est en raison directe de la productivité du capital* (Vol. II, p. 110).

25. "Nous avons vu que la valeur réelle de l'intérêt dépendait *de l'emploi productif donné au capital: puisqu' une certaine plus value est due au capital,* l'intérêt est une partie de cette plus-value présumée fixée à forfait que reçoit le prêteur pour le service par lui rendu" (Vol. II, p. 189).

26. *Traité d'Économie Politique,* 8th ed., Paris, 1880.

27. *Op. cit.,* p. 47.

28. *Op. cit.,* p. 522.

29. *Kleine Schriften staatswirtschaftlichen Inhalts,* Berlin, 1843, p. 566. See also Note 20 on foregoing p. 462.

30. *Op. cit.,* p. 588.

31. *Op. cit.,* p. 576.

32. *Principles of Political Economy,* 5th ed., New York, 1897.

33. Book III, Chap. 4, Secs. 1, 4, 6; Chap. 6, Sec. 1, No. 8; and in numerous other passages.
34. Book I, Chap. 7, Sec. 1, p. 139.
35. Book I, Chap. 5, Sec. 1. p. 95.
36. Book III, Chap. 4, Sec. 4, p. 568. See also Book I, pp. 45 and 213 ff., Book III, Chap. 4 and numerous other references.

37. See foregoing p. 135 ff.
38. See foregoing p. 203 f.
39. Vol. I, pp. 258, 271 and numerous other passages.
40. *Bau und Leben*, Vol. III, p. 273 f.
41. Vol. III, p. 266 f.
42. Vol. III, p. 423; cf. also pp. 330, 386, 428 and numerous other passages.

NOTES TO CHAPTER XIV

1. On the most recent developments see the Appendix to this volume.
2. *Progress and Poverty.* The author quotes from the German ed. translated by Gütschow, Berlin, 1881, and republished in Jena in 1920. [The quotations in this translation are taken from the English "Fiftieth Anniversary Edition," New York, 1929, p. 151 ff. Translators.]
   3. *Capital et Rente;* see foregoing p. 192.
   4. According to George there is another force at work, paralleling the "vital forces of nature" which may be termed the "utilization of differences in the forces of nature and of man *by means of exchange.*" This utilization also leads to an increment "which is in some degree comparable to that produced by the vital forces of nature" (p. 186 f.). I believe I need not enter into a detailed exposition of this rather obscure element, since George himself assigns to it only a secondary role in the origin of interest.
   5. Cf. the comments on "Wealth" in my own *Rechte und Verhältnisse*, p. 80 ff.
   6. See foregoing p. 119 f.
   7. *Die Arbeit und ihr Recht*, Berlin, 1882, p. 195 ff.
   8. *Op. cit.*, pp. 195-201.
   9. *Op. cit.*, p. 203 f.
   10. *Op. cit.*, p. 203 f.
   11. One might perhaps turn the matter as follows: The wool *that has been woven into cloth* is really consumed, and must be charged to the cost of production at its full price; the *replacement* wool must also

be charged to the cost of production; but this *replacement* wool is also temporarily "nonconsumed," it is now "devalued," and hence has a claim to indemnity by reason of nonconsumption. But even when the situation is given this turn, it is obvious that the desired goal still remains unattainable. To detect the error, one need but turn one's attention to the next succeeding period of production. The replacement wool now becomes "specifically" consumed. If it was devalued, then it is charged, during the following period, to the cost of production but at its diminished value. In that case we have the result that was described in the text above. If it was not devalued, then it did not require compensation for devaluation in the preceding period.
   12. *Staatswirtschaftliche Untersuchungen*, 2nd ed., p. 605.
   13. Even the concept of "true capital" as set up in contrast to "concrete capital goods" by Prof. J. B. Clark ("The Genesis of Capital," *Yale Review*, Nov., 1893, p. 302 ff.) seems to me to belong in the same class of mystical conceptual creations. On this subject compare my essay on "The Positive Theory of Capital and its Critics" in the *Quarterly Journal of Economics*, Vol. IX, January, 1895, p. 113 ff., and also the recent interchange of articles between Prof. Clark and myself in the 15th and 16th vols. of the *Zeitschrift für Volkswirtschaft, Sozialpolitik und Verwaltung*, 1906 and 1907; likewise my *Positive Theory of Capital*, p. 55 ff.

NOTES TO CHAPTER XV

1. Written in 1884 before the publication of the 3rd vol. of Marx's *Kapital*. The most recent phase of Marxism makes the matter worse rather than better, by combining the original denial of the decisive differences in value with a belated recognition of them. For the disregard of them is maintained until the decisive erroneous conclusions, which are made possible only by such disregard, have all been drawn. Then the con-

sideration of man's valuation of goods, which has been designedly postponed to this point, finally arrives too late to correct the misconceptions that have been established through disregard of them. Not too late, however, to constitute a self-contradiction. All this makes the system no more correct than before, but it does introduce an additional feature—inconsistency. Cf. Chap. XII, foregoing p. 302 ff.

NOTES TO APPENDIX

1. For the sake of completeness, let us consider at this point the much later writings of Cernuschi. In 1865, in *Mécanique le l'échange* he makes an early reference

to that well-known parallel which writers of old had already drawn. It compares the premium charged for the payment of a sum of money at a different place, with interest which is charged in the case of payment and repayment of goods at different times. But then he adds a special bit of reasoning which leads to a result that is somewhat bizarre and a bit reminiscent of the scholasticists. For Cernuschi proceeds from the assumption that capitals always regenerate their own value, and hence are "everlasting." In the case of a present capital its "perpetuity" begins this very day, while that of a future capital of course does not begin until later. Therefore, the "perpetuity" of a future capital is "shorter" (sic!), hence its time of usefulness is shorter, the amount of its usefulness is less and thus, finally, the value based on that usefulness is smaller than the value of the present capital. I was in some measure reminded of these contentions of Cernuschi's recently by isolated statements by Oswalt in his "Beiträge zur Theorie des Kapitalzinses" in the *Zeitschrift für Sozialwissenschaft*, 1910, p. 100.

2. *Mathematische Begründung der Volkswirtschaftslehre*, Leipzig, 1885; see particularly pp. 5-7, 67 ff., 129.

3. *Grundlegung der theoretischen Staatswirtschaft*, Vienna, 1887, p. 178 ff., p. 313 ff.

4. The "rate of interest charged is based on an estimation of the lesser value possessed by enjoyment in the future, in comparison with equal enjoyment in the present" (Launhardt, p. 129). "The measure of the value of a producers' good . . . is derived from the value of the consumers' good which arises from it. But since the want which is served indirectly by the producers' good is a future want, this imputed value is necessarily smaller than the value which the consumer places on an equivalent consumers' good available in the present. Or, to put the same thing in different words, it is necessarily smaller than the value which the concrete consumers' good, having once become a present reality, will possess for him as a means of satisfying the want which will by that time also have become present. For the value of the future consumers' good, on which the value of the producers' good is based, stems from the future want. And that future want, felt as an anticipated present want, is less potent than the actual present one" . . . "In the difference in value between the producers' good and the consumers' good to which it gives rise lies the so-called 'productivity' of capital" (Sax, p. 317 and p. 321, also cf. p. 178 f.).

5. "The Fundamental Idea of Capital" in the *Quarterly Journal of Economics*, January 1889.

6. See his quite brief but very remarkable essay "Analysis of Cost of Production" in the *Quarterly Journal of Economics*, July 1887, as well as a few later articles in that same *Journal*, October 1890 and January 1892.

7. There is a long series of articles in which this keen and indefatigable theorist, toward the end of the nineteenth century, conducted a research into the theory of capital and interest. The first article of the series is entitled "Capital and its Earnings" and appeared in 1888. Most of his later essays were published in the *Quarterly Journal of Economics*, though single articles appeared in the *Annals of the American Academy* (July 1890) and in the *Yale Review* (November 1893).

8. Macfarlane (*Value and Distribution*, p. xxii, and p. 230 f.) seems anxious to designate it as the "exchange theory." I suspect this is traceable to a certain statement I made myself in my *Positive Theory of Capital*, Book IV, Chapter II, Section 1. A few other economists have since that time adopted the name, including Seager, who uses it on p. 293 of his *Principles of Economics* (1913). However my statement *had not been in reference to the subject of interest* as such, but had concerned itself exclusively with the *nature of loans*. In that connection I had characterized a loan as a genuine exchange of present for future goods, and had espoused that view, as an "exchange theory" in opposition to Knies's presentation of loans in the light of his "use theory." With respect to my interest theory as a whole, I must say I do not find that that name describes it at all well, and so I do not consider it at all apt. However, Bortkiewicz used the name "time-difference theory" in an article in Schmoller's *Jahrbuch*, Vol. XXXI, p. 1289, which I find even less characteristic. In what theory of interest would a "time difference" *not* play a part? Just consider, for instance, the abstinence theory or waiting theory!—And then there is a strange misapprehension on the part of Zaleski, in his *Lehre vom Kapital*, Kazan, 1898. I had given the title *Positive Theory of Capital* to the second volume of my work containing the positive assertion and exposition of my own theory, in contrast to the first volume which contained a history and a critique of the theories of others. But Zaleski interprets my use of the word "positive" as a claim on my part that the adjective characterizes the theory itself!

9. For details the reader is referred to the discussion of this subject which was carried on in the pages of the *Quarterly Journal of Economics* from July 1889 to April 1891. The participants in that discussion, besides Giddings himself, were Bonar, myself, David J. Green and H. Bilgram.

10. *Political Science Quarterly*, Vol. IV, No. 2 (June 1889) p. 342.

11. Thus Seager, for instance, in his *Principles of Economics*, 1913, pp. 295 ff., makes the statement that he can detect "no actual disagreement" between a productivity theory that reflects the spirit of Clark, and my "exchange" theory. An article by Brown appeared recently in the *Quarterly Journal of Economics* (Vol. XXVII, No. 4, August 1913) entitled "The Marginal Productivity vs. the Impatience Theory of Interest." It is a polemic aimed at Irving Fisher, and presents a productivity theory which "essentially" coincides with that of Clark, Carver, Seager, Taussig, Cassel and others. Actually, how-

ever, it shows extended and substantial co-incidence with my own doctrine. And on this same occasion Brown feels it incumbent upon himself to make the statement with respect to my theory, that it is really, like the others, also a productivity theory (*op. cit.*, p. 631). See following text for further comments on this topic.

12. *Rate of Interest*, p. 87 ff.; "The Impatience Theory of Interest," reprint from the periodical *Scientia*, Vol. IX, 1911, p. 386.

13. With reference to Clark see my *Positive Theory of Capital*, Book I, Chapter III, Section 3 and the series of articles quoted there. With reference to Fisher, see especially Essay XII in my *Further Essays on Capital and Interest*.

14. Bilgram, "Analysis of the Nature of Capital and Interest" in the *Journal of Political Economy*, Vol. XVI, No. 3, March 1908, p. 130. Cf. also Farnam's remark in his survey of the "German-American Relations in Economics" appearing in the first volume of Schmoller's *Jubilee Book*, Chap. XVIII, p. 16. In the March 1914 number of the *American Economic Review* (Vol. IV, No. 1, p. 68 ff.) there has just appeared an essay entitled "Interest Theories Old and New" by Fetter. The author engages in an exceedingly thorough and instructive discussion of the various subtle variations of the agio theory which have made their appearance in recent American economic literature. Fetter himself espouses a variant of his own, which he calls the "capitalization theory." This places him on the outermost wing of the purely "psychological" interest theorists—"psychological" as opposed to "technological." He moves into a position far more extreme than the one I occupy, or even the one taken by Irving Fisher.

15. *Studi*, p. 51.

16. See also my Note 82 on p. 472. It is not easy to understand how the three authors mentioned above have unanimously laid at my door the charge that they did. Their indictment runs somewhat as follows. They allege that I base my interest theory exclusively on the "absolute" differences in value between present and future goods. By that they mean the differences which exist between the estimations of value as to present and future goods on the part of a single individual. They point out that an equally material factor—or even more material—in the origin of interest, lies in "relative" differences in value. By that they mean the differing degree to which the various parties to an exchange will place a lower value on future goods. That is especially true, they say, when the two economic subjects are the workers and the capitalists. And these three accuse me of having overlooked this element of the problem or of having neglected it. Cf. for instance Natoli, *op. cit.*, pp. 262-267, p. 311; also Graziani, *Studi*, p. 29 ff.; and Ricca-Salerno, *Teoria del valore*, p. 111. Even a cursory examination of my book will reveal that, as a matter of actual fact, I pointed out in extremely explicit terms that general requirement of

every exchange, even in my general theory of exchange (*Positive Theory of Capital*, Book III, Part B, Chapter II, p. 213 f.). But I went even further. In the subsequent elaboration of my specific interest theory, I used equally explicit terms to show the special application of the "relative differences" to the case of an exchange of present for future goods, and of the origin of interest (*Positive Theory of Capital*, Book IV, Chapter I; Book IV, Chapter II, Section II, p. 284 f., p. 306 ff. and p. 317 ff.). Specifically, I believe I pointed out with entirely adequate clarity, the fact that the wage earners, who are without means, customarily exhibit a stronger preference for present goods than do the capitalists. And I showed why this is so. Could it not be possible that this unanimous accusation, repeated in such similar wording, is traceable to a simple hasty oversight on the part of Ricca-Salerno? Could it not be that it was then taken up, under the blessing of his weighty authority, by the other two otherwise so punctilious and accurate authors, and allowed to slip into their writings without verification?

17. *Les trois notions de la productivité et les revenus* in the *Revue d'Economie Politique*, 1911.

18. Especially in the two well-known and highly esteemed monographs on *Wert, Kapital und Rente*, Jena, 1893, and *Finanztheoretische Untersuchungen*, Jena, 1896. The same is true of his more recent *Vorlesungen über Nationalökonomie* which he published in his native Swedish in Lund in 1901. A German edition was published in Jena in 1913.

19. To a certain degree even Cassel and his adherents might perhaps be included here. I, for my part, have no hesitation in classing Cassel formally and definitely with the opponents of the agio theory, and with the representatives of the use theory and abstinence theory. Indeed, I have set forth that very contention in detail in Essay XIII in my *Further Essays on Capital and Interest*. Yet we are in agreement on so many important factual considerations that I can readily understand how others may regard his theory as a mere variation of the theoretical views for which I stand. Cf. also Bonar's objective and meritorious discussion of Cassel's theory in the *Economic Journal* of June 1904, p. 280 ff.

20. Since I have, unfortunately, no command of the Scandinavian languages, I have been forced to rely on private correspondence, in the main, for the general evaluation registered above. I am indebted in this respect to the kindness of Professor Wicksell in Lund and Professor Jaeger in Oslo.

21. See foregoing p. 203 f.

22. *Grundriss der politischen Ökonomie*, 10th ed., Tübingen, 1913, Sec. 107-110.

23. Cf. particularly, the incisive articles on the doctrines of capital (Spiethoff), interest (Wuttke) and wages (Bernhard).

24. "Beiträge zur Theorie des Kapitalzinses" in the *Zeitschrift für Sozialwissenschaft*, New Series, Vol. I, 1910.

25. *Theorie der wirtschaftlichen Entwicklung,* Leipzig, 1912.
26. See my article entitled "Eine dynamische Theorie des Kapitalzinses" in the *Zeitschrift für Volkswirtschaft, Sozialpolitik und Verwaltung,* Vol. XXII, 1913, p. 1 ff. See also Schumpeter's rebuttal, *ibid.,* p. 599 ff., as well as my concluding remarks, p. 640 ff.
27. "Nouvelle théorie sur l'origine des revenus nets," (*Extrait du Cours d'économie politique,* 1896, 2nd ed., Vol. II, Book II).
28. "L'inesistenza di plus-valore nel lavoro e la fonte del profitto" in the *Giornale degli Economisti,* Vol. XXXII, Series 2, January 1907.
29. "Lohn und Rente," Leipzig and Vienna, 1909; and previously in an article entitled "Kapitalzins" in the March number of Conrad's *Jahrbücher,* 3rd Series, Vol. XXXV, p. 325 ff.
30. For instance, Verryn Stuart in *De Economist,* 1908, p. 476 ff., as well as Oswalt, *Beiträge zur Theorie des Kapitalzinses,* p. 9.
31. "Ertrag und Einkommen," Jena, 1907, p. 12 ff.; "Die Entstehung des Preises aus subjektiven Wertschätzungen." "Grundlagen einer neuen Preistheorie," (*Archiv für Sozialwissenschaft,* Vol. XXXIV).
32. I am almost of a mind to affix the label of "colorlessness" even to the very recently expounded theory of Lehr set forth in his *Grundbegriffe und Grundlagen der Volkswirtschaft,* Leipzig, 1893, Chap. VI, Sec. VII. At least, I have been unable to discern any distinctively characteristic feature in his rather verbose exposition of the problem of interest. He refuses, on the one hand, to subscribe to most of the prevalent interest theories. On the other hand the only positive statements he makes are of one of two kinds. The first consists of references to the factual incontrovertibility or to the appropriateness, justice and fairness of certain phenomena. The second comprises vague intimations of certain exceedingly general motives. An example of the latter is Adam Smith's principle that without the prospect of interest no man would accumulate capital, or utilize it for production, or give it out on loan (p. 332). Nowhere does Lehr, in my estimation, offer a genuine explanation.
33. In Conrad's *Jahrbücher,* New Series, Vol. XVII (1888).
34. *Eléments d'Economie politique pure,* 1st ed., Lausanne, 1874, 2nd ed., 1889. Walras considers interest to be capital's compensation for its *service producteur* which is a special, immaterial good (e.g., pp. 201, 211 and XIII of the second edition). Pareto in his *Cours d'Economie politique,* I, 40 ff., is essentially in agreement with Walras in this concept. However he does drop occasional hints concerning the difference in value between "present and future goods" (e.g., p. 50).
35. I cite as examples the following: Conrad, *Grundriss zum Studium der politischen Ökonomie,* Part I, Jena, 1896, Sec. 67; Dietzel's essay in the *Göttinger gelehrte Anzeigen;* Diehl, *Proudhon, seine Lehre und sein Leben,* Part II, Jena, 1890, p. 240 ff.; M. Block, *Progrès de la science économique depuis Adam Smith,* Paris, 1890, Vol. II, Chap. XXIX; Charles Gide, *Principes d'Economie politique,* 5th ed., Paris 1896, p. 451; there are numerous others.
36. Kazan, 1898.
37. In my *Further Essays on Capital and Interest,* Essay XIII.
38. The page numbers cited in the following pages will, in the absence of express notation to the contrary, refer to Oswalt's *Beiträge,* that is to say, to the volume for the year 1910 of the *Zeitschrift für Sozialwissenschaft.*
39. Oswalt mentions elsewhere this reduction of capital goods which are used up or consumed in the various production periods, to their basic elements, labor and land. That is true also of a concept derived from it, the concept of "average period of production." He repeatedly (e.g., pp. 292 and 296) takes the liberty of branding both of these matters as "devoid of theoretical or practical interest." What Oswalt fails to perceive is, that by so doing he digs out the ground from under a cardinal principle of his own theory. For his own concept of "capitalist method" claims that such method results in a "productivity increase" in the sense that "a quantitative or qualitative increase in the satisfaction of wants" is brought about *per unit of labor and land directly or indirectly employed.* But how could Oswalt arrive at such a distribution of final yield per unit of labor *directly and indirectly* employed, unless he had himself undertaken that proscribed analysis, at least in his own mind—in other words, "theoretically"? And to cap the climax, Oswalt himself writes on p. 85, *"But a theoretical analysis which claims to go to the real root of the matter, . . . must regard every good as the sum total of those elementary goods of which it is comprised."* And still the matter is "devoid of theoretical interest"!
40. On one occasion Oswalt even charges me with failure to observe the presence of interest itself (pp. 5 and 7). For the originator of a theory of interest to have overlooked, as it were, the very goal of his exposition—that is most certainly a very reprehensible "oversight"—that is to say, it would be, *if* he had been guilty of it!
41. Oswalt makes the same insistent claim as Cassel did before him (*Nature and Necessity of Interest,* p. 62). The claim is that this is a mere "description" of the phenomenon which constitutes the problem, and that it does not as yet offer to explain anything (pp. 8 and 100). I cannot fully agree with that contention. It is rather my opinion that the principle of the higher value of present as compared with future goods already represents the first station on the road to an *explanation* of interest, and by no means an unimportant station. But its acceptance signifies a rejection of the explanations offered by most, if not indeed all other interest theories. That is

certainly true with respect to the exploitation theory, the remuneration theory, and the use theory. This acceptance implies endorsement in advance of the proposition that interest is an integral part of the equivalent paid for the present goods themselves, and not a separate equivalent for some postulated separable element. Even Cassel has obviously failed to reason clear through to a realization of his flagrant self-contradiction. He recognizes the higher value of present goods to be a fact, even though it may be a fact that still calls for explanation. That is to say, he acknowledges for instance that it takes not 100 units, but 105 units of a next year's good to count as the equivalent of 100 units of this year's good. And nevertheless he claims that the portion represented by the five units paid as interest can be explained as an extra equivalent for a separate element extraneous to the goods loaned and added to them—an element called "use of capital"!

42. See text, p. 176 f., and Oswalt, p. 5 ff., particularly p. 8. That is the point of origin of the "malobservation" with which Oswalt charges me, and which I have already discussed.

43. Oswalt says in the footnote to his p. 434 that Eulenburg had for that reason described him in plain words as my "spokesman." That is a description which Oswalt apparently and quite justifiably repudiates. It is also one which I, for my part, must reject. That is why I have deliberately refrained from contributing so much as a single word to the voluminous controversies between Oswalt and von Bortkiewicz on the subject of my theory of interest. They appeared in Schmoller's *Jahrbuch für Gesetzgebung*, Vol. xxxi and more recently also in his *Beiträge zur Theorie des Kapitalzinses*. Otherwise there would have been many a well-intentioned "defense" of my theory, against which I should in turn have been obliged to defend myself.

44. Oswalt, *op. cit.*, p. 82 ff., 90 ff., 235 ff., 443 f.

45. Throughout the course of my book I reiterate the reason for the demand for present goods, which outstrips the supply and thus gives rise to interest. That reason I constantly state to be the necessity for providing *for subsistence during the interval which necessarily intervenes* while the time-consuming process of production is completed. That necessity is the very thing which Oswalt calls "requirements of current consumption"!

46. See my *Positive Theory of Capital*, p. 102 ff., and especially p. 371 ff.

47. For instance, *Positive Theory of Capital*, p. 318 f. and *Further Essays on Capital and Interest*, p. 156.

48. I trust I have succeeded by means of later and more detailed explanations in *Further Essays on Capital and Interest*, Essay XII (which was not yet available to Oswalt) in showing that this and similar misunderstandings occupy untenable ground.

49. No one else made so extensive use of this line of reasoning to defend the abstinence theory as did Macfarlane in his *Value and Distribution*, Philadelphia, 1899, pp. 175-177. Others in substantial agreement with him include Loria, with his *La rendita fondiaria*, Milan, 1880, p. 619 ff., Marshall with his "saver's surplus" in *Principles*, 3rd ed., London, 1895, p. 606, as well as Carver, Barone and indeed all those, in general, who recognize the marginal utility theory of value and are at the same time favorably inclined toward the abstinence theory. See also my foregoing p. 183 f.

50. A remark of Macfarlane's (*ibid.*, p. 179) may be said to have reference to this point of mine. Yet I do not feel that it goes to the essence of the matter, but constitutes a mere counterassertion, rather than a reasoned attempt to dispose of the matter.

51. "Analysis of Cost of Production" in *Quarterly Journal of Economics*, July 1887. See also foregoing p. 358.

52. Macfarlane, for instance, feels that in advancing what he calls the "exchange theory" (see Note 8 on foregoing p. 475), with which he is in essential agreement, he is merely presenting mine in improved and more fully developed form. "The theory here proposed is, after all, but an extension of Böhm-Bawerk's analysis" (*op. cit.*, p. 231). And for this improved form he proposes a designation which is likewise improved, and suggests the name "normal value theory." Carver has a similar opinion regarding the relation between these two theories (see later text), as does possibly even Prof. Marshall.

53. Even though Loria's opinions are not completely clear to me, I believe I am not in error in characterizing them as falling into substantially the same category as those of the abstinence theorists. At any rate, the passages in his earlier works which go into the greatest detail seem to point definitely in that direction. This is true of *Rendita fondiaria*, p. 610 ff., and of *Analisi della proprietà capitalista*, Turin, 1889, *passim*. He speaks in the same vein in his more recent and comprehensive *La costituzione economica odierna*, Turin, 1899. He assigns to the *astenzione* (or abstinence) of the capitalists a vital part in the distribution of goods (p. 36 f., p. 75). He follows the same line of thought in his remarks on the motives and limits of accumulation (*Costituzione*, p. 73 ff., p. 98 f.). And yet throughout Loria's works there are statements which lead us to conclude that it is his opinion that exploitation is a material contributing factor to the phenomenon of interest, at least in its present form and extent (e.g., *Costituzione*, p. 34 f., p. 821). It is a well-known idiosyncrasy of Loria's to ascribe to the appropriation of land a peculiarly determining and far-reaching influence even on the origination and magni-

tude of interest (e.g., *Costituzione*, pp. 35, 37, 67 ff.). Graziani has given us a rather detailed exposition and refutation of this opinion of Loria's in his perspicacious *Studi sulla teoria dell'interesse*, Turin, 1898, pp. 46-50. I, for my part, consider Loria's opinion to be entirely erroneous. Nor can I forego this opportunity to make the more general statement that Loria's cogitations in the field of theory often impress me as being far more imaginative than they are precise, and to be frequently interlarded with very superficial misinterpretations of other economists' opinions.

54. *Principles of Economics*, 3rd ed., pp. 142, 662. The fourth and fifth editions subsequently published do not differ from the third in any material respect.

55. *Ibid.*, pp. 142, 622, 751. In these passages, and indeed in all those in which he explains his "productiveness," Professor Marshall quite correctly conceives of it as technological productivity. That is to say, it manifests itself in a surplus of goods which can be produced by an equal expenditure of originary productive powers. In other words, he uses the term to convey exactly the same concept as is covered by the physical or technological productivity of which my interest theory treats. Moreover, Professor Marshall seems to be in further agreement with me in considering capitalist production as production by "roundabout methods." (Compare, for instance, his *Principles*, p. 612; also, however, the footnote on p. 664 which seems to hint at a dissenting view.)

56. *Ibid.*, p. 662.

57. *Op. cit.*, pp. 216, 315.

58. Compare my exposition of Senior's theory on foregoing p. 180 ff.

59. Chapter IX.

60. See foregoing p. 328 f.

61. *Principles*, pp. 195-197; similarly, p. 794 and in several other passages. In this connection Marshall draws a distinction, as clear as it is accurate, between this kind of lower estimate of future gratification, and other differences in estimation which, though connected with a time difference, have their origin in other sources. He contrasts lower valuation, on the one hand, of future gratifications and of future goods which arises from the uncertainty of ultimate realization, with differences in valuation, on the other hand, which arise because an alteration in attendant circumstances effects a change in the nature or the magnitude of the future gratifications themselves. One example would be a probable change in the capacity for enjoyment (such as would attend an alpine journey in one's advanced years); another would be a change in the abundance of supply which would affect the marginal utility (as in the case of eggs stored up for the winter).

62. "Round" because they ignore the compounding of interest. In his *Principles* Marshall supplies a mathematical Note V to his "Appendix" in which he works out an exact algebraic formula.

63. P. 331 ff., Note 1 on p. 429, p. 662, Note 1 on p. 663, p. 668; and indirectly his Note V on p. 794, insofar as "interest" which he explains on other occasions as a "reward of waiting," is here mentioned in connection with the "discounting of future pleasures."

64. In this illustration and in all subsequent ones I am making the assumption, in the interests of simplicity, that the entire sacrifice in labor or money is made all at the same time, and furthermore that that time is the present moment.

65. Marshall's position is shown, for instance, by an illustration involving the construction of a house, the "utility of which when finished" must cover not only the "efforts required for the building" but also an "amount increasing in geometrical proportion (a sort of compound interest) for the period that would elapse between each effort and the time when the house would be ready for his use" (p. 429).

66. On p. 769 Professor Marshall expressly claims a connection between the effect of the "telescopic faculty" and a correspondingly high estimation of "future ills and benefits."

67. Jevons's "endurance of want" in his *Theory of Political Economy*, 2nd ed., p. 254.

68. For example, John Stuart Mill and Jevons in a period antedating Marshall, and in our own day Macfarlane and, it is probably fair to add, Carver. Concerning the last named, see later text.

69. See my Preface to the second edition.

70. Pp. 489 ff.

71. For details see my *Positive Theory of Capital*, pp. 276-278.

72. Cf. Marshall, p. 450.

73. Pp. 662, 663, 665, 666 ff., and footnote, p. 666. In the course of these pages Marshall repeatedly designates the "use" or "services" of capital as the thing for which interest is paid. He explains in detail that there is in this regard "no substantial difference" between hiring a durable good, such as a horse, and borrowing a consumable or fungible good, such as money. And he adds that the distinction made by earlier writers between a lease and a loan, while it is "from an analytical point of view interesting," has very little practical significance. We find Sidgwick offering us a very similar medley of utterances, and we are probably entitled to render the same verdict concerning them. They present an exposition of the abstinence theory in terms which could well be read as an explanation of the use theory (Sidgwick, *Principles of Political Economy*, 2nd ed., [1887] p. 255 f., also p. 167 f., and p. 264).

74. E.g., p. 142 Note 1. See also my Preface to the second edition.

75. "The Place of Abstinence in the Theory of Interest" in the *Quarterly Journal of Economics*, October 1893, pp. 40-61.

76. As the alert reader will soon observe, Carver's reasoning runs parallel for a while

with certain subtle speculations which we have already encountered in Professor Marshall's work. (See foregoing p. 391 ff.) I should like to hazard the guess that Carver derived from these remarks of Marshall the first inspiration for his own theory. Later on, to be sure, he reaches a point where he branches out in an entirely different direction.

77. Very explicit, for instance, in John Stuart Mill's *Principles*, Book II, Chap. XV, Sec. II and Book I, Chap. XI.

78. *Ibid.*, p. 49.

79. *Ibid.*, p. 53.

80. The great bulk of Carver's theory was subsequently adopted by Landry, and some individual features of it by Irving Fisher. On this point see, with respect to Landry, Note 24 to Essay XIII in my *Further Essays on Capital and Interest;* with respect to Fisher, see Essay XII, p. 188 f.

81. I called attention to this very phenomenon myself. See my *Positive Theory of Capital*, p. 371 ff.

82. See also Essay XII, p. 188 f., in my *Further Essays on Capital and Interest* where a parallel is drawn with a very closely related aberration by Irving Fisher.

83. A theory of Giddings which I have already touched upon briefly in another connection (see foregoing text p. 358 f. of this Appendix) shows the closest kinship with this variant of the remuneration theory. But in many respects it displays such marked differences, and is in fact so much more advanced, that I felt obliged to classify it, for the purposes of my survey, with another and more modern group.

84. See Note 18 on foregoing p. 462.

85. *Die soziale Kategorie der Volkswirtschaftslehre*, Berlin, 1896. Subsequently Stolzmann published a second book (of about 800 pages) with the title *Der Zweck in der Volkswirtschaft*, 1909. The second book is, in the main, a polemic defense of the first, and is in fact more particularly aimed at a critique of his first book which I had published in the meantime. Since Stolzmann's second book confirms all the essential and basic views of the first, I trust I may exercise the prerogative of continuing to base my critique on his first book. I prefer to restrict myself largely to his *Soziale Kategorie* because it is more cohesively systematized. I shall avail myself only occasionally of such isolated passages as contain important additions or elucidations. I do not intend to take up more than a few selected points in Stolzmann's polemic. That is partly because its very voluminousness forbids a detailed treatment of it, and partly because the extremely numerous misapprehensions which are strewn throughout its length would have demanded far too detailed and laborious an attempt at clarification. Compare also Note 30 to Book III, Part A in my *Positive Theory of Capital*.

86. On p. 234 of his *Zweck* Stolzmann claims that he deprecates the "pigeonhol-ing" of his value theory with the labor cost theory, and he takes the occasion to include among his remarks one to the effect that he is "not an adherent but an opponent of that theory." In rebuttal I feel I must remind him that on p. 364 of his *Soziale Kategorie* he characterizes as an "irrefutable truth" the statement "that the value of goods (except for rarities) is determined by labor costs of production." And I would have him recall that on p. 329 of the same work he stated that "only a reform, not an abandonment of the labor cost theory" can make it possible to smooth out the true path. Is that the language of an opponent of the labor cost theory? And quite aside from that, it is evident that the detailed content of his doctrine, which he goes on to develop in his text, really marks it as a genuine and indubitable labor cost theory. I feel that both his literal wording and his entire context negate any possibility that Stolzmann's disavowal applied only to the Ricardo-Marxian variant of the labor cost theory. Yet if that possibility were urged, then his polemic thrusts against me would be more than ever without foundation. For, as the next lines of my text above show, there was anything but ambiguity in the emphasis with which I myself pointed out the difference between the Stolzmann labor cost theory and the Ricardo-Marxian version.

87. I expressed myself elsewhere, and in detail, with respect to this opinion. See Conrad's *Jahrbücher*, New Series, Vol. XIII, p. 46 ff., as well as my most recent comments in *Positive Theory of Capital*, p. 196 ff.; also Essay X in my *Further Essays on Capital and Interest*. I wish to adhere to the principle of avoiding rebuttal at this point, and so will not now carry the discussion any further.

88. *Op. cit.*, pp. 31-36; cf. also p. 304.

89. *Op. cit.*, p. 421 ff.

90. E.g., p. 330, where he says: "The value of capital coincides with that of the labor costs expended in accumulating it; the *labor costs* are identical with the *worker's units of subsistence* paid to the workers as wages." Similarly on p. 372, and again on p. 378. In the latter instance he even includes a mathematical exposition of his point. I wish to make the additional observation that these statements do not presuppose a noncapitalistic primitive society, but on the contrary, the existence of capital in a society already fully developed. In my review of Stolzmann's book for the *Zeitschrift für Volkswirtschaft, Sozialpolitik und Verwaltung*, Vol. VII, p. 424, I was prompted by passages like these to accuse Stolzmann of having ignored the influence of the expenditure of unequal amounts of time on the creation of values. On second thought, however, I am persuaded that, from Stolzmann's point of view, these statements represent mere oversights, and that his real opinion is the one presented in the text.

91. Stolzmann does not set up the third hypothesis in those very words, but he implies it with undeniable definitiveness. For he presupposes, in the first place, that each associate "complete from beginning to end" the production of the kind of goods he produces, and that he is, in consequence, at work throughout the entire production period. In the second place, he assumes that "for each consumption period" there is an equal number of pieces of each class of goods "lying ready to be consumed" (p. 31). Consequently it is obvious that the production periods of all goods must be equal to the consumption period, and hence equal to each other. A statement corroborating this picture of the conditions appears also on p. 32.

92. See foregoing p. 317 ff.

93. Strangely enough, Stolzmann wants to hoist me with my own petard and accuse *me* of begging the question. He bases his charge on my presentation of the argument that neither labor time nor waiting time may be regarded as devoid of significance in the matter of wages and value. And yet my exposition was supported, I thought, by a rather detailed structure of pros and cons. It is not my intention to enter into a thoroughgoing rebuttal at this point. I am aware that Stolzmann deals with the subject of the occurrence of more extended periods of production by claiming that any "waiting" can be obviated by skillful interlocking in the schedule of the various steps in production and in the supplying of materials. I merely wish to remark that to me all his attempts to conjure away the time element seem illusory and foredoomed to failure. (See his *Soziale Kategorie*, p. 304 ff., especially pp. 307, 308, 313). No matter how skillfully a blanket may be spread, it cannot be made any longer than it is. Maybe Stolzmann thinks he can blissfully assume, as he does on p. 313, that there simply will "always be a sufficient quantity of present goods lying ready to hand for immediate consumption" and that society is accordingly exempt from any irksome waiting. If he does, then that "sufficient quantity of present goods" must certainly figure in his line of reasoning as a *deus ex machina*. Its "lying ready to hand" would, to be sure, solve all difficulties, but he certainly offers no explanation of the "lying around" and more particularly, no explanation of the confidently assumed "sufficient quantity"!—For further details on this same question as it was treated by Clark some time ago, and by Schumpeter more recently, consult the *Zeitschrift für Volkswirtschaft, Sozialpolitik und Verwaltung*; for Clark's articles see Vol. XVI (1907), p. 19 ff., p. 437 f., and p. 455 f.; for Schumpeter see Vol. XXII (1913), p. 23 f.

94. *Zweck*, pp. 418, 419, 421.

95. Italics by Stolzmann! (*Zweck*, p. 422).

96. On this point compare also the book recently published by Tugan-Baranowsky entitled *Soziale Theorie der Verteilung*, 1913, p. 20.

97. *Progrès de la science économique depuis Adam Smith*, Paris, 1890, Vol. II, p. 319 ff., p. 328, p. 335 f.

98. *Principii di Economia pura*, Florence, 1899 (second impression) p. 301; Pantaleoni's version is given here only in bare outline, but seems to follow the same course as Wieser's theory which is discussed in detail below.

99. *L'intérêt du capital*, 1904.

100. *Quarterly Journal of Economics*, July 1892; cf. also my counterargument, *ibid.*, April 1895.

101. *Distribution of Wealth*, 1899; *Essentials of Economic Theory*, 1907.

102. *Principles of Economics*, 1913.

103. *Grundriss der politischen Ökonomie*, Vol. I, 1893, Sec. 119; 10th ed., 1913, Sec. 108-110.

104. *P. J. Proudhon, seine Lehre und sein Leben*, Part II (Jena, 1890), pp. 216-225.

105. *Sozialismus und kapitalistische Gesellschaftsordnung*, Stuttgart, 1892.

106. *Der natürliche Wert*, Vienna, 1889.

107. *Das Wesen des Kapitalzinses und die Zinstheorie von Böhm-Bawerk*, Breslau, 1904.

108. *Zur Theorie des Produktivkapitalzinses*, Halle, 1908.

109. *Das Kapital*, Innsbruck, 1912.

110. *Kapitalzins und Preisbewegung*, Munich, 1913.

111. See foregoing p. 427 f.

112. One example dates back to 1889, when it appeared in Pierson's *de Economist*, p. 217 f.; later instances are Wicksell's *Über Wert, Kapital und Rente*, p. 86, and Diehl's article in Conrad's *Jahrbücher*, 3rd Series, Vol. XXXV, (1908), p. 551; and among the most recent is Brown's "The Marginal Productivity vs. the Impatience Theory" in the *Quarterly Journal of Economics*, August 1913, p. 631. I myself had many years previously written an article entitled "Zins des Handwörterbuches der Staatswissenschaften." I said in that article that I should not have *much* objection to that designation "provided the use of it were devoid of that deceptive connotation with which it used to be charged by the old productive theorists, and with which even today it is, to the delight of some, so often fraught." And I went on to add, "*except* perhaps, that productivity was, in my opinion, *never the direct* cause, and furthermore *not the only* cause for the occurrence of the phenomenon of interest." And that is still my opinion. If it is merely a matter of wishing to convey the rough idea that the agio theory also derives the chief features of its explanation from the technical (note that word!) productivity of capital, then the designation of "another productivity theory" has my indifferent blessing. But it is not entirely correct. In the first place, this appellation suppresses completely the fact that productivity shares the responsibility for the rise of interest with what my own theory calls the "first reason" and the "second reason." And the

share borne by productivity, though it be a minor one in degree, is fully coordinate in nature. In the second place, it suppresses the very feature which is characteristic of the agio theory and which sets it apart from all other interest theories which may deal with kindred subject matter. That feature is the pervading presence and effect of the common connecting link which runs, like the proverbial red thread, throughout all three originating causes of interest— the connecting link which consists in the difference in value which marks present as compared with future goods. I know perfectly well this is just the feature of my views which constitutes the bone of contention between me and many theorists who in other respects take a position very similar to mine. And yet I feel compelled to maintain, as I already did in the text, on p. 226 f., that this is the one really determinative feature. At least, I cannot see by what other means any explanation of interest could be reconciled with one thought which is certainly almost universally accepted by economic theorists, namely, the thought that the value of capital goods is derived from the value of the goods produced from or by them and is, in principle, equal to the latter in value. If anyone accepts that idea, I do not think he can continue to maintain that there is any such thing as the creation of a *direct* surplus value by that quality of capital which may be termed productivity. Attempts to do so, like Wieser's sometime ago, and a more recent one by Landry must necessarily come to nought. (See following text, and also Essay XIII in my *Further Essays on Capital and Interest*.) Irving Fisher went astray in just the opposite direction. For he made the assumption that the productivity of capital could operate only by means of the subjective reasons which he summed up in the term "impatience." That is to say, he assigned to productivity a position in the explicatory chain one step further back, and thus stationed it *behind* his "impatience." In contrast to that contention Brown is certainly urging the correct one when he places emphasis on the circumstance that productivity and "impatience" are at work in the same *rank*, that is to say, *abreast* of each other, and that hence the influence of productivity is no less direct than is that of "impatience." But both of them certainly affect interest only through the instrumentality of the intermediary link common to both of them, namely, the higher value of present goods. That is the reason why that intermediary link seems to me to be a stepping stone in the way to the real explanation, and not a mere "descriptive" feature. (See also Note 41 on foregoing pages 477-478.) And I believe I must cleave without deviation to the interpretation I have set down here, even in the face of Fetter's most recent statement contained in his very remarkable essay, "Interest Theories Old and New." (See Note 14 on p. 476.)

113. This is true as well of the animadversions of Wolf, which are quite detailed but unrefined, in my estimation. He asserts that "capital is capable of a productivity of value," and then attempts to fulfill his implicit obligation to furnish evidence in support of that assertion. Here he is content to accept reasons which are, "from a to z," nothing more than what I should call paraphrases of the problem itself, rather than corroborations of his assertion or explanations of his theory. He explains the productivity of value which he has claimed for capital as the "ability of capital to yield an income exceeding (1) its own cost, and (2) the cost of the factors of production which are contingently and technologically capable of replacing the original capital." And he claims to be "proving" this thesis by referring to "a fact which everyone can observe," namely, that an excess of proceeds of this kind results whenever certain advantages are gained through the instrumentality of capital. He enumerates, as some of the advantages he has in mind, division of labor, large-scale production, use of machinery and of natural forces which demand an "investment." According to Wolf capital is therefore "doubtless an objective intermediary which enhances productivity" (*op. cit.*, p. 461 ff.).

Well,—yes! There can be no denying that the use of capital as an "intermediary" results in the creation of surplus value. That is the very reason why surplus value, in theory and in practice, is looked upon generally as income from *capital* or as *interest on capital* and not, let us say, as wages of labor or entrepreneur's profit. But that fact is the very subject matter of the interest problem, the one thing that must be explained by any interest theory that is to attain its goal. It is most certainly and definitely not a proof, nor a piece of corroborative evidence of the correctness of some one given theory, such as, let us say, a theory which asserts that capital possesses a quality which may be termed "productivity of value." When it comes to the polemics injected into the matter which Wolf is presenting, even he feels it is necessary to add to his "explanation" a further supplement. So he says that, where the use of capital effects an increase in the quantity of goods produced (say a quadrupling of the former quantity), it is necessary for the consumer, as well, to value the goods more highly. That higher value must exceed that of the capital itself which was consumed, he says, if "the producer is to have any incentive at all to employ his capital." And the consumer will be quite ready, says Wolf, to place that higher value on the goods produced "because, if he does so, he partakes of the advantages arising from the service rendered by capital; for in the absence of that service he would have had to pay a quadrupled price for the quadrupled quantity of the product, whereas he now pays a price that is only doubled or tripled. Now the consumer, who is the one who determines the value of goods, also wants to enjoy an advantage from the producer's employment of capital. To do so, the consumer perforce submits to the logic and the reasonableness of conceding to the capitalist more than the simple replacement of what the latter has consumed. He is compelled, that is, to grant him interest on his capital." That is how, says Wolf, capital's quality of productivity of goods is transmuted into a productivity of value (p. 466).

Indeed? But ordinarily "logic and reasonableness" are known to exert an influence on the actions of both parties to every market transaction, provided effective competition is in operation. That influence tends to reduce the price of goods so that it aproaches cost of production; and the reduction of costs is thus transmuted into a reduction in prices. Why does no reduction occur in Wolf's case, or at least no decline to actual cost? That point certainly deserved a clearer explanation than the one Adam Smith gave so long ago when he struck a patriarchal note by saying the capitalist must have his interest, because otherwise there would be no inducement for him to employ his capital in production! To all appearances, and judging by his more recent compendium, *Nationalökonomie als exakte Wissenschaft*, the Wolf of 1908 retained unchanged his earlier views on the productivity theory.

114. *Über den Ursprung und die Hauptgesetze des wirtschaftlichen Wertes*, Vienna, 1884, p. 139 ff. *Der natürliche Wert*, Vienna, 1889, p. 67 ff., p. 164 ff.

115. *Der natürliche Wert*, Sec. xx.

116. *Der natürliche Wert*, p. 96 ff.

117. *Der natürliche Wert*, p. 85 ff.; and particularly pp. 87, 90, 91 and 92.

118. Consult my comments on this point, set down in some detail in Essay VII in my *Further Essays on Capital and Interest*.

119. *Der natürliche Wert*, p. 123.

120. "In the final analysis, economic theory must assume the burden of proving that capital possesses productivity of value. But to that end it must first establish the existence of physical productivity, which is the framework for the former. Productivity of value presupposes the determination of the value of capital. But it is possible to arrive at a determination of the value of capital only if there has already been a resolution of the question of imputing the shares of the physical product. For the value of capital is based on the imputed share of the product" (*op. cit.*, p. 124).

121. *Op. cit.*, p. 124 f.

122. *Op. cit.*, p. 87.

123. P. 86.

124. P. 113.

125. P. 87.

126. It is conceivable that some producers, especially those who are in business for themselves, may take the point of view that the vital question is whether the return from labor exceeds or fails to equal in magnitude the *irksomeness of labor*. If the benefit which the worker derives as the return from his labor is less than the pain connected with his labor, then it is likewise admissible and relevant to take the point of view that the labor did not pay. Conversely, if the benefit exceeds the pain it was necessary to suffer for its attainment, the excess may be termed a "net benefit." (This is Marshall's "producer's surplus," *Principles*, 3rd ed., p. 217.)

127. *Op. cit.*, p. 125.

128. *Op. cit.*, Sections XXXVI and XXXVII.

129. See foregoing p. 115 ff.

130. *Op. cit.*, p. 130.

131. See foregoing p. 121.

132. *Op. cit.*, p. 134 ff.

133. *Op. cit.*, p. 136; cf. also p. 134 ff.

134. To insure avoidance of any misunderstanding I should like to have one point expressly recorded. Wieser maintains the existence of a physical productivity on the part of capital, but he uses the term "productivity of capital" in a sense which differs from that underlying all the numerous meanings enumerated and expounded in Chapter VII of this book, p. 74 ff. His use of the term also differs from my own as it appears in my *Positive Theory of Capital*, where I have recognized such physical productivity and have made it one of the pillars supporting the structure of my own exegesis. See my *Positive Theory of Capital*, p. 84 f.

135. See foregoing p. 165 ff. and especially p. 169 f.

136. See foregoing p. 158 ff., as well as my *Positive Theory of Capital*, p. 290 f.

137. Details on this topic will be found in my *Positive Theory of Capital*.

138. *Op. cit.*, p. 138. "Yet it is not a matter of indifference whether one comes into possession of it (i.e., a capital) today or not until a year from today *because possession today guarantees one additional return of interest . . . A present sum is always worth more than an equal sum at a later date.*"

139. It is found, *op. cit.*, p. 138, in substantially the same form. He says, "100 which I shall not receive until a year from now, is worth only about 95 today."

140. This book was almost off the press when I received a copy of Wieser's latest book, just published under the title *Theorie der gesellschaftlichen Wirtschaft* appearing as part of his *Grundiss der Sozialökonomik*, Tübingen, 1914. It was impossible for me to do more than devote to it a very hasty and cursory examination. I believe it possible, even so, to recognize that on the whole Wieser has remained loyal to the views on the subject of interest which are to be found in his earlier books. He states that he is not in a position to enter into a detailed polemical defense of his position. I have therefore not been able to ascertain definitely the specific arguments with which he thinks he can meet the many objections

that have been leveled at his theories of imputation and interest. Indeed, Wieser restates his earlier theories without essential change, and so may be said only to furnish evidence of the imperviousness of his convictions to the objections leveled at him, rather than to provide us with any insight into the reasons why he has not yielded to persuasion. Under the circumstances I can unfortunately do nothing but reaffirm the fact that I continue to entertain opinions divergent from his. This difference of opinion on a few of the most important theoretical questions causes a cleavage between me and this outstanding scholar, with whom my personal and professional contacts are particularly friendly. At the moment, however, I am entirely unable to take any action toward a clarification of our relationship.

141. See foregoing p. 303 ff.

142. I compiled a catalogue of these writings on a previous occasion for my monograph "Zum Abschluss des Marxschen Systems" which appeared in the *Festgaben für Karl Knies*, 1896, p. 6. That catalogue comprises the following. Lexis, *Jahrbücher für Nationalökonomie*, 1885, New Series, Vol. XI, pp. 452-465; Schmidt, *Die Durchschnittsprofitrate auf Grund des Marxschen Wertgesetzes*, Stuttgart, 1889; my own commentary on the latter in the Tübingen *Zeitschrift für die gesamte Staatswissenschaft* 1890, p. 590 ff.; another such commentary by Loria in the *Jahrbücher für Nationalökonomie*, New Series, Vol. XX (1890), p. 272 ff.; Stiebeling, *Das Wertgesetz und die Profitrate*, New York, 1890; Wolf, "Das Rätsel der Durchschnittsprofitrate bei Marx" in the *Jahrbücher für Nationalökonomie*, 3rd Series, Vol. II, 1891, p. 352 ff.; another by Schmidt in *Neue Zeit*, 1892 and 1893, Nos. 4 and 5; Landé, *ibid.*, Nos. 19 and 20; Fireman, "Kritik der Marxschen Werttheorie" also in the *Jahrbücher für Nationalökonomie*, 3rd Series, Vol. III (1892), p. 793 ff.; and finally Lafargue, Soldi, Coletti and Graziadei in the *Critica Sociale* from July to November 1894.

143. Of the writings published up to this time it may be worthwhile to mention the following. Numerous essays in the *Neue Zeit*, pre-eminently those by Engels (14th Year, Vol. I, Nos. 1 and 2), by Bernstein and by Kautsky; also Loria, "L'opera postuma di Carlo Marx" in the *Nuova Antologia* for February 1895; Sombart, "Zur Kritik des ökonomischen Systems von K. Marx" in the *Archiv für soziale Gesetzgebung und Statistik*, Vol. VII, No. 4; my aforementioned monograph, "Zum Abschluss des Marxschen Systems," 1896; Komorzynski, "Der dritte Band von Karl Marx' Das Kapital" in the *Zeitschrift für Volkswirtschaft, Sozialpolitik und Verwaltung*, Vol. VI, p. 242 ff.; Wenckstern, *Marx*, Leipzig, 1896; Diehl, "Über das Verhältnis von Wert und Preis im ökonomischen System von Karl Marx" in the *Festschrift zur Feier des 25 jährigen Bestehens des staats-*

wirtschaftlichen Seminars in Halle, Jena, 1898; Labriola, *La teoria del valore di C. Marx*, Milan, 1899; Graziadei, *La produzione capitalistica*, Turin, 1899; Bernstein, *Die Voraussetzungen des Sozialismus und die Aufgaben der Sozialdemokratie*, Stuttgart, 1899; Masaryk, *Die philosophischen und soziologischen Grundlagen des Marxismus*, Vienna, 1899; Weisengrün, *Das Ende des Marxismus*, Leipzig, 1899. See also Bibliography on p. 470, footnote 64, to Chapter XII.

144. "Einige strittige Fragen der Kapitalstheorie," Vienna, 1900, p. 111 ff., reprinted in Vol. VIII of the *Zeitschrift für Volkswirtschaft, Sozialpolitik und Verwaltung.*

145. *Göttinger Gelehrte Anzeigen*, No. 23, 1891, p. 935 and 943.

146. Schmoller's *Jahrbuch*, Vol. XIX, p. 335 ff.

147. Conrad's *Jahrbücher*, New Series, Vol. XI (1885), p. 453.

148. Lexis makes the assumption that the stern pressure of competition assures the leveling of interest at the "normal" rate. And he asserts that the capitalist sellers, despite this pressure, can regularly achieve a "surplus value" in excess of their costs. The latter statement is really the one that we can require Lexis to prove to be a fact. And if it is a fact, it needs, at the very least, to be reconciled with the laws governing value and price, or to be deduced from them in plausible fashion. But nothing that Lexis has yet said constitutes a recognizable attempt to do so. I beg to call attention to the detailed discussion I devoted to this subject in the article I mentioned previously, my "Einige strittige Fragen der Kapitalstheorie," Vienna, 1900, on p. 110 ff. Now since that time Lexis has published his *Allgemeine Volkswirtschaftslehre*, 2nd ed., 1913. It is remarkable that in that book his treatment of the topic of interest is so limited in extent that it can hardly be termed a clearly defined theory of interest. The idea suggested in those aforementioned occasional statements of his is treated with almost greater brevity in this systematically organized work which, in any case, offers nothing like a detailed elaboration of that idea.

149. I expressed myself in greater detail on the subject of this peculiar offshoot of the exploitation theory in the article referred to several times ("Einige strittige Fragen der Kapitalstheorie"). There is another somewhat earlier attempt to present the exploitation theory in combination with a theory of value other than that of the socialists. It is Wittelshöfer's *Untersuchungen über das Kapital*, Tübingen, 1890. While it is interesting, it likewise fails, in my opinion, to sound the depths of the essential problem.

150. *Theorie der reinen und politischen Ökonomie*, Berlin, 1910, 2nd ed., 1911.

151. *Soziale Theorie der Verteilung*, Berlin, 1913.

152. *Op. cit.*, pp. 5 f., 11 f., 81 f.

153. For example, *op. cit.*, pp. 273 f., 415 ff.

154. See foregoing p. 322.

155. See foregoing p. 379.

156. *P. J. Proudhon, seine Lehre und sein Leben*, Part II, Jena, 1890, pp. 217-225, and p. 204.

157. *Principles of Political Economy*, 2nd ed., London, 1887, pp. 167, 168, 264; also 255 ff.

158. *Elemente der Volkswirtschaftslehre*, 2nd ed., Vienna, 1892, p. 282 ff., p. 313 ff., p. 324 ff.

159. See *Progrès*, Paris, 1890, Vol. II, pp. 319, 320, 328, 335 ff.; also pp. 321, 326, 339; finally, pp. 310-322, 348.

160. *Op. cil.*, p. 344; cf. also p. 349.

161. *Principes d'Economie politique*, 5th ed., p. 451, footnote.

162. Nicholson, *Principles of Political Economy*, London, 1893-1897; cf. particularly Vol. I, p. 388 and Vol. II, pp. 217 and 219; Valenti, *Principii di Scienza Econo-mica*, 1906, p. 384 f. In the repeated and marked emphasis on the *servigi produttivi* rendered by capital we hear echoes in Valenti of a dash of the use theory. This is similar to what we find in Pareto.

163. *Göttinger Gelehrte Anzeigen*, 1891, No. 23, p. 930 ff., especially pp. 932-935.

164. *Op. cit.*, p. 933.

165. *Op. cit.*, p. 932 ff.

166. "Einige strittige Fragen der Kapitalstheorie," Vienna, 1900, p. 84 ff.

167. See my Preface to the second edition.

168. In his detailed treatment of my *Positive Theory of Capital* in *The Economist* for March 1889, p. 127, Pierson says, "Our author has both feet planted on the solid ground of the productivity theory"; on the other hand, Macfarlane devotes a separate paragraph (No. 107) in his *Value and Distribution* to a proof that "abstinence is recognized in the exchange theory."

169. *Quarterly Journal of Economics*, October 1898, p. 1.

NOTES TO PREFACES

1. "Dr. Böhm-Bawerk's Theory of Interest," *Quarterly Journal of Economics*, July 1892, p. 339 ff., especially 401-405.

2. *Principles of Economics*, 3rd ed., p. 142 and 664.

3. *Ibid.*, p. 405.

4. *Ibid.*, p. 404 ff.

5. See also my reply to Walker in the *Quarterly Journal of Economics*, April 1895, p. 235 ff.

6. See aforementioned article in *Quarterly Journal of Economics*, April 1895, p. 250.

7. See, *e.g.*, first edition, p. 89 ff., p. 226, 227 para. 2, 227 end, 228 ff.

INDEX OF AUTHORS